The Museum of Renaissance Music

A History in 100 Exhibits

Edited by Vincenzo Borghetti & Tim Shephard

Centre d'études supérieures de la Renaissance de Tours
Université de Tours, UMR 7323 du CNRS

Collection « Épitome musical » dirigée par Philippe Vendrix & Philippe Canguilhem

Image management : Hyacinthe Belliot

Graphic design, layout and music examples : Vincent Besson

Soutenu par

Cover illustration: Hans Ruckers the Elder Flemish, Double Virginal (1581), Musica Dulce Laborum Levamen, MET
Credit Line: Gift of B. H. Homan, 1929
https://www.metmuseum.org/art/collection/search/503676

ISBN: 978-2-503-58856-8
E-ISBN: 978-2-503-58857-5
DOI: 10.1484/M.EM-EB.5.119587
ISSN: 2565-8166
E-ISSN: 2565-9510

Printed in the EU on acid-free paper.
D/2022/0095/263

The Museum of Renaissance Music

A History in 100 Exhibits

Edited by Vincenzo Borghetti & Tim Shephard

Table of Contents

Introduction

*Vincenzo Borghetti & Tim Shephard**

THIS BOOK COLLATES 100 exhibits with accompanying essays as an imaginary museum dedicated to the musical culture of Europe, both at home and in its global horizons, in the fifteenth and sixteenth centuries. As in a physical museum, visiting readers are welcome to follow the flow suggested by the structure of the book, or equally to wander at will among the galleries; to flick through, or to ponder over each exhibit; to stride in with purpose, or to linger at leisure—the collection on display will reward each approach. But the museum is also a book, and like any book that purports—in effect—to tell a history in survey, this project stands on treacherous ground. In conceiving and realising our museum we, its curators, have inevitably made choices and adopted positions in relation to several of the live, and in some cases vexed, issues of Renaissance musicology as it is practiced today; and at the same time we have, we hope, created new opportunities through the counter-intuitive notion of a sonic history told through objects. Although it is our firm intention to let our exhibits be the main actors in this history, to let them speak through the voices of our contributors, it behoves us at the outset to give some account of our decisions.

Defining the Musical Renaissance

Despite the difficulties inherent in defining a period, the boundaries of Renaissance music are conventional, widely agreed upon and understood in theory and in practice, both in musicology and in broader culture. To write of "Renaissance Music" is to refer roughly to the music of the fifteenth and sixteenth centuries. This situation is both confirmed and sustained by textbooks used extensively in the university classroom: there is Allan Atlas' *Renaissance Music: Music in Western Europe 1400-1600* of 1998, for example, and from 1999 both *Music in the Renaissance* by Howard M. Brown and Louise K. Stein, and Leeman L. Perkins's *Music in the Age of the Renaissance*; but also more recent volumes such as Laurenz Lütteken's 2011 *Musik der Renaissance*, Richard Freedman's Norton textbook *Music in the Renaissance* published in 2013, and the seven volumes of the *Handbuch der Musik der Renaissance*, edited by Andrea Lindmayr-Brandl et al., published since 2012 and now approaching completion.

The *Museum of Renaissance Music*, however, is not defined only by two centuries of history: the title deliberately contains the word "Renaissance," because this museum contains something more, and also something less, than a museum dedicated to music between 1400 and 1600. The subject of this museum is not two centuries, but rather an epoch, which, according to a dictionary definition, is "an extended period of time usually characterised by a distinctive development or by a memorable series of events" (Merriam-Webster). The specifics of the definition are in the end banal, but nonetheless they have important consequences for the intellectual project that underlies this book. Even more than a history made out of centuries (itself also the product of conventions neither neutral nor universal, only less obviously so because expressed in numbers), a history made out of epochs places the emphasis on the process whereby the epoch itself is defined—on the fact, that is, that it is the fruit of cultural and historiographical constructions. This does not imply, however, that we are dealing exclusively with a posteriori constructions. The historiography of epochs works with hypotheses of definition founded also, in part, on traces of the consciousness of change, or awareness of some distinctive feature of the period, or of difference from an adjacent period (as, for example, the Middle Ages, which only exists as such after its presumed end), found within the period itself. This is most famously true for Renaissance literature and visual arts, but also to a more limited extent for Renaissance music: some of those involved with it at the time expressed in diverse ways an awareness of differences from the past, or better contributed to a discourse of difference (Owens 1990; Strohm 2001).

Nonetheless the musical Renaissance, perhaps even more than in other fields, is above all a product of the reflections and practices of modern historiography. Nineteenth-century historiography has a fundamental role in emphasising the Renaissance as the definitive surpassing of the Middle Ages (contributing at the same time to the "medievalisation" of the latter) and, in

* The project was collaborative from start to finish, and the editors are jointly responsible for this introduction. Nevertheless, we each took a leading role in researching and writing up particular themes and topics. Vincenzo Borghetti took on primary responsibility for the sections *Defining the Musical Renaissance* and *Who, What, and Where is Renaissance Music?* Tim Shephard was the first author for *The Material Renaissance and the Renaissance of the Material* and *A History in Objects*. Other sections were authored together.

consequence, as one of the key moments of modern Western civilization. The musical Renaissance thus exists in relation to the Renaissance defined by Jacob Burckhardt, its historiography founded ultimately in his *Kulturwissenschaft* (e.g. Schrade 1953; Lowinsky 1954) and the broader discourse it generated.

Recent decades, however, have witnessed growing and justified suspicion of the ideologies enshrined in this nineteenth-century historiography, and in the very notion of the internal coherence of the Renaissance as a period, in musicology as in other disciplines. No longer is a unified Renaissance considered capable of holding together the multiplicity of phenomena that can be found within it, and it is increasingly clear that the concept of Renaissance fits poorly with many of the musical practices that were valued highly in fifteenth- and sixteenth-century Europe. But these critiques have not displaced the utility of epoch-history: rather, Renaissance has often been simply replaced with the epochal designations Late Middle Ages (roughly, the fifteenth century), or Early Modernity (beginning in the sixteenth). These names represent historiographical positions diverging from (the latter) or even opposed to (the former) the notion of Renaissance; they replace the rhetoric of rebirth with a rhetoric of continuity, or of transformation and rupture, but they do not question the assumption that these two centuries span a period of defining change. They too are the product of historiographical and cultural reflections and constructions, and as such are not exempt from the conceptual and methodological difficulties which are always part of a history based on epochs.

For these reasons, despite sustained critique, "Renaissance Music," or "Music in the Renaissance," and similar locutions, are still current and meaningful in contemporary discourse. This is the case because, as with "Late Medieval" or "Early Modern," the historiography of "Renaissance Music" tries to highlight the specificities, the aspects judged "epochal," of the period under consideration—even if this no longer happens in connection with the strict etymological meaning of "Renaissance" (applicable in this sense only perhaps to the diverse manifestations of so-called "ancient" practices, such as singing to the lira, the recitation of Latin odes in ancient meters, chromaticism, the first operas, and so forth), or with the resonances intended by nineteenth-century historiography.

Is the "Renaissance" of our title merely a choice of convenience, then? Yes, and no. Yes, because "Renaissance" as term and as concept enjoys currency, and offers to us as curators of this museum the advantage of referring immediately to a particular period of roughly two centuries, without the need for further details—and this is very useful in a title. The "roughly" is important: "Renaissance," in contrast to a possible "1400-1600," does not impose arbitrary limits, permitting our contributors to consider this epoch in a de-regulated manner, observing phenomena peculiar to these two centuries alongside those that are shared with neighbouring epochs, and thus to interrogate the very category of epochal specificity—one might say, of "Renaissance-ness." Yes, therefore, because these elements of the *longue durée* prompt us to adopt a critical stance from the inside in the debate over the "Renaissance" epoch, considering its artificiality as a construction, stressing thus also the historiographical weaknesses and contradictions that are inevitably entailed in a history by epochs.

But inherent in this position are also the reasons for no: the choice to put "Renaissance" in the title is not only a choice of convenience. If the Renaissance exists today partly, and perhaps primarily, as a creation of the historiography of the nineteenth century, inherited by later historians, our use of this term serves to call attention not only to the objects exhibited as contributions to musical discourse in their historical epoch, but to ourselves and our contributors as integral to the ongoing construction (and critique) of the Renaissance concept, of the epoch and, therefore, of this museum. As we noted at the outset, the remit of the *Museum of Renaissance Music* is not defined only by chronology, and therefore it includes exhibits relating to the discourse of Renaissance music from the seventeenth century up to the present day.

Who, What, and Where is Renaissance Music?

What, then, are the "historical" particularities of the epoch to which this *Museum of Renaissance Music* is dedicated? They are as diverse and numerous as are the stories told by the objects exhibited. They include, for example, the spread and entrenchment of music as an aspect of court culture through the creation or consolidation of princely chapels; the increasing importance of music in the education of sovereigns, of gentlewomen and gentlemen, and the sediments from that process observable in musical discourse; the stories of the genres and manners of the composition and consumption of music, which nourish objects, media, practices, discursive forms (for example changes in the setting of secular texts, of sacred texts, and, for that matter, changes in the supports in which they are textualised; changes in the places, spaces, and social practices into which they are incorporated); the diffusion of musical practice to ever-wider strata of society, and (alongside or perhaps as its precondition) the extension of musical notation to repertories that previously had not made use of it; the expansion of the trade in printed books of music, which emerges in entrepreneurial form only with the sixteenth century, but which is predicated upon an expansion of the music-reading and music-consuming public that occurred during the previous century; the increasing presence of music and musical instruments in domestic spaces, and the development of true "music rooms," which goes hand-in-hand with the invention of new instruments (the harpsichord, for example), the transformation of earlier instruments and their wide dissemination at different levels of society.

This list—a tiny sample of the stories arising from the objects in our museum—has no great role for the words "born" and "reborn," because our project by its nature confronts the homogeneity of the classic historiographical narrative of the Renaissance with the diversity and difference of its exhibits and its contributors, issuing an invitation to interrogate the relationship between each exhibit and the discourse of the Renaissance, both historical and historiographical.

Moreover, the objects displayed in this museum do not only refer to music as textualized or verbalised in the form of notation or of books of and on music. Such documents are certainly important and included, but they are only one part of a museum which embraces a broader view of musical and auditory culture in the relevant epoch. The variety of the exhibits, with differing degrees of "apparent" musicality or sonority, illuminates not only practices that are explicitly musical—those documented by various forms of textualization, musical, verbal, visual, or by obvious tools such as musical instruments—but also the role of music in locations where the echo of its sound has long-since faded (places, spaces, buildings), or where music is present implicitly (metaphors, imagined locations, images, objects). Through the breadth of this approach the *Museum of Renaissance Music* can access a broader social and cultural range of musical practices: not only those of the ruling classes, or those of the musically literate.

Alongside this social and cultural breadth, the organisation of the museum also aims at an expanded geographical representation: the music of Renaissance Europe is both European, and not. However, the global reach of our museum does not extend to the music of all world cultures—a *Museum of Renaissance Music* confers a different brief in this respect to a hypothetical *Museum of Music 1400-1600*. The term "Renaissance" anchors this project in a European perspective, but that perspective is not delimited by the physical geography of the continent; rather, in light of recent debates in musicology and across the humanities, it engages closely with the musical Renaissance in its geographical displacements (European and otherwise) and in its relations with other cultures, exploring the networks and the dynamics of exchange, and offering thus the possibility to reflect upon—and ultimately to reconsider—the phenomena of cross-cultural interconnection that they characterise.

The Material Renaissance and the Renaissance of the Material

In a history dominated by the written text, objects have recently achieved new recognition. As ideas, as products, as possessions, as tools, characterised by shapes, materials, images and inscriptions, made to last, to discard, or even to ingest, objects bear remarkable witness to people, their experiences and practices, and their sentiments and concerns (Motture and O'Malley 2010, 1-4; Hamling and Richardson 2010; Rublack 2013). Although as a field of research material culture is defined by its materiality, the boundaries of the artifact are by no means delimited by its physical structure, or even by its function and use. Artifacts are embedded "into a much wider material world ... relating objects, spaces and people to one another" (Hamling and Richardson 2010, 7). Indeed, in this book we accept spaces and people, and even concepts, to be themselves artifacts, exhibits amenable to display and examination.

It is appropriate that this turn toward the object and its materiality in Renaissance studies has been led by three major museums; and, because of the particular strengths of their collections and their sense of their market among the museum-going public, it has centred largely on Italy. The agenda was set initially at the British Museum, first in Dora Thornton's *The Scholar in His Study* (1997), and then in Thornton and Luke Syson's 2001 *Objects of Virtue: Art in Renaissance Italy*. There followed an extraordinary outpouring of inspiring scholarship from the Victoria and Albert Museum, resulting from the exhibition *At Home in Renaissance Italy* held in 2006 (Ajmar-Wollheim and Dennis 2006; Ajmar-Wollheim, Dennis, and Matchette 2007), and the preparation of new Medieval & Renaissance Galleries which opened in 2009 (Davies and Kennedy 2009; Motture and O'Malley 2010). Simultaneously, a similar approach was taken in the Metropolitan Museum's 2008 exhibition *Art and Love in Renaissance Italy* (Bayer 2008).

The methods associated with this material turn are generally understood to fall into two strands (Motture and O'Malley 2010, 3-4; Hamling and Richardson 2010, 7-12). The first, associated with museums and characterised as curatorial or archaeological, begins with the object and moves outward to broader questions of social and cultural value. The second, located in the academy and in the humanities, begins with research questions which it seeks to answer with the help of different types of evidence, including (but not limited to) objects. The V&A's two projects, and other subsequent efforts, have set out self-consciously—and successfully—to merge the worlds of the museum and the academy, creating a blended scholarship that addresses (in the words of its participants) "the deep connection between our understanding of the materiality of objects and our comprehension of the practices of early modern social life" (Motture and O'Malley 2010, 4).

Medievalists in different fields have been engaged with the materiality of culture for rather longer (e.g. Camille 1985; Huot 1987; Camille 1992; Nichols 1992; Camille 1998, among many others); and medieval musicologists have added their voices to the discussion since the beginning of the century or shortly before (e.g. Tanay 1999; Dillon 2002; Dillon 2012, among others). Over the past decade or so specialists in Renaissance music have also begun to tackle these themes in earnest; indeed, conceived in early 2017, this museum sits within and is the beneficiary of a veritable material turn in the study of Renaissance music. Scholars of music sources have increasingly adopted a material approach, seen for example in Jane Alden's work on the Loire Valley Chansonniers (Alden 2010), and Kate van Orden's on chanson prints in sixteenth-century France (van Orden 2015). Musical practices have also been addressed in these terms, perhaps most intensively in a special issue of the journal *Renaissance Studies* entitled *Musical Materials and Cultural Spaces*, edited by Richard Wistreich (Wistreich 2012). Prominent conferences, projects and publications have considered anew the buildings and spaces used for musical activities through this lens, most notably in the project *Sound and Space in Renaissance Venice* (Howard and Moretti 2009 and 2012), and in studies devoted to urban soundscapes (Fenlon 2008; Fisher 2014; Atkinson 2016; Knighton and Mazuela Anguita 2018, among others), as well as in the conference "Books, Images, Objects: The Media of Secular Music in the Medieval and Early Modern Period" (Verona, 2019). Objects and the musical practices in which they were enmeshed have likewise benefited from the material approach, in the work of Flora Dennis—a pioneer in this field—and more recently also of Matthew Laube and others (Dennis 2010a and 2010b; Willis 2010a; Giselbrecht 2017; Laube 2017). Significantly, several key contributors to this vein of scholarship do not identify as musicologists; indeed, the material approach has been especially fruitful in opening up the study of Renaissance music to scholars of other disciplines, including history (Willis), and the histories of art (Dennis) and architecture (Howard and Moretti; Atkinson).

A History in Objects

"Telling history through things is what museums are for," writes Neil MacGregor at the very beginning of his extraordinary *History of the World in 100 Objects*. This book is a museum, and we its curators, in precisely the same spirit. It is a project that thrives on both the tension and the reconciliation between individual objects and big research questions. At the heart of the book is a set of artifacts—meant in the broadest sense, and referred to here as both exhibits and objects, even if these words and concepts do not apply equally and in the same ways to all the items on display—and their witness to the priorities and activities of people in the past as they addressed their social and cultural world through music. As curators, it is our prerogative to select and assemble these individual witnesses such that together they address fundamental questions about the nature of musical cultures and practices in Renaissance Europe.

The special value of objects as historical witnesses, differing from that of texts, is often noted (Hamling and Richardson 2010, 11-12; MacGregor 2010, xv-xxvi). Just as many social practices in Renaissance Europe (as now) were transacted without the help of writing, we know full well that the surviving notated music constitutes a hopelessly skewed representation of a musical culture that blended notation quite freely with aural and improvisatory practices. Expanding the musicological field of view to encompass not only the most rewarding products of musical and verbal writing, but the much fuller range of material remains that survive, therefore, has the capacity to reach social and geographical groups, and musical practices and panoramas, that are right now gaining greater profile in scholarship.

A history of music in objects is at the whim of accidents of survival, of course, which will tend to favour beautiful, elite objects over plain, everyday ones; the same is true of a history in texts. Because of their rarity and their mundanity, everyday objects are among both the most historically useful, and the easiest to overlook—bringing them to light and setting them alongside their more celebrated elite counterparts is a challenge for this museum and its curators, but the potential scholarly rewards are substantial. However, the materiality of mundanity is not circumscribed by possession, nor restricted to the inexpensive: elaborate public and ecclesiastical spaces, and decorative objects for communal use, fell within the everyday experience of a much larger group of people than those who could pay for their creation.

The history that emerges from this exercise is in many respects a new one, enriched and invigoratingly cacophonous—cacophonous for the diversity of the exhibited objects, and for the diversity of approaches, within an implied and shared material perspective, taken by individual authors in analysing their exhibits. The familiar narrative of Renaissance music, woven around a few Flemish clerics and their notated polyphony, is but one among many competing stories, each with a clear material claim to take its place in our understanding of the period. Far from proposing a neat overarching thread, this is a history by collage, a history of overlapping musical practices, of the messy variety of musicking as seen through its tools. However, this is not a history that eschews big themes and topics; indeed, in critical areas such as devotional practice, sociability, education, identity, social and cultural encounter, and others, it is closely engaged with the broader disciplinary tapestry of Renaissance studies. As a project, then, it has the aspiration, and the potential, to tell a history of Renaissance music that speaks beyond the confines of academic musicology.

A Paper Museum

In organising this book, we have followed our museum metaphor to its logical conclusion and constructed a series of broad thematic galleries or "rooms" in which to display our exhibits—in some cases with integrated sub-rooms addressing more focussed types or topics. Some of our rooms and sub-rooms are defined by object type: the Room of Books and that of Instruments are of this nature, as is the smaller Room of Psalters. Other rooms address particular spaces, including the Room of Sacred Spaces and that concerned with the Public Sphere, with its nested Room of Cities and Room of Travels, as well as the small Room of Imagined Spaces. Practices are thematized, meanwhile, in the Rooms of Devotions, that of Domestic Objects with its integrated Room of Sensualities, and that of Revivals. Finally, in the Room of Experts it is identities that are particularly at stake.

From this categorisation of rooms, both the functionality and the problematicity of our system are already evident, because practices make use of objects; and objects inhabit spaces; and both spaces and identities are socially constructed, negotiated and articulated through objects and practices. And also because some of our neatly identified rooms sit across the rigid categorizations they impose, such that our organizational principles inherently reveal their own conventionality. To give some examples: psalters are of course books, as well as devotional tools; and books are also domestic objects, closely connected with the construction of identities; and sacred spaces are to some extent also public spaces. We puzzled long and hard over where to place the Room of Imagined Spaces: such spaces are often described in the pages of books—that is why they occupy a sub-gallery in the Room of Books—but the specific pictorial representation of heaven discussed in exhibit 44 is evidently not from a book, even if it exists in relation to contemporary descriptions of heaven that do take textual form. This particular case helps to highlight the role of sub-rooms in destabilising the categorisation of themes and objects, and suggesting links between the principal rooms and/or individual objects.

In a physical museum, each gallery features an interpretation panel in which the curators have an opportunity to frame its contents as a whole, and shape their interpretation by visitors. In keeping with our intention to allow multiple voices to present differing views, rather than claiming a single authoritative perspective, we delegated the task of writing introductions to each of the principal rooms to a panel of scholars, most of whom did not also contribute essays on individual exhibits. We gave them carte blanche, so to speak, affording them total freedom in determining their style, approach and emphasis, leaving it up to them to decide how to refer to the individual exhibits in the rooms (and associated sub-rooms) allotted to them, and indeed whether or not to refer to objects in different rooms which connect with the topics under discussion. As a result of this deliberate policy, the rooms' introductions are active not only in clarifying themes and interpretations, but also in highlighting the problems and tensions inherent in the museum's organisation.

The blend of stability and instability created at every level of the conception and disposition of our museum invites readers to trust and at the same time to distrust its organisation, prompting them both to follow and to interrogate the connections suggested by we curators and authors, whilst at the same time exploring and discovering connections we did not envisage.

A physical museum has no index, only a table of contents (in the form of a map, printed on a leaflet or displayed on the wall). This circumstance makes focussed research in displayed collections inconvenient and time-consuming, and at the same time it favours the serendipity, unexpected encounters and provocative juxtapositions that characterise browsing. After wrangling with ourselves for several weeks over the question of whether to align our project with the museum or the book in this respect, we decided that the "map" represented by our Table of Contents is sufficiently explicit, the essays sufficiently focussed and short, that we could follow our museum metaphor through to its conclusion without undue inconvenience to readers.

The collaboration that generated this project can be traced back to 2013, inspired by the lively discussions at the conference "The Production and Reading of Music Sources," held at the British Library and the Warburg Institute under the auspices of Thomas Schmidt's seminal PROMS project. Planning for this museum began in earnest early in 2017, when we, the curators/editors, began a series of long Skype sessions in order to shape this project. As must be obvious, we both admired Neil MacGregor's *History of the World in 100 Objects* and Martina Bagnoli's exhibition *A Feast for the Senses: Art and Experience in Medieval Europe* (2016-17), and wondered what could be drawn from them to throw new and fresh light on the story of Renaissance music.

In the first place we would like to thank the members of our advisory board, colleagues and friends we contacted early on in order to discuss the project in its broad conception and also in its details (themes, exhibits, contributors): namely, Lisa Colton, Flora Dennis, Tess Knighton, Laura Moretti, and Katelijne Schiltz. A special thank-you also to Bonnie Blackburn, who advised in different ways later on in the project, as we tackled the mammoth task of editing over 100 essays. Laura Ștefănescu richly deserves our gratitude for her careful and thorough work proofreading and correcting the complete book manuscript prior to typesetting. Several colleagues were enormously helpful in rooting out digital reproductions of elusive exhibits, particularly in the last stages of the project—we extend our thanks to Catia Amati, Michele Calella, Michele Magnabosco, Laura Ventura Nieto, Rupert Ridgewell, Hector Sequera, and Momoko Uchisaka.

We had the opportunity to present some of the results of this project in themed sessions hosted by the Medieval and Renaissance Music Conferences in Maynooth (2018) and Basel (2019). Our thanks are due especially to Barbara Eichner and Katelijne Schiltz, who happily stepped in to chair some of these themed sessions when last minute changes disrupted our plans. In Maynooth Antonio Cascelli allotted us a room in which to present images of all 100 exhibits spread across a number of tables, where delegates assisted us in developing organisational principles for the rooms of the book/museum.

Whilst the book was under preparation it garnered some media interest. Rai Radio3 followed through, asking us to make a programme out of our book: a radiophonic exhibition presenting 10 of our 100 objects, entitled *La musica del Rinascimento: una mostra in 10 oggetti*, broadcast from 9 January to 2 February 2021. Our great gratitude goes to Monica D'Onofrio, editor of Radio3 Suite, and especially to Gaia Varon and Nicola Pedone (respectively co-presenter and producer), who played fundamental roles in helping us turn a book conceived as a scholarly work into a radio programme.

Inevitably, work on this book was profoundly impacted by the extraordinary events of the coronavirus pandemic in 2020-21. As we all struggled with the practicalities of lockdown, and the consequences for teaching at our universities, or simply with our lives in general, deadlines tumbled and schedules slipped both for some of our contributors and for us as editors. To those contributors who had finished their essays long before, and have waited patiently for so long to see their work in print, we can only offer our humblest apologies. The pandemic has also taken a terrible toll on research infrastructure, causing the long-term closure of libraries and museums, in some cases preventing authors from accessing information on their exhibits. This may have resulted in a certain degree of unevenesses among the essays, especially in the physical descriptions of individual exhibits. In what is already a huge and lengthy project, we have preferred to tolerate some minor imperfections rather than to cause still longer delays in publishing the book.

The publication of this book replete with its full complement of colour images would not have been possible without assistance from the research fund of the Dipartimento di Culture e Civiltà of the University of Verona. We would like to express our greatest gratitude to this institution—particularly to the Head of Department, Arnaldo Soldani, and to the administrative staff, Enrico Maria Cazzaroli and Cristina Iannamorelli—especially given the threats faced by public funding for humanities research at this time. Our most special thanks are due also to Philippe Canguilhem and Philippe Vendrix for accepting this book into the series Épitome Musical, managed through the Centre d'études supérieures de la Renaissance in Tours. We have benefitted enormously from our collaboration with Vincent Besson as typesetter and Hyacinthe Belliot as image editor, both of whom bear a full share of responsibility for the beauty of the finished product. Among many image providers, we are particularly grateful to those museums and libraries who provided high-resolution photographs free of charge.

Besides the scholarly side of working on a book project, there is also a personal aspect, concerning the individuals who in different ways have supported and shared in our work, as scholars but also as partners and friends. I (Vincenzo) would like to dedicate this book to my husband Emanuele Senici: in all the years of the project he patiently discussed with me the issues I was confronted with, putting at my disposal his own experience in book editing and his critical perspectives, particularly valuable precisely because as a musicologist he does not work on the Renaissance. I (Tim) would like to dedicate this book to Philip Weller, who some years ago supervised my first excursions into the world of Renaissance images and objects as my doctoral advisor, and who sadly passed away, unexpectedly, before this project reached completion.

Cremona/Sheffield, May 2021

salue re
gina ma
ter mise
ricordie
uita dl
ce do es
pes nos
tra sal
ue a ti
clama
mos gi
mientis
abisus

I

Devotions

Introduction: The Room of Devotions

Matthew Laube

It is now widely recognised that religious devotion in the Middle Ages and Renaissance was more than a straightforward and interior phenomenon hidden in the minds and hearts of individuals. Illustrated by the work of Caroline Walker Bynum and John Arnold, scholars now accept that devotion—that is, religious worship and observance—was not only filled with complexity, contradictions and paradoxes, but was also shaped and experienced within wide-ranging and dynamic social contexts (Arnold 2005; Bynum 2006). In the late medieval and early modern world, devotion was neither uniform nor fixed. Rather, it was conditioned by such features as a person's language, social networks, and standing. It involved manifold physical spaces and material objects, including altars, paintings, and statues, as well as books, clothing, jewellery, and household items. Like the clergy, lay women and men across the social spectrum harnessed the emotional capacities of devotion, fixing their gaze on the Eucharist, the Virgin Mary, relics, images and statues of saints—even the Word and scripture itself—to activate and channel myriad emotional states ranging from joy, adoration and peace, to pain, humiliation and suffering (Rubin 2009a). Recent work has sought to capture everyday forms of devotion. Moving beyond the institutional cultures of churches and confraternities and the official policies of religious leaders, scholars now emphasise the importance of the Renaissance home and pilgrimage as sites of lay devotional endeavour, and the centrality of devotion to shaping wider human conditions of physical settledness and movement (Brundin et al. 2018; Bynum 2006; Garnett and Rosser 2013).

Devotion was neither intrinsic nor inevitable in late medieval and early modern cultures. Instead, it was actuated through devotional exercises and performance—both ritualised and spontaneous, silent and sounding, individual and communal—which involved changeable combinations of activities incorporating singing, reading, listening, contemplation, drama, dancing, and drumming. Within this multifaceted regime, a range of musical activity and experience became foundational to late medieval and early modern devotion; and for scholars across disciplines, music serves as a multi-focal lens with unique capacities to sharpen and advance current scholarship on devotion.

As the objects in this room illustrate, music throws into sharp relief the social nature of devotion, as music served not just to express religious beliefs, but also to display social identities and cement relationships. The elaborate decoration of music books—including the 1627 edition of *The Whole Booke of Psalmes* (Willis)—reinforced membership in restricted and elite social circles of the English gentry, as much as reflecting a sense of belonging to the wider Church of England. Music cemented social bonds within individual families, as singing and devotional books such the *Prato Haggadah* (Gutwirth) helped families to fashion their own inheritances of sound and matter, which were passed down from one generation to another. Devotional artefacts, including potentially the *Alabaster altarpiece* of the Passion of Christ (Cook, Kirkman, Murat, and Weller), formed an integral part of Renaissance economies of the gift, initiating political bonds and easing tensions across sometimes great geographical distances. As social phenomena, both music and devotion were deeply bodily in nature. Bodies were frequently made the primary focal point of devotional viewing—as with the *Johanneschüssel* (Baert) or the image of the Man of Sorrows in the *Mass of St Gregory* (Nelson)—and representations of the Virgin Mary, including those featured in this room (Bloxam; Nordera; Williamson), were powerfully interconnected with conceptions of celestial music and with widely known song repertories praising the physical role of Mary as bearer of humanity.

Devotional music also bridged spiritual and physical divisions of space, culture, and time. To the creators and Renaissance viewers of the *Madonna of Humility* (Williamson), music bridged the divide between heaven and earth, as the voices of finite earthly bodies could join with unending angelic songs of praise to the Madonna and Child. Vernacular psalms and hymns—such as those contained in *The Whole Booke of Psalmes*—linked parish churches to individual family homes, as singing helped to infuse everyday interactions and activities of domestic life with religious significance. Music also created connections and reflected movement across sometimes considerable geographical and cultural distances, whether it was polyphonic song connecting the Latin schools of Iceland to those of Rostock and Denmark (Ingólfsson), or Armenian psalters linking Christian traditions of East and West (Giovannini).

Neither music nor devotion went uncontested, however. The objects in this room also reveal the limitations of music to forge social bonds, and demonstrate uses of music and religious devotion to express difference and fuel conflict. Even as music helped to negotiate colonial interactions in Mexico and Peru, music never fully effaced meaningful cultural and ethnic differences between indigenous and missionizing European communities (Baker; Candelaria). Indeed, Renaissance communities frequently cultivated devotional music in direct response to conflict and duress, a fact demonstrated especially well in the sub-room *Psalters*. The creation of the Armenian psalter (Giovannini), printed in the turbulent 1560s, took place amidst warfare and the fragmentation of Armenian territories in the South Caucasus. The *Printed Hymnal* in Finnish by Jacobus Finno (Raninen) resulted from the moderate Reformation instituted by the Kingdom of Sweden and their fear of political unrest. But, unlike *The Whole Booke of Psalmes* which became embedded in everyday domestic life, this Finnish hymnal reinforced rather than dissolved existing divisions of literacy and authority, becoming primarily the reserve of literate religious leaders and the wealthy, rather than lay believers lower down the social spectrum.

While some musical artefacts reflected conflict and division, other objects became battlegrounds themselves, triggering a range of competing devotional and musical responses. Fifteenth-century Netherlandish objects like the *Virgin and Child with Angels* (Bloxam), although created initially for Catholic devotion in the home, also attracted the attention of sixteenth-century Protestant iconoclasts whose religious beliefs and musical activities compelled them to destroy, not venerate, such objects, and to view the act of destruction itself as an unambiguous expression of religious devotion.

Above all, the objects in this room illustrate the diversity of musical activity and experience in the global Renaissance. They demonstrate not only a range of musical genres; but, for historians of music today, devotion helps to expose the rich multi-vocality of musical artefacts and paints a vivid picture of the diverse historical agents who cultivated and contested religious music in the Renaissance.

CAPVT IOANNIS BAPTISTE

1. Silence

Barbara Baert

Johannesschüssel (*The Head of St John on a Plate*)
Anon., Upper Rhine, ca. 1480
Wood, 41 cm
Inscribed: DA MICHI IN DISCO CAPVT IOANNIS BAPTISTE MARCI 6
Kremsmünster Abbey
Photo © Bildarchiv Foto Marburg / Ernst Oeters / Carl Ludwig

The *Johannesschüssel*—a popular late medieval devotional image (*Andachtsbild*) of the severed head of Saint John the Baptist on a plate—is an image type that sprang from both text (Mark 6:14-29 and Matthew 14:1-21) and relic (skull relics, the most famous being that in the Cathedral of Amiens). It is an image type that presents death. This death is not an ordinary one; it is the mother of all deaths: the decapitation of the last of the prophets, the forerunner (*precursor*, *prodromos*) and the first martyr (*proto-martyr*) (Gauthier 2012). The functions and uses of the *Johannesschüssel* are complex and heterogeneous, varying according to the period of their production, to the localization of any particular veneration, and finally to the medium and/or material in which the object was fabricated: some were made of the finest materials, others in papier-mâché; some could nod their heads like a pantomime puppet; others contained relics; some were made to hang on the wall of the church; others had a foot for a stand, and so forth. All these different forms and materials are conditioned by their particular uses, environments and functions. Of course, not all these elements and aspects can be treated here; yet a focus on the way the late medieval beholder and user of this specific instrument of devotion (Vanhauwaert and Geml 2015) is mediated by the senses and silences touches upon the larger research questions of this *Museum of Renaissance Music* (Shephard et al. 2017).

As in the main object presented here, the Kremsmünster *Johannesschüssel*, this type of devotional image challenges the viewer to address St John not only through the (paradoxical) tumbling exchange of glances, but also through a "sonoric" communication, or more precisely, from the silencing of his voice. In scripture, to those who ask who he is, the Baptist responds: "Ego sum vox clamantis in deserto" (I am the voice crying out in the wilderness, John 1:22-23). To look at the *Johannesschüssel* is to realise that we can no longer hear his voice. The decapitation has reduced the seat of the vocal cords, the prophet himself, to an acoustic wilderness. The other man, Christ, can at last unveil himself as the true Saviour. This brings me to the phenomenological tension between head and visage, between platter and veil, with a focus on the role of silence(s).

In Indo-European semantics, the root of "head" and "skull" is also the root of dish, platter, pan and recipient (Pokorny n.d. b). Heads and skulls are, archetypically, hollow tools for keeping liquids in a cultic context. Head and platter are essentially equal. The *Johannesschüssel* is then intrinsically a tautology. Further, without the platter John's beheading could never have become an image, become "some-thing." Or rather, without the recipient that catches the head, bears it and hands it over, the moment of the decapitation could not have remained crystalised in the fraction of an instant. The platter is the bearer that has caught up the image and presents it plastically as *memoria*. The platter says: "it has truly happened" (Böhme 1995).

Medusa is the archetypal bridge between beheading and face; of making its gaze "bearable" (Marin 1997, 174). This perspective gives rise to several analogies with the *Johannesschüssel* in terms of form, function, and phantasm. Like the Medusa, the *Johannesschüssel* thematizes decapitation as the genesis of the image. In death itself the image freezes; in a fraction of a moment the head coagulates into an artifact, resulting in the projection of powerful forces. There is a physical analogy to the Medusa with respect to the face: the open mouth, the eyes of death, the gushing neck, and last but not least the snakes and hair fanning out from the head (fig. 1.1). Many *Johannesschüsseln* have pointed tendrils that project on all sides. In the exemplar from Kremsmünster John's hair has become distinctly serpentine. John's prodigious locks are treated as a typical sign of his prophetic "wildness." Nevertheless, this characteristic attached itself to the Medusa as genre by the end of the Middle Ages. With the increasing popularity of the Medusa as a Renaissance motif, we notice a soundless osmosis between the *Johannesschüssel* and the Medusa, between his hair and her snakes, between his neck and her neck, between his blood and hers. This is strikingly evident in the tondo painted in/around 1464-68 by Giovanni Bellini or Marco Zoppo (*The Severed Head of St John the Baptist*, Musei Civici di Pesaro).

Like the Medusa the functions of the *Johannesschüssel* seem to relate to the apotropaic. The uses to which it was put were highly stratified according to the various social experiences of religion: for example, the solstice celebrations of June 24, with their excessive dancing and the many local customs and ramifications brought by the motifs of fire, epilepsy, and solstice anxiety, all rituals that became a portal as an event, a laborious

Figure 1.1: Marco Zoppo or Giovanni Bellini, *Head of St John the Baptist*, c.1465-71. Tempera on panel, 42.5 cm. Musei Civici di Pesaro. Photo courtesy of the Musei Civici di Pesaro.

process that must be coupled with fear and dumb astonishment—that is, with silence or speechlessness (Gaignebet 1986, 351-56).

The silent portal of solstice ritual brings me to the throat as anthropological phantasm. The throat— *gula* in Latin—in most languages makes use of the sound pattern G-R-G. The word *gorgo* is in fact related to this with derivations in *gurgel*, *gurguli*, *gurges*, *gorge* (Pokorny n.d. a). And even today the church of San Giovanni in Venice is called San Gorgo by the inhabitants of its neighbourhood. Again, in Indo-European etymology this phonetic root also means "passage": the throat is a tube, a tunnel, a transition. On the basis of this connotation the throat also reflects the uterus, or the dynamics of what has been swallowed up and can be vomited forth again (Kristeva 1998; Schneider Adams 1976; Veith 1965). In this respect it is most telling that the Hebrew word *nepesh*, a word with a wide semantic range that is often translated as "soul," initially denoted "throat," the physical location of the life breath. To cut the throat of a victim is fundamentally to cut them off from life (Shaw 1996). The exhibitionism of the *Johannesschüssel* concerns thus the opening of all possible openings, with the tube of the throat being the most obsessive opening of all. With this G-R-G phantasm the *Johannesschüssel* opens the breach with life itself, the connecting tunnel that is now cut off.

The connection between throat, John, solstice, and silence is in fact already anchored in a passage from the first chapter of Luke (1:5-45). When the angel announces to the aged Zechariah that he shall have a child, the old man can scarcely believe his ears, and he becomes mute instead. Indeed, Zechariah will only regain his voice at the moment he writes his son's name on a tablet. The voice of Zechariah is given through the name of his son, "the voice" of the new prophet Elijah. Jacobus de Voragine also says Zechariah's losing his voice was a fitting analogy, for the voice was born and allowed the (old) law to remain silent (Ryan and Duffy 1993, 1:329). Silence is truth and is recommended to the seekers of that truth (Kamper and Wulf 1992, 325ff.). When Paul the Deacon, a monk of Monte Cassino, lost his singing voice, he appealed to St John and begged him to give his voice back, as Zechariah was given his (Gaignebet 1986, 356). So it came to pass, and he sang even more beautifully than before. By way of thanks, he wrote the hymn that has been sung in churches on 24 June ever since, and is known today as the origin of Guido of Arezzo's technique of solmization: "UT queant laxis REsonare fibris, MIra gestorum FAmuli tuorum, SOLve polluti LAbii reatum, Sancte Johannes" (So that your servants can sing with free voices the wonders of your deeds, erase sin from their impure lips, Saint John).

The sacral silence is attributed in several cultures to the divine (Prado-Vilar 2013). It is the individual silence of concentration, interiority, and meditation. But there is also another silence. It is a silence modelled after the cosmos, beyond the Pythagorean order of music and the heavenly bodies. Nature astonishes us with such powerful silences in two ways: the silence of zenith and the silence of solstice (Gaignebet 1986, 356).

In archaic Mediterranean culture the moment at which the sun passes the meridian at its zenith is a mystery (De Fraine 1959). Midday is the anxious moment of transition, of the motionless hour, when everything is enveloped in a net of light and astonishing quiet (Chevalier and Gheerbaert 1996, 358). In the landscape all is quiet, because nature has been struck dumb. The silence acquires the thickness of a holy place; the silence becomes a frightening emotional space (*Gefühlsraum*; Schmitz 1981, 264-76). The second silence of the solstice is the "gorgonian" silence, intangibly terrifying but absolutely necessary in order to allow the greatest and most dangerous mysteries: to tilt, to clear the way for the sun, the portal, the transit. The solstice goes through the cosmic "throat" which needs mediation by silence: the anguish (*angoisse*; Gaignebet 1986, 363). This silence is not so much a frightening emotional space, but more of a pause, an interval: the cosmic standstill (Macho 1993).

These reflections become surprisingly concrete in light of the solstice celebrations on St John's day. In Jumièges, the brotherhood of St John, in fact a brotherhood of masons, celebrated their patron on 23 and 24 June (Gaignebet 1986, 363ff.). The chairman was dressed as a wild man in a suit of green leaves and herbs ("le loup vert"). On 23 June processions were held and before midnight a dinner was held during which complete silence was maintained. At the stroke of midnight, the commencement of 24 June, the hymn *Ut queant laxis* was sung. Afterward the participants were permitted to speak freely. The oral mastery of nature also implied the interval of sound and silence.

If we link this back to the multi-sensorial response of the *Johannesschüssel* and its "embodiment of the acoustic system of knowledge" (Baert 2015, 150) we now understand that this system of knowledge also implies silence. The interval that possesses the secret of allowing something to pass—the tube, the transit, the throat, the uterus—makes use of cosmic silence in the fraction of a second: just before the turn. The *Johannesschüssel* seeks the vortex of all the senses, but at the end it brings us to a vanishing point, an interval, a pause: silence indeed.

ADDITIONAL REFERENCES: Baert 2012; Baert 2015; Baert and Rochmes 2017; Brotzman 1988; De Labriolle 1934; De Souzenelle 1991; Didi-Huberman 2000; Ernst 1989; Kilgour 1991; Lupieri 1988; Merrifield 1987; Onians 1951; Pape 1991; Pillinger 2012; Rousseau 2005; Sidgwick 2012.

2. Virgin and Child with Angels

M. Jennifer Bloxam

Anon., northern Netherlands, ca. 1470-1500
Ivory, 13.5 (height) x 8.7 (base width) cm
Inscribed: o dulciz maria
Victoria and Albert Museum, London
Photo © Victoria and Albert Museum, London

O *dulciz Maria—O sweet Mary*! The unknown sculptor of this small ivory relief, carved in the late fifteenth century in the northern Netherlands, inscribed these words in the large book held open by one of the two angels at her feet. Shown upside down and backwards, they are directed not to the viewer but to the angels, whose open mouths confirm their sonic realization. It is not, however, simply the spoken word that carries this fond acclamation to Mary's prominently exposed ear—it is music. Meticulously chiseled note heads above the text evoke a fragment of melody; the celestial lutenist's fingers are frozen mid-performance.

While these angels conjure the sound of music, their large, carefully rendered hands, with long and distinctly articulated fingers, also express the tactile quality common to Virgin and Child ivories. Produced in increasing numbers from the thirteenth through the fifteenth centuries, these luxury objects emphasise virginal maternal flesh in contact with the incarnate flesh of Christ (Sand 2014). Here, the Virgin delicately proffers her breast, a slender thumb and forefinger supporting its milk-heavy weight; her gaze is inward, contemplative. Her other hand grasps the leg of the naked Christ Child, half standing on her hip. He rests his arm on her bosom, but shows no interest in nursing; rather, he looks directly at us, inviting us to join their milk-scented embrace and taste her life-giving sweetness.

O dulciz Maria! Thus the snippet of angelic song that accompanies this image helps activate the viewer's sense of taste and smell as well as her hearing and touch. The sensuous nature of the sculpture is inherent even in the rare and exotic material from which it was crafted. Ivory was a favorite medium for images of the Virgin mother; prized for its pure, creamy white luminosity, it embodied her supreme status as unsullied nurturer of Christ and his church (Sand 2014).

A strong theological current reaching from Clement of Alexandria to Julian of Norwich and beyond understood Mary's breast milk as a Eucharistic metaphor: as a mother provides a child nourishment from her own body, without which it would die, so Christ feeds the faithful with his own flesh and blood in the Eucharist (Berger 2011, 72-88). This baby Jesus, by encouraging us to seek nourishment from the Virgin, actively affirms Mary's intercessory power, most palpably captured in her role as the nursing mother of God, *Virgo lactans*.

The iconographic topos of the nursing mother has ancient roots—the Egyptian mother-goddess Isis, for example, was often depicted breastfeeding her son Horus (Rubin 2009b, 40-42). In the Christian West, the bared female breast long symbolised nourishment and loving care, associations gradually eroded over the course of the Renaissance through its complex transformation into an eroticised and medicalised object (Miles 2008). Nevertheless, the Virgin's milk remained for Catholics the most potent symbol of the mystery of the incarnate God (Warner 1976, 192-200), and consequently droplets of her milk were by far the most numerous of Marian relics, invested with curative and even salvific powers. Stories of miraculous visions were associated with the prayerful contemplation of *Virgo lactans* images (Olson 2014, 155-56), none more widespread or long lasting than that concerning St Bernard of Clairvaux, the Cistercian abbot whose passionate homilies about Christ's mother helped fuel the burgeoning Marian devotion in the ensuing centuries.

The legend is rooted in twelfth-century miracle stories concerning a devout and ailing prelate to whom Mary appears, bares her breast, and bestows three healing drops of milk on his lips. Bernard is first identified as the recipient of this apparition in an early thirteenth-century Cistercian exemplum collection (McGuire 1991, 189-204), and certain striking details relayed in the Bernardine versions in the following centuries reveal much about the dynamic and interactive nature of Marian imagery, the intercessory power attributed to the Virgin's milk, and the importance of music in the multi-sensory matrix of late medieval and Renaissance Marian devotion.

According to the legend, Bernard was kneeling before a statue of the Virgin and Child, praying the *Ave maris stella*, a much-loved hymn beseeching Mary's intercession. At the phrase "Monstra te esse matrem" (Show yourself to be a mother), the carved figure came to life and sprinkled three drops of milk into his mouth. Northern representations of the *lactatio Bernardis* from the decades around 1500 often include the words of this vision-inducing phrase, usually within a speech banderole issuing from his mouth (France 2007, 218-26; fig. 2.1).

Figure 2.1 Jean Pichore, *Lactation of St. Bernard*, early sixteenth century. Oxford, Bodleian Library, MS Douce 264, fol. 38v. Photo © Bodleian Libraries, University of Oxford.

Many Catholics knew the words of the *Ave maris stella* hymn by heart; they were inextricably associated with the melody sung at Marian Vespers throughout the year. Because hymns are strophic in design, the phrase "Monstra te esse matrem," which opens the fourth verse of *Ave maris stella*, was always sung to the familiar opening phrase of the hymn melody. Thus a reader, upon seeing these words in a book or within an image, would be invited to recall the well-known tune. A spiritual encounter with Mary, the story suggests, could be achieved in concentrated prayer facilitated by texts internalised through music and assisted by intense focus on her image.

A viewer contemplating this *Virgo lactans* ivory would have had their musical memory similarly ignited by the text phrase "O dulciz Maria": this is the final acclamation of the beloved and oft-sung antiphon *Salve regina*. Its lengthy text identifies Mary as Queen, Advocate, and Mother of God, and thrice extols her mercy in each role. Although the antiphon's melody is long and ornate, the final "O dulcis Maria" phrase could not fail to impress itself in the singer's or listener's mind, as it recapitulates the memorable initial gesture of the plainsong, sung twice in the opening couplet but not heard again until its return at the opening of the final phrase. What is more, both the opening and closing text phrases extol the sweetness of the Virgin, and the melismas unfolded in the closing acclamation recall those sung at the outset (ex. 2.1).

Example 2.1: Opening couplet and final phrase of *Salve regina* chant compared, from the early sixteenth-century printed antiphoner for the rite of Cambrai Cathedral (Cambrai, Bibliothèque municipale, Impr. XVI C 4, fols. 227v-228r).

The Cistercian order, whose special reverence for the Blessed Virgin was exemplified in Bernard of Clairvaux, fostered and may even have originated the *Salve regina*: it first appears in a mid-twelfth-century Cistercian antiphoner, and the order instituted its use in daily processions after 1218 (Ingram and Falconer 2001). By the late fifteenth century, when this small ivory was made, the plainsong was so widely known and loved that it had become the focal point of music-filled evening assemblies known as *Salve* services. Although popular throughout Europe (Ingram 1973, 31-49), these extra-liturgical devotions were especially brilliant in the Low Countries due to the enthusiastic patronage of large and wealthy lay Marian confraternities in major mercantile centres such as Antwerp and 's-Hertogenbosch (Forney 1987; Roelvink 2002).

In addition to polyphonic settings of the *Salve regina* antiphon, the *Salve* service (also known as *lof*, the Dutch word for "praise" in the Low Countries) featured bell-ringing, organ-playing, additional Marian plainsong and polyphony, as well as prayers offered by a cleric. Held on a weekly or even daily basis, they took place in church, in dedicated side chapels maintained by confraternities that also financed the installation and upkeep of the organ and paid the wages of the organist, choirmaster, and choirmen and boys. A Marian altarpiece or statue usually provided the focal point before which prayers said and sung were tendered, and miraculous powers were often attributed to these images. Although this *Virgo lactans* ivory is too small to have presided over a confraternity chapel (it probably adorned a domestic space or small private chapel as part of a little devotional panel or altarpiece), its direct reference to the *Salve regina* seems designed to spark viewers' memories of larger communal experiences of liturgy and *lof*.

As the production of Marian images surged over the course of the fifteenth century, so too did the creation of polyphonic settings of the *Salve regina* destined primarily for *Salve* services. A trove of 29 such settings, prepared by the workshop of the music scribe Petrus Alamire in the environs of Brussels during the 1520s, is preserved in a manuscript now in Munich (James 2014). Dedicated exclusively to *Salve regina* settings by Dutch, Flemish, and French composers, this unique collection captures the array of stylistic and formal approaches to the text cultivated in the very time and place that gave birth to this *Virgo lactans*. Particularly noteworthy are nine settings that incorporate the tunes of Dutch or French love songs as cantus firmi, signaling the complex interplay of worldly and spiritual desire so often evident in music composed to celebrate the Blessed Virgin during this period (Rothenberg 2011).

The profound influence of Marian veneration on communal devotion and personal piety, as well as musical and visual cultural practices, is reflected in the life and works of the most renowned composer of the Renaissance, Josquin des Prez, whose five-voice *Salve regina* setting (NJE 25.5) is given pride of place in the Munich manuscript. Josquin clearly attached great value to the *Salve* service: his will provided an endowment to ensure that this communal devotion could take place every Saturday and at all vigils of Marian feasts in his local church of Notre-Dame in Condé-sur-Escaut. He also understood the spiritual efficacy of prayers lifted in song before an image of Christ's mother: he left money for his motet *Pater noster* (whose second part sets another cherished Marian antiphon, *Ave Maria gratia plena*), to be sung in all general processions before the statue of the Virgin displayed in the wall of his house in Condé (Fallows 2009, 344-46).

Josquin's much-admired five-voice *Salve regina* stands at the apex of the genre recalled by the "O dulciz Maria" phrase for those who prayed before this small ivory. While characteristic of motet-like settings in some ways (such as its tripartite division of the text and paraphrase of the chant melody concentrated in the superius), its underlying structure is unique (Judd 1992; Milsom 2000, 438-77). Seizing on the distinctive opening four-note "Salve" motive, Josquin creates an ostinato spine in an inner voice which consists of alternating statements of this motive on G and D, each preceded by three bars of rest. He thus crafts a repeating motto unit comprising 7+7 bars sounded 12 times over the course of the piece (ex. 2.2). Beyond the likely symbolic choice of these numbers (seven being the number of Mary's Joys and Sorrows, and 12 the number of stars in the crown of the woman described in Revelations 1:12 [Elders 1994, 151-84]), the sounding effect is mantric, akin to the trance-like iteration of the "Hail Mary" while praying the rosary. Indeed, two early sources introduce the ostinato with a verbal canon from Matthew 10:22, "He that shall persevere unto the end, he shall be saved."

Example 2.2: Motto from Josquin's *Salve regina* (NJE 25.5).

Most affective are the final 12 measures of this setting, devoted to the "O dulcis Maria" phrase. The final statement of the motto unit emerges at the top of the texture as this phrase begins, coming out of its submerged trance to highlight the correspondence between the memorable opening of the first couplet and this closing phrase of the plainsong. The adjective "dulcis" is then heard nine times and Mary's name 11 times in the closing 12 bars, the last imploring call set to one of Josquin's favorite and most poignant gestures, the falling third (ex. 2.3).

Example 2.3: End of Josquin's *Salve regina* (NJE 25.5), mm. 163-177.

The nursing Virgin is seldom explicitly invoked in music, but one intriguing example appears among the many Marian motets by Josquin. A brief, four-voice setting of the *Ave Maria gratia plena* antiphon (NJE 23.4) closes with a surprising appended homage to Mary's breasts ("And blessed be your holy breasts which nursed the king of kings, our lord God") that is certainly not part of the angel Gabriel's salutation. The protracted imitation of a curvaceous motive on the phrase "beata ubera tua" even prompted one writer to suggest that Josquin here aimed to paint the Virgin's breasts in sound (Kirkendale 1984, 84-90; ex. 2.4)! Whatever Josquin's intentions, this little gem would have been perfectly suited for performance before a *Virgo lactans* image, perhaps one posed to listen as attentively as does our small ivory Virgin to the inaudible song offered by angels at her feet.

ABBREVIATIONS: NJE - New Josquin Edition.

ADDITIONAL REFERENCES: Robertson 2015; Sperling 2018; Williamson and Davies 2014, 1: 68-69.

ACKNOWLEDGEMENTS: I acknowledge with gratitude the kind assistance of Michaela Zöschg, the Curator of Medieval Art for the Sculpture, Metalwork, Ceramics and Glass Department at the Victoria and Albert Museum in London, who kindly photographed details of the ivory Virgin and Child with angels that allowed me to better understand and appreciate the object.

Example 2.4: Josquin's *Ave Maria* (NJE 23.4), mm. 45-53.

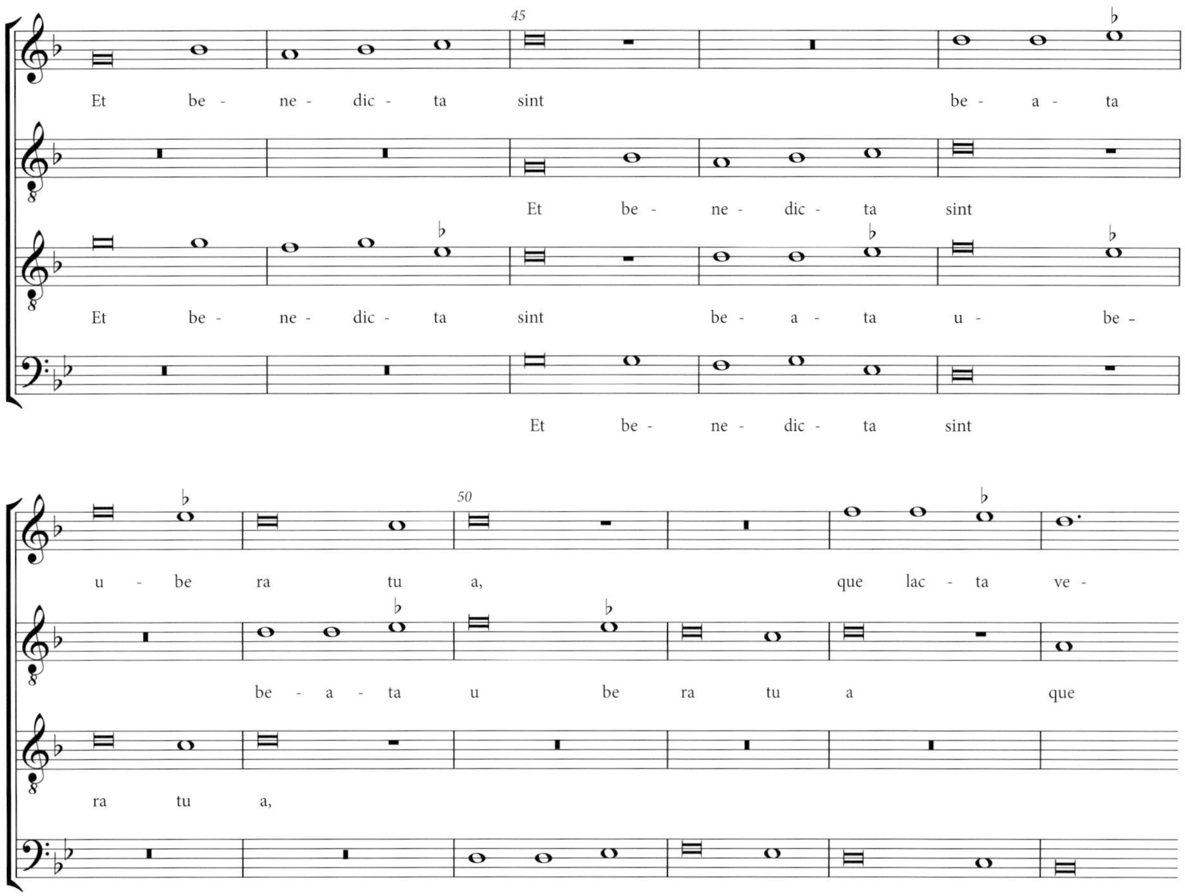

GEMMA
O DECUS OSPETIES OLUX OSTELLA SUPREMI
ETERIS EXAUDI MISERO FAMULO DEPRECANTES
DOMINICUS DOMINI MATREM TE PINXIT ET ORAT MCCCCXXXIII

3. Madonna of Humility

Beth Williamson

Domenico di Bartolo, Siena, 1433
Tempera on wood, 93 x 60 cm
Inscribed:
AVE STELLA MARIS, GEMMAQUE PRETIOSA
O DECUS O SPETIES O LUX O STELLA SUPREMI ETERIS EXAUDI MISEROS FAMULOSQUE PRECANTES
DOMENICUS DOMINI MATREM TE PINXIT ET ORAT. MCCCXXXIII
Adoramus te xp̄e
Pinacoteca Nazionale, Siena
Photo © 2021 Photo Scala, Florence / courtesy of the Ministero Beni e Att. Culturali e del Turismo

Domenico di Bartolo's 1433 painting of the Madonna and Child, now in the Pinacoteca Nazionale in Siena, is an object that offers forth Renaissance music in a visual context. It is not primarily, or obviously, a musical artefact, in the sense that it is not a musical instrument, nor a music manuscript, nor even an instance of visual culture in which music making is the primary iconographical subject. Nonetheless it gives us a variety of ways of thinking about sound, speech, and song, and about vocalising, playing, visualizing, and imagining music in a devotional context in Siena in the early fifteenth century.

The painting depicts the Virgin Mary, surrounded by angels, and seated on the ground, following the composition known as the Madonna of Humility (Williamson 2009). There are several visible indications of angelic music within this painting. Two angels play musical instruments—the one on the far left plays a viella, and the one on the far right plays a portative organ. The angel with the organ appears to look outwards at the viewer of the painting. He is the only figure to do so. The angel on the other side, though his face and his eyes are turned in the direction of the Virgin, does not appear to gaze at her. The small amount of visible white beneath the irises of his eyes seems to show that he directs his eyes upwards, as though trying to recall something, perhaps the music he is playing. And above him, though not obvious at first, is a snippet of music, incised against the painting's gold background, as if it were emerging from his memory.

The painting also suggests what the text that goes with that music might be. The two angels that peer over the Virgin's shoulder are singing. Three words of an inscription, words that must be those of the song that they are singing (*Adoramus te Christe*), can just be seen rising vertically from the conjunction of their brows into the air (fig. 3.1). (The abbreviation used for "Christe" in this inscription is a contraction, commonly used in the late Middle Ages, that combines Greek and Latin: Latin graphic approximations of chi and rho, the first two letters of Christ's name in Greek, combined with the last letter of the Latin "Christe," the vocative case of "Christus," used in a direct address.) *Adoramus te Christe* is the opening of a text known in Siena since the early thirteenth century, which was associated with the liturgy for Good Friday. The words began a Common Antiphon used in the service of the Adoration of the Cross: "Adoramus te, Christe, et benedicimus tibi: quia per sanctam crucem tuam redemisti mundum" (We adore you, O Christ, and we bless you, because you redeem the world by your cross). It had been suggested in the 1990s that the notation on the gold background is reminiscent of the work of the pre-eminent Franco-Flemish composer Guillaume Du Fay who was working in Italy during the 1420s and 1430s (Damiani 1992). But more recent research compares this music with a different repertoire (Dickey 2008).

Figure 3.1: Domenico di Bartolo, *Madonna of Humility* (detail), 1433. Paint on panel, 93 × 60 cm. Siena, Pinacoteca Nazionale. Photo © 2021 Photo Scala, Florence / courtesy of the Ministero Beni e Att. Culturali e del Turismo.

The notation has been transcribed (and completed) by Timothy J. Dickey (ex. 3.1). Dickey has suggested that the melody represents a Sienese *lauda*—a religious song, though originally influenced by secular musical forms. These were commonly sung in praise of the Virgin Mary and other holy patrons by Italian confraternities, lay brotherhoods devoted to religious devotional activity. This painting might well have been owned by such a confraternity, possibly the Company of SS Girolamo e Francesco which met in the crypt of the

Example 3.1: *Adoramus te Christe*, transcribed by Timothy J. Dickey (Dickey 2008).

hospital of Santa Maria della Scala, opposite the cathedral in Siena (Dickey 2008). Confraternities are known to have commissioned panel paintings that were used in their devotions, sometimes carried in processions, and sometimes placed in a chapel. It is sometimes assumed that all such panel paintings would have been placed on altars. However, this is not the case. We need to be careful, therefore, about assuming that any painting commissioned by a confraternity would necessarily have been designed to sit upon an altar. Although Domenico di Bartolo's panel is often described as an "altarpiece," there is no evidence that it was necessarily used in this way. It might have been placed on an altar, but it might also have been fixed elsewhere in a confraternity chapel, such as on a wall.

The musical notation in the painting does not match up with any known version of the *Adoramus te*, but it could represent a hitherto unknown Sienese *lauda* on this text (Dickey 2008). Or it might be intended to evoke a plausible *lauda*, without necessarily referring to a known piece of music. Alternatively, it might be that a contemporary viewer would have read the music in a different way entirely, understanding the musical notation to be offering up the idea of an instrumental accompaniment to the angelic singing, rather than indicating the melody that they themselves sing. The musical praises offered to Christ—depicted in the form of the notation and by the words *Adoramus te xp̄e*—are complemented by other praises offered to the Virgin. Several scrolls, or banderoles, appear within the painting, and offer praises and addresses to the Virgin Mary (Williamson 2013; Ladis 2001). These text scrolls are within the pictorial space, but are oriented to face the viewer outside the picture plane. While the angel second from the left looks up and appears to notice the upper scroll (which addresses the Virgin as the "Star of the Sea"), the words are nonetheless most easily readable by the viewer outside the picture. Similarly, the scroll beneath the Virgin, which pleads for her help and intercession ("Oh Ornament, Oh Splendour, Oh Light, Oh Star of the Highest Ethereal Realm, Listen to the prayers of your miserable servants") is clearly arranged to facilitate reading by the human viewer outside the picture plane.

These textual scrolls draw the viewer in, and suggest for him or her a variety of types of engagement with the Virgin, including both praise and supplication. The viewer is encouraged to speak these prayers, perhaps aloud, or possibly inwardly, in front of the picture. These prayers might be read on multiple occasions by a devotee who returned to this painting again and again, perhaps as a member of a confraternity which used it as the centre of its devotion. They provide cues to the sort of prayerful mindset that such a devotee would be expected to adopt in the presence of an image of this sort. These prayers might also have been communally spoken by members of the confraternity meeting together in front of this painting. The third painted text, also on the lower scroll, but in smaller letters than the "Oh Ornament, Oh Splendour, Oh Light…" prayer, works in a different and particular way. It voices a dedicatory prayer offered by the painter himself: "Mother of God, Domenico painted and prays to you." This is not a prompt to prayer offered to undefined, multiple viewers, but a signature, documenting the production of the painting itself as an act of devotion, and recording a prayer offered once, on a particular occasion by a specific person—the artist himself—at the completion of the painting in 1433.

The music—in the form of the notation and the words of the *Adoramus te Christe*—works in similarly varied ways. An individual could audibly voice the music represented, or might just read it, imagining it only inwardly. For a casual, non-musically literate, viewer the notation might simply denote the *idea* of music. For a member of a confraternity, the notation might actually represent a real melody that they themselves might habitually offer during some of their confraternal devotional activities. So the music and the texts can work in similar ways, encouraging engagement and prayer, both communal and individual, both voiced and silent. However, the music is less obvious. The notation is incised against the gold background, and the words are difficult to discern, running vertically, against the angels' hair. Where the texts on the scrolls are clearly offered to the viewer outside the picture to read, and to voice, the music remains within the picture world, and to some extent "belongs" more to the angels than the human viewers. The devotee in front of the painting can certainly choose to join the angels' Christological praise. He or she can sing, or inwardly recall, the music depicted on the surface of the painting, or perhaps just be prompted to imagine "music" more generally. But this is not the only way that the notation works here. The angels in the painting are singing not just generalised angelic music, but a specific piece. The members of the confraternity may have gathered together in front of this painting from time to time to sing, joining with the angels in voicing musical praises. In this sense, during confraternity devotions the angels and the human devotees make music together. However, the music also suggests the everlasting timelessness of the angelic praises. The visible notation on the painting serves to extend the music. It suggests that the musical praises offered by the confraternity during their services do not stop when the human viewers disperse, and walk away from the painting, because the angels continue to sing, on their behalf.

The painting was steeped in the music that the human devotees offered in front of and around it, just as it might have been enveloped in the smoke of incense and candles. In addition, though, this painting itself also generated music. This could happen both intermittently, and audibly, when the painting encouraged human beings to sing the musical praises that they could discern on its painted surface, and also constantly, and silently, as it depicted a rendering of angelic music being offered eternally in the company of the Virgin and Christ in heaven.

Additional references: Dickey 2008; Ladis 2001; Williamson 2013.

4. Virgin Annunciate

Marina Nordera

Anon., Tuscany, 15th century
Polychromed terracotta, 163 x 53 cm
Museo Stefano Bardini, Florence
Photo © Ines Rodarte

This artefact is an accomplished sculptural example of an Annunciation, an iconographical theme cherished by the visual artists of the Quattrocento. It belongs to a sculptural genre and a figurative tradition of life-size devotional figures, realised in polychrome terracotta or wood during the fifteenth century by Tuscan artists, such as Jacopo della Quercia in Siena and Matteo Civitali in Lucca. Some were installed in a niche, others—especially the wooden examples—could have been dressed in fabrics and transported in processions. In some cases the back could be left rough as it would not be visible, and the upper limbs could be articulated in order to carry props or to be positioned in different gestures. The Virgin could be accompanied by the figure of the announcing angel, both being conceived as a sculptural group representing the whole Annunciation scene (Brunini et al. 2008; Caglioti 2004; Seidel 2010).

The author of the Virgin Annunciate (without angel, so far as we know) of the Bardini Museum is still unidentified, its provenance and history unknown. And yet the authenticity of this statue has never been questioned by scholars—despite the fact that between the nineteenth and twentieth centuries, at the time in which the Florentine restorer, collector, connoisseur, and art dealer Stefano Bardini acquired this artefact for his collection, the practice of reproducing or recreating works of arts in Renaissance style was flourishing at commercial scale (Caglioti 2017).

The moulded clothing of this Virgin Annunciate, perfectly three-dimensional, reproduces an elegant tunic, decorated with purple floral patterns symbolising fertility. She is bareheaded, with gathered hair, as appropriate for a maiden. Her corporeal attitude tells her whole story in a brief moment: she holds a closed book in her left hand because she was reading a prayer before being suddenly moved, in the sense of being affected but also put in motion, by the angel's announcement. At the same time, as the gesture of her right hand and her facial expression show, her attention turns within herself as she becomes aware of having already conceived the son of God in her womb.

This figure's balanced organization of mass and weight activates the representation of movement through realistic kinetic parameters. The main support on the left foot and the protrusion of the right knee, just bent, confer their dynamics to the drapery of the lower part of the dress. The asymmetry of the shoulder plane and the slight inclination of the head suggest an attentive attitude, which is activated by listening and by perception of space through the skin, rather than by sight. The colouring and the accuracy of the modelling accentuate the tactility of the surface, intensify the realism and, in reflecting the light, give it a surprising effect of presence. The eyelids, slightly lowered in an introspective glance, draw attention to the intensity of the relationship between the face and the right hand placed on the breastbone. The grave concentration of the whole figure activates the surrounding space, as it were inhabited by an auditory aura. Just like some other sculptural portraits of women of the same period, this female figure occupies a liminal position as both image and body, together amounting to an assertion of presence (Kohl 2010).

The function of this symbolically dense devotional object, intended to be exposed to a large audience, was primarily performative (Stevenson 2010a). The effect of presence that it releases places it at the crossroads of different discourses about body, movement, and gesture in Quattrocento culture and, in a way that has rarely been remarked upon in devotional objects, it makes visible the representation of embodiment and perception as it was conceived in dance manuals and conduct books of the time (Nordera 2017). Its corporeal attitude effectively offers a synthesis of contemporary notions concerning bodily awareness and perception, the listening attitude and the listener's relation to music, as well as of feminine behaviour.

In the first part of his manual *On the Practice or Art of Dancing* (Sparti 1993), while explaining the fundamental principles of dance practice to an implied male reader, the Italian dancing master Guglielmo Ebreo da Pesaro describes an exercise in which the dancer performs a saltarello (a short sequence of steps and jumps) in conflict with a musician who, in playing, tries to bring the dancer back to the beat. Guglielmo invites the dancer who experiments with this exercise to be "freely master of his *persona* and of his foot." In emancipating himself from music, dominating himself (his "persona") and controlling changes to his weight support (his foot), the dancer develops a mastery of bodily movement that makes him free to act and aware of his gestures in relation to music.

As he does in this passage, when he needs to indicate the body Guglielmo always uses the term *persona*. Etymologically, this Latin term has been interpreted as meaning "that sounds through" (*per-sono*), in its earliest use indicating the theatrical mask amplifying the voice of the actor. The term then entered into the Roman legal lexicon, assuming a metaphorical meaning to suggest an individual who plays a specific role in expressing his opinion. Referring to the practice of artful public oratory, in Cicero's writings the *persona* is embodied in a concrete and singular individual who can temporarily play the part of others without losing his own individuality; in this sense it assumes performative values. Renaissance Humanism, reaffirming the centrality of this concept in Christian thought as a primary and indivisible substance, theorises the *persona*—constituted of body, spirit and reason—as free and responsible, even in its dependence upon the divine. Read in the context of this intellectual history, the occurrences of the term *persona* in *On the Practice or Art of Dancing* define the body not only as a generic biological entity, but also as a corporeity and awareness in action. Therefore, the term *persona* does not refer to a body given by nature or by God, but to an embodied subjectivity, having a specific weight distribution in posture, a recognizable gait in carriage, and a kinetic style in gestures (Bolens 2012).

Using the term *persona*, Guglielmo underlines the fact that some aspects of bodily movement and gesture cannot be reduced to a simple biomechanical phenomenon. The dancer, collecting his thoughts and paying attention to the measured and concordant music, with his whole *persona* performs gestures and steps, which are the results of the bodily elaboration of complex proprioceptive and perceptive stimuli. In this way the term *persona* integrates the natural predisposition of bodily movement with technical acquisitions and cultural dispositions that identify the bodies and distinguish them in society in terms of age, gender, and status (Nordera 2017; Robichaud 2018).

The *Chapter on the Regulation of Women*, which concludes the theoretical part of Guglielmo's treatise, advises women to follow all the rules already provided for men, but with more modesty and discretion. Like a man, a woman should be able to understand measure and should be skilled in music, as well as attentive and able to remember it. She has also to be aware of the space around her. Her carriage must be dignified and stately, sweet and gentle, her movement humble and meek, her gestures light and shapely. Her gaze should not be haughty, nor roaming, but modestly turned towards the ground, eyes lowered, while the head should be carried upright, aligned with the body as required by nature. In dancing, she must be skilful, graceful, temperate, shrewd, suitable, human, while keeping her intellect always attentive to music and measure (Sparti 1993, 108-11).

These behavioural qualities describe the image of a discreet and contained femininity, a body without weight and enclosed in itself, moved by its inner virtues. These qualities correspond to consciously elaborated cultural and social norms as they are described in the treatise *On Wifely Duties* by the Venetian humanist Francesco Barbaro (Barbaro 2015). Written in Latin probably between 1415 and 1416 whilst the author was in Florence, and dedicated to Lorenzo di Giovanni de' Medici on the occasion of his marriage to Giulia Cavalcanti, this treatise was an immediate success among contemporary secular and ecclesiastical intellectuals. It later spread to numerous manuscript editions and was reprinted several times both in Latin and in the vernacular (Kravina 2018).

Barbaro's treatment of the theme of the choice of a wife and the education of children, largely depending on Plutarch, unfolds through arguments drawn from common morals. His attention to the female body, which is always the body not only of a woman but of a wife, is linked to the ethical value of the external signs of the soul, and is built around the concept of modesty. This quality, according to Barbaro, is a certain kind of shyness that comes from the manifestation of the desire of the female subject to be irrelevant. Modesty is a virtue concerning the soul that makes itself visible through the body. As such it has a specific value in terms of personal as well as relational ethics, in that it helps a woman in constructing a body image that allows her to be admired and respected by those around her. Modesty is revealed in gestures, words, clothing, in daily occupations, but especially in the gaze, which reflects even the most secret movements of the soul (Bochi 1961; Frick 1989; Knox 2000; Zarri 1996). Modesty is the result of bodily self-control carried out under the banner of gravity, slowness, immobility; in contrast, the attitudes to be avoided have to do with the qualities of speed, excessive movement, instability. This sort of sculptural remoteness must not, however, become an external sign of pride, but an indication of meekness, in accordance with the two meanings of this term: submission and civility.

Barbaro proposes to the good wife a specific method for improving the control of her body image, taken from the art of oratory and in particular from Demosthenes' habit of correcting everyday expressions and gestures in front of a mirror (Barbaro 1915, fols. 44-46). This invitation to think of oneself as a reflection is very significant in the process of constructing a self-image that proceeds from the outside to the inside, and exemplifies the theory according to which the soul is positively affected by discipline of the body. The woman must therefore learn to express her irrelevance through silence, as well as through precise and targeted gestures: the eyelids lowered and the composure of the limbs, avoiding any surprising movements and stifling laughter. For Barbaro, this capacity of improving self-control and self-management is also the precondition to women's participation in public life—albeit in the company of their husbands, of course.

The Virgin Annunciate as figured in this sculptural artefact represents the embodiment of behavioural norms concerning women's agency in public space in the fifteenth century, as they are formulated in Barbaro's treatise. Simultaneously, it is the central figure of the miracle of the incarnation, celebrating the crucial instant in which past, present, and future interpenetrate each other in order to write the seminal narrative of the history of Christianity. And finally, this exhibit offers some sensory hints about the perceptual context—visible, palpable, and audible—in which fifteenth-century bodies were immersed, not only in spaces for social dance but also in those designed for devotion and liturgy, where the performativity of the body acquired crucial symbolic and functional meanings.

ישראל בפרך

ונצעק

אל יי' אלהי אבותינו וישמע
יי' את קולנו וירא את ענינו
ואת עמלנו ואת לחצנו

ונצעק

5. The Prato *Haggadah*

Eleazar Gutwirth

New York, Jewish Theological Seminary, MS 9478
Spain, ca. 1350-1450(?)
Manuscript on vellum with tempera, gold and ink illuminations, 85 fols., 21 x 14 cm
Image: fol. 14r, detail. Photo courtesy of The Library of The Jewish Theological Seminary.

The hooded musician at the top left of the margin gazes pensively at a page of the *Haggadah*, the text normally read on the nights of the year in which the Passover Seder—sometimes described as the model of the Christian Easter—is celebrated, commemorating the Exodus from Egypt to the Promised Land. The instrumentalist is depicted in a fantastical form: the top half of the body is human, the bottom half animal. This striking representation is hardly improvised or accidental. Preparations for a Hebrew manuscript codex and its illuminations could take years—as is particularly visible in this, the Prato *Haggadah*, which was never finished. Thus, for example, we can see the original drawing, and the preparation of the parchment for gold leaf by applying an under-layer of *gessum*, or the preliminary employment of blue before other colors (Cohen 1992, 439-51).

Like other illuminated Hebrew codices, this one—whose last private owner belonged to the family of the Chief Rabbi of Rome, David Prato, hence its name—was meant to be enjoyed by Hispano Jewish families before the 1490s expulsions from Iberia. The dating of this codex changes frequently: it was once thought to be thirteenth-century, then ca. 1300, then 1330s, then 1330-45, or even ca. 1450 (Kenter 2014). Whichever dating we accept as the Prato *Haggadah*'s point of origin, once acquired, such Hebrew manuscripts were intended to be used by successive generations of the family (Gutwirth 2014). Families deserve mention in the context of this codex not only because of this, and because family celebration is the subject of illustrations in manuscripts of Iberian *Haggadot*, but also because halakhic or juridical authorities, whether ancient (Talmud, before 500 CE) medieval (Maimonides, 1170-80) or early modern (the sixteenth-century *Table* by the famous codifier Joseph Caro), explicitly (and in detail) encouraged parents to keep their children attentive during the celebration.

This insight might offer us a way to understand the more whimsical aspects of the art here. One of these aspects is that the musician seems to be riding—not side-saddle but astride—a snail. The snail, of course, was one of the creatures forbidden by Jewish dietary laws. Yet it was not a complete stranger to Jewish texts, even if medieval exegetes such as Rashi or Ibn Ezra had doubts about the identity of the mollusk alluded to in Psalm 58:9 (their legitimate doubts would not have been suspected by readers of the King James Version's translation: "Let them be as a snail which melteth and passeth away"). Certainly the snail was an extremely common motif in Christian manuscript illuminations in the Middle Ages and the Renaissance. Famously, Lillian M.C. Randall found over 70 snail images in 29 manuscripts produced in Northern France at the end of the thirteenth century (Randall 1962). But this trend was not limited to France, nor to Christian manuscripts. Snails appear also in late medieval illuminated *Haggadot* from Spain—for example, a late medieval Spanish *Haggadah* (Manchester, John Rylands Library, MS Heb. 6, fol. 29b) presents a grotesque at the *Dayenu*, a song for the Passover Seder: half long-bearded man, half snail. Other media also make their contributions to the molluscan iconography: wooden carvings on Spanish cathedral choir misericords and armrests offer further examples.

If we observe the silhouette and the compositional play of vertical and horizontal, upper and lower—and especially the hooves, we might compare our fantastical motif with that of the musician as centaur or faun. The centaur/faun is a central element of Greco-Roman or pagan mythology, where it is understood as representing unbridled lust, chaos and barbarism, as in the numerous tales of centaurs violating women. The allusion to the centaur in this Jewish context is far less shocking than it sounds: centaurs appear in the decorations of late-antique synagogues such as Chorazin, Dura, or Sephoris, where we find the mosaic of Sagittarius. This association with the Zodiac was still the main resonance in the fifteenth century, as demonstrated in Alfonso de Palencia's *Universal vocabulario en latín y en romance* published in Seville in 1490 (Palencia 1490, "centauro"). Astronomy and astrology were intensely cultivated by the Jews in medieval Spain, and illuminated Hebrew manuscripts followed convention in representing Sagittarius as a centaur. These approaches (both literary and visual) would continue in the Renaissance (Gutwirth 2015, 157-82).

In our Prato *Haggadah*, in contrast, we see the once-lustful centaur relocated in a book pertaining to a family context, a book directly linked to the ceremonial family meal, a foil for fulfilling a sacred or religious duty. It is, perhaps, a particularly apt image for the Passover Seder for other reasons which fourteenth- or fifteenth-century Jews—the same people who commissioned and for generations used this particular kind of book—would not have suspected. Indeed, in the 1950s, Sigmund Stein opened a new era of *Haggadah* studies when he drew attention to extensive, detailed analogies (including musical analogies) between the Seder and the pagan Hellenic or Hellenistic institution of the Symposium (of which Plato's is only the best known example). In this context, the Seder's music—and also other elements—could be seen as sacralized vestiges of a Hellenized age and place (Stein 1957). And yet, one also recalls the music of the Levites during the ceremony of the paschal lamb at the Temple of Jerusalem, as a possible Jewish precedent for the Seder's song and music. As in the case of the *epikomon* (final piece of matzah at the end of the Passover meal) the two traditions fused almost seamlessly in medieval and later practice.

To return to the musician on the top margin of fol. 14ʳ, he is a *gaitero*, a bagpipe-player, playing music *a lo divino* (a cultural category to be discussed later in the essay) which we cannot hear. The instrument belongs to the *gaita* family, which in the Iberian peninsula has variants in Aragon, Navarre and Galicia. The image in the Prato *Haggadah* is closer to what is known as an *odrecillo* (a small bagpipe): despite the predominant anti-realism, and as in other medieval illuminations, the artist took the trouble to make us see the holes on the *canutos* (pipes) and the long, uneven *puntero* (mouthpiece). The *gaitero*-centaur-faun holds the *odre* (bag) under his right arm, as seen in other contemporary Iberian visual representations of the *gaitero* both in illuminated manuscripts and sculptures, such as those that survive in Galicia and Portugal.

Recent work has underlined that in late medieval Spain ethnic, religious, or national identities (e.g. Arabic or French) were ascribed to the *gaita/odrecillo* and similar musical instruments, as seen in the writings of contemporary authors (Gutwirth 1998). Similar is the association of the *gaita* with the tavern. We find this in the fourteenth and fifteenth centuries, as for example in evidence from the 1490s in which the bagpipe is related to the tavern's *folía* (Maldonado 1935, 153). Conversely, in 1348, the *Poema de Alfonso Onceno* refers to the *gaita*'s subtlety, which, it says, pleases everyone (Alfonso XI 1991, 122).

A valuable source for discussing the associations and resonances of such musical instruments in the fifteenth century is the corpus of *Biblias romanceadas* (translations of the Bible into Ibero-Romance languages; Gutwirth 1988) preserved in fifteenth-century manuscripts such as Ajuda (Biblioteca de Ajuda, 52-XIII-1) or E3 (Real biblioteca del Monasterio de San Lorenzo de el Escorial, I.i.3). These are usually seen as works ultimately emanating from medieval Jewish communities in contact with the Hebrew language of the originals. It should be stressed that some translators, such as Rabbi Moses Arragel, avoided mention of the *gaita* when translating the Biblical Hebrew terms for musical instruments into the *romance*. They preferred to employ Ibero-Romance terms of Arabic etymology for such musical instruments (Gutwirth 2015b, 187-212). In contrast, Ajuda and E3 saw nothing incongruous in Laban the Aramean talking to the patriarch Jacob about *gaitas* in Genesis 31:27, or in writing that, at the coronation and anointment of King Solomon, the people were playing their *gaitas* (I Kings 1:40). In a sense, these sources could be seen as elevating the instrument of the tavern to a role in sacred scriptures.

In Spain, music *a lo divino* is part of a large cluster of Renaissance creative endeavors *a lo divino* in areas such as theatre, painting, religion, the lyric in poetry, mysticism, agriculture, and economics, all of which recast a secular phenomenon in a religious sphere. This process—despite well-known parallels such as *Kontrafaktur*—can be understood as characteristic of culture in the sixteenth and seventeenth centuries. Fifteenth-century precursors of particular note include the poets Fray Iñigo de Mendoza OFM and Alvarez Gato: the former was a royal courtier famous for his villancicos (lit. songs of the villagers) or Christmas carols, and both would have been perceived at that time and place as New Christians (*conversos*). This transition from medieval to Renaissance paradigms, this movement from low to high or from secular to sacred which we see in the vernacular lyric and music of the *conversos*, had a long history in other languages current in Hispano-Jewish communities. The same prosodic forms—such as those of the "dangerous," scandalous, or licentious *muwashshahat* (strophic poems), whose music was seen by Maimonides, for example, as detrimental to religion (Farmer 1933, 867-84; Seroussi 2002, 126-35)—were used for liturgical or sacred poetry.

Iberian Jewish authors contemporary with the *gaitero*, such as Profayt Duran and Salomon Alami, testify to the attraction evidently felt by synagogal congregations and their precentors to melodies from Christian erotic and other songs in fifteenth-century Spain. A liturgical poem or *piyyut* by Salomon Bonafed in the genre of *reshut* (the liturgical introductory poems sung by the precentor who begs "permission") is explicitly said to be based on a pre-existing song in the *romance*—that is, a non-sacral vernacular song/music. This phenomenon continues to be mentioned amongst the exiles from Spain (such as the musician and precentor Israel Nájera of Safed) in the Ottoman Empire in the sixteenth century and beyond (Gutwirth 2016; Gutwirth 2004). It is perhaps no coincidence that in such cultures of Iberian exiles as were present in the sixteenth-century Ottoman Empire, there flourished an analogous paradigm of elevation from the non-spiritual to the spiritual, founded in the specific, religious and mystical ideal of the need to "raise the fallen sparks" whose roots are already present in medieval Spain (Idel 2013, 196-240).

Unlike the comparable Sarajevo codex, the Prato *Haggadah*, due to the codicological contingencies of the mise en page, contains, in the text of one and the same page, two *Haggadah* references to The Scream ("And *we cried out* to the Lord, the God of our fathers, and the Lord heard *our voice* and saw our suffering, our labor and our oppression"; Deuteronomy 26:7). In the manuscript, both textual references are selected and presented by the artist in painted rectangular frames and are therefore very prominent on the page. These repeated references to sound or "voice" in this page of the *Haggadah* are complemented by the evocative illumination of the *gaitero* which accompanies them and whose varied meanings we have attempted to explore here.

TOR
CAN

LOS CANTORES DE LAS TA

yglecia enpedidos de taza

dotrina

los

6. The Musicians of the Holy Church, Exempt from Tax

Geoffrey Baker

El primer nueva corónica y buen gobierno (The First New Chronicle and Good Government)
Felipe Guaman Poma de Ayala, Peru, ca. 1615
Manuscript on paper, 1189 pp., 21.7 x 14.7 cm
Copenhagen, Det Kongelige Bibliotek, GKS 2232 4°
Image: Pen drawing, p. 666. Photo courtesy of Det Kongelige Bibliotek, Copenhagen.

Written in the first decade and a half of the seventeenth century by the indigenous Peruvian nobleman Felipe Guaman Poma de Ayala, *El primer nueva corónica y buen gobierno* is one of the most significant sources for colonial Andean history. Alongside nearly 800 pages of text, this chronicle includes 398 large drawings; among several of interest to music historians is *Los cantores de la santa iglesia impedidos de tasa* (*The Musicians of the Holy Church, Exempt from Tax*; Guaman Poma 1980, 680). It shows five church musicians, clearly identifiable as indigenous by their clothing and hairstyles, playing the *Salve Regina* on recorders. The combination of indigenous and European elements makes this drawing a potent image of the mixing of cultural worlds, and it illustrates key aspects of colonial music in Spanish America around 1600, including musical instruments and capacities, the centrality of indigenous musicians, and social and economic aspects of the music profession.

Some of the earliest interactions between native Andeans and Spanish missionaries in the sixteenth century involved musical performance. Visual and aural pomp were considered vital elements in convincing the local population of the superiority of the new faith. Drawing on the precedent of the missionary campaigns in Mexico, music was harnessed as an evangelical tool: an effective means of capturing the attention of native populations, bypassing the language barrier, and teaching doctrine in memorable form.

From then on, there were sustained efforts to train Andeans in the performance of European ecclesiastical music. By involving Andeans in religious rituals, priests sought to inspire greater devotion and commitment on the part of their charges. Numerous official decrees and recommendations relating to music were issued in the late sixteenth century. The Third Council of Lima, in 1583, encouraged the establishment of music ensembles and schools for singing and playing instruments in all native parish churches. The Franciscan Jerónimo de Oré, in his 1598 *Symbolo catholico indiano* (1992, fol. 56), recommended that in each Andean parish "there should be a school, with a master, and selected singers who are paid a sufficient salary, where the children may learn to recite the doctrine, and to read and write, sing, and play instruments."

As Guaman Poma's drawing illustrates, a corpus of indigenous musicians thus emerged and established itself in the newly created *doctrinas de indios*, or indigenous parishes. The head figure was the *maestro de capilla* or *maestro de coro* (chapel- or choir-master), whose duties, according to Guaman Poma (1980, 636), included leading the singers every morning, at the afternoon *Salve* (pictured), and at evening Vespers, as well as teaching music alongside basic literacy. The *maestro de capilla* was in charge of the *cantores* (musicians) of the parish, who conventionally numbered around four to six, though some churches were served by a dozen or more.

The *cantores* typically sang and doubled on wind instruments. Inventories refer to collections of recorders, curtals, shawms, cornetts, and sackbuts, including consorts of up to seven instruments. Churches often had an organ, in some cases two, and harps were commonplace. References to the purchase of written music and music stands, mirroring Guaman Poma's drawing, underline that these musicians were literate.

The presence of so many musical instruments in parishes suggests not only the employment of musicians but also the performance of polyphony. This was certainly the intention of the church authorities: Franciscans such as Jerónimo de Oré (1992, fol. 51) and Diego de Córdova Salinas (1957, 159) both exhorted and recorded the performance of polyphony with instruments in the *doctrinas* of their order. Juan Pérez Bocanegra, the priest of Andahuaylillas (a village near Cuzco), included in his *Ritual formulario* of 1631 the first piece of polyphony to be printed in the New World, the four-part *Hanacpachap*, with a text in the indigenous language of Quechua. Bocanegra spent more than 40 years in the Cuzco region teaching doctrine to the native population (Stevenson 1976; 1980. On music in Cuzco, see Baker 2008). He thus had a deep knowledge of the musical skills of Andean parish church musicians, for whom this piece was intended.

Guaman Poma painted a contradictory portrait of music and musicians in the colonial Andes; he perceived them to hold considerable power, both positive and negative. On the one hand, he wrote about fine polyphonic singers and instrumentalists who were also prime examples of good, loyal Andean Christians, worthy even of joining the priesthood

(1980, 764). He believed that daily performances by church musicians served to assuage God's wrath as manifested in the form of natural calamities (631). He concluded his chapter on the *maestro de coro* with the words: "If possible, there should be a school and Christianity and *policía* in every village, large or small, throughout the realm" (635). The notion that consolidating not only education but also the central colonial concept of *policía*—order, good government, Christianity, and civilization (Kagan 2000)—was a responsibility of the choirmaster illustrates the importance of this figure in the development of colonial Andean society and culture.

On the other hand, Guaman Poma felt that some musicians abused their position, writing that "the *cantores* of the church are very free in the absence of the fathers. They do not celebrate Vespers nor Matins nor None nor *Alba* [dawn Mass] nor the *Salve* nor do they bury the dead" (1980, 631). When musicians and other indigenous church assistants did lead church services in the absence of the priest, they sometimes had ulterior motives: "on Wednesdays and Fridays they perform the service at night with the aim of committing sins with the girls and single women" (626). He also took a dim view of the way that some musicians came to exercise authority over others, accusing them of behaving as though they were Inka nobles (857).

Pace De Oré, it appears that *cantores* were not generally paid in cash but rather in kind. They sometimes received a small bonus payment for participating in parish or confraternity ceremonies, for instance on the feast of a patron saint, but church records rarely show a salary. Rather, they were *impedidos de tasa*: exempt from tribute payments and labour levies. As such, they were not obliged to participate in the *mita* (forced labour system). The *mita* to the silver mines at Potosí was the most notorious, but the draft to the mines at Huancavelica and Cailloma was equally feared, as was the coca leaf *mita* in Paucartambo. Conditions in many of the region's textile mills were little better, and all these forms of labour left large numbers of Andeans dead or crippled by disease or injury.

The appeal of music to Andeans undoubtedly had much to do with the privileges that this path could bestow in the new society emerging after the Spanish conquest. Faced with the choice between fulfilling their community obligations in the choir or in the mines, textile mills, or haciendas, it is not hard to see why many Andeans might have opted for the former. Guaman Poma (1980, 736) claimed that indigenous leaders used community posts such as that of *cantor* as an officially sanctioned way of shielding their friends and allies from the *mita*. Exemption from tribute, meanwhile, would have spared musicians the wage labour to which many Andeans were driven in order to pay their taxes. *Impedidos de tasa* are thus three crucial words for understanding colonial music culture.

Church service offered protection from the greatest burdens and most oppressive aspects of the colonial system: not only forced labour and taxation, but also rapacious officials known as *corregidores*. Furthermore, in many rural areas the colonial enterprise rested largely on the Catholic Church, and the pursuit of music gave Andeans the opportunity to occupy a position in the ecclesiastical hierarchy and a role in religious ceremonies. Serving the church was considered an honour, and assistants derived social status from their position within the colonial system as intermediaries between the Andean and Spanish worlds.

It is perhaps unsurprising, then, that some *doctrinas* had larger musical forces than those stipulated by official recommendations. In some villages that were subject to the *mita*, we find 10 to 18 *cantores*. Colonial Peru thus reveals a distinctly decentralized musical culture, with a proliferation of permanent and self-sufficient ensembles, capable of singing and playing polyphony, on the urban periphery and in rural areas.

That said, some churches were too poor to offer much support for such musical activities. As a result, some priests contributed to the cost of music out of their own pockets. In other cases, it was local indigenous leaders and communities that paid for more expensive music servants such as *maestros de capilla* and organists, providing them with cash, food, animals, and/or land. In many ways, the two groups' objectives coincided, since a flourishing musical life benefited both the priests, who could take pride in the celebration of rituals in their churches (while impressing inspectors and boosting their chances of promotion), and the indigenous leaders, who could use the church musicians to enhance their prestige and reinforce their authority. It also benefited the musicians themselves, as already noted.

In this light, colonial music culture looks less like an instrument of domination or a cultural conquest than like the result of negotiations between Spanish authorities, native leaders, and indigenous communities. Indeed, the impressively rich musical life of indigenous parishes on the periphery of the Spanish empire reflected both colonial policies and the support that Andean communities gave to their musicians.

The abundance of music in these parishes was promoted and regulated by the highest religious and secular authorities. Peru's viceregal government repeatedly defended musicians' rights to exemptions from tribute and labour levies. That viceroys, bishops, and the Crown should have intervened over such matters is a clear indication that music retained its position at the core of Spanish policies towards Peru's indigenous inhabitants.

Spanish policy alone cannot, however, explain the strength of parish music. The cooperation and active participation of indigenous communities was essential to maintaining musical activities in their churches. The prevalence of non-salaried musicians in indigenous parishes might be seen as rooted in long-standing Andean traditions of mutual support between communities and religious servants. While the model of parish musical organization was imposed by the Spanish colonists, its implementation was shaped by the Andean concept and practice of reciprocity. The organization of musical provision was adapted from a professional European model to one that was more flexible and better suited to the local traditions and economic conditions in the Andes.

Furthermore, it would be a mistake to view Andean enthusiasm for European music as purely strategic. Performance and ritual were also central to pre-Hispanic Andean religious traditions. Music was associated with important royal occasions in Inka society; performers enjoyed high honours, considerable rewards, and superior status. It is thus understandable that, from the earliest days of the conquest, members of the native population should have gravitated towards music and ceremony.

Colonial musical practices, too, show continuities with pre-Hispanic traditions. For example, Guaman Poma's drawing of the *cantores* reveals considerable similarities with his illustration of the indigenous fiesta of the Collasuyos (326); in both, native wind-players are prominent. Continuity is particularly apparent in the use of wind music in rituals of death. In many pre-Hispanic cultures in Peru, wind instruments were associated with death, transcendence, or communication between mortal and immortal realms (Olsen 2002). After the Conquest, wind instruments became a characteristic feature of Andean church music, as Guaman Poma illustrates, and one of the prime responsibilities of indigenous parish musicians was the collection and burial of the dead. Ultimately, then, Guaman Poma's image represents not so much the acculturation of the indigenous population as the emergence of colonial musical practices through processes of transculturation.

6. The musicians of the Holy Church, exempt from tax

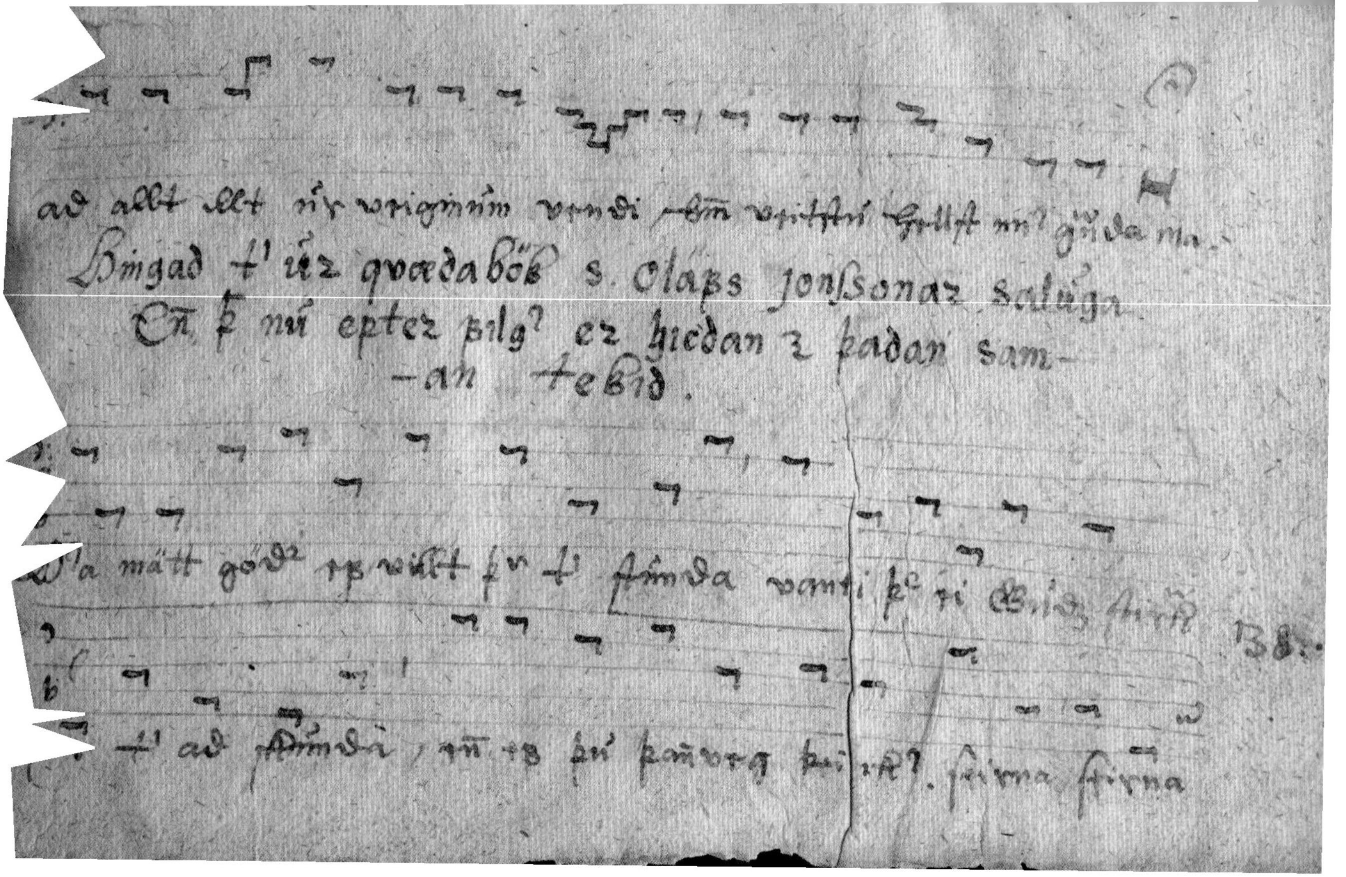
Hingad t'ur quædabok s. Olafs Jonssonar saluga
En þ nu epter filg' er hiedan z þadan sam-
-an tekid.

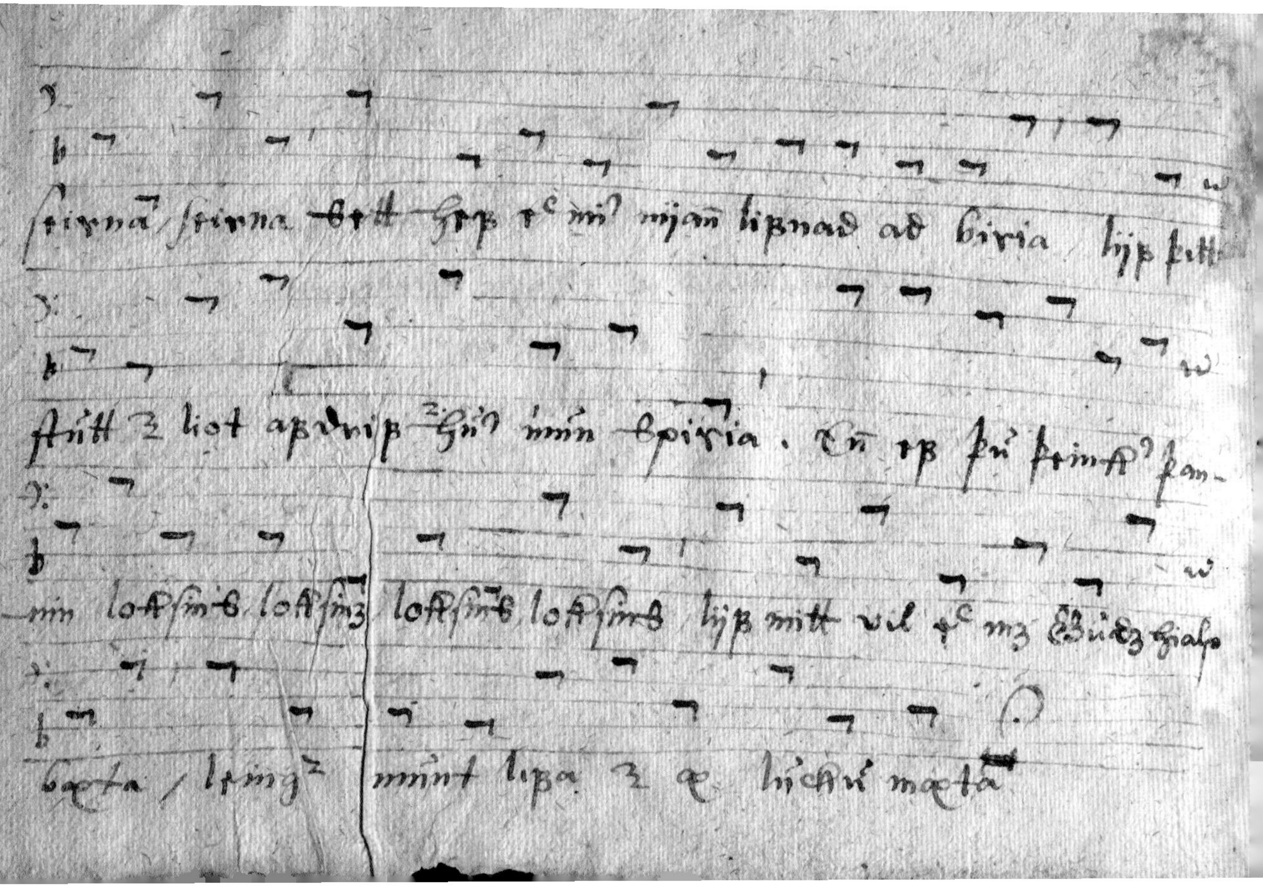

7. A Devotional Song from Iceland

Árni Heimir Ingólfsson

Madonna io t'haggio amato et amo assai / Esse bonum licet / Vera mátt góður
Francesco Corteccia / Ludwig Helmbold / Anon. Icelandic, ca. 1660
Copenhagen University, The Arnamagnæan Collection, Department of Nordic Studies and Linguistics, Rask 98, fol. 43r-v
Manuscript on paper, 95 fols., 11.3 x 16.4 cm
Photo: Suzanne Reitz, used with permission

ICELAND was a remote part of Europe during the medieval and early modern periods. Travel by sea from Denmark took around three weeks and ships only made the journey twice a year, in spring and autumn (Jónsson 1998, 191). Most of the inhabitants, estimated at ca. 50,000 in 1600, lived on farms scattered along the coast. There were only two small villages: the hamlets surrounding the cathedrals of Skálholt, in the South, and Hólar, in the North, each numbering roughly 100 people. To most Europeans, Iceland must have seemed a strange, even frightening place. Pope John XXIII, in a letter dating from 1413, referred to it as "insula maris in finibus mundi"—the island at the end of the world (Þorkelsson 1906-13, 23).

Yet, while it may seem that Iceland was a place unconnected to developments in continental music, the surviving sources tell a different story. Around 100 fragments of liturgical chant manuscripts survive from prior to the Reformation, as well as over 150 music sources from the early modern period. There must once have been many more; after all, Icelanders had valorized writing and manuscript production since the Middle Ages.

One manuscript songbook in particular, now in the Arnamagnæan collection at Copenhagen University, provides a compelling glimpse into the traditions of music in Iceland during the early modern age. It was written around 1660-70 and is known by its shelfmark, Rask 98, since in the early nineteenth century it belonged to the noted Danish linguist Rasmus Christian Rask, who probably acquired it during an extended stay in Iceland from 1813-15 (Hjelmslev 1941, 171). This is the most substantial Icelandic music manuscript of the seventeenth century to have survived and it contains a total of 223 songs, over half of which are unique to this source. The manuscript's heading announces this to be a book of imported songs in translation: "MELODIA. A few foreign tunes to Icelandic poetry, many of them useful for spiritual entertainment." The heading is not entirely accurate, since 11 of the songs have Latin texts, one is in Danish, and one has no text at all. Rask 98 is a notably eclectic manuscript, bearing witness to the variety of music-making in seventeenth-century Iceland. It contains hymns from local and foreign hymnals, secular songs, chant in Latin as well as in Icelandic translations, and archaic two-part polyphony, all in non-rhythmic notation. It also contains single as well as multiple parts from four-part polyphonic pieces by continental composers, including—in the exhibit presently under examination—the Florentine *maestro di cappella* Francesco Corteccia.

Among the "foreign tunes" in Rask 98 is *Vera mátt góður* (*You must be good*; no. 138, fols. 43^{r-v}). The "Bass-like" characteristics of this piece—notated in F-clef and mostly moving by fourths and fifths—were already remarked upon in the early twentieth century, although its origins remained elusive at that time (Þorsteinsson 1906-09, 281). As it turns out, this is the Bass part to Corteccia's *Madonna io t'haggio amato et amo assai*, one of the 16 pieces printed in Adrian Willaert's popular collection of *Canzone villanesche alla napolitana* in Venice in 1544/45 (see fig. 7.1; Cardamone 1978). As the name for this secular genre suggests, the "canzone villanesca" (or "villanella") was a simple, homophonic piece, easily sung even by amateurs, and thus presumably at a level that Icelandic schoolboys, far away from the European cultural centres, were able to manage.

Yet the story of the Italian song's journey to Iceland is more complicated than this. In the Lutheran heartlands of Saxony and Thuringia from the 1570s onwards, as Stephen Rose has shown, pastors and teachers were repelled by the erotic texts of Italian villanellas and madrigals, yet could not resist the singable qualities of the repertory. Seeking to purify these settings by replacing the Italian texts with devotional or moralistic words, they hoped to create morally uplifting pieces suitable for schoolboys (Rose 2016). The first such collection, *Cantiones suavissimae*, printed in Erfurt by Georg Baumann in 1576, contained contrafacta of Italian songs edited by the Magdeburg cantor Leonhart Schröter with Latin texts by Ludwig Hembold, a teacher in Mühlhausen. Item no. 19 in this anthology is Corteccia's villanella, set to a Latin contrafactum (*Esse bonum licet*) that encourages the singer/listener to immediately embrace a virtuous life. It is this text that appears to Corteccia's Bass part in Rask 98, in an anonymous Icelandic translation. It partly reads:

> if you think: "later, later I have resolved to begin my new life," your short life and ill fate will be known to all men, but if you think: "at

Figure 7.1: Adrian Willaert, *Canzone villanesche alla napolitana* (Venice: Antonio Gardano, 1545), Bassus partbook, p. XIII (Francesco Corteccia, *Madonna io t'haggio amato et amo assai*). Munich, Bayerische Staatsbibliothek, 4 Mus.pr. 96#Beibd.14 / urn:nbn:de:bvb:12-bsb00071912-2. Photo courtesy of the Bayerische Staatsbibliothek.

> last, at last with help from God I shall make my life better," you will live longer and ever find fortune.

Several features of Rask 98 suggest that this manuscript was written at Skálholt, the cathedral of the southern diocese in Iceland and also home to a Latin school of roughly 24 students divided into two classes. Among the contents of Rask 98 are pieces only known from one other manuscript, written nearly a century earlier by the Bishop of Skálholt himself; it also contains hymns known to still have been in the cathedral school repertory in the eighteenth century. This earlier manuscript transmits Tenor and/or Bass parts to pieces by Paul Hofhaimer, Ludwig Senfl, Jacobus Clemens non Papa, and Corteccia, as well as the fashionable *Susanne un jour*, and settings from the widely used Buchanan psalter, a volume of Latin psalm paraphrases in classical meters by the Scottish humanist George Buchanan, set to homophonic four-part odes by the Rostock cantor Statius Olthof (Widmann 1889).

While the scribe of Rask 98 did not copy the Soprano and Alto parts, evidence suggests that four-part singing was practiced at the Skálholt school in the second half of the sixteenth century. One of the schoolmasters there, Erasmus Villatsson, was born in Denmark and studied there before relocating to Iceland. The chronicler Jón Halldórsson writes in his 1719 *Chronicle of the School-Masters at Skálholt* that Villatsson was "an outstanding singer, the first to use Discant and such singing in this land. Many of his descendants are also fine singers" (Halldórsson 1916-18, 16; Guðmundsson 2000, 159). The term "discant" seems to be employed here to refer to four-part music in a general sense; it is also used in three Icelandic manuscripts in its more common early modern meaning, to designate the highest part in four-voice polyphony. It would hardly be surprising if Villatsson, the teacher who introduced discant (in these senses) to Icelanders, had brought with him a handful of recent music prints when arriving from Denmark to take up his new post at the Skálholt Latin school.

But Villatsson only held the post of schoolmaster from 1561-64; he then became a priest in one of the diocese's most sought-after parishes, and subsequently married the bishop's daughter. It seems unlikely that he would have been responsible for bringing the 1576 Erfurt print back to Iceland, since he is not known to have made further trips to the continent. But Iceland was in frequent contact with Germany and Denmark, and several natives are known to have studied at German universities in the last quarter of the sixteenth century. For example, Oddur Stefánsson studied in Copenhagen and Rostock in ca. 1583-90 and immediately took the post of schoolmaster in Skálholt upon his return to the island. He was considered among Iceland's most learned priests, and one source relates that his nephew spent a year with him after completing the Skálholt school, "to study music" (Benediktsson 1909-15, 536). Two other schoolmasters were noted for their fine knowledge of music: Gísli Guðbrandsson (schoolmaster 1583-85) and Sigurður Stefánsson (schoolmaster 1595), but where they attended university (presumably in Germany and/or Denmark) is unknown. Any of these three priests, scholars, and singers could easily have brought back a volume of Italian villanellas edited for use in German schools. They must then have set to work on translating the texts in order to introduce them to their Icelandic students, or enlisted the aid of one of their school colleagues to do so. The extended travels of Corteccia's *canzona* serve as a reminder both of the strong influence of Italian culture in sixteenth-century Europe, and of the fact that music travelled far and wide—in this case from Italy to Germany and on to the farthest North, the very edge of the world itself.

The Icelandic version of *Vera mátt góður* enjoyed an unexpected and unusual revival in the twentieth century. The contents of Rask 98 were published for the first time in 1906-09, in a hefty tome (almost 1000 pages) entitled *Íslenzk þjóðlög* (*Icelandic Folk Songs*), which contains transcriptions of vernacular singing made by the priest and composer Bjarni Þorsteinsson and his colleagues, as well as his transcriptions of music from old Icelandic manuscripts. He rendered *Vera mátt góður* in triple meter (whereas the original is in duple time) and described it as a "kind of a bass solo, and thus very different from the other songs in this book" (Þorsteinsson 1906-09, 281). Writing during Iceland's final push for independence from Denmark (achieved in 1918), Þorsteinsson emphasised that even though Rask 98 contained "foreign songs," according to its title page, they had "lived with the country for hundreds of years and therefore deserve to be called Icelandic" (Þorsteinsson 1906-09, 207).

In its triple-meter guise, *Vera mátt góður* was included in a 1960 volume of Icelandic folk songs arranged for voice and piano by the Austrian pianist Ferdinand Rauter, and it was released in 1978 on a popular LP of Icelandic folk songs performed by the progressive rock/folk band Þursaflokkurinn (The Flock of Trolls), where it was performed as a bass solo just as Þorsteinsson had implied in his volume (Lund 1960; Hinn íslenzki Þursaflokkur 1978). It has since appeared on several other albums, including a performance by the Danish-Swedish folk singer Hanne Juul (Juul 1993), as well as in instrumental and choral arrangements by Icelandic composers. In Iceland, the story of Corteccia's 1545 song seems to be an ongoing saga.

ADDITIONAL REFERENCES: Ingólfsson 2003; Ingólfsson 2012.

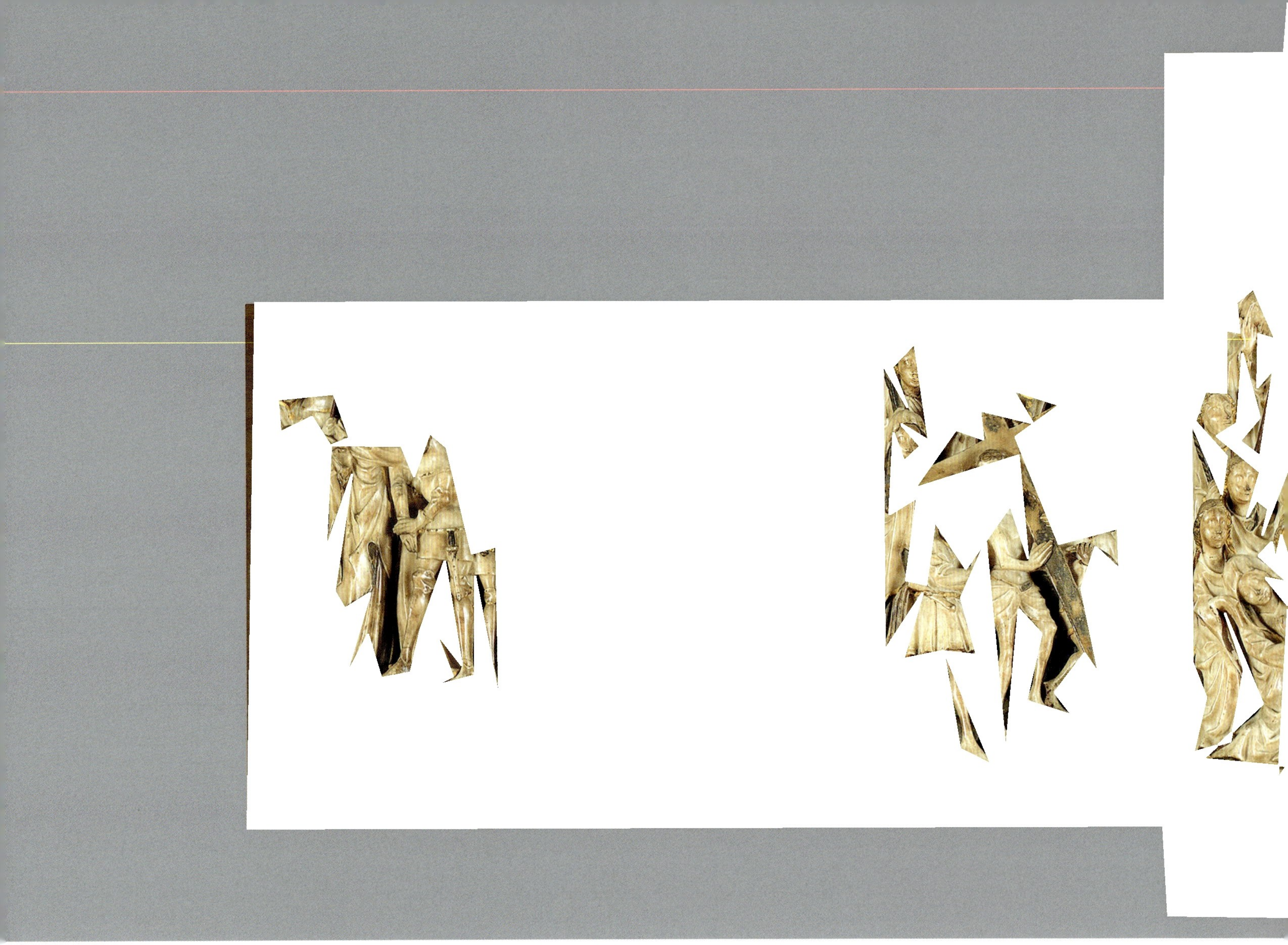

8. Alabaster Altarpiece

James Cook, Andrew Kirkman, Zuleika Murat, and Philip Weller

Anon., English Midlands, ca. 1470-80
Alabaster with remnants of gilding and polychromy, 73 x 25 cm (central panel), 40 x 22 cm (each side panel)
Musei Civici d'Arte Antica, Palazzo Schifanoia, Ferrara
Photo courtesy of the Musei di Arte Antica del Comune di Ferrara

To enter the sacred space of all late-medieval and Renaissance churches and chapels was, by definition, a multidimensional experience. Spatial, architectural, and lighting effects were enriched with the temporal and expressive effects of sound, smell, and music, in both a localised and a broader, immersive way. The rituals and devotions, and also the political and civic events, that took place within such spaces all unfolded within a rich, highly developed multisensory environment. This was the human and cultural "religious theatre" for which sacred art of all kinds was created: specifically designed, crafted, installed, and experienced.

Such an environment offered unique artistic-and-religious experiences that were the only such live experiences available to many people; and it provided for an encounter between art and music that, within the given sacred and architectural framework, was both highly focused and widely dispersed. Convergence between music and visual imagery was a given: visual artefacts and images "received" music just as they received prayers, veneration, and diverse kinds of ritual; and music was given focus and "purchase"—in terms of spatial orientation and human cognitive attention—by the presence of sacred images and the particular articulation of the sacred space.

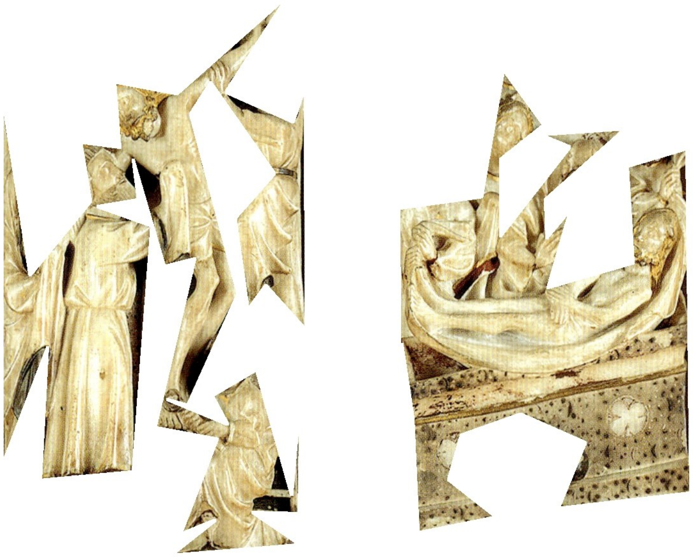

The English alabaster altarpiece surviving in Ferrara depicts in seven panels the Passion of Christ, with a Eucharistic focus on the taller panel of the Crucifixion placed at its centre. The Ferrara of the Estensi was one of the premier centres for the evolution of Renaissance culture across the arts and other disciplines during the fifteenth and sixteenth centuries, and has been inscribed as a UNESCO World Heritage site since 1995. Both its musical and its artistic culture were at the forefront of Renaissance developments, accommodating and (re)elaborating both local and international traditions. Stylistic and typological evidence suggests that the alabaster panels date from around the middle of the fifteenth century, perhaps as late as the 1470s. In all probability, they originated as the primary altarpiece of the Este princely chapel, which was the physical location of the sacred *cappella ducale* institution of the Ferrarese princely household (Scalabrini 1773, 306; Tuohy 1996, 90-95).

In its original state, the altarpiece would have had a horizontal box frame enriched with colour and decoration and brief Latin inscriptions (Nelson 1920; Cheetham 1984, 24-26. See also Cheetham 2003). The panels themselves would have been carefully finished and polychromed with a range of lustrous pigments and gold, as can be ascertained from many comparative examples, including the roughly contemporary altarpieces on the same subject which survive in Naples (Museo Nazionale di Capodimonte) and Venafro (Museo Nazionale del Molise, Castello Pandone).

The Ferrara Passion altarpiece is one of a number of such altarpieces, carved in alabaster quarried from the English Midlands and fashioned there (Ramsay 1991), which survive to this day in Italian museums, having typically been commissioned, purchased, or presented in the fifteenth century. These altarpieces—and also a number of individual panels, most of which probably come from dismembered altarpieces of similar type—show striking evidence of the interest of certain kinds of Italian (especially aristocratic) patrons in art of non-Italian provenance (Murat 2016; Murat 2019), at this richest of all periods for the flourishing of native Italian sculpture and painting.

The Ferrarese altarpiece may conceivably have been a diplomatic gift from England (Varese 1985), in which case it would have carried a special political as well as religious significance. In any event, some degree of contact between the aristocratic ruling families of the northern and central Italian states and the royal houses of France and England was formative, almost axiomatic, at this period. Our purpose is briefly to consider the apparent reasons for this special visual and cultural interest in English work among Italian patrons and institutions, but more importantly to chart and evoke this Ferrarese altarpiece's intrinsic relationship to music within its specific sacred setting.

The altar is the main spatial and religious focus of any sacred Christian space (Williamson 2004). Together with any formal image placed upon or in front of it, it has a special relationship to the surrounding area, to the liturgical performances focused upon it, and to all participants in any devotional or ceremonial event that takes place within its surrounding forcefield (Williamson 2013; Kirkman and Weller 2017; Kirkman and Weller 2019). Sacred images, indeed, mark and denote a sacred presence, just as, in the Mass especially, the altar itself does—most obviously at the Consecration, Transubstantiation and Elevation of the Host. So the visual aspect of an altarpiece has a special technical and ritual function at certain points in the liturgy, moments which are marked by particular actions and words, and almost always by music as well (whether in the form of plainchant or polyphony, with or without instrumental accompaniment). Music and art converge and interact intensively at these key points.

Altarpieces also exude a general aura of presence over the sanctuary and chancel area where they are located, and by extension over the whole church or chapel space. Thus they stand as an all-seeing, all-hearing witness not simply to the various liturgical enactments, but to the music in which so many of these enactments are not just clothed but embodied. This function is a more generalised, but in its way equally important one. Art and image tend to dominate the space whose focus they occupy, even as the music articulating the sacred utterance is diffused throughout the building.

The Ferrara altarpiece thus stood witness, potentially, to all the wide range of music that was sung within the chapel of the Este princes over the period of a century and a half (Lockwood 1984; Cavicchi 2006; Nugent 1990). If the altarpiece's origins go back to the final years of the reign of Borso d'Este (r. 1450-71) or, more plausibly perhaps, to the early years of Ercole I (r. 1471-1505), it is nevertheless not really clear when, if at all, it might have been removed from the ducal chapel. The likelihood is, however, that it would have been left *in situ* until Ercole's new chapel was replaced by a still newer one in the 1590s. After that, the altarpiece was apparently moved to the Ferrarese church of Sant'Andrea, as witnessed by local writers in the eighteenth century (Murat 2016, 410). In any case, the Estensi lost control of Ferrara itself to the pope in 1598, following the death of Duke Alfonso II without heirs.

As elsewhere, including all the most prestigious *cappella musicale* institutions of the later medieval and early Renaissance period, plainchant would in the Este chapel have been sung alongside polyphony, and would have formed by far the greater part of the chapel music, despite the generally much higher public profile enjoyed now by polyphony and its most gifted exponents. Polyphony is, in this period, an essentially aristocratic, princely tradition, with the Ferrara of Ercole I standing at the forefront. There is a very substantial quantity of manuscript (and, later, printed) musical repertory surviving that would have been available for Ferrarese performances in the fifteenth and sixteenth centuries. Three manuscripts in particular need mention as playing clearly more than a random or arbitrary role in the linkage between music and art.

One important manuscript shows very clearly just how highly prized English music was at this period, how enthusiastically its lead was being followed by continental patrons and musicians, how closely it was tied into the European scene, and how tangibly it stands in parallel to the widespread continental "adoption" of English alabaster sculptures: the source Modena, Biblioteca Estense Universitaria, α [alpha] X. 1. 11, known as ModB. This codex had its origins in and around the papal chapel while it was in residence at Florence around 1440, and thence moved into the private ownership of the Estensi, probably in the late 1440s during the reign of Leonello (Dean 2017). More than 30 years later a further musical work was copied into it at or just after Ercole I's accession in 1471, revealing that it was still in use during the altarpiece's early years in Ferrara, assuming those to coincide with the beginning of Ercole's reign.

ModB is one of the precious group of large-scale sources from south of the Alps which preserve a great deal of English music, dating from the earlier fifteenth century through to the 1460s and 70s. So we find a situation in which a major musical manuscript, with substantial English as well as continental repertoire, is physically present in Ferrara from before mid-century, concurrently with a major ritual altarpiece of English workmanship. This, we believe, is a near-unique—or at least very rare—conjunction that is demonstrable within the cultural history of the time. It is certainly true that English music was highly prized in Continental Europe, with both English works and other pieces demonstrating English influence found in abundance (Cook 2019). The point here, however, is that the situation in Ferrara is unique in allowing us to observe the possible presence of music from England in the same spaces as (and perhaps in immediate interaction with) sacred art also from England.

Another manuscript may give us further indications that English music was used at Ferrara and elsewhere in the North of Italy during the middle and later years of the fifteenth century. Florence MS Magl. XIX 112 *bis* is a middle-sized paper-and-parchment manuscript, probably assembled and copied ca. 1460/70 by Antonius (de) Januë, a musician apparently from Genoa who may very well be the "Antonio da Genova" recorded at Ferrara Cathedral in 1462 (Kanazawa 2001). Besides a group of his own compositions, this source comprises items (mainly Office music and antiphons) by Du Fay and Binchois, along with a quantity of material by Dunstaple, Power, and Walter Frye (Kanazawa 1974). There is no final proof of close or extended involvement of Januë at Ferrara, but this example does reveal the kind of repertoire that could be found in circulation in the 1460s to 1480s, and that might have been available to Ferrara beyond ModB.

Finally, we need to acknowledge the presence of the very striking and important choirbook ModF, a specially produced volume containing polyphonic Masses by Josquin des Prez and Jacob Obrecht, with just one additional Mass by Johannes Ockeghem. Lockwood and others have very plausibly seen this source as a memorial volume to Obrecht, who succumbed in the city to plague in 1505 (Lockwood 1984, 253-54). Its relevance here is that it is the unique source for Obrecht's *Missa Caput*, a piece modelled compositionally on the (anonymous) English antecedent *Caput* Mass and chant—and revealing also knowledge of the only other *Caput* Mass, by Ockeghem. The possible convergence of music and art under ritual conditions, as proposed here within the Ferrara princely chapel, suggests that this Obrecht Mass and its companions, along with many others by Josquin's and Obrecht's colleagues and successors, must have been performed in the presence of our English altarpiece—but its presence here in Ferrara may also say something more pointed than has been noted hitherto concerning its relationship to its English model, and hence to English musical style more generally, in the Ferrarese context.

Both the alabaster altar and the music (of ModB and to some extent of ModF) came from a royal court—that of England, one of the most influential in the cultural and specifically musical panorama of the time—and contributed to establishing the princely discourse of the Este family from Leonello onwards. Our Passion altarpiece from the English Midlands was thus the silent, observant witness to the performance of all this music at one of the most distinguished cultural centres of the Italian Renaissance. The relationship between the two expressive media—sculpture and music—would have been further enhanced originally by common textual links provided not just by liturgical and devotional texts but also by such features as the inscriptions traced on the wooden frame box of the alabaster altarpiece and on the long scroll which appears in the central Crucifixion. Short written cues of this kind abound in late-medieval art, and alabaster carvings of many types, not just those of Christ's Passion, were often equipped with just this kind of feature, showing how image and music converged not least through their reference to similar, or complementary, texts and narrative indicators.

With its narrative images, the alabaster altar makes the story of Christ visible and makes Christ's presence in the Eucharist concrete. The music that accompanies this celebration, of whatever type it may be, makes this very presence something alive, realised in front of those who attend the celebration thanks precisely to its musical elaboration. The result is therefore not only a Eucharistic ritual, but a Eucharistic ritual that becomes sensual and thus memorable, its recollection linked to the vivid experience of sound and vision, its interpretation assisted by the commonplace textual inscriptions.

In sum, the Ferrara Passion altarpiece would have been one of the most important—visual, ritual, and spiritual—points of focus within the Este ducal chapel from the 1470s through into the sixteenth century. Until its removal in 1590, it would have been a witness to all forms of music deployed within the Este chapel, which during that period housed one of the most significant performing ensembles of the entire musical Renaissance in northern and central Italy. If these sculptures could speak ("se le pietre potessero parlare…"), we would be in a position to learn an enormous amount about the sound and usage of plainchant, polyphony, and instrumental music, both ritual and devotional, in a major court chapel in those years. There is a lot to learn even by interrogating those objects and spaces that at first glance seem "silent." The silence of the sculptures "calls for" music, which scholars and performers can try to reimagine and reconstruct with the help of a wealth of contemporary testimony. Convergence between music, art, liturgy, and devotion responds both to a tangible, documentable historical situation, and simultaneously to a modern-day artistic necessity: to make this form of multisensory experience real and accessible to modern viewers and audiences, and hence to give each of its individual components what we believe is their fuller historical meaning.

9. The Mass of St Gregory

Bernadette Nelson

Anon., Spain, ca. 1490-1500
Oil and gold on wood, 72 x 55.5 cm
The Metropolitan Museum of Art, New York
Photo © CCo

The Mass of Saint Gregory was one of the most widely circulated devotional images in early modern Europe—either within books of hours or as an independent painting or engraving. The subject fundamentally combined or conflated more than one iconographical tradition. One, which was especially associated with the early *Imago pietatis* mosaic icon in the Basilica di Santa Croce in Gerusalemme, Rome, shows the Christ surrounded by Instruments of the Passion (*Arma Christi*). In another, this idea was to become embedded in a "new narrative image" (Rudy 2016, 103), which shows Pope Gregory's vision at Mass of the consecrated host transmuted into the physical body of Christ (and depicted as the Man of Sorrows), thus affirming the doctrine of transubstantiation—and indeed the intimate unity of the Passion and the Eucharistic miracle, one of the most widely advanced themes of the *Devotio Moderna*, which swept through Europe from the fifteenth century onwards. Contemplation of these images and the sacred relics embedded within them, together with reciting accompanying indulgenced prayers, was widely believed to play a significant role in the onlooker's (soul's) journey towards redemption, a theme that was recreated in many other cultural manifestations, including in medieval and Renaissance Passion plays (Sturges 2015, 32-50).

This large Spanish painting of the *Mass of St Gregory* encapsulates some two or more of these sets of narratives and pictorial formulae: one showing the pope (here, represented as a Franciscan friar) at Mass assisted by clerics at the moment of elevation of the chalice; the other showing the Man of Sorrows standing on the altar, this time directing blood from his right side into the Eucharistic chalice, and set against a counterpoint of selected *Arma Christi*. It was clearly inspired by the Northern European *Mass of St Gregory* iconographical tradition in books of hours and by such early painters as Robert Campin, Israhel van Meckenhem, and others. However, whereas only two deacons are in attendance in this Spanish image, Meckenem's pictures, for example, might embrace a broader array of clergy that included, besides Gregory, the Church Fathers Augustine, Ambrose, and Jerome. Topically, these four Doctors of the Church were especially associated with teachings on the doctrine of transubstantiation, and in fact often entered other artistic manifestations connected with the Passion and the Eucharist composed in the spiritual and intellectual atmosphere of the *Devotio Moderna* movement: not only visual (including notably Raphael's famous *Disputa* in the Vatican Palace, for example) but also literary, embracing Spanish and Portuguese Passion poetry and plays some with musical components, as explored below.

In this painting, the liturgical setting is shown in minute detail. Two richly coped deacons holding candles are depicted raising the splendid damask chasuble of the celebrant pope at the moment of elevation, as he kneels and holds the chalice with both hands in receipt of blood from the *Imago pietatis*, or Man of Sorrows. On the altar, the already consecrated host is seen resting on a paten to the pope's right, whilst to the pope's left, a missal is open at an illumination depicting the crucified Christ with his mother and St John. In the far left-hand corner sits the pope's triple-tiered tiara. Slightly below the altar to the right are two small jars of water and wine.

What is striking is that at this dramatic moment frozen in time, the eyes of all three celebrants are directed towards and apparently meet the gaze of the Man of Sorrows looking down at them from his elevated position. This actual perspective and participation in the celebrants' experience in the painting, however, is denied to the viewers, although their vantage point is one that is normally denied to non-clerical attendants. Moreover, their own eyes are simultaneously drawn to the Veronica icon looking directly at them from the top of the riddel curtain to the left of the altar, the same height as the head of the Man of Sorrows. This is pinned up along with other *Arma Christi* that include the hammer, the holy sponge, the dice, the spear and, resonating with the two liturgical jars and the chalice, the jug of water used by Pilate to wash his hands. Other Instruments of the Passion—the Cross, the pair of keys, and the nails—are integrated into the golden retable (albeit partially obscured by the *Imago pietatis*). In addition, repeated insignia with the five wounds of Christ (to which the Franciscans had a special devotion) grace the borders of the riddel courtain.

These instruments all exist as cues for a larger narrative: the humiliation, torture, pain, and suffering of Christ's

Passion. Thus, whilst the viewers are not actual participants in the drama depicted, they are enjoined, though absorption and meditation on these mnemonic prompts and the wounds of the post-crucified Christ (simultaneously shown in the image of the Man of Sorrows), to empathise with and participate in his suffering. Further, and owing to the artist's purposeful design, the onlookers are also reminded of a further essential theological concept. Drawn by the lines of perspective of the angles of the pillar bases and the altar to where they converge at the point of infinity, they are directed to the image of the Virgin and Child in the stained glass window on the far wall, and thereby simultaneously invited to meditate on the mystery of the Incarnation of Jesus Christ, the Word made flesh, and its resonance with the Eucharistic miracle at the altar.

Identifying with and meditating on such images, as strongly encouraged by the *Devotio Moderna* movement, would very likely promote a certain "performance literacy" (Stevenson 2010b; Ramakers 2015, 142) and enable further interaction with other devotional forms, rituals and expressions by way of contemplation and deeper cognitive understanding, and beyond to a nurturing on a profoundly experienced spiritual level. Performance in religious theatre, in which a spectator was invited to witness and therefore identify with the central protagonists' own staged drama and perhaps even spiritual journey, would have played a significant role in this. For example, the Passion dramas that developed in the fifteenth and sixteenth centuries in the Iberian Peninsula were similarly often tangible expressions of or responses to devotional fervour incited by the *Devotio Moderna*, especially through emotive subjective texts such as Ludolph of Saxony's *Vita Christi* (second half of the fourteenth century, and translated into Castilian and Portuguese in the late fifteenth century), which indulged in graphic descriptions of the pain and suffering experienced by Jesus Christ on the road to Calvary. These descriptions became the source of inspiration for a number of newly composed Latin prayers, many of which were used as motet texts, whilst others may have been written for special Offices for some of the Instruments of the Passion or the Sacred Wounds. Such prayers may also even have been combined with the contemplation of actual *Arma Christi* used as props in two- and three-dimensional form on stage, promoting an intensity of response, and drawing the spectator into an intimate engagement with Christ's Passion.

Gómez Manrique's *Representación del Nacimiento de Nuestro Señor* (1458-68) and Alonso del Campo's *Auto de la Pasión* (1485-86) are among the first-known productions to highlight selected Instruments of the Passion as tangible objects of contemplation on stage, and Lucas Fernández's *Auto de la Pasión* (early 1500s) is the first drama in which these objects are also commented upon musically, with settings in four-part polyphony. Near the beginning of this play, an "Ecce Homo" (presumably an image of the Man of Sorrows) is produced, before which the actors kneel and sing *Ecce Homo, Ecce Homo, Ecce Homo* in four parts; then part way through the play, a Crucifix is likewise manifested and, kneeling, the actors sing a polyphonic version of *O crux, ave spes unica*. Right at the very end of the play, before a reconstruction of the Monument, they then sing the villancico, *Adorámoste Señor* (Knighton 2007, 72-73).

This combination of religious drama, contemplation of sacred image with accompanying sung Latin text, and reconstructed liturgical ceremony characterises a number of early modern Iberian religious (Passion) plays, including a number by the Portuguese court playwright Gil Vicente. Moreover, the correspondence between the Passion and the Eucharistic miracle, which interweaves Fernández's *Auto de Pasión*, is the comparable framework of Vicente's allegorical *Auto da Alma* (*Play of the Soul*, ca. 1508) in which a Soul is invited, through a sequence of vignettes of the via crucis and Christ's Passion, to undertake his own salvific journey. As in Fernández's play, selected *Arma Christi* are dramatically revealed one by one for their immediate evocation of Christ's pain as a kind of initiation, through prayer and contemplation, into the necessary suffering that must precede (eventual) redemption. In general, prayer in various forms played a very important role in Vicente's plays (Delgado Morales 2014, 227). This particular play was clearly inspired by Ludolph of Saxony's *Vita Christi*, one of the most profoundly influential texts of the *Devotio Moderna*, of which Vicente was an adept (Perkins and Earle 2009, 63).

Vicente's *Auto da Alma* was first performed in 1508 at the royal court in Lisbon before King Manuel I and members of the royal court on the eve of Good Friday ("noite das Endoenças"). The main protagonists are the Soul (Alma), his Guardian Angel, Mother Church, four Doctors of the Church—Ambrose, Augustine, Jerome, and "Thomas" (i.e. Gregory—Révah 1949; Moser 1966, 98), and two tempting devils. The drama focuses on the journeying Soul's invitation to take rest in an inn ("a rest for souls," represented by Mother Church) and to take nourishment from the table (the altar), being both assisted by the angel, and goaded and tempted by the devils. Here, she is attended and directed spiritually by the four Doctors of the Church—especially Augustine and Ambrose—who, at the climax of the play, enter carrying four cooking pots covered by cloths, singing the hymn *Vexilla regis prodeunt*. The remainder of the drama is structured from a sequence of five symbolic vignettes centred on a small selection of *Arma Christi*, which Jerome offers one by one to the Soul, as tangible objects, for "feasting on" and contemplation, as a means towards obtaining purification and spiritual transcendence. With each one, the doctors sing an appropriate Latin prayer of devotion, presumably as a polyphonic setting, beginning, when the Veronica towel is flourished from above the pots, with the famous associated indulgenced prayer, *Salve, sancta facies* (similar, perhaps, to the three-voice setting in the Segovia manuscript: Segovia Cathedral, Archivo Capitular, s.s. [antiguo18], fol. 148[r]), in which they are joined by Mother Church. This is followed by the successive presentation of three chosen Instruments of the Passion from inside the pots—the whip, the crown of thorns, and the three nails. Each time, the Soul is invited to "eat" or "chew" upon them "sorrowfully" or "slowly, in contemplation of the Lord's suffering," whilst the doctors successively sing *Ave flagellum, Ave corona spinarum* and *Dulce lignum, dulcis clavos*.

With this idea of meditation and prayer, which embraces the idea of eating and ingestion while the Soul gazes upon the object, Vicente would appear to be drawing upon the metaphor used in the *Lectio Divina* (as advocated by masters of the *Devotio Moderna*) in the recommended structured practice of reading, meditation, prayer, and contemplation: "Reading as it were puts whole food in the mouth, meditation chews it and breaks it up, prayer extracts its flavour" (Ayres and Volpe 2019, 353). In this context, the process is crystallised in the accompanying, sung Latin verses, with the motet as an integrated part of the three-fourfold *Lectio Divina* principle. The musical-aural element introduced here would thereby encourage a further dimension of response and interaction in the audience or onlookers, that might be transferred to or from their responses in their contemplation of otherwise silent or mute devotional and religious images.

Finally in the play, and as a fitting climax to this intense contemplation of stages of Christ's Passion, St Jerome recalls the Incarnation and birth of Christ ultimately "given as offering"—"Entrusted first in mystery, to a holy Virgin came from Heaven this secret thing … then to the Eternal Father given as offering" (Bell 1920)—and draws a crucifix out from between the pots. At this, all players kneel in adoration and sing a prayer beginning *Domine Jesu Christe*. The inclusion of this particular Latin incipit is highly significant—not only for its clear association with Passion motets by Iberian composers (notably Juan de Anchieta), but equally also for its close connection with the famous St Gregory versed prayer, [*O*] *Domine Jesu Christe*, known also in a setting by Josquin (Blackburn 1997, 599-603), which became so intimately connected with the *Mass of St Gregory* painting and attendant indulgences (Corbin 1951, 14; Blackburn 1997, 595; Rudy 2016, 107-10). While the text of Anchieta's polyphonic motet—which might well have been sung at this point in the play—relates to the Hours of the Passion (Knighton and Kreitner 2019, 84-85, 88-91), the words *Domine Jesu Christe* indeed open a number of prayers ("Oratios") at the ends of chapters in Ludolph of Saxony's *Vita Christi*, the likely inspiration for the introduction of the prayer at this point in the play. Finally, all players exit in procession to adore the Monument (traditionally reserved for the sacred Host for the Good Friday ceremony)—"the fruit to end this feast"—singing the *Te Deum*.

Additional references: Grande Quijgo 2003; Hand 1992; Rivera 2014; Robinson 2013; Wardropper 1950.

I

Devotions

Psalters

PSALMODIA

CHRISTIANA, Y SERMONA-
rio delos Sanctos del Año, en lengua Mexicana:
cópueſta por el muy. R. Padre Fray Bernardino
de Sahagun, de la orden de ſant Franciſco.
Ordenada en cantares ò Pſalmos: paraque canten los
Indios en los areytos, que hazen en las Igleſias.

EN MEXICO.
Con licencia, en caſa de Pedro Ocharte.
M.D.LXXXIII. Años.

10. Bernardino de Sahagún's *Psalmodia Christiana*

Lorenzo Candelaria

Mexico City: Pedro Ocharte, 1583
[4] + 236 fols.; 21 cm (4°)
The University of Texas at Austin, Nettie Lee Benson Latin American Collection, OCLC: 21357732
Photo courtesy of the Nettie Lee Benson Latin American Collection, University of Texas Libraries, The University of Texas at Austin

The *Psalmodia Christiana* is the first book of vernacular song published in the Americas and an outstanding example of Hispanic devotional literature published during the first Christian century in the central valley of Mexico (then New Spain). Bernardino de Sahagún, a Spanish priest and missionary of the Franciscan order, composed it between about the mid-1560s and 1579. Pedro Ocharte, a native of Rouen active in Mexico from 1563-92, printed the work in Mexico City in 1583. The *Psalmodia* is one of at least 131 distinct titles of Mexican incunabula now in public libraries throughout the world, a work of 236 folios containing 333 short religious songs (*psalmos*), and 54 illustrations of Christ and canonized saints of the Roman Catholic Church.

Designed as an aid to inculcate the native Mexica (more widely known as the Aztecs) with Catholic doctrine, Sahagún composed his songbook in Hispanicized Nahuatl, the missionary language of Mexico's central valley following the Spanish occupation that began in 1519 (Candelaria 2014). There is evidence that Sahagún was aided in the work's early stages by a cohort of native assistants who were fluent in Latin, Spanish, and Nahuatl. Four reliable names have come down to us: Antonio Valeriano (of Azcapotzalco), Martín Jacobita (of Tlatelolco), Alonso Vegerano, and Pedro de San Buenaventura (both of Cuautitlán). They had been instructed in grammar by Sahagún himself at the College of Santa Cruz de Tlatelolco, where he taught in the early 1560s.

Fray Bernardino ranks among the most important writers on life and culture in the New World. Educated at the prestigious University of Salamanca, he entered the Franciscan order around 1522, then traveled to New Spain in 1529. He died there in 1590, having taught the Christian faith to the Mexica for over 60 years. In the course of that time, Sahagún studied and richly documented their native language and culture. Celebrated by subsequent generations as a pioneering anthropologist in Mexico, Fray Bernardino's reputation today rests largely on his monumental *Historia general de las cosas de Nueva España* (*General History of the Things of New Spain*, also known as the Florentine Codex—Sahagún 1950-82), an illustrated encyclopedia recording detailed aspects of life and culture among the Mexica. For all the renown the *Historia general* has rightly garnered, however, the manuscript was never published during Sahagún's lifetime and only became widely known in the nineteenth century. The *Psalmodia Christiana* is the only work that he ever saw in print.

Books to advance Catholic doctrine in New Spain were common in the sixteenth century and many of them utilised an indigenous language. Sahagún's *Psalmodia* is unique, however, in that all of its doctrinal lessons were meant to be sung and danced. This singular feature of the book is explicit in the full title of the frontispiece:

> Christian psalmody and sermonary for the saints of the year in the language of the Mexica [Nahuatl] written by the Very Reverend Friar Bernardino de Sahagún of the Order of Saint Francis. They are arranged in canticles or psalms for the Indians to sing in the *areítos* they perform in the churches.

Spanish missionaries broadly applied the word *areíto* (probably first learned from the Taínos of the Greater Antilles around the turn of the fifteenth century) to a dynamic form of religious singing and dancing cultivated by the Mexica prior to European contact (Stevenson 1968). Contemporary accounts agree that the *areíto* was a song and dance ceremony in which the indigenous, richly adorned with feathers, flowers, and jewelry, gathered shoulder to shoulder into large concentric circles, moving and chanting to the beat of two sacred drums that were central to pre-Hispanic worship among the Mexica, the *huehuetl* and *teponaztli*. Prior to the Europeans' arrival, these were performed on religious festivals that occurred about every 20 days. They could involve thousands of dancers singing throughout much of the day and well into the night, either in the grand plazas before their major temples of worship (*teocalli*) or in large courtyards called *patios* that were attached to the palaces of Mexica nobility.

Singing and dancing were central to Mexica religious ceremonies before the Spanish occupation and remained so afterward. The practice of Christianizing the pagan *areíto* goes back to Fray Pedro de Gante in the 1520s. De Gante was a Flemish laybrother of the Franciscan order (and possibly a relative of Emperor Charles V) who arrived in New Spain in 1523. He was attached to the convent of San Francisco el Grande in Mexico City from about 1527 to 1572, building and sustaining there an educational program for native youths in the convent's Indian chapel of San José de los Naturales (St Joseph of the Natives) where he taught reading, writing, and music. Sahagún is documented at the convent of San Francisco between 1565 and 1568 and must have had regular contact with de Gante at that time. Interestingly, Sahagún's writings share that he was then at work revising and making a clean copy of a body of *cantares* (songs) that may be related to the *Psalmodia*. Whether or not de Gante had a direct hand in that work is unknown.

The structure and *cursus* of the *Psalmodia Christiana* reflect a methodical approach to fostering Catholic orthodoxy among the Mexica. Of the 333 *psalmos* that comprise the volume, the first 13 present a short catechism on fundamental prayers and tenets of Christianity including the Sign of the Cross, Apostles' Creed, Our Father, Hail Mary, and the Ten Commandments. The next 320 psalms make up a comprehensive sermonary (arranged calendrically from January to December), distinctively weaving the feasts of the temporal cycle (focused on the life of Christ) and sanctoral cycle (focused on the lives of the saints) into a seamless presentation of 54 feasts drawn from the greater church year. Easter, Pentecost, and Christmas are assigned psalms over three days to reflect the custom of celebrating those solemnities with a three-day sabbath, a custom observed well into the eighteenth century.

The sound of the *Psalmodia Christiana* in performance remains a matter of conjecture since the volume entirely lacks musical notation. In that sense, it is much like the first edition of the famous *Bay Psalm Book*, published in Cambridge, Massachusetts, in 1640. Unlike that first publication of the North American British colonies, however, Sahagún's Nahua canticles are neither rhymed nor metered. Beyond that, Sahagún's writings leave no instruction whatsoever regarding their performance, possibly on the simple assumption that the singers and dancers would know what to do.

For subsequent students of the *Psalmodia*, two manuscripts of possibly related Nahua songs may offer important clues about musical style: the sixteenth-century *Cantares mexicanos* and *Romances de los señores de la Nueva España*, preserved now at the Biblioteca Nacional in Mexico City and at the University of Texas at Austin (Bierhorst 1985; Bierhorst 2009). The *Cantares* refers to several songs as *melahuac cuicatl*, a phrase that designates the plainchant style of the Roman Catholic Church. The *Cantares* and *Romances* both indicate two-tone drumming patterns for the performances of songs (fig. 10.1). The drum cadences are indicated by various combinations of four syllables—"ti, to, qui, co," the lower pitches presumably represented by the rounder "to" and "co," and the higher ones by the more incisive "ti" and "qui." These were probably rendered on the *huehuetl* and *teponaztli* that were central to Mexica ritual and ceremony.

While missionaries found useful tools for the Mexica's evangelization in their pre-conquest cultures of song and dance, the Catholic hierarchy found cause for concern. An Ecclesiastical Conference of 1539 determined that *areítos* should be discouraged wherever possible and, if permitted, should only take place under the close supervision of an approved Christian observer who was fluent in Nahuatl and thus capable of understanding what was being sung. The First Provincial Council at Mexico City cathedral in 1555 affirmed the cautious stance taken in 1539 toward the *areíto*. Francisco Cervantes de Salazar, professor of rhetoric at the Royal and Pontifical University of Mexico, noted around 1559 in his *Crónica de la Nueva España* that "if there is no one around who happens to understand the language well" the natives performing the Christianized songs "blend in the songs of their pagan ways and, better to conceal the eternally damned song, they begin and end with words pertaining to God, interposing the pagan things in between" (Candelaria 2014, 637). Beyond a risk of heresy in the sung word, the rituals themselves bore an association with the human sacrifices they had accompanied in the not too distant pre-Christian past. Sahagún's own *Historia general* records often startling contexts for music and dance that included the ritualized killing of children during the first four months of the Mexica calendar to help ensure abundant rainfall.

Sahagún's prologue to the *Psalmodia Christiana* offers the work as a definitive solution for the vexing problems that had provoked such distrust and cynicism: "So that this mischief can be easily remedied, in this year of 1583, these songs have been printed, which are in this volume, which is called *Psalmodia Christiana* in the language of the Mexica, so that the old songs may be completely abandoned" (Candelaria 2014, 639). The front matter of the volume relates that on 5 July 1578 a review of the manuscript was made by Dr Hernando Ortiz de Hinojosa, vicar general of the archdiocese of Mexico, who certified that he had examined the *Psalmodia Christiana* on the order of Archbishop Pedro Moya de Contreras and determined that it was, in his judgment, "a Catholic book, clean of all suspicion and error or heresy" (Candelaria 2014, 643). Perhaps for safe measure, marginal indications throughout the *Psalmodia* indicate references or direct translations in the Nahua text of numerous Biblical passages, antiphons, responsories, and hymns that course through the collection of songs.

Ironically, two centuries later, Fray Francisco de la Rosa Figueroa, librarian of the convent of San Francisco and a re-

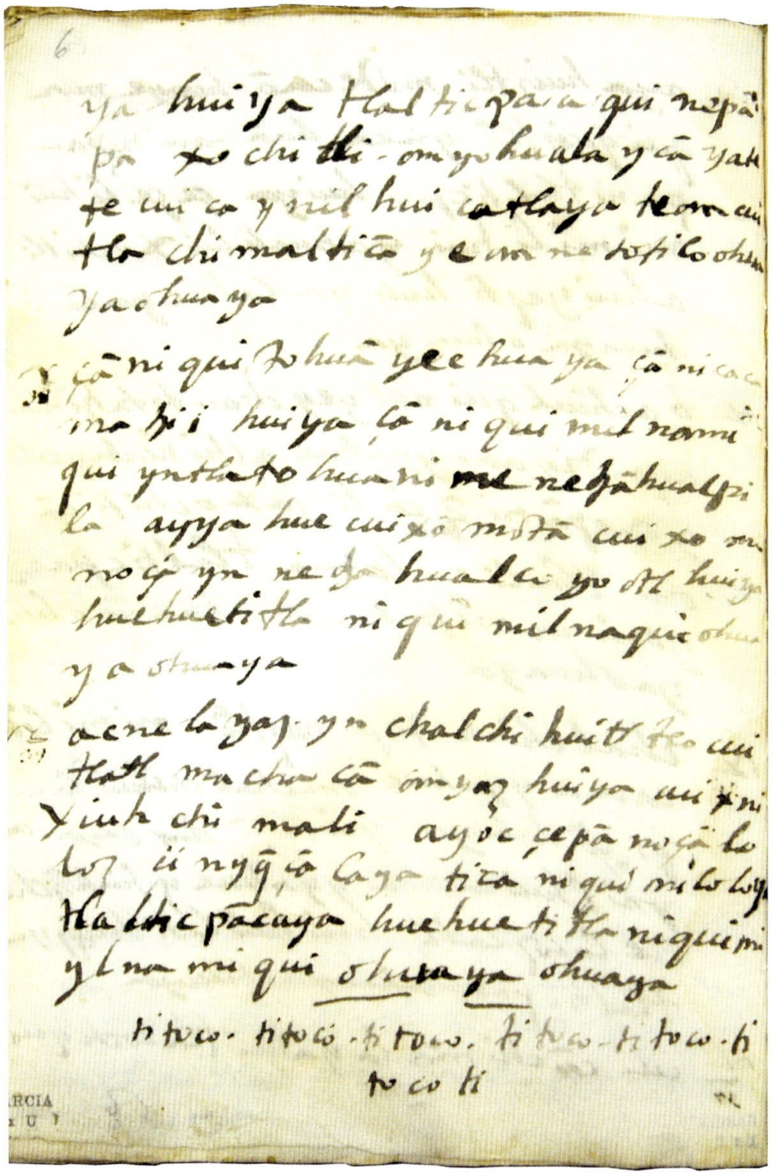

Figure 10.1: Page with a drumming cue (ti to co - ti to co - ti to co) in the *Romances de los señores de la Nueva España*. The University of Texas at Austin, Benson Latin American Collection, Ms. CDG-980 (G-59), fol. 6v. Photo courtesy of the Nettie Lee Benson Latin American Collection, University of Texas Libraries, The University of Texas at Austin.

viewer of books for the Inquisition, denounced the *Psalmodia* outright on account of a more recent rule that forbade translations of Holy Scripture into vernacular languages in Spain and all of her dominions. The rule was subsequently relaxed, but in the meantime, surviving copies of the once popular *Psalmodia* would be subject to denunciation and, likely, to deaccession. Of the seven exemplars that have been positively identified and located in Mexico, Spain, and the United States, the most complete and pristine copy is now at the Benson Rare Book and Manuscript Library at the University of Texas at Austin. Along with the *Cantares mexicanos* and *Romances de los señores de la Nueva España*, Sahagún's *Psalmodia Christiana* of 1583 presents us with a principal source of Nahua song dating from the sixteenth century. It stands alone as the first vernacular songbook printed in the Americas and a cornerstone in the early history of Mexican Catholicism.

Additional references: Candelaria 2014; Sahagún 1993; Tomlinson 2007.

Աւրհնութիւն երից մանկանցն հնոցին

Benedictus es Dñe Deus Patrum nostr[orum] etc.

1 Աւրհնեալ ես տր ած հար
ցն մերոց աւրհնեալ փա
ռաւորեալ անուն քո յաւիտեան։

2 Յիրաւունս ամն ցուցեր զայս ամ ընդ
մեզ արդար ես դու տր եւ ամ գործք քո
ճշմարիտ են։

3 Ճանապարհք քո ուղիղ են եւ ամ դա
4 տաստանք քո ուղիղ են։

11. The Սաղմոսարան of Abgar Dpir Tokhatetsi

Ortensia Giovannini

Venice: Abgar Dpir Tokhatetsi, 1565
272 fols., 15 x 10 cm
Milan, Veneranda Biblioteca Ambrosiana, S.P.XII.77
Image: *The Song of the Three Holy Children*, woodcut, fol. 262r. Photo © Veneranda Biblioteca Ambrosiana / Mondadori Portfolio

The periods known to Europeans as their Renaissance and Enlightenment are thought of by Armenians, in contrast, as among the harshest episodes of their history. During the sixteenth century, warfare between the Ottoman Empire and Safavid Iran fragmented Armenian territories in the South Caucasus, imposing oppressive measures that brought about a large-scale migration and the establishment of Armenian communities in countries all over the world (Uluhogian 2009, 45-47; De Morgan 1981, 245).

Although in these troubled times Armenians saw few avenues for cultural expression in their homeland, nonetheless diasporic Armenian communities found and took new opportunities, including those represented by the printing press. Starting in 1513 with the printing of Hakob Meghapart "The Sinful"'s *Calendar* in Venice, Armenians established printing presses in almost all the major urban centres that had a substantial Armenian presence, and continued to develop printing techniques outside Armenian territories proper up to the mid-eighteenth century (Uluhogian 2009, 47-48; Grigoryan 2014, 8-10). The content of their printed books reproduced that of medieval manuscripts; and Armenian presses were almost all led by clergymen, thus religious texts dominated the field. These religious scholars depended on the support of so-called port Armenians, long-distance merchants constantly in motion. Armenian merchant colonists of this kind conducted what world historians have called "cross-cultural trade," and resided for the most part in the great port cities of their age (Aslanian 2012, 7-12).

The Սաղմոսարան (romanised as *Saghmosaran*: psalter) of the *Dpir* (sacristan) Abgar Tokhatetsi ("of Tokhat," in northern Anatolia) conserved in Milan's Ambrosiana library, as well as the life of Abgar himself, are significant historical witnesses of the culture of Armenian communities, both in Europe and in Western Asia, during the Renaissance. Sources revealing the biographies of the earliest Armenian printers are terse and widely dispersed, presenting significant challenges to historians. Nonetheless, it is possible to establish that Abgar the Scribe—as he calls himself in the colophons of the books he printed—was a cleric and diplomatic envoy, arriving in Venice with his son Sultanshah in 1564 on route to Rome (Magno 2013, 112-13; Grigoryan 2014, 10-14).

The Armenian Church and its head, the *Catholicos* in Etchmiadzin, were the only surviving institutions representing a distinctive cultural and intellectual tradition for Armenians worldwide. Armenians' struggle for independence and cultural survival was fought under the banner of the Church, because the national cause intermingled with the desire to maintain an independent Armenian Apostolic Church in the face of occupation by Muslim states. During a synod in 1552, Catholicos Michael and the highest bishops of the Armenian Church decided to send a delegation headed by Abgar to Pope Pius IV and to the European princes, in the hope of raising support for their cause as Christians living under Muslim rule. Abgar's embassy met with some success: the pope sent him back to Armenia with a Catholic bishop and presents. However, the bishop died in Cyprus, and the gifts were returned to Rome; ultimately no help was forthcoming from either sacred or secular European authorities (Magno 2013, 112-13; Grigoryan 2014, 10-14). In this the fate of Abgar's mission was characteristic of a broader trend in Armenian relations with Europe. Since the fourteenth century, and especially following the fall of Constantinople in 1453, repeated attempts had been made to gain assistance from European leaders. However, issues between the Eastern and Western Christian Churches dating from the schism of 1054, as well as commercial competition with the Republic of Venice, resulted in a lack of political will in Europe.

Whilst political leaders in Europe showed little interest in the affairs of Christians in Ottoman-dominated Western Asia, the same was not the case for European humanists. Alongside Eurocentric and orientalist perspectives on the Ottoman sultans, a large group of scholars showed great interest in studying the languages and traditions of the Christian East as components of a shared ancient heritage. This interest is conspicuous in the annotations appearing in the Ambrosiana's copy of Abgar's psalter. Rather than documenting liturgical or musical usage of the book, the annotations instead indicate what has been called a "Catholic Orientalism" (Barreto and Županov 2015), engaging with the Christian traditions of the Armenians in order to build bridges between Roman Catholicism and the distinct branches of the Oriental Orthodox faith. Indeed, this interest is responsible for the survival of the psalter in Milan: Near-Eastern studies have been a focus of the Ambrosiana since its foundation by Cardinal Federico Borromeo, nephew of Pope Pius IV and archbishop of Milan, in 1609 (Uluhogian 2016, 327; Magno 2013, 112-13).

In Venice, Abgar printed a perpetual calendar and then the psalter, both in 1565. He remained in the city until 1567, when he transferred his press to Constantinople, home to a larger Armenian community (Hacikyan 2005, 44). The colophons and woodcuts of the psalter document his activity and his relationships with Italian personalities. In the Latin inscription in the woodcut at the beginning of the psalter, in addition to the year of publication, is a representation of Pope Pius IV blessing Abgar and his son, together with four prominent Italians, among them Cardinal Borromeo. In a second woodcut Abgar is received by Girolamo Priuli, the doge of Venice (Uhluhogian 2016, 319). These woodcuts represent, above all, a way to thank Abgar's sponsors, and they probably also functioned as a way to hide the true reason for his mission to Rome from Ottoman officials, demonstrating that he met prominent Western leaders merely to ask for support in his printing enterprise.

The psalter is a small volume, comprising 34 gatherings of eight sheets each. The printer used typefaces in two sizes, the larger for psalms, and the smaller, half the size, for prefatory and concluding elements. Following the practice in Armenian manuscripts, animals, birds, and floral motifs ornament the initials, and human figures populate the margins; the 12 woodcuts, in contrast, are Italian in style (Uhluhogian 2016, 318-20). The third woodcut indicates the allocation of the psalms, and it is dedicated to King David, traditionally identified as the author of the first book of Psalms, who is represented with his harp.

As one of the oldest Christian cultures in the world (Pane 2011, 11), Christianity was wholly integrated into Armenian identity and experience; it became an inalienable habitus, a complex notion that defines Armenian-ness. In common with other early Churches, the book of Psalms was the principal element in the Armenian Offices, and the singing of psalms was long established as a core component of Armenian identity. Of course, the psalms were also fundamental to Western Christian cultures of the period, both Catholic and Protestant; therefore, this publication would have served well as a bridge between Armenian and European cultures.

Abgar's psalter contains no music notation, most likely because it was not intended for practical use, but rather as a luxury object for wealthy Armenian merchants, or for use as a gift for influential Europeans (Grigoryan 2014, iii). Even so, most scholars would agree that music is intrinsic to the concept and practice of the psalms in Armenian culture, using melodies of great antiquity associated with folk tradition and aural transmission. Even today the chanting of the psalms, as well as the Liturgy of the Hours, is based on a monophonic tradition constructed on an unequal temperament that tends to use natural intervals, especially in relation with an accompanying drone (Utidjian 2009; Kerovpyan 1996; Kerovpyan 2001).

In the Armenian tradition, just as in medieval Europe, psalters circulated separately from the rest of the Old Testament, intended both for use in church and for private devotion. In the manuscripts and the earliest printed psalters, the psalms from 1 to 147 were divided into eight *canons*, or books, to which corresponded eight modes termed *dzajn* (voice), with canticles from the Old Testament inserted at the end of each book (Mearns 1914, 31). Then came Psalms 148-50, followed by the *Prayer of Azariah* and the *Song of the Three Holy Children* (from the Armenian version of the book of Daniel), the latter portrayed in the last woodcut of Abgar's psalter (Sanjian 1999, 5). Since the earliest years of Christendom, Armenians have chanted this last prayer on the eve of Christmas and Easter as an anticipation of Christ's birth and resurrection. It recalls the story of the children who refused to worship a golden statue of Nebuchadnezzar, and survived their punishment in a furnace by singing prayers to God. After this passage, considered deuterocanonical in some traditions but of central importance in the Armenian tradition, there followed three canticles from the New Testament, the additional Psalm 151, and the apocryphal *Prayer of Manasseh* (Sanjian 1999, 4).

The psalms were intended to be performed in unison by the whole congregation. The chanting of each psalm was probably constructed on traditional melodic recitation formulae, developed on the basis of the structure of the words in the text. This practice created a system of melodic and tempo variation according to the lyrics, which was used for ritual purposes and organised into complex cyclical structures where the chants that belonged to particular melody types were carefully distributed across the daily, weekly, and annual cycles of the liturgical calendar. The composing elements at play were the language in song (the *krapar*, in classical Armenian), the pronunciation, the sonority, and the vocabulary of melody and ornament (Kerovpyan 1996; Kerovpyan 2001; Findikyan 2006).

The modal system of Armenian liturgical music as heard today contains many intertwined layers of historical development and change. Although notation systems have been used throughout the history of Armenian chant, the role of oral transmission from master-singers (*tbrabed*) to the choristers (*tbir*) of the novitiate was, and remains, essential. The structure of this system was built upon the monastic network, and it developed in the complex relationships between teacher and student, body and voice. Traditionally chanted by men alone, without accompaniment, the psalms are experienced as music and gesture, the leading voice conducting the others through small hands movements, a sort of chironomy that promotes learning by imitation, without being conscious of the precise practice (Kerovpyan 1995-96).

Whilst Armenian liturgical song is a continuous and continuing tradition, it has also been the subject of projects aimed at revival and preservation in the modern day. A traditional, or historical, approach to Armenian chant has especially been championed by Aram Kerovpyan, as director of the Armenian liturgical chant ensemble *Akn*, as head of the Centre for Armenian Liturgical Chant Studies in Paris, and as the former master-singer of the Armenian Cathedral of Paris. Kerovpyan's work has led to the production of recordings with *Akn* and with the Armenian Mekhitarist Congregation of Venice. The objective of this last initiative in particular was to safeguard the musical heritage preserved by the Mekhitarists, whose role as curators of Armenian culture dates from their foundation on the island of San Lazzaro in the Venetian lagoon in 1717. The efforts of the Mekhitarists, and from 1771 also the Armenian Church at Etchmiatzin, to propagate an authentic and ancient Armenian literary culture through the medium of print played a large role in the *Zarthonkh* (Awakening), the national renaissance and liberation movement that Armenians associate with achieving modernity (Uluhogian 2009, 49-50).

ADDITIONAL REFERENCES: Giovannini 2016; Kushnatyan 2016.

Muutamat Dawidin Psalmit wirsixi tedhyt.

Ensimäinen Psalmi.

Beatus vir qui non abijt.

AUtuas se quin ei käyskele
Jumalattomitten retkel
Eick synnisten tiellä astele
Eick istu pilcaitten keskel

12. A Printed Hymnal by Jacobus Finno

Sanna Raninen

Stockholm: Andreas Gutterwitz, ca. 1583
[92?] fols., 14.8 x 9.3 cm (8vo)
Uppsala University Library, Sv. Rar. 10:227
Image: fol. 5r. Photo courtesy of Uppsala University Library.

Most of the area comprising modern-day Finland was part of the newly formed Kingdom of Sweden in the sixteenth century. Although the religious Reformation was embraced by Sweden and its new king Gustav Vasa from 1523 onwards, the considerable size of the kingdom coupled with its sparse population and the potential for political unrest against the new hereditary rule held the theological and liturgical changes to a moderate pace. The use of the vernacular for worship did not fully replace the use of Latin for the next hundred years, and although Swedish was the main language of administration, other languages were also spoken.

This first-known printed hymnal in Finnish was the creation of Jacobus Petri Finno, the headmaster of the cathedral school in Turku. Finno was commissioned in 1578 by King John III of Sweden to translate "some useful books" into Finnish; in response, Finno translated a catechism, a prayerbook, and a hymnal, all of which were printed by Andreas Gutterwitz at the royal printing press in Stockholm. In addition, together with Theodoricus Petri Rutha he published a collection of songs in Latin known as *Piae Cantiones*, which was printed in Greifswald in 1582 (Juva 1952, 73; Lehtonen 2016, 194). Although literary culture had reached Finland already in the medieval period, the written languages in use were Latin, German, and Swedish (Heikkilä 2010, 347-49; Kallio et al. 2018, 31-35). The first printed books in Finnish had appeared only a few decades prior to Finno's publications, written by Mikael Agricola.

Only one defective copy of the hymnal survives, held at Uppsala University Library. As both the frontispiece and colophon are missing, both the exact year of publication and the book's original title remain unknown, but it was presumably printed ca. 1583, around the same time as Finno's other translated devotional books (Collijn 1932-33, 3-5; Lempiäinen 1988, 367-68). The hymnal was printed in upright octavo format; the original size has shrunk somewhat, as a folded margin on fol. 43 reveals the pages were once 15.3 cm in height, before being trimmed in its current binding. The unique copy is missing 30 of its pages in their entirety, with an additional ten pages surviving only as fragments (Kurvinen 1929, 15; Lempiäinen 1988, 377). The final surviving page is fol. 86, but based on the surviving quire markings of the print it most likely contained at least 92 folios in total in its original state. The surviving copy belonged at some point to Andreas Jacobi from Paimio, who has written his name in the surviving flyleaves; however Andreas did not give a date, and no details of his life or profession are known. The book contains additional written notes in the margins as well as complete handwritten pages to compensate for the missing ones, but no further legible names or dates appear in the book. It is first recorded in the possession of Uppsala University in a library inventory of 1796 with its old siglum 28:597.

In its intact form the hymnal contained 101 hymns, translated to Finnish and organised into nine categories: Biblical canticles (1-5), psalms (6-22), hymns for the Gospel (23-26), catechism hymns (27-37), hymns for Mass (38-44), hymns for special feast days (45-74), hymns for a "few Christian doctrines" (Wirdhet muutamist Christillisen opin Cappaleist) containing Gradual hymns (75-83), hymns for prayer and thanksgiving (84-96), and lamentations (98-101) (Kurvinen 1929, 16). The order and format of the contents was modelled after *Then swenska psalmboken*, a hymnal in Swedish that was published in 1572 (Lehtonen 2016, 194). Finno did not use this as his sole point of reference however, but based his translations on a variety of sources in Latin, Swedish, and German, often mixing influences rather than relying on a strict translation of any one source (Kurvinen 1929, 88-89, 25-312; Lempiäinen 1988, 363). He consistently gives metrical translations of these hymns, whereas his prayer book contains prayers without a particular poetic measure (Kallio 2016, 137; Kallio et al. 2018, 121-22).

Lutheran hymns are distinguished for their importance in the musical expression of mutual worship by the whole congregation, as well as their key presence in domestic lay devotion (Brown 2005; Leaver 2007). Despite Finno's claims in the preface for using his book in various congregational meetings and feasts, the first Finnish hymnal was not received as a book destined for the hands of all the congregation, nor for moments of private devotion in an average Finnish home. Levels of literacy were low among the Finnish-speaking population in the sixteenth century, and books of any kind were mainly in the use of the educated few. The clergy obviously benefited from the new translated material for conducting worship, and hymnals could also be possessed by the few wealthy laymen: a surviving inventory of the estate belonging to nobleman Arvid Tawast mentions a hymnal among his possessions, although there is nothing to suggest that the book was Finno's publication specifically (Koskinen 2010). Even in the late seventeenth century the use of books by the congregation was seemingly rare, despite new efforts to raise levels of literacy, as following parish visitations in 1697 Bishop Johannes Gezelius the younger threatened punishments for members of the congregation who laughed at others for using books for singing (Lempiäinen 1988, 360-61).

A music book is often distinguished from other literature by the presence of some form of notation as a visual device, and many of the printed German hymnals especially towards the end of the sixteenth century included a melody printed along with the text (Brown 2005, table 1.1). Finno's book contains no printed notation, although a later user of the book has added melodies in the margins for the hymns *Christus cäski sanans saarnatta* (fol. 34ʳ) and *Christityt nyt iloitcam* (fol. 36ᵛ). Lutheran hymnals without notation are not altogether unusual, and earlier Swedish printers of liturgical and devotional books before and after the Reformation had printed empty staves which the book's user could fill with appropriate notation. Rather than being seen as a sign of technical inadequacy on the part of the printing house, this approach provided a diplomatic way of accommodating the different melodies and their variants used around the kingdom.

If general levels of literacy were low among sixteenth-century Finnish-speakers, the musical literacy required for reading notation was a skill possessed by even fewer. Much of the hymn repertory was transmitted in writing or orally by a small network of clergymen and their immediate professional collaborators, and the melodic variation in liturgical music and hymns continued after the Reformation without any apparent agenda for uniformity (Vapaavuori 2003, 46; Tuppurainen 2005, 53). The small group of readers for this hymnal, then, were able to source the melodies through other means, rather than expecting them to be printed alongside the text. The royal printer Andreas Gutterwitz did not include printed notation in his books until *Then swenske psalmboken* of 1586, which is thought to be the first book with printed notation from Sweden; even then Gutterwitz chose to include notation only for the Credo in both Swedish and Latin (Davidsson 1957, 21 and 93). Despite the availability of technical means, a Finnish hymnal with notation did not appear until 1702, under the title *Yxi tarpelinen Nuotti-Kirja*. Amund Laurentsson—a royal printer preceding Andreas Gutterwitz—had printed staves from woodcuts for the new Reformation liturgical books in both Swedish and Finnish, even in octavo format for his *Parabolen om Samaritaner* in 1572, but Gutterwitz did not use Laurentsson's stave blocks for any of his prints. In contrast, the woodcut images used by Laurentsson were kept in use: for example, fol. 5ʳ in Finno's hymnal features an image of David with his harp (shown in the main image), apt for the beginning of a category of psalm translations; the same image can also be seen in *Rucouskiria* by Mikael Agricola printed in 1544.

Liturgical music manuscripts copied in the region by sixteenth-century clergymen attest to the successful adoption of Finno's translations, as well as to the adaptation of printed sources in personal manuscripts. Although printed books were available from the 1540s onwards, the clergy still relied on making their own books to suit their own needs, which might vary in format, style, and choice of language according to personal preferences, professional requirements, and available materials. The surviving music manuscripts from sixteenth-century Finland were written by clergy for conducting liturgy and worship. It is commonly the case that one codex contains many scribal hands, as the clergymen collated a variety of material considered useful not only to themselves but also to their professional associates and successors, who continued working from the same written material. Many of the liturgical melodies used prior to the Reformation were retained, with some adjustments as needed to accommodate the different syllabic structures of Latin and Finnish (Tuppurainen and Hannikainen 2010; Hannikainen and Tuppurainen 2016, 157-78).

The most popular translations copied from Finno's hymnal are unsurprisingly those connected with the essentials of the annual liturgy, such as *O Jumala sinua me kijtämme* (the *Te Deum*), and sequences for specific feasts such as *Tule pyhä hengi* (*Veni creator spiritus*) for Pentecost and *Caicki Christityt iloitcan* (*Laetabundus*) for Christmas. Other alternative translations continued to circulate after the publication of Finno's hymnal, and several translations of a single Latin text are occasionally incorporated into the same anthology manuscript. The scribe of an octavo manuscript from the end of the sixteenth century (Helsinki, National Library, C.ö.III.20) has even added Finno's translations of *Laetabundus* and *Jesus Christus vhrix meille* (*Victimae paschali laudes*) as additional options underneath earlier versions; as the metrical structures vary somewhat between the two versions, the melody does not always fully match Finno's translation. Many of the manuscripts contain the most important liturgical music excerpts in Swedish and Latin as well as in Finnish; often all three are copied consecutively, with the melody tailored to fit the metrical patterns of the three very different languages.

Very often the text from Finno's hymnal is copied without fitting it to notation. Most notably, one surviving composite manuscript (Helsinki, National Library, C.III.20) has Finno's translations carefully copied by two scribes in octavo books with similar dimensions (max. 16.8 x 10 cm). Although the scribes observe the headings as well as indentations for phrase structure, some more intricate typographical features are not replicated. Gutterwitz set Finno's text with two fonts: gothic for Finnish and roman for occasional titles and passages in Latin. Particularly in the Christmas hymn *Piltin synnyt Bethlehem* (*Puer natus in Bethlehem*), the two languages tend to merge in the page layout, the Finnish translation alternating with the original text in Latin, and the two fonts provide a clear distinction between the languages.

Being the first in something often warrants a special position in historical perspective, and Finno's translation work and the fortuitous survival of this one copy of his hymnal certainly form an important moment in Finnish literary, poetic and musical history. Finno's hymnal did not revolutionise late sixteenth-century song traditions in Finland, as it continued to rely on and blend with the existing oral/aural learning and transmission of songs. Yet, the evidence of Finno's contemporary success is witnessed in the manuscript copies, in which his translations merged into the mosaic of a rich manuscript culture of various formats and styles that embraced the new aspects of worship, incorporating them into practices familiar from the pre-Reformation era.

ADDITIONAL REFERENCES: Knuutila 1997; Suomalaisen Kirjallisuuden Seura n.d.; Virtuaalikatedraali n.d.

University Library, Birmingham.
But vouchsafe me to keepe,
From those infernall foes:
And from that lake so deepe,
Whereas no mercy growes.
And I shall sing the songs,
Confirmed with the iust:
That unto thee belongs,
Which art mine only trust.
FINIS.
THE PSALMES OF DAVID.
Beatus vir. Psalme j. T. S.
This Psalme is set as a Preface to exhort all godly men to study and meditate the heavenly wisedome. For they be blessed that so doe, but the wicked contemners thereof at length shall come to misery.
The man is blest that hath not bent
to wicked rede his eare: Nor led his
life as sinners do, nor sate in scorners
chaire. But in the law of God the Lord
doth

13. *The Whole Booke of Psalmes*

Jonathan Willis

London: imprinted for the Company of Stationers, 1627
[64], 226, 239-375, 378-400, 399-461, [65] pp., 8 x 5 cm (8vo), with contemporary silver thread binding and silver clasps
University of Birmingham, Cadbury Research Library, d 16.B5

Upper image: Binding with clasps.
Lower image: Opening of the first psalm, *Beatus vir*, sigs. D[7]v - D[8]r.
Photo courtesy of the Cadbury Research Library: Special Collections, University of Birmingham.

This tiny 1627 edition of *The whole booke of Psalmes. Collected into English meeter by Thomas Sternhold, Ioh. Hopkins, and others* is in octavo format (meaning it was printed from a single sheet of paper folded in half three times to make eight pages, or leaves), and measures just over 8 cm tall by 5 cm wide. Enclosed within a contemporary embroidered binding with silver thread and silver clasps, the delicate physicality of the artefact belies the fact that *Sternhold and Hopkins* (as the book was commonly known) ushered in a revolution in the religious and musical cultures of Reformation and post-Reformation England, in the twin arenas of public worship in the parish church, and domestic devotion within the household.

Sternhold and Hopkins was not simply a reproduction of the same prose texts that could be found in successive English translations of the Bible from Coverdale's onwards, in the Old Testament book of Psalms. Rather, it was a metrical psalter, containing rhyming paraphrases of the psalms arranged in verses so that they could be sung as hymns. English metrical psalmody had its origins in experimental publications by reformers during the reigns of Henry VIII and Edward VI. The *Goostly psalmes* published in the 1530s by the Biblical translator Miles Coverdale were publicly burned by the conservative Henrician regime in the 1540s, but during the reign of the young evangelical King Edward VI metrical psalms started to become fashionable in court circles (Leaver 1991, 62-84, 117-21). Ironically, it was not until the reign of the Catholic Queen Mary I that metrical psalms started to be sung by English congregations in exile on the continent, influenced by the practice of Protestant communities in cities such as Strassburg, Frankfurt, and Geneva (Duguid 2014, 13-48). The returning exiles brought the practice back to England with them, and it seems to have become instantly popular. The former exile and first Elizabethan bishop of Salisbury, John Jewel, wrote to his friend and mentor Peter Martyr Vermigli on 5 March 1560 that "you may now sometimes see at Paul's Cross, after the service, six thousand persons, old and young, of both sexes, all singing together and praising God" (Jewel 1842, 71). Eleven days later, on 17 March, the conservative clothier and diarist Henry Machyn confirmed that after the sermon at Paul's Cross "they songe all, old and yong, a salme in myter, the tune of Genevay ways" (Nichols 1848, 228).

Theologically, the Church of England under Edward VI and Elizabeth I was part of the Reformed family of Protestant Churches, a distinct offshoot of the Protestant family tree separate from the Lutheran confession. The influence of the Strassburg reformer Martin Bucer, the Zurich reformer Heinrich Bullinger, and the French author of the Genevan reformation John Calvin, was therefore much stronger than that of the Wittenberg reformers Martin Luther and Philip Melancthon. Luther himself and other Lutheran reformers embraced the musical arts unreservedly, and wrote original hymns to communicate Lutheran doctrine, such as the resounding *Ein feste Burg ist unser Gott* (*A mighty fortress is our God*) (Buszin 1946, 97). Calvin did not object wholeheartedly to music, and saw it as a valid aspect of prayer and praise, but he placed much stricter limits on the forms which religious music might legitimately take. In particular, he rejected instrumental music, and insisted that the only subject matter which should form the basis of a true Christian's song was the word of God; in other words, texts taken from scripture, and primarily the Psalms. Calvin also recommended that religious music be sung to tunes that were sober and appropriate to their subject matter. He warned that "the song be neither light not frivolous," and insisted that "there is a great difference between the music which one makes to entertain men at table and in their houses, and the Psalms which are sung in the Church in the presence of God and his angels" (Garside Jr. 1951, 568 and passim). It was therefore sober *a cappella* metrical psalmody, rather than lavishly accompanied Lutheran-style hymnody, which formed the essential soundtrack to the English Reformation.

The metrical psalms were not the only form of religious music to emerge out of the English Reformation, although history could have played out very differently. During the 1562 meeting of the Convocation of Canterbury, the synodical assembly for the southern Province of the Church of England, a group of religious extremists in the Lower House proposed the abolition of "all curious singing and playing of the organs," while a less radical proposal that "the use of organs be removed" was defeated by only one vote (Le Huray 1967, 35-36). However, more elaborate forms of Church music had a staunch defender in none other than Queen Elizabeth I herself. The forty-ninth of the 1559 Royal Injunctions referred to music as a "lawdable science," and sought to preserve musical livings in cathedrals and collegiate churches and chapels. In stylistic terms the Royal Injunctions aimed both to have their cake and eat it, by referring to "the comforting of such as delyte in musicke" with "the best sort of melodye and musicke that maye be convenientlye devysed," while at the same time requiring "a modeste and destyncte songe so … that the same maye be as playnely understanded as if it were read without singing" (Elizabeth I 1559, sig. Civ^{r-v}).

The English Reformation therefore witnessed the growth of a crowded and lively musical marketplace, in which reformed traditional musical forms (organ music and choral polyphony) evolved, and competed (and even interacted) with new genres, such as metrical psalmody. The metrical psalms had no formal place in the services outlined in the *Book of Common Prayer*, but they came to occupy a relatively secure position in church where they were habitually sung before and after the sermon, before and after morning and evening prayer, and occasionally even during communion (Quitslund 2012, 237). Cathedrals therefore resounded with the stately melodies of the metrical psalms almost as often as parish churches, and there is suggestive evidence that some parish churches may have occasionally enjoyed choral as well as congregational performances of metrical psalms, accompanied by organ as well as *a cappella* (Willis 2010b, 121-28). For the first time, English congregations were able—encouraged, even—to play an active, participatory musical role in public worship. Before the Reformation, the Dutch humanist Desiderius Erasmus had complained that there was a threefold barrier between church music and the people, consisting of non-participation, the use of the Latin language, and the kind of stylistic elaboration (e.g. melisma) that might make words difficult to understand (Willis 2010b, 46). Simple congregational, vernacular, monophonic metrical psalmody removed those three barriers, and allowed people to connect with their religion in powerful new spiritual, sensory, and emotional ways.

To a large extent, once their texts and tunes had been learned and memorised, the metrical psalms became part of a popular oral tradition. Nevertheless, the psalms were also an early modern publishing phenomenon. From the first complete metrical psalter issued by John Day in 1562, more than 470 editions had been published by 1640, equating to quite possibly a million copies in circulation (Green 2000, 509). Ian Green has estimated that *Sternhold and Hopkins* "was probably published more often than any other work in the early modern period" (Green 2000, 503). During the reign of Elizabeth, most editions of the metrical psalms were published as large folio or medium-sized quarto volumes, whereas the tendency into the middle decades of the seventeenth century was towards publishing smaller and smaller editions: octavo (8vo), duodecimo (12mo), 16mo, 24mo, and 32mo, in a mixture of one-column and two column formats (Green 2000, 513). Larger size metrical psalters were commonly bound with other religious or liturgical texts, such as Bibles or copies of the *Book of Common Prayer*, and may have been intended for public use at church or in the home. Smaller editions, such as our exhibit, featured only the text of the metrical psalter, and were clearly intensely personal items, small enough to be carried in a bag or pocket or hung from a belt.

Alec Ryrie has noted that post-Reformation Protestants valued books not only as texts, but as physical objects, complicating our traditional sense of Protestantism as a purely logocentric (word-centred) religion. Religious books such as Bibles or psalters became "palimpsests layered with meaning" and might represent a range of personal, emotional, spiritual, and even magical forms of significance and power (Ryrie 2013, 292-97). We do not know who purchased d. 16.B5, who owned it, who embroidered it lovingly with a floral design, highlighted with silver thread and secured with silver clasps, who thumbed through its delicate pages, and read, mediated upon, and sang the verses contained therein. But this was clearly a precious object, both in terms of the raw materials and labour of its construction, and the social, cultural, and religious significance with which those materials and labour imbued it. Susan Frye has argued that learning about women's lives and textualities in the early modern period "requires embracing a broader sense of text than the literary," including "visual texts like drawings, paintings, and needlework" (Frye 2011, 9). It is not hard to imagine d 16.B5 as the property of a woman of gentry status or higher, and that the act of embroidering this tiny psalter in precious silver thread was itself a species of devotional activity, just as much as singing the psalms contained within its pages. As such, a psalter like d 16.B5 may be viewed as a form of what Alfred Gell has described as "distributed personhood": "as social persons," Gell writes, "we are present, not just in our singular bodies, but in everything in our surroundings which bears witness to our existence, our attributes, and our agency" (Gell 1998, 103). This beautiful psalter was a physical extension and manifestation of the piety and devotion of the young woman who decorated and possessed it, and of her economic and social status as well.

In addition to aiding the public performance of congregational metrical psalmody in church, therefore, metrical psalters like d 16.B5 were part of the physical and cultural landscape of personal and domestic devotion. Protestant ministers and authors encouraged both lay and clerical households to participate in an expansive round of private, conjugal, and household devotions, including prayer, table graces, reading devotional guides, Bible reading, godly fellowship and conference and, of course, the singing of psalms. We have already seen how Calvin equated psalm-singing with prayer, and Beth Quitslund has demonstrated that psalm singing was also promulgated as "healthful recreation, especially in the specific sense of restoration" (Quitslund 2012, 244). Psalm-singing was probably one of the more enjoyable and sociable aspects of this kind of domestic devotion, and the periodic publication throughout the later sixteenth and seventeenth centuries of polyphonic arrangements of the psalms, occasionally with instrumental accompaniment, demonstrates how differently the psalms might be performed in a domestic versus an ecclesiastical setting. Richard Alison's 1599 *Psalmes of David in meter the plaine song being the common tunne to be sung and plaide upon the lute, orpharyon, citterne or base viol, severally or altogether* is a good example of such an arrangement (Alison 1599).

This tiny decorative metrical psalter therefore offers a small window onto a powerful series of transformations in religious music and religious cultures more broadly, as a result of the tumultuous events of the English Reformation. The reign of Elizabeth I was not only the era of Byrd and Tallis: it also bore witness to the coming of age of congregational song within the English Church, and of a common musical culture of domestic devotion, both embodied in the form of the humble metrical psalter.

TVTVS

II

Domestic Objects

Introduction: The Room of Domestic Objects

Paul Schleuse

A TABLE, A CANOPIED BED, a decorative cabinet. A statue, a tapestry, a panel painting. We can imagine the furnishings of this "period room" arranged as they might be in an aristocratic home. These objects and a variety of smaller handheld ones—a knife, a book, a fan, and a deck of cards—are suggestive of the everyday life of (primarily elite) Europeans from the late fifteenth to the early seventeenth centuries, and as such draw us into a space resonant with music and meaning. Europeans of the Renaissance sang, played, and listened to music in various spaces: public, courtly, and ecclesiastical, but nowhere did these activities reflect and construct their intimate relationships and emotional identities as in the private home. Domestic sociability and musicking were just as performative as were public activities, and the personal sphere fostered nuanced discourses about the power of sound to affect the body and soul, inspire love or lust, and to articulate the shades of social class that structured early modern societies. In this room we encounter both practical and decorative items that told their owners and viewers (and can tell us) what music could mean, and what musicking could do.

As a pendant to the main room we encounter four items that contextualize the sensual powers of intimate music in Renaissance culture, and some of the anxieties this power provoked. Both the allegorical engraving *Venus* (Shephard) attributed to Baccio Baldini and the manuscript fragment of Vitsentzos Kornaros' poem *Erotokritos* (Hatzikiriakos) depict music's power to inspire love. Yet in different ways each also speaks to humanist erudition and intellectual histories: *Venus* through evocations of classical teachings on love and harmony, and *Erotokritos* through a literary heritage traceable to medieval romance, troubadour song, and Orphic legend. Other items remind us that music's sensuality is also dangerous. The panel painting *Death and the Maiden* (Butler) warns us of the vanity of life's pleasures, which slip away as quickly as a lute's dying sound. The sirens depicted in the *Balet comique de la Royne* (Refini) commemorate another such vanity: the spectacular display of power at the French court. Just as Jacques Patin's scenic designs dazzled the eyes, his sirens (and Girard de Beaulieu's music) beguiled the ears. Ulysses, lashed to his ship's mast, could safely indulge in music's pleasures; we must be always on our guard.

Upon entering the room itself we encounter the god of music, Apollo, in the form of an ancient *Statue* (Moretti). As a beautiful object and a prized remnant of classical Greece it draws us in just as it did visitors to Mario Bevilacqua's palazzo, itself a kind of museum where private and public activities merged, creating a stage for the performance of identity—and of music—decorated with objects that articulate their owner's magnificence, virtue, and erudition. One of the most astonishing early modern objects in our room is Philipp Hainhofer's *Cabinet of Curiosities* (Körndle), with its miniature renderings of hundreds of everyday implements in precious materials, and its seemingly magical concealed music automaton decorated with the Muses.

Of course, musical erudition is displayed not only through collecting and craftsmanship but through performance. The sounds of recreational music-making in a private home are powerfully evoked by the so-called Eglantine *Table* (Bank), whose inlaid surface offers trompe l'oeil music books and instruments along with cards and boards for chess and backgammon: images that playfully evoke and interact with the kinds of activities that might be enjoyed around such a table. Like games, recreational music-making provides a structure that controls and directs conversation towards the display of virtuosity and harmony. Harmonious conviviality is scripted more directly—and just as wittily—by the *Knife* (Dennis) engraved with musical notation, one of a set that collectively present a four-part blessing. As a venue for social performance, the dinner table was no less a stage than the music room, and while the musical knife is a luxury item suggestive of a ceremonial function, some of the surviving examples show signs of practical use by servers or diners as well.

Other objects in the room also present musical notation in novel contexts that evoke recreational musicking: the function of the printed *Playing Cards* (Schiltz) is transformed by the owner's addition of unique music on the reverse sides of each card, rendering them virtually useless for gaming (since the cards can be identified by their music), but refashioning them as an unbound set of partbooks that can only be put to use by sorting the cards by suit and rank. The Rothschild Chansonnier, a kind of musical *Commonplace Book* (van Orden), interleaves printed images from Ovid's *Metamorphoses* with manuscript pages that reflect the unknown compiler's personal tastes in poetry, music, and instrumental practice, effecting a transformation worthy of its Ovidian material. Both the cards and the chansonnier reveal how domestic pastimes like gaming, reading, and collecting were pursued parallel to music.

The room's two tapestries depict music-making in allegorical contexts whose resonances are as powerful as their specific meanings are open-ended. The contemplation and interpretation of such objects would have been both instructive and provocative for early modern conversationalists. The female organist in the *Tapestry* (Zecher) represents Hearing in the most widely accepted reading of the *Lady and the Unicorn* series, but both individually and as a set the connections to medieval romance, Marian devotion, and heraldic imagery remain characteristically multivalent. As artworks of great aesthetic value and practical portability, such tapestries lend themselves to close reading in multiple contexts. The Garden of Love portrayed in the tapestry *Valance* (Butler) conveys a more specific meaning since it decorates a bed—the site of consummation for the amorous activities it depicts, including music and dance.

As luxury decor, marvellous objects, and displays of humanist learning, the items in this room are connected almost exclusively to elite culture. By attending to rare surviving material and textual artifacts, museums always risk overemphasizing society's most powerful makers and consumers. The erasure of commoners' non-literate musical lives is all the more likely since their music is all but irrecoverably silent. Two items in our room point, if indirectly, toward popular musical practices. Camilla Cavicchi proposes that the anonymous *Painting* of dancers in a vineyard depicts the musical therapy of tarantism, whose rustic origins in Puglia stand behind the learned medical descriptions and poetic allegories possibly evoked here. Finally, a true piece of musical ephemera, the paper *Fan* (Dennis) is of a type sold cheaply by urban street vendors to members of all social classes, and often decorated with printed images or poetry. Our fan has *La canzone della violina*, a popular tune referred to in multiple literary sources as having been sung widely in northern Italy in the years around 1600. The tune itself is known from Adriano Banchieri's setting in *La pazzia senile* (1598), where it forms an epilogue to the work. While ephemeral material like this fan and its music sometimes found its way into elite spaces and media—and thus survived—a significant part of its value lies in what it can tell us about music in streets, homes, and public spaces distant from the aristocratic setting of this room.

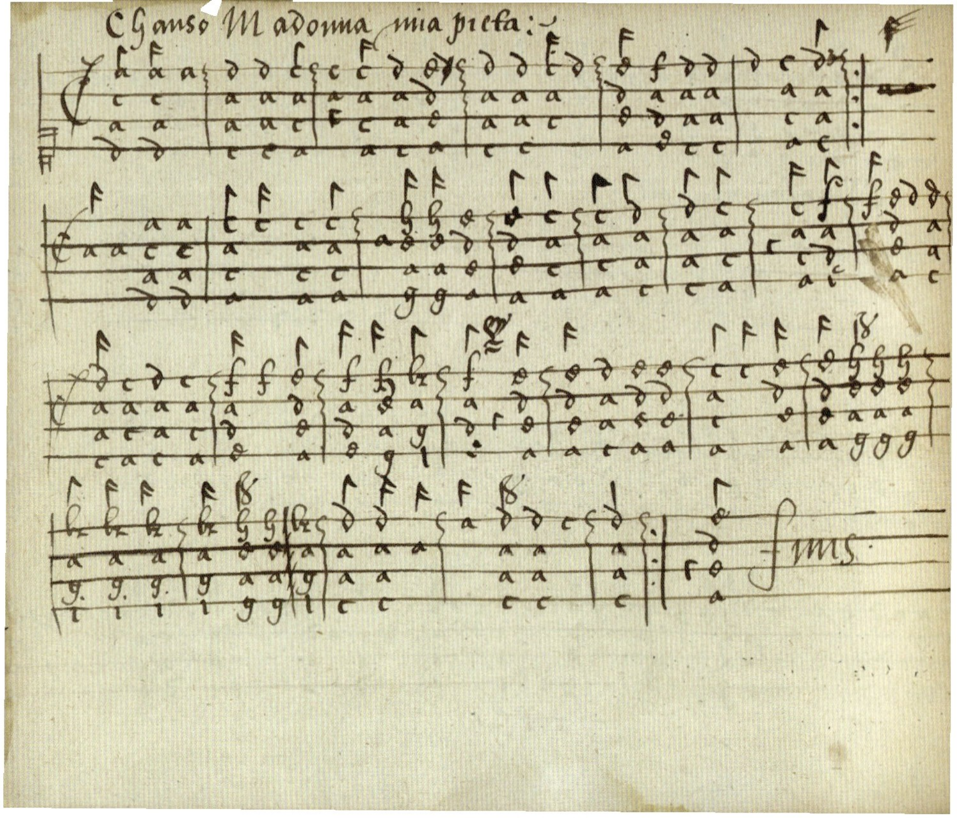

14. Commonplace Book

Kate van Orden

Left side:
Orlando di Lasso, *Madonna mia pietà*, intabulated for cittern
Anon. copyist, possibly Burgundy, ca. 1582

Right side:
Virgil Solis, *Neptune and Coronis*, woodcut
Printed in Johann Posthius, *Tetrasticha in Ovidii Metam. Lib. XV* (Frankfurt: Georg I Rab, haer.Weigand Han & Sigmund Feyerabend, 1563), p. 29

Both: Paris, Bibliothèque nationale de France, Rothschild 411, fol. 23v – p. 29

In the sixteenth century, printed books were sold unbound or tied into simple paper covers, and it was up to owners to decide if and when to have them bound. The book in this exhibit is a mongrel of the sort that resulted from the creativity of readers, who could assemble printed matter into bound books as they chose. Half manuscript, half print, the book catalogued as Rothschild 411 and held at the Département des Manuscrits of the Bibliothèque nationale de France is an album created by interleaving a series of woodcuts depicting Ovid's *Metamorphoses* with blank pages that were filled with music, poems, and love letters (Picot 1967, 1:219-26).

The opening shown here contains the song *Madonna mia pietà* in manuscript, arranged for cittern, across from a depiction of the princess Coronis morphing into a raven as she flees from Neptune's unwanted advances. Such striking juxtapositions are representative of the entire volume, in which facing pages put songs and instrumental music into conversation with mythological scenes of transformation. In addition to its extraordinary amalgam of visual, literary, and musical genres, the book stands as a remarkable witness to cultural mobility in the late sixteenth century, for it joins songs in French, Italian, and Spanish to a bilingual synopsis of Ovid's epic poem in both Latin

and German. Thus even a cursory biography of Rothschild 411 must touch upon the cultural transactions that aligned music with the visual arts, the social pastimes during which the book was put into action, and the polyglot environments presumed by its several tongues. Such an approach views the book caught in a web of cultural practices and human interactions that extends well beyond its textuality: as an object, it bursts with past voices and encounters that ultimately require histories of oral transmission, travel, and international commerce to adequately explain. In the words of Natalie Zemon Davis, we should consider the book "not merely a source for ideas and images, but as a carrier of relationships" (Davis 1975, 192).

Rothschild 411 projects multiple relationships, the boldest of which links Ovid to music through the material form of the object itself, which began with a copy of the 1563 *Tetrasticha in Ovidii Metam. Lib. XV* in which Ovid's poem is summarised in quatrains by Johann Posthius (Kinney and Styron 2018). Ovid had been a staple of commercial printing from the very start, with a dozen Italian editions of the *Opera* issued between 1471 and 1498, and two dozen editions of the *Metamorphoses* by 1500, including vernacular translations into French, Italian, and Catalan (ISTC; USTC; Moss 1982). Beginning in 1493, Antoine Verard's Parisian editions bore the title: *La Bible des poètes, Methamorphoze*, marking Ovid's centrality as a Latin author and the importance of the *Metamorphoses* as an all-in-one source for classical mythology. Indeed, many sixteenth-century editions were designed as textbooks, which could be interleaved with blank folios for note-taking (Blair 1989).

Ultimately, the *Metamorphoses* became a bible not just for poets and students, but for artists as well (Allen 2002). The privileging of image over text in editions like this one expanded across the sixteenth century as growing publics for print avidly consumed graphic depictions of laurel branches sprouting from Daphne's fingertips and Coronis growing wings. The woodcuts in Rothschild 411, made by Virgil Solis, seem to have been instantly popular, since they were issued in multiple editions in 1563 alone; this second (or third) edition is all about the illustrations, which crowd out the quatrains jammed in above and below the elegant strapwork frames that replace the commentaries present in other editions.

If the popularity of illustrated Ovids makes the appeal of this "bible" of classical mythology virtually self-evident, the same cannot be said for pairing it with music, for whereas the *Metamorphoses* would ultimately be mined by centuries of opera librettists beginning with Ottavio Rinuccini's *Dafne* (1598), sixteenth-century musical settings of Ovid gravitated toward the *Heroides*, when Ovid was sung at all (McKinnon and Anderson 2001). None of the songs in Rothschild 411 bears any thematic connection to the scenes they adjoin, and even the amorous epistles on folios 62, 65, and 79 make no references to the *Metamorphoses*. A few songs refer to "Cupido" or "Cupidon" in a generic way common in love lyric, but none is paired with the engraving of Cupid shooting Pluto as he emerges from hell (p. 63).

Intriguingly, the logic that led the book's owner to stockpile songs, dances, and love lyric within its covers is not governed by Ovidian themes, but by the practicalities of book design. The oblong format used for the *Tetrasticha in Ovidii Metam. Lib. XV* was highly unusual: then, as now, books tended to be printed in upright formats (as was the first edition to include Solis' woodcuts, which are padded out in this edition with frames that rationalise the oblong orientation). The great exception to this general rule of upright formats was music printing. From the outset defined by Ottaviano Petrucci's *Odhecaton* (Venice, 1501), music books were regularly printed in oblong. Although Venetian music printers gradually transitioned to upright quarto in the last decades of the century, in the North, oblong formats for music persisted into the seventeenth century (van Orden 2015, 8-11). An early owner of Rothschild 411 appears to have been Laurent de Sainct Seigne, who signed it on fol. 6^r^ of the manuscript portion, where the cittern tablature begins. If Laurent was indeed from Sainct Seine, in Burgundy, oblong partbooks of vocal polyphony and tablature from Paris, Lyon, and the Low Countries would have been most familiar. Thus the format of *Tetrasticha in Ovidii Metam. Lib. XV* triggered musical associations, prompting Laurent to copy out songs and dances on the broad blank pages of the book. In some sense, Ovid was a glorious extra to what ultimately doubled as a musical commonplace book. The evolution from Ovid to musical repository is not unlike the metamorphoses that can be spotted in some textbooks that survive from the Renaissance, in which blank pages intended for note-taking are sometimes taken over by musical pastimes. A copy of *Aristotelis ad Nicomachum filium de Moribus, quae Ethica nominantur, libri decem* (Paris: Denis du Pré, 1576), for example, also preserved at the Bibliothèque nationale de France, is interfoliated with blank pages filled with lecture notes and music for lute and cittern. Though we can only guess, it seems quite probable that Sainct Seigne was a university student at Louvain or Dijon: the collegiate song *Nous sommes une bande de jeunes escoliers* (fols. 81^v^-82^r^) is signed "Vive Laurent. Fait le 13 d'ap 1581."

The music collected in Rothschild 411 has all the traits of a little compendium of choice pieces, a sort of personal library of favorite music drawn from popular repertory. The Superius parts in mensural notation that open the volume (numbers 1-6) were likely excerpted from the extraordinarily popular *Septiesme livre de chansons*, a hit-parade of four-voice songs first issued in 1560 by Pierre Phalèse and reedited at least 27 times (Vanhulst 1978). This is the origin of the Spanish- and Italian-texted songs in Rothschild 411. Many of the cittern pieces that follow are likewise concordant with books of music from the presses of Phalèse, who issued arrangements of favorite songs and dances for four-course cittern: the intabulation of Orlando di Lasso's *Madonna mia pietà* shown in this exhibit may well have been copied from the *Hortulus Citharae* of 1582 (Vanhulst 1982). Phalèse specialised in music for students and amateurs, something visible in the simplicity of the *Septiesme livre* and the little treatise included in the *Hortulus Citharae*, which explained how to read tablature and how to tune and play the cittern (van Orden 2015, 209-13). Some of the numbers in Rothschild 411 are cittern duos, which would have been perfect for lessons with a teacher.

The cittern itself locates Rothschild 411 in a musical culture defined by maximum accessibility, for these rugged instruments with bodies carved from a single block of wood and strung with durable wire were cheaper by far than lutes and viols. Moreover, the four-course diatonic cittern for which these intabulations were designed was the easiest type to play, with missing and shortened frets that facilitated reaching chords otherwise uncomfortable for the right hand.

The range of notations in Rothschild 411—mensural notation and French tablature—certainly witnesses the musical literacy of its owner and copyist, but we might also note that the material form of the book in some cases prevented musicians from using it in performance. One cittern duo has the Superius and Bassus parts copied on versos of the same folio, making it impossible to read both at the same time; other songs have music on one page and lyrics copied out in a different section of the volume. The last section of the manuscript (fols. 62-87) contains lyrics for which melodies were well-known from polyphonic settings or as timbres (van Orden 2001), which were cited in rubrics such as "La Complainte de madame d'Aumalle sur la mort du sieur d'Aumalle, son mary, *sur le chant* La Parque est si terrible" (fol. 75ʳ), and "Chanson de la complainte des pauvres laboureurs et des gens de village, *sur le chant* Dames d'honneur, je vous prie" (fol. 77ʳ) (emphasis added).

More aide-mémoire than performance parts, this small octavo book stands at the intersection of multiple practices that cross back and forth from oral to written as lyric poetry was set by polyphonists like Lasso, learned by heart, sung from memory, and reworked into instrumental numbers. Just as the stripped-down presentation of Ovid's epic—reduced to quatrains and evocative depictions—fuelled storytelling and after-hours pastimes in college rooms and salons, we might hear in *Madonna mia pietà* the echoes of a lover's plaint or street-worthy Italian serenade with strummed accompaniment on the cittern. "Take mercy on me, my lady," he pleads, begging his mistress to put out the flames of love consuming him. Built on seven common chords, it is a little Petrarchan gem, perfect for courtship and fun, and the book containing it full of conversation starters and tokens of friendship from a student's college years, reminiscent of *alba amicorum*, the autograph books in which students collected drawings, poems, messages, and other mementos of friends and classmates.

ABBREVIATIONS: ISTC – Incunabula Short Title Catalogue, https://data.cerl.org; USTC – Universal Short Title Catalogue, https://www.ustc.ac.uk.

15. Knife

Flora Dennis

France(?), 16th century
Etched steel blade and ivory handle, 29.1 x 3.6 cm
Inscribed: i⁹ Tenor / Pro tuis deus beneficiis gratias agimus tibi / Quae sumpturi sumus benedicat trinus et unus
Victoria and Albert Museum, London

THIS EXHIBIT is simultaneously a knife and a piece of music. Both sides of its broad blade bear a clearly legible musical inscription: a blessing of the table (*Benedictio mensae*), to be sung before a meal, and a prayer giving thanks (*Gratiarum actio*), to be sung when the meal has ended (Dennis 2010a, 156-84; Bouvet 2003, 138-47; Corry at al. 2017, 20-21; Bagnoli 2016, 219). Above each of the staves is marked the voice part, "primus Tenor." The rest of the blade and its handle are richly decorated with scrolling foliage; gilding and green stained bone add colour and brilliance to this distinctive object.

Why was this knife made and how was it used? It is not the only one of its kind to survive. At least 18 examples are known, inscribed with "Superius," "Superius secondus," "Contratenor," "Tenor," "Tenor secondus," and "Bassus" voice parts. At first glance, it appears that these 18 knives, with their coherent decoration, originally formed a single, large, polyphonic group. When their music is transcribed, however, it swiftly becomes clear that there are in fact two groups of knives, one a setting for four voices and one for six voices (Dennis 2010a, 179-84). Visually similar, these knives are musically different.

Establishing even the most basic facts about where, when and why the knives were made is not straightforward. A single capital letter "N"—or possibly a "Z"—appears on ten of the knives, which may signify that their blades were produced in Nuremberg or Schwabach in southern Germany, where engraved decoration on knives was a speciality (Tebbe et al. 2007, 1:500-06; Pagé 1896-1905, 6:1405). Very similar scrolling foliage decoration is found on sixteenth-century sets of hunting or pruning implements, some of which were made in France (Blair 1974, 175-78; *Highlights of the Untermyer Collection* 1977, cat. 333). The music knives' distinctive shape, however, and heraldic imagery potentially link them to an Italian context. The Latin motto "Infracta virtus ad sidera tendit" (Unbroken virtue tends towards the stars) appears at the base of the blades of two *Bassus* knives, together with a device consisting of three trees flanked by stars. But neither inscription nor emblem have yet been identified as belonging to a particular individual, family, or institution. Their placement is, however, similar to a number of other Italian knives: at right-angles to the horizontally written musical text, so that the knife has to be held upright for them to be read and recognised (Salvatici 1999, 91 n100 and 92 n102).

These knives have been previously described as refectory knives, table knives, dessert knives, bread knives, carving knives, and *presentoirs* (broad, flat knives for serving meat) (Dennis 2010a, 169). In fact, their shape falls somewhere between that of the *presentoirs* and a type of carving knife used in Italy that has a sharp point for penetrating and breaking joints of meat (Scappi 1570; Scappi 2008; Cervio 1581; Giegher 1639). They may originally have been used to carve or present meat, or their distinctive profiles may refer symbolically to these acts. Some of the knives have clearly been used heavily, others remain pristine.

The texts and music do not provide us with any further help in pinpointing their original contexts. The exact wording of the Benediction prayer, "Quae sumpturi sumus benedicat trinus et unus" (May the three-in-one bless that which we are about to eat), or the Grace, "Pro tuis deus beneficiis gratias agimus tibi" (We give thanks to you God for your generosity), are not found in other contemporary sources. For each of the two musical groups of knives, the predominantly homophonic settings are typical of a generic style of sixteenth-century European chordal polyphony, offering no further clues as to their origins. A number of longer polyphonic settings of the Benediction and the Grace in Latin, French, and German were published across Europe during the sixteenth century, by composers including Cipriano de Rore and Orlando de Lasso (Sprague Smith 1965, 236-82; di Lasso 2006, 13).

Blessing the table at the beginning of a meal and giving thanks to God at its conclusion had long provided a formal structure to the experience of collective dining in monastic communities. The Benediction and Grace were written in the first person plural; they express the idea of uniting collectively to share food. The knives similarly needed to be united in a social context for their music to be performed. At the same time, however, the knives symbolise a contradictory impulse to dismember and divide. By slicing meat, the knives permit it to be shared between the gathered company in the same way that dismembering and scattering the musical text across the knives enabled a group to share the music. The acts of uniting to say the Benediction and Grace, uniting to eat, and uniting to sing are intertwined with those of separating, dividing, and sharing both meat and music.

Just as the meal was framed by blessing the table at its start and saying grace at its end, so witnessing the spectacle of carving formed a means of articulating the meal (Grieco 2006). The role of the professional carver or *trinciante* took on greater emphasis during the sixteenth century; their technical virtuosity was discussed in a series of published treatises (Messisbugo 1549; Romoli 1560; Scappi 1570; Cervio 1581; Evitascandolo 1598; Giegher 1639). This almost theatrical multisensory performance, including elements of smell and the prospect of taste, formed a counterpoint to the musical entertainments we know often accompanied such banquets (Mayer Brown 1975).

Where, when, and why the knives were made remains a mystery; what can we determine about how they were used? The knives had to be held in different ways to fulfil their different roles: in the left hand for the music to be viewed correctly, in the right for carving or eating. This might suggest some symbolic transition between the moment of eating and the prayers that flank it, if, indeed, the knives were intended for practical use. They may originally have been used by professional musicians, singing to an audience of diners, most likely at a court or in the household of a wealthy patrician, or the diners might have used the knives themselves. Singing and eating communally could reflect symbolically a sacred or secular form of brotherhood. The polyphony on the knives is not complex; a basic musical literacy is sufficient to sing the parts. If used repeatedly, the musical texts may have merely acted as prompts for memory. Possible contexts in which the knives might have provoked song and a sense of community would have included a monastic refectory, a confraternity, or an academy.

These knives are objects over which a musical text has been scattered. This parallels a material shift in the primary location of polyphonic musical texts: from the single, central choir book, in which all voice parts were written out together on a double-page opening, to sets of separate part-books, each containing a single voice. This shift undermined the gravitational pull of the choir lectern, not only facilitating the development of increasingly complex polychoral music, with singers and instrumentalists positioned in different locations within a church, but also enabling amateur musicians to sit together around a table or a room. Notated music was materially fragmented across partbooks, only able to exist fully when the set was brought together. This permitted the representation of individual voice parts on a range of diverse objects in a way that was previously conceptually impossible, radically expanding the material contexts in which musical texts could exist. Music was not just restricted to the manuscript or the printed page, but could spill over the surfaces of embroidered table-cloths, ceramic dishes, and knives (Laube 2017; Dennis 2010a, 175-77; Dennis 2006).

These extraordinary and enigmatic knives are therefore more than just a curiosity. They reveal the intimate connections between sociability, dining, and music; they encapsulate the rituals and rich sensory experiences of the meal and spiritual belief in the sixteenth century; and, most importantly, they expose an important conceptual shift in music's relationship to material culture.

16. Playing Cards

Katelijne Schiltz

Peter Flötner (designer) and Franz Christoph Zell (printer and painter), Nuremberg, ca. 1540
47 coloured woodcuts, 10.5 x 5.9 cm
Nuremberg, Bibliothek des Germanischen Nationalmuseums, Sp 7418 1–47 Kapsel 516

Left image: Peter Flötner, 5 of Acorns with parody of the St George legend.
Remaining images: reverse of selected cards showing Bassus parts; at top right is the reverse of the 5 of Acorns with the Bassus of the song *Was soll ich thun*.

Among the treasures of the Germanisches Nationalmuseum in Nuremberg is a deck of hand-painted cards that was designed by Peter Flötner around 1540. The reverse of each card is neither blank nor covered with geometrical figures, as contemporary convention would dictate; rather, it carries musical notation yielding four-voice *Lieder* (songs). Among the six surviving copies of the set—the others in Berlin (Kupferstich-Kabinett), Paris (Bibliothèque nationale de France), London (British Museum), Oxford (Bodleian Library, Douce Collection), and New Haven (Beinecke Rare Book Library, Cary Collection)—the Nuremberg deck is the only coloured copy, and also the most complete: only one card, the 2 of Acorns, is missing. The set in Berlin bears the initials F C Z upon this particular card, which in all probability stand for the woodblock-cutter Franz Christoph Zell, who in a document from 1527 is named "Christoff Kartenmaler" (Cristoph the Card Painter).

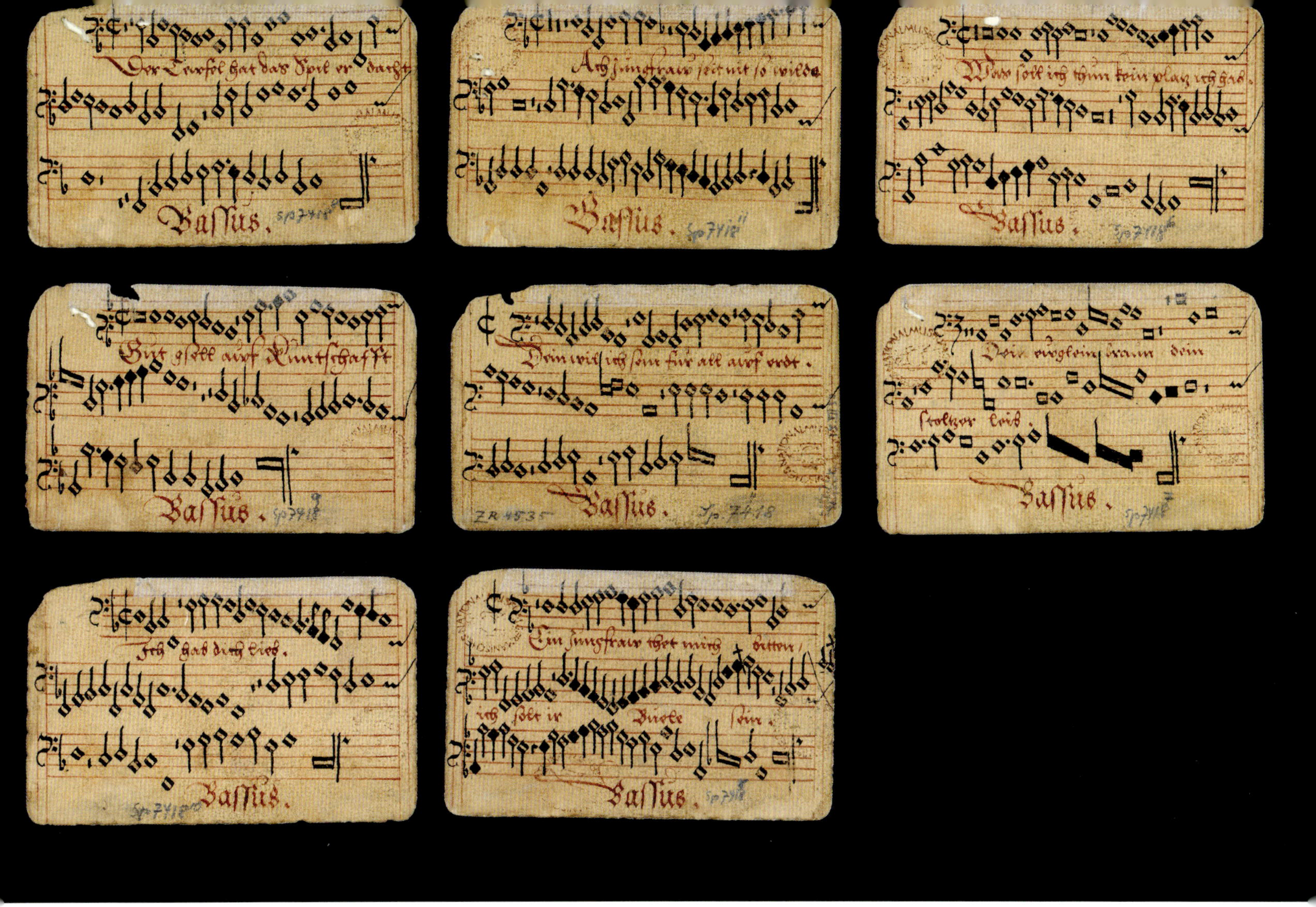

Alongside Augsburg and Ulm, Nuremberg was one of the major centres of card manufacture in Germany in this period. Although the city boasted a tradition of *Kartenmaler* dating back to the first half of the fifteenth century, the Reformation must have been instrumental in encouraging prominent artists to move into this area of work. Now that a market for devotional images by and large had ceased to exist, famous names including Hans Sebald Beham, Erhard Schön, Hans Schaufelein, Peter Flötner, and Jost Amman found they had to turn their attention to other forms of printed graphic work, such as pamphlets, mythological, and allegorical pictures—and playing cards.

For Flötner, playing card design was just one of his many artistic endeavours, in an oeuvre that embraces sculpture, medals, and relief plaques, as well as designs for furniture, panels, and book illustrations. Although the exact date of these playing cards is unknown, they seem to have been created at a time when Flötner produced a number of woodcuts, among them an anthropomorphic alphabet, a human sundial, and the satirical *New Passion of Christ* showing Christ being beaten and mocked by members of the clergy. The latter two woodcuts are especially interesting, as they contain elements that can be linked with the deck of cards: scatological humour and faecal fantasies on the one hand (Kammel 2007), and anti-Catholic propaganda on the other.

According to the typical German playing card system, each of the four suits (Hearts, Bells, Leaves, and Acorns) has 12 cards, comprising King, Upper Knave (or over-valet), Under Knave (or under-valet), Banner (10) and 9 through to 2. The Deuce cards (German *Daus*, from the French *deux*) bear a coat of arms, which according to Schadendorf belongs to Francesco d'Este, youngest son of Duke Alfonso I of Ferrara and his wife Lucrezia Borgia (Schadendorf 1960). This hypothesis gains plausibility from the fact that Francesco visited Nuremberg in 1541 in the company of Emperor Charles V—both were on their way to the Imperial Diet that was to take place in Regensburg in the same year. Flötner designed a triumphal arch (*Ehrenpforte*) on the occasion of Charles' visit, and the idea to produce playing cards for his Ferrarese companion might well be related to this event. What is more, Charles V figures on one of the cards, the King of Leaves, joined in that rank by the Turkish sultan (King of Hearts), the Indian potentate (King of Bells), and a King of Acorns who has been variously identified as Emperor Maximilian I and Charles V's brother Ferdinand. Russell Crosby (Crosby 1967) suggests the four Kings stand for the Austrian (Acorns) and Spanish branch (Leaves) of the House of Habsburg, the New World (Bells) and the Orient (Hearts).

Careful thought has clearly gone into the other categories and divisions of the deck also. Flötner marks an obvious social distinction between the Upper and Under Knaves, depicting a townsman, a scribe, a cup-bearer, and a trombonist as the former; and a messenger, a cook, a butcher, and a fool—all of them with caricature-like features—as the latter. The four suits in general each have a thematic focus: whereas pigs dominate the suit of Acorns and fools populate the suit of Bells, Leaves and Hearts focus on peasants and townsmen respectively. Wulf Schadendorf hypothesizes that Flötner's own features can be discerned upon the 6 of Hearts, the artist having taken the *Bürgereid* (citizen's oath) to become a citizen of his adoptive home town (Schadendorf 1960).

Scholars have interpreted the pictures and purpose of Flötner's cards in various ways. Laura Smoller highlights the *mundus inversus* as a recurring theme: "Fools pull a sled in which more fools ride; rabbits capture a hunter; wives beat their husbands; and boars sniff at heaps of excrement. All of these themes relate to a carnivalesque triumph of folly over reason and of the lowly over the exalted" (Smoller 1986, 193). Satirical elements also include a parody of the St George legend (5 of Acorns), which takes the form of a hunchbacked dwarf sitting on a goat and attacking a pig with a lance (see upper image). Another scholar highlights "the obsession and insatiability of his sexual and fecal fantasies, which led Flötner to constantly new inventions" (transl. from Schoch 1993, 71; Kammel 2007). At the same time Rainer Schoch situates the card game in a broader cultural context, in which games also played a role in the moral education of the people who used them, thus contributing to the building of healthy social habits, even through an activity wrought with moral peril such as a card game. Schoch rightly stresses that already in the fifteenth century, most prominently in Ingold Wild's *Das guldin Spil* (*The Golden Game*) from 1432-33, various types of game were associated with the seven deadly sins (chess with pride, board games with gluttony, cards with lust, etc.) and were—more broadly speaking—part of the iconography of the vices. Against this background, Flötner's deck of cards can indeed be said to contain a moral message.

And then there is the music on the back of each card. The fact that a deck consists of four suits makes this medium almost ideally suited to the presentation of four-part music in a format similar to a partbook, albeit on small loose leaves. The music occupies three systems, with staves in red, and each suit is related to a voice (Acorns: Bassus; Leaves: Tenor; Bells: Altus; Hearts: Discantus). The *Lieder* all have approximately the same length of between 20 and 25 breves (with 5, *Was soll ich thun / kein platz ich hab* [see lower image], and 2, *Du bist allein meins herzens Kron*, being slightly longer), which suggests they were composed specifically for the cards. Nuremberg is a likely point of origin for these songs, as for the cards themselves, given that the city was an important centre for the production and printing of *Lieder* around the time Flötner's deck was created: famous contemporary collections include *Hundert und ainundzwanzig newe Lieder* and *Hundert und fünfftzehen guter newer Liedlein* (Nuremberg: Hans Ott, 1534 and 1544) and Georg Forster's "teutsche Liedlein" (published in five parts between 1539 and 1556).

Unfortunately, we only have the incipits of the texts, which raises questions as to whether these *Lieder* were known to the persons using them—and, more generally, as to the performance context of the music. On the basis of the *Lieder*'s incipits, Schadendorf sees a coherent programme lying behind the order of the songs in the set, which he describes as a gradual progress: from the lover praising the beloved as the crown of his heart (as in *Lied* 2), to the sufferings and joys of the lover, to the lover indulging in self-pity.

In his 1967 edition of the *Lieder*, C. Russell Crosby suggests similarities with existing melodies, pointing to possible traces of Wilhelm Breitengraser's *Sich hat mein herz dir geneigt* in the Discantus of 9, and of the Lutheran chorales *Aus tiefer Not schrei ich zu dir* and *Wie schön leuchtet der Morgenstern* in the Tenor of 5 and 10 respectively. Most of the *Lieder* have a polyphonic texture; some of them start with a homophonic passage (especially striking in the series 6 to 9).

An intriguing question remains when one reflects upon the relationship between the two faces of each card. As the organisation of songs and voice-parts is tied to the organisation of ranks and suits in the deck, with some experience it would be easy to know the obverse of each card from a view of the song on its reverse. For example, if you saw the Discantus of *Du bist allein meins herzens Kron* in a player's hand, you could deduce that the player has the 2 of Hearts—as the Discantus voice-part is related to the suit of Hearts, and this particular song appears on the Deuce cards. In other words, the music betrays which cards a person has in their hand, subverting the secretive aspect of the game. Schadendorf even comes to the conclusion that the cards were more playful than playable (Schadendorf 1960, 147). What both sides of the cards clearly have in common is their ludic intent: both can be considered as pastimes in the company of kindred spirits. One also wonders when the *Lieder* were sung: were they intended to be performed before, during, or after the card game, or maybe even independently? I like to think of them as the culmination of and reward after the game, underlining the collective act of playing together after all the participants had finished playing for themselves—*ex discordia concors*. The addition of music could thus help in highlighting the moral value of the game: singing together—or even just seeing polyphonic music scattered across the cards—reminded the players of the importance of harmony as a symbol for a well-ordered society, a harmony that good citizens should never forget before starting a card game, never lose during it, and eventually always be able to restore after it.

ADDITIONAL REFERENCES: Hoffmann 1993; Röttinger 1916.

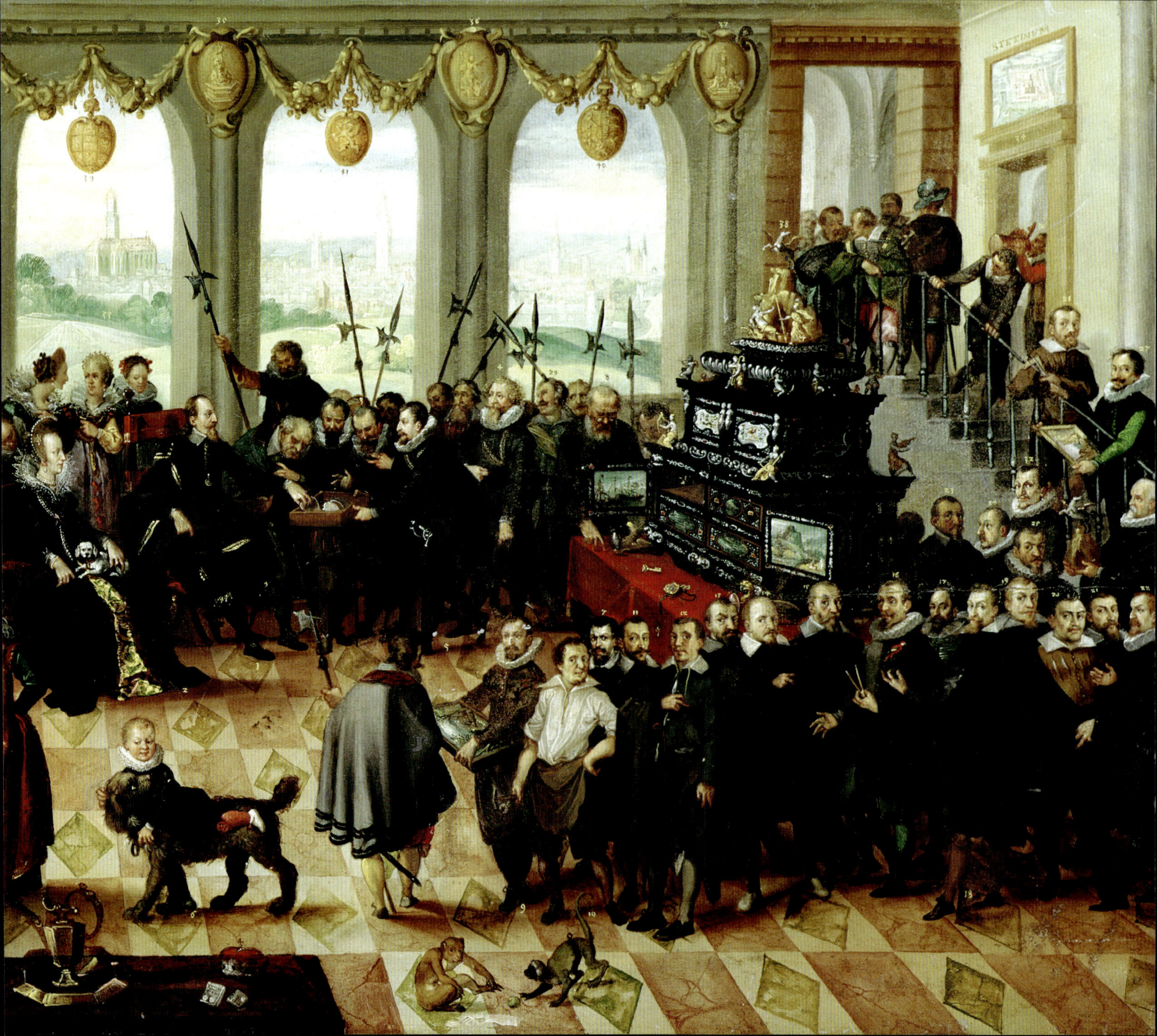
STETINUM

17. Cabinet of Curiosities

Franz Körndle

Pommerscher Kunstschrank
Ulrich Baumgartner et al., Augsburg, 1610-17
Exterior of ebony with fittings and inlays of silver and gems; interior of sandalwood and red leather; 148 (h.) x 102 (l.) x 86 (w.) cm
Kunstgewerbemuseum, Staatliche Museen zu Berlin (remnants—partially destroyed in WWII)

Image: Anton Mozart, *Presentation of the Pomeranian Kunstschrank to Duke Philip II of Pomerania in 1617*, ca. 1617. Oil on wood, 39.5 x 45.4 cm. Kunstgewerbemuseum, Staatliche Museen zu Berlin. Photo © Staatliche Museen, Berlin / Bridgeman Images.

The *Pommersche Kunstschrank* (Pomerian art cabinet) was an elaborate piece of furniture commissioned in 1610 by the art dealer and diplomat Philipp Hainhofer from Augsburg carpenters and artists under the responsibility of Ulrich Baumgartner. After its completion, it was delivered in 1617 to Duke Philip II of Pomerania. The art cabinet with its silver ornaments was not only remarkable for the finesse of its exterior; inside, it was endowed with many valuable and curious items, decorated with various gems, gold, and silver. For this reason, experts have discussed it as a miniature cabinet of curiosities. Its contents included about 300 objects. There were iron tools such as pliers, drills, a rile, a rasp, a hammer and anvil, watches, a compass and other geometric instruments, quadrants, an astrolabe, a ruler, board games such as nine men's morris and chess, and dice, chalk and sponge, as well as playing cards made of silver. Equipment from the realm of hygiene included a small pharmacy with cans, small bottles and glasses, and a balance, of course lozenges and a bezoar. Furthermore, several surgical instruments were included for bloodletting, cupping, or injection, and also toothpowder. For a shave, one could find razors, a strop, hair scissors, beard curling tongs and combs, toothpicks, mirrors, and brushes. Cutlery and crockery were as much a part of the inventory as pans and small jugs. Also present were writing utensils, with quills and scissors, erasers, inkwell, castor, letter opener, ruler, and of course sealing wax, as well as prayer books and other books. Finally, at the bottom of the cabinet was a small organ housed as a musical automaton.

The exterior of the cabinet was decorated with figures. On the top there was a sculpture representing the mythical winged horse Pegasus on mount Parnassus, the home of the Muses. At the foot of the mountain were Pallas Athena (standing on the right) and a muse or nymph (seated on the left). The latter has several musical instruments around her (lira da braccio, rebec, shawm and other wind instruments). Between the two figures lay a music book (Gottron 1959, 466-67). On the open pages could be read a two-part song with the text "Dum vivo spero" (As long as I live I hope—derived from Cicero's *Letters to Atticus* 9.10) and a four-part canon with the text "Miscentur tristia laetis" (Joy mixes with grief; Ovid, *Fasti* 6.463). Beneath Parnassus were the figures of the Muses made of gilded silver, holding musical instruments; of the six figures still extant before the destruction of the cabinet, five played trombone, lute, cornet, violin, and harp, the sixth was apparently also playing but her instrument had already been lost. A series of engravings with the Muses shows clear parallels. Lucas Kilian had designed the models, which his brother Wolfgang Kilian engraved in copper (Kilian 1612). To explain the content, Philipp Hainhofer added a booklet with a description (Lessing and Brüning 1905, 32-57).

The production of artworks containing musical automata had a long tradition in the free imperial city of Augsburg. Most likely this tradition traces back to a visit of the cathedral organist Erasmus Mayr to Tivoli in the year 1576, where he encountered the self-playing organ in the famous garden of Villa d'Este. Mayr observed the technique used to create this instrument, and shared the information with the craftsmen of Augsburg upon his return, among them Hans Meitting and Hans Schlottheim (Schmid 1941, 135-37). In the instruments produced in this tradition, pins and bridges were installed on a cylinder, and when the cylinder turned the pins and bridges pressed the keys of an organ or a spinet. Like a clock, the motive force was produced by a strong spring, which could also power the organ's bellows to supply the pipes with wind (von Stetten 1779, 184-85 and 190).

Soon the Augsburg gold- and silversmiths adapted this idea and began to build musical automata into artificial replicas of ships, buildings, or animals. For example, a clock built by Hans Schlottheim in 1602 for Christian II, Elector of Saxony (who gave it to his wife Hedwig the following year) takes the form of a tower upon the galleries of which are brass ensembles (Grünes Gewölbe, Dresden; Protz 1939, 38-39). The musicians with their shawms and trombones wear an outfit in red, green, and white, the colours of the Augsburg city pipers. The sound of the music is produced by a small organ in the tower's substructure using 17 open and stopped pipes of wood.

Some of these Augsburg artworks were particularly attractive because they were set up so that they could move. In 1585, Schlottheim constructed a ship of gold and silver for Emperor Rudolf II's cabinet of curiosities (Kunsthistorisches Museum, Vienna; Haspels 2006, 197). On the deck of the ship is a group of trumpeters who can lift their instruments to blow. The audible signals, produced by a miniature organ with small reed pipes, are modelled on traditional trumpet fanfares. Mechanical beats on a membrane simulate the sound of kettle drums. Additionally, a short musical piece is played on metal pipes, apparently as an imitation of military pipers. Afterwards, the ship sets in motion on built-in wheels. Finally, coming to a standstill, cannons are fired.

The visual aesthetics of musical automata changed during the first quarter of the seventeenth century. The concept was now to integrate the instruments—organs or even spinets—within larger cabinets. It was the Augsburg patrician Philipp Hainhofer who propelled the taste for these ornate pieces of furniture. A very well educated man, he had studied law in Padua, Bologna, and Siena from 1594. On his later travels he not only expanded his already enormous linguistic skills, but also gained knowledge of the political situation in Europe and the current state of the arts. He documented his impressions of the important cabinets of curiosities in Munich, Innsbruck, and Dresden in his extensive travel diaries. The descriptions of performances and remarks on the instruments contained therein also testify to his keen interest in music. Several books from his collecting dating to 1603 and 1604 contain music for the lute (now in the Herzog-August Library in Wolfenbüttel), which he himself mastered very well (Lüdtke 2001). Before long collectors were seeking his advice, and therefore he began to act as an agent in the purchase and commission of art objects. Due to the city's excellent trade relations, Hainhofer's home in Augsburg proved extremely favourable for these activities and their attendant international correspondence. He therefore became a central figure in the collection and art politics of early seventeenth-century Europe.

Hainhofer commissioned designs for several of these cabinets, and himself wrote descriptions of them, looking for wealthy buyers. He distributed incoming orders among the Augsburg carpenters, gold- and silversmiths, as well as makers of automata and musical instruments. In some cases, his negotiations were successful. In the years 1619-25, after the *Pommersche Kunstschrank*, another cabinet was made for Archduke Leopold V (Museo degli Argenti, Florence; Orth 2018, 27), and in 1625-31 a third example was bought by the City Council of Augsburg to be handed over to King Gustav Adolf of Sweden in 1631 (Universitets Konstsamlingar, Uppsala; Boström 1994, 555, 562).

The *Pommersche Kunstschrank* was completed in 1617 and delivered to Duke Philip's principal city, Szczecin. Even before this occasion, most likely in 1615, Hainhofer ordered a painting from Anton Mozart showing the act of the presentation—the very same painting that is on display alongside this essay, in the absence of the object itself. The visible interior of the ducal castle was fictitious. On the left one can see Duke Philip of Pomerania with his wife Sophia and Philipp Hainhofer. On the right, the craftsmen who were involved in the production are arranged around the cabinet.

The painting was accompanied by a small plaque on which the names of the 24 participating artisans are recorded. To aid identification, both the names on the plaque and the individuals in the painting are numbered. Number 9 is Achilles Langenbucher, a well-known manufacturer of musical automata, who some scholars have therefore identified as the maker of the cabinet's small organ (Protz 1939, 39-49; Mundt 2009,155-56). On the plaque, however, Langenbucher is called a "Muggenman" (a maker of tiny metal animals), whereas number 17, Marx Genser, is identified as an organ builder. Taking everything into account, the most likely situation is that Langenbucher assembled the mechanical action and placed the pins and bridges on the cylinder, whilst Marx Günzer built the small organ with 21 wooden pipes.

The cylinder was prepared with several compositions to be played by the organ. As with other musical automata from Augsburg, the music began with descending triads in order to clarify the tonality. Three pieces followed, first a prelude (*Praeambulum*), then richly ornamented elaborations of the chorale-melody *Allein nach dir, Herr Jesu Christ*, and finally a fantasia. When Hainhofer delivered the cabinet built for Archduke Leopold V in 1628, he mentioned in an accompanying letter the same musical pieces as could be heard from the Pomeranian cabinet, adding that they were composed by Christian Erbach. Adam Gottron has suggested that Erbach was also responsible for the two canons depicted in the music book on the lid (Gottron 1959, 466).

The *Pommersche Kunstschrank* was undoubtedly the most spectacular object of its kind. Its conception incorporated many aspects of the great tradition of the cabinet of curiosities. Furthermore, the integration of musical instruments shows that it was not just a matter of gathering special features and curiosities from nature and the visual arts. In search of new marvels, makers of musical automata even tried to overcome the ephemeral character of music. The sound of a performance given by singers or instrumentalists ends as soon as the last chord has faded away. By recording compositions and their performance parameters on the cylinder of a self-playing instrument, it is not only possible to hear pieces without the participation of musicians, but to repeat them as often as desired. People afforded the privilege of viewing the art cabinet could not only admire the magnificent exterior, but as an audience they noticed how the hidden organ automatically produced musical compositions. The mechanical parts of the musical instrument are not on display; they serve as a hidden medium for the representation of life and nature. Perhaps an intention to address all five senses was a conscious part of the cabinet's design: art for the eyes; the objects inside for smell and taste as well as the sense of touch—including tools, cutlery, plates, and mugs as well as incense, spices, and salt; and an organ, which not only filled the ears with music, but completed all the aspects as a representation of cosmic harmony.

In 1684 the *Pommersche Kunstschrank* ended up in Berlin, where it found its place in the Kunst- und Raritätenkabinet of the Electoral Palace. From there it came in 1876 to the new Königliche Kunstgewerbemuseum. In 1934 Hans Cürlis directed a documentary film showing how the cabinet could be disassembled and what was kept inside (Savoy 2014). In 1938, Albert Protz was able to examine the cabinet and to take photographs of the organ. In addition to a detailed description, he precisely transcribed the positions of the pins and bridges on the musical cylinder into modern musical notation. Protz' documentation is carefully executed and even captures aspects of performance practice. The spacing of the pins, for example, indicated a ritardando in cadences.

During World War II, the cabinet's case, including the organ, was put into the safe of the Neue Münze. There it burned in a bombing raid on 11 March 1945 (Hannes 1990; Hinterkeuser 2014). The objects once stored inside, however, had been relocated to Wiesbaden during the war, thus they could be saved, silent witnesses of a beautiful dream of cosmic harmony now forever destroyed.

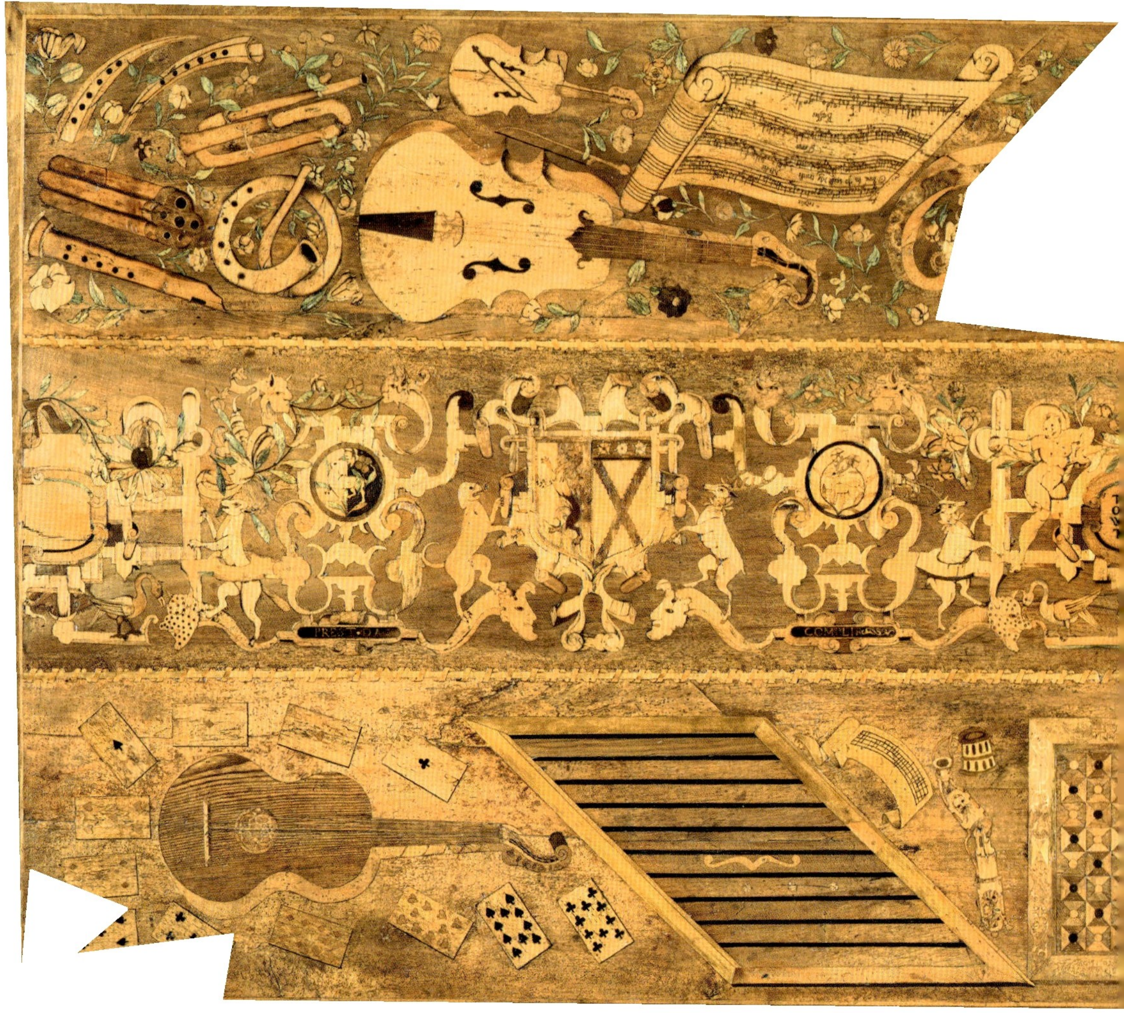

18. Table

Katie Bank

The Eglantine Table
Anon., London, ca. 1568
The top walnut, limewood and fruitwood veneers on a deal core, inlaid with various woods; the base of ash with painted decoration to the stretchers; 90 (height) x 302 (length) x 129 (width) cm
Inscribed: THE * REDOLENT * SMLE * / * OF * AEGLENTYNE / WE * STAGGES * EXAVET * / TO * THE * DEVEYNE
The National Trust Hardwick Hall, Derbyshire
Photo © National Trust Images / John Hammond / Bridgeman Images

In 1567, Elizabeth of Hardwick, known as Bess, married her fourth husband, George Talbot, sixth Earl of Shrewsbury. As a part of the marital arrangement, Bess agreed for two of her children from her previous marriage to William Cavendish to marry two of Shrewsbury's. In 1568, Bess' 12-year-old Mary Cavendish was married to 16-year-old Gilbert Talbot, and Bess' eldest, 18-year-old Henry Cavendish, was married to 8-year-old Grace Talbot. The so-called Eglantine Table, now located at Hardwick Hall, was probably crafted in 1568 to commemorate this merger between three of England's most powerful families. The centre panel bears the arms of Hardwick, Cavendish, and Talbot in various impaled arrangements symbolising the marriages. The central inscription reads, in modern English, "the redolent smell of Eglantine, We Stags exalt to the Divine." Simon Jervis observes that the stags on either side of the central couplet are Hardwick stags, asserting that Bess herself is the focus of the table (Jervis 2016, 96-97). While there remains some controversy about when the table found its way to Hardwick Hall, Mark Girourd surmises the table was crafted for the Great High Gallery or Great High Chamber at

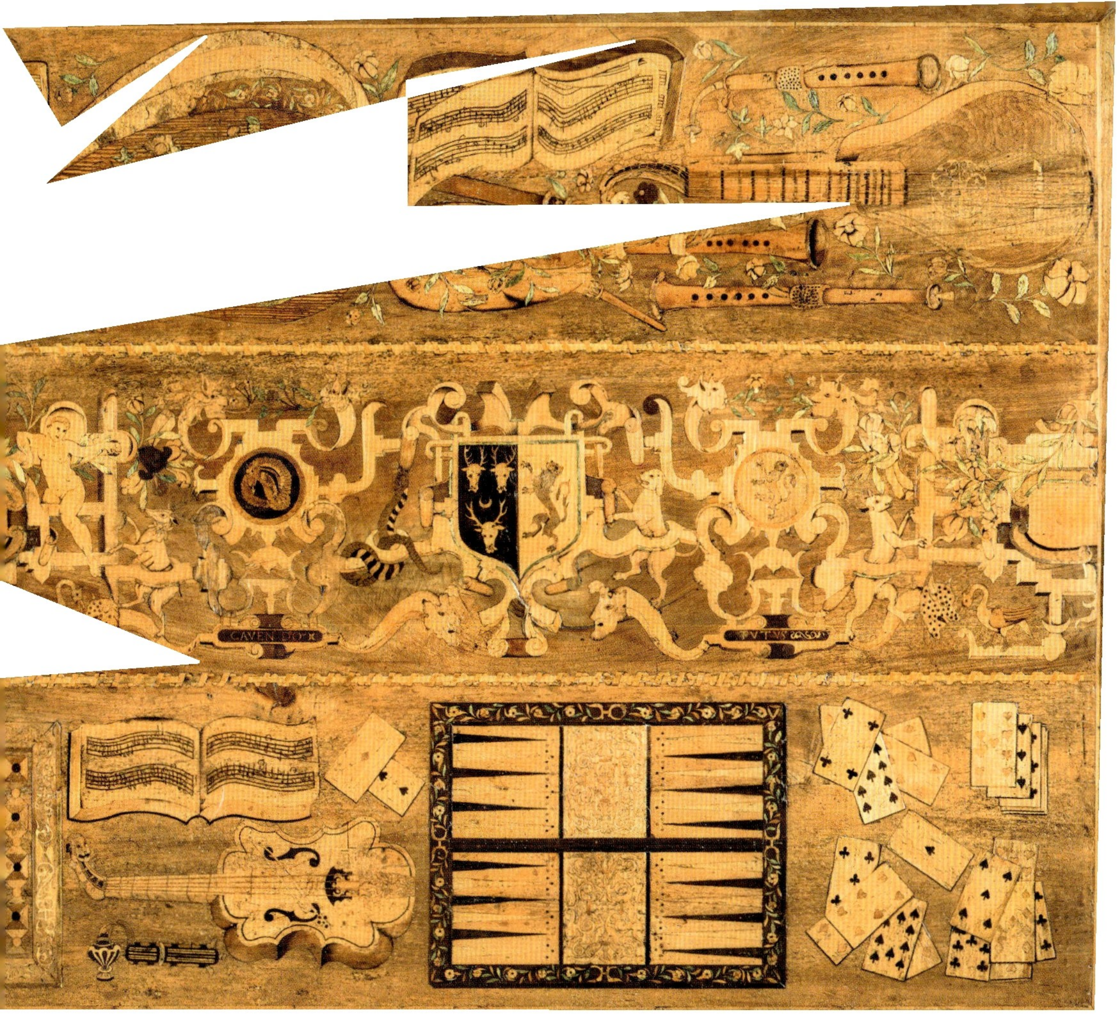

Chatsworth, the Cavendish estate, and brought to Hardwick at an unknown date (Girouard 2006, 90). As Girouard points out, high chambers and galleries were often used for eating special meals with guests, plays, masques, dancing, and playing games like cards, dice, and backgammon in between meals. Their musical function meant that such rooms were often adorned with musical iconography.

Representations of the objects of domestic recreation—including those pertaining to music—dominate the table's intricate inlay. As a common symbol of marital harmony, an object decorated with musical iconography makes an appropriate wedding gift. Decorating the upper and lower friezes are 15 musical instruments, various music books and scrolls, a four-part harmonization of *Lord, in thee is all my trust* by Thomas Tallis, board games and playing cards, and other items. Coloured floral inlay dots the upper frieze, including two instances of Tudor roses. In an attempt to account for the variation in construction materials—walnut for the central panel, fruitwood and limewood for the friezes—some have speculated that the central board may have been conceived as an independent panel, for a wall or some other household use, and the two outer boards added when it was turned into a table. But as Jervis concludes, "it seems much more likely that such an ambitious inlaid table required a measure of structural ad-hocism … and that its design was simply original and experimental" (Jervis 2016, 97-98). Perhaps future investigations into the table's iconography will shed further light on this question, if conclusions drawn from a focus on structure and design remain uncertain (Fleming and Page 2021).

Anthony Wells-Cole has convincingly demonstrated that design ideas for the strapwork of the centre frieze were adapted from prints published in Antwerp in 1566-67 by Flemish artist Jacob Floris, demonstrating that the table's design was sharply on trend when it was created (Wells-Cole 1997, 249-

50). But in spite of these continental design elements, it is thought the table was crafted and designed in London. Benno Forman has demonstrated that at least 405 foreign craftsmen skilled in marquetry, mostly from the Low Countries, settled in Southwark between 1511 and 1621, as it was outside the jurisdiction of the London Joiners' Company (Forman 1971, 105-20). This, combined with the fact that the floral slips of the upper frieze are distinctly Elizabethan in taste, give strong evidence suggesting London craftsmanship.

A central theme of the Eglantine Table, evident in its decoration, is the idea of play. Games and music were centrepieces of contemporary domestic recreation. Johan Huizinga's work on the phenomenon of play argues that play is not an element *in* culture, but an element *of* culture (Huizinga 1949, 10). Huizinga highlights play as a dominant mode of culture formation, as well as emphasising the significance of the physical space in which play occurs, as play is often spatially and temporally demarcated. He suggests that play is not only an integral part of culture and culture-forming, but also reciprocally shapes the spaces in which it takes place.

The games and musical objects featured on the table were all commonly played in the homes of the nobility. By the sixteenth century, all the board games featured on the table—cards, backgammon, chess, and dice—were long-standing aspects of English culture. Dice games had been in England since the Roman occupation, and table games like backgammon and chess first appeared in England in the twelfth century. Card games were the relative newcomers, first appearing on record during the third year of the reign of Edward IV. On the right lower panel, four hands of cards are casually laid on the table, as if in mid play. Patrick Ball believes that the game depicted here is Triumph (or French Ruff), and that this would have been apparent to Elizabethans (Ball 2021).

David Collins has identified and described the musical instruments of the table, making observations about structural accuracy (Collins 1976). Minus one small scroll next to the dice board, which had been heavily damaged, Collins also transcribed the notation, including the lute tablature and the song by Tallis. Since then, the remaining staff notation has been identified by John Milsom (Milsom 2021). The most well-known musical feature of the table is the score-like harmonization of a tune ascribed to Tallis, *O Lord in thee is all my trust*. The tune was widely known as a monophonic devotional song and was included in Sternhold and Hopkins' widely-reprinted metrical psalter (see exhibit 13). Though the tune is unascribed in the psalter, a four-part harmonization attributed to "M Talys" was in existence as early as 1550. Milsom suggests the Eglantine Table version, one of three main sources for the piece, may have been intended for instruments, on account of the unusually wide ranges and ornamentation.

While there is thorough existing scholarship on *what* the Eglantine Table depicts (most recently and comprehensively, Fleming and Page 2021), this essay hopes to explore what is revealed about contemporary domestic recreation from *how* meaning was produced in the table's iconography. Material historians, art historians, and anthropologists have productively explored how the intricacies of human relationships, social values, and even systems of thought, are embedded in objects. As sound and experience are ephemeral, one must turn to an examination of the objects within spaces, in addition to the spaces themselves, as the objects are often the only evidence of those daily practices and activities that imbued space with meaning. For this reason, a look beyond the provenance and physical characteristics of the Eglantine Table proves a fruitful venture in further understanding the meaning of play or recreation in contemporary domestic life.

What this exhibit offers to our understanding of domestic spaces concerns the idea that an object, in icon and function, can do more than statically represent activity. If the friezes of the table were hung on a wall, they would still be a part of the domestic space. But as a functional object that could have played a literally supporting and central role in gaming or music activities, activities which often surrounded a table, the iconography is imbued with additional meaning. It demonstrates contemporary thought about recreation and how those practices shaped domestic spaces and the objects in them. Unlike a plainer table, the explicit iconography of the Eglantine Table in effect insists on a consideration of the playing that formed the space, thereby also drawing attention to the table's own nature and function in those recreational activities.

Additionally, the artist has done their best to make the play in this table seem full of motion. For example, the four hands of cards left casually mid-game demonstrate the objects in use. The book of lute music is displayed not flat, but with curls in both corners. Whether this is to demonstrate it mid-turn, or just with wear from heavy repeated use, it gives the image dimensionality, rooting the representations of those objects in their use in daily life. The music book in the upper right top panel is similarly depicted mid-page turn. The left page is curled in a strangely un-naturalistic fashion, the right page floating up. It is unclear if the bagpipe plays a role in this page's position, but either way, it appears on its way to turning, whether abiding the laws of physics or not.

The table also displays two sets of penners and ink pots, perhaps for notating music or for keeping score in a board game. Given the open penner and unstopped ink horn are in proximity to the scroll of music, the former seems more likely. The open inkpot and possibly unfinished scroll might further contribute to the idea of "activity signalled" that is suggested by the in-play card game and the implied motion of the music books. The pens are out, the ink pot is open, waiting for the hand that animates them.

There are obvious challenges in capturing a practice, experience, or motion in static art. Most often, visual imagery of music is given its action through representations of humanoid subjects mid-song, as the many singing angels of the period amply demonstrate (see, for example, exhibits 2, 3, and 44). But this table presents no human figures to imply the action of musicking. Moreover, the subjectless motion and use depicted in these music books were unusual for Tudor artwork, which more often depicted books in pristine condition with subjects using them, as in the contemporary painting of *Death and the Maiden* hanging elsewhere in this museum (exhibit 26). Some continental paintings of music books show inference of motion in their pages, as in Caravaggio's *The Lute Player* (ca. 1596, Wildenstein Collection). But crucially, most paintings depicting music-making also show a central figure who acts as a probable source of motion for the music.

In the Eglantine Table, the absence of a represented subject leaves a vacancy which insists that viewers contemplate the practice and action of an *implied* subject, one that instigates reflection on one's own play experiences. Alternatively, as Bess herself is the heraldic centre of the table, one might also suggest that this iconography is an extension of Bess's wider architectural and political prowess. Perhaps the iconography situates Bess and her children as the active subjects and realisers of the activities.

Additionally, the fact that the Tallis song appears in a score-like form means the music is performable from the table. Rather than stopping at an iconographic reference to musical notation, as a depiction of a single partbook in a portrait might do, this object presents an implied performance of a potentially recognised piece. Though a fundamentally different kind of signifier than the iconology of the objects of recreation, notation also carries with it the potential to be realised as an embodied activity. As Richard Wistreich has argued,

> the act of reading musical notation (and, in the case of songs, its associated words) "back into sound" is, by comparison with most other literary texts, almost always physiologically quite spectacularly dynamic … As such, it admirably fulfils Roger Chartier's dictum that "Reading is not uniquely an abstract operation of the intellect: it brings the body into play, it is inscribed in a space and a relationship with oneself and with others" (Wistreich 2012, 3).

The iconography and notation of the Eglantine Table do exactly this. Meaning is derived from the combination of performable notation with iconography that strongly invokes the action and experience of play, but crucially without a represented subject. This thrusts the subject viewing into the implied action, bringing their own body into play. Moreover, the table's practical function as the central arena of play reinforces the iconography's emphasis on practice and action.

Understanding the relationship between a historical space and human activity requires a degree of informed imagination. As Huizinga and other theorists have concluded, space is a practiced place. Play is not a marginal part of life, but a significant way in which we form culture. The Eglantine Table offers insight not only into how the meanings behind recreation shaped domestic spaces and objects, but also into contemporary approaches to subjectivity. The table's musical iconography raises promising possibilities for further study on the iconology of musical experience.

Additional references: Arcangeli 2003; Bank 2020; Buckley 1998; Chan 2020; Fleming and Page 2021; Milsom 2021; Motture and O'Malley 2010; Otis 2017; Tallis 1993; Wistreich 2012.

19. Statue

Laura Moretti

Praying Boy ("*Adorante*") also known as *Apollo*
Anon. in the manner of Lysippos, ca. 300 BC, arms added in the 18th century
Bronze, 128 cm
Antikensammlung, Staatliche Museen zu Berlin
Photo © BPK, Berlin, Dist. RMN-Grand Palais / Johannes Laurentius

In a list of medals, coins, and bronze and marble statues possessed by the Veronese collector and patron of the arts Mario Bevilacqua, dated 1589 and possibly drawn up by their owner, we find a reference to an "Apollo giovane," a bronze statue six palms in height with no arms (Franzoni 1970, 161). It was by some distance the most precious object included in the list, valued at 600 *scudi d'oro*. The statue is now preserved in the Antikensammlung of the Staatliche Museen in Berlin, where it is reputed to be one of the most important objects in the collection, and one of the few which must never leave the museum (Zimmer and Hackländer 1997).

The antique bronze, originally from Rhodes, was brought to Venice at the beginning of the sixteenth century. On 28 September 1503, the musical instrument maker Lorenzo Gusnasco, also known as Lorenzo da Pavia, wrote to his patron and regular correspondent Isabella d'Este to announce the arrival of the statue (Brown 2002, 176-77). Although it was missing part of its arms and left foot, and its hair "could have been better [executed]," Lorenzo expressed genuine enthusiasm, claiming that he had "never [seen] a more beautiful thing." The statue was then in the hands of Andrea de Martini, member of the Knights of St John of Jerusalem and friend of Taddeo Albano, Isabella's agent in Venice.

Upon landing in La Serenissima, the statue quickly became one of the most admired artworks in the city. As Enea Vico attests in his *Discorsi sopra le medaglie degli antichi* (1558), Pietro Bembo offered a piece from his own collection in Padua for the restoration of the missing foot. In January 1549, Pietro Aretino wrote a long and appreciative letter to de Martini describing the statue in detail and praising its beauty, while Francesco Sansovino referred to it as "a marvel" in his *Delle cose notabili* (1561) (Perry 1975).

In the mid-1570s, a replica was made and placed first in the treasury of San Marco and later, in 1613, in the Statuario Pubblico in the Antisala of the Biblioteca Marciana. Today this copy can be found in the Museo Archeologico Nazionale in Piazza San Marco.

At a certain point, presumably during the second half of the 1570s, the statue passed into the hands of the famous Venetian collector Leonardo Mocenigo. Francesco Sansovino, in his *Venetia città nobilissima et singolare* (1581), lists Mocenigo's collection of antiquities as one of the most important in the city. When Leonardo died, the collection passed to his son Alvise, who started to sell several items to make good on the extensive debts incurred by his father over years spent acquiring valuable and rare objects. Consequently, the bronze statue formed part of the "antique things" sold by Alvise Mocenigo to Mario Bevilacqua, most probably in the second half of the 1580s (Brown and Lorenzoni 1999, 62).

Bevilacqua was one of the greatest collectors and patrons of literature and the arts in the second half of the sixteenth century. Born in Verona on 8 October 1536 to Gregorio and Giulia Canossa (niece of Girolamo Canossa, another important Veronese collector), Mario grew up in a cultured and refined environment. A true lover of literature and the arts, he had a particular fondness for music and an innate attraction to antiquities. After studying in Padua and Bologna, from which he graduated in 1567, he returned to Verona, where he settled in the family palazzo, on today's Corso Cavour, which had been renovated at mid-century by the Veronese architect Michele Sanmicheli. In 1588 Mario married Isabella Giusti, daughter of Count Agostino Giusti, another famous Veronese collector and patron of the arts. In the years following his return to his native city, Bevilacqua transformed his residence into a museum open to the public. In it, visitors could admire paintings and sculpture, drawings and prints, coins and medals, manuscripts and printed books, as well as musical instruments, objects to which Mario dedicated much of his time and resources, and which he had collected within the span of about 25 years. The library was considered one of the richest in the city, while the *galleria* contained masterpieces by Tintoretto and Paolo Veronese, among others, as well as antique statues and busts of Roman emperors. The famous *ridotto*, in which salaried musicians were employed, was regularly frequented by citizens and foreigners and enjoyed an international reputation.

An all-round patron of the arts, Bevilacqua was celebrated for his generosity and magnanimity. Many literary works of the 1570s and 1580s were dedicated to him by, among others, Andrea Grazioli, Adriano Valerini, Francesco Mondella, Felice Figliucci, Battista Peretti, and Federico Ceruti, as were a large number of printed music books, from at least 1574 on (Cecchi 2002, 444-45; Moretti 2020, 249-61). The long list of composers who dedicated their works to Bevilacqua included local maestri, like Gabriele Martinengo, Paolo Masnelli, and Leone Leoni, but also well-known names, including Claudio Merulo, Orazio Vecchi, Maddalena Casulana, Girolamo dalla Casa, Giovanni Bassano, Orlando di Lasso, Philippe de Monte, and Luca Marenzio. In terms of numbers, the dedicatory letters in editions of printed music addressed to Mario Bevilacqua were surpassed only by those directed at princes and sovereigns such as Alfonso II d'Este and Guglielmo Gonzaga.

Upon his death, Bevilacqua left a large collection of sculptures, paintings, drawings, medals, books, and musical instruments in his palace. According to an inventory drawn up in August 1593 shortly after the death of Bevilacqua (Enrico Paganuzzi in Franzoni 1970, 145-46), the *ridotto* housed a huge collection of musical instruments and portraits of composers and instrumentalists. The document lists 78 instruments—including keyboards, wind and brass instruments, bowed and plucked string instruments—56 portraits and six additional paintings of unspecified subjects, in addition to about 50 printed musical scores and 14 manuscripts stored in an armoire, a "walnut crescent for singing" (most likely a music stand), four painted chests—probably for the storage of instruments—a small table, five chairs, 65 stools with and without backrests, ten benches, eight gold leather panels used for wall decoration, and andirons for the fireplace. The room was obviously spacious and furnished to accommodate a significant number of both performers and listeners. Several of the musical instruments stored in the *ridotto* Bevilacqua were rare and valuable objects, as for example was the "regale a sette registri" (regal with seven stops), the "claviorgano," the "clavacimbano doppio" (double harpsichord), and the "bassanelli" (double-reed instruments)—which appear here for the first time in a sixteenth-century Italian inventory (Castellani 1973).

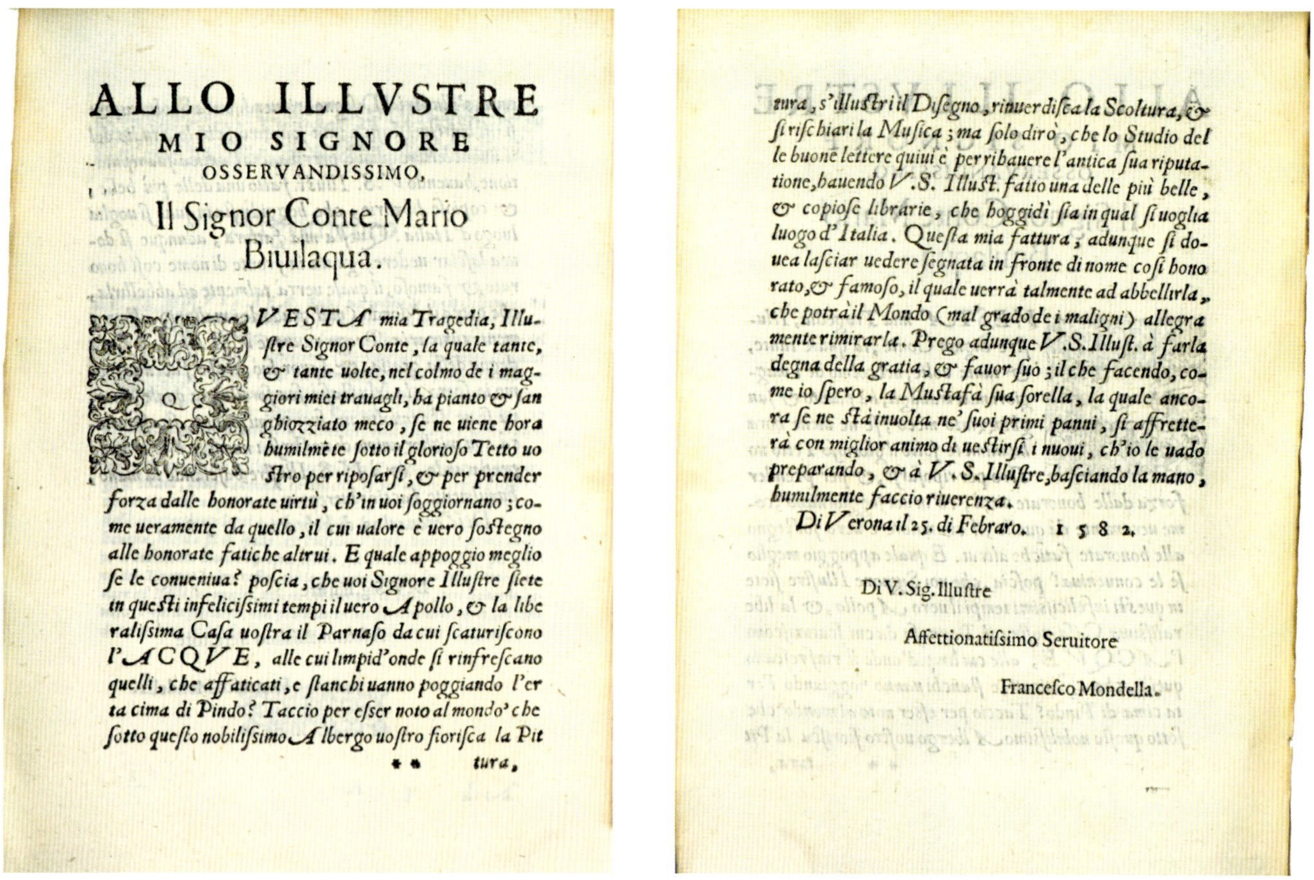

ALLO ILLVSTRE
MIO SIGNORE
OSSERVANDISSIMO,
Il Signor Conte Mario
Biuilaqua.

QVESTA mia Tragedia, Illuſtre Signor Conte, la quale tante, & tante uolte, nel colmo de i maggiori miei trauagli, ha pianto & ſanghiozziato meco, ſe ne uiene hora humilmẽte ſotto il glorioſo Tetto uoſtro per ripoſarſi, & per prender forza dalle honorate uirtù, ch'in uoi ſoggiornano; come ueramente da quello, il cui ualore è uero ſoſtegno alle honorate fatiche altrui. E quale appoggio meglio ſe le conueniua? poſcia, che uoi Signore Illuſtre ſiete in queſti infeliciſsimi tempi il uero Apollo, & la liberaliſsima Caſa uoſtra il Parnaſo da cui ſcaturiſcono l'ACQVE, alle cui limpid'onde ſi rinfreſcano quelli, che affaticati, e ſtanchi uanno poggiando l'erta cima di Pindo? Taccio per eſser noto al mondo' che ſotto queſto nobiliſsimo Albergo uoſtro fioriſca la Pittura, s'illuſtri il Diſegno, rinuerdiſca la Scoltura, & ſi riſchiari la Muſica; ma ſolo dirò, che lo Studio delle buone lettere quiui è per ribauere l'antica ſua riputatione, hauendo V.S. Illuſt. fatto una delle più belle, & copioſe librarie, che hoggidì ſia in qual ſi uoglia luogo d'Italia. Queſta mia fattura, adunque ſi doueua laſciar uedere ſegnata in fronte di nome coſi honorato, & famoſo, il quale uerrà talmente ad abbellirla, che potrà il Mondo (mal grado de i maligni) allegramente rimirarla. Prego adunque V.S. Illuſt. à farla degna della gratia, & fauor ſuo; il che facendo, come io ſpero, la Muſtafà ſua ſorella, la quale ancora ſe ne ſtà inuolta ne' ſuoi primi panni, ſi affretterà con miglior animo di ueſtirſi i nuoui, ch'io le uado preparando, & à V.S. Illuſtre, baſciando la mano, humilmente faccio riuerenza.

Di Verona il 25. di Febraro. 1582.

Di V. Sig. Illuſtre

Affettionatiſsimo Seruitore

Franceſco Mondella.

Figure 19.1: Francesco Mondella, *Isifile tragedia* (Verona: Sebastiano and Giovanni Dalle Donne, 1582), fol. 1r-v. Munich, Bayerische Staatsbibliothek, 4 P.o.it. 176#Beibd.4 / urn:nbn:de:bvb:12-bsb10166017-6.
Photo courtesy of the Bayerische Staatsbibliothek.

A list drawn up most likely before 1601 places the *Apollo* in the *galleria* (Franzoni 1970, 164-65). Cross-referencing the available data, it emerges that the statue was located in the spotlight, close to the entrance to the *ridotto*, at the intersection of the paths leading to the main reception areas accessible to visitors upon entering the palace (Moretti 2015; Moretti 2020). Here the statue acquired a particular value and meaning, and revealed the role it played in this specific context—that of a point of convergence, a pivot and major attraction. Anybody who came to the palace to admire Bevilacqua's collections, visit his library and participate in learned conversation, or listen to the regular musical performances held in the *ridotto*, would have seen and appreciated its beauty, and, by extension, the excellent taste and exceptional wealth of its owner. In their dedicatory letters, authors and composers often referred to Bevilacqua as Apollo and his residence as Mount Parnassus, the home of the Muses. The playwright Francesco Mondella, for example, in the dedicatory letter prefacing his 1582 *Isifile tragedia* (see fig. 19.1), calls Mario the "true Apollo" and defines his palazzo as Mount Parnassus, from which pour forth the waters that quench the thirst of tired climbers (an obvious reference to Mario's surname).

Apollo remained in this location until the beginning of the seventeenth century; thereafter, an adventurous life awaited him. In his will dated 30 July 1593, Mario Bevilacqua left the statue to his maternal uncle Claudio Canossa (Franzoni 1970, 111). A few years later, in 1598, Canossa in turn left it to his brother Ludovico. The object became part of the controversies which arose among Mario's heirs (Moretti 2020), and was sold by Galeazzo Canossa to the Gonzaga in Mantua in the early seventeenth century, and from them—by way of the merchant and antiquary Daniel Nijs—it entered the collection of Charles I of England at Whitehall Palace, where it remained for about 20 years.

By 1651, the statue was at the Château de Vaux-Le-Vicomte; it was probably at this point that Nicolas Fouquet—finance minister of Louis XIV—commissioned replacements for its missing arms. It then passed into the collections of Prince Eugene of Savoy and subsequently to his niece Anna Victoria, who sold it to the Venetian collector Anton Maria Zanetti, who, in his turn, gave it to Prince Wenzel of Liechtenstein. Upon his nomination as ambassador to the court of Frederick II of Prussia, the prince gave the statue to the sovereign, who placed it in his residence in Potsdam. Since 1786, the statue has remained in Berlin, save a sojourn at the Musée du Louvre in Paris in the early nineteenth century, and another in St Petersburg during World War II.

Apollo took on particular significance and meaning when displayed and viewed in the context of Palazzo Bevilacqua. We know that Mario acquired several works of art related to music and depicting singers and instrumentalists. Among the most important we can mention Tintoretto's *Paradise* now at the Louvre (ca. 1564), a painting identified as "Zorzon dal lauto grande" in the inventory of 1593 (Moretti 2015), in addition to the numerous portraits that adorned the *ridotto*. In the case of our bronze statue, it was Bevilacqua himself who identified him as Apollo, the god of music, reinterpreting the object according to the role that he intended to attribute to him in his own residence.

SELECTED REFERENCES: Howard and Moretti 2009; Howard and Moretti 2012; Moretti 2010; Moretti 2015; Moretti 2017; Moretti 2020.

20. Valance

Katherine Butler

Anon., English, Scottish or French, ca. 1570-1600
Embroidered in tent stitch with silks and wools on linen, with details in stem stitch and couched work, 56 x 218 cm
Victoria and Albert Museum, Dundee
Photo © Victoria and Albert Museum, London

This embroidered panel was one of a set of valances that would have hung around the top of a late sixteenth-century bed, decorating and hiding the join between the canopy and the curtains. Such valances often acted like friezes depicting two or three scenes from a Biblical, classical, or historical narrative, or portrayed allegorical figures and courtly tableaux. Yet as the figures were usually depicted in contemporary dress in the setting of a formal garden, identification is not easy (Little 1941, 183).

If a story is being told in this valance, it is not readily identifiable; however, the design is rich in potential allegorical meanings. The main tableaux of figures in fashionable, late sixteenth-century, courtly dress is set in a garden. The distant trellis fence and gateway, the high sculptured hedges, and the bower that encloses the central couple draw on the imagery of the *hortus conclusus* or enclosed garden. Inspired by a passage in the Song of Songs 4:12—"A garden enclosed is my sister, my spouse; a garden enclosed, a fountain sealed up"—the *hortus conclusus* had sacred connotations as a symbol of Mary. Yet a parallel secular and courtly imagery developed in medieval romances such as the thirteenth-century *Le Roman de la Rose*, in which the *hortus conclusus* became a private and intimate garden, a setting for sensuous pleasures and amorous activity (Barnett 2009, 139-40; Philips 1992, 205-11). This secular imagery became an established pictorial tradition in the early Renaissance, and the garden depicted in this valance contains many elements typical of such Gardens of Love: an ornamental fountain, pairs of young lovers, musicians, pairs of birds, and abundant flowers and wildlife. The roses too are symbolic of love as the flowers of Venus (Levi D'Ancona 1977, 330).

The sensuousness of this Garden of Love is further alluded to through allegorical depictions of the five senses. The musical trio on the right represent hearing, and the lady with the mirror by the fountain, sight. Both the lady with the dog and

the lady holding the flower on the far right could represent smell. Touch is symbolised in the central pair of lovers holding hands, while taste is alluded to through the strawberries growing beneath them.

The three musicians play the viol, the lute, and the flute. This combination of plucked and bowed string instruments with a soft wind instrument is a miniature variant of the six-part mixed consort, which was closely associated with the outdoor entertainments of aristocratic households (Holman 1993, 132-35). Although courtly conduct books such as Castiglione's *Il libro del cortegiano* (translated into English in the sixteenth century as *The Courtyer*) counselled against women learning to play wind instruments (Castiglione 1561, sig. Cc.i^{v}), in fact quite a number of sixteenth-century continental portraits depict female flautists, often in consort with other women viol-players, lutenists, or singers. Indeed a sixteenth-century valance in the Metropolitan Museum of Art that shares many themes with this one from the Victoria and Albert Museum—fountains, formal gardens, a lady with a mirror and figures in contemporary dress, and allegorical representations of the senses—also includes a female flautist, again with a lutenist and a music book (fig. 20.1; Hayward 2016, 35). As female music-making was strongly associated with beauty and seduction (Austern 1989), this group of female musicians adds to the amorous atmosphere and sensual enchantments of the scene. Moreover, both the flute and the lute carried particular bodily and erotic connotations: the flute as a phallic symbol, and the lute as the pregnant belly or vagina (Craig-McFeely 2002, 300-01, 312; Zecher 2007, 139-41). Nor is the flute the only potential phallic symbol in the scene—the casually propped sword of the gentleman in the central pair of lovers is also suggestive.
Holding the music for the trio of instrumentalists is a small black boy, whose moving legs imply he may also be dancing, causing the viol player to strain to see the page. Black servant boys (technically, there was no legal basis for slavery in Britain or France—Kaufmann 2017, 48-49, 60, 99) were regarded as a fashionable accessory and a courtly status symbol among the European aristocracy. Indeed the black page became a motif

Figure 20.1: Probably British, *Valance*, 1580-1610. Canvas worked with wool and silk thread in tent and satin stitches, 53.3 x 172.7 cm. Metropolitan Museum of Art, New York. Photo © CC0.

in European Renaissance art, with young black children appearing frequently in portraits of noblewomen (Massing 2011, 222-29). These children might be adorned with pearls and gold jewellery that emphasised their exoticism or—as on this valance—dressed in white to emphasise their black skin. Black pages were used iconographically as signs of wealth and status, or to set off the beauty of a white, female sitter. Moreover, black Africans were regularly associated with music and dance; there are other examples of paintings depicting black boys holding music (Massing 2011, 241; Bindman et al. 2010, 123-25), and indeed black musicians were employed in both the English and Scottish courts in the sixteenth century (Kaufmann 2017, 8-12), as well as in other parts of Europe (see exhibit 64; Spohr 2019). In this garden, the black boy is symbolic of musical ability, courtly fashion, exoticism, and luxury.

Yet the Garden of Love depicted in this valance is not solely a depiction of courtly amour. To the left of the fountain stands a lady holding and gesturing to a pair of tablets. The French text on these appears to read "un dieu sur toutes choses & ton prochain comme toy mesme," an allusion to the two central commandments of the New Testament to love your God, and to love your neighbour as yourself. Moreover, this lady with the tablets turns her back on the other two women at the fountain, and indeed upon the Garden of Love as a whole, instead showing her tablet to the two male figures on the right. Her piety and religious devotion therefore appear to be placed in opposition to the secular love of the garden.

This depiction of sacred or divine love in the garden opens up other interpretative layers, encouraging the viewer to search for what other types of love might be portrayed. In addition to their role in the allegory of the senses, the other two ladies at the fountain might also be interpreted as allegories of types of love, with the dog representing fidelity or faithful love, and the mirror self-love. The two pairs of lovers also seem to be in different stages of amorous engagement. The woman in the central pair wears an open-breasted dress typically worn by unmarried women. In the right-hand pair of lovers, the lady wears a high-necked dress and carries a pink or carnation, a symbol of a newly wedded couple (Levi D'Ancona 1977, 81). The musical consort might equally be read as symbolic of marital harmony.

The most mysterious part of the embroidery is the two male figures on the left to whom the lady with the tablets is turned. In contrast to the youthful figures in the garden, these men are older, and they are dressed, not in contemporary fashions, but in more classical garb. They also appear to be outside of the garden in a less cultivated landscape of fields, trees and a natural stream, open to the mountains in the distance (as opposed to the flowers, green architecture, formal fountains, and enclosed boundaries of the garden). The gesturing of the two figures suggests a narrative or reaction. The man on the right gestures to the garden and its figures, while his right hand points upwards and bids his male companion to take note of the scene. Yet the man at the far left of the valance, while also gesturing towards the garden scene, seems to be turning his back on it.

Allegorical motifs also appear to be present in this part of the valance. The lion was typically symbolic of fortitude (though it is particularly small here) and the oak tree on the far left was also a symbol of strength and endurance. Both are masculine virtues, in contrast to the effeminate lovers and female-dominated garden scene. While the Garden of Love was an attractive and desirable place, in many Renaissance romances it was also a dangerously alluring one. In Edmund Spenser's *Faerie*

Queene (1590/96), for example, Sir Guyon (embodying the virtue of temperance), destroys the "Bower of Bliss" in which the sorceress Acrasia has captured the youth Verdant. Her garden shares many features with the one depicted in the valance: enclosing walls, a fountain, floral abundance, shady groves, roses, birds, young maidens, and musical harmony (Book II, Canto XII). Perhaps a similar reflection on duty and temperance is intended here. The older, classical figures and the pious lady with her tablets certainly provoke the viewer to reflect on the morality of the Garden of Love. There is little in the image to suggest that there is any impropriety about the secular lovers; indeed the lush scene seems to celebrate their fertility and harmonious unions. Yet in contrasting this secular and passionate amour with other kinds of love, and in introducing these external observers to the scene, the image does prompt the viewer to contemplate the relationship between its sacred and secular, virtuous and potentially licentious forms.

Hung in the bedchamber, the valance's amorous theme would be most appropriate. The curtained bed becomes a parallel to the enclosed Garden of Love depicted on the valance, and within this curtained space the eros only subtly evoked in the embroidery can reach its fulfilment. The abundance of the embroidered garden symbolises the fertility of the union. The married and unmarried lovers evoke memories of real courtship, and past, present, and future joys. Yet alongside this celebration of the sensual pleasures of the Garden of Love, the scene might also prompt moral contemplation of the virtuous pursuit of love, and remind the viewer of the sacred love that transcends the earthly.

21. Painting

Camilla Cavicchi

Musical Allegory
Giovanni Battista Cavalletto(?), Bologna, ca. 1490-1500
Tempera on wood, 42.3 x 62.5 cm
Muzeul National de Arta, Bucharest
Photo © Cameraphoto Arte Venezia / Bridgeman Images

THIS PAINTING shows a bucolic scene. A musical event is taking place in a vineyard, graphically simplified, and the colours are warm and florid. The picture space is horizontally divided into two layers: the green of the grass, a natural element, and in the background a reddish orange wall, which recalls ancient Roman paintings—a device favoured contemporaneously by painters such as Cosmè Tura and Ercole de' Roberti. The orange background encloses the space, blocking any view of the sky or the surroundings, and focuses the viewer's attention instead on the action of the figures. The scene is framed by two trees; that on the left bears yellow fruit—it is a quince, whose fruits ripen in September. A vine with bunches of green grapes climbs upon the trees and across a support formed of two sticks—a practice typical of northern Italy (Badiali 2011). A golden plaque, now blank, and a coat of arms with two sheaves of wheat (five ears in each sheaf, probably a reference to the month of August, as in Schifanoia's frescoes in Ferrara), and an unidentified symbol below are hung on the bunches.

In this environment, adults and children are dancing, singing, playing, and lying on the ground. In the centre of the scene, two adult couples dance, hands clasped, with two further male dancers at their left, one of whom reaches out as if competing for the attention of the woman in pink. The men wear nothing but vine wreaths, whereas the women wear loose classicising attire similar to that worn by the Muses in Mantegna's contemporary *Parnassus* (Louvre, Paris); one of the women gazes up to the sky, her mouth open in an attitude suggesting she is singing. Their dance is imitated in a playful register by a pair of putti in the left foreground. The adult dancing group is flanked by two pairs of musicians. On the right, one musician engages the viewer with his gaze and holds something in his left hand, perhaps a book, whilst the other faces away and bows a viella; both have their mouths open in song. On the left are two instrumentalists: one stands playing the lute, whilst the other is seated playing a *vihuela da mano*; both are dressed *all'antica*. In the foreground, along the length of the panel, a woman and child lie prostrate on the grass, whilst beside them a recumbent man adopts a more dramatic and agitated posture.

The painting was partially repainted between the end of the nineteenth century and the 1970s, as a comparison with the picture published by Bachelin in 1898 shows (Bachelin 1898, plate 8). Drapes and vine leaves which covered the genitals of the dancers were removed, and their faces were retouched. A surviving anonymous sixteenth-century copy of this painting may record the figure's original attire (private collection; see Sotheby's 2004, lot 302).

Over the years there has been some dispute as to who painted this work. It was first attributed to Luca Signorelli (Bechelin 1898), and then to Giovanni Francesco Maineri (Zamboni 1975, 43-44). Most recently, it has been given to Giovanni Battista Cavalletto (Bauer-Eberhardt 1999; Medica 2008a and 2008b), an artist from Bologna specialising in miniatures who also worked in Ferrara, Mantua, and Rome. The painting shows similarities to other dance scenes, such as those painted by Mantegna around the same time (Bauer-Eberhardt 1999; Medica 2008a-b). The choice of the figurative theme of naked dancers is clearly inspired by Antiquity, perhaps by the numerous reliefs discovered in Rome in that period, as well as their modern interpretations by Donatello—the dancing putti in the cantoria of Santa Maria del Fiore in Florence (1433-38), and the frescoes with naked dancers by Antonio del Pollaiolo in the Villa La Gallina at Arcetri (ca. 1465), for example. Cavalletto's scene seems to have a very close relationship with Pollaiolo's frescoes, especially in terms of the ritual and the popular connotations of the dance.

Nevertheless, doubts remain over the subject of Cavalletto's painting, which must form a pair with another panel of similar dimensions and style preserved in the same museum. This latter work features a nativity scene in front of an arch which should probably be understood as the entrance to a temple. Indeed, over the years, art historians have proposed that they be identified with the iconographic themes *Paganism* and *Christianity* (Bachelin 1898), *The Good Omen* and *The Bad Omen* (Busuioceanu 1937; 1939), *The Sleep* and *The Nativity* (Ragghianti 1938), and *Eros Protheurytmos* and *Amor Dei* (Stoichiţă 1978).

There is no doubt, however, that this is a dance scene in a vineyard: the energetic actions of the figures are led by the rhythm of the music of voices and instruments provided by the two duos. Although the scene is set in Antiquity, the music-making represented in the painting is characteristic of Italy at the end of the fifteenth century. The duo of lute and *vihuela da mano*, or other similar plucked instruments, is well documented (Polk 1990; Kirnbauer 2005; Cavicchi 2015). The most famous Italian lutenist of the late fifteenth century, Pietrobono dal Chitarrino, spent the majority of his career based in Ferrara, a town familiar to both Cavalletto and Maineri. He is known to have accompanied dancing, together with a duet partner known as a *tenorista*. The practice was widespread, though; for instance, it can also be seen in representations of weddings festivities on fifteenth-century Florentine *cassoni* (wedding chests).

As regards the dance itself, some elements suggest that the six figures at the centre of the picture are dancing a *moresca* (Moorish dance; Premoli 1991), but some other aspects—and in particular the man writhing on the ground—point towards a different practice: the healing of tarantism. Tarantism is a phenomenon based on the belief that people bitten by the tarantula (or *phalangium*) spider would sicken and die unless cured by a long and intense musical therapy session. This is an ancient rite which involves music and expansive dance moves, particularly common in southern Italy where it is documented since Antiquity.

The symptoms of the illness first manifested as catalepsy, during which the sick fell into a deep sleep (De Martino 1996), which would explain the woman and child apparently sleeping in the foreground. To wake the patient, a group of musical therapists would attempt to stimulate their senses by playing a series of songs. They had to explore their repertoire to find the precise melody that would act as an antidote to the venom of a particular spider. For this reason, the musicians had to stay close to the sick, forcing them to listen to the melody. Cavalletto's painting represents this quite closely. The musicians on the left in particular seem focused on the people on the ground. The seeming agitation of the man in the foreground reflects the second stage of the tarantism cure, in which the stricken patient begins to move, and eventually dance. The dance itself normally had two phases (Carpitella 1996): a "mimetic phase" in which the afflicted imitated the spider, lying on the ground and moving their arms and legs; and a more frenetic phase, involving exaggerated movements, jumping and cartwheels—perhaps exemplified by the energetic figures in the background.

During the Renaissance this musical therapy against the spider venom, although particularly characteristic of the Puglia region, was well known right across the Italian peninsula (Mina 2000). Fifteenth-century literary sources describe the illness as a feeling of melancholy, sometimes accompanied by vomiting and stomach pains, and always associated with a compulsive need to dance. Administering healing to the afflicted was a difficult and responsible task: should the musical therapy not be properly conducted, the patient would surely die. According to Leon Battista Alberti:

> Musicians caress the ears of the afflicted with various forms of harmony, and when they hit the right one, the victim will leap up as though startled, and then, through joy, straining every nerve and muscle, will keep time to the music in whatever manner takes his fancy. Some of the victims will, as you may see, try to dance, others to sing, while others will exert themselves attempting whatever their passion and frenzy dictate, until they are exhausted; they continue to sweat for several days more, and only recover when the madness, which had taken root, has been totally satiated (Alberti 1988, 15; Alberti 1966, 41-43).

Marsilio Ficino also mentions tarantism in his *De vita* first printed in 1489, writing that people "stung by the phalangium spider became stunned and lay half-dead until they listened to their proper music. For then, they dance along with that melody in the convenient way, and sweat and then get well" (Ficino 1989, 362-63).

In other literary sources, the melancholy produced by the spider's venom was associated with the melancholy of love. Two poems emerging from the Italian courtly milieu in the late fifteenth century treat this link as a commonplace. In a sonnet entitled *Comparatione de li intarantolati* (*Comparison of those afflicted by tarantism*), the Milanese court poet Gaspare Ambrogio Visconti suggests an analogy between the bite of the spider and ensuing madness of tarantism, and the prick of Cupid's arrow and ensuing madness of love. Just as those afflicted by tarantism will recover upon hearing the right melody, so it is only the sound of the beloved that can heal the lover (Visconti 1979, 184). Similarly, in a sonnet by the immensely popular poet-musician Serafino Ciminelli detto l'Aquilano, the lover indulges in a dance to the death, seeking refuge from an affliction caused by a bite received in the company of his beloved; he will be reborn only when he hears the sound of a love-inspired verse (Rossi 2005, 197):

Serafino Aquilano, *Similitudine della Tarantola*

Mercé, madonna, ahimé, ch'io son infermo
de non so che, che un dì fra voi mi morse,
e da quel primo dì che 'l caso occorse
più non mi allegro e più non so star fermo.

Credo fu el morso de quel crudo vermo
che offeso alcun desia nel ballo porse,
perché al venen che al cor subito corse
sol col ballar ci fu reparo e schermo.

Dunque al ballar, ché questo tempo è perso,
già che tu puoi saper di che mi pasco,
ché così vole amor crudo e perverso.

E se pur nel ballar qui morto casco
Non ne stupir, fa' pur ch'io senta el verso
Che amor mi diè, che subito renasco.

Comparison of the Tarantula

Mercy, my Lady, alas, as I am ill with
I don't know what, which one day when I was with you bit me,
and since that first day it is the case
that no longer am I cheerful and no longer do I stay still.

I think that it was the bite of that brutal worm
which when it bites drives one to dance
because the poison which courses straight to the heart
is only repaired and blocked by dancing.

So while dancing, as this is a waste of time,
you can understand on what I feed myself,
as this is what Love, harsh and perverse, wants.

And even if I fall down here dead while dancing,
Do not be surprised, let me listen to the verse
which love gave me, and I will immediately become reborn.

A look at some other images by Giovanni Battista Cavalletto seems to confirm that this comparison was also familiar to painters. For example, his miniature for Francesco Petrarca's *Trionfo d'Amore* shows the lover as a half-dead man, lying on the ground like the figures in the Bucharest painting (Madrid, Biblioteca Nacional, cod. Vitt. 22.3., fol. 142^{v}). Furthermore, some elements of the setting for the dance scene in our exhibit—including the vine, the crown, the bunches of grapes and the golden tablet—are also found among the traditions attached to the ritual space prepared for musical therapy (De Martino 1996, 127-31). Perhaps most tellingly of all, later, more explicit representations of the tarantism dance, such as that by Athanasius Kircher in 1673, demonstrate considerable continuity with Cavalletto's model in terms of both the ritual space and the dance (Cavicchi 2013). No bad omen then; rather, Cavalletto's painting very likely represents an age-old southern Italian version of musical therapy, and perhaps even a cure for lovesick hearts.

CANZONE

SOPRA LA VIOLINA

E Di quala vogliamo dire, ù, ù,
Che diremo de la Violina, fa la li lon la.
Che suo Padre gli diceua, ù, ù,
Maritarla à vn ricco vecchino, fa la li lon la.
E lei dice fatemi degna, ù, ù,
D'vn leggiadro, e bel giouinino, fa la li lon la.
Che mi facci compagnia, ù, ù,
Che stia sempre al mio piacere, fa la li lon la.
E poi in capo di noue mesi, ú ù,
Partorisca vn bel fantino, fa la li lon la.
Che gli ponaremo nome, ú, ù,
Gioan francesco di valentino, fa la li lon la.
Chi sara nostro compare, ù, ù,
Il Signore Febo Trentino, fa la li lon la.
Chi sara nostra comadre, ù, ù,
La Signora di Francolino, fa la li lon la.
E che arte vogliam che'l faccia, ù, u,
Il Sartore, ò il Barberino, fa la li lon la.
Che l'impara di sonare, ù, ù,
Di chitara, e di violino, fa la li lon la.
Che l'impara di balare, ù, ù,
E che'l porta il penacchino, fa la li lon la.
E che'l possa braueggiare, ù, ù,
Con la spada, e co'l pugnalino, fa la li lon la.

publice[tur] [illegible] vic. inq. Bonon

22. Fan

Flora Dennis

Canzone sopra la Violina
Giulio Cesare Croce, Bologna, early 17th century
Printed paper, 21.4 x 30 cm
Bologna, Biblioteca Universitaria, Ms.3878.Caps.LIII.T.XVI.n.13

At first glance, this image appears to show a late sixteenth- or early seventeenth-century print. The A4-sized sheet of paper is divided into two. On the left is a woodcut image of a well-dressed, seated woman, her hair teased and twisted into fashionable twin "horns," her dress trimmed with lace and an open, standing ruff. She stares implacably ahead as she clutches a lace-trimmed handkerchief in her hand. On the right are printed the lyrics to a popular sixteenth-century song: *La Violina* (Dennis 2010b, 194-98).

This is not a decorative print, but a rare survival of a particular type of paper fan. Known as a *ventola* or *ventarola*, these fans were used extensively in Italy from the 1520s onwards, folded and glued, sometimes over cardboard, around a wooden stick (Milano 1987; Milano and Villani 1995). They were often elaborately decorated: "Most of them are very elegant and pretty things," writes the Englishman Thomas Coryat, "the paper…is on both sides most curiously adorned with excellent pictures, either of amorous things tending to dalliance, having some witty Italian verses or fine emblems written under them or of some notable Italian city" (Milano 1987, 3). Sold in the streets by ambulant pedlars, they were available to a wide range of people. One poem opening "My name is fan" (Mi chiamo ventarola) states "I serve everyone / Men, women, and children" (Croce 1639, fol. 4[r]), while another, "In praise of fans," declaims that they are loved and respected "by the low, by those in the middle, and by Heroes" (Croce 1639, fol. 3[v]). In summer, people used them to cool down and to shoo away insects—one fan illustrates on one side a fly-plagued gathering of fan-less folk, and on the other the happy company with fans in their hands, untroubled by insects (Fortini Brown 2004, 151); while in winter they protected people from sparks from the fire. Produced cheaply and in large quantities, these fans were not durable. Their use weakened and wore them out. The rare examples that survive today have been "hidden," bound, and catalogued in libraries as books of poetry or in collections of popular prints, making them difficult to locate. The largest collections of such fans survive in Milan as part of the Civica Raccolta delle Stampe "Achille Bertarelli," and in Bologna within the collections of the Biblioteca Universitaria and the Biblioteca comunale dell'Archiginnasio.

This fan is typical in its combination of woodcut decoration and poetry. What is notable is that the poem was a widely-known song. *La Violina* was popular in Italy over a period of at least 70 years. In a fictional account of a Bolognese party published in 1599, the host asks his son to "Sing whatever song you like, as long as it's short." The son's reply, "I'll sing *La Violina*," is met with the disdainful response "Oh no, that's an old one" (Croce 1599, 9). A kitchen maid, serenaded by her gluttonous lover in a poem of 1612, promises him that "If you come with the sound / of your dear and sweet little guitar / To sing *La Violina* / or *La Girometta* / I'll give you a meatball as well" (Rivani 1612, fol. 1[v]). At least four late sixteenth- and early seventeenth-century editions of *La Violina* survive, with a number of textual variants. These editions are all small printed books or pamphlets, of the type usually sold by professional street singers (*cantimbanchi* or *cantastorie*) after their performances in public spaces, such as town squares (Degl'Innocenti and Rospocher 2019). Although they contained no musical notation, the title pages of these books often state that the contents were to be sung, to melodies that were probably transmitted orally. We know from numerous sources that Ariosto's epic poem the *Orlando furioso* was performed across Italy in this way, to stock melodies that subsequently became universally popular: in Giovanni Bardi's words from 1583, "loved by the old, the young, women, the most learned of men; they resound through the city and travel to the country" (Haar 2004, 2:183; Haar 1981). A "Reply" to *La Violina*, printed alongside it in one surviving pamphlet, proclaims "Everyone's singing *La Violina* / From night until morning," noting the various places in which it was sung: "in the houses and in the streets / At the market stalls and the morning serenades" (Grotto 1590). Giulio Cesare Croce, the author of the poem, was known to have been himself a *cantimbanco* and it is quite likely that this poem was one he performed regularly (Zanardi 2009).

A fleeting echo of *La Violina*'s melody survives today. As with the tunes of comparable sixteenth-century songs such as *La bella Franceschina* or *La Girometta*, which were quoted self-consciously in printed madrigals (Kirkendale 1972; Kirkendale 1988), a snippet of *La Violina* can be heard at the end of Adriano Banchieri's *La pazzia senile* (1598) (see fig. 22.1).

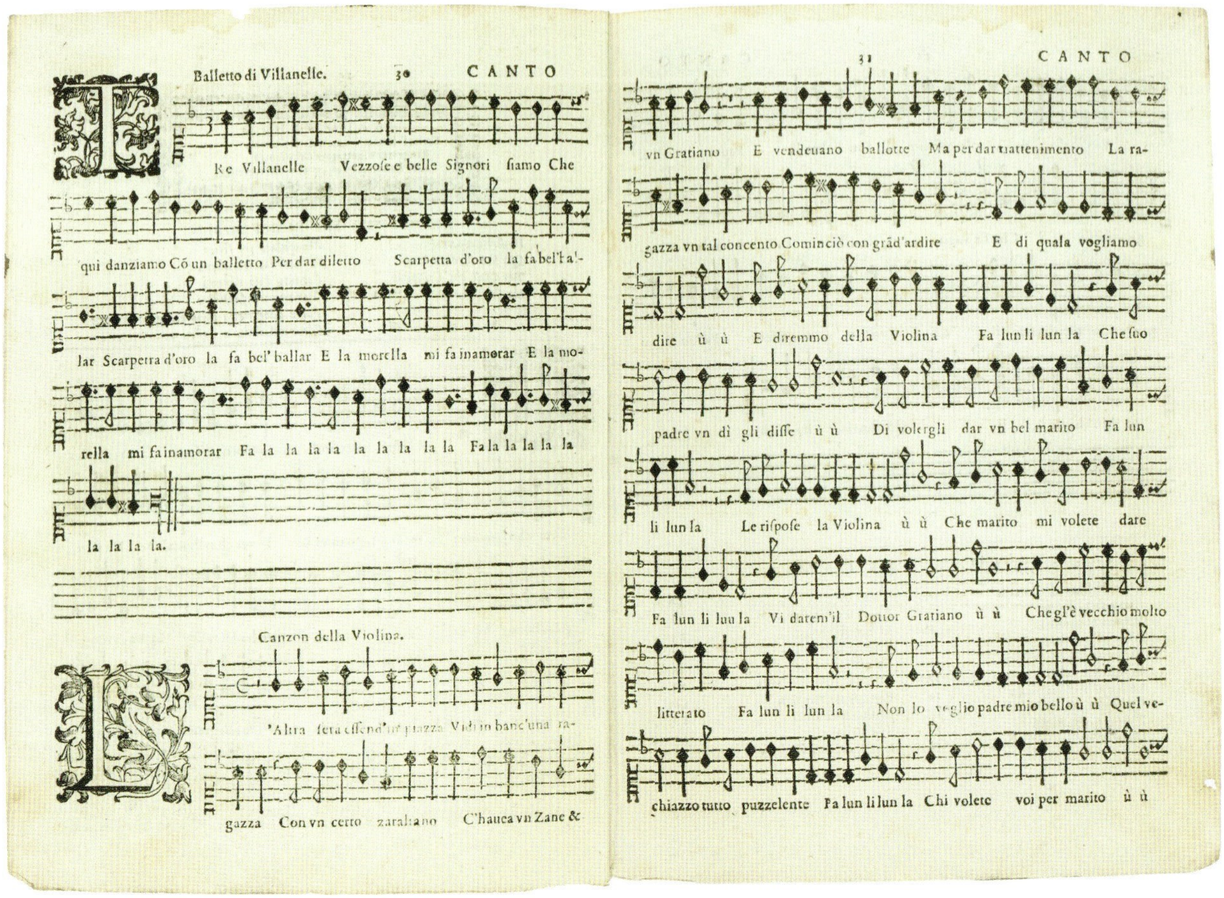

Figure 22.1: *La Pazzia senile, ragionamenti vaghi, et dilettevoli, a tre voci, di Adriano Banchieri,... novamente ristampati* (Venice: Ricciardo Amadino, 1604), 30-32 (*Canzon della Violina*). Paris, Bibliothèque nationale de France, département Musique, RES-123. Photos: Bibliothèque nationale de France.

Beyond this echo, there is no evidence to suggest that its melody was ever published independently in notated form. This suggests that, for all those who knew it, the lyrics of *La Violina* would have triggered memories of a particular tune.

When the relationships between fans and music are explored in more depth, finding song lyrics on a fan is not entirely surprising. A fan-seller in a contemporary poem cries "Here you see beautiful sonnets / Verses, rhymes and learned sayings / Madrigals and villanellas, and *capricii* and lovely things" (Milano 1987, 6). Several surviving fans include musical imagery. A maiolica dish, now in a private collection, shows a woman gently fanning herself as the man next to her strums his lute.

Although making specific links between fans and particular social practices is difficult, it seems that fans played a role in domestic entertainments. Literary evidence describes fans being carried at parties and being used as tokens of exchange during games (Croce 1601, fol. 2[v]; Welch 2009). *La Violina* is not the only song text to appear on a fan: other song lyrics noted in literary accounts of sixteenth-century domestic musical and theatrical performances can also be found on surviving fans. Several Bolognese examples feature verses known as *mascherate* (Bellettini, Campioni, and Zanardi 2000, 34-43). A frequent ingredient of sixteenth-century sociable gatherings, the *mascherata* was a type of musical charade-like game in which the participants impersonated stock characters. In a fictional description of a late-sixteenth century Bolognese party or *veglia*, the person in charge of the games instructs the others present to perform *mascherate* as a range of characters, from wet nurses, French cooks, and mourning widows, to the well-known comic characters Gratian and Pantalone. Fans survive that bear similar or identical verses for these various

characters, and which are illustrated with woodcuts depicting these figures. For example, Giulio Cesare Croce's *Mascherate piacevolissime* (Croce 1604) includes the texts "Vedove, che vanno piangendo i mariti" and "Pantaloni innamorati," which also appear, with illustrative woodcuts, on fans (*Vedove, che vanno piangendo i loro mariti morti* and *Pantaloni innamorati*, both printed in Bologna in 1613). In addition to *La Violina*, the text of the *Serenata, overo cantata del Dottore Gratiano, e Pedrolino in lode delle loro innamorate* appears on a fan, complete with woodcut illustrations, and is also described as being performed in a fictional account of a Bolognese party or *veglia* (Croce 1599, 41).

In the Bolognese party described above, one guest has to sing a peasant girl's song; another is told, "Marino, I want you to be a chimneysweep" (Croce 1601, fol. 3v; Dennis 2010c, 225). Marino's response—"Oh, oh, chimneysweeps, who, lovely ladies, has a chimney to sweep?"—is almost indistinguishable from a text set to music and published by the Bolognese composer Filippo Azzaiolo (Azzaiolo 1557; Marshall 2004, 2:65-66). Fans, it seems, could function as prompts for the singing of poetry, playing an active role in domestic theatrical performances and games. The jaunty syllables of *La Violina*'s refrains—"ù ù" and "fa la li lon la"—made the song both catchy and convivial.

This object allows us to understand the unrecognised breadth of material supports for musical activity. Making music did not just rely on reading notation from the pages of printed books or manuscripts. The most ephemeral—even disposable—objects could play a significant role in musical performance during the sixteenth century.

Acknowledgements: My thanks to Paul Schleuse for pointing out the appearance of *La Violina* in Banchieri's *La pazzia senile*.

23. Tapestry

Carla Zecher

The Lady and the Unicorn: Hearing
Anon., Paris, ca. 1500
Wool and silk, 370 x 290 cm
Musée national du Moyen Âge, Paris

The tale of a French lady and a captive Turkish prince? Christian iconography, representing the miracles of the Immaculate Conception and the Incarnation? A meditation on the development of the human soul? A depiction of medieval *fin'amor*, known today as courtly love? A display of the heraldry of the Parisian Le Viste family? An allegory of the five senses? From the moment of their discovery by the writer and archaeologist Prosper Mérimée in 1841, moldering in Boussac castle in the Limousin region of France, the six *Lady and the Unicorn* tapestries have inspired numerous scholarly interpretations and generated artistic expressions in media ranging from novels to film to adventure games. Legend has it that only a virgin can capture a unicorn. And that the unicorn's horn can purify water and counteract poison. There is a rich tradition of literary and pictorial depictions of ladies and unicorns that dates back to Classical Antiquity, with vestiges still remaining in the hunting mythology of the Caucasus Mountains (Hunt 2003). But the *Lady and the Unicorn* tapestries, which have been a centerpiece of the collection of the Musée de Cluny (the national museum of the Middle Ages) in Paris since the 1880s, are surely the most famed instance of that tradition.

Woven in Flanders in about 1500, from French designs, each of the tapestries depicts a graceful, elegantly-attired woman posed—poised—between a lion on her right and a unicorn on her left, set against a luxurious millefleur background. In each scene she engages in a different activity: holding up a handmirror so that the unicorn can see itself, playing a portative organ, touching the unicorn's horn, receiving sweets, being presented with flowers, and standing under a pavilion as she places her jewels in a casket. A female attendant plays a significant role in several of the scenes, perhaps none more than the one in which she pumps the bellows of the small organ. Without her assistance, the instrument would remain silent.

The assumption that the Cluny tapestries present an allegory of the five senses has gained the widest acceptance over the years. But what, then, is the sixth sense, the one represented by the mysterious final tapestry in the series, which prominently displays the text "A mon seul désir" (To my one/only desire)? Does it sum up the others in some way, by constituting wisdom or cognition or memory or emotion? Perhaps it simply sets them aside, in favor of the heart, as some believe. To further complicate matters, the use of heraldry in the images suggests that the sixth tapestry was not necessarily displayed at the end of the sequence, as has often been assumed. Various orderings of the tapestries may have been utilised originally, depending on the nature of the wall space available, as their owners moved from one residence to another (Nickel 1982, 14).

In our own encounters with the tapestries, whether in museums or their many reproductions, it is easy to lose sight of the ways in which their original owners, the Le Viste family ("quick," like the unicorn), would have experienced them using their own senses. They would of course have viewed the tapestries from various distances and angles, taking in the active scenes but also the decorative details. They must have reached out to touch them, feeling their lush textures and the warmth they brought to cold walls. They may even have smelled them, not only imagining the floral scents depicted in the images, but perhaps on a damp day noticing the odours of the wool and silk of which they were woven. Even the image depicting the sense of hearing would have been very sensual, since it would have stretched the acoustic imagination much less in the late Middle Ages and early Renaissance than it does now. Courtly viewers at the time would have had the sound of a portative organ readily in their ears.

Living in Paris just after the turn of the twentieth century, Rainer Maria Rilke recorded his impressions of the tapestries in his semi-autobiographical novel, *Die Aufzeichnungen des Malte Laurids Brigge*, published in 1910 (*The Notebooks of Malte Laurids Brigge*; the first English title was *Journal of My Other Self*). Rilke first takes in the ensemble as a whole, then pauses before each individual scene to absorb its details. Arriving at the sense of hearing, he ponders,

> Should not music enter into this stillness, is it not already there, subdued? Gravely and quietly adorned, [the lady] has gone forward (how slowly, has she not?) to the portable organ, and now stands playing it. The pipes separate her from the maid-servant who is blowing the bellows on the other side of the instrument. She has never yet been so lovely… The lion, out of humour, unwillingly endures the sounds, biting back a howl. But the unicorn is beautiful, as with an undulating motion (Edinger 1948, 166).

Rilke reminds us that although tapestries serve to muffle sound rather than amplify it, we need to bring our ears, as well as our eyes, to the contemplation of the lady and unicorn tapestries, especially the one depicting the sense of hearing.

Beginning in the 1970s, an impressive and eclectic series of musicians and composers have brought the tapestries to life in musical sound—not the sound of a portative organ but of voices and instruments more favored in modernity. British folk guitarist John Renbourn gave the tapestries the voice of finger-plucked strings in his 1970 best-selling album *The Lady and the Unicorn*. The American all-female a cappella quartet called Anonymous 4 used one of the tapestries as the cover image for *Love's Illusion*, their 1994 recording of courtly love motets from the thirteenth-century Montpellier Codex. Welsh composer Alun Hoddinott's *Lady and Unicorn* (op. 110, 1984) is a six-part cantata—one movement for each tapestry—for four-part (SATB) chorus and piano, setting a text by Ursula Vaughan Williams, wife of the composer Ralph Vaughan Williams. The tapestries also inspired the six movements of the Finnish composer Kaija Saariaho's clarinet concerto *D'om le Vrai Sens* (2010). She wrote it for the world-renowned clarinetist Kari Kriikku, who premiered and recorded it with the Finnish Radio Symphony Orchestra. Saariaho's French title, which roughly translates as *Man's true sense*, is an anagram of "A mon seul désir."

The lady and unicorn series also is among the eight masterpieces of visual art featured in poems by the American postwar poet Jorie Graham in her 1983 collection, *Erosion*. As the scholar Bonnie Costello has pointed out, Graham's poem, although titled *The Lady and the Unicorn and Other Tapestries*, never mentions the central subjects of the tapestries, because Graham is more interested in their decorative impulse than their symbolism. Graham's opening lines express her "measured faith in 'stitching'" as a means by which the ephemeral world is woven into permanence:

> If I have a faith it is something like this: this ordering of images within an atmosphere that will receive them, hold them in solution, unsolved.

The "unsolvability" of the tapestries, Costello explains, is that they are like a still life, fixed, resistant to erosion, and also that they depict a paradox: the lady and the unicorn, chastity and virility, as companions (Costello 1992, 381-82).

Over the past 150 years the lady and unicorn tapestries have left their Cluny home only four times. They were spirited away from Paris during World War II to protect them from perhaps being looted. More recently, they have toured three times to other continents, and each voyage has brought them into dialogue with cultures radically different from the one that produced them. The exhibition of the tapestries in New York in 1973 was the most historically informed, providing an opportunity to compare them in situ with a similar series, *The Hunt of the Unicorn*, in the permanent collection of The Met Cloisters. In Japan in 2013, the lady and unicorn competed for attention at the National Art Center in Tokyo with an exhibition on *California Design, 1930-1965: Living in a Modern Way*. The juxtaposition was less bizarre than it might seem. After all, in commissioning the creation of the tapestries at the end of the fifteenth century, the Le Viste family was exercising its own claim to modernity. In the National Museum of Art, Osaka, the lady and unicorn rubbed elbows, incongruously, with an exhibition on Japanese and Western postwar sculpture. Finally, in 2018, they traveled to the Art Gallery of New South Wales, in Australia. Julie Ewington, writing of the exhibition in *The Monthly*, remarks that:

> Each exquisite image is replete with significance; a woven world captures meaning in every thread. "You can look and look and look," murmurs the woman beside me.
>
> That's the point: one never tires. The unicorn seems knowing, the lion mildly baffled, the little dogs completely spoilt. All else aside, the tapestries are a compendium of medieval design: a lovely table-covering under a portable organ; gorgeous dresses and jewellery; a hardy woven basket holding flowers in the tapestry devoted to the sense of smell; the distinctive lettering on the tent canopy spelling out Mon seul desir (My only desire) (Ewington 2018).

To celebrate their return to their Cluny home in July 2018, the tapestries, while awaiting the completion of a major renovation of the museum in 2020, were featured in an exhibition titled *Magiques Licornes*. The exhibition made excursions into modern media, ranging from a display of ballet costumes by Jean Cocteau, to Tomi Ungerer's satirical poster *Virgin Milking a Unicorn*. Yet it also re-anchored them in the late Middle Ages by juxtaposing them with representations in other media which, like tapestries, were favored at the time, such as sculptures and illuminated manuscripts. Most important, it brought to new life the tapestry depicting the sense of hearing, in a concert called *L'ouïe retrouvée* (*Hearing recovered* or *refound*), presented by Christophe Delignes and Catalina Vicens, on two portative organs. Here was an opportunity to listen, as well as look.

ADDITIONAL REFERENCES: Chevalier 2004; Godden 1937; Sand 1844; Taburet-Delahaye and Pastoureau 2013.

II

Domestic Objects

Sensualities

VENERE ESEGNO FEMININO POSTO NELTERSO CIELO EFREDDO EVMIDA TENPERATA LAQV
ALE AQVESTE PROPIETA AMA BELLI VESTIMENTI ORNATI DORO EDARGENTO ECHANSONE EG
ADII EGVCHI ET ELASCIVA· EA DOLCE PARLARE EBELLA NEGLIOCHI ELIELLA FRONTE EDICORPO LEGGI
ERI PIENA DICARNE EDIMESANA STVRA DA ATVTTIOPERE CIRCA ALLABELLESSA ET SOTTOP
OSTO ALLEI LOTTONE ELSVO DI EVENERDI ELA PRIMA HORA 8 15 ET 22 ELANOTTE SVA
EMARTEDI ELSVO AMICO EGIOVE ELNIMICO MERCVRIO ET ADVA ABITASIONI ELTORO D
IGORNO ELIBRA DINOTTE EPERCHONSIGLIERE ELSOLE ELAVITA SVA ESALTASIONE
E ILPESCE ELAMORTE EVMILIASIONE EVIRGO EVA IN 10 MESI 12 SEGNI INCOMIN
CAND DALIBRA EIN 25 GIORNI VA VNOSENGNO EINVMGIORNO VA VNO GRADO
E 12 MINVTI ENVNA, ORA 30 MINVTI

24. Venus

Tim Shephard

Baccio Baldini(?), Florence, ca. 1464
Engraving, 32 x 21.5 cm
Inscribed: VENERE; TORO; BILANCE; OMNIA VINCIT AMOR; AMES DROIT
The British Museum, London
Photo © The Trustees of the British Museum

At the top of this engraving Venus, simultaneously a goddess and a planet, rides through the heavens accompanied by her son Cupid. Upon the wheels of their car are the constellations over which Venus rules, Taurus and Libra. In the landscape below, young women drop flowers from a castle of love upon a group of courtly revellers, who sing, dance, feast, and flirt. Further back on the right, in the shade of a tent, three figures bathe together in a frankly erotic embrace. An inscription above the entrance to the castle declares that "Love conquers all." At the foot of the page a further inscription explains that:

> Venus is a feminine sign placed in the third sphere and [of] cold and moist temperament, which, because of these properties, loves beautiful clothes ornamented with gold and silver, and song and festivities and games, and is lascivious. She is sweet in speech and beautiful in the eyes and face, and of graceful body full of flesh and of medium height, given to every work concerned with beauty.

There follows a summary of the times and circumstances under which her influence holds sway.

This picture, together with the other six in the same set, arose within a Europe-wide vogue for so-called Children of the Planets images, many of which are closely related in their design (Blume 2004). Essentially such images represent the characteristic activities and behaviours of those born under the influence of each sphere in turn, as a concise and accessible astrological guidebook. The same information, given in much more detail, could be found in a standard astrological encyclopedia such as Guido Bonatti's *Decem tractatus astronomie*; indeed, the 1506 Venetian printed edition of Bonatti's tome borrows elements from the Baldini engravings as decoration (Bonatti 1506). Of course, in this period astrology was a legitimate science, indistinguishable from astronomy, and entirely compatible with Christian doctrine—it was considered an effective means of discovering the will of God, who moved the heavens (Dooley 2014).

A useful point of comparison in many respects is provided by the enormously popular geographical encyclopedia entitled *The Globe* (*La sfera*), written around 1400 by Florentine merchant Gregorio Dati, which circulated in hundreds of manuscript copies and also ran through many printed editions during the fifteenth and sixteenth centuries in Italy (Dati ca. 1475). In *The Globe*, astronomical/astrological information on the heavenly spheres is presented alongside explanations of the elements, topographical features, the weather, tides, the seasons, the four humours, continents, rivers, cities, and countries. Each topic is allotted one or two stanzas of *ottava rima* in Italian, not Latin, a concise format that certainly meets the needs of accessibility—Gregorio himself, although a very capable man, was not highly educated. The geography of *The Globe* shows a leaning toward topics and regions that might be relevant to the interests of a Florentine merchant engaging in trade on the Mediterranean. However, the nautical information provided is not accurate enough to use, suggesting that the book was intended as a coffee-table compilation of general knowledge—the kind of trivia that one might aspire to have on the tip of one's tongue in order to appear well-informed in conversation. In all respects, our engraving, and the set from which it is taken, should probably be understood in the same way.

The engraving is attributed to the enigmatic Florentine artist Baccio Baldini, identified by Giorgio Vasari as a student of the "inventor" of engraving, Maso Finiguerra. Baldini is credited today with the authorship of a large number of mid-fifteenth-century engravings, although direct contemporary evidence is lacking. Accepting, for the sake of argument, that the engraving is at least Florentine, its viewers would have immediately seen a similarity with Garden of Love scenes, popular on Florentine wedding chests (*cassoni*) and birth trays (*deschi da parto*) in the first half of the fifteenth century (fig. 24.1; Watson 1979). Such scenes find their origins in a literary topos deployed most famously in the French thirteenth-century *Roman de la Rose*, a dream narrative in which the protagonist, Amant (Lover), enters a walled garden owned by Deduit (Pleasure), and falls in love with a rose (see exhibit 42). An Italian paraphrase of the *Rose*, *Il Fiore*, has been attributed to Dante, and the influence of the French original is obvious in some of the most enduringly popular of all Italian verse: Brunetto Latini's *Tesoretto*, Petrarch's *Trionfo d'Amore*, and above all Boccaccio's *Amorosa Visione*, *Teseida*, and *Decamerone*.

Boccaccio specifically connects Venus with feasting, dance, and music in his mythographic compendium, *Genealogy of the Pagan Gods*, a work which enjoyed a print circulation through-

Figure 24.1: Florentine, *Garden of Love* (desco da parto), ca. 1430. Tempera on panel, 57.5 cm. Princeton University Art Museum. Photo courtesy of Princeton University Art Museum - artmuseum.princeton.edu.

out the fifteenth and sixteenth centuries, with the addition of a useful index by Domenico Bandini. Citing as his sources the widely-read medieval Persian astronomer Albumasar (Abu Ma'shar al-Balkhi), and his own teacher of astronomy Andalò di Negro, Boccaccio writes:

> Venus signifies the beauty of the face, attractiveness of the body, and an adornment for every thing, and so the use of precious unguents, fragrant aromatics, games of dice and calculation, or of bandits, and also drunkenness and feasts, wines, honeys, and whatever seems to pertain to sweetness and warmth, equally fornication of every kind and wantonness and a multitude of coition, the guardianship of statues and pictures, the composition of wreaths and wearing of garments, weavings with gold and silver, the greatest amusement in song

and laughter, dancing, music by stringed instruments and pipes, weddings, and many other things (Boccaccio 2011, 382-55).

Also citing astronomical authorities, Mario Equicola gives a similar summary in his *Book on the Nature of Love*, printed in 1525, noting that Venus "Loves games, feasts, songs, pictures, perfumes, cheerfulness, and lovers' tokens" (Equicola 1525, fol. 63^r).

For Equicola, as for other Italians, the relationship between Venus and music was an aspect of a broader connection between music and love. In his *Compendium of the Effects of Music*, written around 1470 in Naples, the musician and cleric Johannes Tinctoris lists music's capacity "to attract love" as the seventeenth in his catalogue of music's 20 characteristic effects. In support of this contention he cites Ovid:

So Ovid advises girls desirous of attracting men's love to learn singing. Indeed, in *Ars amatoria* [3.315-16] he says:

"Song is seductive: girls should learn to sing (her voice,

And not her face, has many a girl's procuress been)."

That is why poets record that when Orpheus strummed sweetly on his lyre, many women were fired with love for him (Cullington 2001, 64).

Ars amatoria (*The Art of Love*), essentially a guidebook for seduction, was one of the most popular classical texts in Italy, and one of the first to be printed in Italian translation. At its opening Ovid elegantly disowns the poet's usual patrons—rational, virtuous Apollo and the Muses—invoking instead the assistance of Venus and her son in crafting what he repeatedly calls his "song," the purpose of which is to teach others how to achieve their erotic desires. In a neat conundrum, he names himself Venus' *vates* (meaning a poet in receipt of divine inspiration), whilst in the same line citing his experience as the source of the work—implying, of course, that his experience in love was itself inspired divinely, by Cupid's arrows.

The circulation of a quote from a popular text which suggests that musicianship makes women sexually available is obviously in conflict with the contemporary requirement that women remain chaste. Baldassare Castiglione notes with regret in his famous *Book of the Courtier* that

we ourselves, as men, have made it a rule that a dissolute way of life is not to be thought evil or blameworthy or disgraceful, whereas in women it leads to such complete opprobrium and shame that once a woman has been spoken ill of, whether the accusation be true or false, she is utterly disgraced for ever (Castiglione 1967, 195).

In a rather conservative treatise on education written by the Vatican administrator Maffeo Vegio in 1433 and printed in 1491, the same quote from the *Ars amatoria* is used to caution parents against letting their daughters associate "with unknown girls … who indulge in singing love songs with passion, so that your daughters do not follow their example" (Lorenzetti 2011a, 10). The first printed guidebook on young women's conduct, the *Decor puellarum* of 1471, warned similarly against allowing daughters to acquire a reputation for "singing and playing like a whore" (*Decor puellarum* 1471, fol. 57^r).

Although moralists found the association of music with love troubling, to poets it was a gift, providing a range of elegant metaphors for amorous attraction. Most popular was the analogy of reciprocal love to the musical phenomenon of sympathetic resonance. Players say that, when two lutes are tuned well and to the same pitch, whoever plucks one, where the other is close by and facing it, both respond in the same way; and that sound which is made by the plucked lute, the same sound is made by the other which is not plucked by anyone, explains Pietro Bembo in his *Gli Asolani* printed in 1505. "Oh Amor, what lutes or what liras could respond to one another more harmoniously than two souls of yours that love one another?" (Bembo 1961, 120). In a sonnet of the 1480s, Lorenzo de' Medici uses sympathetic resonance to describe the effect upon him of a portrait that calls to mind his beloved. Just as a plucked string will excite another tuned to the same note, so the sight of a similar face will echo in his heart as the face of his beloved (Medici 1913-14, 1:205). Blending the preoccupation with amorous subject matter with Ovid's Venereal poetics, on the title page of a 1510 poetry edition the author, the famous poet and musician Serafino dell'Aquila, is represented singing his *strambotti* whilst assailed by Cupid's arrows (fig. 24.2). A contemporary biography claims that Serafino learned to compose verse and sing specifically in order to "better enflame the breasts of beautiful young women" (Calmeta 1959, 69).

If Venereal musicianship used music's affective power to seduce, the metaphor of sympathetic resonance also relied on music's parallel identity as a rational discipline founded in the Pythagorean mathematics of proportion, an earthly imitation of the proportional harmony of the heavenly spheres. Owners of Baldini's Children of the Planets engravings could find music exemplified in its mathematical guise under the patronage of Mercury (fig. 24.3). The inscription at the foot of the image explains that Mercury is "eloquent and inventive" and "loves the mathematical sciences and the study of divination." His children pursue activities appropriate to this characterisation: on the left are a painter, a goldsmith, and a sculptor; on the right, writers, an engineer, and an organist; and in the centre a group of astrologers. The different lengths of the organ's pipes, required to produce the different pitches, are a neat demonstration of the principles of harmonious proportionality identified by Pythagoras.

Although the Pythagorean mathematics of harmony, a system that embraced not only sounding music but the inaudible music generated by the movements of the heavenly spheres, created a clear connection between music and astrology, most astrologers made little explicit use of it. The key exception to this rule is represented by the Florentine priest Marsilio Ficino, famous for his translations and studies of Platonic philosophy. Ficino built upon the connection a sophisticated strategy for arousing beneficial celestial influence through song, and brought it to a broader public in his *Three Books on Life*, first printed in 1489. "Tones first chosen by the rule of the stars and then combined according to the congruity of these stars with each other," he explained, "make a sort of common form, and in it a celestial power arises," which "wonderfully arouses our spirit upwards to the celestial influence and the celestial influence downwards to our spirit." To prompt such celestial beneficence one must sing the right song, at the right time, in the right spirit—for the musical character of each sphere is different. Jupiter's music is "deep, earnest, sweet, and joyful with stability," whilst the songs of Venus are "voluptuous with wantonness and softness." Songs that are "reverential, simple and earnest" belong to the Sun (Apollo), whilst those of Mercury are less austere, but "vigorous and complex" (Ficino 1989, 362-63).

ADDITIONAL REFERENCES: Blažeković 2003; Dennis 2010; Mirimonde 1977; Shephard 2015; Shephard et al. 2020; Tomlinson 1993; Trottein 1993; Voss 2002.

ACKNOWLEDGMENT: The research presented in this essay was completed within the project "Music in the Art of Renaissance Italy 1420-1540," funded by a Leverhulme Trust Research Project Grant. I gladly acknowledge the assistance and stimulating dialogue of my project colleagues, Patrick McMahon, Annabelle Page, Sanna Raninen, Serenella Sessini, and Laura Ştefănescu.

Figure 24.2: *Opere dello elegante Poeta Seraphino Aquillano* (Venice: Giorgio Rusconi, 1510), title page. Photograph courtesy of the Fondation Barbier-Mueller pour l'étude de la poésie italienne de la Renaissance, Geneva.

Figure 24.3: Baccio Baldini, *The Seven Planets: Mercury*, ca. 1464. Woodcut, 21.8 x 32.4 cm. British Museum, London. Photo © The Trustees of the British Museum.

Figure des Sereines.

25. Sirens

Eugenio Refini

Jacques Patin
Engraving from *Balet comique de la Royne*
Paris: Le Roy and Ballard, 1582
[7] + 75 + [1] fols., 4°
Paris, Bibliothèque nationale de France, RES4-LN27-10436, fol. 10v
Photo © Bibliothèque nationale de France

In book 12 of Homer's *Odyssey*, Circe warns Ulysses against the dangerous song of the sirens. Duly instructed by the enchantress, the hero manages to sail past the rock of the sirens without falling prey to their deadly seduction. Ulysses hears their honeyed voices promising a wealth of knowledge and is tempted to reach them, but, bound to the mast of the ship, he resists their call. The poet does not describe the sirens, thus contributing to the ambiguous charm that these creatures have continually exerted. Typically represented in Classical Antiquity as birds with female heads—the result of one of the many punitive metamorphoses that populated Greek mythology—the sirens later faced further transformations: plunging them into the sea, medieval culture gave them several monstrous and hybrid shapes, including that of fishtailed women, which tended to prevail over other iconographies in the centuries that followed (Smart 2010; Holford-Strevens 2006).

As fishtailed women, three sirens made their appearance in the *Balet comique de la Royne* held at the Hotel de Bourbon in Paris on 15 October 1581. Commissioned by Catherine de' Medici as a display of political power on the occasion of the wedding of Anne de Baternay, Duke of Joyeuse, and Marguerite de Vaudemont, sister of Queen Louise of Lorraine, the *Balet* was meant to celebrate the many virtues of the Valois court at a moment of political and religious turmoil (McGowan 1963, 42-47; Aercke 1994, 27-28; Anthony 2001, 41-44; McGowan 2008, 114-18). Revolving around the figure of Circe, as a powerful embodiment of the ties that bind men to vice and sin, the spectacle involved the direct participation of members of the court. Indeed, by performing different roles within the staged narrative, the courtiers contributed to the defeat of the enchantress and to the triumph of harmony. As such, the *Balet comique de la Royne* is an outstanding example of the festivals that, as Frances Yates and others have noted, were used by the princely patrons of early modern Europe to showcase political propaganda and create consensus within and outside their courts (Yates 1947). In conjunction with the poetical and musical experimentation fostered by the Pléiade and, more specifically, by the members of the newly founded Académie de Poésie et de Musique (renamed Académie du Palais during the reign of Henry III), the *Balet comique* marked a turning point in the history of Renaissance festivals. Led by the Italian choreographer Baldassarre Baltazarini di Belgioioso (also known as Balthasar de Beaujoyeulx), the creative team included Nicolas Filleul de La Chesnaye (author of the text, possibly in collaboration with Agrippa d'Aubigné), Jacques Patin (set and costume designer), Girard de Beaulieu (composer of the music), and Jacques Salmon (music master).

As suggested by Beaujoyeulx himself in the preface that opens the printed edition of text and score, the *Balet comique* revolved around a single narrative plot ("it has the unity of a comic play"), a feature that made it the first French courtly divertissement to possess dramatic unity (McGowan 1982; Anthony 2001, 42-43). The main narrative line—that of Ulysses escaping from Circe's garden of dangerous delight—unfolds through a series of choruses, monologues, and dialogues that, while making room for visually outstanding scenes, do not compromise the progress of the action. The sirens appear on stage after Circe's complaint about the escape of Ulysses. They redirect the attention of the audience towards the king who, unsurprisingly, is presented as antithetical to the malevolent enchantress. Within an allegorical frame that highlights the virtuous effects of the king's rule, the laudatory song of the sirens (*Océan, père chenu—Ocean, ancient father*) holds a special place—and doubly so. On the one hand, as personifications of cosmic harmony (see below), the three sirens praise the king's justice and his divine nature, which is said to surpass even Jupiter's. The text of the third verse of the *Chanson des sereines* is explicit in this respect: in contrast with pagan Antiquity, where the rule of the world was divided among different gods, France has a unique ruler in charge of preserving cosmic harmony.

Iupiter n'est seul aux cieux,	Jupiter is not alone in the heavens,
La mer loge mille Dieux:	The sea hosts a thousand gods:
Un Roy seul en France habite,	Only one king lives in France,
Henry, grand Roy des François,	Henry, great King of the French;
En peuple, en justice, en loix	In matters of the people, justice, and law,
Rien aux autres Dieux ne quitte.	He concedes nothing to the other gods.

(*Balet comique*, fol. 13^{v})

On the other hand, however, the sirens' performance is not devoid of ambiguity, for the beauty of their harmonious singing goes hand in hand with the beauty of their exposed naked bodies. To be sure, this all-too-physical kind of charm is justified by the context of their appearance: namely, a maritime triumph that includes tritons, naiads, and dolphins, as well as godlike figures such as Glaucus and Thetis. Furthermore, displays of nudity in similar contexts were not new—three naked girls playing the role of sirens, for instance, greeted King Louis XI on the occasion of his entry into Antwerp in 1461 (Wolfthal 2018, 87). Not necessarily meant to evoke notions of lust, the Renaissance nude should be understood within the multifaceted aesthetics of the time, where the beauty of a naked body could convey ideas of both sublimation and debasement (Kren, Burke, and Campbell 2018; Burke 2018b). Yet, the ambivalence intrinsic to the naked female body as a site rich in sexual undertones haunts the sirens' performance in the *Balet comique* and reminds the audience of their dangerous past.

In fact, even when reduced to merely decorative bystanders, hence pleasing and harmless, the sirens inevitably raise cultural associations that stem from the double nature of the mythological figure: seductive and deadly (as per Ulysses' experience), but also in charge of the music of the spheres (as in Plato's *Republic*). Attempts to distinguish between earthly and heavenly sirens were often made in the Renaissance. The confusion between the two kinds of sirens, though, proved more seductive than any clear-cut distinction, weakening the boundaries between sinful pleasure and spiritual delight. This dynamic was particularly productive within those liminal contexts in which the realm of poetry encountered the charm of music and vocal expression. While the siren's song is taken as an allegory of indisputable evil in canto 19 of Dante's *Purgatorio* (Jones 1994), Petrarch does not eschew the ambiguity of the mythological figure in his *Canzoniere*: indeed, Laura's voice haunts the imagination and mind of the poet as the voices of sirens typically do. Needless to say, as recalled in sonnet 167 (*Quando Amor i belli occhi a terra inchina—When Love inclines her lovely eyes to earth*), Petrarch's muse is a heavenly siren ("questa sola fra noi del ciel Sirena"/that sole Siren from heaven who's among us). However, the distracting allure of her charm does not result in spiritual elevation until the poet's fixation on her earthly beauty is sublimated into a higher (that is, spiritual) engagement (Calogero 2006, 141-42). Closer in time to the *Balet comique*, poets such as Torquato Tasso complicated this tradition further, turning to the image of the siren on several occasions as an index of the potentially threatening nature of poetry and vocal expression, a feature that would also translate into musical and theatrical adaptations of various sorts throughout the Renaissance and the Baroque (Volterrani 1997; Refini 2018).

The ambiguity intrinsic to the image of the siren is often visualised through iconographic attributes that expand the eminently musical nature of her traditional equipment: usually portrayed with instruments—visual emblems of their musical skills—sirens are also frequently represented holding mirrors. This is the case for the three sirens that appear in the *Balet comique de la Royne*. With music being played not by the sirens themselves, but by other musicians, the three female creatures are free to hold objects other than musical instruments. The choice to have them hold mirrors is of the utmost interest: in fact, the image of the mirror is traditionally associated with negative meanings, first and foremost *vanitas* and vainglory. As such, mirrors are not rare in medieval and early modern representations of sirens, where the attribute is meant to signify the evil creature's connection to falsehood and simulation (Holford-Strevens 2006, 36). Yet, the mirror is also a symbol of uncovering: one can, for instance, be reminded of one's real nature by the image reflected in a mirror (Shuger 1998). Deceit and revelation are thus intertwined and the twofold nature of the mirror fits the likewise double status of the siren.

Holding their golden mirrors and accompanied by an escort of tritons, the Parisian sirens of the *Balet comique* praise the king. The "daughters of Achelous," as they are called by the chorus that responds to their song from the vault, were often believed to be also daughters of the Muse Melpomene, from whom they likely inherited poetical and musical skills. When they perform at the Valois court, they embody a contamination of traditions—poetical, iconographic, philosophical—that is the result of centuries of mythmaking. Before Paris, the sirens had been singing on the Florentine stage as part of the nuptial festivities for Cosimo I de' Medici and Eleonora of Toledo (1539), when they performed a madrigal by Francesco Corteccia, as well as in Fontainebleau on the occasion of the royal entry of Charles IX in 1564 (Minor and Mitchell 1968; Hoogvliet 2003, 120). Consistent with their newly established decorative status, which had reduced their dangerous charm to the aesthetically pleasing experience of their beauty (physical and acoustic), the performances of these sirens aimed to inspire wonder in the audience. Summoned back to Florence in 1589, they put aside their fishtails and reacquired the birdlike nature they had in Antiquity: the "celestial sirens" that sing the music of the spheres in the *Intermedi della Pellegrina* do not show their chests and are unequivocal images of cosmic harmony, the embodiment of a sophisticated iconographic and musical program that attempts to combine the hedonistic experience of the festival with an occasion for erudite invention (Warburg 1999 [1895]; Ketterer 1999, 202-07).

Returned to the Platonic spheres, sirens do not disappear from the earthly world. Through a further metamorphosis, their sensual and powerfully ambiguous charm is taken over by the new sirens of early modernity. Some of them, as is the case with cloistered nuns, amazed the listeners from within the enclosed space of the convent, exposing their angelic voices as heavenly sirens, but not their bodies (Kendrick 1996). Others—actresses and singers often celebrated as the sirens of the stage—posed a threat to the impressionable ears (but also to the sensitive eyes) of their audiences. If the virtuous nature of the Princess of Lorraine—whose emblem on the occasion of the *Balet comique de la Royne* was a siren accompanied by the motto "Siren virtute haud blandior ulla est" (There is no siren more charming than virtue)—was uncontested, siren-like performers were deemed much more dangerous. As recommended in Cornelis Schonaeus' distich for the allegory of hearing printed by Jan Saenredam after Hendrik Goltzius in 1595, people should not open their ears to "the enchantment of the sirens, which is often harmful through the sweet charm of their singing" (fig. 25.1; Hollstein 1993, 695). The engraving, which is part of a famous series on the five senses, represents an elegant woman playing a clavichord. The lutenist who accompanies her is apparently very sensitive to the charms of his fellow musician. By warning the observer, the engraving and the distich enter the same ambiguous realm of potentially disruptive seduction that was at the core of the myth of the sirens. Originally shapeless (or rather invisible to the eyes, but present through the ears), their song was given a hybrid body that simultaneously made them appealing and stressed their supernatural status. Reduced to a visually enticing emblem, as is the case with royal festivals such as the *Balet comique*, the Sirens regain their dangerously seductive power when transformed into the embodied metaphor of sung performance.

Figure 25.1 Jan Saenredam after Hendrik Goltzius, *The Five Senses: Hearing*, 1595. Engraving, 17.3 x 12.3 cm. Rosenwald Collection, National Gallery of Art, Washington. Photo: Public Domain

MORS VLTIMA LINEA
RERVM EST.

26. Death and the Maiden

Katherine Butler

Anon., England, ca. 1570
Oil on wood, 65 x 49 cm
Inscribed: MORS ULTIMA LINEA RERUM EST
Shakespeare Birthplace Trust, Hall's Croft, Stratford-upon-Avon

At first glance, this painting depicts a conventional image of a young and richly attired gentlewoman playing her lute, with a music book open on the table in front of her. In Elizabethan England music increasingly formed part of a young noble or gentlewoman's education. Having the time for such a leisured pursuit was a sign of status, while music's associations with female beauty and attractiveness meant that it was also seen as improving a woman's marriage prospects (Austern 1989, 429-31).

Yet the eye is quickly drawn to the skull that is being held directly behind her head, and then to the older gentleman who holds it, standing in the shadows. He ignores the viewer and instead fixes his attention firmly on the young woman, for whom he is positioning a mirror so that she might see the reflections of both her face and the skull behind. The painting is no mere portrait, but an allegory that challenges the viewer to contemplate its layers of meaning in relation to their own morality and musicality.

Depictions of women playing music (rather than simply being depicted with an instrument) are rare from Elizabethan England; the other well-known surviving portrait of a lute-playing woman is a miniature of Queen Elizabeth I painted by Nicholas Hilliard in ca. 1580 (Butler 2015, 15-18, 42). One reason for the reluctance to portray women with instruments may be the challenges of depicting a musical woman in a positive light without opening up the possibility of more negative connotations. An allegorical painting of a musical woman, however, could openly address the complexities of music's morality. The inspiration for this painting may have been continental, as its basic composition is nearly identical (though reversed) to several anonymous sixteenth-century Flemish paintings, including one sold at Christie's in 2007 (Christie's 2007; Mirimonde 1978, 119-20), and various versions of *An Allegory of the Transience of Earthly Beauty* (NationalMuseum, Stockholm; Christie's 2006). The reversed composition perhaps suggests that an intermediary engraving served as the model for this English version.

In this English painting, a motto above the gentleman's head suggests the lesson that he is trying to impart: "mors ultima linea rerum est," or "death is the last thing in line," taken from Horace's first book of *Epistles* (16.l.79). The motto, the skull, and the contrasting ages of the figures all place the painting in the *memento mori* tradition, which reminded viewers that all life ultimately ends in death. The phrase "last in line" can be read as evoking both the chronological line from youth to age to death, as well as the compositional alignment that links the books, lute, and the woman's face with the skull. The gentleman and his mirror stand apart from this main axis of the painting, emphasising his differing perspective from that of the young woman. While the gentleman's gaze is focussed on the skull and the contemplation of morality, the young woman looks out at the viewer, more concerned to gain our attention and admiration.

Many elements of the young woman's portrayal can be linked with the iconography of *vanitas* or the idea that all earthly life, possessions, and pleasures are empty and ephemeral (Ariès 1985, 193). The lady's rich red gown and bodice embroidered in gold with a fine damask underskirt, slashed sleeves, and ruff, together with her carefully manicured hair with a small headdress and feathered hat, were fashionable in the 1570s (Hewitt 2014, 255) and evoke the vanities of appearance and wealth (Hewitt 2011). Yet, the skull's direct alignment with the young woman's head unmasks her beauty by alluding to its ultimate decay.

If the lady's appearance appeals to the eye, then the lute playing refers to the pleasures of the ear. Peter Forrester has argued that the lute depicted is specifically the smaller treble lute, designed for playing in duets and consorts (Forrester 1994, 12-13; Spring 2001, 180-81), though in the context of domestic performance its use may have been more fluid in practice.

Musical objects were common features of *vanitas* imagery, both because music is a transient, sensual pleasure that soon fades to silence, and because musical instruments were often symbolic substitutes for the human body, their sound for breath. Human death was implicit in the instrument's dying sound (Austern 2003). When the characters of Protestant theologian Thomas Becon's *The Iewel of Ioye* (1550) turn to discussing vanity, their first example of how soon "carnal delectation[n] & worldli ioy vanish awai" is music (sig. E.viii^{r}). The character Philemon asks rhetorically, "though we delite never so greatly in the[m], doeth not the sownde strayghte waye perysh, & we receyve none other commoditie then losse of tyme?" (sig. Ev.iii[v]). Even the education and learning represented by the books depicted in the painting will ultimately be revealed as vanities, as death comes to all regardless.

Mirrors too were often symbols of vanity. Here the mirror is held not by the young woman, but by the older man. Rather than reflecting her beauty, he holds the mirror such that she could see the skull he holds and reflect on the moral he is trying to impart. If the young woman with her accoutrements might be read as an allegory of vanity, then the gentleman with his long, white beard and mirror might be truth or wisdom. He may also allude to the duty of elder family members in moral instruction. When Charles Butler addressed the accusation that music was a mere vanity, his approach was not one of denial—as the same was true of fine buildings, gardens, wealth, wisdom, indeed all possessions and actions, and humanity itself (Butler 1636, 129)—but rather to place the burden on "grave Elders and chief men of each place" to prevent abuses. This included "bringing them [the young] up in the nurture and admonition of the Lord," being present to make sure that they "demean themselvs civilly and modestly at their sports," and ensuring "that they take times alloued and convenient for such exercise." In other words, those who are older and wiser should emulate the gentleman of the painting in educating their young women not just in how to present themselves visually and aurally in ways appropriate to their status, but also in distinguishing between the use and abuse of such attributes.

Indeed the painting itself may have formed part of a young lady's moral instruction. The *memento mori* and the *vanitas* traditions aimed to draw attention to the transience of earthly life and pleasures. Although absent from the image itself, pious Elizabethans would have recognised the invitation to turn away from such fading pleasures in favour of the promised eternal joys of heaven. As the poem *Our Pleasures are Vanities* (various attributed to Daniel Sands and William Hunnis) in Richard Edwards' *The Paradyse of Daynty Deuises* advised readers: "Have mind on brittle life, whose pleasures are but vayne, / On death likewise bethink, how thou maist not remaine, / And feare thy Lord to greeve, which sought thy soule to save" (Edwards 1576, 1).

Yet the young woman in the painting is refusing to look into the mirror, turning away instead to the viewer as she continues to play. She is too concerned with her performance to pay attention to the elder man's lesson. In this way the painting problematizes not only music's transitory and worldly nature, but its potential to distract from more serious matters. In the discussion of vanity in Becon's *Iewel of Ioye*, the protagonists specifically discuss the care with which music must be used. The character Theophile quotes a phrase from Ecclesiastes 40:20: "wine and minstrels reioyce the hert" (Becon 1550, sig. E.viii[v]); however, Philemon points out that the passage goes on to state that "the love of wysdome" excels both. A third character, Cristofer, then laments that "many delyghte in Musike, but fewe in the love of wysdome. Many covet to excel in singyng, playng and dauncing, but in the knowledge of Gods worde very fewe" (sig. F.i[r]). Although Theophile briefly argues (following St Paul) that a Christian's melody should consist of heart not song, ultimately Philemon concludes the discussion more moderately by asserting that music is indeed "vain and transitory" but when "soberly exercised as a handmaid to virtue it is tolerable" (sig. F.iii[r-v]).

The characters' debate in Becon's *Iewel of Ioye* is typical of music's ambiguous position in early modern culture. Music was simultaneously an earthly, sensual pleasure and a foretaste of the angelic heavenly chorus. Spiritual songs could inspire virtue and spiritual fulfilment, or music might provide a remedy for melancholy; alternatively, love songs and dance tunes might inspire lust, frivolity and wantonness (Austern 1989, 422-24, 434-35; Austern 2003, 310-12). The painting, like Philemon in *The Iewel of Ioye*, seems to promote the moderation not the prohibition of pleasures. The gentleman is still finely dressed with fur-trimmed clothes, and he shows care for his appearance in his neatly trimmed beard. Nevertheless he chooses more muted colours, and there are no such extravagances as gold embroidery and feathers, as the young woman displays.

Similarly, the painting alludes to the delicate balance that an Elizabethan gentlewoman must maintain in her music-making also. Her lute playing is not in itself a vice, but her preference for music-making over the moral lesson the elder gentleman is trying to teach certainly is. That the gentlewoman's music-making is not a sign of wisdom or deep learning is suggested by the books on the table. Their oblong format suggests music-books, but in fact the pages are blank—the books are just for show. Her talents do not extend to musical literacy, but she performs from memory or improvises. The lack of notation further underlines the vanity of her music-making, no trace of which will remain when the sound fades.

The boldness with which the gentlewoman meets the eye of the viewer as she plays indicates a further layer of moral and social impropriety in her conduct. In that most influential guide to courtly conduct, Baldassare Castiglione's *Il libro del cortegiano* (translated into English by Sir Thomas Hoby as *The Courtyer* in 1561), the character Lord Julian argues that a musically talented gentlewoman should

> be brought to it w[ith] suffringe her self somewhat to be prayed, and with a certein bashfulnes, that may declare the noble shamefastnes that is contrarye to headinesse. She ought also to frame her garmentes to this entent, and so to apparaile herself that she appeere not fonde and light (sig. Cc.i^{v}).

Indeed with such a lack of modesty the gentlewoman in this painting risks aligning herself with such morally depraved, musical temptresses as the mythical Sirens, or the real-world courtesans. The lute was the badge of trade for the infamous Venetian courtesans, and the fact that the Flemish for lute, *Luit*, was also the word for vagina meant that lute-playing courtesans were frequently the subject of continental paintings (Craig-McFeely 2002, 300-01, 312). The young woman's immodesty opens her up to the criticism that her music-making is a sign of lust and sexually manipulative intentions.

In the home of a wealthy, well-educated family, the kind of domestic space in which this modestly sized painting hung may also have been a space for actual musical performance. As the family made music, the picture would have encouraged self-reflection on its virtuous use. A young gentlewoman might be prompted to reflect on whether she held her appearance and musicality in too high esteem and whether it served as a distraction from more virtuous pursuits. For a young gentleman, the skull unmasks the seductive powers of female beauty and music for the transient sensual pleasures they are, and might cause him to reflect on the attractions of more lasting virtues. Older family members might be prompted to consider whether they were fulfilling their duties in morally instructing their youths. To guests, the painting combined a display of the family's status and accomplishments with a show of moral virtue and piety. The allegory captures the ambiguous and precarious place of music in Protestant Elizabethan culture, but by openly acknowledging the vanity of music, the owning family might also assert that they knew its proper place and use.

αι μὴμ πορόντας να βαστᾶ το μάκρος ὀχειμχόρη,
ἐβάλθηκε της πόρτας να σιδερνᾶ ὅσε μπόρη.
Κ μόνε κρυφὰ κ' δροσερὴ καθ' ἄνθρωπ' ἀναπέβη,
κ' καθεζὸ να κρυμῆ το πο μαυρὶ γυρέβη,

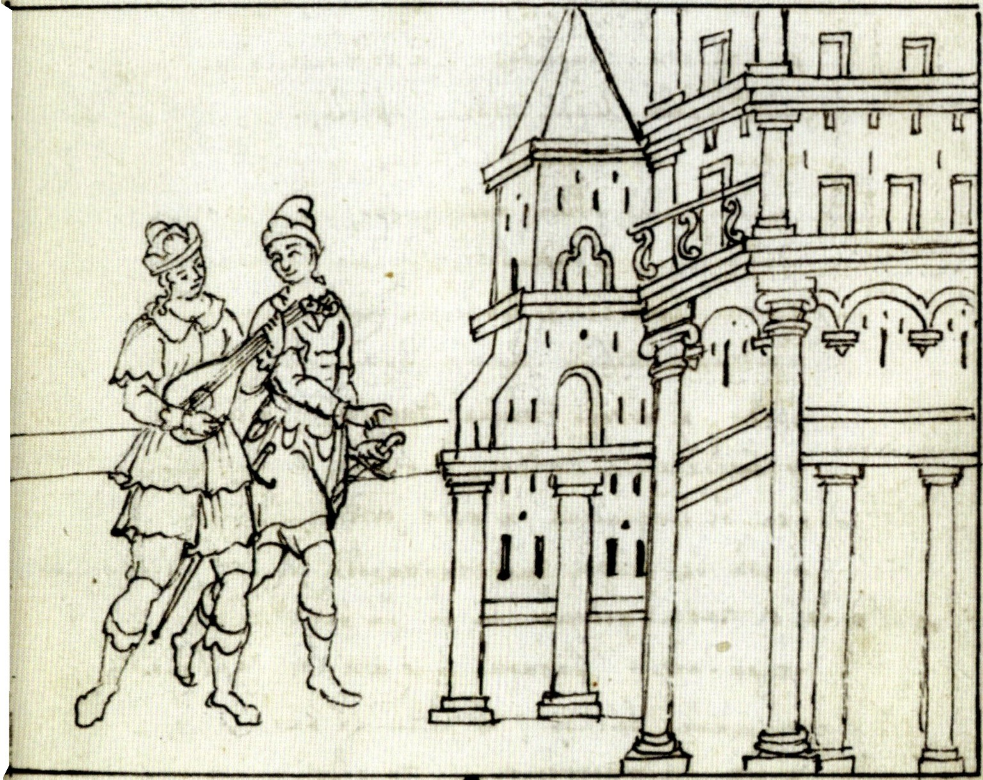

περνεῖ το λαβοῦτο, κ' σιγανὰ ἐπορπάτη,
κ' ἐχτύπατο γλυκὰ γλυκὰ ἀγνάντια σο παλάτη.

Του ἐχέρα

27. Erotokritos Sings a Love Song to Aretousa

Alexandros Maria Hatzikiriakos

Erotokritos, lines 1.389-402
Vitsentzos Kornaros, Crete, ca. 1590-1613

Image: London, British Library, ms. Harley 5644, fol. 19r. Pen drawing. Manuscript on paper, 264 fols., 22 x 15 cm. Photo © British Library Board. All Rights Reserved.

EVERY NIGHT, a young lover takes his lute, stands beneath the window of a princess, and serenades her until dawn. The tunes he plays are sweet and melodious, but the words of the songs are sad, and make everybody listening melancholic, including the princess herself.

> When the cool night gave rest to every mortal,
> and every beast sought to find a place to sleep
> he took his lute, went out silently
> and plucked it very sweetly opposite the palace.
> His hand was as sugar. He had a voice like the nightingale.
> On hearing him, every heart sobbed and wept.
> He recounted and told of the sufferings of passion:
> how he was entangled in love and how he languished and withered.
> At such an exceedingly sweet voice every heart, even if it was like snow,
> was kindled when it came near.
> He tamed everything wild. What was hard grew soft.
> What he sang lingered sadly in one's mind.
> The complaint he uttered devastated hearts,
> split marble and made ice boil.
>
> (Kornaros 2004, 7)

Despite the similarities, these lines are not taken from a medieval romance, and nor does the image illustrating the scene represent a trouvère or a troubadour singing a *canso* (song) to his lady. In fact, both text and illustration are taken from a Greek chivalric poem entitled *Erotokritos*, written by the Cretan nobleman Vitsentzos Kornaros (or Vicenzo Corner) between the end of the sixteenth and the first decades of the seventeenth century. The poem narrates the story of the forbidden love between the young knight Erotokritos and the princess Aretousa, daughter of the King of Athens. The story is set in an anachronistic pre-Christian Greece in which classical culture is mingled with elements derived from the Byzantine heritage and the Western feudal world, as well as the contemporary Italian Renaissance. *Erotokritos* represents the epitome of the so-called Cretan Renaissance (1453-1669), a prolific period of the history of Crete, which was then under Venetian rule. From the fall of Constantinople until the late seventeenth century, Crete flourished as one of the most important cultural centres of the eastern Mediterranean. The island was ruled by a cultured and enlightened aristocracy, mostly composed of Hellenised families of Venetian origin, actively involved in the arts, theatre, literature, and, of course, music. This was the context in which the Cretan school of icon painting flourished together with the art of El Greco, humanist *accademie* such as Gli Stravaganti in Herakleion, or the Neoplatonic Accademia dei Vivi in Rethymnon, as well as Cretan comedies, tragedies, and theatrical intermedi, and many other works of literature of considerable importance—among them *Erotokritos*.

This exhibit seems to lead us to the very edge of the European Renaissance, since the Byzantine and the modern Greek world are not conventionally included in the chronology and geography of the period. However, as a liminal object, *Erotokritos* synthesises and creatively elaborates elements from both early modern Italy and Byzantine culture. Even if it was written at the eastern edge of the Venetian dominion, *Erotokritos* is deeply rooted in the Western European world. A first glaring example of such a cross-cultural aesthetic is offered by the image which illustrates this exhibit. This image is taken from the only extant manuscript copy of the poem, MS Harley 5644 in the British Library, which was compiled and decorated in Corfu in 1710, a few years before the first Venetian printed editions. Clearly, the illustrator of the manuscript imagined the world of *Erotokritos* to be more like a Venetian city than an ancient Greek polis. The Athens depicted in the 121 images in MS Harley 5644 is far from being authentic—in fact it resembles a Renaissance utopia. All the lavish clothes and armour of the characters, as well as the abundance of architectural elements, visibly recall the costumes and scenography used in early modern Italian theatres. Apparently, the artist sought to create a theatrical illusion, having in mind not only the dramatic tradition of early modern Crete but also the architectural conception of contemporary Italian spectacles, especially Sebastiano Serlio's scenography. Furthermore, although the manuscript was compiled in the Ionian island some decades after the fall of Crete, there is nonetheless a striking relationship with the works of the Cretan icon painters. A very similar Italian architectural influence can be found in the orthodox icons by Georgios Klontzas, a contemporary of Kornaros, or even in many of the *anthibola* (working sketches) from the eighteenth-century Ionian masters—today preserved at the Byzantine and Christian Museum of Athens—which could have served the artist of MS Harley 5644 as models.

Hybridity also characterises the story of *Erotokritos*. Indeed, the plot of the poem is taken from a Venetian translation of the fifteenth-century French *roman Paris et Vienne*, by Pierre de La Cépède (Mavromatis 1982). This was one of the most popular late medieval stories, translated in several languages including Italian, English, Romanian, Turkish, Catalan, Yiddish, and Swedish (Babbi 1991, 123-24). However, far from simply being a translation, *Erotokritos* constitutes a re-creation of the late medieval story in an early modern setting. The fictional persona of Erotokritos encloses within himself all the values of the ideal Renaissance man. Not only is he a valiant and courtly knight, who defends his homeland in battle, as well as in tournaments; he is also a refined courtier, musician, and intellectual. An accomplished scholar, he cultivates the arts and sciences in a private *akrivokamara* (literally: a precious chamber), a finely decorated room located in the corner of a blooming garden, not dissimilar to the Italian *studiolo* (Kaplanis 2014). Furthermore, he proficiently practices painting, poetry, and music, gathering together a list of virtues that would easily fulfil Castiglione's requirements for the perfect courtier (Lasithiotakis 2008).

Amongst this embarrassment of riches, music is the art he prefers for communicating his emotions:

> My friend, I have taken to song and lute
> so that they may heal me quickly in my distress.
> When I sing and speak of the pain which torments me
> it seems that water is quenching the fire within me.
> (Kornaros 2004, 7)

Singing allows Erotokritos to give voice to his love anguish and to relieve his pain; but more importantly, it is also a way to express and perform his own identity. Indeed, the name of the protagonist is a charactonym: it literally means "tormented by love" (in Cretan Greek έρωτας, love, and κρίνω, to torment).

Thus, love-torment represents the actual self of Erotokritos; and it is also the trigger of all the major events in the poem. Sounding out his identity through songs allows him not only to soothe his heart, but also to affect, or better infect, his listeners with the same illness. This aural contamination will eventually help him to pursue his main aim, which is to have his love reciprocated by the princess Aretousa. The sweetness of the melody and the sadness of the song enchant the princess, so she falls in love with a person she has never seen before. Indeed, Erotokritos manages to keep his identity secret, singing unseen and hidden by the darkness of night—like an ante-litteram *acousmêtre*.

Notably, the forcefully emotional and almost magical power of Erotokritos' songs goes beyond the usual skills that one could expect from a typical courtly lover. The effects of his song are equally out of the ordinary:

> At such an exceedingly sweet voice every heart, even if it was like snow,
> was kindled when it came near.
> He tamed everything wild. What was hard grew soft.
> What he sang lingered sadly in one's mind.
> The complaint he uttered devastated hearts,
> split marble and made ice boil.
> (Kornaros 2004, 7)

Erotokritos' sweet lament possessed supernatural capacities, affecting animals and even inanimate objects. Savage beasts could not escape the seduction of his formidable singing; stone cracked and ice melted at the sound of his voice. It is clear in this excerpt that Kornaros' point of reference for the vocal and poetical skills of Erotokritos was the mighty musician Orpheus.

Erotokritos' Orphic features, entirely absent in the Venetian translation of Pierre de La Cépède's *Paris et Vienne*, are among the most interesting innovations brought by Kornaros to the original plot. In the Venetian version, as well as in the French original, the serenade scene does not occupy an equivalent position in the economy of the story, and the account of the event seems nothing more than a conventional, if not a ready-made, description: "And for this reason he sustained much pain, having no other solace or remedy except to go with Adoardo under the room in which Viena slept: and so sweetly they played and sang, that every other playing and singing was nothing in comparison." (Babbi 1991, 165).

There is a further, striking, difference between the bittersweet music of *Erotokritos* and the night song of its French and Venetian models. The songs made by Paris and his friend are excellently performed, but they are only generically labelled as "sweet" ("dolcemente sonavano"). In contrast, Erotokritos' songs are far more sophisticated and complex performances. He sings sweetly, like Paris; but also, in an extremely mournful manner. Furthermore, singing to the lute is essential to Erotokritos, not only to recover his spirits, but also to convey his identity into sound, and to penetrate the ear and heart of his beloved with his melancholic self.

No more than a century divides Kornaros from Pierre de La Cépède and his anonymous Venetian translator, and yet they evince radically different conceptions of song and of voice, and of the different ways they can affect the human soul. In the original French *roman*, Pierre de La Cépède explicitly describes the serenades made by Paris and his friend with the phrase "faisant oubades de leur chanssons" (making serenades of their songs; Kaltenbacher 1904, 397), in which *oubades* refers both to the classic troubadour *alba* (dawn song) and to the practice of night singing, typical of this genre. Despite the great importance that the song scene has in the *roman*, the description of Paris' musical skills is short and concise, like a stereotypical troubadour *vida*. In contrast, Kornaros gives a new meaning and new cultural resonance to the musical qualities of the protagonist. If Paris still sings like a late medieval trouvère, Erotokritos is instead represented as a Renaissance Orpheus.

Thanks to the humanist re-discovery of the myth of Orpheus as a poet and song-maker, the Thracian demigod became a paradigm of the early modern idea of music—especially of the art of singing to the lute or any other string instrument (Shephard 2014, 73). Indeed, in Renaissance Italy Orpheus was considered the poet-singer par excellence, and his rhetorical and musical skills served as a model for monophonic singing and theatrical music, from the early sixteenth-century frottole and *strambotti*, to the first operatic efforts of Peri, Caccini, and Monteverdi (Pirrotta and Povoledo 1969). It is not by chance, then, that in the same period Kornaros was working at *Erotokritos*, Italian courtly and academic circles were taking the first steps towards opera. Despite its location at the geographical borders of Western Humanism, Crete was not a peripheral cultural centre. Veneto-Cretan intellectuals, such as Kornaros, were actively involved in the artistic experiments and theoretical discussions of contemporary Italian literature, philosophy, art, and music. Thus, the voice and songs of Orpheus, which were a major source of inspiration for music and philosophy in Renaissance Italy, also gave shape to the main character of the first masterpiece of modern Greek literature.

Additional references: Alexiou 1985; Holton 1991a; Holton 1991b; Maltezou et al. 2009; Panagiotakis 1988; Panagiotakis 1989.

disi Tu es singularis virgo

III

Books

Introduction: The Room of Books

Elisabeth Giselbrecht

Books and museums were intimately linked from the very beginning. When in the 1560s Duke Albrecht V of Bavaria founded his *Kunst- und Wunderkammer*, arguably the origin of the museum concept, he did so in parallel with his library. Fuelled by the theories of his artistic advisor Samuel Quiccheberg, the cabinet of curiosities and the library mirrored each other in portraying all areas of knowledge, and many books, in fact, were included within the *Kunstkammer*. Almost 200 years later, Sir Hans Sloan's collection of artefacts and books provided the foundation for the British Museum. Still today, the Enlightenment gallery in the British Museum shows this symbiosis, with the book collection quite literally supporting the building to house the artefacts.

Books make attractive items for museums in manifold ways. As material objects, they fascinate with their beauty, their size, elaborate bindings, elegant writing; their physical properties also providing an account of each era's materials and technologies. As a container of knowledge they span every imaginable area of human interest. They tell us about individuals, both as personal accounts of lives and imagined worlds of their authors, but equally of the lives, thoughts, and experiences of their users. Beyond the individual they are evidence of shared experiences—be it the long-common communities of readers or, as is the case for much of music and theatre, as the basis for a performance, which was then to reach audiences far beyond those who would ever see the physical book. This is why books appear in many of the rooms in this museum—as items of devotion, in private spaces, or containing the intellectual worlds of experts.

We find these attributes amply represented in this room specifically dedicated to books: beautiful objects, such as the stitched motets KK 5370-5373 (*Embroidered Partbooks*, Lodes), personal items, such as the *Chansonnier of Margaret of Austria* (Borghetti), telling us about the lives of their owners and stories of communal experiences. Importantly, they often contain the rare evidence of an otherwise lost musical repertoire—such as the pre-Reformation English choral music in the *Eton Choirbook* (Williamson), or Czech vernacular music of the Hussite movement in the *Jistebnice Cantionale* (Hlávková). Underlying all of this is also the story of how music was put on the page, reflecting broader technological developments, but also the relationship between material, form, and meaning, as the *Musical Staff* shows (Alden). The three large books of polyphony, the *Liber selectarum cantionum* (*Coat of Arms of Matthäus Lang*, Giselbrecht), the *Liber quindecim missarum* (Gancarczyk), and the aforementioned chansonnier appear, on first sight, rather similar. Upon closer inspection, however, the different processes involved in making them (multiple impression printing, woodblock printing, manuscript) are both a result of and a testament to their widely different identities and the identities they were meant to shape.

Specifically in this room of books, however, our exhibits also reflect on their own materiality and history, and on the relationship, in particular, of music with written culture in all its developments, technological changes, and also its limitations. Three dichotomies in the relation between sonic and written experience run through these exhibits:

First, the simultaneous limits and opportunities of capturing sound on the page. There are limitations, for sound can never be fully represented on the page—notation is merely an aide-mémoire, a script; sound itself cannot be captured. At the same time, though, there is great opportunity. Recent research has opened up our thinking to sound off the page, though still encapsulated in written forms. This is, on the one hand, sound that is made when expanding or improvising using written notation. The *Saxilby Fragment* (Colton and Cook) in this room is a rare and early example of a simple noted polyphony, as taught at a young age and closely linked to practices of improvisation. Beyond, the written word or image can lead us to aural experiences beyond the page, as is the case in *Le Jardin de plaisance* (Taylor) and in the *Hypnerotomachia Poliphili* (Privitera), which without a single note evoke musical practices and performances through literary texts and images. Conversely, sometimes musical notation on the page does not actually represent physical sound, but the role of music and harmony in philosophical or theological thought, as is the case, for example, in the notated music as part of the illuminations in the *Bible of Borso d'Este* (Sessini), invoking, Sessini argues, Boethius' celestial harmony. Similarly, music, depicted with instruments and dance, allows a vivid (and terrifying) portrait of something that words can only partially evoke without music, such as death as represented in Hans Holbein's engravings for *Les simulachres et historiées faces de la mort* (Schiltz).

This idea is further explored in the side gallery of Imagined Spaces—here music's role as an allegory, a mode of transport into unknown spaces, a way of depicting what cannot be depicted, is most explicit. It is clearly apparent in the role of music in visually narrating paradise (through instruments, for example, in *Heaven*; Ştefănescu) or the Garden of Delight (through depictions of singing and dance in *Deduit's Garden*; Huot), and in the way music is implied as a natural component of the mythical Arcadia of Guarini's *Pastor Fido* (Gerbino). The latter, even without music in its definitive print, could rely on the reader's experience of the music associated with its verses, and, for a selected group, of the music used in its stagings and recalled by the images.

Our second dichotomy concerns books' ability to demonstrate both uniformity and individuality. Printing in particular was long associated, following Elizabeth Eisenstein's work, with the opportunity for standardisation and, thus, imposing uniformity. To some extent, this cannot be denied, as it was now possible to produce the same (or seemingly the same) content in multiple copies. Recent research, however, has shown how individualism was still maintained and valued in the sphere of music printing. While printed books of liturgy might seem the ideal opportunity for standardisation, the *Constance Gradual* (Gillion) in this room is just one example of how such standardisation was often lacking or not even desired. Numerous liturgical books of the incunabula period were printed with staves only, specifically to allow for individualisation of each copy. The extent to which uniformity was an illusion also becomes clear in the *Liber selectarum cantionum*: not only were there two versions made from the outset (one set of presentation copies with a coat-of-arms printed in colour, the others in black), but no two surviving examples of this publication are exactly the same, with the numerous small stop-press corrections subverting the idea of quick, identical reproduction. Uniformity becomes even more of an illusion when one considers what happens to books in the hands of their users, as in the case of the *Liber quindecim missarum*, or the *Commonplace Book* (van Orden) on display in the previous room.

Finally, the items in this room also portray the tension of the music book being both a rather specific item (limited, often to those who could read notation, circulating in a smaller market), while at the same time being books like all others. Recent research has pointed to music books' status as books—produced, often, by the same individuals as all types of other books, circulated as part of the wider book market, needing to make a profit, collected, and stored. This dichotomy is represented here through the *Grande Musique* typeface of Plantin (Hunter-Bradley), one of the most industrious printers, publishers, and distributors of books in the late sixteenth and early seventeenth centuries, for whom music was part of this wider economic enterprise.

The items in this room, then, encapsulate not only the many faces of music books, but in fact of music itself: highly individual and yet a shared experience, a commodity and yet a luxury item, a fleeting moment, impossible to capture, and yet with an ability to endure.

ue sanctissima Mari a
Mater dei re gina celi Porta para
ue sanctissima Ma ri a
Mater dei regina celi Porta para

28. Chansonnier of Margaret of Austria

Vincenzo Borghetti

Brussels, Bibliothèque Royale de Belgique Albert 1er/Koninklijke Bibliotheek Albert I, MS 228
Workshop of Petrus Alamire, Habsburg-Burgundian court of the Low Countries, main corpus ca. 1515, later additions ca. 1519
Manuscript on parchment, 73 fols., 36.5 x 26 cm
Image: fols. 1v-2r. Inscribed: Memento mei. Photo © KBR-Cabinet des Estampes.

THE MANUSCRIPT 228 of the Royal Library of Belgium is the chansonnier of Margaret of Austria, created for her by Petrus Alamire, copyist and supervisor of the musical scriptorium of the court of the Low Countries, around 1515 (Hofmann 2019). A cultured woman, lover of the arts and of music, Margaret was the daughter of Mary of Burgundy and the Emperor Maximilian I, and hence aunt of the Emperor Charles V who was the son of her elder brother Philip the Fair and Juana of Castile. Born in 1480, Margaret lost her mother at two years of age. As was typical for high-born women of the time, Margaret was soon used by her father, and later on by her brother, as a pawn for political ends. At the age of three she was promised in marriage to the French Dauphin, Charles VIII. Rejected by him in 1491, in 1497 Margaret was married to Juan of Castile, heir to the Spanish crown. Juan's sudden death a few months after the wedding left her a widow at the age of seventeen. Also of brief duration was her next marriage, in 1501, to Philibert, Duke of Savoy, who died in 1504 during a hunt. Margaret had no surviving children from her two marriages, and took no husband after Philibert. Unusually for a woman of her era, she sought and ultimately obtained political office: from 1508 to 1515 and from 1519 until her death in 1530 she was governor of the Low Countries (Eichberger 2005a). What role her precious chansonnier played in this achievement will be the subject of this essay. Before focussing on her beautiful music book, however, it will be useful to comment further on a few details of her biography.

The tragic events Margaret experienced deeply affected her life, but not necessarily in a negative way. Even for a princess like her, being a widow without children was the only way for a woman to have access to an inheritance, and therefore to gain a degree of autonomy not available to a wife or a widow with living issue. After the death of Philibert, Margaret became financially independent: this is the main reason why she was able to resist other matrimonial projects of her father and brother—the chosen candidate was the elderly Henry VII of England (Wellens 1982). Margaret's autonomy was not based solely on her financial independence, however. The culture of the time granted widows a special status among women. Scripture, the Fathers of the Church, later theologians, and religious authorities all acknowledged widowhood as a virtuous state for a woman, under specific circumstances. To uphold that virtue, convention required that a widow should be pious and remain faithful to the memory of her late husband(s)—a kind of nun living outside a convent. In Margaret's day, only as such a virtuous widow could a single woman obtain a certain degree of autonomy and social recognition, and eventually—as a kind of new incarnation of the Biblical widow Judith—aspire to an official political role, if such a role was desired. And Margaret certainly did desire it (Eichberger 2005a and 2005b; Welzel 2005, 103-13).

We come, then, to her chansonnier (henceforth: 228). An initial and interesting document in the history of 228 is found in the 1523 inventory of Margaret's library, where the entry describing it begins thus: "A big book of music" (Debae 1995, 11). It may seem curious today that the book's first feature of note was its dimensions. Looking at the image opposite—the first two pages of the manuscript—one might imagine that for visitors to this Museum the richness of the decorative apparatus would have much greater importance for its identification within Margaret's library than the manuscript's size. And yet, the prominence the inventory gives to it is not only the result of a distant book culture, or of the detached routine of librarians interested solely in the most superficial aspects of the books that they wanted to include in a list. There is already something revelatory in the beginning of this standardised description, something that we can use as a key to better understand not only the peculiarities of this chansonnier when compared with other music books of the period (including the other three examples in Margaret's library), but also Margaret herself, who she was and who she wanted to be, and why music and this book in particular were so important to her.

As a matter of fact, at the beginning of the sixteenth century "a *big* book of music" was not a common way of describing a chansonnier (a music book containing mainly, but by no means exclusively, secular polyphonic music). The 1523 inventory terms the other chansonnier in Margaret's collection (Brussels, Bibliothèque Royale, MS 11239) differently: "A *small* book of music" (Debae 1995, 480). In fact, at the time chansonniers were usually rather small, and sometimes very small.

228 is considerably larger than a typical chansonnier; its size (36.5 x 26 cm) is closer to that of choirbooks containing sacred music, which were the largest polyphonic music books of the period (Meconi 2010, 19-20; see also exhibit 88). The inventory's entry does not connect 228 with the other chansonnier, but rather with the only choirbook of sacred polyphony in Margaret's library, also listed as a "big book" (Borghetti 2018, 56; Debae 1995, 11 and 61).

The dimensions are not the only surprising features of this chansonnier. As the image shows, 228 opens with a motet by Pierre de la Rue, *Ave sanctissima Maria*. It was common for chansonniers to begin with a sacred piece at the time (Rothenberg 2011, 123-58). These are generally three-voiced cantilena-motets—chanson-style compositions with devotional texts—and therefore similar to most of the music that follows in terms of both style and number of voices. Opening 228, Margaret and/or her guests would have seen a typical beginning for a chansonnier: three voices notated on the page, as in a chanson. Indeed, 228 would have presented itself as a particularly unassuming chansonnier, since by the second decade of the sixteenth century the standard number of voices for such compositions had risen to four. Careful attention was needed to find the *signa congruentiae*, the little signs indicating that each part is to be sung by two singers, one starting from the beginning, the other starting where the signs indicate, and thus discover that *Ave sanctissima Maria* is not a three-voiced cantilena-motet, but rather a grand canonic motet for six voices, almost twice as long as the pieces typically featured at the beginning of a chansonnier. The motet *Ave sanctissima Maria* opens not a choirbook, but a chansonnier; this chansonnier, though, resembles a choirbook in terms of size; at first glance *Ave sanctissima Maria* presents itself as a three-voiced cantilena-motet, which, however, it is not (Borghetti 2018, 56-57).

Following the conventions for presentation manuscripts, as the initial composition *Ave sanctissima Maria* is accompanied by the richest decoration found in the book, featuring Margaret's portrait and her coat of arms. Atypically for a woman in manuscripts of the time, Margaret is the only human figure present, and yet she does not present herself on her own. Beneath her portrait is her coat of arms, impaled with the cross of the late Philibert of Savoy, and therefore identifying Margaret as a widow. At the same time, however, Margaret also presents herself as a ruler, a ruler *because* a widow: the portrait shows her wearing the typical Flemish widow's ruff, but together with a gold gown lined or trimmed with ermine, a form of attire suited to a queen, thus combining elements referring to her widowhood with symbols of power (Eichberger 2002, 33-42; Meconi 2010, 15-19; Borghetti 2018, 57-58).

Together with Margaret's portrait and coat of arms, on the initial pages of 228 we see a monkey and a child. As symbols of primitive or imperfect humanity, they are located on the *bas de page*, in a position opposite to that held by Margaret. Their occupations are also opposite: while Margaret, at prayer, can look at herself in the spiritual mirror of the Immaculate Virgin, termed by medieval tradition "speculum sine macula" (mirror without stain), the monkey sees itself reflected instead in a worldly mirror, which by contrast is "cum macula." The black stain at its centre is at the same time the monkey's reflection and an allegory of the sin resulting from its vice-ridden activity. The child is also doing something purposeless: he plays with whatever is at hand, and like the monkey appears not to notice the apparition of the Virgin (Borghetti 2018, 59-60). The monkey and the child are not just beautiful decorations, amusingly enliving the borders. Both ostensibly unaware of the high moral ends that may be served even by enjoyable activities, they are placed at the book's opening as an admonishment to Margaret herself not to cede to the temptation of taking mere pleasure in her sumptuous chansonnier: this is a serious book of music, not just some pretty chansonnier for fancy and vain ladies.

The musical content of the book contributes significantly to this image of 228 as a serious chansonnier. After *Ave sanctissima Maria* we find almost exclusively pieces in a doleful tone, presenting over and over again the themes of death, sadness, regret, and grief. Mingled with classic courtly chansons on the theme of love spurned, we find compositions mourning the death of family members such as her brother Philip (d. 1506) or father Maximilian (d. 1519), of close court associates such as Jean de Luxembourg (d. 1519), and of her much-loved pet parrot (d. 1505). As a collection of mostly sorrowful pieces, 228 speaks for Margaret: along with elements of the decoration, its music makes a decisive contribution to the definition and performance of her identity as a mourning and faithful widow (Borghetti 2018, 55).

This chansonnier, then, did not only state Margaret's interest in art-music, a privilege typical of persons of her rank; it was rather an important tool for constructing and promoting Margaret's identity as a pious and strong widow—a woman stricken but not bent by fortune—and therefore a tool for making claims to power, exploiting for this purpose the interaction of all the elements offered by music and its media.

The difficulties for a woman, even one as privileged as Margaret, in creating for herself an autonomous discursive space in a world dominated by men, were many. 228 constitutes an example of her success in this enterprise, but also of the limits which Margaret, as a woman, could not exceed. Her book remains a chansonnier, suited to the more private sphere of chamber music rather than the public one of chapel music, which was run instead by the men of her family. The large dimensions of this chansonnier and the large compositions located in prominent positions within it, such as *Ave sanctissima Maria*, concretely exemplify the compromises Margaret as a woman had to make to attain her position of preeminence: 228 does indeed exceed the form and conventions of a chansonnier "for women," but it does not quite equal those of a church choirbook; *Ave sanctissima Maria* is indeed a grand canonic motet, but it hides behind the appearance of a typical cantilena-motet "for a chansonnier," which is to say, a form of motet suited "for women." Margaret's music book was thus in the end a book "for women." And it was important for Margaret to be able to show that she knew how to keep to the place which, as a woman (albeit a member of a ruling family), was allotted to her by a patriarchal society. With 228 she presented herself as a good Christian widow who, although in possession of a precious chansonnier, did not use it for her personal vanity, but to perform her proper devotions (as in *Ave sanctissima Maria*), and to read, to hear, and perhaps to sing music meditating on the sorrows of her existence, those which had allowed her to achieve a position of command (the melancholic compositions; the arms of her dead husband).

All this, though, was not enough. To be credible as both widow and sovereign, Margaret had to show her awareness of the fact that, as a woman, even her virtuous occupations were thought to be more exposed than those of a man to the dangers of sin. The opening pages of her chansonnier served emphatically to reaffirm, to herself and to the world, that there was nothing frivolous in her beautiful music book. The monkey and the child were put right at the begininning at the bottom of the page, in order explicitly to remind herself and the world that she was able to keep afar from the sins of which her sex was traditionally accused. This was the price that even a high-ranking woman had to pay to be a ruler without necessarily having a man by her side (Borghetti 2018, 61-62).

Dnica prima aduentus Dnica
Ad te leuaui animam meam
deus meus in te confido non
erubescam neque irrideant me inimi ci me i
etenim uniuersi qui te exspectant nō confū dent
Vias tuas domine demōstra mihi et semitas
tuas e do ce me Uniuer si
qui te exspe ctant nō confunden tur domine

29. The Constance Gradual

Marianne C.E. Gillion

Southern Germany(?): Printer of the Constance Breviary(?), ca. 1473
160 fols., 30.8 x 22 cm
London, The British Library, General Reference Collection I.B.15154
Image: fol. 1r. Photo © British Library / Bridgeman Images.

The invention of the printing press in the second half of the fifteenth century opened up a world of possibilities to printers and prelates alike, centring around the publication of the books necessary for the celebration of the sacraments. Ambitious entrepreneurs recognised the lucrative market, while astute archbishops realised the opportunity to engender reform and to consolidate their political and ecclesiastical power. Liturgical incunabula appeared quickly, in both official and unofficial versions (Nowakowska 2011; Duggan 2018; Gillion 2021). However, there remained a hurdle in terms of their production. A number of books, either partially or completely, contained notated monophonic music (see VDM). The plainchant repertoire was melodically and notationally complex, and could vary significantly between geographical and ecclesiastical regions (Bloxam 1992, 141-43). The first printers often left blank space or included empty printed staves, which allowed users to add the chant melodies themselves (Duggan 1992, 13-17; VDM). These methods were practical for books that contained a limited amount of music, but precluded the production of books for the choir. The core problem—the difficulty of printing notes upon staves—required a solution. The first large-scale attempt at printed musical notation is found in an anonymous gradual, most likely produced in southern Germany around 1473. The only complete copy of the *Graduale* resides at the British Library, although seven leaves are held by the Universitätsbibliothek Tübingen (De 378.4°). This deceptively modest book was a technical and conceptual breakthrough, and offers tantalising insights into the purpose and power of printed liturgical music.

The anonymity of the *Graduale* is one of its most intriguing features. The incunable's geographical and chronological provenances have been deduced from its internal evidence. It was bound in Augsburg by Ambros Keller, whose name is stamped among the decoration of the cover (*Catalogue* 1912, 2:401). The print starts without preamble on the first Sunday of Advent (fol. 1ʳ, pictured), the beginning of the church year, and continues for 160 folio pages. Analyses of the watermarks undertaken by Mary Kay Duggan concluded that similar sheets appeared throughout the southern German-speaking lands between 1467 and 1482 (Duggan 1992, 13). The text type was used in an edition of the psalter and of the breviary for the diocese of Constance, the latter of which was rubricated in 1473 (Hyatt King 1973, 1221). The *Graduale* cannot be tied to a specific institution; its pages contain no reference to any former users. The book ends almost as abruptly as it begins. There is no colophon, although the words *finit feliciter* occur after the last textual and musical phrase (fol. 160ʳ). Given the complexity of the printing process, the anonymous printer (or their compositor) was justified in this small celebration of the *Graduale*'s happy and successful completion.

Before work on the *Graduale* could begin, preparatory work was required for the innovative music printing method. A gothic plainchant type was commissioned, designed, and produced in the same manner as a text type (Hyatt King 1973, 1223). The type created for the *Graduale* embodies a mixture of crudity and sophistication. A range of notational forms occur, as well as *F*, *C*, and *Gamma-ut* clefs, custodes, and accidentals. The four basic notes are the *punctum*, *bistropha*, *virga*, and *clivis*. The latter two occur in different heights relative to their positioning on the staff. Additionally, the *punctum*, *clivis*, and *virga* appear in multiple versions in order to facilitate the creation of compound neumes. For example, the *pes*, which denotes an upward movement from one note to another, is formed by setting a *punctum* with a curlicue next to a *virga*. The ornate *punctum* is only rarely used separately. The *torculus* and *porrectus* are created in an equivalent fashion, by combinations of *clives* and *puncti* or *virga*. The shapes of the notes, while irregular, are reasonably elegant. The notational complexity is indicative of the care and planning that went into the type's creation, and also a desire for precision. This goal, however, was not always attainable due to technical limitations.

The *Graduale* was printed using a multiple impression process. Out of long metal rules, the compositor created five-line staves bound with double margins. These, along with the text, were printed first in black ink. The notes, clefs, custodes, and woodcut initials were printed in a second impression, also in black ink. This technique allowed the notes to be printed upon the staves, but it was time-consuming and required considerable accuracy by the compositor (Hyatt King 1973, 1223). The difficulty of aligning the musical and textual elements can be seen on the first folio. The syllables are carefully spaced in relation to the number of notes they receive. However, in phrases with a large amount of text and low melodic density, the syllable-note correlation can become unclear. This is partially due to the relatively poor quality of the text type (Duggan 2010, 20). The space around the letters in the form was not tightly packed, and as a result the words stagger unevenly across the page. Conversely, the notation sits precisely on the staves, although the clefs and custodes sometimes float within the double margins. The wet sheets were not always treated carefully between impressions. Many have instances of ink transfer, appearing as faintly overlapping notes, clefs, and letters on the affected pages. Visual incongruencies notwithstanding, the successful calibration of the various elements in multiple impressions was an impressive achievement.

After the sheets came off the press further work was carried out by hand. The compositor had left space for liturgical instructions, foliation, ornate initials, headings, and other decorations. Once the printed sheets were dry, a rubricator went through and provided these missing elements. They also traced over every *F*-line in red ink, a common practice in manuscript chant books during this period. Further, there is evidence that the *Graduale* was proofread by someone with musical knowledge, although it is unclear whether the rubricator fulfilled this role. On fol. 11^{v}, a missing word and its music are added in red ink in the bottom margin of the page. Similarly, a typesetting error in which a syllable and its music are set twice—once at the end of the final staff on fol. 139^{v}, and again at the beginning of the first staff on fol. 140^{r}—is corrected, again in red ink. The proofreading, however, was sporadic. An instance of clef misalignment on fol. 84^{v} is uncorrected, as are many of the textual and grammatical errors that occur throughout the book. It is uncertain whether the latter stemmed from the exemplar used, or from errors by the compositor, who would not necessarily have been literate in Latin.

Once the *Graduale* was printed, rubricated, and bound, it was theoretically ready to be used in sung celebrations of the Mass. Yet was it sufficient for its liturgical purpose? When the contents of the *Graduale* are examined, a curious fact comes to light. It contains the expected constituent elements: a *Temporale* (proper of time), *Sanctorale* (proper of saints), *Commune Sanctorum* (common of saints), *Sequentiale* (collection of sequences), and *Kyriale* (collection of Mass ordinary chants). Yet the *Temporale* is incomplete. Two of the four Sundays in Advent are lacking, as are the three Sundays after Epiphany, two of the three Sundays of Septuagesima, two of the four Sundays in Lent, and all of the Sundays after Easter and after Pentecost. These are not glaring omissions on the part of the compositor, as the text and music of the celebrations that do appear run smoothly. Therefore, the *Graduale* appears to be abbreviated by design (Gillion 2015, 79-81). This drastic curtailment could have stemmed from the copytext. It might also reflect a conscious decision on the part of the printer. A full gradual spans hundreds of pages and contains over 1,000 pieces of plainchant. The creation of such a book would have been a daunting prospect for someone experimenting with a new printing technique and assessing the demand for a new product. Moreover, the venture would represent a substantial financial risk, especially if the printer assumed the expenses himself. The production of an abbreviated gradual would lower the cost for printer and purchasers alike. The consequence of this course of action was that the *Graduale* could never completely supersede an institution's pre-existing manuscripts; it could only supplement them.

The celebrations in the *Sanctorale* provide further evidence of the provenance and intended audience of the *Graduale*. The inclusion of saints venerated in Bavaria, such as Ulrich, Laurence, and George, has led book historians to reassign the *Graduale* from the diocese of Augsburg to that of Constance (Duggan 1992, 11). New analyses of the proper chants for certain saints and celebrations challenge this view. The rubricated Masses do not have exact concordances in early missals printed for Constance, Augsburg, or their archdiocese of Mainz (table 29.1). Key areas of difference concern the assignment of alleluias and sequences. The alleluia for Saint Katherine, for example, represents a localised practice with no known textual concordances (Schlager 1968-67, 2:674-77). *Gaudete iusti*, the alleluia used for St George in the *Graduale*, was used in Mainz and Constance. Conversely, the sequence for St Ulrich, and both alleluias for the Visitation were used in Augsburg. Two of these three chants, *Alleluia In Maria benignitas* and *Laude dignum sanctum* occur in the first printed edition of the *Graduale Augustense* (Basel: Pforzheim, 1511). A comparison of the alleluia melodies reveals similar melodic profiles, although the version in the *Graduale* is less melismatic. The liturgical and musical evidence confirms that the exemplar used originated in the archdiocese of Mainz, but from a region closer to Augsburg than Constance. The specificity of the *Sanctorale* limited the potential market for the *Graduale*. It also contrasted with contemporary trends towards liturgical reform evident in the archdiocese. The ability to print liturgical music could bolster ecclesiastical power structures, but could also—whether intentionally or not—subvert them.

Table 1: Concordances among early printed service books for the Archdiocese of Mainz

Saint or Celebration	*Graduale* (ca. 1473)	*Missale Moguntiense* (Basel: Wenssler, ca. 1488)	*Missale Constantiense* (Augsburg: Ratdolt, 1504)	*Missale Augustanum* (Dillingen: Sensenschmidt, 1489)	*Graduale Augustense* (Basel: Pforzheim, 1511)
George	**Al. Gaudete iusti**	**Al. Gaudete iusti** Al. Christus resurgens Al. Surrexit pastor bonus	Al. Letabitur iustus **Al. Gaudete iusti**	Al. Letabitur iustus Al. Christus resurgens	*Not present.*
Visitation of the Blessed Virgin Mary	**Al. In Maria benignitas** **Al. Spes datur**	**Al. In Maria benignitas** Al. Ave stillens melle	**Al. Spes datur**	**Al. In Maria benignitas** **Al. Spes datur**	**Al. In Maria benignitas**
Ulrich	**Sq. Laude dignum sanctum**	*None given.*	Sq. Gaude mater	**Sq. Laude dignum sanctum**	**Sq. Laude dignum sanctum**
Katherine	**Al. Ista est speciose martyr**	Al. Beata virgo katherina	Al. Ex tumba	Al. Beata virgo katherina	*Not present.*

The often overlooked *Graduale* is a foundational publication. Its production marked a technical breakthrough in the field of printing. The multiple impression process that allowed notes to be printed upon staves was soon used throughout Europe: mainly for books of liturgy and theory, but also for polyphonic and instrumental music. The ability to print plainchant added a new dimension to the publication patterns of liturgical works. Prelates' attempts to control worship through textual revision and regularisation could extend sonically to the music of the Mass and the Office. Their efforts, however, would be undermined by opportunistic printers who printed unauthorised or universally applicable editions. The medium of print rendered standardisation possible, but not always probable; diversity continued to exist (Gozzi 2013, 50-54; Gillion 2019). The *Graduale*, although anonymous, bears traces of those who created it and the audience for whom it was intended. The innovative chant type indicates the skill of the cutter; the painstaking composition of the page, the care of the compositor; and the handwritten elements, the contributions of the rubricator and proofreader. The surprising contents of the *Graduale*, with its abbreviated *Temporale* and specific *Sanctorale*, reveal the printer's cautious approach to his envisaged regional users. The technical and conceptual complexities of the *Graduale* would be reflected in subsequent publications as prelates, publishers, and the public explored the power of printed liturgical music.

ABBREVIATIONS: VDM - Verzeichnis deutscher Musicfrühdrucke, http://www.vdm.sbg.ac.at.

GENESIS

30. The Bible of Borso d'Este

Serenella Sessini

Modena, Biblioteca Estense, V.G.12=Lat. 422 and V.G.13=Lat. 423
Taddeo Crivelli, Franco de' Russi and collaborators, Ferrara, 1455-1461
Manuscript on parchment; vol. 1: 311 fols., vol. 2: 293 fols.; 37.5 x 26.5 cm
Image: vol. 1, fol. 5v. Photo © Heritage Images / Fine Art Images / akg-images.

Over 1000 miniatures appear in the incredibly rich decorative and illustrative ornamentations that populate the lavishly illuminated borders of each of the over 600 folios of the Bible commissioned by Borso d'Este, Marquis then Duke of Ferrara (r. 1450-71). Among them one regularly encounters a wide range of Biblical characters (dressed in fifteenth-century clothes), fantastic creatures, a variety of animals and flowers, and devices and emblems of the Este house (see *La Bibbia di Borso d'Este* 1997). Music appears in several instances, both in illustrations of the numerous Biblical scenes that involve music-making figures, and, less often, in the decoration—for example, a musical putto, angel, or mythical figure. Musical notation, however, is rare.

This musical miniature decorates the initial *I* of the sentence that opens the book of Genesis. The initial *I*, a pink and green twig, is enclosed in a rectangular box framed with roses, and stands out from a golden background. Two winged dragons, one green and one blue, hold the initial with their mouths, while a dog and a youth seem to be attempting to hold them back. Below, a hybrid creature with bird's legs and tail and a human upper body spreads his arms to grab the ends of a musical scroll, which seems to have fallen from above, becoming entangled in the process (fig. 30.1). Twelve scenes from God's creation fill the borders of Genesis' double-page opening (fols. 5v-6r), together with a number of devices of the manuscript's patron, Duke Borso d'Este, including a diamond ring and a unicorn (Fava and Salmi 1950, 90-91).

This opening is rather emblematic of Borso d'Este's commission. His chamberlain, Galeotto dell'Assassino, signed a contract with the artists Taddeo Crivelli and Franco de' Russi, dated 11 July 1455, stipulating that "each book should have a magnificent opening made, as this Bible deserves" (Treccani degli Alfieri 1942, 69; Toniolo 1997a, 297; Milano 1997, 25). Thanks to Crivelli's creative invention and splendid execution, these miniatures are among the finest in the whole work (Toniolo 1997, 158-59; Toniolo 1997a, 398), perhaps because they were among the last pages to be illuminated by the miniaturist towards the end of his contract (the quinternion including fols. 2r-11r was the last to be completed).

Figure 30.1: Musical scroll—detail of Crivelli, *Initial I* (*Genesis*). Photo © Heritage Images / Fine Art Images / akg-images.

A comparable scroll appears elsewhere in the Bible, on a page that includes the end of Paul's Epistle to the Hebrews, a Prologue to and the beginning of the Acts of the Apostles (fig. 30.2). This design, with a putto (or an angel) in the act of disentangling one of his legs from a musical scroll, was repeated by Crivelli in some of his future works, including the Gualenghi-d'Este Book of Hours (Los Angeles, J. Paul Getty Museum, MS Ludwig IX 13, fols. 3v and 172v), illuminated around 1469 (Shephard et al. 2017). The two-line musical staff is reused in

Figure 30.2: Taddeo Crivelli, musical scroll. Modena, Biblioteca Estense, V.G.13=Lat. 423, fol. 215v. Photo courtesy of the Ministero della Cultura / Gallerie Estensi, Biblioteca Estense Universitaria.

several works by the artist; it appears, for example, in a book of hours made for a member of the Faletti family between 1461 and 1463 (New York, Pierpont Morgan Library, M.227, fol. 92r), and in another from around 1465 (Basel, Universitäts-Bibliothek, AN VIII 45, fol. 112r).

The notation on the Genesis scroll, arranged on a two-line staff, does not reflect a real composition, and is rather a suggestion of music; but the note shapes are those specifically of neumatic notation, used for plainchant. This indicates that Crivelli had some familiarity with plainchant and neumes, knowledge that he had probably acquired by illuminating service books—between 1453-54 Crivelli illuminated at least two antiphonaries and two missals (Bertoni 1925, 16).

This miniature might be seen as rather cryptic at first, as it cannot be classified as a narrative scene, nor as a mere decoration, but it can be better understood thanks to the particular position it occupies in Borso's Bible. As noted by Federica Toniolo, a link can sometimes be established between the Biblical text and the decorative apparatus, such as on fol. 185r of the second volume, where the image of the unicorn triumphing over a dragon can be associated with the divine wrath against sin, which is expressed in the facing text from the second chapter of Paul's Epistle to the Romans (Toniolo 1997a, 494-95).

Our musical miniature appears at the opening of the book of Genesis, on the very first page of the first book of the Bible. Why did Crivelli choose a musical scroll to illustrate this section? The first sentence of the book, of which the scroll decorates the initial *I*, reads: "In principio creavit Deus coelum et terram" (In the beginning, God created the heavens and the earth). Directly above the initial, a miniature shows God creating the Firmament. Directly below, God separates the light from the darkness and sets the sun and the moon in the sky. The celestial leitmotiv seems at this stage obvious, and it induces a musical association that would have been familiar to fifteenth-century readers equipped with an elite education. The Pythagorean concept of the music of the spheres was described and developed most paradigmatically by the sixth-century Roman philosopher Boethius in his *De Musica*, in which he identifies three categories of music, among them a *musica mundana* consisting in the sounds produced by the motions of the spheres, inaudible on earth but comprehensible through the rational investigation of consonance.

That the notion of celestial harmony was still very much alive in the fifteenth century is demonstrated in a multitude of sources. In Giorgio Anselmi's *De Musica* of 1434, for example, it appears as a *harmonia celestis* in which each sphere is governed by an angel. Anselmi practised medicine in Ferrara in the 1420s, and it is likely that his works were known to the Este (Shephard 2014, 46). Even more compelling, in Ugolino of Orvieto's *Declaratio musice discipline*, probably composed in Ferrara between 1430 and 1435, *musica caelestis* (which includes the Boethian categories of *musica mundana*, *musica humana*, and *musica instrumentalis*) is seen as a higher harmony that is at the foundations of all music. A copy of this treatise is recorded as being kept in the sacristy of Ferrara's cathedral in library inventories of 1462 and 1466, and more copies were made in Ferrara in the mid- and late fifteenth century (MacCarthy 2014, 411; Lockwood 2009, 88-89; Palisca 1985, 163-64). One of these was illuminated by Giorgio d'Alemagna and Guglielmo Giraldi for Rinaldo Maria d'Este, younger half-brother of Borso, in 1453 (Biblioteca Apostolica Vaticana, Ross. 455; MacCarthy 2014, 416-22).

Even though these books are not among those listed in the inventory of Borso's personal library (carried out in 1461 and edited in 1467), the duke had access to other treatises that explore the topic, such as Boethius' *De consolatione philosophiae*, and Dante's *Divine Comedy*. It is well-known that Borso's knowledge of Latin was fairly limited, so it is notable that in his library there were two copies of Boethius' treatise, one in Latin and one in French, and two copies of Dante's text, which was written in the vernacular and therefore accessible to the duke (Bertoni 1926, 705-28). In Boethius' work, the reader could find references to the *musica mundana*, and indeed the whole work has an implicit musical theme (Chamberlain 1970, 80). Although *musica mundana* is mentioned in this treatise in terms of its visible rather than its sonic properties, the text is infused with philosophical and spiritual ideas, and the author states that God is the one responsible for this celestial motion (Chamberlain 1970, 81, 89; Hicks 2017, 254). In Dante's *Comedy* the author perceives the *musica mundana* during his otherworldly journey to Paradise, where he hears "sweet musics" that "render sweet harmony among these spheres" (*Paradiso* VI, 124-26; Smythe 1926, 87, 90-91).

Borso was likely familiar with this concept and would have been able to recognise the invocation of celestial harmony on Genesis' illuminated opening. Given that Borso's limited knowledge of Latin meant that he would not have been able to read the text, the Bible's images take on an additional importance, guiding the duke's navigation and comprehension of the Creation story. In equal parts a work of piety and an ostentatious display of magnificence, the Bible was shown to visiting dignitaries and other guests. In August 1467, the Bible was shown to a group of Bolognese ambassadors, while in April 1471 Borso took it to Pope Paul II in Rome on the occasion of his investiture as duke of Ferrara (Milano 1997, 28; Rosenberg 1981, 62). The presence of the Genesis miniature at the opening of the first volume must have given it a special prominence on such occasions, as the first impression in an encounter with Borso's Bible that seems unlikely to have been detailed or comprehensive, whilst the sophistication of such audiences implies a familiarity with the concept of the music of the spheres.

The book of Genesis also includes the first mention of music in the Bible (Genesis 4:21): Jubal, a descendent of Cain, is described as the ancestor of those who play *cithara* and *organo* (as the Vulgate has it; harp and organ in the Douay-Rheims translation), establishing him as the inventor of music. Crivelli's musical scrolls in the Gualenghi-d'Este Hours have been associated with the concept of silent music in private devotional practice, where the notation is suggestive of music but does not imply audible song (Shephard et al. 2017). In this Genesis, the same idea is taken even further, as the musical scroll is here evocative of cosmic music, the supreme example of inaudible music. Between the music of the spheres created by God and human music invented by Jubal, we can see this miniature as a symbol of an emblematic "birth of music." At the same time, perhaps, it imputes a musical character to the divine utterance through which creation took form. God's act of creation set the spheres in motion, and their harmony expresses the essential nature of divine order, the endless but inaudible resonance of his own higher realm echoing throughout the whole of creation.

31. The Jistebnice Cantionale

Lenka Hlávková

Prague, Knihovna Národního muzea (Library of the National Museum), Ms. II C 7
Prague(?), 1420s
Manuscript on paper, [6] + 132 fols. + [5], 31 x 21 cm

Image: fols. 50r-v. Anon. (music) and Jan Čapek (text), *Ktož jsú boží bojovníci*, 1420s. Photo courtesy of the Knihovna Národního muzea, Prague.

On 14 August 1431 the Hussite army dispersed the Crusaders near the town of Domažlice (Taus) in western Bohemia (Turnbull 2004, 14, 40; Čornej 2000, 555-56). This memorable victory was celebrated by the contemporary poet, a master of Prague University, Laurencius de Brzezova in his 1431 *Carmen insignis Corone Bohemie* (*Poem of the Illustrious Crown of Bohemia*; Hrdina and Ryba 1951). His testimony states that after hearing sounds coming from the military positions of the Hussites three miles away, their enemies ran away, frightened by the thunder of military wagons, neighing horses, shouting soldiers, blowing bugles, and the vigorous singing of the Hussite army:

Honoris iam inmemores	Forgetful now of their honour,
divites necnon pauperes	rich and poor
metu vexilla deserunt	alike desert the banners through fear and
et ut amentes fugiunt	flee like madmen,
nondum conspecto agmine,	not yet having seen
hostis obvii specie –	the army or met the sight of the enemy –
nam mei tunc ab hostibus	for at that point
tribus distabant millibus –	my men were three miles from the foe –
solo audito strepitu	but only having heard the creak of cart,
rede, equorum sonitu	the din of horses and
tumultuque horribili	the dreadful tumult
vociferantis populi,	of a noisy crowd,
classicorum sonancium,	of trumpets sounding
populorum cantancium.	and the people singing.
(Hrdina and Ryba 1951, 48)	trans. Henry Howard

Although there is no direct evidence, the *cantio* (battle song) *Ktož jsú boží bojovníci* (*You who are the warriors of God*) is traditionally connected with this scene. Its text, written by the Hussite priest Jan Čapek, is a summary of the Hussite approach to war, and it may have worked as an efficient means to rouse the spirits of warriors at the beginning of combat. Since the Czech national revival in the nineteenth century, this song, understood as a symbol of the Hussites and the Czech nation, has been quoted and arranged by several Czech composers in their compositions, with a clear patriotic or historic message—for example, by Bedřich Smetana in *Tábor* and *Blaník* from the cycle *Má vlast* (*My Country*); by Antonín Dvořák in *Husitská* (*Hussite*); by Leoš Janáček in his opera *Výlety páně Broučkovy* (*The Excursions of Mr Brouček*); and by Karel Husa in *Music for Prague 1968*.

Thanks to the ambitious politics of the Holy Roman Emperor and King of Bohemia Charles IV, Prague became the capital of the Holy Roman Empire in the fourteenth century, the residence of an archbishop and also, with the founding of the University, the most important intellectual centre in late medieval Central Europe. This inspiring atmosphere was also expressed in the composition of many new pieces of music, mostly new chants for the liturgy as well as sacred songs (Curry 2011, 171). The expanding *Devotio Moderna* spiritual movement, which promoted and supported the ideas of individual spiritual experience and understanding of the Christian faith, prompted the creation of sacred songs not only in Latin, but also in vernacular languages. As we know from contemporary sources, songs in Czech were very popular and they were often sung in churches at the turn of the fourteenth century. In 1408 singing in Czech was restricted by a document issued by the Prague synod and only four songs were then permitted to be performed within the Mass (Hlávková and Vlhová-Wörner 2014, 476-77). The communal singing of the lay community brought a new dimension of spiritual experience into the church. Despite the restrictions, new songs in Czech were composed at this time and they became an important medium for the dissemination of critical and reformist perspectives on the Roman Church.

After the death at the stake of the popular preacher and University teacher Johannes Hus in Constance in 1415, the so-called Hussite war began. It lasted for 15 years (1419-34) and came to an end thanks to the Compacts concluded at the Council of Basel. This document confirmed that in Bohemia and Moravia everyone who should request it had a right to obtain communion in the form of both Bread and Wine (Šmahel 1996)—that is, under both kinds, or in Latin *sub utraque specie*, from which is derived "Utraquists," referring to moderate Hussites and their followers after the war.

Hussitism was arguably the first European Reformation (Soukup 2013). Intellectuals who held Hussite views translated liturgical texts for Mass and Office for selected feasts of the liturgical year, and adapted the plainchant melodies to the structure of the new Czech texts. They elevated a vernacular language into the position of a sacred liturgical language, assigned until then exclusively to Latin (Vlhová-Wörner 2019, xii-xvii). Songs in Czech, mostly of sacred character, also played an important role in the life of Hussite communities. In some song texts we can even follow theological discussions from the beginning of the fifteenth century, or see historical issues through contemporary eyes (Holeton 2019, 61-64). The collection of songs preserved in the Jistebnice Cantionale from the 1420s also contains sung prayers for the Holy Trinity and the Virgin Mary which follow the older tradition. But most of the compositions discuss the principal ideas of the Reformation, such as communion under both kinds, which, in Hussite thought, was a necessary condition for each believer to achieve salvation. Other songs reflecting basic principles of the Christian faith, such as the Ten Commandments, were used as an effective means of lay education.

The so-called Jistebnice Cantionale is the only preserved "Hussite songbook" source known to us today. The modest manuscript of 31 x 21 cm consists of 132 paper folios and originates, according to recent research, from the 1420s, most probably in Prague. The *Cantionale* is a unique testimony to the first attempt in Europe to translate and transform the repertory of liturgical chants into the vernacular. Unfortunately, several folios of the original collection are lost, and some chants and songs with them. The second life of this book began in 1872 in the south Bohemian village of Jistebnice, near Tábor. Leopold Katz, a 17-year-old student of the Gymnasium (grammar school) in Tábor, found an old book hidden in the library of the parish office. He informed his teacher, and his report reached the historians Martin Kolář and František Palacký, prominent representatives of the Czech cultural elite. They recognised the exceptional value of the *Cantionale*, and in 1874 the book became a part of collections of the National Museum in Prague (Kozina and Kozinová 2005, 29-36). However, the title "Jistebnice Cantionale" is rather misleading, as it is not a collection of songs from the village of Jistebnice. The book contains, most importantly, Czech translations of liturgical chants for selected feasts of the liturgical year. The song collection only occupies about a quarter of the total number of folios, but scholars from the end of the nineteenth and the beginning of the twentieth centuries found them to be the most interesting and valuable part of the collection, and therefore began to call it a songbook. The significance of the song collection included in the Jistebnice Cantionale is supported by the high quality of the song tunes: some of them were of older origin, reused in a new context or with a new Czech text, but many were composed anew by Hussite authors and show a highly developed taste for melodic structures. Hussite authors also introduced a regular refrain, which served to underline the main ideas expressed in the song text, and also made it easier to integrate the laity into communal singing.

Recent research connects the Jistebnice Cantionale with the Emmaus monastery in Prague, which was closely linked to Hussitism and was one of only a handful of Bohemian monastic communities to maintain full continuity during the Hussite wars. A striking textual relationship between the *Cantionale* and the *Glagolitic Bible*—a translation of the Bible into Old Slavonic—has been observed; and furthermore, it may well be in the hands of the last Utraquist abbot of the monastery, Pavel Paminodas Horský, who served as priest in Jistebnice, that the book found its way from monastery to village in the late sixteenth century (Vlhová-Wörner 2019, xv-xvi).

The Jistebnice Cantionale also contains a few battle songs, which later paradoxically became the most popular parts of the whole collection; and among them *Ktož jsú boží bojovníci* has emerged as carrying particular national significance. The text of the song is inspired by the Books of the Maccabees, the oldest Czech *cantio Svatý Václave* (*Saint Wenceslas*), and the military order of Jan Žižka, the leader of the Hussite army. In penning the text, Čapek clearly had number symbolism in mind: he composed stanzas of 14 verses and periods of 14 syllables, referring to the fourteenth verse of the fourteenth chapter in the first Book of Moses, which speaks of Abraham's army of 318 soldiers—it is no coincidence that the text of *Ktož jsú boží bojovníci* has exactly 318 syllables (Boubín 2014, 508-09). The musical form implies that more experienced singers were needed to perform the rhythmically complicated first part (*versus*), then the community might have joined in with the much easier second part (*repetitio*) (Černý et al. 2005, 167-69)—does this arrangement fit with the explosive atmosphere just as a battle is about to commence, as tradition has determined?

The song was known even before the discovery of the Jistebnice Cantionale in 1872, but in a slightly different shape. If we compare the Hussite version with those preserved in songbooks from the sixteenth century onwards, it becomes clear that its melody and rhythm underwent several changes. The rhythmic pattern of the fifteenth-century version, in triple metre with an upbeat, was transformed into a marching duple metre (Černý et al. 2005, 167-69; Vlhová-Wörner 2019, 212-14). The newer pattern has come to act as an audible sign of the Hussites in Czech musical culture (as, for example, at the beginning of the symphonic poems *Tábor* and *Blaník* from Smetana's *Má vlast*), but it has nothing to do with the original shape of the *cantio* as it was sung in the 1420s. Thus one of the most recognisable national musical symbols is in reality a fiction, based on a later version of what was once a Hussite song.

Jan Čapek, *Ktož jsú boží bojovníci*: original text and translation

Ktož jsú boží bojovníci
a zákona jeho,
prostež od Boha pomoci
a ufajte v něho,
že konečně vždycky
s ním svítězíte.

Kristusť vám za škody stojí,
stokrát viec slibuje,
pakli kto proň život složí,
věčný mieti bude,
blaze každému,
ktož na pravdě sende.

R° Tenť pán velíť se nebáti
záhubcí tělesných,
velíť i život složiti
pro lásku svých bližních.

Protož střelci, kopiníci
řádu rytieřského,
sudličníci a cepníci
lidu rozličného,
pomnětež všichni
na pána štědrého.

Nepřátel se nelekajte,
na množstvie nehleďte,
pána svého v srdci mějte,
proň a s ním bojujte
a před nepřátely
neutiekajte.

R° Dávno Čechové řiekali
a příslovie měli,
že podlé dobrého pána
dobrá jiezda bývá.

Vy pakosti a drabanti,
na duše pomněte,
pro lakomstvie a lúpeže
životóv netraťte
a na kořistech
se nezastavujte.

Heslo všichni pamatujte,
kteréž vám vydáno,
svých hauptmanóv pozorujte,
retuj druh druhého,
hlediž a drž se
každý šiku svého.

R° A s tiem vesele křikněte,
řkúc: Na ně, hr, na ně,
braň svú rukama chutnajte,
Bóh pán náš, křikněte

Vlhová-Wörner 2019, 212-14

You who are the warriors of God
and of his law,
beg God for help
and trust in him
that you will win with him
the final victory.

Christ warrants of your losses,
he promises a hundred times more,
if one lays down his life for him,
he will have an eternal one,
blessed is everyone
who falls <in battle> for truth.

R° This lord commands <us> not to fear
those who kill the body
and commands to give up even one's life
for the love of one's neighbour.

Therefore you archers and spearmen,
you of knightly order,
you with pitchforks and flails,
you sundry people,
you all remember
the munificent Lord.

Do not fear the enemies,
disregard the multitude,
keep the lord in your hearts,
fight for and with him,
and do not run away
from the enemies.

R° From time immemorial Czechs
have said in proverb
that the ride is as good
as is its lord.

You plunderers and guards,
remember your souls;
do not squander lives
through avarice and robbery,
do not stop
for booty.

You all remember the password
that was issued to you,
obey your captains,
save one another,
let everyone mind
and hold his rank.

R° And then cheerfully exclaim,
saying: Against them, hurrah against them,
grab your weapon in your hands,
exclaim: "God is our Lord!"

Vlhová-Wörner 2019, 301-02

Additional references: Cermanová et al. 2014; Kolár et al. 2005.

Acknowledgements: This essay was written within the research project EXPRO 19-28306X *Old Myths, New Facts: Czech Lands at the Center of 15th-Century Musical Developments*, funded by the Czech Science Foundation.

Atrē omnipotentem factorē celi t tre visi
liū Et ī vnū dnm ihm xp filiū
ex prē natū ante omnia secula genitū nō factū
quē oīa facta sūt Qui ppť nos homines t ppť
tē descendit de ce lis Et incarnat' ē de spū
scō ex maria virgine t homo fac tus est
Atrem omnipo ten tem factorē ce li t tre visibi liū
omniū t ī visibilium Et in vnū dnm ihm
xpm fi lium dei vni genitū t ex prē natū
añ omnia secla consubstancialē prī
p quē omnia facta sūt

32. The Saxilby Fragment

Lisa Colton and James Cook

Lincoln, Lincolnshire County Archive, Saxilby Parish 23/1
Lincoln(?), ca. 1450–75
Manuscript on parchment, 2 fols., 43 x 32.5 cm
Image: fol. 1r. Photo © Lincolnshire County Council.

In museums, one is often drawn to the most sumptuously decorated objects, items that seem to have been designed to impress and be remembered. These display items can, however, be only indirectly representative of the objects with which rank-and-file musicians interacted. The Saxilby Fragment, as it is commonly known, conveys evidence of pragmatic methods devised to compose, teach, notate, and perform vocal music.

Before the English Reformation, musicians were highly skilled in diverse improvisatory practices that over time disappeared. Song in as many as five or more parts could be performed without being committed to slate, parchment, or paper. Musicians' professional skills were fundamentally based on developing strong ear training, and aurally led contrapuntal skills, hand in hand with memorisation. Many musicians did not need notation, not least those engaged in ceremonial instrumental music or minstrelsy; rather, the mark of their prowess lay in both their knowledge of a vast repertory of vocal or instrumental melodies, and their ability to improvise new lines of music above or around a given set of notes. The music that was committed to manuscript or early print contains few obvious traces of either the skills of such musicians, or the ways in which oral and written musical skills were learned in churches, monasteries, and cathedrals.

The Saxilby Fragment is not the most conventionally beautiful of sources. It contains two unusually notated pieces of music which seem originally to have formed part of a choir book used as part of services. The two pieces are a Credo and a fragmentary Sanctus, both of which would have been performed at Mass as part of a series of polyphonic movements. The leaves have survived through an act of recycling: as is typical of out-dated sources of English music, their original book was reused to cover what was probably an account book from Saxilby parish. The relative availability of parchment for such rebinding purposes makes it likely that the leaves had not travelled far, but there is no evidence of the specific institution that originally made use of the music. Among local centres associated with polyphonic music, Lincoln Minster and its major parish churches remain plausible sites for the pieces' scribe and/or composer.

What might the idiosyncratic notation tell us? Two forms of pared-down notation, known as "stroke" and "strene," are rarely found in surviving manuscripts, but their presence in more than one source suggests common strategies in circulation for the simplified notation of polyphony. Stroke notation seems to have been a "shorthand or popular version" of more complex systems of its time (Bent 1969, 149), in which the basic note value was represented by a stroke which equalled a semibreve (whole note); longer durations were represented through repeating the same symbol in groups of two or more semibreves. Strene notation uses two note lengths, strenes and breves; it is named after the note shape with two tails described by John Merbecke in his *Booke of Common praier noted* of 1550 (Benham 1993, 153).

The contexts for pared-down notations might be understood as quite broad. What sort of musicians might have wanted or needed to use them to create polyphonic performances? An obvious opportunity was in teaching, not least of boys learning the various skills that might prepare them for a life as a chorister or priest. Similarly, one can imagine their use for teaching women in nunneries where other forms of simplified texts were in common usage, such as the reduced liturgies employed at Syon Abbey (Bagnall Yardley 2006), or religious texts translated into the vernacular (Bell 1995). In musical education plainchant notation was presumably introduced first; this explains how these adapted notations have come to use symbols that would be recognisable from chant manuscripts, including staves, clefs, and pitched note-heads. As Bent and Bowers speculated: "It is, perhaps, no accident that music so notated could almost certainly be deciphered and successfully performed by singers whose acquaintance with musical notation was limited to that of plainsong" (Bent and Bowers 1981, 2, 7).

Finally, we should remember that adult singers, both male and female, may not have regularly had need to refer to sources of written polyphony, and that for those who seldom used such books, a system that was reduced to essential elements—but could still create three- or four-part music—would have been attractive. These notations, and the sources that preserve them, are evidently not high-status books: they are working copies of pieces that speak to their singers' skills at that point in their training. Stoke notation was not limited to British sources: the Saxilby Fragment is comparable to examples from Germany and the Low Countries that are understood to preserve music associated with singers developing their experience, including secular music (Haggh 1997, 128).

The use of divisi notes in the Credo at the very last chord of "mortuos" (bar 39) suggests the need for more than one voice per line, and that the opportunity to exploit this, in final sonorities, was expected by the scribe. Such practices had been documented from the fourteenth century (in Durham Cathedral, MS C.I 20, edited in Harrison and Lefferts 1980, item 34), and are known as "gymel," with one line splitting into two for final cadences (Sanders 2001). Several English discant pieces in the Old Hall Manuscript (first layer, copied ca. 1410s) include added thirds at or before cadences, typically in the middle line of the texture. This split voice part might reinforce the case for the Saxilby Fragment's music as having been performed by a choir of more than one voice per part; it also presents a point of contact with the written-out discant practices found in Old Hall, extensions of improvised traditions that could no longer cope without some form of visual, notated prompt.

At Durham Cathedral, these sorts of skills were valued in polyphonic song. Visitation records (ca. 1390) indicate that: "There used to be paid clerks singing the organum and assisting the monks in the song that is called 'trebill,' and they are no longer there, to the great inconvenience and frustration of the brothers singing in the choir" (Crosby 1992, 35; trans. Colton).

"Trebill" might refer to three-part singing in general, the need for a clerk to sing the uppermost part (Bowers 1995, 17), or the reinforcement of the uppermost "triplum" part. More local to the provenance of the Saxilby Fragment, the foundation charters for Epworth, a small chantry chapel on the Isle of Axholme, Lincolnshire, indicated the need for four singers: "one tenor, one middle-range voice, and two who know how to sing competently on the treble line" (Lincoln, Lincolnshire Archives Office, Archives of the Dean and Chapter, MS Dij 51/3(4); cited in Bowers 1983, 178). Given that the Saxilby Credo is already in four parts (in ranges roughly equivalent to the modern choral scoring SATB), the minimum number of voices performing it would be five (two Trebles; Mene; Tenor; Contratenor-bassus, or modern SSATB).

The Saxilby Fragment remains the most impressive example of a piece of music that uses just one rhythmic symbol (apart from rests) but that results in a satisfying, four-part texture (Bent and Bowers 1981, 7). Rob C. Wegman noted the survival of "The Saxilby Mass" in some manuscript fragments now in Bologna originally described by Charles Hamm (Wegman 1996, 418; Hamm 1968). Whilst this concordance has not gone unnoticed among scholars, the full ramifications of the discovery, which provides large sections of all five movements of the Mass, are yet to be explored. It has been argued that the Italian fragments represent Italian compositions, produced by an Italian scribe (Hamm 1968), but this is clearly only partially true. Certainly the Mass is English, since it corresponds well to English stylistic features, but it does seem to have been translated into more conventional notation by an Italian scribe: the stroke notation of the original instead literally becomes groups of semibreves repeated in twos or threes.

Bent and Bowers (1981) have previously noted that, unlike in the case of a *Salve Regina* setting, uniquely preserved in stroke notation in the Ritson manuscript but elsewhere given in fully mensural notation, there is no evidence that the Saxilby Fragment preserves a simplified version of a pre-existent mensural work. Instead, the work could be a written-out approach to the improvised practice of English Discant, which provides for certain consonant intervals over a pre-existent plainsong producing simple improvised polyphony. Whilst most contemporary theorists discuss discant as a purely two-voice phenomenon, Pseudo-Tunstede discusses its application in three voices, whilst also noting the difficulties presented by improvising two voices independently against a given line. The survival of many more written-out discant compositions for three voices than for two, despite the opposite theoretical testimony, is surely testament to the difficulty of realising this as actual improvisation. Whilst the Saxilby Mass has much in common with discant compositions—from its almost constant consonance, to its vocal parts which correspond roughly to the "sights" in discant of Treble, Countertenor, Plainsong, and Counter—it does not follow the practice exactly. The opening and closing pitches generally do not follow the usual rules of the practice, even if the rest does correspond well to the intervals allowed in English Discant. The musical language, like the notational form of the work, therefore speaks to a desire to produce simple polyphony, drawn from a practice that was taught at an early age to singers, before the practice of learning written mensural polyphony.

As far as it is possible to discern, the Mass follows the typical English mensural pattern of the period: opening in triple time, moving to duple, and then closing again in triple. It even seems to correspond to an absolutely strict textural groundplan: each movement begins with the same opening motif, and proceeds in an identical succession of textures. This basic idea of similarity between movements in structure, length, and mensural practice seems to be at the heart of most English

Mass cycles from the mid-fifteenth century, but is almost always treated with a lighter touch than is here displayed. The Credo corresponds, to an extent, to another English habit, arguably stemming from the same priority to create similarity between movements. Despite the extreme length of the Credo text, in comparison to that of other movements, the Saxilby Credo is not much longer since it omits several lines of text. In most English Mass cycles, the Credo sets different lines of text simultaneously in different voices. In continental copies of these works, scribes often text only the upper voice, consequently producing a work with textual omissions. If such "telescoping," as the practice is usually called, was ever intended here, it has subsequently been ironed out by the Saxilby scribe.

The Saxilby Fragment was considered "lately discovered" a century ago (Hughes 1924, 153), but it awaited the detailed consideration of Margaret Bent and Roger Bowers for wider awareness. Like many sources discovered only in the twentieth century, its full significance can only truly be understood within a network of contemporary sources, none of which can properly be considered "typical." The Fragment's relationship with other sources of Mass music of the period, with music that uses stroke notation, with the music of Lincolnshire, and with contemporary performance and pedagogical practices, has much more to stimulate our curiosity than might appear at first glance.

Additional references: Bent 1968; Bowers 1999; Owen 1971.

Sans tenir ne chemin ne voye
Sinon en ensuiuant la voix
De refroidie et morte ioye
Apres hault vouloir cheuauchoie
Et les autres semblablement
Et tousiours la voie escoutoye
Qui tant se plaignoit asprement

Tant cheuauchasmes que nous veismes
Parmy la grant forest espesse
Celluy que de si loing oysmes
Naure au cueur a grant destresse

Par fortune et par sa rudesse
Dont il se plaignoit malement
En la blasmant par grant aspresse
Ainsi ou bien semblablement

¶Lamant sans partie

¶Comment lamant se complaint a for-
tune/et les autres lescoutent mucez derrie
re vng buisson

He fortune ie te doy bien maldire
Quant a moy seul es plus cruelle
q̃ au demourãt de ceulx q̃ sõt sur terre
Helas amours que me vault a le dire
Fors seulement a degorgier mon ire
Qui mallement par sa fureur ma terre
Dueil recele le poure cueur me serre
Si serrement que riens ne le deserre
Fors pleurs et cry nourry en desplaisance
Je ny scay plus autre conseil requerre
Fors a moy mesmes entreprendre vne guerre
Pour racompter au long ma doleance
Vray dieu damours ie suis de mon enfance
Tien ligement et de foy et dõmaige
Et tay seruy de toute ma puissance
De corps/de biẽs/de vueil ⁊ de courage
Et ay souffert que par ton doulx messaige
Aies assis mon cueur a ta plaisance
Mais ma fortune est fierement sauuaige
Car ie ne puis auoir que desplaisance
De toy mon dieu ne me vueil pas plaindre
Mais ie te pry escoute ma complainte
Jay tant ame sans en amours me faindre
Quen paradis neut oncques saint ne saincte
Qui tant aymast de son gre sans contrainte
Que iayme celle que ie tiens a ma dame
Dont desplaisir me donne telle estrainte
Quen chascun iour cent mille foys me pasme

33. *Le Jardin de Plaisance et Fleur de Rhétorique*

Jane H.M. Taylor

Paris: Antoine Vérard, ca. 1501-02
267 fols., 26 x 19 cm (40)
Paris, Bibliothèque nationale de France, RES-YE-168
Image: sig. g vi^{v}. Photo © Bibliothèque nationale de France.

In 1501, the great Parisian printer and bookseller Antoine Vérard published a volume he called *Le Jardin de Plaisance et Fleur de Rhétorique* (*The Garden of Delight and the Flower of Rhetoric*), and which is the very first printed anthology of French lyric verse. It is a remarkably handsome, large-format, luxurious publication: small in-folio, consisting of some 258 leaves, with spacious page lay-out, an elegant, very legible typeface, and a suite of pleasing woodcut illustrations. Vérard was, in 1501, at the height of his powers and his reputation (*Le Jardin de Plaisance* 1910-25; Kovacs 1994; Winn 1997; Sewright 2008); his books were bought and treasured by courtiers and judges, merchants and officials, and kings and princes accepted beautifully illuminated presentation copies—indeed, Vérard had a copy of the *Jardin de Plaisance* printed on vellum and lovingly illuminated, perhaps for Louis XII; this copy is now in the Kongelige Bibliotek, Copenhagen (Perg. Haun. 18 2°).

The *Jardin de Plaisance* offers the reader no fewer than 672 pieces of verse: of these, 33 are longer, narrative, or moralising, or expository, and an astonishing, torrential, and unrelieved 639 are the shorter, lyric pieces, traditionally medieval, that crowd into earlier manuscript anthologies (Taylor 2007): ballades, rondeaux, virelais, and so forth—"torrential," because at first glance they seem simply to be accumulated, nearly all anonymous, untitled, or at most labelled "Ballade" or "Rondel" or "Chançon," and "unrelieved," because although some of them, as we shall see, are in other manuscript collections set to music, here, in the *Jardin*, a typical double-page spread lays out as many as ten consecutive lyrics.

An indigestible outpouring, then, and to us certainly so—but the *Jardin de Plaisance* enjoyed a considerable publishing success. Vérard himself brought out a second edition in 1504, a third in 1505; his competitors and successors saw a market and brought out a further six editions before 1530 (Lachèvre 1922, 3-11; Pettegree et. al. 2007). And indeed Vérard, canny merchant that he was, had not attained his level of success and publishing prestige without considering the tastes of his readers. There are, I said, 33 longer, narrative or moralising pieces—and with those, Vérard has constructed a rudimentary if very conventional narrative to hold his unwieldy collection together: in a pleasure garden which is the haunt of elegant ladies and gallant knights and squires, a "povre amoureux" (poor lover) falls in love with a lovely lady; he declares his love only to be roundly rejected; he laments his fate, is banished from the garden by Malebouche (Evil Tongue); his chosen lady dies—and lamenting her, he too dies. Conventional enough, of course—and, it must be admitted, not all the longer poems quite fit the story-line—but providing, crucially, a rudimentary framework in which to fit the 639 fixed form lyrics which constitute the bulk of the *Jardin de Plaisance*.

For the central conceit of the book, as its title indicates, is indeed a pleasure garden: a *hortus conclusus*, the enclosed garden which is in the Middle Ages and the Renaissance, by literary convention, an arena of recreation and creativity, of playful encounters and social display. The lady, the lover (the "chevalier oultré d'amour"—the knight undone by love), and the remainder of the protagonists, we are told, live a cultured and sophisticated life, led in particular in a pleasure garden where they spend their time composing, reciting, singing, and responding to "choses joyeuses," light-hearted rondeaux and ballades, centring, as the rubric on sig. i i^{r} shows, on performance:

> How the lovers in the said pleasure garden, having listened to the debate between the Heart and the Eye, joyfully amused themselves by composing many ballades and rondeaux for the ladies present; some verses were made in honour of the ladies, others to condemn them. And with them, the responses of the said ladies to their lovers, and many other very enjoyable things.

And it is here, perhaps, that the woodcut illustrations come into their own.

Vérard has made use of a particularly innovative technology, the technique for which he borrowed from a German publisher, Jean Grüninger, and which he had made use of recently, somewhere between 1499 and 1501, for an edition of Terence's plays (Kovacs 2001). The two images accompanying this essay demonstrate how flexible and creative Vérard could be. Rather than have a craftsman create a series of single scenes, Vérard has commissioned a series of interchangeable smaller blocks, of the same height, which can be combined to create a particular scene—so for instance in fig. 33.1, we are given three separate figures of dapper young men, one labelled with a banderole saying "Le cueur" (the Heart; the motif had already

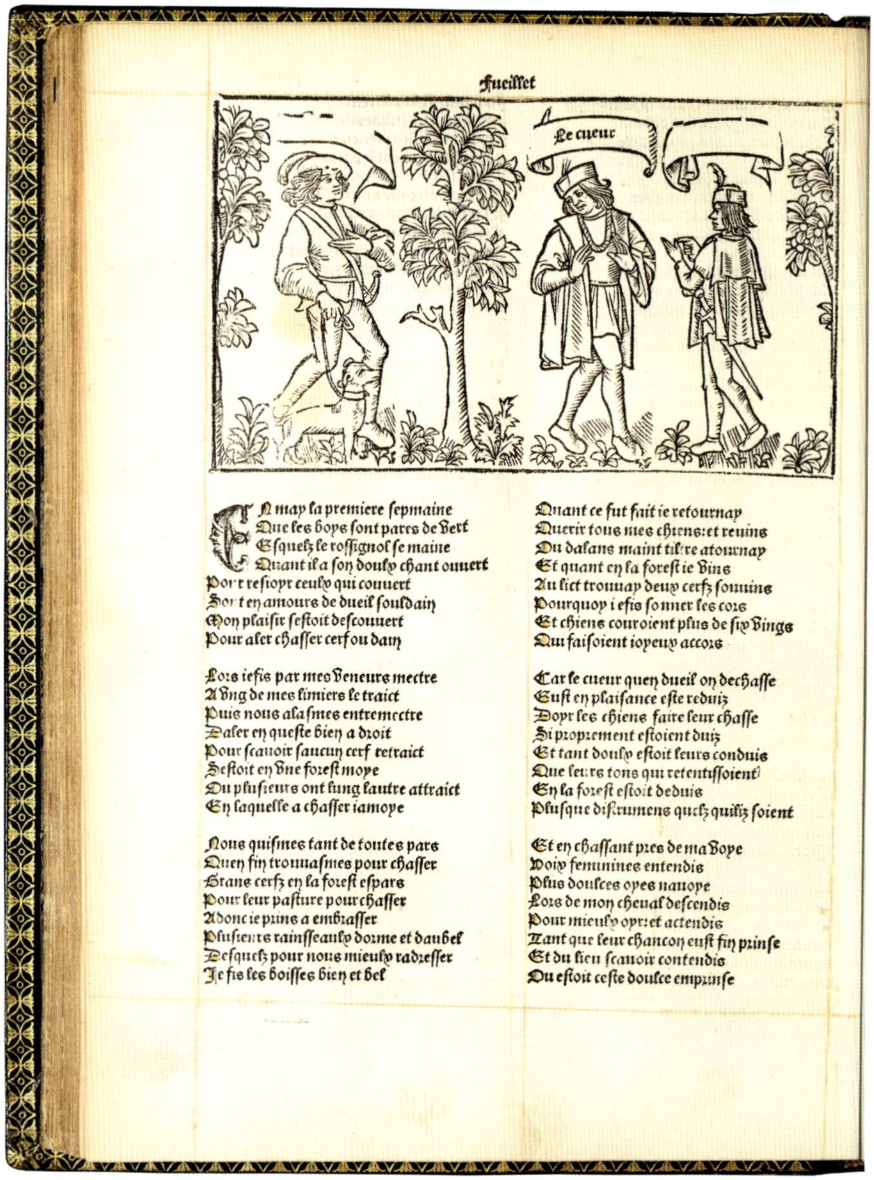
Fueillet

Le cueur

En may la premiere sepmaine
Que les boys sont pares de vert
Esquelz le rossignol se maine
Quant il a son doulx chant ouvert
Por t resioyr ceulx qui couvert
Sont en amours de dueil souldain
Mon plaisir sestoit descouvert
Pour aler chasser cerf ou dain

Lors iefis par mes veneurs mectre
A ung de mes limiers le traict
Puis nous alasmes entremectre
Daler en queste bien a droit
Pour scavoir saucun cerf retraict
Sestoit en une forest moye
Ou plusieurs ont lung lautre attraict
En laquelle a chasser iamoye

Nous quismes tant de toutes pars
Quen fin trouvasmes pour chasser
Grans cerfz en la forest espars
Pour leur pasture pourchasser
Adonc ie prins a embrasser
Plusieurs rainsseaulx dorme et daubel
Desquelz pour nous mieulx radresser
Je fis les boisses bien et bel

Quant ce fut fait ie retournay
Querir tous mes chiens: et revins
Ou dalans maint tiltre atournay
Et quant en la forest ie vins
Au lict trouvay deux cerfz souvins
Pourquoy i efis sonner les cors
Et chiens couroient plus de six vings
Qui faisoient ioyeux accors

Car le cueur quen dueil on dechasse
Eust en plaisance este reduiz
Oyr les chiens faire leur chasse
Si proprement estoient duiz
Et tant doulx estoit leurs conduis
Que leurs tons qui retentissoient
En la forest estoit deduis
Plus que diftrumens quelz quilz soient

Et en chassant pres de ma voye
Voix feminines entendis
Plus doulces oyes navoye
Lors de mon cheval descendis
Pour mieulx oyr: et actendis
Tant que leur chancon eust fin prinse
Et du lieu scavoir contendis
Ou estoit ceste doulce emprinse

Figure 33.1: *Le Jardin de Plaisance et Fleur de Rhétorique* (Paris: Vérard, ca. 1501-02), sig. i i[v]. Paris, Bibliothèque nationale de France, RES-YE-168. Photo © Bibliothèque nationale de France.

appeared in our main image, there labelled "L'amant"—the Lover), each standing on grassy turf, and three trees, one complete, two halves, the latter designed to book-end each image: six blocks combined, here, into a single garden scene, but then remake-able, recombine-able, to suit the different scenarios that the *Jardin de Plaisance* imagines. So the main image recycles one of the half-trees, and the image said in fig. 33.1 to be "Le cueur," is here re-baptised "L'amant." The figure of Fortune, in the main image, will recur elsewhere, as "Envie" (Envy) or "La dame" (the Lady); the right-most of the male figures in fig. 33.1 will recur, among other things, as "Le non-marié" (the Bachelor) (*Le Jardin de Plaisance* 1910-25, 2:29-34). Vérard, in other words, is creating a composite image of the pleasure-garden and some of its habitués.

The combinations, moreover, are not randomly chosen, not merely decorative: as the opening poem below the image in fig. 33.1 shows, Vérard's image reflects, carefully, the setting: the month of May, the "boys parés de vert" (the woodlands decked in green). And the stances of the characters are also studiously reflected in the disposition of the blocks: the two characters to the right, we are told, are "mucez derriere ung buisson," hidden, in other words, behind that rather rudimentary tree [bush] at the centre, with a half-tree on the right which also appears in the main image; the rubric here reads "How the Lover lamented to Fortune, and the others hid behind a bush and listened to him." But not only that: might the gestures of the characters in fig. 33.1 be designed to suggest the performance, perhaps indeed the singing, of the poems concerned (the rubric tells us that as the lovers walked in the garden, one recited a "complainte": the left-most figure with his hand on his heart, the right-most figure counting out the rhythm?). The *Jardin de Plaisance* gives no musical settings—but Kathleen Sewright's admirably meticulous research (Sewright 2008) shows that a surprisingly large number of the fixed-form lyrics (ballades, rondeaux, virelais) in the collection do indeed have musical settings in other late-medieval and Renaissance manuscripts: she finds settings for 78 of the lyrics, many anonymous, many, however, composed by major composers of the fifteenth century like Binchois, Ockeghem, Busnois, or Du Fay.

And in the rubrics which are the contribution of Vérard himself, or of his editors, the emphasis is very much on composition, on performance, and hence no doubt on song; more particularly on a shared creativity of poem and response, a dialogue of lovers and ladies. In the rubric (fol. 60^r), for instance, that introduces fig. 33.1, the rubricator insists on just this: "How the lovers present in the Jardin de Plaisance revel in composing many ballades and rondeaux for the ladies there present, along with the ladies' responses to their lovers." The implication is, of course, that the ballades and rondeaux were performed, were public compositions—sung, perhaps, as contrafacta: is it implied that our lovers and ladies borrow existing, familiar melodies and simply substitute their own words? Yolanda Plumley and others (Plumley 2013; Di Bacco and Plumley 2013) have shown how prevalent such manoeuvres were in the Middle Ages and the Renaissance: how freely and unapologetically poets might appropriate even sacred melodies as settings for their own poems, or, in the case of their anthologisers, for the poems they collect.

In the case of the *Jardin de Plaisance*, such a suggestion might be underlined precisely by the stress on dialogue: clearly, in the garden, young men and women are expected to perform—sing—their poems with ease and confidence; thus each lyric has a generic title—rondeau or ballade—and some, with titles like *Rondeau en chant*, or *Balade faicte de plusieurs chançons* (*Sung rondeau* or *Ballade constructed from a number of chansons*), make song explicit. And Vérard has kindly provided, as the second item in his collection, a treatise he designed, perhaps, as a handy guide to successful composition and performance, an *Instructif de seconde rhétorique* (*Instructions in the art of second rhetoric*, that is, for vernacular verse), composed by someone who calls himself "L'Infortuné" (the Unlucky one): many believe (*Le Jardin de Plaisance* 1910-25, 36-40; Sewright 2008, 191-98) that "L'Infortuné" was actually responsible for the anthology as a whole; they suggest that he is to be identified with a rather obscure poet called Regnault Le Queux who was responsible for the next item in the collection. Sewright (2008, 191-98) is inclined to agree; most other critics less so, notably those responsible for the most recent edition of the *Instructif* (Monferrand et al. 2015, 19-27). The *Instructif* lays out, usefully for any aspiring lover, the mechanisms of the fixed-form lyrics of the late Middle Ages—the ballade, the rondeau, the virelai—and provides "en briefz jours" (in just a few days) what he calls the "tresprecieux vestement" (most precious ornamentations) which will enable the aspiring amateur to shine. He must—most important of all—master the principal features which govern the poetic structures essential for performance: rhyme, of course, and most in detail, in all its complexities, and also rhythm. Interestingly, "L'Infortuné" includes as the final chapter of his treatise a segment on poetry "par personnages," performed in character, and hence theatrical—but are we also to see this as a description of and instructions for embodied poetry, poetry made public, performed for an audience (Kovacs 2001; Buron 2015)? Might the collected verses that Vérard has put together serve also as a handbook to different forms: to demonstrate how to compose a "Balade amoureuse" (love ballade) or a "Balade de bergerie" (pastoral ballade), or a "Rondel de refus" (refusal rondeau) (*Le Jardin de Plaisance*, lyrics 7-39; Sewright 2008, 251-53)?

The *Jardin de Plaisance* remains intriguing: Vérard's daring in publishing so large and elaborate—and pioneering—a collection speaks to his belief that there was an enthusiastic readership for verse and for the skills to compose, to perform, to sing it: to sing a poem to a new melody, or perhaps, as we saw, as a contrafactum, using an existing melody. It speaks too of his, or a compiler's, assiduity simply in collection: in ensuring, perhaps, that the late-medieval lyric repertory might flourish, and propagate.

Finito che la nympha cum comitate blandiſſima hebbe il ſuo beni
gno ſuaſo & multo acceptiſſima recordatiõe, che la mia acrocoma Polia
propera & mãſuetiſſima leuatoſe cum gli ſui feſteuoli, & facetiſſimi ſimu
lachri, ouero ſembianti, & cum punicante gene, & rubẽte buccule da ho
neſto & uenerãte rubore ſuffuſe aptauaſe di uolere per omni uia ſatiſfare
di natura prompta ad omni uirtute, & dare opera alla honeſta petitionẽ.
Non che prima peroe ſe poteſſe cælare & dicio retinere alquãto che ella
intrinſicamente non ſuſpirulaſſe. Ilquale dulciſſimo ſuſpirulo penetroe
reflectendo nel intimo del mio, immo ſuo core, per la uniforme conue-
nientia. Quale aduene a dui parimente participati & concordi litui. Et
ciaſcuna cum diuo obtuto reſpecta intrepidulamente, cum quegli ludi-
bondi & micanti ochii, Da fare (Ome) gli adamanti freſi in mille fragmẽ
ticuli. Cum pie & ſummiſſe uoce, & cum elegantiſſimi geſti decentemen
te reuerita ogni una, ritornoe al ſuo ſolatioſo ſedere ſupra il ſerpilaceo ſo
lo. La initiata opera ſequendo ſellularia. Cum accommodata pronunti

atio-

34. *Hypnerotomachia Poliphili*

Massimo Privitera

Venice: Aldo Manuzio, 1499
234 fols., 22.5 x 13.4 cm
New York, Metropolitan Museum of Art, 23.73.1
Image: sig. z ix^{v}. Photo © CC0.

This airy and seductive representation of a garden of delights comes from the *Hypnerotomachia Poliphili*, a magnificent volume printed with great care in Venice by Aldo Manuzio in 1499. The book's 172 beautiful woodcuts, as well as its multifaceted enigmatic character, have made the *Hypnerotomachia* one of the causes célèbres of Renaissance literature (Colonna 2009).

A central enigma of the book is the author's name. Although it is not stated directly in the volume, many contemporary readers knew that the first letters of the book's 38 chapters generate the acrostic "Poliam Frater Franciscus Columna Peramavit" (Friar Francesco Colonna loved Polia). Since Polia is the name of the protagonist's beloved and the book is the adventurous tale of their reciprocal loves, a Friar Francesco Colonna must be the author. But around 1499 Francesco Colonna can be identified either as a Venetian friar, according to Giovanni Pozzi (Casella-Pozzi 1959), or as a Roman patrician, according to Maurizio Calvesi (Calvesi 1996). At the present state of research it seems impossible to affirm with certainty which of these is the author of the *Hypnerotomachia*.

Another enigma concerns the woodcuts. Although it is clear from internal textual evidence that the majority of the images are modelled on sketches made by Colonna himself, the actual authors of the woodcuts have not been identified. Certainly they belonged to an important Venetian workshop, since the monograms [b] and [•b•] which are to be found in some of the *Hypnerotomachia*'s woodcuts also appear in numerous other illustrated Venetian books printed between 1490 and 1499 (Ariani-Gabriele 2004, xcix). However, the individual identities of these engravers are not yet known (Essling 1874-1914, 4:239-40).

About 20 of the volume's vignettes have musical implications with various meanings. This demonstrates that music—understood broadly as sounds, voices, instruments, dance—plays an important role in the economy of the book (Gallo 1987; Morelli 1987; Gabriele 2007; Zara 2010; Lorenzetti 2011b). Among them, the image discussed here may be the most interesting and significant, placed as it is at a strategic point in the text.

The *Hypnerotomachia* is the tale of a dream experienced by a man called Poliphilo, and of the remarkable things he sees in it; a dream that is in fact an initiatory journey from sensual love to elevated, spiritual love. In the process Poliphilo experiences extreme and opposing states of mind, passes through many different landscapes, and comes across several ancient buildings, often in ruins, with hieroglyphics, allegorical statues, and inscriptions in various languages. (In fact, language is another enigmatic aspect of the book, since it is written in a Latinized Italian with insertions in Latin, Greek, Hebrew, and Arabic—quotations in the present essay are taken from the modern English translation: Colonna 1999; references to this translation are preceded by citations of the 1499 edition).

Poliphilo meticulously describes everything he sees, and a large proportion of the woodcuts present illustrations of the monuments he encounters. Poliphilo also meets magnificent people, such as Queen Eleuterillide who represents Free Will, and many other figures, always young and beautiful, mainly pretty damsels in splendid dresses who he identifies as nymphs. At a certain point in his journey Poliphilo meets his beloved, Polia; together they visit the priestess of Venus, who blesses their love, and finally reach the island of Cythera where they meet the goddess in person. With the exploration of Cythera we arrive at the end of the first part of the *Hypnerotomachia*. The second part comprises Polia's tale of her love adventures, at the end of which she embraces and kisses her beloved. At that point Poliphilo awakes, and the book ends.

Our image of the garden of delights is found at the very end of the first part of the book. Poliphilo and Polia have been walking through Cythera, accompanied by nymphs. Finally they arrive in a wonderful garden with a beautiful fountain. Here there is the grave of Adonis, Venus' beloved, who was killed by a boar at the instigation of the goddess' jealous lover Mars. The nymphs narrate that every year, at the calends and at the ides of May, Venus attends the grave in their company to accomplish "such memorable and curious mysteries;" and once the rite has finished the whole of this famous day is dedicated strictly "to pleasure, to choiring, playing and singing" (sig. z viii^{v}; 376).

Once they have finished their tale, the nymphs began to make music again. They sang, with great sweetness and delight, a metrical version of the stories they had told and the things that had occurred, and for a long time they danced in a circle about the spring; then they all sat with folded knees on this comfortable ground with its lovely verdure (sig. z viii^{v}; 376).

Their songs of Venus and Adonis have an irresistible erotic effect. Poliphilo places his head upon Polia's scented bosom, continuing: "I kissed ardently her milk-white hands and her snow-white breast that shone like pure ivory; then our kisses became mutual, for it was clear from her looks she was not unresponsive, but equally possessed by the voluptuous impulses of love" (sig. z viii^{v}; 376). Here we witness the most perfect fulfillment of Love, completely reciprocal, physical as well as spiritual, blessed by God, and celebrated by the community. It is at this perfect moment that "the players laid themselves and their melodious instruments down on the pleasant lawn, and the singers shut up their mellifluous voices in their delicious bosoms, and fell silent" (sig. z viii^{v}; 377).

Why do the nymphs become silent? The mutual fusion of the two lovers is so perfect because it comes after a long struggle, originating in Polia's misunderstanding of Poliphilo's feelings. There is no perfect happiness without suffering; and the nymphs stop the music and ask Polia to tell them their "love's labour's lost." The two lovers look at each other, and the memory of their past pains leads them to a deep sigh; but now it is a shared feeling, "such as occurs between two trumpets when they share an identical tuning" (sig. z ix^{v}; 378).

The woodcut is particularly effective in representing the many facets of such an affective dynamic within the frozen space of a vignette. The setting respects the medieval tradition of the *locus amœnus*, with its trees, fountains, and pergola. It represents sweetness and pleasantness, reinforced by the love allegorized in the statue of Venus in the background. The composition of the figures is symmetrical: six nymphs sit on the right side, six on the left. Polia stands and walks toward Poliphilo, who sits at the centre. At the same time there is a certain randomness in the individual positions of the nymphs that gives movement to the ensemble. The result is a happy mixture of order and freedom.

The instruments highlight the musical character of the scene. However, since they are abandoned here and there, evidently the nymphs are not about to play; rather, they have already played, and then set the instruments aside. Nonetheless the spirit of music lingers on, and lends its tone to the conversation, generating a feeling of harmony and gaiety.

The choice of instruments is significant, even though the accompanying passage of text does not name them. In the *Hypnerotomachia* different kinds of musical instruments are mentioned—winds, strings, and percussion—both as real objects and as metaphors (for example, at sig. i vi^{v}; 147, Colonna says that Poliphilo's heart palpitates like a raucous drum). They are also represented in some of the vignettes, especially those depicting triumphal floats (sig. k iii^{v} and ff.; 158 and ff.) where the text refers to the instruments using classical names and defines them as "veterrimi"—the oldest. Yet, apart from a tambourine at the bottom right, our vignette only includes stringed instruments: two harps, a kithara, a lira da braccio, and a lute. The kithara evokes Orpheus and Apollo, ancient divine prototypes of the inspired poet-musician. The harp also has strong symbolic resonances (from David's harp to the troubadours), but at the same time it is a real contemporary instrument (represented as such, for example, in Martin Le Franc's *Champion des dames*—Paris, Bibliothèque nationale de France, MS fr. 12476—where Guillaume Du Fay is shown with an organ and Gilles Binchois with a harp). But the instruments most familiar to the everyday experience of readers in Italy in 1499 are the lira da braccio and the lute. The lira was beloved of elite amateurs, as well as humanists such as Marsilio Ficino, to accompany the sung declamation of all types of verse (Ficino called it the "lyra orphica"; see Bugini 2008). But it is the lute that stands out as the most important instrument of the fifteenth and sixteenth centuries, and lute virtuosos of the Quattrocento, such as the "divine" Pietrobono dal Chitarrino, were idolized and celebrated by chroniclers, poets, and theorists (Gallo 1995, 86-97). The lute was considered the most perfect accompanist of the voice: in 1536 the printer Francesco Marcolini writes that the voice "will expand her sweetness given to her by nature and art when she combines her tones with the sound of the lute" (*Intabolatura de liuto de diversi* 1536). Hence, the engraver's choice to represent a selection of instruments commonly used to accompany song and recitation tells us that this garden is placed under the auspices of voices singing amorous poetry, that is to say, the very essence of the *Hypnerotomachia* (Pozzi, in Colonna 1980, 2:8).

The association between music, love, poetry, and love poetry was completely ubiquitous in this period, as several other exhibits in this museum attest (exhibits 24-27). Underpinning that link, and giving it an ethical dimension highly conducive to the kind of Neoplatonic thinking of which the *Hypnerotomachia* is full, is the musical concept of harmony, used very commonly in European Renaissance culture as a metaphor for the proper ordering of all kinds of systems according to laws that are both aesthetically and ethically correct, and indeed consonant with God's own ordering of the universe. In this harmoniously-designed woodcut, partnered with its accompanying text, these themes are brought together to give a visual commentary upon a crucial moment in the journey of Polia and Poliphilo—a journey which is both romantic and spiritual in nature. The nymphs' music-making both symbolises and facilitates the lovers' transition from sensual to spiritual consummation of their love; once that turning point is reached, the music has fulfilled its role and the instruments are left aside—in their new-found transcendence, both erotic and religious in character, Polia and Poliphilo are now attending to the silent music of the beauty of the divine as it is reflected in their own perfect love.

TENOR:
CONTRA TENOR
DISCANTUS
ECCE · VENIT · CAROLUS ·
PERSTITIO ·

35. Embroidered Partbooks

Birgit Lodes

Vienna, Kunsthistorisches Museum (on permanent loan to Schloss Ambras, Innsbruck),
KK 5369 (belt pouch); KK 5370-5373 (motet *Martia terque quater*); KK 5374-5377 (song *Aus gutem Grund*) Innsbruck, 1530
Silk thread on linen, with silver, gold and pearls; KK 5370-5373: 21 x 16 cm; KK 5374-5377: 14 x 19 cm

Image: KK 5370, fols. 3v and 4r. Ludwig Senfl(?), *Martia terque quater*. Photo © KHM-Museumsverband.

The fifteenth and sixteenth centuries saw experimentation with ingenious ways of writing down music in a variety of media: in manuscripts and prints of different types and decorations (e.g. exhibits 28, 29, 31, 32, 38, 39), in paintings (exhibits 3, 30), on maiolica dishes (Slim 1984), on wood panelling for walls or ceilings (Reese 1968), on playing cards (exhibit 16), on tables (exhibit 18) and tablecloths (Laube 2017), and much more besides. It is against this backdrop that we should set the idea of embroidering specific pieces of music with silken thread on linen. Three matching partbook sets have survived—two discussed here, the third dated ca. 1545 and containing a motet by Josquin Baston (Munich, Universitätsbibliothek, Cim. 54)—and the existence of five further sets is reported in archival evidence (four in Tröster 2013; the fifth located by Grantley McDonald, documented in the possession of Bishop Georg von Slatkonia). All these partbooks have in common that only a single, specific composition was embroidered in each case. This was an exclusive and expensive medium that was, evidently, not intended for duplicate production: neither duplicate copies of the same piece, nor embroidered booklets with multiple pieces are extant. Most probably, the specific composition was selected in each case for its suitability as a gift for a particular recipient.

The partbooks were manufactured using materials of the highest quality: musical notation and text are embroidered in black silk; voice designations, capital letters, and the edges of pages even with gold. The title pages are executed with threads in silver and other colours as well as with pearls. In addition, some of these sources are clearly personalised, the coat-of-arms of the recipient appearing on the title page—as in the (lost) sets for Raimund Fugger and Count Palatine Ottheinrich or, particularly impressive, the four partbooks for the newly crowned Emperor Charles V whose title pages bear the imperial insignia (Tröster 2013, 170-2). Finished as presentation objects and with a personal touch, the embroidered partbooks stand as prize gifts among the aristocracy and the powerful—much like the famous and, of course, much more extensive illuminated manuscripts from the scriptorium of Petrus Alamire associated with the Hapsburg-Burgundian court. The pertinence of this comparison is also evident from the circle of recipients: except for Georg Slatkonia and Count Palatine Ottheinrich, all known presentees of embroidered music books also possessed manuscripts from the Alamire scriptorium—namely, Emperor Charles V, Queen Anne of Bohemia and Hungary, Mary of Hungary, and Raimund Fugger. Thus the partbooks, which were doubtless produced in southern German regions, joined an established tradition of musical gift-exchange among the ruling classes of the empire, translating it, however, into a yet more exclusive medium. The majority of the embroidered partbooks were created in 1530, evidently within the context of the Imperial Diet at Augsburg which was attended by all the named parties (apart from Slatkonia). Additionally, the surviving evidence reveals that these embroidered partbooks, like some of the Alamire codices, were not typically stored with the music-books of the respective court chapel but rather in the cabinet of curiosities.

It has often been suggested that it is not possible to sing from these sources, but in fact the opposite is true, as has been demonstrated in modern performance. The embroidered partbooks from Ambras, for example, are certainly large enough to sing from, they supply very good musical readings, notate *custodes* and *signa congruentiae* and also, occasionally, accidentals. In addition, physical aids to help with turning the page (gilt buttons) are affixed to the edges of the openings in the sets. Moreover, the text is very accurately underlaid—for every strophe in the case of *Aus gutem Grund* (see fig. 35.1; see also Tröster 2013, 165)—a provision that is rare in the song repertory of the time. It is thus my assumption that the embroidered composition was actually sung when the gift was presented; for example, on the occasion of an official *adventus*.

Two of the surviving embroidered partbook sets are housed today at Ambras Castle, stored inside a belt bag of the same historical epoch. They transmit Ludwig Senfl's six-voice motet *Martia terque quater* (Gasch et al. 2019, *M54; Lodes 2013, 206-23 and 241-54) as well as the aforementioned four-voice *Aus gutem Grund* (Gasch et al. 2019, S 29). Several theories have been proposed concerning the origin of these partbooks. Since preeminent embroiderers were particularly active in Augsburg,

Walter Salmen (1992, 75) considered it likely that they were produced there; Moritz Kelber (2018, 187-88) has subsequently suggested they were commissioned by the city of Augsburg. It seems to me more plausible, however, that the Bavarian Duke William IV was behind the two gifts (Lodes 2013), especially as Senfl, the Bavarian court composer, most probably composed the two works specifically for this purpose.

Following the coronation of the Emperor Charles V in Bologna by Pope Clement VII on 24 February 1530, a summit of non-Protestant rulers lasting several weeks was organised in Innsbruck. Attendees, besides the Emperor Charles V and his brother King Ferdinand I, included Duke William IV of Bavaria, Count Palatine Frederick II, as well as Mary of Hungary (the sister of Charles V). The prime purpose of the gathering was to coordinate their somewhat divergent interests in preparation for the upcoming Imperial Diet at Augsburg. The text and music of the motet *Martia terque quater* were freshly and specifically composed for the reception of Charles V within the imperial realm, which he had not visited for nine years. As host, the music-loving Queen Anna of Bohemia and Hungary, wife of King Ferdinand, apparently received on this occasion the four-voice paean *Aus gutem Grund*, a customised composition by Senfl bearing the acrostic A-N-NA (fig. 35.1). Furthermore, Sonja Tröster has argued persuasively that Count Palatine Frederick II had Senfl's song *Mag ich dem Glück nit danken viel*, with the acrostic MA-R-IA, embroidered as a token of love for Mary of Hungary, to be presented on the same occasion (lost—formerly in the Koninklijke Bibliotheek in Brussels; Tröster 2013; Gasch et al. 2019, *S 218). This was probably inspired by the presentation of the other embroidered sets, Frederick having accompanied the emperor on his journey to Bologna and onwards into the imperial realm. Moreover, since the "double marriage" in Vienna in 1515, Mary (married to Anna's brother, King Louis II of Hungary and Bohemia) and Anna (married to King Ferdinand, Mary's brother) had been educated together (from 1517 at court in Innsbruck).

Figure 35.1: KK 5375, fol. 2r. Ludwig Senfl, *Aus gutem Grund*, beginning of Tenor voice. Photo © KHM-Museumsverband.

The presentation of the two partbook sets for Emperor Charles V and Queen Anna of Bohemia probably took place in Innsbruck, the seat of government of Charles's brother Ferdinand and his wife Anna (Lodes 2013, 198). After his successful proclamation in Bologna, one of the most pressing tasks for the emperor was to bolster the peace and unity of the Holy Roman Empire of the German Nation, which had been sorely weakened by the Reformation. The poetic text of the embroidered motet *Martia terque quater*, newly written and highly polished, appropriates formulations and images from Classical Antiquity: the new Emperor Charles is addressed as the bringer of peace in the tradition of Augustus Caesar and the *Pax Augusta*. Charles's role in re-establishing imperial unity was viewed in close connection with the potent old prophecy of a "last emperor," which foretold that a descendent of Charlemagne, a "Carolus redivivus," would appear after a phase of religious conflict to renew and reform the Church (Tanner 1993, 119-30).

Mārtia tērque quatēr | Germānia plāude triūmphans Cēsar ab Ītaliā | Cārolus ēcce venīt!	Applaud three times, martial Germany, See here, Emperor Charles comes with triumph from Italy!
Āurea quī terrīs | revehāt regnāta parēnte sēcula Sāturnō | Cārolus ēcce venīt!	He who may bring back to the countries the Golden Ages Reigned by Father Saturn, See here, Charles comes!
Vāna supērstitiō | procul ī discōrdia dēmens pācifer āc vindēx | Cārolus ēcce venīt!	Vain is superstition, and foolish persistent discord, The peace-bringer and vindicator, See here, Charles comes!

(Translation from Salmen 1992, 80, adapted by Jeremy Llewellyn)

The structure of the lines in elegiac distichs provides the guideline for the musical organisation; the motet is thus not shaped according to syntax or meaning, but on the basis of the poetic caesuras (penthemimeres, as well as line-endings). In addition, the musical setting notably replicates the verse quantities beloved of humanist scholars: Senfl sets long quantities with long note-values and shorts with shorts (with particular consistency in the canonic voice; see main image). He applies this principle on two temporal levels, and thus—in comparison to his stricter settings of odes—manages to retain a compositional freedom. In this way, a dactyl can either be rendered by a breve and two semibreves or else as a semibreve and two minims. Senfl's motet *Martia terque quater* therefore not only mimics the panegyrics for rulers of Antiquity in its text (content, as well as classical metre), but also foregrounds them sonically in polyphony.

A further point of particular interest is the consistency with which Senfl works musically with the prominent triplicities of the text. The number three may refer symbolically to the fact that Charles V was the third Habsburg emperor after Frederick and Maximilian. This was repeatedly the subject of contemporary commentary, and echoes a Burgundian tradition which interpreted the emperor, king, and son (or grandson) as the Holy Trinity (e.g. Molinet, ed. Doutrepont, vol. 1, 535; Lodes 2016). Senfl constructed his three-part motet *Martia terque quater* with a strict three-voice canon throughout (in the Discant, Contratenor, and Tenor, each time at the distance of the fifth) along with three free voices. The fact that the music for the three canonic voices is given only once—but with three different clefs (D, T, and Ct)—had a symbolic meaning: three different voices are brought together in a single unity. Given that Senfl had already deployed this musical symbolism several times in motets and settings of the Proper for the Holy Trinity (Lodes 2006; Gasch 2013, 194-96), when used in *Martia terque quater* it seems to cross-reference the popular Trinitarian metaphors associated with the Habsburgs. Moreover, the canon emphasises in a figurative sense the central message of the text that the religious discord across the land may be set aside through the advent of the newly crowned emperor, and peace—that is, unity in its broadest sense—may be reestablished (Lodes 2013, 201).

The title pages of the motet *Martia terque quater* are (in contrast with the song *Aus gutem Grund*) not labelled with the names of the voices, but lavishly decorated. The cover page of the canonic voices displays—in embroidery of gold, silver, and coloured silk together with pearl additions—the coat-of-arms of Charles V with the imperial crown (fig. 35.2a). The other cover pages feature the imperial orb (fig. 35.2b), the imperial sceptre (fig. 35.2c), and the imperial sword (fig. 35.2d). Thus the decorations feature precisely those insignia which had been ceremonially handed to the emperor during his coronation in Bologna, in which context their function had been to underpin and represent the sovereign's legitimacy. In a manner similar to the paintings, printed leaflets and numerous texts disseminated across Europe in relation to the coronation (Burke 2000), these representational title pages communicated a clear political message: Charles V is addressed as the legitimate emperor, and the gift-giver publicly acknowledges him in this function. Such an act is significant at a time when it was not so much the emperor's election, but rather the coronation and, above all, the *acclamatio* of the people that authenticated the claim to the imperial throne (Stollberg-Rilinger 2015, 59-60; Petersohn 1997, 182); and even more significant in light of the precarious acceptance of this actual "coronation," which could not even take place in Rome.

In this context, it makes sense that the closing acclamation of each stanza—"Carolus ecce venit!" (See here, Charles comes!)—musically comprises around half of each of the three *partes*. Moreover, the phrase is set three times in different ways, and through the successive, slightly varied entries of the *soggetto* one seems to hear the exhilarated cries of the crowds. Thus in the musical texture of this panegyric the acclamatory *laudatio*, rather than the *narratio*, comes to the fore.

Viewed in light of this reading, it is clear that the embroidered motet was planned as a Gesamtkunstwerk: the programme of illumination in the four partbooks is not simply

Figure 35.2: Title pages of the embroidered partbooks: a) KK 5370 (imperial crown with coat of arms); b) KK 5371 (imperial orb); c) KK 5372 (imperial sceptre); d) KK 5373 (imperial sword). Photos © KHM-Museumsverband.

decoration, but corresponds to the core affirmation of the text, the musical organisation and, above all, the contemporaneous propagandistic reports and artistic representations of the imperial coronation. In performing the customised composition from this extravagant partbook set, its special meaning was conveyed effectively in sight and in sound. Thus, this exhibit is the product of an initiative to create a new form of multimedia panegyric that would emphatically underscore the idea of the last emperor and universal sovereign who will usher in a new golden age. This was achieved through the allusions to classical texts, but more so by the felicitous combination of ingenious polyphony (with the canon symbolising unity) and a poetic delivery with classicizing quantification. Behind this concept lay the idea of a musical *translatio artium*: to translate the metrical declamation of imperial panegyrics from Antiquity into a "modern" polyphony.

ADDITIONAL REFERENCES: Lodes 2017; Panagl 2004; Stollberg-Rilinger 1994; Tröster 2019.

36. "Grande Musicque" Typeface

Louisa Hunter-Bradley

Hendrik van den Keere, Antwerp, 1577
Steel punches and copper matrices, 5 lines, 25.5 mm
Museum Plantin-Moretus, Antwerp
Photos courtesy of the Museum Plantin-Moretus

The Plantin-Moretus Museum contains the equipment, correspondence, and accounts for the Officina Plantiniana, one of the most important and influential printing and publishing houses in Europe in the second half of the sixteenth century. Among its many sets of movable type are the punches and matrices for the *Grande Musicque* font, which would be used in all grand folio choirbooks of polyphony published by the Officina Plantiniana from 1578 to 1644. The 39 punches and 4 counterpunches (ST 68) include staves, clefs, time signatures, notes, sharps, flats, pauses, rests, bar lines, and directs. The negative impressions of these symbols are found in the 71 extant matrices (MA 91a). The font was exceptionally elegant as shown by the intricate curves at the top of its G clef, the directs and tails of the quaver notes, as well as the delicate diagonals of the sharp signs (fig. 36.1).

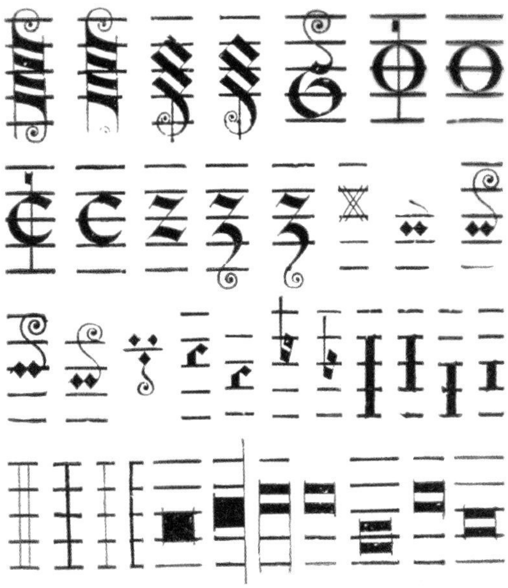

Figure 36.1: Printed examples of the Grand Musique typeface. Photos courtesy of the Museum Plantin-Moretus.

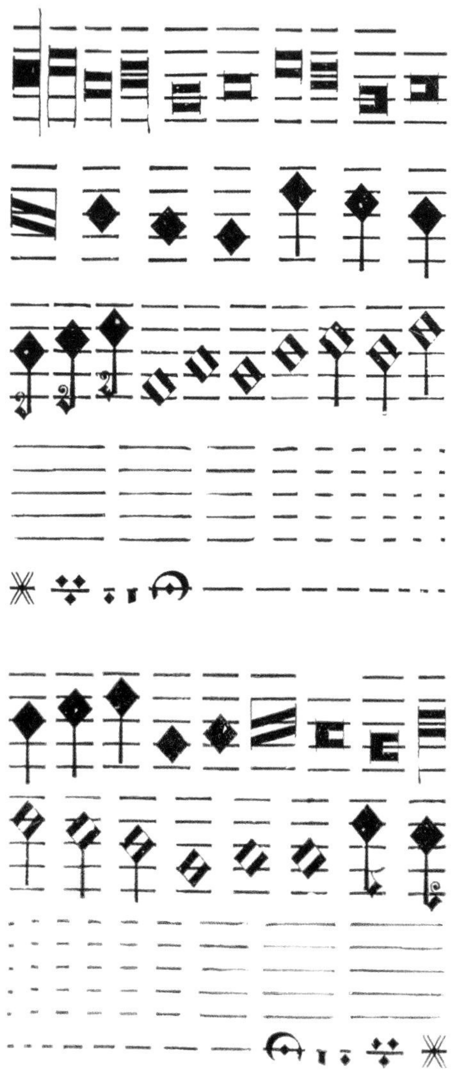

To create a typeface, a punch—a bar of steel with the symbol filed at one end in relief—was made for every symbol required. The punch was then struck on a piece of copper or brass producing an impression (a "strike") of about 1.5 mm depth. To make the impressions a uniform depth, the faces of a strike were filed or "justified" to form a set of matrices, from which the pieces of type would be cast in lead. The process of justification involved adjusting the margins to make the rectangular pieces parallel and evenly aligned. Finally, a mould was made in two halves, so that one half formed the body of the piece of type in a certain aperture width and the upper face of the type was formed in the matrix. Once the type was cast, the foot was broken off and filed to remove the rough edge, as well as the sides rubbed to create a clean surface. The piece of type was then ready to use.

In 1576 Christopher Plantin, owner, editor, and publisher at the Officina Plantiniana, commissioned Hendrik van den Keere to design and cut his *Grande Musicque* font. Correspondence between van den Keere and Plantin illuminates the process of commissioning a new music type; in particular a letter sent from van den Keere dated 16 January 1576 (fig. 36.2). Although the letter is addressed to the typecutter under the name "Henri du Tour," van den Keere is more commonly referred to by his Flemish name as he originated from Ghent.

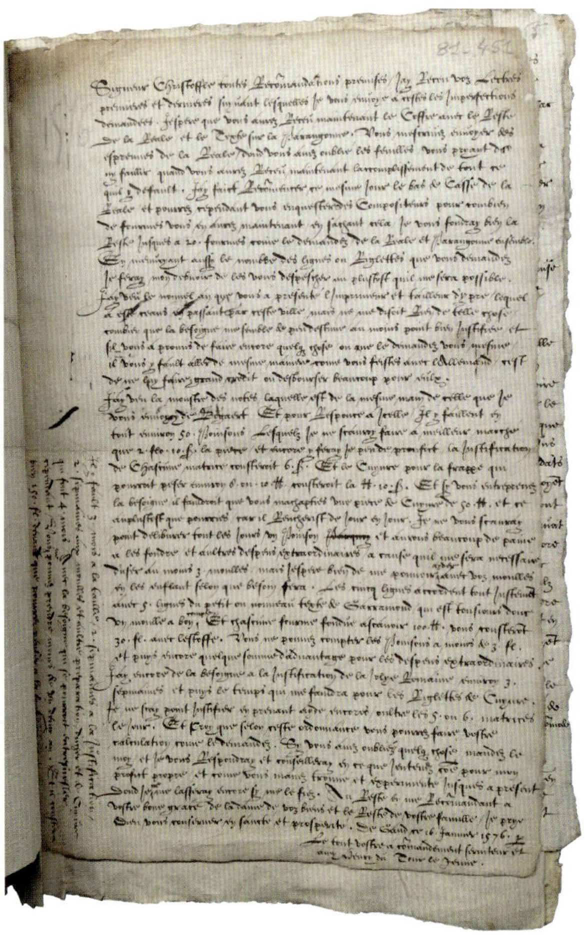

Figure 36.2: Hendrik van den Keere to Christopher Plantin, 16 January 1576. Antwerp, Museum Plantin-Moretus, MPM ARCH 81, fol. 451r. Photo courtesy of the Museum Plantin-Moretus.

The first half of van der Keere's letter addresses some aspects of general type production, including the maintenance of a set of type, the printing of samples, and required staffing levels. Then van den Keere outlines the making of a new music font as follows:

> I have seen the large music [font], the one which is by the same person as the one I sent you from Bogard. To make a type like it would mean about 50 punches in all, which I could not make at a better price than 2 florins, 10 stuivers apiece. And even then I wouldn't be making much profit. Justifying each matrice would cost 6 stuivers. And the copper for an impression, which could weigh between 8 and 10 pounds, would cost 10 stuivers per pound. And if you decide to go ahead, you will need to buy me a 50 pound piece of copper, as quickly as possible, because the price goes up on a daily basis. I absolutely wouldn't be able to deliver a punch every day and would have great difficulty in casting them, and there will be additional costs, such that it will be necessary for me to use at least 3 moulds. But I very much hope that it might be possible to help by reusing your moulds as required. The five staff-lines match exactly with the 5 lines of the small or new text of *Garamond*, whose mould is still in good condition. And each fount of a forme weighing 100 pounds will cost you 30 florins with the material. You are looking at, at least 3 florins per punch and then a bit more on top of that for unanticipated costs. I still have work to do on justifying the *Jolye* Romaine [font], approximately 3 weeks, and then have to be able to take the time for the copper rules. I cannot justify more than the 5 or 6 matrices a day, even with taking on more assistance. And I believe that according to this arrangement, you are able to make your calculation as requested.

Regarding the design of this new music type, van den Keere explained that he had seen another large music font, by the same designer as a font he had sent to Plantin from Jean Bogard, printer, bookseller, and editor in Douai. Susan Bain (Bain 1974, 141) has suggested that the other music types in the Plantin-Moretus Museum's collection (including the Granjon types) may have been acquired as models or simply as additions to the collection. When mentioning the Bogard music font as a model, van den Keere did not state that he would copy the design of the preexisting type, but that to make a comparable type would require "about 50 punches in all." As may be seen in the latter part of the letter, van den Keere explained that he hoped to use previous moulds owned by Plantin to keep the costs down as much as possible, and here specifically, the "new text of Garamont" as the staff lines matched the five lines of this type exactly.

Unlike previous type-cutters and their all-inclusive costings for type, van den Keere calculated separate prices for punches and matrices, with the copper either provided by the printer or charged as an extra. Van den Keere initially gave a charge of 2 florins, 10 stuivers per punch, later modifying it to 3 florins or "possibly a little more." Justifying each matrice would add a charge of 6 stuivers. Van den Keere offered a complete cost of 30 florins for each forme of 100 lbs including the material, and the final sentence in the margin provided a figure of approximately 150 florins as a total cost "before a font may be cast." Although a number of sixteenth-century registers of fonts have been preserved in the Plantin-Moretus Museum (MPM ARCH 153), unfortunately there is no record of the number of pieces of type that were ordered for this *Grande Musicque* typeface or the firm's other music fonts.

Van den Keere's estimates for the cost of the Grande Musicque font can be compared with the actual costs recorded on the invoice in Plantin's archives (MPM ARCH 42). These accounts for the *Grande Musicque* typeface demonstrate the variety of elements required in the manufacture of a new font. They show that the final cost was increased by half from the quoted amount of approximately 150 florins, with a final sum totalling 229 florins 14.5 stuivers. The cost of 4 florins, 6 stuivers for transporting 16 lbs of type was not mentioned in the outline of costs in the letter, nor were imperfections factored into the estimate, for which a figure of 9 florins, 3 stuivers was recorded in the accounts. The accounts also show that the cost for the justification of matrices increased by only 12 stuivers in total and the increase in cost for the punches was significant, up from the estimated 3 florins to 4 florins per punch (a total increase of 38 florins for the punches alone). Other additional elements in the accounts included costs of 6 florins for justification for the moulds as well as 1 florin for paper used in the impression of the type. The other considerable cost within the commission was for the copper required; Van den Keere suggests that Plantin act quickly to purchase a 50 pound piece of copper as the price rises "on a daily basis." This figure is not given in the account as it was provided by Plantin separately.

The letter also indicates the timespan for making a new font. In the margin of this letter, van den Keere wrote that it would take three months for the cutting, two weeks of justifying, and two weeks with the moulds and other preparation of the materials, equating to four months in total. He then remarked that with any work that may intervene, one may expect that the font would take no less than half a year. It seems that the work on this font was challenging; van den Keere asserts that "I absolutely wouldn't be able to work on it every day and would have great difficulty in casting them." Leon Voet (Voet 1969-72, 2:81) hypothesises that van den Keere's warning that he would not be able to deliver one punch every day implies that one punch per day would be the normal tempo of work with average sized fonts. This slower rate of manufacture may reflect the size and complexity of the design.

The date of this letter outlining the requirements for manufacture of the *Grande Musicque* type is January 1576, and yet the account for payments to van den Keere was not compiled until July 1577, with further charges for imperfections and related sundries dated up until 10 December 1577, two years after the date of the letter. The printing of the first book to use this type, George de la Hèle's *Octo Missae*, commenced a month earlier than this final account, on 9 November 1577, and was completed on 12 July 1578 (MPM ARCH 32, fol. 277^{v}). The dedication of this choirbook was dated October 1578. Thus it took 33 months from van den Keere accepting the commission to the publication of Plantin's first book using the new type.

It is no wonder that printers were keen to use standard fonts, given the time and cost involved in commissioning one anew. Almost three years after the commission and following an investment of more than 229 florins, Plantin was finally able to showcase the *Grande Musicque* font in his first publication of polyphonic liturgical music in choirbooks of grand folio format; Plantin's strong trade in liturgical publications enabled such an investment in his less lucrative music publishing enterprise. Despite the substantial lead-time and cost involved in commissioning the type, Plantin was keen to use such new fonts, to distinguish his publications from his peers and add to his reputation for works of the highest typographic quality.

ADDITIONAL REFERENCES: Bowen and Imhof 2008; Hellinga 1962; Krummel and Sadie 1980; Nave 1996; Parker 1958; Stellfeld 1949; Updike 1922; Vervliet 1968; Voet 1980-83.

37. Coat of Arms of Matthäus Lang von Wellenburg

Elisabeth Giselbrecht

Hans Weiditz (designer?), Grimm & Wirsung (printers?), Augsburg, 1520
Colour woodcut, 27.4 x 20.6 cm
The British Museum, London

This single-sheet woodcut in the Department of Prints and Drawings at the British Museum, printed in 1520, depicts the coat of arms of Matthäus Lang von Wellenburg, cardinal and prince-archbishop of Salzburg and one of the most influential clerical and secular leaders in the empire of Maximilian I. It was printed—not painted—in seven colours, including gold (Giselbrecht and Upper 2012). Both this colour woodcut and the context in which it appeared—the extraordinary music book *Liber selectarum cantionum*—challenge our understanding of how and why print technology was used in the early sixteenth century. The complexity and ambition of this coat of arms and the music book demonstrate how understanding an item's materiality and production techniques leads to new insights into both the producers and users of printed material in early modern Europe.

Particularly in the eighteenth and nineteenth centuries, colour prints were considered an oddity for the time of Dürer (and beyond), as late medieval and early modern prints were hailed for the purity of their black-and-white aesthetic. Recent research, however, has unearthed thousands of colour impressions from sixteenth-century Germany, demonstrating that they were much more common than previously assumed (Savage 2015a). Within this growing body of colour prints, the vast majority of which were printed from two blocks and thus with two colours, this single sheet holds a unique place: Made from seven blocks, one each for red, pink, grey, green, blue, black, and varnish for gold leaf, it is the most complex woodcut of its time and the number of blocks was not rivalled until the revival of colour woodcut in the nineteenth century (Giselbrecht and Upper 2012, 24). The high number of woodblocks not only added to the complexity and required unprecedented skill, it also made the printing more likely to fail and the process more costly and precarious. The sheet had to run through the press separately for each block, increasing the risk of mis-registration. This risk was exaggerated by the use of gold, an expensive material that was unusual in printed material.

Only five other single-sheet German prints from this time survive that were "printed" with gold, whether using gold ink or gold leaf laid on printed varnish (Savage 2015b, 9). The unique palette of this unsigned woodcut complicates the search for its makers. The image has previously been linked to various designers, and Hans Weiditz (active Augsburg 1518-22, Strasbourg 1522-36) is the most likely option (Giselbrecht and Upper 2012), but identifying the woodcut's printer is more complicated.

The printers might be assumed to be Grimm & Wirsung by circumstantial evidence, even though this would have been their only colour woodcut. But this woodcut was not produced as an autonomous artwork, a single-sheet coat of arms which the archbishop might have given to his contacts or used as decoration. Instead, it originally adorned the opening page of the *Liber selectarum cantionum*, a collection of 24 motets for four to six voices printed by Grimm & Wirsung in Augsburg in 1520. Curiously, it was the last book they printed, but their first colour woodcut and their first to contain music from type, giving rise to the speculation that the colour woodcut might have been printed by someone else. The book exists in two versions, one with the colour frontispiece, and a simpler version with the coat of arms printed in black and white. It has previously been assumed that the British Library sheet was the only colour frontispiece produced, expensively made to adorn the presentation copy to the archbishop, the dedicatee of the music book. Recent research has shown, however, that multiple copies of the colour-printed version existed (Giselbrecht and Upper 2012, Appendix 1, 57-58). Of the 20 surviving copies of the *Liber selectarum*, six still contain the colour print, while the first folios were removed from five copies (suggesting that they might also have contained the colour version). The remaining surviving copies contain the black-and-white version. This colour woodcut, then, was used to distinguish some copies of this publication as more luxurious versions, a discovery which sheds new light on an already unique book of music.

Like its frontispiece, the *Liber selectarum* holds a special place in the history of early printing. The printing of polyphonic music was still quite new north of the Alps—only ten earlier examples are known—and it was the first motet book to be printed there. Moreover, it comes in a rather unusual size and layout. As a choirbook, with all voice parts laid out on one opening, it was the exception in music printing, where the partbook format had quickly become the norm. For an entire choir to sing from it, therefore, it needed to be rather large, and each of the *Liber*'s 270 folios measures ca. 44.5 x 28.5 cm. At more than 500 pages in length, the size made the book not only impressive to see but also expensive to produce (see fig. 37.1).

Figure 37.1: *Liber selectarum cantionum* (Augsburg: Grimm & Wirsung, 1520), fol. 14r. Staatliche Bibliothek Regensburg, 999/2Liturg.69. Photo courtesy of the Staatliche Bibliothek Regensburg.

The only other early printed book of polyphony in this format was the *Liber quindecim missarum*, a collection of 15 Masses printed by Andrea Antico in Rome in 1516 and dedicated to Pope Leo X. While superficially rather similar—both large printed choirbooks of sacred music dedicated to important church leaders—the two books come with one important difference: their printing technique. Antico's Roman *Liber* was printed entirely from woodcut and it took three years to produce the volume (Weeks-Chapman 1964). The *Liber selectarum* from Augsburg, however, is printed from moveable type with two runs through the press, the so-called "double impression" technique. In one run, the stave lines were printed; in another, the notes were printed on top, set from individual pieces of type which, like letters, could then be taken apart and set again for the next page.

Printing notation from moveable type was quickly becoming the norm for polyphonic music and books of liturgical music. Woodcuts were still used throughout the sixteenth century, for example in printing musical examples within music theory books, but no music book on the scale of the Roman *Liber quindecim missarum* was ever printed entirely from woodblocks again. While the Augsburg *Liber selectarum cantionum* used the more common method, however, its immense scale brought particular challenges. With no precedent of comparable size, the creators of the *Liber selectarum cantionum* had to have a new music font made specifically for this publication. Oddly, despite the costs involved in commissioning and casting a new font—the inherent benefit of which lay in repeated use—it appears to have been created solely for this publication; no other music books survive in which the same font has been used. Not only was the frontispiece a unique and expensive technical feat, but considerable money and skill were lavished also on printing the music of the *Liber selectarum cantionum*.

Considering the frontispiece in combination with the music book to which it was originally attached reveals four specific respects in which the history of music printing is just now undergoing re-evaluation, thanks to the adoption of interdisciplinary methods in scholarship: the materiality of the printed matter; the "artistic" style of the notation and/or its visual context; the publication's collecting and usage history; and an emphasis on understanding each copy as a unique item. Each of these perspectives has its own contribution to make to our understanding of the *Liber selectarum cantionum* and its history.

Among the distinctive features of this publication is the clear focus on the printing technique—that is, on how both the coat of arms and the rest of the music book are produced. An elaborate coat of arms could easily have been hand-coloured in one or a number of presentation copies, a practice known from numerous other cases. Instead, a complex and highly risky process was used to produce a printed version. Similarly, considerable effort went into creating a beautiful book of music from moveable type, produced—as the epilogue puts it—with "great labour and at no little expense." Not only did the printers specifically commission a music font, evidently they also took great care over the appearance of each of the pages. A comparison of surviving copies has revealed an astonishing number of stop-press corrections, many of which were not essential to the reading of the music or the text, but were rather purely aesthetic considerations (Picker 1998, 154; Bator 2004).

The interest the book's makers took in the specific printing technique and its meticulous execution have once more opened the question of for whom this music book was made. Its repertoire—grand motets by composers such as Ludwig Senfl and Heinrich Isaac—clearly link it to the Imperial chapel of Maximilian I. So do the individuals involved in making the book: Senfl, who had been employed at Maximilian's court, was the editor; and the humanist Konrad Peutinger, involved in many of Maximilian's print projects, wrote the epilogue. However, its publication in October 1520—more than a year after Maximilian's death—has previously discouraged all suggestions it might have been made for the Emperor himself. It seems clear, though, that such a publication must have taken months to prepare, especially with the creation of a new music font; and with the specific focus on printing technique, a link to Maximilian, who had a particular interest in printing and its possibilities, seems likely after all. This is corroborated by the use of gold in the frontispiece, as all other known uses of gold in prints of the period have imperial links. Even though a direct commission or close association with Maximilian for the *Liber selectarum cantionum* cannot be established as a certainty, numerous considerations arising from the production methods of the book and its unusual frontispiece raise the probability of Maximilian's involvement, at least in the initial stages (Giselbrecht and Upper 2012, 50-51).

Both the colour woodcut and the music book demonstrate the close visual and conceptual links between print and manuscript cultures. The coat of arms with all its behind-the-scenes complexity gives the impression of hand-colouring and makes no effort to distinguish itself from this (much cheaper) practice. Similarly, it has been observed that this music book emulates the style of music manuscripts, in particular those written for the court in Munich (Picker 1998, 156). This is in keeping with Maximilian's taste for cutting-edge applications of the emerging technology of printing that used anachronistic medieval imagery, which communicated both the contemporary power and historical roots of his imperial office.

The existence of two issues of the first and only edition of the *Liber selectarum cantionum*, one with the complex colour print and the other with a simpler black-and-white version, points to the different markets and uses for music books in early modern Europe. Copies of the same publication could have been made for presentation, to impress a ruler in the hope of financial reward, whilst others might have been aimed at a different group of buyers, perhaps churches or choirs. The two versions, however, should not lead to a false assumption that there was a clear split between the beautiful, pristine presentation copy and the less elaborate copy destined for everyday use. A survey of the surviving copies and some early modern inventories clearly suggests that the distribution and use of this book did not respect these imagined boundaries (Giselbrecht and Upper 2012, 53-56).

The frontispiece and the much-corrected *Liber selectarum cantionum* remind us that each copy of a publication is a separate, individual material object, in clear contradiction of the oft-assumed uniformity of the printed item and the claim of "identical" products. This individualisation starts not only after the book leaves the printshop, but is already part of the production process, where the story of each material object begins.

Additional references: Senfl 1520; Bartrum 1995; Dogson 1903; Savage 2018; Strauss 1973.

Willimus

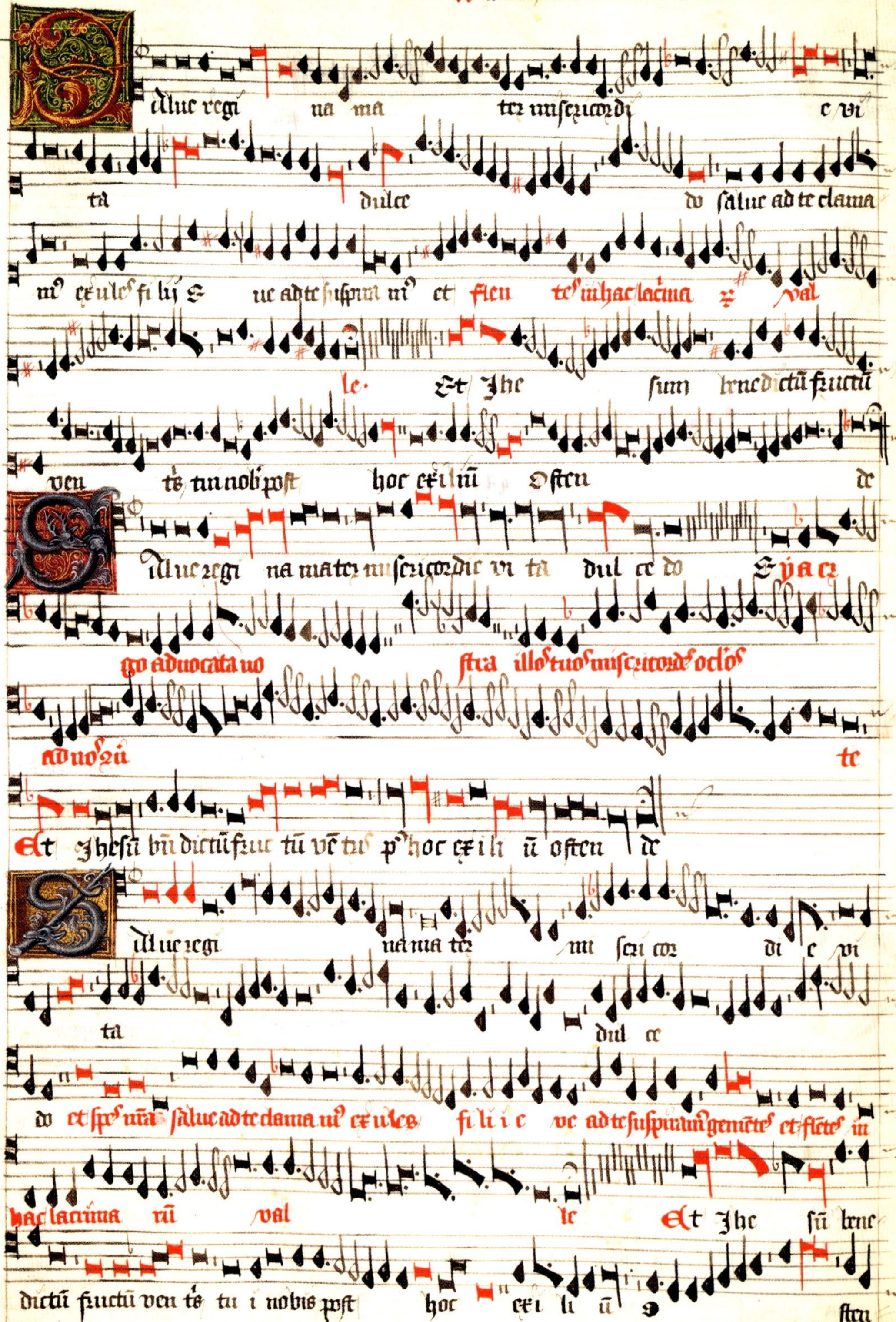
Salue regi na ma ter misericordi e vi
ta dulce do salue ad te clama
mus exules filii Eue ad te suspira mus et flen tes in hac lacrima rum val
le. Et Ihe sum benedictum fructum
ven tris tui nobis post hoc exilium osten de
Salue regi na mater misericordie vi ta dul ce do Spes nostra
ergo aduocata no stra illos tuos misericordes oculos
ad nos conuer te
Et Ihesum benedictum fructum uentris tui nobis post hoc exili um osten de
Salue regi na ma ter mi seri cor di e vi
ta dul ce
do et spes nostra salue ad te clama mus exules fili i e ue ad te suspiramus gementes et flentes in
hac lacrima rum val le Et Ihe sum bene
dictum fructum ven tris tui nobis post hoc exi li um o sten

to O Dul
cis Mari a Sal
ve
to O
Dul
cis maria Sal
ve
to Et pro no
bis flagellato spinis punc to fel le pota
to O Dul
cis ma ri a Sal
ve

38. The Eton Choirbook

Magnus Williamson

Eton College, MS 178
England, ca. 1504
Manuscript on vellum, [2] + 126 + [2] fols., 59.5 x 42.5 cm
Image: fols. 29v-30r. William Brygeman, *Salve regina* (fragmentary). Reproduced by permission of the Provost and Fellows of Eton College.

INSCRIBED IN THE UNESCO Memory of the World Register in summer 2018, the Eton Choirbook captures more than any other manuscript the sonic traces of English piety at its pre-Reformation zenith. When complete, the manuscript comprised 224 vellum folios disposed across 28 gatherings, from *a* to *ee*, on which were copied 93 pieces (24 settings of the Magnificat, 67 Latin anthems, a Matthew Passion, and a thirteen-part round on the Apostles' Creed). Two surviving indexes show that 29 pieces are entirely lost; Brygeman's *Salve* is one of a further 21 fragmentary and incomplete pieces. Copied for use in a lavishly-endowed late-medieval chantry college, in effect a production line of prayer, the Eton Choirbook symbolises the forgotten ancestry of the English choral tradition. In the 1440s, Henry VI had stipulated that the Marian antiphon *Salve regina* should be recited by Eton's choristers daily during Lent: such veneration of the Virgin Mary was one of the first ceremonies to come under attack when the Protestant vernacular liturgy was created after 1547.

The image shown here is visually less elegant than other sections of the same manuscript, and it depicts an incomplete piece, but it is inversely informative. William Brygeman was a lay clerk at Eton College for three terms in the academic year 1503-04. At some point thereafter, perhaps immediately, he moved to Bristol where he served as parish clerk at All Saints parish church; he was there by 1516 and he bequeathed a large collection of polyphonic music to All Saints on his death in 1524 (Burgess 2004, 283-84). This collection included repertory of courtly origin, including music by Robert Fayrfax of the Chapel Royal, as well as Brygeman's own Mass *Ascendo ad patrem*, and items that he probably copied while at Eton and subsequently took to Bristol.

Unlike his contemporary Robert Wylkynson who probably spent his entire working life singing at Eton, Brygeman was therefore only briefly on Eton College's payroll. The college accounts for 1502-03 are lost (most unfortunately, as this is probably when most of the choirbook was copied), but Brygeman had recently arrived by 21 September 1503 when he was bequeathed bedding by a local priest. He left in June 1504, and the brevity of this sojourn therefore provides an end-date for the choirbook's copying. The gradual evolution of the principal copyist's hand, and the last-minute inclusion of Brygeman's *Salve* in the first of two indexes of the choirbook's contents, show that it was a late-comer to what was by then a far-advanced project. Coincidentally the very first piece to be copied, William Horwood's *Salve regina*, can be seen in shadowy form by way of show-through on the right-hand side.

By this stage the choirbook nearing completion. Ruling, notation, and texting are done with accomplished ease; text underlay is ornamented with hairlines; the alternation of red and black ink, so characteristic of early-Tudor choirbooks, is carefully maintained; painted initials follow a standard type of floral, foliate, and serpentine figures, more sober and uniform than the mixture of styles seen during earlier phases (exemplified by the ghostly strapwork "U" showing through from fol. 30^{v}). However, there are signs of scribal ennui as a major copying project in its final stages: stave lines here are proficient and systematic but slightly slapdash, while the irregular black text underlay on fol. 29^{v} suggests a scribe of great experience but waning enthusiasm.

Like the majority of Eton pieces, Brygeman's *Salve* is scored in five parts: we see on fol. 30^{r} the part-names of Medius (II) and Bassus (V), in their customary positions on the right-hand side. The Eton copyist left the voices undesignated on the first opening of each piece, hence the lack of part-names on fol. 29^{v}, where the Triplex (I) appears first, with Tenor (IV) immediately below it and Contratenor (III) straddling the gutter from lower-left to upper-right. Although unlabelled, the Tenor part (middle LH) is instantly identifiable by virtue of its page location and the presence of the cantus firmus in long notes on the sixth and ninth staves. This is the antiphon *Omnes electi*: "All you elect of our God, remember us before God: that, helped by your prayers, we may be worthy to join your company." *Omnes electi* was sung at First Vespers on the feast of All Saints (30 October), and recited throughout the year within private devotions to All Saints. Like *Salve regina* itself, *Omnes electi* was a favoured item in books of hours: as a musical vehicle for such widely-circulated devotional texts, the Eton Choirbook spanned high culture and popular piety.

Returning to vocal scoring, the most frequent clef combination found in Eton produces a stack of perfect fifths between the voices: above the Bassus (F4 clef), the Contratenor and Tenor shared C4 clefs, notionally a fifth higher; above them sits the lower of the two boys' voices, Medius (with clef C2, again a fifth higher), and, another fifth above that, the Triplex (G2 clef). This, the "Great Compass," is not used by Brygeman here: instead, his five-part chorus is topped by a low-lying Triplex with C1 mezzo clef. Glancing at these clefs, an early-Tudor singer would quickly apprise the number and voice-types of singers needed to perform this piece. As a failsafe, the overall compass, from highest to lowest note, was written on the now-lost side, *f.*7R, along with the surname "Brygeman" (facing his forename "Willimus" which can still be seen on fol. 29^v). The same information is given in the index, in alternating black and red text: "Salve Regina – *5 parcium* – Brygeman – *f. 7. 19*": in other words, "if you turn to opening *f.*7 you will find Brygeman's five-part *Salve regina* which has an overall compass of 19 notes." The larger-scale pieces had compasses of 22-23 notes, so Brygeman's *Salve* might be useful if sickness depleted the ranks of Treble voices.

Among Eton's fifteen *Salve reginas*, this is the only incomplete one. Between the two surviving sides, *f.*7L and *g.*1R, were a further two folios comprising *f.*7R, *f.*8L-R, and *g.*1L. The lost folios tell their own story. The choirbook acquired its definitive modern foliation in the 1890s when M. R. James catalogued the manuscripts of his alma mater (James 1895, 108-12). This foliation is written in pencil at the foot of each recto; around the middle of the sixteenth century, an earlier foliation had been made in ink (and later duplicated in pencil) at the top RH corner. This shows that 78 folios were lost by the 1550s when the choirbook was re-bound (by the same craftsman who bound another iconic Tudor music book: British Library, Additional MS 30513, the Mulliner Book). The reconditioned manuscript remained relatively intact thereafter, losing a further 20 leaves between the 1550s and the 1890s; unfortunately, Brygeman's was among the pieces affected by these later losses.

Additional references: Bowers 1987; Harrison 1956-61; Williamson 1997; Williamson 2010; Williamson 2015.

LIBER QVINDECIM MISSARVM ELECTARVM QVAE PER EXCELLENTISSIMOS MVSICOS COMPOSITAE FVERVNT.

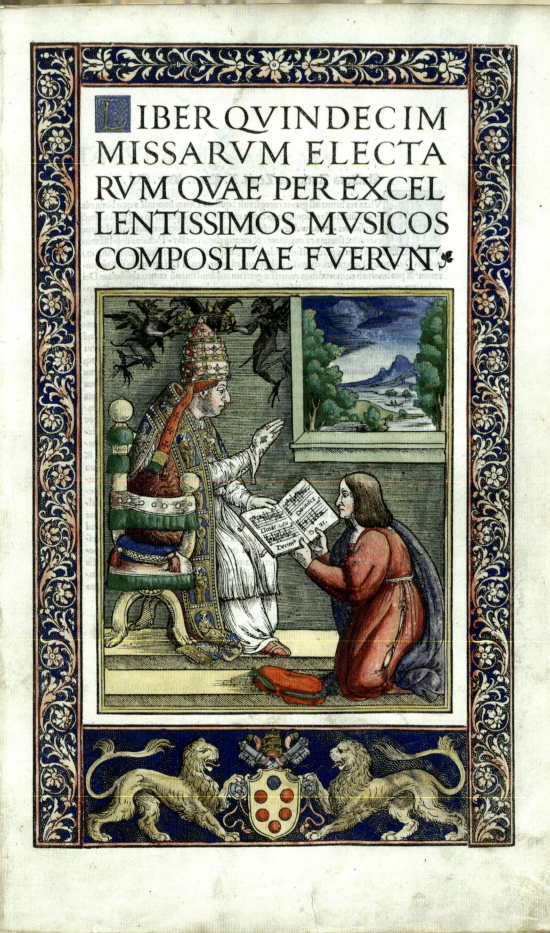

39. *Liber Quindecim Missarum*

Paweł Gancarczyk

Rome: Andrea Antico, 1516
162 fols., 42.5 x 28 cm (20)
Illuminated/coloured by anon., Königsberg(?), after 1525
Toruń, Biblioteka Uniwersytecka, VI 32
Image: Title page. Photo © Biblioteki Uniwersyteckiej w Toruniu.

Liber quindecim missarum (*The book of fifteen Masses*) is one of the best known early music prints, frequently reproduced and commented upon. It appeared at a time when the market for polyphonic music publications was beginning to take shape, gradually extending to include more centres and countries. Ottaviano Petrucci with his printing house was a pioneer in this area; his activities began in Venice, but later he moved to his hometown of Fossombrone. Starting from 1501 he published chansons, motets, frottolas, Masses, and other pieces for more than one part. For a while, Petrucci's carefully produced and elegant editions had no rivals, and neither did his method of printing using the multiple-impression process. It was not until the second decade of the sixteenth century that the first competitors appeared. The most important among them was Andrea Antico who settled in Rome. In contrast to his Venetian predecessor, Antico did not use moveable typefaces for printing music, but engraved musical notation on wooden blocks. In this he was a true master, and nobody before or since has succeeded in achieving such magnificent effects using woodcuts (Fenlon 1995, 28-35).

Antico started printing in 1510, obtaining successive privileges for his business from Pope Leo X. *Liber quindecim missarum* appeared on the basis of a privilege granted early in 1516, concerning the printing of polyphonic music in "magno volumine ac regalis Chartis," i.e. in a large volume of royal folio size. This was a significant innovation, since until then editions of such music, including Petrucci's prints, were published in smaller sizes, most often in quarto. However, many musical ensembles needed large choirbooks, better suited to church interiors, from which music could be read by a larger group of singers. The tradition of creating such volumes existed in, among others, the Sistine Chapel, whose manuscripts became the main point of reference for *Liber quindecim missarum* (Raninen 2018, 123-25). Referring to these models, Antico created a large, richly decorated book, containing, as the title promises, 15 Mass cycles composed by the "most splendid musicians," such as Josquin des Prez, Antoine Brumel, Pierre de la Rue, and others. He created a new model of musical edition, referred to by later music printers, particularly in Rome; while his successors used different materials and techniques, they continued to duplicate similar solutions (Raninen 2018, 125-32; Signer 2020). This also applied to the title page of *Liber quindecim missarum*, where we see Pope Leo X on a throne, blessing the book being handed to him by a kneeling figure. This figure is most likely Andrea Antico himself, and the book being offered represents the *Liber quindecim missarum*, even though on its open pages we see not a Mass but a short canon praising the pope with the words "Vivat Leo Decimus, Pontifex Maximus" (Long Live Leo X, High Priest). This scene is reproduced on the title pages of editions of Masses by Cristóbal de Morales (1544) and Giovanni Pierluigi da Palestrina (1554) printed in Rome by Valerio Dorico, the appearance of the pope and the figure offering the book changing in each case.

Thus Andrea Antico's venture was a success, something that can also be measured in terms of the number of copies printed and sold. While the print runs of Petrucci's editions generally did not go above 300 (Boorman 2006, 360-66), the number of published copies of *Liber quindecim missarum* was as high as 1008. It sold at a price of 20 *giulii*, many times more than the price of smaller editions (Heartz 1969, 109). In spite of its expense it found numerous purchasers throughout Europe, and also in colonialized New Spain (Stevenson 1964, 343), as evidenced by the copies extant today and by surviving inventories of lost collections. It seems that this book satisfied the needs of church and court choirs, and its authority was undoubtedly strengthened by the pope's *imprimatur*. And thus, for the first time in history, singers in different parts of Europe, and beyond, performed music using the same sheet music and admiring the same woodcuts. We might regard this as one of the first steps towards the globalisation of musical culture (Gancarczyk 2015, 128-37).

However, the use and significance that *Liber quindecim missarum* carried with it could look quite different at each location to which it found its way. This is illustrated by the copy from the music library of Duke Albert of Prussia in Königsberg (now Kaliningrad in Russia), now preserved at the University Library in Toruń (Poland). It is the only copy of *Liber* known to me that has been illuminated; all the initials and borders

Figure 39.1: *Liber quindecim missarum* (Rome: Antico, 1516), p. 81. Opening initial K of Jean Mouton's *Missa Dictes moy toutes vos pensees*. Photo © Biblioteki Uniwersyteckiej w Toruniu.

Figure 39.2: *Liber quindecim missarum* (Rome: Antico, 1516), title page, detail. Photo © Biblioteki Uniwersyteckiej w Toruniu.

in the book have been coloured with great precision (see fig. 39.1). This makes the volume unique, giving it even greater resemblance to its models and forerunners, the luxury manuscript choirbooks. The value and visual attractiveness of the book are made even greater by its expensive binding, and the sumptuous exlibris with the ducal coat of arms and his titulature testifies to it being part of the ducal collection.

As mentioned above, the visual symbol of *Liber quindecim missarum* is the woodcut on its title page, depicting papal authority with all its attributes. Here also the illuminator coloured the smallest details, but in this case he was very much more inventive. He went beyond the content of the Antico woodcut and above the pope sitting on the throne he added two devils who, floating in the air, place a flaming crown on the papal tiara (fig. 39.2). The interpretation of this scene leaves no room for doubt: the pope is crowned as the Antichrist, the flames symbolise hellfire, and their number—ten—may refer to St John's Apocalypse (13:1) and the description of the ten-horned beast. How did this astonishing visual commentary come to appear in a book that is meant to express homage to the Roman Church and Pope Leo X?

Identifying the pope or, more generally, the papacy with the Antichrist has a long tradition in Christianity. It was linked to various currents of criticism of the Roman Church, but gathered strength after the theses of Martin Luther. Of particular significance for the imaginarium of supporters of the Reformation was the pamphlet *Passional Christi und Antichristi* (Wittenberg: J. Rhau, 1521), which put together suggestive pictures by Lucas Cranach the Elder and brief German texts of the theologian Philipp Melanchthon. Neighbouring pages juxtapose the simple and holy life of Christ with the vainglorious and corrupt life of the pope, referred to here as the Antichrist. The pamphlet was a reaction to the papal bull of 1520, *Exsurge Domine* (*Arise, O Lord*), which threatened Luther with excommunication, and to which the latter responded with the text *Adversus execrabilem Antichristi bullam* (*Against the Execrable*

Bull of the Antichrist). The figure of the pope as the Antichrist appears in many later pamphlets, including songs (Oettinger 2001, 171-201).

Luther's ideas, assisted by the expansion of print, quickly reached many corners of Europe. They also found their supporters in the State of the Teutonic Order in Prussia, which at that time was in the midst of a political and spiritual crisis. The origins of this state reached back to 1226 and were linked to the mission of spreading the faith among the pagan Prussian tribes, supported by successive popes and emperors. At its peak the state governed enormous swathes of today's northern Poland, the Kaliningrad region of Russia, and the Baltic countries. Its further expansion threatened the neighbouring Kingdom of Poland and the Grand Duchy of Lithuania, and was halted when the Teutonic army was defeated by the combined armies of Poland and Lithuania during the battle of Grunwald (Tannenberg) in 1410. The Teutonic Order gradually lost its lands and its political significance. The crusader ideology underlying its existence also lost its purpose, since the pagans who inhabited the Prussian lands were either brutally exterminated or converted to Christianity. Successive grand masters residing in Malbork (Marienburg) and later in Königsberg gradually moved away from the mode of life of the monk-knights, and their courts increasingly resembled those of secular rulers (Biskup and Czaja 2008). This also applied to musical life; even before 1410 an ensemble of three-four musicians playing shawms and slide trumpets (called the *alta cappella*) was maintained at Malbork, while during Mass at the castle chapel in the presence of Anna, grand duchess of Lithuania, one could hear the playing of a fiddler (Gancarczyk 2012, 193). Albert of Prussia was the last grand master of the order and, because of the growing secularising tendencies, like many other brothers he abandoned his monk's habit and became a Lutheran. He was already a secular duke when in 1525 he pledged liege homage to the king of Poland, becoming the ruler of the first Lutheran state in Europe (Wijaczka 2019).

Albert of Prussia attached great significance to music, and one of his protégés was for many years the famous lutenist from Transylvania, Valentin Bakfark. We may suppose that *Liber quindecim missarum* had been purchased for the duke's collection prior to the secularisation of the Prussian part of the Teutonic Order, that is, prior to 1525. It was only illuminated later, and Leo X's likeness on its title page, now an object of hate for supporters of the Reformation, changed from a Holy Father to the Antichrist. Popes aside, the musical repertory performed by the Lutherans was based to a great extent on the earlier Catholic repertory, a phenomenon we can observe in many locations in Europe. At a later time the musical library in Königsberg was enriched by a sizeable collection of printed choirbooks published in Augsburg, Paris, Lyon, and Leuven, unfortunately lost during World War II (Müller-Blattau 1923/24, 219-23). It included two volumes of Masses by Cristóbal de Morales, published in the years 1546 and 1551 by Jacques Moderne in Lyon. These prints also referred to the model of *Liber quindecim missarum*, although the pope as Antichrist is absent from their title pages.

The *Liber quindecim missarum* in Albert's collection bears no traces of intensive usage: it is highly unlikely that the duke's musicians would have sung from it. Why, then, was so much importance attached to it, even though it represented a kind of homage to the pope, a figure of hate for the Lutherans? Why illuminate it, bind it, give it the ducal exlibris, instead of consigning it to oblivion or passing it to a new owner? *Liber quindecim missarum* was not only an object worth 20 *giulii*, it was also part of a larger collection, systematically supplemented and expanded. Every collection has special non-material value, regardless of whether the items that are part of it are of any practical use. As Krzysztof Pomian has put it:

> the creation of libraries or collections, is one of the procedures which transform utility into significance and allow the person who occupies a high rank in the hierarchy of wealth to achieve an appropriate position in the hierarchy of good taste and knowledge, since the elements of the collection are [...] signifiers indicating membership of a social class or indeed superiority (Pomian 1987, 53).

In possession of a music library with such extraordinary works as *Liber quindecim missarum*, Albert of Prussia could hope to be seen as a splendid, well-educated monarch, an objective to which an Antichrist pope presented no obstacle.

ACKNOWLEDGEMENTS: This text, translated from the Polish by Zofia Weaver, was produced as part of research project no. 2018/31/B/HS2/00479 "Music in the Teutonic Order State in Prussia: Sources, Repertoires, Contexts," funded by the National Science Centre, Poland.

Les ſimulachres & HISTORIEES FACES DE LA MORT, AVTANT ELEgammẽt pourtraictes, que artifi-ciellement imaginées.

A LYON,
Soubz l'eſcu de COLOI
M. D. XXXVII

Væ væ væ habitantibus in terra.
APOCALYPSIS VIII
Cuncta in quibus ſpiraculum vitæ eſt, mortua ſunt.
GENESIS VII

Malheureux qui uiuez au monde
Touſiours remplis d'aduerſitez,
Pour quelque bien qui uous abonde,
Serez tous de Mort uiſitez.

40. *Les simulachres & hiſtoriées faces de la mort*

Katelijne Schiltz

Lyons: Melchior and Gaſpar Trechsel, 1538
Hans Holbein (engravings), Jean de Vauzelles (text), and Gilles Corrozet (text)
48 fols., 17.6 x 12.1 cm
Paris, Bibliothèque nationale de France, RES-Z-1990

Upper image: title page.
Lower image: sig. Cii^{v}.
Photos © Bibliothèque nationale de France.

When, somewhere between 1523 and 1526, Hans Holbein the Younger made the drawings for what in 1538 would appear under the title *Les simulachres & hiſtoriées faces de la mort*, it was not his firſt encounter with the Dance of Death. Literary and visual depictions of dancing skeletons, leading people to their grave regardless of their age, class, and gender, were part of a long tradition throughout Europe. Numerous texts, paintings, frescoes, woodcuts, miniatures, and sculptures from the fourteenth century onwards reminded people of the imminence of death, while at the same time calling on them to do penance.

While working in Basel in the 1520s, Holbein muſt have been familiar with the fifteenth-century fresco on the cemetery wall of the Predigerkirche, which came to be known as the "Basler Totentanz" (Basel Dance of Death; Hiſtorisches Museum Basel—now fragmentary). The mural painting was made shortly after the city had been afflicted by the plague, thus making it a powerful symbol of Basel's pride and renewed consciousness of death.

In fact, Holbein produced satirical reflections on the vanity of earthly life more than once. Apart from the drawings for *Les simulachres*, he portrayed the danse macabre on a dagger sheath—an object certainly apt for the topic—engraved by Urs Graf in 1521. Holbein's pen and wash drawing is now kept at the Berliner Bauakademie, and a copy of it survives in the Basler Kunſtsammlung. Furthermore, he created a series of 24 initials, showing people from all levels of society, in hierarchical order, accompanied by one or more skeletons. This Dance of Death alphabet, with woodcuts by Hans Lützelburger, was firſt used in the 1524 edition of the Greek New Teſtament *Tēs Kainēs Diathēkēs hapanta = Novi Teſtamenti omnia* (Basel: Io. Bebelivm).

Lützelburger also made the woodcuts for what Alexander Goette has termed the "großer Totentanz," i.e. the one that was included in *Les simulachres & hiſtoriées faces de la mort*, published in Lyons by the Trechsel brothers in 1538 (Goette 1897). The print opens with a prefatory letter, entitled "Épiſtre des faces de la mort" by the humaniſt and cleric Jean de Vauzelles (Kammerer 2013), which is addressed to Jeanne de Thouzelles, the abbess of the proſperous convent Saint-Pierre-les-Nonnains at Lyons. Vauzelles raises the queſtion of how something invisible (i.e. death) can be represented by something visible. It is in this context that he introduces the term "simulachres." Vauzelles explains that the drawings by Holbein serve as an attempt to visualise the abſtract nature of death: "Simulachre they are moſt correctly called, for simulachre derives from the verb to simulate and to feign that which is not really there." He also ſtresses that images, more than words, have a ſtrong impact on the recipient: they have the capacity "to imprint the memory of Death with more force than all the rhetorical descriptions of the orators ever could" (Holbein 1538, A iii^{r}).

At the heart of the *Simulachres* are 41 woodcuts after drawings by Holbein—whose name and authorship, it should be added, are mentioned nowhere in the print. Intereſtingly, the very medium of the book causes Holbein to deviate from the classical representation of the danse macabre, as it was generally known. For whereas people and skeletons were usually lined up in single file, physically connected with one another, Holbein choses individual scenes and settings inſtead. Moreover, each page is conceived as an emblem with a tripartite ſtructure: a Latin quotation from the Bible serves as *inscriptio* (motto) for Holbein's drawing (the emblem's *pictura*), while a French quatrain underneath functions as *subscriptio* (epigram). The quatrains, authored by Gilles Corrozet, explain and deepen the connection between the Biblical verse and the woodcut, drawing the reader into a self-reflective examination of his own mortality. The texts accompanying our image of the Dance of Death can serve as an example:

Motto (*inscriptio*)	
Vae vae vae habitantibus in terra APOCALYPSIS VIII	Woe, woe, woe to the inhabitants of the earth. Revelation 8
Cuncta in quibus ſpiraculum vitae eſt, mortua sunt. GENESIS VIII	And all things wherein there is the breath of life on the earth, died. Genesis 8

Epigram (*subscriptio*)

Malheureux qui uiuez au monde Tousiours remplis d'adversitez, Pour quelque bien qui uous abonde, Serez tous de Mort visitez.	Unhappy are those who live in the world always full of adversities, for every benefit with which you abound, you will all be visited by Death.

(Holbein 1538, sig. Cii^v^)

Biblical imagery also dominates the beginning and the end of the series. Holbein starts with four scenes from Genesis, showing the creation of man and woman, the Fall, Adam and Eve's expulsion from paradise (from which point a skeleton is always present), and their tilling of the earth. At the very end we find two drawings showing the Last Judgement and the escutcheon of Death, urging the reader to look at it as often as possible if he wants to live a life free of sins: "Si tu ueux uiure sans peché / Voy cest imaige a tous propos" (Holbein 1538, G iv^v^). The series thus has a clear narrative frame, which connects the beginning and the end of time. As Elina Gertsman has put it,

> The Fall and the Last Judgement mark the first and the last instance of mortal, human history: the former establishes the moment Death came into the world, and the latter is the culminating moment in the history of humanity, when all the deceased—victims of Death—will rise again to be judged (Gertsman 2010, 170-72).

In-between the extremes of this conceptual framework comes the actual Dance of Death, with an outdoor concert (so to speak) given by a group of skeletons serving as the opening of the dance. People from various backgrounds and classes are then shown roughly in hierarchical order, from the pope and the emperor to the senator and the priest to the peasant and the child. No one can escape the clutches of Death, who "comes upon his victim in the midst of the latter's own surroundings and activities" (Zemon Davis 1956, 101), like the abbess holding the rosary, the preacher delivering a sermon from a pulpit, or the peasant working in the field. The hourglass that figures prominently in many of the woodcuts underlines the fact that life can end in the twinkling of an eye.

Especially in the case of high-ranking political and religious figures, the emblems also serve to criticise social injustice and deplorable vices, such as avarice and the lust for power. People are often caught in the midst of nefarious activities, as with the judge who is being bribed by a rich man, the cardinal who is trading in benefices and indulgences, the greedy mendicant friar who is trying to escape with a bag full of money, and so forth.

In most cases and contrary to the age-old tradition, however, Death is not really dancing (or engaging his unfortunate partner in a dance), but rather dragging away his victims. Indeed, Death can appear in various guises, be it as a cardinal among the entourage of the pope, as a cupbearer of the king (who clearly looks like Francis I), as court jester to the queen, as a rival (wearing his chain mail) of the knight, or as a horse driver of the ploughman.

Given the fact that dancing does not play a prominent role, it is not surprising that musical instruments occur on only eight woodcuts—this low figure is quite striking compared with projects like Heinrich Knoblochtzer's late fifteenth-century *Doten dantz mit figuren* (*Death dance with illustrations*), which has instruments on nearly all images. The outdoor performance mentioned above is by far the noisiest musical scene, in that it combines kettledrums, crumhorns, shawms, straight trumpets, and a hurdy-gurdy (see lower image). A similar setting opens Holbein's Dance of Death alphabet, which is also otherwise lacking in musical instruments—apart from the letter A, the concert, only for the queen at letter G is Death playing the flute. In *Les simulachres*, a xylophone occurs twice in a similar context: its sounds accompany both the old man and the old woman to their graves. For the approaching death of a noble couple, a skeleton plays the drum; a lira da braccio announces the death of the duchess. There is an interesting instance where the instrument is not played by a skeleton, but a human being: the lute-playing lover who sits on a bed to serenade a sinful nun—a clear expression of the sensuous and lustful side of music.

In four short treatises that conclude the *Simulachres*, Jean de Vauzelles reflects upon death from various perspectives. He presents views on death from the Bible, philosophers, Church Fathers, and pagan writers, and ends with an essay on the necessity of death. In later editions these were replaced by other texts, such as French translations of Lutheran writings. Natalie Zemon Davis, who has investigated the reception of the *Simulachres* in confessional terms, was able to show that its surrounding paratexts (the opening prefaces and the concluding sermons) were adapted to different political and religious leanings. She concludes that "both Catholics and Protestants wished, through the pictures, to turn men's thoughts to a Christian preparation for death" (Zemon Davis 1956, 126).

Although the sharp criticism of social wrongs in general and the clerical estate in particular is inherent in the Dance of Death tradition, the first edition of the *Simulachres* was listed in the *Index of Prohibited Books*; later editions were banned by major universities such as those of Paris and Louvain. However, this could not prevent the success of the project. Soon after 1538, translations appeared in Italian (e.g. *Simolachri, Historie, e Figure de la Morte*, Lyons: Jean Frellon, 1549) and Latin (variously entitled *Imagines de morte* or *Icones mortis*), and more people were added to the Dance of Death (a soldier, a drunkard, a beggar, a gambler, a robber, etc.). Above all, well into the nineteenth century, artists continued to copy and reinterpret Holbein's drawings.

With his series, Holbein was able to illustrate the *memento mori*—to put it somewhat paradoxically—in a particularly vivid way. He shows Death's victims in different expressions, costumes, and situations, making the arrival of Death all the more shocking. Together with the Biblical quotations and the French verses, the *Simulachres* offer their readers a multi-layered opportunity for contemplation on the transient nature of earthly life and the equalising force of Death.

ADDITIONAL REFERENCES: Bätschmann and Griener 2014; Gundersheimer 1971.

t du vergier du tout atire
a facon vous rediray puis
out ensemble dire ne puis

De chanter nestoiēt iamais l
La doulceur et la melodie
Me mist au cueur grāt reshau

La karole du vergier

Mais quāt ie escoute vn poy
les oyseaux. tenir ne me poy
Q' dan deduit veoir nalasse
ar a saison moult desirasse

Son contenemēt et son estre
Lors men alay tout droit a d
Par vne petiote sente
Plaine de faneul et de ment

III

Books

Imagined Spaces

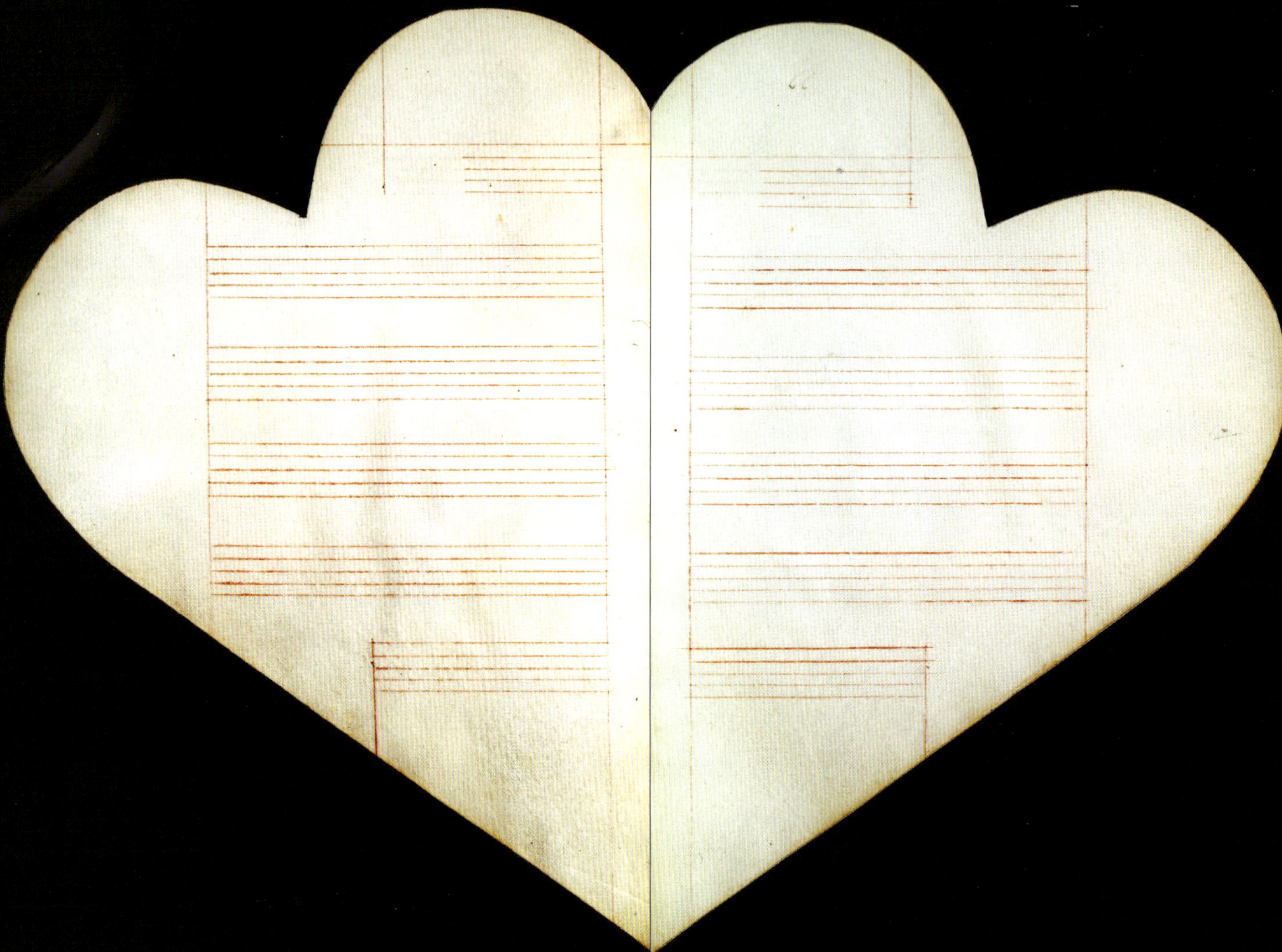

41. The Musical Staff

Jane Alden

Paris, Bibliothèque nationale de France, MS Rothschild 2973 (I.5.13), fols. 65v-66r
Chansonnier Cordiforme (Chansonnier de Jean de Montchenu)
Savoy, ca. 1475
Manuscript on parchment, [4] + 68 fols., 21 x 30 cm (total width)
Photo © Bibliothèque nationale de France

Imagine if this were the only opening to survive from the Chansonnier Cordiforme. With the physical object on hand, it would be possible to turn over this folded leaf (a bifolium) to see the other side, which would reveal itself to be identically ruled and similarly devoid of notation. But what could be discerned of the parent source if all that remained was this digital image of two conjoined parchment hearts? The only manuscript to survive in this distinctive double heart shape (although two survive in the shape of a fleur-de-lys—Kraemer 2008, 12-13), it is disheartening to imagine a world without the most famous of fifteenth-century songbooks. An object of extraordinary symbolism: a single heart closed, it opens to join two hearts. But even without notation, these digital leaves reveal their intended function through one decisive aspect: their ruling.

This bifolium was evidently prepared using a laborious process of soaking, scraping, and stretching. Its pelt was pumiced and chalked to achieve the smooth, pale quality of parchment characteristic of deluxe manuscripts. Given Cordiforme's unusual shape, it seems likely that copying and decoration would have been completed before the manuscript was trimmed. Accordingly, it must have been deemed complete, even though the entire final gathering is without notation.

But the person who ruled these leaves would not have anticipated that decades (and indeed centuries) later they would remain unfilled. The matching ink color suggests that all of the staves in the Chansonnier Cordiforme were ruled (without a *rastrum*) at the same time, ahead of any copying. The staves were ruled exactly back-to-back, so that the viewer's eye is not distracted by any bleed-through lines from the other side (Fallows 2008, 15). This precise positioning was made possible by pricking holes that guided the ruling and indicated where the parchment should be cut into its double heart configuration (Thibault and Fallows 1991, xlviii). The contours must have been decided before the leaves were pricked, and similarly the decision that this was to be a musical manuscript (with musical staves). Indeed, all those who pricked, ruled, copied, and decorated the Chansonnier Cordiforme would have known the manuscript's intended final appearance, even though they worked on uncut leaves.

The chansonniers produced in France and French-speaking areas in the 1460s and 70s are noticeably smaller than those copied some years later in Italy. The recently-discovered Leuven Chansonnier measures only 12 x 8.5 cm, whereas the slightly later Italian sources (which contain much of the same French repertory, but with incomplete texts) are around 21 x 14 cm (Burn 2017; Alden 2010). The Chansonnier Cordiforme is of Savoyard origin. Closed and positioned with the spine forming a y-axis, the cover measures 21.5 cm from the top of the uppermost scallop to the x-axis. In this orientation, the cover extends 15.5 cm from the perpendicular, but the diagonal cuts make this manuscript more perusable than a rectangular codex measuring 21.5 x 15.5 cm. From the point at the bottom, the trimmed leaves span 21 cm to the edge of each scallop and 18.5 cm to the central notch. The widest part of each leaf measures 16 cm, although Cordiforme's mise-en-page (arrangement of notation, initials, and border decoration) reduces the copying space.

Although the Chansonnier Nivelle de la Chaussée has eight staves per page, the Copenhagen, Dijon, Laborde, and Wolfenbüttel Chansonniers were each ruled with seven (measuring 8-9 mm and separated at intervals of 7 mm), as were many of the Italian sources. In contrast, the Chansonnier Cordiforme leaves were ruled with only six staves, each measuring approximately 11 mm and separated by about 10 mm (Alden 2010, Appendix A). The Leuven Chansonnier was also ruled with six staves (8 mm, 6.5 mm apart), which helped prevent the writing space becoming overcrowded in this smallest of chansonniers. Cordiforme's six staves may have been determined by the manuscript's smaller copying space, but the result is that the staves have a spacious quality that contributes to the overall elegance of the leaves.

In order to accommodate the notch of the double heart outline, the first staff on each leaf is only 32 mm wide. The following four staves each span 88 mm, but the diagonal cut required the sixth staff line, at the bottom of each leaf, to be only 51 mm. To demarcate the boundaries of musical staves, the Chansonnier Cordiforme was ruled with vertical lines 15 mm from each inner gutter and 46 mm from each outer extreme. In addition, the shorter first and last staves have their

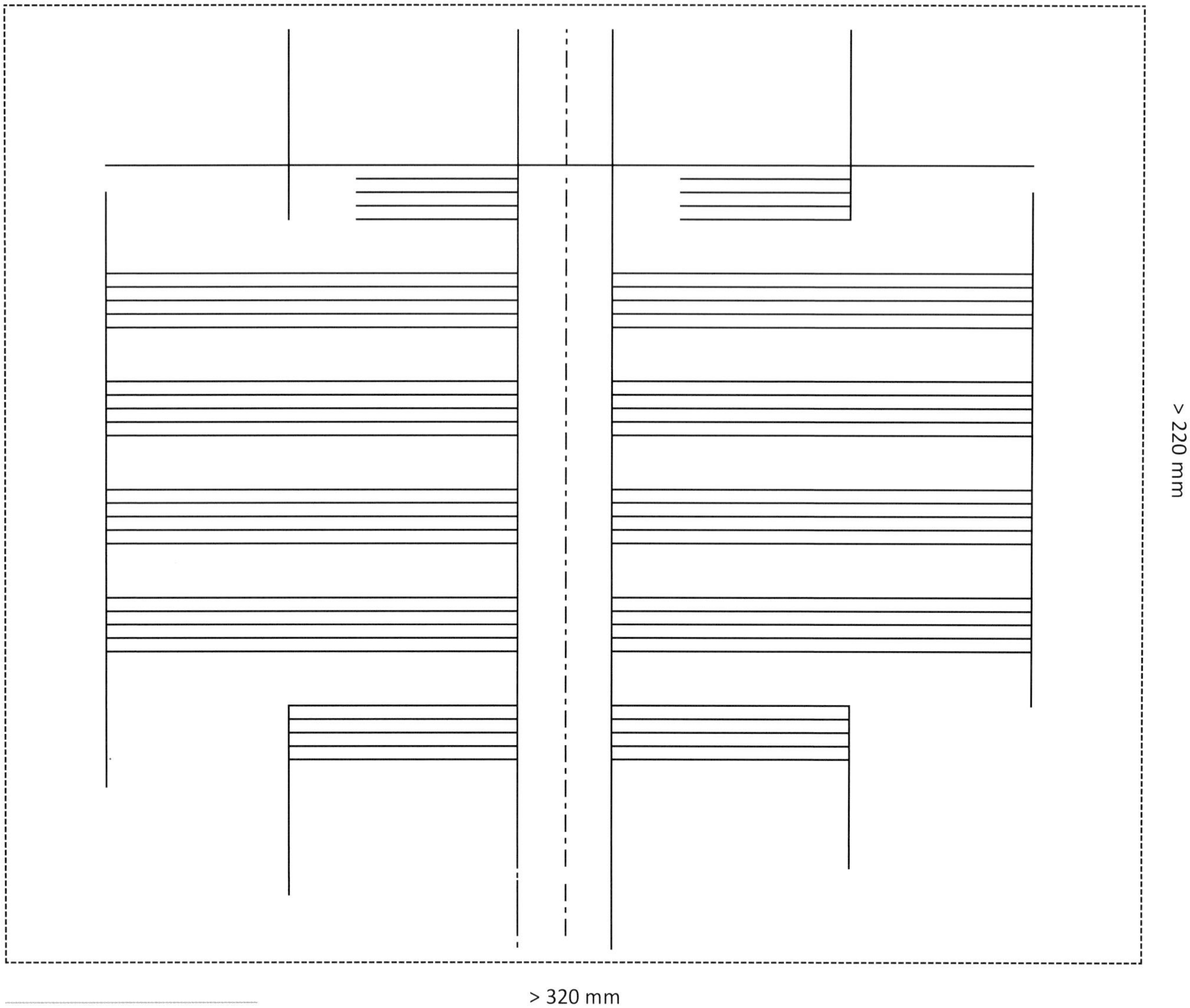

Figure 41.1: Hypothetical ruling of the Chansonnier Cordiforme.

own vertical bounding lines. These eight vertical lines would have been drawn ahead of the horizontal ruling.

Cordiforme must have been cut from bifolio leaves measuring at least 32 x 22 cm (see fig. 41.1 for a hypothetical reconstruction of the ruling prior to trimming). The horizontal line at the top, and the absence of pricking holes in the inner margins, suggest that Cordiforme was ruled straight across. This procedure indicates that the manuscript's layout was fixed at an early stage of its preparation. The fact that the Leuven Chansonnier was also ruled straight across implies that the number of leaves needed and the repertoire to be included in this manuscript were also known ahead of copying.

That the person ruling the staves was familiar with the chanson repertoire, or had been instructed by someone who knew the standard layout of voices, is clear from the spaces left for decorated initials. Fifteenth-century chansonniers were typically presented in so-called choirbook layout, with the Discantus and Tenor copied on facing sides of each opening. (The Tenor voice, from the Latin *tenere*, to hold, was the contrapuntal foundation, the "fundamentum relationis," according to the theorist Johannes Tinctoris' *Terminorum musicae diffinitorum* of ca. 1475.) Although the Contratenor was generally copied below the Tenor on the recto leaf (the right-hand side of each opening), in Cordiforme, this voice begins on the short bottom staff of the verso (left-hand) leaf and continues on the lower staves of the facing recto (see fig. 41.2). Spaces were left for Discantus and Tenor initials to be added. As no equivalent spaces were left at the beginning of the Contratenor voice, its decorated initial "C"s were added between the boundary line and the edge of the page. The offset presentation of Contratenor initials helps to reinforce the greater importance of the Discantus part, whose initials belong to the song texts; the Tenor and Contratenor initials, in contrast, indicate each respective voice part.

The discrepant staff lengths in the Chansonnier Cordiforme draw attention to three key aspects of these songbooks. First, this is music to be understood in a polylinear (rather than vertical) fashion; at 88 mm across, the central four staves on each leaf of Cordiforme offer more horizontal space than other early chansonniers, whose staves are 55 mm (Leuven), 57-60 mm (Laborde), 63 mm (Wolfenbüttel), and 68-70 mm (Copenhagen and Dijon). Second, chansonniers invite browsing, both between songs and around the pages of each opening. These are not books to be read from the top left-hand corner of the first leaf through to the bottom right-hand corner of the last; instead, one's eye is encouraged to dart around the decorated initials, the poetic verses, and the borders, as if in a garden of flowers. David Fallows has observed that the Cordiforme scribe rarely copied later strophes for rondeaux spread across two openings on the appropriate opening, relative to the music (Fallows 2008, 45); perhaps the turning to and fro this necessitated was a deliberate choice, encouraging browsing. Third, chansonnier contents draw on the courtly love tradition: this is music of, about, and (here quite literally) written on the heart (Jager 2000). Cordiforme's unusual shape necessitates the short staves, which in turn provide a visual focus on the *formes fixes* incipits (see *Ma bouche plaint*, in fig. 41.2, where each voice part represents the incipit on its short first staff). Tracing each of these three aspects, the reader follows a path, whether it be the sweep of the musical line, ocular wandering around the page, or the emotional/literary journey to the heart. Given the etymology of the word "staff" from the Old English *stæf*, a stick carried in the hand to aid walking or climbing, it is quite appropriate that the short staff lines in Cordiforme offer extra guidance.

The five-line staff was not new in the fifteenth century. The person credited with popularising the ruling of spaces for musical notation, the eleventh-century monk Guido of Arezzo, did not specify the number of lines in a staff, and the earliest manuscripts reflecting his ideas present three, four, and sometimes five lines (Haines 2008; Hiley 2001). But as polyphonic pieces started to be copied in greater number, and with wider ranges, the five-line staff became standard, offering a clear visual scaffold with enough space to accommodate larger melodic leaps. From the thirteenth century onwards, northern French sources of polyphony consistently use five-line staves, ruled in red or black ink. The Copenhagen and Wolfenbüttel Chansonniers were both ruled with red, Dijon and Leuven with brown, Laborde with tan-colored, and Nivelle with rose-colored staves. The staff lines in Cordiforme were probably ruled in red ink, which has faded to a delicate mauve color.

Although musical staves had been incorporated into lavishly-decorated secular manuscripts from the thirteenth century onwards, new in the fifteenth century were these diminutive chansonniers, small enough to fit snugly into a reader's hands. The poetry, music, and decoration are all replete with associations—chivalric contests, literary traditions, the private contemplation of books of hours, sung performance—and underline the status of these manuscripts as objects of leisure.

Reinforcing the distance between nobility and peasant workers, leisure was the defining quality of medieval aristocracy. A deluxe book of love songs was as much a signifier of nobility as owning hunting hounds. With the means to escape into the allegorical world of courtly love, the book's owner could enjoy this private type of *amor*, in solitude or intimate company.

Many of the surviving chansonniers bear witness to early changes in ownership and scope. From the outset, they were crafted in ways that meant they could be expanded by later users. The bifolium exhibited here is the middle leaf of the final gathering of the Chansonnier Cordiforme. Although these staves remain empty, they fill the imagination, by inviting consideration of potential music-making, in all forms. Perhaps this is the message to be taken to heart.

Figure 41.2: Chansonnier Cordiforme, fols. 46v–47r, first opening of *Ma bouche plaint*. Photo © Bibliothèque nationale de France.

41. The Musical Staff

Quant elle m'avoit defferme
Le guichet du vergier rame
Des ores si com je sauray
Vous compteray comment jouiray
Premier de quoy deduit servoit
Et quel compaignie il avoit
Sans longue fable vous vueil dire
Et du vergier du tout a tire
La facon vous rediray puis
Tout ensemble dire ne puis
Mais tout vous compteray en ordre
Que on ny sache que remordre
Grant servise doulx et plaisant
Aloient ces oiseaux faisant
Lais damours souef et courtoys
Chantoient en leur serventoys
Lungs en hault et lautre bas
De chanter nestoient jamais las
La doulceur et la melodie
Me mist au cueur grant reebaudie

La karole du vergier

Mais quant jey escoute un poy
Les oyseaux tenir ne me poy
Que dan deduit veoir nalasse
Car a savoir mout desirasse
Son contenement et son estre
Lors men alay tout droit a destre
Par une petiote sente
Plaine de fanoul et de mente

42. Deduit's Garden

Sylvia Huot

Boethius Master, *Cortoisie invites the Dreamer to dance*
Miniature from *Le Roman de la Rose*, Paris, Bibliothèque nationale de France, MS Fr. 19153, fol. 7r
France, ca. 1460
Manuscript on parchment, 150 fols., 34.2 x 25.3 cm

THIS IMAGE occurs in the fifteenth-century manuscript Bibliothèque nationale de France fr. 19153 (ca. 1460), fol. 7^{r}, and illustrates the carol scene in the *Roman de la Rose* (Lorris and Meun 1973-75). Begun by Guillaume de Lorris ca. 1230 (vv. 1-4028), and continued by Jean de Meun about 40 years later (vv. 4029-21,750), this allegorical poem narrates a young man's dream of entering the walled Garden of Delight, falling in love with a rose bud that he sees reflected in the Fountain of Love, and seeking, through his encounters with a host of allegorical figures, to approach and possess the Rose.

Having been admitted to the Garden by Oiseuse (Idleness or Leisure), the Dreamer decides to seek out its owner, Deduit (Delight), whom he soon finds in the midst of a festive carol: a dance form, especially popular in the twelfth and thirteenth centuries, in which participants held hands and danced to their own singing, sometimes accompanied by instrumentalists. This profusion of music and dance sets a tone of aristocratic opulence and amorous flirtation and desire. It is Leesce (Joy) who leads the song. We are told that singing is her favourite occupation (737-40), underscoring the strong association between song and gaiety. The carol, a highly ornate affair, also includes professional musicians: *fleüteors* (pipers), *menestreus* (minstrels)—presumably other instrumentalists and/or singers—and *jugleors*, possibly dancers or acrobats (745-46). There are female drum and tambourine players (*timberesses* and *tableteresses* [751-52]); this particular manuscript also notes female acrobatic dancers, amending v. 752 to read "Tumberesses et timberesses" (fol. 7^{v}, see fig. 42.1). Two female dancers, around whom the line of carolers circles, dance around each other in a movement that involves a close approach face to face, as if kissing, and then receding, only to repeat the move (757-69).

Before encountering the carolers, the Dreamer has been entranced by the bewildering profusion of birds—three times as many as in the whole of France (480-81)—with 13 different species enumerated in as many lines (643-55). The birds themselves are described as singing "lais d'amors et sonoiz cortois" (amorous lays and courtly songs [701])—a line amended in the current manuscript to "l'art d'amours souef et courtoys" (the sweet and courtly art of love [fol. 7^{r}]), as if the birds are somehow vocalising the poem itself, characterised in its Prologue as one in which "l'art d'Amors est tote enclose" (the art of love is completely contained [38]). Hearing them makes the Dreamer happier than he has ever been before (679-80). When he comes to the carol, with Joy herself leading the song, and the God of Love as a principal figure, it is as though the affective associations of the birdsong—a natural phenomenon, but one that seems increasingly crafted as the description goes on—have taken on visual form, embodied in the cluster of allegorical personifications.

The main participants in the carol are the masculine Amors (Cupid, God of Love) and Deduit, along with the feminine Leesce, Cortoisie (Courtesy), Biauté (Beauty), Richece (Wealth), Largesce (Generosity), Franchise (Openness or Liberality of Spirit), Oiseuse, Joinece (Youth), and their chivalric partners. In effect, it is a pattern of words—courtly and amorous concepts and ideals—in endless, repetitive motion. A living *chanson courtoise*, it moves and changes, yet stays the same, mirroring, interweaving. Emmanuèle Baumgartner notes of the carol that the "interplay of repetitions… isolates an eternal present and fixes it in the space of the text": one in which the female dancers "repeat their acrobatic movements like automata" (Baumgartner 1992, 27-28). If birdsong has metamorphosed into courtly love lyric in the form of an allegorical dance scene, the carol will further serve as the means by which the Dreamer enters into the vortex of erotic desire, becoming the central figure in an allegorical love narrative in which he is inspired, aided, or hindered by the very qualities and ideals represented in the carol itself.

The miniature depicts the moment in which Cortoisie invites the Dreamer into the dance. We see him in a moment of transition, as he moves from spectator to participant in the central activity of the Garden. Once the Dreamer has entered into the narrative of desire, the carol has served its purpose and we hear no more about it as such; but it is still the iconic moment that informs the imagery of snares, musical entrapment, and the lure of desire running throughout the poem. The Dreamer's captivation in the intertwining line of dancers subtly foreshadows his later entrapment when he is snared by the metaphorical *laz* (snares) and *engins* (devices) that Cupid has laid around the perilous Fountain of Love (1589-90). His attraction to the music

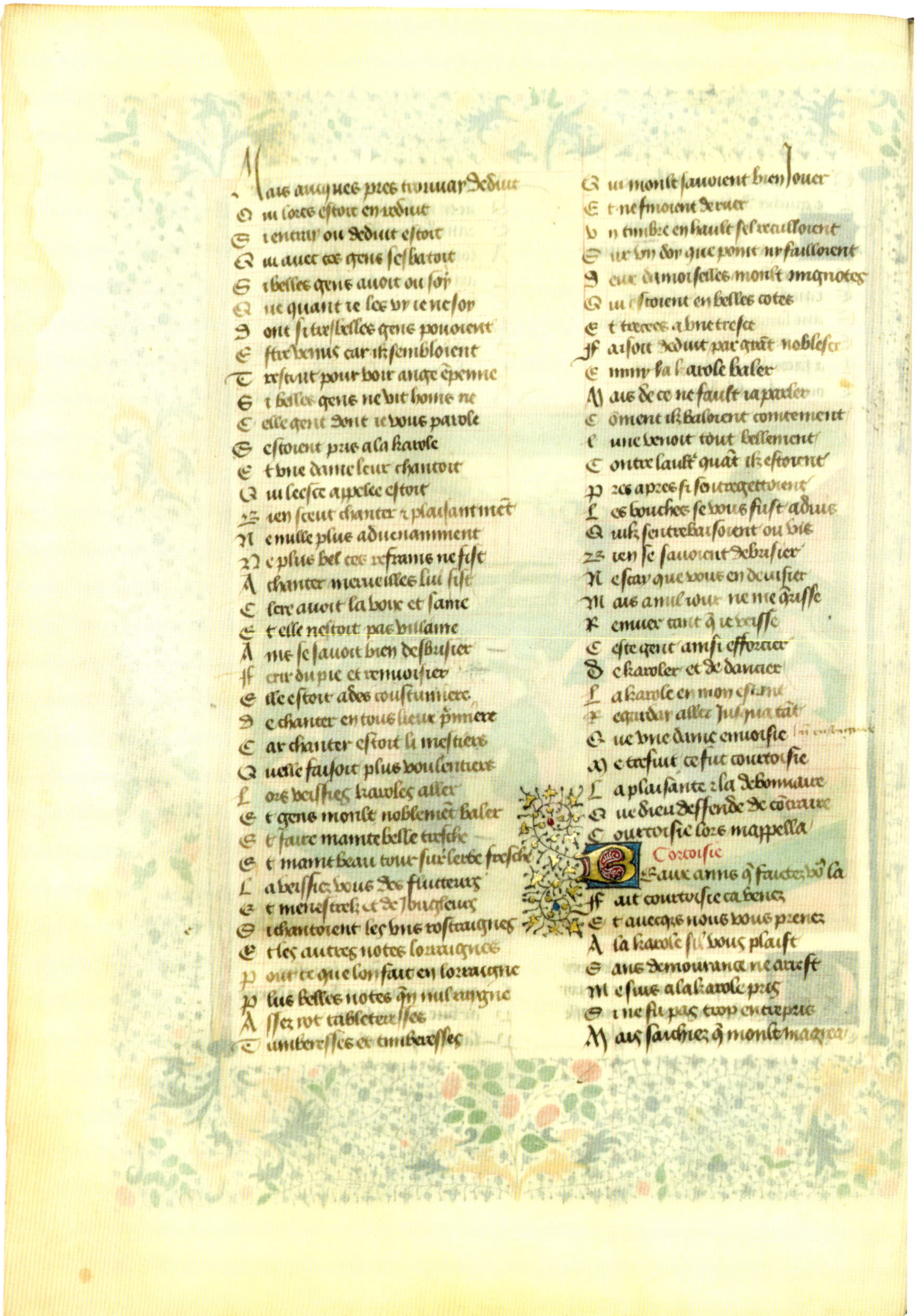

Figure 42.1: Paris, Bibliothèque nationale de France, MS Fr. 19153, fol. 7v. Photo © Bibliothèque nationale de France.

provided by the *fleüteors* and other minstrels, in turn, is echoed in the poem's closing comparison of wily seducers to *fleüsteürs* who captivate naïve maidens with their sweet words, and hunters who lure birds with the "douz sonez" (sweet trills) of false bird calls (21,436; 21,463—Morton 2018).

But the motif of the carol extends beyond the Dreamer's personal experience of seduction. The Golden Age described by Ami (Friend), for example, features simple, uncorrupted folk whose lives are given over to *jeu d'amors* (love-making), *jolivetez* (merriment), and *queroles* (carols) (8404; 8413; 8409), carried out in fields and groves replete with flowers and shaded by lush green trees: a rustic precursor to the artfully constructed Garden of Delight, with its exotic trees imported from the *terre Alixandrins* of the eastern Mediterranean (590-91), in which the dream narrative is set. If Ami's vision of primeval innocence already casts an ominous shadow of corruption and duplicity on the carol led by Deduit, this impression is only heightened when Ami conjures up a Jealous Husband, castigating his wife for spending too much time caroling, dancing, and singing like a Siren (8429-44): in his view, the carol is a scene of adulterous temptation and debauchery. Towards the end of the poem, Nature's priest Genius proffers his heterodox vision of a Heaven reserved for those who participate in procreative sexuality, explicitly constructed in opposition to the Garden of Delight. His sermon places the Elect in a celestial meadow, where they will spend eternity singing "motez, conduiz et chançonnetes, / par l'erbe vert, seur les floretes, / souz l'olivete querolant" (motets, conductus, and little songs, on the green grass, amidst the flowers, caroling beneath the olive tree—20,627-29): a far cry, Genius claims, from the temporal carolers of the Garden, doomed to death and decay (20,325-26) as they persist in their sterile subservience to a desire that is never consummated in sexual reproduction. The motif of the carol not only informs our understanding of the original pleasure-garden, but also provides the foundation for a series of reworkings by both poets, as they probe the mysteries of human sexuality and desire.

The carol is illustrated in the majority of the approximately 300 surviving manuscripts of the *Rose*, befitting its importance in setting up the love allegory to follow; but with considerable variation across manuscripts (see the *Roman de la Rose* digital library, romandelarose.org). Virtually all agree on a line of dancers, alternating men with women, and accompanied by one or more musicians. Some artists, however, choose one or more wind instruments—shawms, trumpets, bagpipes, pipe, and tabor—while others settle on lute, vielle, or harp. No doubt the choice of instruments accorded with contemporary practices familiar both to the artists and to their patrons. Occasionally the dancing girls at the heart of the carol are shown, but not often. The freedom with which artists executed an image of such importance to the overall iconography and tone of the allegorical text, indicates that the precise nature of the musical performance is far less important than the fact of there being one. Similarly, there is little or no effort by the illuminators to depict the dancers in accordance with the detailed descriptions provided in the text, and the current image is no exception. Rather than the richly jeweled belt that adorns Richece in the narrator's account, or the Oriental purple of Largesce's gown, we see clothing that reflects fashions contemporary with the manuscript itself. The fur trim on the men's robes, their pointy-toed shoes, and the elegant conical hats on the ladies with their swept up hair, are clear signs that this is an aristocratic elite: a gathering of such splendour that the Dreamer feels they seem no less than "angres empenez" (winged angels [723]).

The setting is equally variable, sometimes including the Dreamer in the act of joining the dance and sometimes depicting only the carolers. Occasionally they are placed on a kind of paved dance floor, perhaps even with a gallery for viewing by an audience; most often, they are on the lawn. Sometimes the rest of the Garden is visible around them. In this case, the carol takes place in a set-off area within the garden; one can see pathways under the trees, hinting at a more extensive landscaping that is not drawn in detail. We see no spectators or bystanders: to be within this verdant Garden of Delight is to take part in the dance that operates at its heart. The musicians stand on a turf-topped wall above the dancers, who are in a sunken area just large enough to accommodate them. The masonry surrounding the dance is the same as that of the outer wall, locating the carol in a walled space within a walled garden. The concentric frames of lush lawns in different shades of green, contrasting with the reddish brick or stone of the double set of walls, serve to focus attention on the carol, making it the vital centre of the Garden. The choreographed movements of these courtly ideals, like the inner workings of a music box or the verbal and metrical play of an intricate poem, express the values of amorous intrigue and aestheticized desire that underwrite the youthful initiation into love.

ADDITIONAL REFERENCES: Bagnoli 2016; Brownlee and Huot 1992; Dillon 2018; Huot 1993.

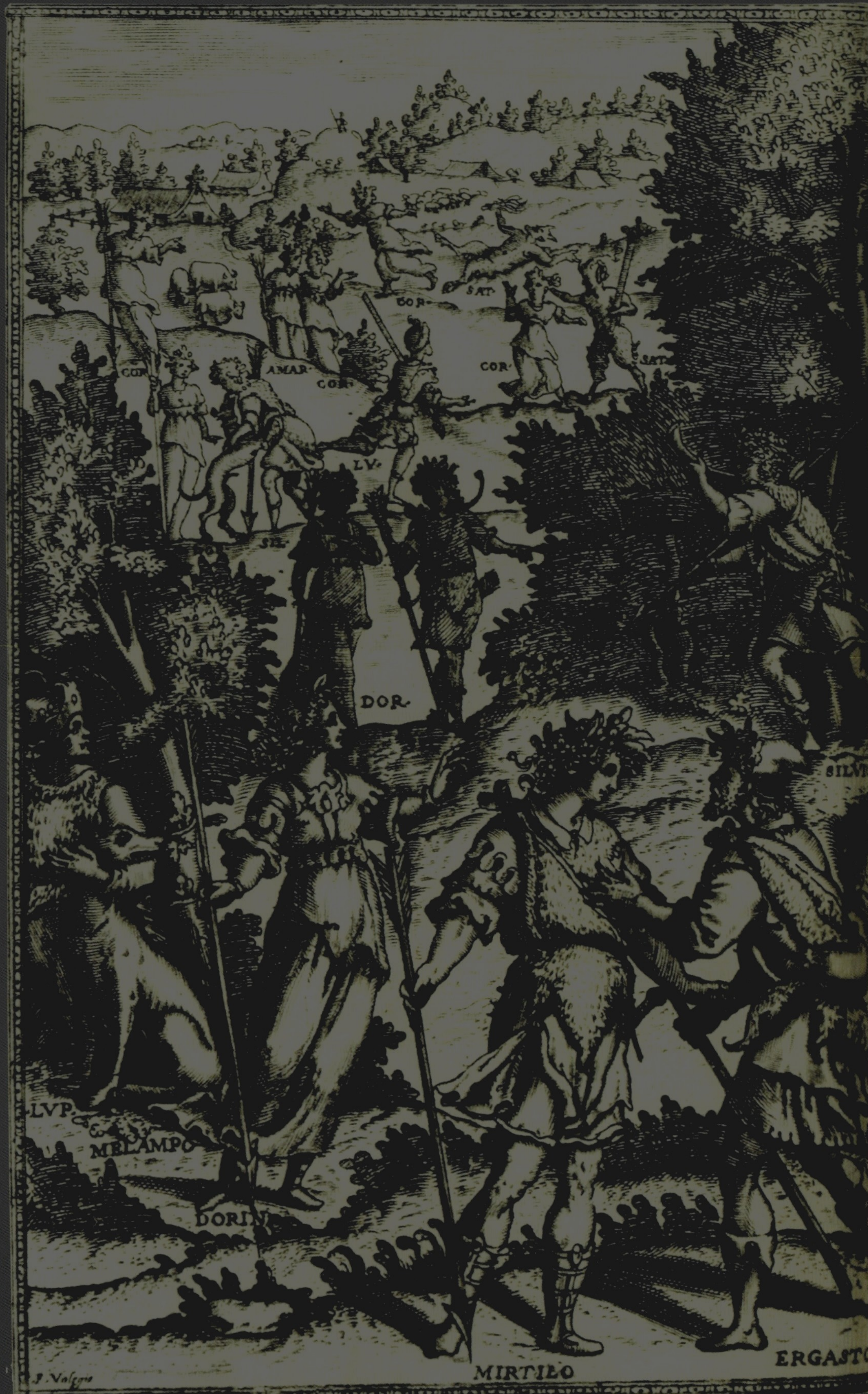
AMAR
COR
SAT
LV
DOR
LVP
MELAMPO
MIRTILO

43. Arcadia

Giuseppe Gerbino

Francesco Valesio [Valegio]
Engraving from Battista Guarini, *Il pastor fido: tragicommedia pastorale*
Venice: Giovanni Battista Ciotti, 1602
[30] + 488 + [10] + 64 pp.; 20 x 15 cm
Williamstown, Sterling and Francine Clark Art Institute Library, Julius S. Held Collection of Rare Books, N6915 G83, p. [74]
Photo: Public Domain

Battista Guarini's play *Il pastor fido, tragicommedia pastorale* (*The Faithful Shepherd, A Pastoral Tragicomedy*) was one of the most influential and controversial works of the late Renaissance. A heated polemic accompanied its gestation and publication, turning the vicissitudes and misfortunes of the inhabitants of Arcadia into the last great literary controversy of the sixteenth century. For Giason Denores, professor of Moral Philosophy at the University of Padua and Guarini's first and most severe critic, pastoral tragicomedy was a monstrous and disproportionate work (Denores 1586, fol. 38v). The trouble, as any literary theorist of the time knew well, was that the new pastoral drama forced together tragedy and comedy into an ambiguous amalgam, thus destroying the dual archetype of the representation of human behavior and fate inherited from Classical Antiquity. As for its pastoral setting, nothing of moral value could be gained from the unrealistic manners and amorous intrigues of shepherds and nymphs. Guarini offered a first defense of his play in 1588 (Guarini 1588). Denores counter-attacked in 1590 (Denores 1590). Guarini retaliated three years later (Guarini 1593). In the meantime, others joined the fight, and by 1613 supporters and detractors of *Il pastor fido* could count on no fewer than 11 new titles (Perella 1973). The turbulent popularity of Guarini's pastoral tragicomedy proved to be a boon for music. Hundreds of madrigals inspired by the play gradually flooded the music market. Some of Claudio Monteverdi's *Pastor fido* madrigals became the subject of a controversy of their own. Indeed, the history of secular music between the Renaissance and Baroque could in part be written along the lines of the pastoral vogue fueled by Guarini's provocative masterpiece.

The first edition of *Il pastor fido* appeared in December 1589. It went through several reprints before the publication of the definitive version by the Venetian printer Giovanni Battista Ciotti in 1602. The new edition marked a watershed in the defense and consecration of the so-called third genre of theater. Bound together with the *Compendio della poesia tragicomica*—Guarini's final word on the topic of tragicomedy—it included additional notes on the text by Guarini himself as well as six full-page illustrations by Francesco Valesio. The dedication to Duke Vincenzo Gonzaga linked the print to the lavish performance that took place in Mantua in 1598, with music by Giovanni Giacomo Gastoldi for the *Ballo della cieca*, a sung and danced choreography in Act 3. Technically, this was not the premiere, but it was certainly the most important full-scale production following a long series of failed attempts to stage the play, starting from the 1580s, both in Mantua and in other cities (Fenlon 1980, 149-61). The occasion—the visit of Queen Margaret of Austria, who had recently celebrated her marriage to Philip III of Spain by proxy in Ferrara—symbolically ended the controversy with the seal of approval of courtly taste and authority (Sampson 2003). Valesio's engravings accompanying the prologue and each of the five acts might offer a glimpse into the costumes and set designs of the 1598 Mantuan performance. With their labyrinthine perspective, they also stand as visual icons of the complex double-plot mechanism that miraculously lead to the just union of the two pairs of star-crossed lovers, Mirtillo and Amarilli, and Silvio and Dorinda, as well as the lifting of the punishment that the goddess Diana had imposed on Arcadia.

Theoretical justification within the Aristotelian canon and public recognition in the arena of court culture merged in the 1602 Ciotti edition. On closer inspection, this was not a mere strategic move on Guarini's part. At the core of his defense of pastoral drama was indeed the claim that the new theater represented the expression and ratification of a modern sensitivity, a modern way of understanding human nature that rejected the pagan desperation of the impenetrable abyss of tragedy in favor of a representation of love suffering redeemed by love and, in a perspective of social and religious cohesion, marriage. To paraphrase Guarini's Aristotelean argument, pastoral tragicomedy is tragic only in potency, but not in act. Love's agony, understood in Petrarchist terms, but only as a temporary plunge into emotional distress from the safe space of theatrical fiction, became the measure of this modern sense of the tragic. In a sense, *Il pastor fido* equated love suffering, but not the irreversible annihilation of the self, with the tragic spirit of the moderns. Somewhat paradoxically, the poetic and emotional eloquence of shepherds and nymphs, which the critics of the new genre regarded as ridiculously implausible, fulfilled the need to give dramatic voice to a typically Renaissance understanding of human desire in its natural state. Revising Aristotle's famous dictum on catharsis, for Guarini the end of the new pastoral tragicomedy was the purging of melancholy—the true malaise of his time—through the bittersweet pleasure engendered by the experience of a subtly orchestrated balance of negative and positive emotions (Guarini 1601, 22; Gerbino 2009, 378-99).

Guarini's psychology of tragic pleasure found natural expression in music. The passionate lyricism in dramatic garb of his *Pastor fido* infused the Petrarchist tradition of love poetry, which had shaped the affective palette of the musical madrigal, with new theatrical vividness. His reflection on the changed state of tragedy had an echo in early opera. The battleground of contrary emotions depicted in the speeches and laments of Mirtillo, Amarilli, Silvio, and Dorinda became the source of inspiration for some of the most experimental music of the late Renaissance. Musical adaptations of texts related to the play began to circulate during the second half of the 1580s, but the musical fortune of *Il pastor fido* took a sharp turn in the years 1594-95, when Luca Marenzio and Giaches de Wert, two giants of the musical madrigal, published an extensive selection of highlights from Guarini's pastoral drama. In 1594, Marenzio featured four settings in his sixth book for five voices. The following year, Wert, who had been involved in the preparations for a failed production of the play in Mantua in 1591-92, released four compositions in his eleventh book for five voices, including an impressive five-part madrigal on Mirtillo's soliloquy *O primavera, gioventù de l'anno*. The dedication to Francesco Gonzaga, the eldest son of Duke Vincenzo, is signed 18 August 1595. Within a few months, on 20 October 1595, Marenzio signed the dedication of his seventh book of five-voice madrigals to Don Diego de Campo, the private "cameriere" of Pope Clement VIII. With 12 texts drawn from *Il pastor fido* (including the madrigal *Deh, dolce anima mia* by the Florentine composer Antonio Bicci), the book seems to have been conceived as a monothematic collection. Marenzio turned again to the play in his eighth book for five voices of 1598. By 1600, composers such as Philippe de Monte began to publish madrigal books entirely devoted to *Il pastor fido*. Both Marenzio and Wert were associated with patrons who showed a nearly obsessive interest in Guarini's work. It is possible that their engagement with the play reflected private readings and discussions fostered in aristocratic and academic circles and, at least in Wert's case, through direct contact with Guarini.

Marenzio's settings exemplify the array of stylistic responses stirred by the encounter with Guarini's theater. They range from the tapestry of harsh and disorienting dissonances accompanying the dark emotional landscape of texts such as *Cruda Amarilli* or *Arda pur sempre o mora*, to the exploration of a supple but intense declamatory polyphony in the madrigals of his eighth book. Pushing the polyphonic language of Marenzio and Wert to new limits, the most controversial music born out of Guarini's controversial play is without doubt found in Monteverdi's fourth and fifth books of madrigals (1603 and 1605). In Ferrara, in the same days that saw the celebration of the marriage between Margaret of Austria and Philip III of Spain, the Bolognese canon Giovanni Maria Artusi launched his famous attack against Monteverdi from the house of Antonio Goretti, where he had an opportunity to hear some new compositions, just a few days before the Mantuan performance of Guarini's play. Two years later, three of Monteverdi's *Pastor fido* settings, *Cruda Amarilli*, *O Mirtillo*, and *Anima mia perdona*, were singled out for public reproach, without mentioning their composer, in Artusi's first dialogue on the imperfection of modern music of 1600 (Artusi 1600; Palisca 1994). In particular, *Cruda Amarilli* was criticised for what Artusi considered an incorrect treatment of dissonances, and *O Mirtillo* for an unorthodox admixture of musical modes (Ossi 2008; Coluzzi 2013). The Artusi-Monteverdi controversy, an iconic moment in the last season of the polyphonic madrigal, brought into focus issues and concerns that were to dominate the transition to the so-called Baroque period, including Monteverdi's influential definition of a "second musical practice" superseding the "prima practica" codified in the polyphony of the early sixteenth century. Scholars have pointed out the parallels between the Artusi-Monteverdi controversy and the Denores-Guarini controversy, especially their respective claims to modernity, as they have also noticed the convergence of the events surrounding the 1598 performance of the play (Tomlinson 1987). Although not every detail can be reconstructed with precision, it is clear that different literary and musical traditions, as well as social and political forces, uncannily merged into *Il pastor fido*, turning Guarini's pastoral tragicomedy into a catalyst for the avant-gardes of the late Renaissance.

ADDITIONAL REFERENCES: Chater 1997; Coluzzi 2014; Schneider 2008; Selmi 2001.

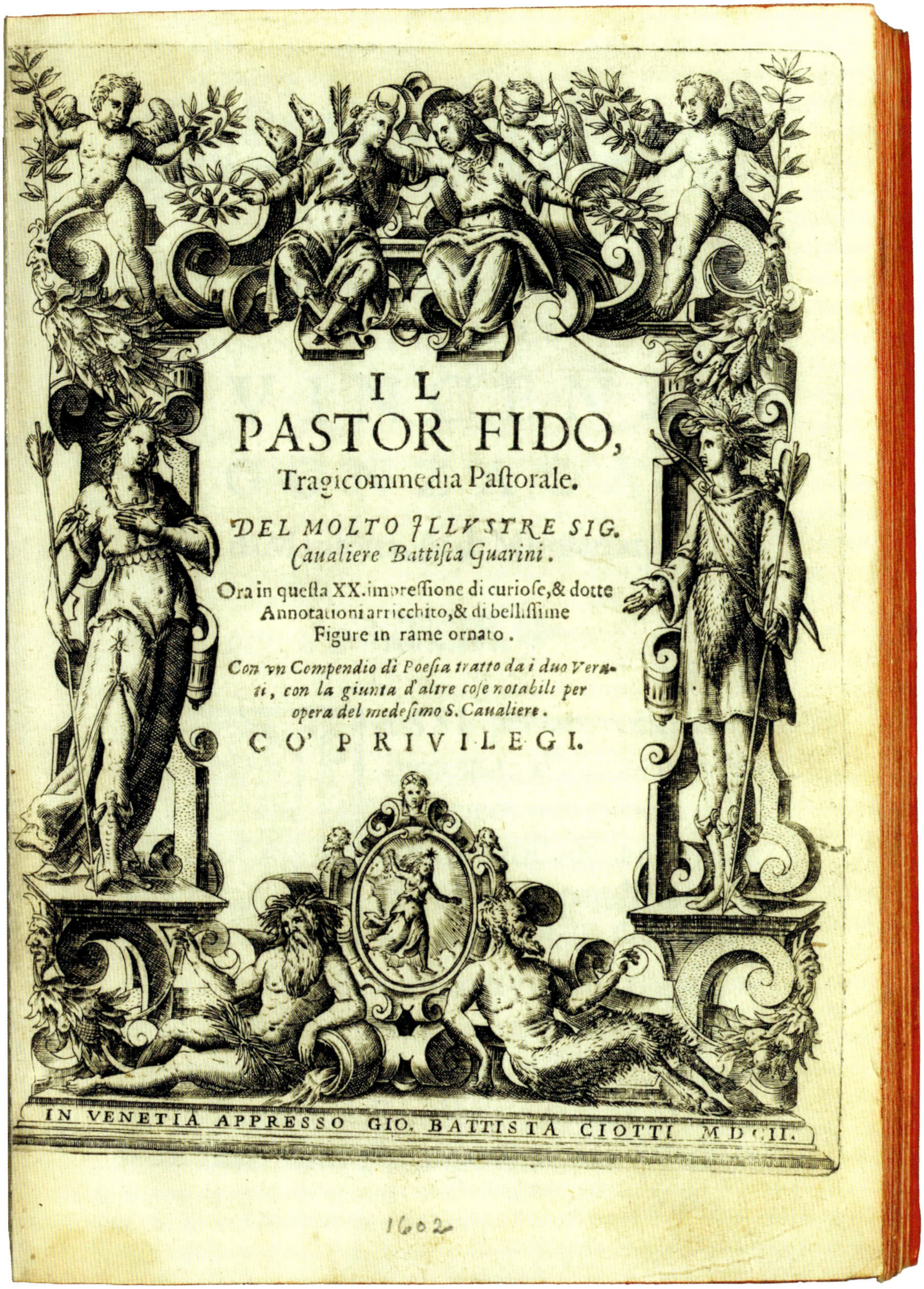

Figure 43.1: Battista Guarini, *Il pastor fido* (Venice: Ciotti, 1602), title page. Williamstown, Sterling and Francine Clark Art Institute Library, Julius S. Held Collection of Rare Books, N6915 G83. Photo: Public Domain.

DELPHICA
SIBYLLA
CVMANA
SIBYLLA

44. Heaven

Laura Ştefănescu

Assumption of the Virgin
Filippino Lippi, Rome, 1488-93
Fresco
Basilica of Santa Maria sopra Minerva, Rome
Photo © Luisa Ricciarini / Bridgeman Images

On 26 August 1488 the Florentine painter Filippino Lippi was travelling to Rome, carrying with him the heavy baggage of a rich visual culture. On Lorenzo de' Medici's request, as recorded by Giorgio Vasari (Vasari 1878-85, 3:467), he had abandoned work on Filippo Strozzi's funerary chapel in Santa Maria Novella in favour of Cardinal Oliviero Carafa and his demands for a final resting place. In exchange, Lorenzo's son, Giovanni, future Pope Leo X, would be made cardinal at a very young age (Geiger 1986, 48). In 1493 Filippino returned home, leaving behind a satisfied patron in his freshly-painted chapel, to contemplate, among other marvels, a heaven that shined, sang, danced, and smelled divine, a glimpse of a desired afterlife. Sitting in his chapel in Santa Maria sopra Minerva, the cardinal could lift his gaze above the altarpiece and see the Virgin's Assumption into paradise, a festive and joyful episode, and one which he hoped his soul would imitate once it had left his body behind to rest eternally in the adjacent burial chamber. These heavenly festivities delighted even papal eyes, such as those of Alexander VI who issued a papal bull for those worshipping in front of the sacred images (Geiger 1981, 62, 71).

Filippino had painted on the walls of Oliviero Carafa's Roman chapel a Florentine visual and musical spectacle that belonged as much to this world as to the next, an essential element of the Quattrocento imaginary. Several scholars have discussed the influences of Roman art upon Filippino's style (La Malfa 2005; Nelson 2011, 41), from the foreshortened angels of Melozzo da Forlì's frescoes in the basilica of Santi Apostoli (Berti 1991, 67), to the decorations of the Sistine chapel (Nelson 2004, 530). But alongside these Roman references Filippino's *Assumption* remains impregnated with elements of Florentine visual culture, and some consider that even after his encounter with Roman art Filippino stayed true to his native style (Neilson 1972, 79). In the fifteenth century there was an established tradition of Florentine painters working for Roman cardinals and popes (Geiger 1986, 47), a tradition continued by Carafa in this commission. Whether or not we accept the idea that the cardinal wanted a work specifically in the Florentine style (Berthier 1910, 152), his choice dictated by artistic preferences, it is clear that such motivations were accompanied by political considerations, as the insignia of the Medici are depicted next to those of Carafa, alluding to an alliance between the two families (Vitiello 2003, 57). The result, however, brought a glimpse of the Florentine heavenly choirs to the walls of a Roman chapel.

The Virgin's Assumption allowed for paradise to be represented to the eyes of devotees—a space frequently depicted in the art of the Quattrocento, particularly in its musical guise, appearing everywhere from private chapels to altarpieces, and even theatrical representations. Earlier debates about the impossibility of representing the invisible or the inaudible (Kessler 2000; Krüger 2017) were soon forgotten in favour of a luxurious sensorial experience, licensed by the use of the superior spiritual senses that belonged to Augustine's *homo interior* (Taylor 1989, 127-42; Cary 2000; Lootens 2011). If in the thirteenth century Umiltà da Faenza recognised the unsingable quality of angelic song, "sweet melodies which nobody else knows how to make" (Umiltà da Faenza 2005, 68), in 1504 the monk Celso Maffei wrote of a heaven in which the blessed were able to match the perfection of divine performers, because there the sense of hearing, just like all the other senses, would be "better than it was in the present life" (Maffei 1504, sig. A.IV^{v}).

This change from a paradise that was impossible to perceive to one characterised by an augmented sensory perception is specific to the heaven of the Quattrocento, a visual space markedly defined by an evocation of the five senses, sometimes in exaggerated forms. In Filippino's *Assumption* the angels hold torches that blind the eyes, they play on instruments that confound the ears, and even the small cherubs hidden in the cloud participate in the feast of the senses by swinging thuribles meant to dissipate their fragrance unto nearby nostrils. Whenever the viewer's perception is thus assaulted by sensory stimuli, one may be certain of having entered the realm of eternal delights.

In order to better understand Filippino's heavenly construction and the sound of an Italian fifteenth-century paradise we must travel back to Florence, where we find our painter absorbed in a very different commission, preparing performance materials for the religious festivities and mystery plays that were the pride of the city. Vasari wrote that at his funeral Filippino "was mourned by all those who had known him, and particularly by the youth of this noble city, which in public festivities, masquerades, and other spectacles always used, with great satisfaction, the ingenuity and creativity of Filippo, who had no equal in such things" (Vasari 1878-85, 3:476). Gail Geiger has observed the influence of Florentine *sacre rappresentazioni* on Filippino's *Assumption* (Geiger 1986, 155), an influence which becomes even more meaningful in light of his actual participation in the creation of these earthly enactments of heavenly space.

In the Carafa chapel, each angel sits on his own narrow cloud, identical to the wooden platforms covered in cotton, known as *nuvole*, on which the angels of Florentine sacred plays were suspended (Buccheri 2014, 51). The Virgin is placed on a sturdier construction, much larger in size, required not only by the importance of her figure, but also by the necessity to support the cherubic mandorla that surrounds her. Although in the painting the mandorla is apparently as light as smoke, in religious processions and festivals it must have weighed much more, revealing its solidity and earthly materiality. Florentine confraternities used to parade their patron saint, often the Virgin Mary, sitting on a *nuvola*, and surrounded by a mandorla, "all covered with cotton, and cherubim, and lights, and other ornaments," as described by Vasari in the life of Il Cecca (Vasari 1878-85, 3:200).

If the setting of the Virgin's *Assumption* is reminiscent of the scenography for *sacre rappresentazioni* to which Filippino apparently contributed, the sounds of his heaven must also derive from these theatrical productions. To understand the bizarre combination of musical instruments used in Quattrocento angelic concerts it is necessary to take into account the symbiotic relationship between painted heavens and those embodied in theatrical performances. If imagining paradise visually can be initiated by both arts, it is only on stage that the question of what heaven sounds like is concretely addressed. The musical heaven in the visual arts alludes to sound; one can imagine it, but perhaps not hear it distinctly. However, when a curious audience awaits bedazzlement by a theatrical earthly paradise with incarnated angels, the importance of creating sound that stretches the bounds of the human whilst remaining accessible to the available technical and musical resources becomes acute.

After enjoying the Annunciation festivities in Florence in 1439, Abraham, the Russian bishop of Suzdal and a participant in the Council of Florence, entered the church of Santa Maria del Carmine to witness the Ascension mystery play. As heaven opened up, he wrote of having seen "a throng of little children who represent angels with pipes and lutes and lots of tiny bells" (Newbigin 1996, 1:61-62). Abraham described what he heard as "deafening music and sweet singing" (Newbigin 1996, 1:61-62), concluding that the sight and sound of the Florentine heaven "is a wonderfully joyous spectacle that no man can describe" (Newbigin 1996, 1:6). In Filippino's *Assumption* the angels play all sorts of instruments, both real and invented, from what might be the earliest known accurate depiction of a trombone (McGee 2006-07, 6), to percussion instruments, as well as strings and winds (Geiger 1986, 152), exactly as in a *sacra rappresentazione*. To show the unimaginable performance of heavenly musicians, Filippino even has the angel in red on the left play a stringed instrument and a pipe simultaneously.

The combination of loud (wind) and soft (string) instruments belonged more to angelic ensembles than to Quattrocento human ones, and such a choice has puzzled scholars and provoked debate (Winternitz 1963, 458-59; McGee 1985, 75-76; Powers 2004, 54). According to the documentation provided by the staging of *sacre rappresentazioni* in Florence (Newbigin 1996, 1:82), the heaven of theatrical performances was accompanied by both *strumenti grossi* (brass and woodwind instruments) and *strumenti sottili* (string instruments). Therefore, the visual juxtaposition of contrasting instruments in painted heavenly ensembles may well derive from the creative solution devised by confraternities when confronted with the problem of angelic music. To materialise a music unheard on earth, all types of musical instruments were required, creating the "deafening," unimaginable sound of the fifteenth-century Italian heaven described by Abraham of Suzdal. The Florentine festivities were the pride of the city, in which all were involved and for which all confraternities laboured. As a Florentine, Filippino most likely had seen and heard these human attempts at singing like the angels, the performers lifted up on solid, wooden clouds. If Cardinal Carafa might not have had the opportunity to hear the sounds of the Florentine theatrical heaven, Filippino brought the marvellous spectacle with him to Rome and imprinted it on the walls of his chapel.

The animated poses, fluttering drapery, and circular arrangement of the angelic figures also make reference to another Florentine theatrical marvel, designed by Filippo Brunelleschi for the Annunciation *festa* in San Felice in Piazza, namely the round-dance of the angels (Meyer-Baer 1970, 130-88; Olson 1981). The heavenly figures, through their peculiar music-making and unusual dancing, point to the theatrical origins of the Quattrocento iconography of paradise as a space defined by sensory references and constructed particularly as a musical realm. The importance of processions, *feste*, and *sacre rappresentazioni* for the life of the city transforms theatrical productions into a religious visual language that permeates the art of the time.

Filippino, just like other contemporary painters who worked as scenographers, depicts heaven in the manner in which the Florentines had imagined it. This distinctive and luxurious idea of heaven, developed in religious theatrical productions, was the product of Florentine lay society, organised into confraternities which were responsible for these spectacles. The particular circumstances of devotional culture in fifteenth-century Florence, which allotted to the laity an exceptional role in leading the religious life of the city, gave to religious art unprecedented tonalities. Although the decoration of Cardinal Oliviero Carafa's chapel was filled with references to church doctrine, the musical heaven toward which Filippino's Virgin is carried was a lay invention, echoing festivities staged on the streets of Florence.

The juxtaposition of the Assumption fresco above an altarpiece of the Annunciation is uncommon in the art of the time (Geiger 1986, 150). Perhaps it occurred because of the value of integrating a heavenly scene into the decoration of a burial chapel, as a reminder of the afterlife. Fifteenth-century Italians were drawn towards the heavens, embodied either by fortune-giving stars, ancient gods, or angelic musicians. The afterlife was a continuous presence, and was not only for the church to define and imagine. The whole of society contributed, through its rituals and the images they generated, to the creation and popularity of a heaven suited to its concerns and aspirations. Filippino's musical angels, which Oliviero Carafa hoped would greet and carry aloft his soul after death, offer testimony to the importance of this space in the religious life of Quattrocento Italy, and to a cultural product created by a lay society thirsty for an enhanced sensory perception of heavenly delight.

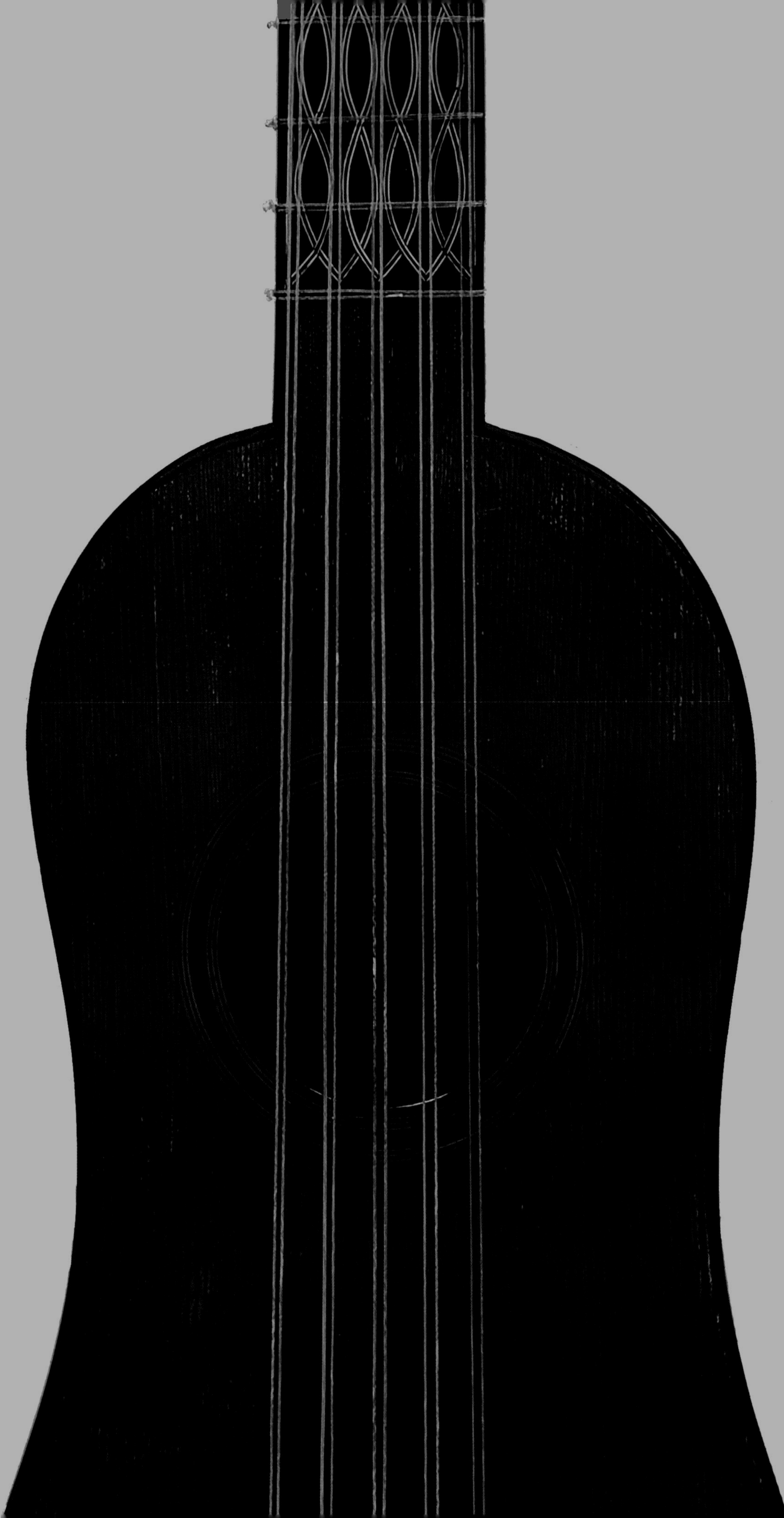

IV

Instruments

The Room of Instruments

Emanuela Vai

The instruments represented in this room, each in their own way, provide valuable windows onto the social, cultural, and material worlds of Renaissance music. Virginals, bagpipes, trumpets, and horns are just some of the instruments that the reader will encounter in this curated collection. These instruments appear in myriad forms and media: as material musical objects; as items listed in inventories; as images in paintings, hanging scrolls, printed texts, and woodcuts. The accompanying essays draw on approaches from across disciplinary fields, showcasing the potential of musical instruments as generative sites for cross-disciplinary dialogue, where multiple perspectives can meet to deepen and diversify our understandings of Renaissance musical cultures. This short introduction presents some overlapping themes that the objects collected here bring into view. The aim is not to anchor these heterogenous objects in any kind of totalising narrative, but to explore and examine the resonances that the reader might encounter as they navigate the room.

Despite their current stillness—both in their respective museums, galleries, and archives, and as images on these printed pages—each entry in this room draws our attention to musical instruments as lively, moving objects. Purchased, inherited, and traded on international networks, instruments were entangled in the flows of commerce and can shed light on the back-and-forth of cultural transmission. David R.M. Irving's analysis of a Japanese hanging scroll featuring a woman playing a *vihuela da mano* reveals instruments as rich sites of intercultural contact (*Lady Playing Vihiela da Mano*). Music-making was an essential part of European missions in Japan, and representations of European instruments in Japanese artworks provide unique platforms for discussions of cultural hegemony and hybridity. In Kate van Orden's study of Danish printmaker Melchior Lorck's woodcut we see that instruments from non-European contexts also circulated within Renaissance Europe's spheres of print-making and picturing (*Kös*). Another example of the geographical and cultural circulation of musical instruments comes in the form of the double virginals discussed by Moritz Kelber, which made its way from the Low Countries to Peru and, eventually, to the Metropolitan Museum of Art in New York City (*Double Virginals*). Amidst imperatives to decolonise Renaissance studies, by "following" musical instruments as they moved through the world in their various material and symbolic forms, we can expand our understandings of the distribution and circulation of Renaissance music in global contexts.

Perhaps more than anything, the objects included in this room remind us that musical instruments are infused with social meanings. Musical instruments materially articulate class structures, social status, gender inequalities, and shifting aesthetic values. John Thompson's analysis of Thomas Fella's bagpiper drawing, for example, highlights the many symbolic associations that were attached to the bagpipe in early modernity (*Bagpipes*). The Renaissance period saw innovations in technology, knowledge production, and labour and artisanal practices. This led to growth in the production of musical instruments, making them more widely available to a broader social stratum of amateurs, collectors, and enthusiasts. The domestic sphere emerged as a new social and spatial context for music-making and consumption, with musical instruments appearing as household objects in inventories, as Emily Peppers' essay shows. Peppers' analysis illustrates how historical documents, such as notary records, can provide us with a glimpse into the presence of music in private homes, even if such records do not speak to the enjoyment, entertainment, or companionship these instruments provided (*Inventory after the Death of Madame Montcuyt*). Visual representations of instruments can shed valuable light on the everyday social lives and spatial contexts of Renaissance music-making cultures and practices. As instruments entered the home, they became signs of affluence but they were also highly gendered objects. The gendering of musical instruments is present in a number of the essays collected here, but is perhaps most clearly demonstrated in Laura Ventura Nieto's exploration of the role that the virginals played within the private musical lives of "well-bred" young women (*Girl Playing the Virginals*).

In a growing culture of leisure and consumption, musical instruments emerged as luxury goods. They were aesthetic objects and artworks, evaluated according to changing tastes and fashions, as well as the scientific principles of geometry, proportion, and harmony. This is something that John Griffiths explores here in his essay on a Portuguese *vihuela*/guitar from the late sixteenth century, the craftsmanship of which, he notes "would satisfy both the eye, ear, and mind in the most discerning Renaissance musician." Here Griffiths draws our attention to the multi-sensorial dimensions of musical instruments, which were valued for their visual and physical appearance as well as acoustic performance (*Vihuela*). Indeed, musical instruments were not purely sounding objects to be played, but also things to be dis-played in a variety of viewing contexts, from cabinets of curiosity to their depiction in paintings. We therefore cannot detach these instruments from the Renaissance period's traditions of collecting and the particular modes of looking, classifying, cataloguing, representing, and displaying in which they were embedded. Martin Kirnbauer's analysis of Archduke Ferdinand II of Tyrol's collection at the castle of Ambras illustrates the ornamental value with which musical instruments were endowed, and reminds us that instruments were investments and status symbols. Many of the instruments that survive from the Renaissance period are those that were collected by wealthy elites, but Kirnbauer's exploration of this horn, which perhaps once belonged to shepherds or herdsmen, is suggestive of the windows that instruments can open onto the worlds of Renaissance music at lower social levels (*Horn from Allgäu*).

By bringing together objects that would otherwise be studied separately (paintings, hand scrolls, inventories, drawings, and physical musical instruments), this room offers a heterogeneous space within which to explore the resonance of musical instruments as points of entry for historical enquiry. The essays here engage with the objecthood and material culture of music from a variety of perspectives and provide a contextual richness that highlights the more-than-musical capacities of instruments, including their social, biographical, visual, and material dynamics. Taken together, the musical instruments represented in this room build up a picture of the complex and multifaceted lives of these objects as multi-sensory material goods and as symbolic forms. Musical instruments are by no means static, inert objects. Rather, they epitomise the conjunction of materials, embodied and technical expertise, social structures, cultural meanings, aesthetics, and economic investments. As such, they are ideal objects through which we can enrich our thinking about Renaissance music.

45. Lady Playing the Vihuela da Mano

David R.M. Irving

Fujo-dankin zu
Nobukata(?), Nagasaki, ca. 1600
Hanging scroll, 55.5 x 37.3 cm
Yamato Bunkakan, Nara
Photo courtesy of the Museum Yamato Bunkakan

In several late Renaissance-era paintings from the Land of the Rising Sun, angels and humans are depicted making delicate sounds on plucked string instruments. Most of these artworks are landscapes that display stereotypical vistas of idealised European views. They were produced in the art schools attached to schools and seminaries established by the Society of Jesus in Japan during the second half of the sixteenth century. In these institutions, the arts of Europe—painting, instrumental and vocal music, drama, literature—were taught by Jesuit missionaries as part of their broader objective to introduce Christianity to Japan. Roman Catholicism was the fastest-growing religion in Japan in the last decades of the sixteenth century, with an estimated 200 churches and 150,000 converts by 1580 (Boxer 1951, 114). Music was an essential part of liturgical rituals and devotional practices, as well as a demonstration of cultural life in Europe. Jesuit music teachers taught vocal plainchant and polyphony, and the playing of European instruments such as lute, viola da gamba, organ, clavichord, shawm, and *vihuela* (Harich-Schneider 1973a, 474-75; Kambe 2000; Woodfield 1995, 184). Members of other missionary orders, especially the Franciscans, also taught music.

Japanese paintings with musical instruments form the backdrop of a remarkable period of deep intercultural fascination between Japanese and European nations in the second half of the sixteenth century. The first known arrival of any European visitor to Japan was documented in 1543; in 1549 Francis Xavier landed, and it was at this point that the Jesuit mission began. Music was an essential part of the mission (Waterhouse 1997; Bloechl 2019). Within the space of just a few decades, Japanese and Europeans arguably matched each other's levels of xenophilic interest in their respective cultures (Boxer 1951). Missionaries used European arts to attract the interest and attention of the Japanese population, and Japanese rulers and subjects responded with curiosity to the unknown cultural practices and objects brought by the Portuguese traders and the missionary orders (Takao 2019). Europeans demonstrated their desire for access to the wealth in trade and Japanese arts (especially lacquering, known as "japanning"). When missionaries began to teach the arts of Europe to Japanese converts and students, they used the results of these labours to demonstrate to religious authorities in Europe the success of their mission. Four Japanese youths who were skilful musicians travelled to Europe in the 1580s as part of a Jesuit delegation organised to advocate for the mission in Japan (Harich-Schneider 1973b; Minamino 1997; see exhibit 78). They played keyboard, viol, lute, and rebec, as well as being proficient singers, and it is likely that they were able to perform on a range of related instruments, including *vihuela* (Waterhouse 1997, 360-64).

The visual arts were an important part of the mission to Japan. As Hiroyuki Minamino has discussed in a study of Japanese paintings with musical instruments, the Jesuits relied on visual imagery to explain and teach their religious doctrines. Although they imported many paintings at the beginning of the mission, local production was soon initiated due to the number of paintings required, and around 20 Japanese painters ("dogicos pintores") were active in this area by ca. 1600 (Minamino 1999, 44). Artworks featuring non-religious or secular scenes were also produced, presumably for aesthetic pleasure and appreciation, and many of these include depictions of musical instruments. This painting on a hanging scroll of a Japanese lady playing a European string instrument, attributed to a painter signed as Nobukata (dates unknown), is one of the most intriguing and arresting images of cultural exchange, adoption, and absorption. It is a rare glimpse of the transculturalism in musical practices that flourished in Japan at the time (see Takao 2019). The physiognomy of the player appears more Japanese than European, and her posture and physical gestures frozen in paint suggest a certain sprezzatura or effortlessness in performance. Two other paintings include a lady with a similar posture playing what seems to be an identical instrument, whereas other paintings show a lady in a similar posture playing a lute with a round body (van Ooijen 2011); it is possible that Nobukata's painting is modelled on one of these, or on a lost original. The instrument itself is a *vihuela da mano* with nine strings (four double-strung courses and one single-strung course), and Minamino has speculated on the possibility of this iconographic representation displaying a hybrid instrument formed of structural characteristics drawn from several different types of *vihuela da mano* (Minamino 1999, 47-48).

The *Fujo-dankin zu* is one of the best-known visual icons of cross-cultural musical currents in sixteenth-century Japan. But if this painting is simply a copy of another artwork, is it at best an imagined or idealised representation of what such artworks represented? Or does it reflect some reality of the conditions of musical exchange and hybridity in late sixteenth-century Japan? Yoriko Kobayashi-Sato observes that "most of these paintings were mere copies of the Western models," but qualifies that "there existed some exceptions … executed by a painter who signed some paintings as "Nobukata." He splendidly mixed the Japanese and Western manners and created an original style" (Kobayashi-Sato 2010, 164).

We could speculatively ask: what kind of music might the painter have imagined emanating from this player and instrument? Could it have been a European piece typical of the period, or a Japanese melody? Alternatively, could it have been a Japanese melody adapted to European tastes, or would it have reflected the typical kinds of vocal pieces sung by players of the Japanese *biwa* (fretted lute), including recent Christian converts (see Takao 2019, 188-94)? Significantly, the absence of a landscape background behind the player (which is present in the other representations of this instrumentalist) seems to indicate the recontextualisation or at least the intended neutrality of presentation, thereby implying acceptance or absorption of a foreign inspiration into the Japanese host culture. A comparable example can be observed in Mughal India, a couple of decades later, where the focal figure from an original Flemish painting is reproduced against a neutral or void background: King David with a harp, painted by Manohar in 1610-20 (Welch 1987, 65). In that painting the depicted figure (revered as a prophet in Islam) was embraced fully as a constituent element of familiar culture, even though the instrument with which he is shown was organologically different from local chordophones. In similar terms, Nobukata's painting of a lady playing a string instrument (albeit an instrument exotic to Japan) could theoretically have been accepted within Japanese culture as a recognisable form of visual expression of a female performer.

It is important not to underestimate the symbolic power of analogous practices being recognised and considered in parallel in contexts of intercultural encounter in the early modern world. When lutes and *vihuelas* were first introduced to Japan, local musicians would likely have compared this new instrumentarium to the Japanese *biwa*, and other chordophones. Although European instruments were clearly different, they were not considered irrevocably incommensurable, as can be seen in the tendency to compare and contrast them. The fascination with differences or similarities between Japanese and European cultures is borne out in a 1585 treatise on the customs of Japan, by Jesuit Luis Fróis, which mentions singing, instrumental music, and dancing, among other practices (Fróis and Schütte 1955). The often playful, but sometimes disparaging, treatments of cultural difference in this treatise of comparative ethnography seem to point to a desire for identifying cultural parity, or at least a thirst for knowledge about cultural difference.

Fróis states: "Our violas [plucked string instruments] have six strings, besides the double courses, and are played with the hand; those of Japan [have] four, and are played with a kind of comb [plectrum]" (Fróis and Schütte 1955, 246). He also points out the different social roles of string instruments: "Amongst us, noble people pride themselves in playing violas [this could imply plucked instruments as much as bowed viols]; in Japan it is the occupation of the blind, just like the players of hurdy-gurdies in Europe" (Fróis and Schütte 1955, 246). This last observation highlights intercultural contrasts in the social symbolism of a person's talent for instrumental practice. Thus the presence of paintings that depicted skill in playing a lute or *vihuela* as the lofty and exalted cultural practice of the higher echelons of European society was in direct contrast to the social status of players of plucked string instruments in Japanese society of the time. Significantly, some of the blind Japanese *biwa* players became key to the dissemination of religious doctrine in the early days of the Jesuit mission (Ruiz-de-Medina 2003; Takao 2019, 190-94).

From the late 1590s, the practice of Christianity was periodically banned in various regions of Japan. A few decades later, the complete suppression of the religion and the closure of Japan to all outsiders (except the Dutch) in 1639 resulted in the almost complete disappearance of European musical practices from the country. Besides bringing its own theological framework, the introduction of Christianity was seen by some Japanese rulers to imply changes in social perspectives, political philosophy, and cultural practices. The music introduced by Catholic European missionaries in Japan was considered inherently linked to their evangelistic endeavours; it was viewed as both an outward symbol of cultural and religious hegemony, and an expressive practice that could have internal power over one's emotions. Thus it could not be extricated or considered separately from the cultural system that had introduced it, and was considered complicit in the potential hegemonic intentions of the Portuguese and other European nations. A few Dutch musical practices in the quarantined trading factory of Deshima in the bay of Nagasaki became known to the Japanese population during the period of *sakoku* (the virtual closure of

Japan to outsiders between 1639 and 1853), but they had relatively little wider impact. Thus the iconographical and documentary relics of European music in Japan from the 1550s to ca. 1640 are today endowed with a considerable level of symbolic value, and viewed with great historical curiosity for their demonstration of a unique set of conditions for long-distance cultural exchange in the late Renaissance era.

Given that remnants of art and culture from the so-called Christian century in Japan are rare, how did this painting survive? Was it rolled up and secreted in a bamboo tube, and hidden when the purges of Portuguese cultural influence took place? Or was it taken out of Japan and then returned? Some objects relating to Portuguese influence survived in exile, or were represented or included in European reminiscences of this period of cultural exchange, while performed practices of liturgical and devotional chant went underground. In the "crypto-Christian" or "hidden Christian" (*kakure Kirishitan*) communities of Ikitsuki, fragments of Gregorian chant are incorporated within syncretic chants that blend elements of Christian, Buddhist, and Shinto practices (Minagawa 1990). The instrumental practices of Europe that were introduced to Japan in the late sixteenth century certainly fell out of use, and the *vihuela* later fell out of use around the world until its revival in the early twentieth century. Today Japan is a prominent centre for the early music movement, which has swept around the world, and it is important to acknowledge that for more than half a century in the late Renaissance many Japanese musicians were enthusiastic participants in the study and performance of the musical arts of Europe, which they adopted as their own. Nobukata's intriguing and beautiful painting of a Japanese lady playing a *vihuela da mano* in ca. 1600, painted in a style that bridges European and Japanese aesthetic conventions, is a poignant and telling reminder that Renaissance music was as international and heterogeneous a phenomenon in its own times as it is now.

46. Double Virginals

Moritz Kelber

Hans Ruckers the Elder, Antwerp, 1581
Pine, beech, poplar, mahogany, paint, gesso, metal, parchment, and brass; 182.2 (width) x 49.5 (depth) cm
Inscribed: HANS RVEKERS ME FECIT 1581
The Metropolitan Museum, New York
Photo © CC0

From the sixteenth century to modern times stringed keyboard instruments have remained a central element of private musical life. Starting from the late Middle Ages, various designs of European keyboard instruments entered circulation, carrying many different names. Because of the complex contexts of its use, the virginals is among the most interesting keyboard instruments of the pre-modern period. The term "virginals" usually describes a basic instrument in rectangular form with a single string per note. Like all instruments from the harpsichord family, the virginals generates its sound with small plectra mounted on jacks. Thus, its sound is very similar to that of a plucked string instrument like a lute or a cittern.

The origins of the term "virginals" remain a mystery. One peculiarly interesting theory links the term to the word "virgin" or to the Virgin Mary in particular. According to this hypothesis, "virginals" is used to refer to the gender of the instrument's players and to the purity and nobility of its sound.

Indeed, the virginals has been seen as a female instrument (Busch-Salmen 2000, 42). A great number of sixteenth- and especially seventeenth-century portraits show young women sitting at an object that looks exactly like a virginals. The most prominent of these are by Johannes Vermeer. Two of his iconic paintings—*Lady standing at a Virginals* and *Young Woman Seated at a Virginals*—are today kept in the National Gallery in London (see fig. 46.1). Both works date from around 1670 and not only show female musicians: they reflect on the sexuality of music-making itself by showing a cupid or an intimate musical scene on a painting in the background. Learning to play a keyboard instrument was a key component in the basic education of aristocratic and bourgeois women. In *The Book of the Courtier* Baldassare Castiglione emphasised the importance of music education for all courtiers, women and men alike. However, according to Castiglione, women should be more reserved than men when making music in public, and they should carefully choose their musical instruments, avoiding drums and wind instruments (Haar 1983, 177). Thus, the soft, lute-like tone of the virginals might have been seen to represent late medieval and early modern female virtues of silence, obedience, and chastity. The latter is also expressed in the modest posture of a person playing a virginals.

The sixteenth century was a time of technological experiments: in different parts of Europe instrument makers, watchmakers, gold and silversmiths collaborated in creating a variety of different automatons and musical instruments—from organs to stringed keyboard instruments (see exhibit 17).

Figure 46.1: Jan Vermeer, *A Young Woman Standing at a Virginal*, 1670-1672. Oil on canvas, 51.7 x 45.2 cm. National Gallery, London. Photo © National Gallery, London / Bridgeman Images.

Figure 46.2: Italian, *Rebecchino*, 15th c. 37.5 x 9 x 6.5 cm. Kunsthistorisches Museum, Vienna. Photo © KHM Museumsverband.

Among technological enhancements affecting our exhibit is the so-called double virginals, produced most commonly in Flanders. A handful of these instruments from the sixteenth century survive in their original form, among them this beautifully decorated instrument made by Hans Ruckers in Antwerp in 1581. One of the earliest known Flemish keyboards of its kind, this virginals has been kept at the Metropolitan Museum of Art in New York City since 1929.

Double virginals are two-in-one instruments: hidden in a compartment within the body of the main virginals is a second, smaller one which can be played independently. Contemporaries named the larger instrument "mother" and the smaller "child." The gap of an octave in the tuning of mother and child may have been a motivation for this metaphorical nomenclature. More evidently, however, the design of the instrument could have had a role, since the smaller virginals can be completely extracted from the larger one, thus anthropomorphically resembling a child emerging from its mother's womb. This design enables a special feature: the two instruments can be coupled by placing the child on top of the mother. In this way, each jack of the larger virginals moves one of the smaller, creating two simultaneous sounds at the interval of an octave.

The analogy between human and machine, between musical instruments and living beings was deeply rooted in medieval and early modern thought. It can be traced from early examples of organ building right through to seventeenth-century philosophy (Kelber 2019). String instruments in the form of female bodies, or wind instruments shaped like dragons, were kept in late-medieval and early modern art collections (as was the fifteenth-century Italian *rebecchino* in fig. 46.2). In the introduction to Thomas Hobbes' *Leviathan*—one of the fundamental works of political philosophy from its publication in 1651—this analogy is vividly conceptualised in the description of a mechanical body of state:

> why may we not say, that all Automata (Engines that move themselves by springs and wheeles as doth a watch) have an artificiall life? For what is the Heart, but a Spring; and Nerves, but so many Strings; and the Ioynts, but so many Wheeles, giving motion to the whole Body, such as was intended by the Artificer? Art goes yet further, imitating that rationall and most excellent worke of Nature, Man. For by Art is created that great Leviathan called a Commonwealth, or State, (in latine Civitas) which is but an Artificiall Man (Hobbes 2004, xxxvii).

To illustrate his idea of the state as a body, Hobbes uses the example of automata, which were extremely popular all over Europe from the late sixteenth century. According to the philosopher, man and machine work in similar ways: the heart of a human is nothing other than the spring of an automaton. Although Hobbes is not explicitly referring to instrument-making, he outlines the philosophical backdrop to instruments like our Hans Ruckers virginals. In light of his comments, anthropomorphic musical instruments may even be seen as early attempts to create forms of artificial life.

Unlike similar instruments from late sixteenth-century Antwerp, which were decorated with printed ornamentation, Ruckers' double virginals was elaborately decorated by hand (Pollens 1997, 87). The centrepiece is the painting on the inside of the soundboard. Such paintings were common for all kinds of keyboard instruments, but this instance is of exceptional artistic quality. It shows a garden party in the park of a country château. On the left hand side courtiers in late sixteenth-century clothing arrive by boat to dine in an arcade, to dance to the music of a small group of pipers, or to play a game that resembles golf. The most evident characteristic of the painting is the omnipresence of music and musicians, with a particularly large number of string instruments, which might be seen to correspond to the sound of the virginals itself. In the centre of the painting one can see a couple sitting at a table inside the arcade. Interestingly here a woman plays the lute: this detail might be read as a reference to the assumed gender of the instrument itself and of its sound.

On the virginals' dropboard one can read the Latin motto "MVSICA. DVLCE. LABORVM. LEVAMEN" (Sweet music eases work). This short phrase explicitly addresses the person playing the instrument. She or he is evidently not a professional musician. For the player, music making is not a profession but a relief from labour. Other decorative elements include two gilded medallions on the front board of the larger instrument. They are copies of popular examples showing Anne of Austria and her husband King Philip II of Spain. This has been interpreted by various scholars as an indication that the object may have been a presentation piece given by the king of Spain to a member of the nobility (Pollens 1997, 87; Pollens 1998, 138; Moore et. al. 2015, 58). The visual presence of Philip and his wife adds another dimension to the "double" quality of the virginals. The two paired instruments not only represent the mother-child dualism but also the marital harmony of a man and a woman, with the octave coupling as a parallel to the difference between female and male voices.

In its more than 400 years of existence, Hans Ruckers' New York virginals has had a rather turbulent history (S. G. B. 1916). In 1916 it was discovered in Peru in the chapel of a country mansion near Cuzco which once belonged to the marquises of Oropesa. In 1929 the Metropolitan Museum acquired the instrument, which was at the time somewhat damaged, although the decoration and the mechanism were still intact, unusually for keyboard instruments of that period. It is not known how the virginals came to Peru in the first place. Interestingly, the use of wood from South America for some parts of the instrument indicates that it had been repaired there at least once—a task that required significant craftsmanship (Pollens 1997, 90). Although we do not know how Ruckers' virginals travelled to the New World it is likely that it arrived there during the early modern period. Perhaps it was a gift from the Spanish royal family to ambassadors or emissaries in the Spanish colony. Virginals seem like the perfect instruments for travelling: their small rectangular shape—usually they were built without legs—made them very easy to transport on coaches or on ships. Furthermore, their soft tone made them perfect for playing music in confined spaces.

Hans Ruckers' New York virginals affords insights into various important aspects of early modern music history which have been underrepresented in traditional musicological scholarship. It documents a more private musical life beyond the large courtly and urban institutions in which female musicians played an important role. It is a product of a time of technological endeavour—when builders of musical instruments started to experiment with all kinds of new designs. And it opens our eyes to the mobility and the wide horizons of European music in the age of early colonialism.

ADDITIONAL REFERENCES: Fenlon 2005; O'Brien 1990; Vandervellen 2017.

47. Horn from Allgäu

Martin Kirnbauer

Southern Germany, end of 16th century
Pinewood, covered with birchbark; 52 cm (overall length), 5.5 cm (diameter bell)
Kunsthistorisches Museum, Vienna
Photo © KHM-Museumsverband

In the world-famous collection of Renaissance musical instruments housed today in the Hofburg in Vienna one might be surprised to discover a rather plain-looking wooden object: a tightly-wound cylindrical tube, with a straight mouthpipe at one end, and a slightly flaring bell at the other. The mouthpiece is not detachable, because it has been turned out of the wood at the top end of the mouthpipe. The diameter of the coiled tube is about 30 cm, but uncoiled its length would measure an impressive three meters; along most of its length it is wrapped in birchbark. At first sight this curiously-shaped instrument made of simple pinewood looks strange in comparison to the other, more richly finished objects in the same collection, such as the engraved silver trumpet with gold-plated fittings by Anton Schnitzer (Nuremberg, 1581), or the highly-decorated cittern by Girolamo de Virchi from 1574, one of the most precious musical instruments preserved from the sixteenth century. Strangely enough, however, these apparently incongruous objects all share the very same provenance: the collection of Archduke Ferdinand II of Tyrol at the castle of Ambras, sometimes called "the oldest museum in the world."

This epithet points to the vast collection of weapons, books, paintings and many other objects, which Archduke Ferdinand II collected during his lifetime, and finally displayed in specially-designed buildings at the summer castle of Ambras near his residence in Innsbruck. This place and its collections became an attraction for foreign travellers (such as Michel de Montaigne, who however failed to gain admission owing to his French nationality), with guided tours arranged for paying visitors. There were other similar collections at other locations, but it was Archduke Ferdinand who coined the famous term "Kunst- und Wunderkammer" (cabinet of art and curiosities) by which such collections became known (Primisser 1777, 16-17). The idea behind a *Kunst- und Wunderkammer* is perhaps best described by Francis Bacon in his *Gesta Grayorum*, speeches accompanying a play held at Gray's Inn in 1594 in the presence of Queen Elizabeth I as part of the Christmas festivities. Here, "The Second Counsellor, advising the Study of Philosophy," is recommending four principal tasks to a prince: "First, the collecting of a most perfect and general library"; next, a spacious garden with all kind of plants and animals, birds and fishes—"and so you may have in small compass a model of universal nature made private." Third is "a goodly huge cabinet, wherein whatsoever the hand of man by exquisite art or engine had made rare in stuff, form or motion." Fourth and last is "such a still-house, so furnished with mills, instruments, furnaces, and vessels, as may be a palace fit for a philosopher's stone." So, after having studied all these natural and artificial wonders, the prince "shall be left the only miracle and wonder of the world" (Bacon 1862, 335). Thus, the *Kunst- und Wunderkammer* has its centre and vanishing-point in the person of the princely collector and owner, who is using and showing his *sapientia* (wisdom) through the collection. By collecting a microcosm of the world, he is acting in analogy to God's act of creation, becoming an *alter deus* (a second god or creator). From this point of view a *Kunst- und Wunderkammer* is an instrument of princely education and self-fashioning.

Ferdinand II began his collection with suits of armour worn by famous personalities and a corresponding collection of drawings and portraits ("Armamentarium Heroicum"), but later added books, manuscripts, and objects of all kinds. His collection was housed at Ambras in a great hall, contained in 20 great cabinets standing back-to-back in the middle of the room, two of them placed at opposite ends. On the walls "really artful and beautiful portraits and paintings" were presented, and mounted exotic animals and birds hung from the ceiling. There was a certain order intended, mostly according to material or manufacturing technique. Samuel Quiccheberg—a Belgian physician, and scientific and artistic adviser to the Duke Albrecht V of Bavaria—gave a detailed description of the organising principle of a notional *Kunst- und Wunderkammer* in 1565, its contents arranged into "Artificialia" (precious works of art created by artifice), "Naturalia" (rare natural objects), "Scientifica" (scientific instruments), "Exotica" (objects from foreign countries), and "Mirabilia" (wonders such as fantastically formed plant roots or superbly turned goblets; Quiccheberg 1565).

According to an inventory of the collection made following Ferdinand's death in 1596, the *Kunst- und Wunderkammer* in Ambras also included some musical instruments—kept in the fourth cabinet, which was painted white. The adjacent third, red, cabinet contained so-called "Handsteine," i.e., samples of ore from the mines owned by the archduke; the fifth, buff-coloured cabinet displayed clocks and mechanical automatons (the meaning of the different colours of the cabinets remains unknown). In between, in the fourth cabinet, we find the trumpet by Schnitzer and the cittern by de Virchi mentioned above, an organ with intarsia, a large lute with two necks and a lute made of ivory, wind instruments in the form of dragons (called "tartöld"), and so forth (Boeheim 1888, cclxxxv). Our coiled horn is not mentioned in 1596; only in a second inventory from 1613 we find as the last entry: "Ain Allgeyisch khrumbs Waldthorn" (a coiled forest horn from Allgäu). It can be distinguished from another instrument, called "Ain groß Allgeyisch Waldthorn" (a big forest horn from Allgäu), which was apparently neither bent nor twisted (Vienna, Kunsthistorisches Museum, Kunstkammer, inv. 6653 [*Ambraser Hauptinventar*], 56-57). But what is the exact meaning of "Waldthorn" and what of "Allgeyisch"?

The latter is easy, designating the topographical area called Allgäu in southern Germany, covering a region in the south of Bavaria, south-eastern Baden-Württemberg and parts of Austria. "Wald" (forest) points to the sphere of hunting, which was certainly a royal prerogative. The coiled form of the horn would assist its use during a hunt, as with the metal hunting horns of later times. This interpretation seems to be confirmed by Marin Mersenne (1588-1648) in his *Harmonicorvm Libri XII* (Paris: Guillaume Baudry, 1648), who described a particular type of horn as "buccina vel cornu Venatorium" (hunting trumpet or horn), or in the French edition "Trompes & Cors, & particulierement ceux qui seruent à la Chasse" (trumpets or horns used particularly for hunting) (Mersenne 1648, 102-03; Mersenne 1637, 244-46). Mersenne even depicts a coiled instrument very similar to the "Allgeyisch khrumbs Waldthorn" and adds the commentary "rarior est vsus" (rarely used) (fig. 47.1). So it seems that Ferdinand—or his successor—collected an item pertaining to the hunt, curiously enough not a notably precious object. But it may be that hunting is a red herring leading us to the wrong explanation.

Long before the entry of the object into the Ambras collection, in the first ever printed treatise on musical instruments by Sebastian Virdung, the *Mvsica getutscht und auszgezogen* (Basel: Michael Furter, 1511), a similar coiled horn is illustrated. Here it is called "Acher horn" (field horn), pointing perhaps to herding. It is interesting that Virdung considers this horn among the "dorlicher instrumenta" (rustic instruments), being a "göckel spill" (literally a cock's or juggler's plaything; Virdung 1511, sig. [$D3^{v}$-$D4^{r}$]). Virdung had very strong opin ions about the usefulness of musical instruments: he was only

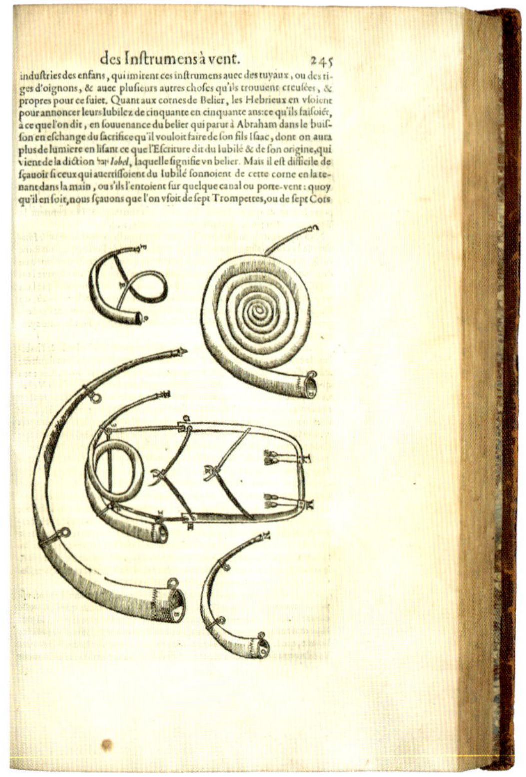
des Inſtrumens à vent. 245

induſtries des enfans, qui imitent ces inſtrumens auec des tuyaux, ou des tiges d'oignons, & auec pluſieurs autres choſes qu'ils trouuent creuſées, & propres pour ce ſuiet. Quant aux cornes de Belier, les Hebrieux en vſoient pour annoncer leurs Iubilez de cinquante en cinquante ans: ce qu'ils faiſoiét, à ce que l'on dit, en ſouuenance du belier qui parut à Abraham dans le buiſſon en eſchange du ſacrifice qu'il vouloit faire de ſon fils Iſaac, dont on aura plus de lumiere en liſant ce que l'Eſcriture dit du Iubilé & de ſon origine, qui vient de la diction יובל *Iobel*, laquelle ſignifie vn belier. Mais il eſt difficile de ſçauoir ſi ceux qui auertiſſoient du Iubilé ſonnoient de cette corne en la tenant dans la main, ou s'ils l'entoient ſur quelque canal ou porte-vent: quoy qu'il en ſoit, nous ſçauons que l'on vſoit de ſept Trompettes, ou de ſept Cors

Figure 47.1: Marin Mersenne, *Seconde Partie de L'Harmonie Universelle* (Paris: Pierre Ballard, 1637), 245. Paris, Bibliothèque nationale de France, RES-V-588 (2). Photo © Bibliothèque nationale de France.

interested in instruments which could be learned and played by non-professionals, the presumed buyers of his book. From this point of view a horn blown by shepherds and herdsmen is of course rather a "göckel spill." However, during the sixteenth century a growing interest in the pretended picturesque and naïve life of rural people can be observed in aristocratic and learned circles, leading to what we can call a pastoral fashion. A letter from 1598 documents this interest in a particularly direct manner—and it even mentions an "Allgeyer horn." Duke Wilhelm V of Bavaria asked Count Eitel Friedrich IV of Zollern-Hechingen to send him a capable shepherd with a boy for his sheep farm, and some specific equipment necessary for sheep tending (including bells), which was not in use in Bavaria ("die bey uns etwan nit breichig"). And then he adds: "also a herdsman or assistant, who can play the *Allgeyer horn* well" (also auch einen hierten oder zuhelfer, welcher das Allgeyer horn gar wohl blasen khindt). Apparently Duke Wilhelm was interested in a complete setting for his sheep farm, including the soundtrack (Schmid 1948, 142).

With this information, both the "Allgeyer horn" as well as the "Allgeyisch khrumbs Waldthorn" can be unmasked as a type of alphorn, nowadays associated almost exclusively with Switzerland thanks to the efforts of Swiss tourism marketing. In fact, such long wooden trumpets or horns were used in pastoral communities in many places across Europe, including Switzerland, but by no means only there. The very long, straight alphorn can be folded for practical reasons—or even coiled, as in the "Allgeyisch khrumbs Waldthorn." Its sounding length of about three meters would allow playing up to the eighth or perhaps tenth harmonic, and is therefore musically attractive. It can be assumed, then, that Archduke Ferdinand first included a "groß Allgeyisch Waldthorn" in his collection not out of simple curiosity, but as a sample of a local tradition, comparable to the "Handsteine" in the neighbouring cabinet. Later, a second example in coiled form was added to the collection. The shape of this coiled instrument must have prompted comparisons with other objects typically included in cabinets of curiosities: its complex manufacture with examples of fine woodwork, its shape with that of ammonites, the extinct molluscs known only as fossils. Thus, in a single object the different aspects of a *Kunst- und Wunderkammer* are perfectly represented, oscillating between "Artificilia," "Naturalia," and "Mirabilia."

ADDITIONAL REFERENCES: Emsheimer 1969; Giselbrecht 2017; Huber 1995; Schlosser 1920; Schlosser 1978; Seiple 2001.

Instrumens de musicque

Ungz regalles avec fleustes [illegible] flustes [illegible] estropietz

Une espinette double

Une espinette simple

Ung manicordion double

Troys ou quatre simples

Huict vyollez

Ung lucz avec lestuy

Deux flustez dallemant avec leurs estuitz

Une orloge de fer [illegible] mouvementz [illegible] estropietz
et [illegible]

Une harpe

Une espinette organisee [illegible] le Roy [illegible]

Ung [illegible] de musicque

48. Inventory after the Death of Madame Montcuyt

Emily Peppers

Rouen, 3 July 1557
Rouen, Archives départementales de Seine-Maritime, G. 2816, fol. 5r
Photo courtesy of the Archives départementales de la Seine-Maritime

Transcription:

Inventaire faicte au iii du juillet mil L^{c} Lvii aprez le decez de ma femme qui fut le xxiieme jour du moys de may procedit ledit jour par moy guillaume montcuyt et anne ma fille ainsy quil ensuyt de tous les bonez meublez estantz en mon logis…

Instruments de musique
unez regallez avec l'estuy les soufflez et contrepoitz
une espinette double
une espinette simple
ung manycordion double
troys ou quatre simples
huict vyollez
ung lucz avec lestuy
deux flustez dallemant avec les estuytz
une orloge de fer mouvement cloche contrepoitz et estuy
une montre
une espinette organisee chez le R__ [quil] m___ de s musique.
(G 2816, fols. 1^{r}, 5^{r})

Translation:

Inventory made on the third of July, 1557 after the death of my wife, who died the twenty-second day of the month of May, completed on the aforementioned day by me, Guillaume Montcuyt and Anne, my daughter and so follows all the goods and furniture in my home.

Musical instruments
a regal with case, pipes and counterweights
a double manual spinet
a single manual spinet
a double manicordion
three or four single manuals
eight viols
a lute with case
two German flutes with cases
an iron clock with counterweight movement
a watch
an organised spinet ___
___ of ___ music.

This after death inventory, found in the official documents of the Cathedral of Rouen, lists the household goods of the Montcuyt household and was recorded during the summer of 1557 after the death of Guillaume Montcuyt's wife. This document is quite unusual for two reasons: first, it records a snapshot of the household goods while the male head Guillaume was still alive; and second, it documents a large personal collection of musical instruments, including eight viols, an unprecedented number among French inventories of the period that are known to scholarship. Montcuyt was the cathedral organist, in which capacity he appeared in annual payment records from 1539 until the 1550s (Rouen Archives G. 2540-51, 1539-55). By 1555 there exist many documents in which Montcuyt can be found acting in an official capacity for the cathedral, overseeing payments to workers (Rouen Archives G. 2629, 1555). His last year of recorded employment as an organist was in 1555/56, where he is listed as "Montcuyt, organist at a wage of 40 livres" (Rouen Archives G. 2551, 1556).

The introduction at the start of the inventory declares that it was made by Montcuyt and his daughter Anne, in what we can only surmise to have been a sombre exercise to tally the objects present in the house during a time of great sorrow. Yet the practice of conducting an after-death inventory soon after the passing of a "head" of the household—typically the adult male or his widow—was a common and necessary occurrence in the days or weeks after a death. It is notable that in this case Madame Montcuyt was not a widower, and Guillaume would have continued to be the owner of the house contents.

Inventories were completed by a notary, an official post found in every city and town across France. Notarial records are an invaluable and extensive resource for the modern historian, providing a unique window into the everyday lives of the Renaissance man and woman. Inventories officially recorded debts, titles, and property that was then used by the surviving family to determine how the deceased's estate was to be split among family members, or sold, either for profit or to pay outstanding debts. Relatives were present as the inventory was conducted and provided their signature (in name or symbol) at the end of each day. The largest collection of notarial records in France is found at the Minutier central des notaires at the

Archives nationales in Paris: 170,000 articles in 122 studies, spanning some 21 linear kilometres. Notarial records include legal acts, commercial contracts, and inventories of household goods, like ours, recorded after a death. Inventories are important to the study of music and music-making as amongst the lists of household goods—pots, pans, clothing, and furniture—musical instruments are occasionally recorded.

There are limitations, however, to using after death inventories in the study of domestic music. Inventories do not record, for instance, how the instruments were used or in what ensemble arrangements, if instruments were brought to the house to complement what existed there already, if servants played the instruments, if the musical instruments were recently acquired or if they had lain gathering dust for several decades. Inventories do not record women's roles in private music-making, or the extended family that may have participated in musical activities. In terms of charting musical trends or fashions for newly popular instruments, inventories' witness to the wide dispersal of a particular instrument may be substantially delayed, coming perhaps decades after the instruments were first purchased and used. Meanwhile, instruments that had once been owned but had subsequently been sold, given or thrown away would not appear in the records.

As a reliable source of information regarding sixteenth-century domestic space, a great many issues could have prevented a realistic portrayal of objects in the house. In the case of musical instruments, the accuracy of the data recorded by the individuals completing the inventory was obviously constrained by the quality of the information and relevant expertise available to them at the time. Wrongly-identified musical instruments, garbled descriptions and very approximate valuations are probably quite common in after death inventories of the period. The Parisian inventory of priest Nicole Masseron, completed during the same summer of 1557, is a rare example where the notary (or notarial scribe) was corrected mid-record: "Item ~~seven viols~~ six viols and a broken violin ~~the aforementioned~~ priced together lx Sols Tournois" (Paris Archives MC ET LIV 226/D, fol. 2^{r}, 1557). Faced with a set of bowed string instruments, the notary began by describing them as seven viols, but was apparently corrected by someone who knew the difference between a viol and a violin.

The overwhelming majority of extant inventories record valuations of musical instruments as part of a total estimation of the net worth of the estate. The end goal of the surviving relatives in such cases may have been to liquidate the deceased's assets. Yet the inventory from Rouen does not include valuations, claiming to have been completed by Guillaume Montcuyt himself and his daughter, rather than a notary. What could have been the point of recording the household collection at this time? Was it completed for another purpose, such as for the original owners of the instruments?

Montcuyt's instrument collection featured a broad range of keyboard instruments, the most numerous type of instrument identified in after-death inventories of mid-sixteenth-century France. As a musician of high status, Montcuyt's collection reflected his personal and professional interest in keyboard instruments, with no less than eight or nine examples. Of the instruments mentioned, the regal was a small portable organ, and "espinette" or spinet was the term used at the time for plucked keyboard instruments such as the virginals or harpsichord. The "manicordion," or clavichord, could have been the small table-top version of the instrument or a larger free-standing example, while the "espinette organisee," or organised spinet—later, in the seventeenth century, to be termed a "clavecin organisée" or "claviorgan"—was a large keyboard instrument combining the plucked strings of a harpsichord with the pipes and bellows of an organ. Although these instruments are not valued in the inventory, it can be assumed that many of them, and especially the organised spinet, would have been very expensive. Organised spinets identified in other inventories of the period have been valued at nine livres, almost a quarter of Montcuyt's annual wages (Paris Archives MC ET LIV 215, fol. 3^{r}, 1551).

The viols, eight in total, are of particular interest in Montcuyt's inventory as they are present in the largest quantity yet identified in a private French collection of the period. The number of viols may reflect their use in consorts of four; the inventory may record the presence of two sets of four, perhaps even matching sets. It could equally have been an uneven collection, comprising instruments of different sizes purchased as Montcuyt or members of his household took up what was a relatively new fashion. Alongside the viols Montcuyt possessed a set of two "German" or transverse flutes, and a lute, all with their cases. A musical clock is also mentioned specifically among the musical instruments. The viols, lute, flutes, and keyboard instruments would have enabled flexible combinations of instruments to enjoy polyphonic music of the period, with or without voices, and could have provided many a pleasant evening's entertainment in the Montcuyt household.

There are several factors which make it unclear as to whether Montcuyt owned these instruments for himself or they were owned by the church and used in relation to his professional role. A musical man, apparently growing in importance in the church, it is certainly plausible that Montcuyt owned the instruments himself as part of a distinguished personal collection. The lack of valuation does not necessarily signify or confirm a separate owner, as in the case of this inventory none of the items listed were assigned monetary amounts. A separate Parisian inventory completed five years earlier further reinforces the likelihood that Montcuyt himself was the owner of this instrument collection. Robert Leroy, seigneur de la Motte, *valet de chambre ordinaire*, had within his collection a spinet that was specifically identified as the property of the duke of Nivernais, in whose service he was employed: "Item a spinet also covered in leather banded with tin priced 6 Livres Tournois / The aforementioned spinet [ ] belongs to Monsieur the Duke of Nivernais" (Paris Archives MC ET III 303, fol. 6^{r}, 1552). No such phrase is to be found in Montcuyt's inventory, and this omission is important. When read as an official, transparent, and legally binding notarial record, after death inventories required full disclosure of any discrepancies in ownership within the property—Montcuyt's musical collection would undoubtedly be listed as belonging to its rightful owner (the cathedral for instance), if it did not belong to him. This case is more complex, however, because the inventory was included as part of a larger inventory of the cathedral's possessions which also did not feature valuations, nor were they completed by an official notary. In the end, despite the apparent certainty of a legal document, the identity of the owner of the instruments listed by Montcuyt is lost to the past.

As a snapshot at the end of someone's life, after-death inventories limit the historian to rather sterile entries in official documents recorded at a time of grief; they do not speak of the enjoyment or companionship of musical soirées in years and decades past. Terms and valuations recorded relied upon the knowledge, interest, and conventions of the inventory creators—notaries, scribes, and family members in attendance—and may have fallen victim to inaccuracies. These inventories, however, provide a unique glimpse into the private lives and homes of individual men and women living almost 500 years ago, during a period when musical knowledge and ability was considered to communicate a cultivated aesthetic and was a fundamental part of a well-rounded education in the Liberal Arts.

Additional references: Greffe and Brouselle 1997; Jurgens 1982; Lesure 1954; Woodfield 1984; Zecher 2007.

CATERINA DE HEMESSEN
PINGEBAT 1548
ÆTATIS SVÆ 22

49. Girl Playing the Virginals

Laura S. Ventura Nieto

Catharina van Hemessen, Antwerp, 1548
Oil on oak panel, 30.5 x 24 cm
Inscribed: CATERINA DE HEMESSEN; PINGEBAT 1548; ÆTATIS SUÆ 22; HABET [E]R[GO] MINVS
Wallraf-Richartz-Museum, Cologne

This small painting depicts a 22-year-old woman against a dark background, dressed in a high-necked black bodice with red sleeves decorated with lace, her dark hair covered by a double-layered cap tied under her chin. Gazing away from her viewer, she is playing a polygonal virginals, its case decorated with dark foliage over a golden background, with the Latin words HABET ERGO MINUS inscribed on the inside. Overall, the painting conveys a very sober tone.

Signed and dated on the top right corner of the panel, this portrait is one of the few extant paintings that can be attributed unmistakably to the Flemish painter Catharina van Hemessen, daughter of the painter Jan Sanders van Hemessen. Active in Antwerp between 1548 and 1552, her artistic skills attracted the attention of Mary of Hungary, who invited van Hemessen and her husband (the organist Kerstian de Morien) to join her court, first in the Netherlands and later in Spain (Guicciardini 1567, 100). Like many other sixteenth-century courts across Europe, the court of the governor of the Habsburg Netherlands emulated the ideal court constructed by Baldassare Castiglione in *The Book of the Courtier* (1528), where courtiers and ladies were skilful in all manner of genteel accomplishments, such as music, literature, and the arts.

The young woman in the portrait perfectly embodies the role of the musical lady of the court advocated by Castiglione's book. Her demeanour shows a "sweet mildness" (soave mansuetudine) that was considered becoming in courtly ladies. Moreover, her posture in front of the virginals is relaxed and neutral, not betraying any effort used to acquire her musical skills, or indeed necessary to play her musical instrument. Most importantly, her sober black dress and timid gaze not only convey propriety, but also suggest an affluent background. Her choice of musical instrument is also consonant with Castiglione's preference for keyboard instruments as suitable for well-bred ladies—and in the case of virginals even the name of the instrument would make it most perfect for properly educated and behaved women.

It is unsurprising that in translating Castiglione's advice into this portrait van Hemessen used elements that were readily available within her own context. Indeed, the city of Antwerp was famous for its keyboard industry and, in the same year the portrait was executed, the German builder Joes Karest constructed one of the earliest extant Flemish virginals, now in the Musical Instruments Museum in Brussels (fig. 49.1). This instrument, polygonal and thin-cased, is quite similar in appearance to that depicted by van Hemessen, even including a Latin motto on the inside of the instrument's case as part of its decoration. Karest's virginals has been linked to a series of sixteenth-century Flemish family portraits featuring keyboard instruments, among them van Hemessen's painting, on the basis of the decorations and mottos on the instruments, and thus instruments represented in paint have played a significant role in writing the history of early keyboard manufacture in Flanders (Ripin 1977, 67-75).

As can be seen in the Karest virginals and other sixteenth-century Flemish instruments (both extant and depicted), it was not unusual for mottos to be included as part of their decorations. In this example, the three words inscribed inside the virginals imply the Latin sentence "Omnia dat Dominus non habet ergo minus" (The Lord gives everything and still has as much left), which encapsulates the Catholic concepts of selflessness, protection against avarice, and belief in the afterlife, as exemplified in the parable of the rich man and Lazarus (John 16:19-31). These ideas were in vogue in the Habsburg Netherlands through the writings of the Spanish humanist Juan Luis Vives and the Flemish Carmelite Adrien du Hecquet amongst others. In fact, the motto seen in this painting can be found in at least two other sixteenth-century paintings produced in the Low Countries: on the one hand, *The Schoolboy* attributed to Jan van Scorel (1531; Museum Boijmans Van Beuningen, Rotterdam); on the other hand, the anonymous *Portrait of Pierre de Moucheron, his Wife Isabeau de Gerbier and their Children* (1563; Rijksmuseum, Amsterdam), which also depicts a young woman playing a virginals that closely resembles both the Karest instrument and the keyboard in our portrait. In van Hemessen's example, the moralising content of the inscription adds an extra layer of sobriety to the young woman's attitude, as she is reminded of God's endless kindness whilst being encouraged to live a selfless life.

Figure 49.1: Joes Karest, *Virginals*, 1548. 20.5 (height) x 150 (length) x 50 (depth) cm. Musée des Instruments de Musique, Brussels. Photo © Creative Commons CC BY - MRAH/KMKG.

Catharina van Hemessen's depiction is regarded as one of the earliest portraits featuring a young woman playing a keyboard instrument (Austern 2005, 31). This trend, namely that of fashioning female identity through musical accomplishments, proved to be especially successful in the Low Countries, as can be seen in the substantial number of extant portraits using this trope well into the seventeenth century: for example, Jan Sanders van Hemessen's *Young Woman Playing the Clavichord* (ca. 1530; Worcester Art Museum), *Lady Playing the Clavichord* by the Master of the Female Half-Lengths (ca. 1530; National Museum, Poznań), and Frans Floris's *Family Portrait* (1561; Stadsmuseum Lier), just to name a few. Outside the Low Countries, the mask of the amateur keyboardist was adopted also by the Cremonese painter Sofonisba Anguissola to fashion two of her self-portraits, both of which closely resemble van Hemessen's portrait (Caroli 1987, 212). Although both Anguissola and van Hemessen were ladies-in-waiting in the Spanish court at different times during the 1550s, we cannot know for sure whether they ever met. The iconography of the female self as musician was reworked further during the last quarter of the century by the Bolognese painter Lavinia Fontana, who probably knew of Anguissola's self-portraits (Cantaro 1989, 74). Whether as a depiction of the self or a construction of the other, the image of the female keyboardist was widely adopted in both Italy and the Low Countries as a successful iconographical solution to construct female portraits, regardless of the sitter's own musical skills.

Citizens of Antwerp provided their daughters with an upbringing designed to turn them into perfect wives for their merchant husbands: piety, genteel accomplishments, basic arithmetic, reading, and writing would have been useful skills to run business, home, and family (Forney 1995). Such a training, broadly speaking an adaptation of that conceived by Vives for the princess Mary Tudor (Vives 2000), was criticised by the Italian writer Giovanni Michele Bruto, only seven years after this painting was executed, as superfluous and morally dangerous: "For as musicke […] under a colour of vertue […] it hath in it a secret baire that leadeth to grievous mischiefes, and those of great consequence." (Bruto 1598, sig. $H4^{v}$-$H6^{r}$). Respectable, musically educated and God-fearing, the young woman constructed by van Hemessen in this depiction matches the image of the accomplished merchant daughter of Antwerp, a model of womanhood admired by some but open to moral critique.

A young woman of the age and status of van Hemessen's sitter was most likely either engaged to or recently married to one of the merchants that populated the city of Antwerp. Seen in this light, we might imagine that the portrait was painted for her parents, as a lasting reminder of their success in bringing up their daughter to make a suitable and advantageous marriage; or perhaps it served to manifest her husband's pride in having secured such an accomplished wife. However, the sitter's precise identity remains uncertain, although some scholars have identified it as a portrait of Catharina van Hemessen's older sister Christina (Harris and Nochlin 1976, 105). Close female relatives were subjects for representation in paint that women artists could access easily within their own domestic realms, a circumstance that favours this identification. Moreover, the physical similarities between both women and the dimensions of both panels have been used to consider this portrait as a pendant of van Hemessen's 1548 self-portrait at the easel kept now at the Kunstmuseum in Basel (Gaze 1997, 1:68). If the two paintings were conceived as a pair, these two highly accomplished women might have invested in their painted representation for their own ends, as symbols of their own pride, not only someone else's. Regardless of the sitter's identity, this portrait has been crafted carefully to construct the image of an ideal marriageable woman who, even though she seems to be showing off her musical skills, cannot be accused of stepping outside the rightful place that patriarchal society has assigned to her gender.

50. Vihuela

John Griffiths

Belchior Dias, Lisbon, 1581
Back of kingwood(?), front veneered with brazilwood(?) with decorations of ebony and boxwood, neck and top-block of ebony, 77.1 (length) x 19.9 (width) cm
The Royal College of Music, London
Photo © Royal College of Music / ArenaPAL

An object of elegant simplicity, this *vihuela* (or guitar) is one of the few Iberian plucked instruments surviving from the sixteenth century, built in Lisbon in 1581 by Belchior Dias. It is the epitome of grace and elegance in Renaissance instrument building, but in recent times it has also been the centre of considerable controversy. The dispute concerns a seemingly innocent matter of names, the vexing question of whether this instrument should be considered a *vihuela* or a guitar. The matter of its identity erupted into an acrimonious argument as a result of an observation around 2006 by luthier Alexander Batov that the instrument, previously considered a guitar, had an additional eleventh hole reamed in its pegbox, thus raising the possibility that it was, in fact, a *vihuela*.

Resolving the quandary requires perspective. As an artefact, this instrument owes its survival to having been preserved in a museum. By their nature, museums encourage us to regard objects historically, usually looking backwards from the present into the past. Unsurprisingly, scholarly research usually proceeds in the same direction, with the same retrospective vision. An alternative approach, sometimes more illuminating, is to remove the artefact from its museum and allow it to run free in its natural habitat, like a captive animal returned to the wild. This emancipation opens up the possibility of apprehending the object of study from the opposite direction, looking from its past towards its future, often with astonishing clarity. This is the case regarding the guitar and *vihuela*.

Thousands of *vihuelas* and guitars similar to the Dias instrument were built on the Iberian peninsula during the sixteenth century (Griffiths 2009, 355; Griffiths 1999). Early in the century many appear to have been built in the old way, with a shallow body hollowed out from a single block of wood. With the importation of expensive woods from the Americas, *violeros* invented the new technique of building instruments with separate back and sides, the method still used today for making guitars. Belchior Dias' instrument represents a further stage of development in construction style that has not previously been delineated and that appears to have been introduced in the 1570s or 1580s. Its essential feature is the arched back of fluted ribs. Other *vihuelas* described in inventories from the same period corroborate this new fashion. A 1580 post-mortem inventory of the belongings of Count Rodrigo Sarmiento de Villandrado, for example, lists a "vihuela de ébano alaudada," that is, an ebony "luted" *vihuela* (Archivo Histórico Provincial de Valladolid, Protocolos, legajo 386, fol. 587). Instruments of this type were an expensive luxury due to the intricacy of their construction. To make such a back, Dias would first have had to cut thin flat ribs of 2 mm or less, and then wet, heat and bend them around a cylindrical tube as many times as necessary. Once fluted, the ribs had to be bent gradually backwards onto a mould of the instrument's body. This requires consummate skill, and results in instruments that are not only wondrous feats of joinery, but also remarkably rigid and light, requiring no further reinforcement. The only other surviving late sixteenth-century *vihuela*—an anonymous instrument at the Musée de la Musique, Paris—also features a vaulted back built of fluted ribs. This new body design added bass resonance by increasing the internal air volume in the sound box and reducing the total weight of the instrument. Even though this style of construction did not become standard practice, it persisted throughout the seventeenth and eighteenth centuries in the wire-strung Italian *chitarra battente*, and is still preserved today in a similar type of guitar used in traditional music in southern Italy.

To resolve the issue of names, let us return to fifteenth-century Spain where the bowed *vihuela* (fiddle) was being transformed into a larger multi-purpose instrument played either with a bow or plucked, usually with a quill. It was not until the last decade of the century that it was separated into distinct bowed and plucked instruments, the *vihuela de arco* and the *vihuela de mano* (*viola da mão* in Portuguese) respectively. Each now had its distinct design and stringing in function of its playing technique, for the first time allowing them to be used as solo instruments. In contrast, the fifteenth-century *guitarra* (gittern) was a small lute played throughout Europe, notably as the discant instrument of the lute-gittern duo for which players such as the Italian Pietrobono "detto il chitarrino" were renowned. In Spain, however, it seems that small figure-of-eight shaped *vihuelas de mano* usurped the role of the *guitarra*, including its name, becoming known as *guitarra* due to its function rather than its morphology (Rey and Navarro 1993, 43-44). The sixteenth-century *guitarra* was thus nothing but a small version of the *vihuela* with four courses of strings rather than six, built by the same makers, made by the same craftsmen using the same tools, construction techniques, and processes, finished with the same varnish, and strung with the same strings. This contrasts with the more usual explanation of the difference between the *vihuela* and guitar that comes from a retrospective approach that separates the two instruments on the basis of the style of their music, without considering constructional and other similarities. In the sixteenth century, the guitar is clearly a subset of *vihuela* and the dispute about names is reduced to a storm in a teacup.

In its present state, it is not possible to determine exactly whether the Belchior Dias was initially built as a four-course *guitarra* or a six-course *vihuela*, although the evidence tends to support the latter. Modifications to the original instrument are the main obstacle, especially the new soundboard, moustached bridge, and nut that were added around 1730, allowing it to be used as a contemporary five-course guitar. For this reason, the number of holes in the pegbox is crucial evidence: five holes along each side and an extra hole in the centre of the pegbox close to the nut. This rules out the possibility of having been built as a four-course guitar, but admits the possibility that it originated as a five-course *vihuela* of the kind for which Miguel de Fuenllana composed ten pieces (Fuenllana 1554, fols. 90, 158-162). If the eleventh hole were to be for an additional tuning peg, then the instrument may well have been originally built as a small six-course *vihuela* with a single *prima* and then five double courses (Batov 2006-2017). Given its 55.4 cm string length it is likely to have been tuned in A (A–d–g–b–e'–a'), rather than the standard G tuning, a tone lower, to which Juan Bermudo referred as the "common *vihuela*" (Bermudo 1555, fol. 28).

Resistance to the Dias instrument being called a *vihuela* is not just a matter of the number of strings, but also of size. Among the small number of surviving *vihuelas*, this one is by far the smallest, but should not be excluded on this ground. I have long argued the likelihood that smaller six-course *vihuelas* like the Dias instrument became common in the mid and late sixteenth century. Anyone who has attempted to play the music of Fuenllana and Esteban Daza published in the 1550s and 1570s will be familiar with the technical complexities that arise from the music's dense polyphony (Fuenllana 1554; Daza 1576). This music is much better suited to small instruments with a shorter string length and narrow neck that, in combination, make it easier for the player to define the linearity of each polyphonic voice.

The Dias *vihuela* is one of the most beautiful guitar-shaped instruments to survive from the sixteenth century. Its exquisite elegance and balance are no accident. Renaissance instrument makers, like others of their time, understood the Pythagorean conception of music as the perceptible embodiment of the harmony of the spheres and the natural order of the world. Just as contemporary musicians tried to mirror the harmony of the universe in their compositions, makers believed that their instruments should themselves also embody the same proportion and balance. While the earliest records of the guilds of *violeros* in Seville (1527), Granada (1552), Lisbon (1572), and Madrid (1578) do not go into esoteric detail, more can be derived from the ordinances promulgated in Toledo in 1617, which detail the examination of apprentices (Romanillos and Winspear 2002, Appendix). To become a master craftsman, an apprentice was required to build a *vihuela*, a harp, and a violin, within a span of six months, in the workshop of one of the examiners (González 2007, 175). In making the *vihuela*, the apprentice was not allowed to use preexisting designs, but had to work from scratch using only ruler, compass, set square, and knife—tools that strongly suggest the role of geometry in designing an instrument.

With the apprentice's workbench in mind, we can attempt to reverse-engineer the Dias *vihuela*, uncovering—hypothetically at least—the geometrical plan followed by the *violero* (fig. 50.1). Dias may have started by drawing a square the width of the lower bout (19.9 cm, shown in blue), then a second square above it forming a ratio of 5:6 with the width of the first. This established the proportional ratio of the upper bout to the lower bout, and the length of the body to the bouts, and also determined the position of the lower edge of the sound hole. The division of the lower square into three, both horizontally and vertically, would serve to position the bridge and would establish the diameter of the curves of the upper and lower bouts (the green circles). A larger circle (red) whose radius was equal to the length of the large initial square gave the curve for the lower end of the sound box; and a further two circles of the same diameter were drawn, centred upon the widest point of the lower bouts. These contribute to tracing the perimeter of the sound box, and are completed by a further two larger circles (magenta). This analysis shows how nearly every aspect of the design, including the length of the neck and pegbox, could all derive from the same starting point and form part of the same set of proportional relationships.

Thus, not only through the technical and tonal affordances of its design, but also through the harmony of its proportions, Belchior Dias built a *vihuela* that would satisfy both the eye, ear, and mind of the most discerning Renaissance musician.

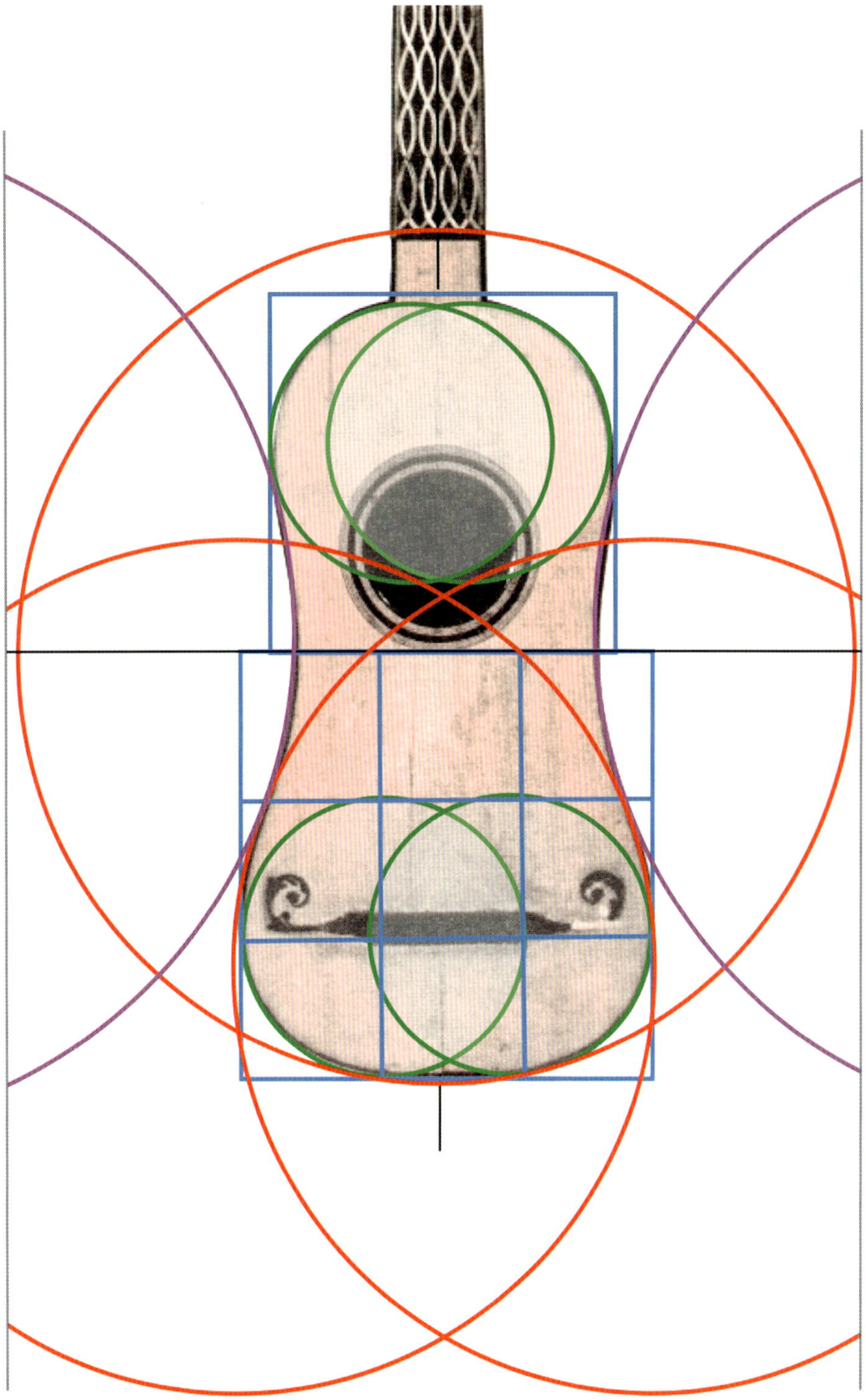

Figure 50.1: Geometrical design of the Belchior Dias vihuela.

Let nothing
cause thy harte
to quayle
launce out thy
boate hale vppe
thy sayle. put
from the shore

And at the last
thou shalt obtayn
vnto the porte
that shall remayn
for ever more

Ille seruus qui
cognovit volun
tatem domini sui
et non prepara
vit. nec fecit se
cundum volun
tatem eius.
plagis vapulabit
multis. /

Studemus igitur ingredi in illam requiem nequis eodem occidat incredulitatis exemplo vivus est enim sermo dei et efficax et penetrantior quovis gladio vtriumque inciden te ac pertingens vsque ad divisionem animæ simul ac spe ritus compagumque et medullarum et discretor cogita cionem et intentionum cordis nec est ylla creatura que non manifesta sit in conspectu illius sed omnia nuda et resu pinata occulis eius ad quem nobis est sermo. /hebrues 4.

51. Bagpipes

John J. Thompson

Thomas Fella, *Bagpiper*
From *A booke of diveirs devises and sortes of pictures [...]*, Washington DC, The Folger Shakespeare Library, MS V.a.311, fol. 29r
Halesworth, ca. 1592-98
Manuscript on paper, 81 fols., 20 x 15 cm
Photo courtesy of the Folger Shakespeare Library

The image of the bagpiper in *A booke of diveirs devises and sortes of pictures, with the alphabete of letters, deuised and drawne with the pen [...] devised and made by T.F.* (fol. 29r) stands at a fascinating transitional point in the representation of this musical instrument by Elizabethan writers. The image is used to decorate the letter L in Thomas Fella's calligraphic alphabet (fols. 18v-42r), occupying about a third of the space available in his small book of illustrated emblems, proverbs, poems (including a verse calendar on the seasons and months of the year), and naturalistic border decoration, mostly written and drawn by Fella in the last decade of the sixteenth century (Sanford and Blatchly 2012). Fella was a draper and copyist from Halesworth, Suffolk, who obviously had an interest in professional writing and drawing skills and whose career was based in Halesworth and the surrounding district. Among other paralegal activities, such as the drawing up and execution of local wills, Fella was responsible, in 1611, for the setting up and maintaining of the records of income and expenditure of a local charity offering poor relief.

Although *A booke of diveirs devises* seems an idiosyncratic production that never appears to have strayed far from its local Suffolk area during Fella's lifetime, it demonstrates a range of quintessentially Elizabethan post-Reformation tendencies in its choice of writing sources and drawing models. Fella obviously had access to a substantial library of printed works, and, with perhaps the exception of some parts of his border work, few, if any, of his carefully and usually expertly hand-drawn illustrations are either entirely original or, necessarily, taken directly from his observation of Suffolk life. As such, Fella has derived the figure of the bagpiper from a woodcut illustration in John de Beau Chesne's *A booke containing divers sortes of hands, as well the English as French secretarie with the Italian, Roman, chancelry & court hands [...] Imprinted at London by Thomas Vautrollier, dwelling in the blackefrieres* (London: Thomas Vautrollier, 1570—reissued many times). De Beau Chesne was a Hugenot writing master, in London from ca. 1565, where he was resident in the ward of Farringdon Without, and, since 1567, had worked professionally for William Bowyer, Keeper of the Records in the Tower of London (Wolpe 1980). *A booke containing divers sortes of hands* is a quarto volume that has the distinction of being the first copybook of sample alphabets and texts covering a range of current handwriting styles to be printed in English (Heal 1931). The illustrated alphabet in Fella's little *booke of diveirs devises* can thus be considered alongside several surviving near-contemporary sixteenth-century prints produced in direct imitation of de Beau Chesne, and sometimes borrowing the same woodcuts. The difference is that Fella produced a handmade book, of course, one that has, perhaps, more of the character of a commonplace book than of a professional writing manual intended for widespread reproduction, distribution, and copying.

The English verse written alongside and to the right of Fella's bagpiper image is derived from another similarly iconic Elizabethan printed source that reveals a particularly important formative influence on Fella's reading, writing, and drawing interests and achievement. The text reads:

> Let nothing cause thy harte to quayle
> launce out thy boate hale vppe thy sayle
> put from the shore
>
> And at the last thou shalt obtayn
> vnto the porte that shall remayn
> for evermore.

It is derived from a stirring verse epistle that forms part of Robert Smith's own account of his examinations, imprisonment, and martyrdom, now preserved in the first edition of John Foxe's *Actes and monuments of these latter and perillous dayes, touching matters of the church* (London: John Day, 1563). Foxe describes Smith as a gifted semi-professional artist working as a clerk in Windsor until he was removed from his post and brought before the Marian bishop of London, Edmund Bonner, then imprisoned at Newgate before, finally, being sent to his fiery death at Staines in July 1555. In the 1563 edition, particular attention is drawn to the short verse quoted above from Fella's version, because it immediately follows a woodcut depicting Smith and his fellow protestants in Newgate entitled "a Picture describynge the maner and place of them whiche were in bondes for the testimonye of the truthe, conferrynge together among themselues." It is entirely typical of both text and image in Foxe's *Acts and monuments* that the figure of a Protestant martyr such as Smith should capture the communitarian spirit of the persecuted formerly associated, in a liturgical sense at least, by celebration of the Mass (Rust 2013).

Foxe's gargantuan work—his so-called Book of Martyrs—underwent much textual adaptation and change in the course of its reprintings as an Elizabethan bestseller (King 2006). Following their appearance in the first edition, Smith's verse epistles were subsequently omitted from the text for 20 years, until Day's fourth edition—the last in Foxe's lifetime—in 1583: *Actes and monuments ...Newly reuised and recognised, partly also augmented, and now the fourth time published*. By then, the short verse corresponding to Fella's version has been characterised as "robert smith to all faithfull seruants of Christ, exhorting them to be strong vnder persecution," thereby confirming Smith's importance as a key figure among the early Protestant martyrs, and, obviously also, a person whose inspirational writings were of some interest to Thomas Fella as he worked on the varied post-Reformation sources for his own homemade book in Suffolk.

In addition to borrowing the textual extracts from *Actes and monuments*, and the illustrative materials from his de Beau Chesne printed source for the bagpiper image, it is worth noting that Fella can also be shown more generally to have copied a good number of the figures illustrating other parts of his book directly from a range of the woodcuts he must have found in his Foxe print. While it has already been demonstrated that Fella borrowed and copied many other short texts and illustrations from the variety of different early printed sources to which he had access, there is much to suggest that he was particularly fascinated by Foxe's *Actes and monuments* and possibly even attempted through his own handmade book to emulate some of the circumstances in which he imagined Foxe's illustrated printed text had originally been assembled. Such an assumption implies that it is worth investigating further whether some kind of iconic significance might be attached to the bagpiper image and accompanying English text on fol. 29r.

There is plenty of visual and textual evidence to suggest that bagpipes were often present in a range of formal and informal communal settings where music was called for as part of particular forms of late medieval and early modern social interaction (Thompson 2010). It is clear too that bagpipe images were often pressed into service for a number of quite contradictory religio-didactic and other ideological purposes. On the lowest level, the bagpipe was often represented as a vulgar instrument, associated with the rural life, the rough and ready existence of the lower orders, riotous assemblies of pilgrims making holidays of holy days, and, by extension, sometimes, with animal crudeness, discord, and loud unpleasant noise. The instrument's shape reminded some medieval Biblical commentators of the distended stomach, or even the male organ, and as a result the bagpipe was readily and enthusiastically associated with the sins of gluttony and lechery. On another more elevated level of late medieval artistic representation, the bagpipe was often placed together with other musical instruments and associated with the celebration of earthly and heavenly concordance at great moments in human history, such as the adoration of the infant Christ at the Nativity, and, by extension, at great royal and civic occasions, where music was performed by the city waits and perhaps other professional musicians in addition to royal trumpeters and pipers as part of a public commitment to and demonstration of the ties that bind church and state, courtly and civic life, the king and his people. Nativity scenes where bagpipes are present and played by angels or shepherds were a commonplace in English later medieval art and decoration, but not in the later early modern period.

The association of bagpipes with other musical instruments is less common but still apparent throughout the later medieval and early modern period. In the early fourteenth-century Gorleston and Macclesfield Psalters, for example, images of bagpipes are presented alongside representations of trumpets, fiddles, pipes, tabors, and horns in a variety of settings (Montagu 2006). The six carved angel musicians in Manchester Cathedral, dating from the 1460s and now heavily restored, on the south side are shown playing mainly string instruments while on the north side mainly wind instruments, including a portative organ, a shawm, a trumpet, a recorder, and bagpipes with arm bellows, a single drone and two chanters (Merryweather 2001). Similarly (but at a much later date), carved into the Eglantine table at Hardwick Hall in Derbyshire—made to celebrate the marriage in 1568 of Elizabeth Hardwick to the Earl of Shrewsbury—is an elaborate inlay of courtly games, flowers, heraldic devices, and musical instruments (see exhibit 18). The latter includes images of two viols, a harp, a guitar, two cornets, trumpets, shawms, a recorder, and a bagpipe, here perhaps representing an early example of a new tradition in English pastoral based on classical models where the pan-pipe is displaced by an English equivalent.

In terms of bagpipe playing in civic and court life, the extant account of the music for the 1474 royal entry of the infant Prince Edward into Coventry reveals that the so-called *haut* music played at the fifth station where the three kings of Cologne (the Magi) were encountered on the prince's route through the city consisted of bagpipe playing, perhaps on instruments that were the predecessors of the Northumbrian small-pipes (Rastall 1975). The extant court records also show that Edward II and Edward III had pipers at the English court, and that Henry VIII's inventory of musical instruments, made posthumously, included "pipes of ivorie and a bagge couered with purple vellat" (Collinson 1975, 95).

Thomas Fella's representation of the bagpipe in *A booke of diveirs devises* implies a context where the musical instrument has been shorn of its pre-Reformation significance in terms of any close association with the spectacle of either earthly or heavenly adoration of the infant Christ at the Nativity, or any other association that might be drawn between the musical instrument and the idea of pilgrimage or holy days. There is also no suggestion in Fella's illustration that the bagpipe was a favoured instrument for important public royal or civic occasions, or that it was well on the way to becoming a pastoral instrument based on classical models. For Fella, the bagpipe instead seems to have retained its ubiquitous presence in late medieval and early modern popular culture as a robust musical instrument with predominantly rural associations, but one that since Foxe's *Acts and monuments* might also help promote the idea of communal solidarity and reformed church bonhomie among like-minded readers, artists, writers, and other Suffolk fellow travelers in Elizabethan England.

52. Kös

Kate van Orden

Anon., Ottoman, 17th century
Copper, leather and hide; 36 (height) x 52 (maximum diameter) cm
Badisches Landesmuseum, Karlsruhe
Photo © Badisches Landesmuseum / Thomas Goldschmidt

The drum in this exhibit is a Turkish kettledrum or *kös*, now in the Badisches Landesmuseum in Karlsruhe Palace, Germany. It is one of several types of drum employed by the *mehterhâne* of the Janissaries, an elite Ottoman infantry corps that had its own official musical ensemble. As a military band destined to serve in open air ceremonies and on the battlefield, the mehter was a "loud band," with shawms (*zurna*), trumpets (*boru*), and drums, both double-headed drums (*ṭabl* or *dawul*) and kettledrums of two sizes: the smaller *naḳḳāre*, played in pairs, and the larger *kös*. Cymbals (*halīles* or *zīls*) and the crescent-shaped *čewgān* with jingling bells filled out the percussion section with their distinctive timbre, audible today in the cymbals of the Avedis Zildjian company, whose patented alloy and manufacturing process were devised in Constantinople in 1623.

According to Walter Feldman, the official mehter had three specific functions: to play continuously in battle, to greet the sultan each afternoon with a musical performance accompanied by prayers for his well-being and that of the state, and to play each day before morning prayers and after evening prayers (Feldman 2012). In an account of the Topkapı palace complex written around 1665, *Serai Enderum, cioè Penetrale dell'Seraglio*, the musician ʿAlī Ufuḳī (aka Albert Bobowski) describes the daily routine of the *mehterhâne* in the following way:

> In the afternoon the masters of the field music come [to the palace] and there they do the same as the others. Their instruments are pipes, Turkish *zurna*, and trumpets, *boru*. They play them to the beat of the drum, *davul* or small nakers, *kudüm* or *dümbelek* and cymbals *zil*, and there they also learn to play the bronze drums [*kūs*], which are carried on a camel before the Grand Signor (Haug 2019, 416-17).

The *kös* was by far the largest of the drums used in the *mehterhâne*, and at their most magnificent they could measure up to 1.5 meters in diameter (Pirker 2001; Mersenne 1636-37, 2:52 depicts a *kös*-like drum). Consisting of a copper basin and camel skin head tightened with lashings of thong, they were indeed carried on military campaigns by musicians mounted on camels (even though the Janissaries were an infantry division). The French traveler Jean Palerne, who witnessed the ceremonies for the circumcision of the son of Sultan Murad III in 1582, describes a huge ensemble over one hundred strong: "some of them had large drums, that they struck with heavy clubs, big enough to knock out a steer: these drums are so heavy that they carry them on camels when they go to war" (Palerne 1606, 446). The illustration accompanying this exhibit, a 1576 woodcut by Melchior Lorck (fig. 52.1), shows a drummer astride a regally harnessed and caparisoned camel, playing a *kös* draped in fabric with two large mallets (Rasmussen 2014). From the reins dangle open and closed bells that added metallic sparkle to the thunderous drumbeats.

Lorck's woodcut provides crucial context for the drum in our exhibit, for the *kös* player he depicts bears two insignia of military command: the horsetail standard (*tügh*) and a small flag. *Tügh*s were posted before the tents of generals, in increasing numbers according to rank (Goodwin 1994, 71-72). The strong association of the *kös*—unique to the *mehterhâne* of the Janissaries—and the *tügh* is affirmed by the title given to viziers, provincial governors, and local lords: "ṭabl-u ʿalem ṣāḥibi" (possessor of drum and standard). They too had mehter ensembles, though far smaller than the sultan's (Feldman 2012). According to the *Seyâhatnâme* (*Travelogue*) of Evliyā Çelebi, who calls the musicians of the official mehter "Mehterán Kúsjián" (beaters of the kettledrum), in 1630 the *mehterhâne* had 150 pairs of kettledrums (a number that probably included the smaller *naḳḳāre*), with the largest being transported by elephant during the Battle of Khotyn in 1621 (Evliyā Çelebi 2012, 1:226). The historian Godfrey Goodwin relates that four extremely large *kös* were sounded only in war (Goodwin 1994, 83), and it may be that the mammoth and battle-scarred *kös* preserved in the Istanbul Military Museum is one of these legendary battle drums.

Like many items in the collection at Karlsruhe, the *kös* in this exhibit was probably acquired when armies under the command of the Polish king Jan Sobieski broke the siege being waged at Vienna by Kara Mustafa Pasha in 1683. On the battlefield, the drums of the Janissary mehter would have played continuously during engagement, giving signals to the troops, enflaming courage, and providing a sonic rallying point near the company's standard (Feldman 2012). Hence this *kös* was not a curiosity or your average bit of loot, but a trophy from the battlefield and a symbol of the Janissaries disarmed. So

Figure 52.1: Melchior Lorck, *A Kettledrum Player Riding a Camel*, 1576. Woodcut on paper, 20.4 x 16.9 cm. The British Museum, London. Photo © The Trustees of the British Museum.

catastrophic was the rout of Mustafa Pasha's army that the Ottomans abandoned virtually everything as they fled, leaving behind "300 guns, 5000 tents, pay, provisions, and all the banners and horsetails except the sacred Standard of the Prophet" (Goodwin 1994, 176).

Although the Karlsruhe *kös* represents an Ottoman defeat, we might also hear in this exhibit the fearsomeness of the Janissary corps. Whereas Western European infantries consisted of ragtag groups of conscripts and effective but often unscrupulous mercenaries, in the fifteenth century the Ottomans created a permanent army, of which the Janissaries were a signature component. Rigorously trained and highly disciplined, Janissaries were career professionals who lived in splendid barracks, ate well, and were uniformly dressed, well equipped, and salaried. On military campaigns, Ottoman camps were pitched by an advance guard of servants who set up small cities of splendid tents, field kitchens, latrines, and roads, the whole provisioned by a massive supply train of camels carrying grain, cloth, weapons, and other goods (Goodwin 1994, 83-85). At every level, little elsewhere could compare to Ottoman military order. Indeed, it was only in the early seventeenth century that generals such as Maurice of Nassau began to institute regular drill for foot soldiers, a practice that—not incidentally—made drummers central to the chain of command (van Orden 2005, 209-10).

The significance of objects is culturally constructed, something beautifully exemplified by the Karlsruhe *kös*, which was forged by elite coppersmiths in Constantinople, galvanised the Janissaries during their campaign, and was left behind in retreat. Its displacement and transfer from one culture to another occurred at a turning point in geopolitical relations between what became West and East, and we should note that those very divisions between "Europe" and its Others were elaborated in performances of musical difference that featured instruments of the *mehterhâne* centre stage. The Battle of Vienna inspired musical celebrations from Hamburg to Madrid and operatic treatments of the victory included *Il gran Tamerlano* (Venice, 1689), which promised spectators "Balli...con istromenti Turcheschi" (Corradi 1698, 8; Wolff 2012, 19-22). Now, centuries later, the dilapidated and unpolished state of the *kös* further accentuates its alterity by making it appear rustic and homespun. Its inclusion in our museum, however, is designed to remind readers that Orientalist discourses, which characterised the Ottomans as decadent, weak, and in need of Western governance, are a relatively modern phenomenon that should not be casually projected onto the more distant past.

V

Sacred Spaces

Introduction: The Room of Sacred Spaces

David Fiala

Christianity was the majority but not the only religious practice current in Renaissance Europe. Iberia, where before 1492 Christian, Jewish, and Muslim communities lived side by side, provides a particular diversity of sacred spaces, as well as examples of the sharing and blending of architectural and decorative elements between faiths, achieved willingly or by force. The Cathedral of Cordoba, for example, began life as a mosque, and served the needs of Christian worshipers from 1236 up to the sixteenth century before significant structural alterations were deemed necessary. Craftspeople from all of Iberia's faith communities worked for clients of all faiths—resulting, for example, in the use of textiles bearing Islamic motifs and inscriptions in Christian contexts. Nonetheless, although music connected with the religious practices of Jewish, Muslim, and other faith communities are highlighted elsewhere in this museum (the Rooms of Devotions, Psalters, the Public Sphere, Cities, and Travels), the notated choral polyphony that has come to define Renaissance musical style for modern ears was a product of Catholic and Reformed Christian liturgies, and Christian sacred spaces were the matrix of its development; therefore, they are the focus of this room.

Christian religious buildings are associated with specific materials (stone, glass, fabrics), and often comprise multiple linked volumes of space. Thus their acoustic properties are both singular and complex, giving a particular character to musical and other sounding performances, a topic that has been explored in a particularly systematic way in relation to Venetian churches (Howard and Moretti 2009), and tapestries in the Sistine Chapel (Pon 2015). In some instances it can be shown that the design of a church was specifically influenced by acoustic considerations linked to musical performance: this is the case for the nuns discussed by Barbara Eichner (*St Katherine's Convent Church*), who took extreme steps to ensure their new church favoured the ease and beauty of their singing. Also of considerable relevance to sound, churches came in very diverse sizes, from chapels and parish churches of a few dozen square meters, to huge cathedrals, pilgrimage basilicas, or collegiate churches. One of the largest in Europe, the Basilica of San Petronio in Bologna, is more than 130 m long, 60 m wide, and 44 m high, for an estimated volume of 170,000 m3—large enough for more than 25,000 people. The *Chapel of King Sigismund* discussed by Paweł Gancarczyk, in contrast, measures a mere six meters square, placing severe limitations on the number of musicians and listeners that can be accommodated, and affecting the acoustics.

The sacrality of Catholic and some Protestant Christian spaces is defined and materialised by the presence of an altar, a table traditionally of stone, which acquired its sacred quality through rituals of consecration that allow the main sacrament of Christianity, the Eucharist, to be celebrated upon it. The immediate surroundings of this main altar, called the sanctuary, can host other sacred objects, such as the tabernacle in which the hosts are held, and reliquary shrines, tangible forms of sanctity. Sometimes elevated by a few steps or adorned with a retable, the altar can also be isolated from the rest of the space by mobile curtains. This small, hidden, even secret space, usually located at the east end of the building, is the centre of a spatial hierarchy that governs the architecture, arrangement, use, and decoration of many church buildings.

The most general structural principle of Catholic liturgical space is the division between the nave, which can be accessed by the laity, and the choir, for the clergy only. The whole clergy of the church, and in monastic contexts the whole community, numbering from a few persons to several dozens, gathers in the choir every day to attend Mass and Office. The usual physical structure of a choir organises participants into two groups facing each other, in carved wooden stalls arranged face-to-face, at right-angles to the main altar. The heavy furniture of the stalls, with its fixed seating arrangement for holders of different ranks and offices, is a spatial incarnation of the ecclesiastical order, reflecting the celestial hierarchy. But it also plays an essential acoustic function: in the largest churches, it both retains and concentrates the sound, acting as a resonance chamber.

The carving of the stalls offered a plethora of decorative opportunities, both in the round and in relief, and musical subjects are common, especially in proximity to seats occupied by musical office-holders such as the precentor and vicars choral, and the lectern on which the service book was placed (Allen 2009). Misericords, which offered a welcome perch to clerics required to stand for long periods while singing, also sometimes featured carved musical scenes, as in the example discussed by Frédéric Billiet (*Misericord*). From the thirteenth to the seventeenth century, the boundary between the nave and the choir was materialised by structures ranging from the slightest railings to the most massive choir screens. A choir screen was one of several possible locations for a gallery accommodating singers and organist, a common feature of chapels and churches with the resources to appoint professional musicians. In the case discussed by Sophia D'Addio (*Organ Shutters from the Cathedral of Ferrara*), the organ was initially installed at the centre of the choir, but later moved into the nave, where its painted shutters would have enjoyed a larger audience.

With rare exceptions, in Catholic churches ceremonies celebrated at the main altar remained inaccessible to the laity. It is probably to redress this situation that the practice of founding and consecrating secondary altars across the rest of the church space developed, creating an impressive flood of celebrations. Around 1470, the chapter of canons of the Dijon Saint-Chapelle, an important collegiate church, was proud to declare that within their walls at least 15,000 low Masses (spoken), and 2000 high Masses (sung in chant, whether or not with polyphony and instrumental music), were celebrated each year. In his thick description of the *Basilica of the Santissima Annunziata*, Giovanni Zanovello emphasises the ways in which the overlapping sonic interventions generated by the church's many altars were characterised by different musical practices, helping to "zone" the space. In the case of monastic foundations, that zoning extended from the church to the cloister, with its more private, domestic spaces; musical practices, whether sounding or imaginative, were also relevant here, as Tim Shephard notes in his analysis of the decorations of a Cremonese convent library (*Ceiling with the Muses and Apollo*).

Zanovello emphasises the centrality of private, secular patrons to the funding of sacred spaces and their associated observances; indeed, the penetration of secular power into sacred spaces was highly characteristic of Renaissance Catholic churches, and a key issue in both Reformation and Counter-Reformation. If the Medici family were able to take an important Marian shrine under their wing at Santissima Annunziata, and King Sigismund to establish a funerary chapel within Wawel Cathedral, for the Princess of Éboli and her heirs it was necessary to adopt a parish church in its entirety to create a suitable representation of the family's piety. As Iain Fenlon recounts (*The Funeral Monument of the Princess of Éboli*), the family used their influence to have the pope elevate the institution to the status of a Collegiate Church, and set about providing it with ornaments, furnishings, and musical resources commensurate with their status. Here the overlap is particularly apparent between the Room of Sacred Spaces and that of Devotions, among whose exhibits are several that occupied space within a church or chapel, and several also which result from private sponsorship and piety. The case of the bequest of York bell-founder and politician Richard Tunnoc, however, as illuminated by Lisa Colton in the present room (*The Bell Founder's Window*), illustrates the potential fragility of such arrangements in the longer term: following the conversion of York Minster to the Anglican confession, all that remained of Tunnoc's elaborate memorial was the window he sponsored.

The Reformation brought significant changes to the design and use of churches in Protestant localities—including to their soundscapes, with the removal of privately endowed chantries, the re-orientation of liturgy away from the choir and towards the nave, and the encouragement of congregational singing. Although the bells whose manufacturing techniques are depicted in Tunnoc's window remained integral to the sound of the Anglican York Minster, the chantry founded in his memory did not. Monastic foundations fared particularly badly: only three decades after its completion, the new church attached to St Katherine's convent in Augsburg was closed by the newly Protestant city council. On the other hand, there were also significant continuities. The moral messages and Biblical commentary conveyed by the murals with their curious bestial musicians at the Church of Härnevi in Sweden, for example, discussed by Mattias Lundberg, remained relevant when its worshipers converted to Lutheranism (*A Sow Playing the Organ*). Indeed, even newly built Lutheran churches retained important similarities to those of the Catholic confession, as Inga Mai Groote underlines in her account of the *Hauptkirche Beatae Mariae Virginis, Wolfenbüttel*.

The architecture and decoration of Renaissance churches were primarily guided by liturgical, devotional, social, and ideological concerns. But an overall aesthetic agenda is no less obvious, to which the continuity of singing, as a symbol of the permanent presence of the divine, was integral. As these essays demonstrate, wall paintings, carved furniture, sculptures, stained-glass windows, tapestries, and many other surfaces and objects, offered visual representations of musical subjects, and spatial articulations of musical practices. As such, they both underline the general coherence of the aesthetic program of the sacred space, and enhance the musical experience of it, perpetuating it even when sounding musical performances were not actually taking place.

CCCCLXXVII ET HVIVS

53. The Basilica of the Santissima Annunziata, Florence

Giovanni Zanovello

Leon Battista Alberti, Michelozzo di Bartolommeo, et al., ca. 1250 with alterations and additions in the 14th, 15th and 17th centuries
Piazza della Santissima Annunziata, Florence

Millions of tourists visit Florence every year and many of them explore the city's churches. These buildings are ancient, grand, and beautiful. They are decorated with precious materials and house some of the greatest masterpieces of Italian art. Some, like San Marco or Santa Maria Novella, have become museums. Others are still officiated, balancing (as it were) their original function and present cultural interest. The Servite sanctuary of Santissima Annunziata is one of these churches, at once the most important Marian shrine in Florence and one of the top tourist destinations for art lovers. Preserved inside this dusky monument at the core of the city centre is a miraculous fresco of the Annunciation. The face of the Virgin Mary, according to an old tradition, was painted by an angel during a night in the thirteenth century, after the inexpert painter Bartolomeo gave up on the impossible task of representing the mother of God (Holmes 2013, 80-83 and 240-47; Oen 2011). Pilgrims young and old come from all over the world to join the veiled local worshippers and kneel in prayer before this medieval Madonna. Around them, sun-burned tourists in tank tops shoot selfies, while art lovers take in the architecture of Leon Battista Alberti and pay reverence to the paintings of Andrea del Sarto and Jacopo da Pontormo.

Mass tourism is a relatively recent phenomenon, but at Santissima Annunziata people of different nationalities, social class, and religious sensibilities dwelled side by side for centuries. Indeed, the church's very internal organization, as the Servite friars finalised it in the late fifteenth century, breaks the space up into different areas, where specific groups met and fulfilled distinct ritual functions. If this is common to virtually all monastic and cathedral churches from the time, highly unusual is the documentation that survives for Santissima Annunziata, allowing us to reconstruct the kinds of music that defined each area.

The church retains all the elements it had at the end of the fifteenth century, though the decoration is more recent. As we enter past a small covered cloister, we can pause just a few steps inside the main door. If we mentally erase the layer of marble and the wonderful Baroque ceiling, we can imagine ourselves to be in the Renaissance. The miraculous fresco is on the counter-facade behind us, just outside the picture. Before us, with chapels on both sides, the single wide nave ends in a transept and a triumphal arch leading to the Rotonda. The Rotonda is a round section where the main altar and the choir are placed, surrounded by nine more chapels, though these are only partly visible from our vantage point (fig. 53.1).

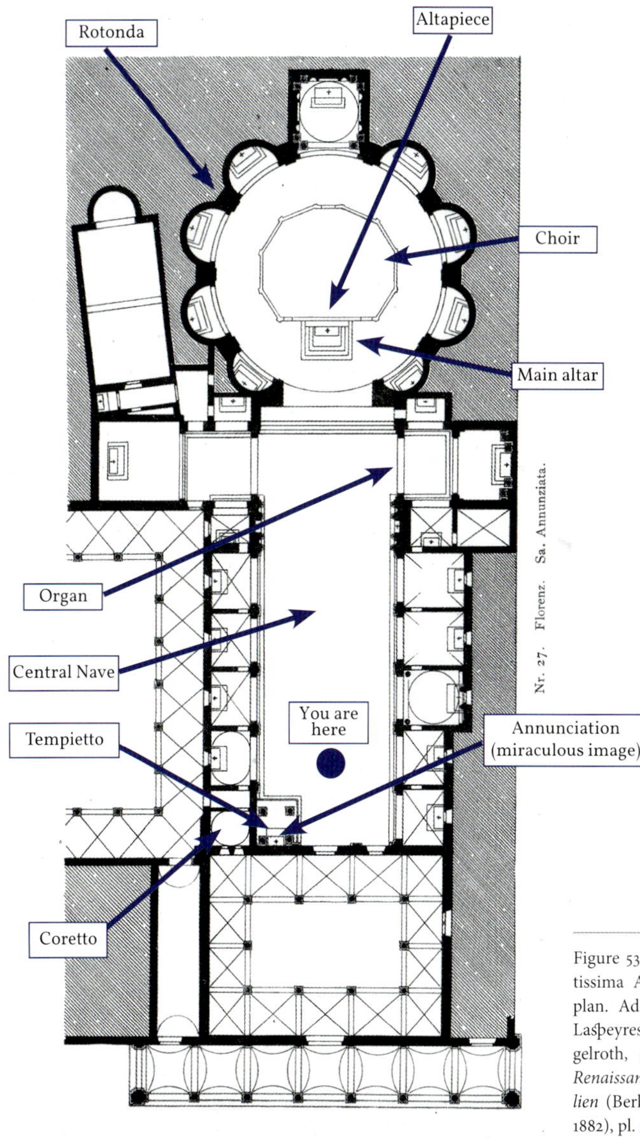

Figure 53.1: Florence, Santissima Annunziata, floor plan. Adapted from Paul Laspeyres and H. Angelroth, *Die Kirchen der Renaissance in Mittel-Italien* (Berlin: W. Spemann, 1882), pl. xi n. 27.

As is often the case with ancient churches, the floor plan of Santissima Annunziata results from multiple alterations that occurred at various times between the thirteenth and the fifteenth century. The first church was in existence in 1250, when the friars Servants of Mary received it and had the Annunciation fresco painted on a side wall. In 1290 the Falconieri family supported the completion of a much larger new church. Construction intensified during the following century (Taucci 1942; Verdon 2005), and in the fifteenth century special areas were remodeled by two well-known architects with the sponsorship of new wealthy patrons. Michelozzo di Bartolomeo created the Tempietto, an internal structure sheltering the Annunciation fresco, on a commission from banker Piero di Cosimo de' Medici (Morolli 1998, 148-63). Decades later, Marchese Ludovico III Gonzaga of Mantua charged architect Leon Battista Alberti with reforming the presbytery and choir area—a project completed in 1480 (Pacciani 2006, 185-91).

One may look at the plan and wonder why there were so many chapels—who could need over 25 altars under the same roof? In fact, the different areas of the church had specialised functions and served different constituencies. Instead of considering the church as one space, we should see it as a collection of different, connected places, each hosting rituals, participants, and sounds. The vast majority of the altars were located in the chapels on the sides of the nave, at the extremities of the transept, and around the choir. These were private places, in the possession of individual families who had donated the most money to the friary. Here, they buried their deceased and had the friars celebrate memorial Masses on behalf of their souls (Gardner von Teuffel 2005, 387; Landau 1975). These chapels were enclosed by locked gates that precluded access to anyone but members of the family and the friars. The substantial donations given by chapel holders effectively fueled the century-long construction. On any given day most chapels would be empty and dark with the exception of one or two, in which a friar celebrated a memorial service. There we would see the flickering light of candles and hear a simple spoken Mass, or possibly one sung in plainchant. In some cases a handful of family members would be present, though often the celebrant would be alone.

Certain chapels were used differently. The one at the right hand side of the transept, for example, was rented to the Confraternity of Santa Barbara, a pious association of northern immigrants living in Florence, who met there regularly (Liscia-Bemporad 1996). The Tempietto with the Annunciation fresco and the adjacent chapel were nominally under the patronage of the Medici family, but celebrations there were directly managed by the friary (Ames-Lewis 1993; Fantoni 1989; Finiello Zervas 1988; Liebenwein 1993). Every day the Servites engaged in a marathon of spoken and chanted Masses from well before dawn into the night, as part of their liturgical schedule but mostly in response to requests from devout individuals and families.

Plainchant, however, was not all people would hear in this part of the church. Starting in the early 1480s, the most sophisticated polyphonic music was deployed to decorate the Lady Mass on Saturday morning, which had long constituted the high point of the *Reverences for the Blessed Virgin Mary*, the set of rituals that the Servites dedicated to their patroness (Crociani 1987; Dal Pino 1953). Many extant documents help tell the story of this weekly Mass. Scholars have found contracts signed by French and Flemish singers committing "to sing the Mass of figural music in the Chapel of the Annunziata on Saturday morning" (D'Accone 1961, 334). Singers made these agreements with the prior, who was responsible for their salary and for procuring suitable repertory. In contrast, no private bequests in favor of polyphonic music are known.

We also have tantalising information about the repertory performed in the Tempietto. An exceptional notebook compiled by prior Antonio Alabanti (first half of the fifteenth century-1495) generically lists three-voice Masses, along with a Mass based on the *L'homme armé* melody and a Mass on the song *De tous biens plaine*. Numerous settings exist for each of these compositions, including those by Antoine Busnoys, Guillaume Du Fay, and possibly Jacob Obrecht (Zanovello 2014, 401-03). The musical manuscripts used at Santissima Annunziata to record polyphonic compositions have disappeared, so we may never be able to pin down the exact compositions performed there. Regardless, this kind of repertory sung by professional singers was normally associated with princely chapels and great cathedrals. By adopting it as part of their *Reverences*, the Servites sent a strong signal of artistic excellence (Gori 1981).

We should now move our gaze towards the nave, the only part of the church accessible to everyone. If this central area did not host liturgical celebrations in itself, people standing here would hear the sounds coming from the Tempietto, the main altar, the choir, and the private chapels. At certain times of the day, the nave also possessed its own soundscape, with organ music as one of its distinctive features. The organ tradition at Santissima Annunziata was illustrious, boasting one of the oldest instruments in the city and the memory of a Trecento virtuoso—celebrated Servite organist and composer Brother Andrea da Firenze (D'Accone 2001, 321; Fischer 1992, 142; Morelli 1997).

The nave also featured the singing of *laude*, or vernacular devotional songs. Although this music had been part of the Servite tradition for centuries, beginning in 1475 the priors of Santissima Annunziata gathered an updated repertory and hired local virtuosi like Ser Firenze di Lazzaro da Cortona to teach their novices. By the 1490s they also paid soloists—talented boys such as Baccino di Michelagnolo (alias Bartolomeo degli Organi), Zacharia d'Antonio, or Francesco di Smeraldo, who would sing from the organ loft, possibly accompanied by the instrument (Morelli 1998; Wilson 1992, 106). *Laude* were symbolically fitting for the nave, as they immediately conveyed the special devotion that moved the local people, the "regulars" of the church who were denied access to other areas. Their mostly chordal and melodic style evoked a musical and ritual language aimed at the urban mercantile and working classes, in contrast with the plainchant Masses sung in the private chapels of the wealthiest citizens, the dazzling polyphonic Saturday Mass, and the Divine Office—a ritual associated with the ordained community.

If we look straight, beyond the massive triumphal arch, we see the Rotonda, which was a separate building until 1480. This is the sanctuary, with the main altar, the friars' choir, and nine private chapels. In the Renaissance its access was restricted and only the friars and chapel holders could enter it, though the main altar is (and was) visible from the nave (Fastenrath Vinattieri and Schaefer 2011). Here the daily conventual Mass took place, mostly sung in plainchant or simple polyphony, the performance practice in which musical formulas were applied to chant melodies to create a richer sound, mostly proceeding by parallel intervals. From the nave, two doors are in view at the sides of the altar, leading inside the walled-in choir. Several times a day, dozens of friars wearing black robes would enter the church from the left side of the transept and walk in line through the choir doors to sing the Divine Office. Prior Alabanti probably instituted a polyphonic celebration of the Office. In the early 1480s professional singers joined the friars, though within a couple of years the latter were able to sing polyphony on their own. A page in the prior's notebook lists 21 friars divided by voice type, and the names of the teachers who helped each section rehearse (Gori 1981, 16-19; Smith 2002). As in the case of the music for the Tempietto, we cannot pin down this repertory. Yet we know from the account books that the priors bought and commissioned music for the choir at least until 1488, when Heinrich Isaac was paid for composing polyphonic psalms evidently used for the Office (Nádas 2014, 49).

The church is a meeting place. Tourists are a recent addition, but Santissima Annunziata was as bustling in the Renaissance as it is today. Friars were busy with their liturgical schedule, rich chapel-holders walked through it along with the artists they commissioned to memorialise their family's burial places. Pilgrims rich and poor expressed their devotion to the Virgin Mary in front of a century-old painting, perhaps hoping for a miracle that would change their lives. Then, as now, different people sought different things in this complex and venerable building, symbolically articulating the church with sounding rituals and musical styles.

ADDITIONAL REFERENCES: Benassi, Dias, and Faustini 1987; Böninger 2006; Brown 1981; Bulman 1971; Canali 2006; Casalini 1995; Casalini et al. 1987; Dal Pino et al. 2002; Ircani Menichini 2004; Nelson 1997; Strohm 1993, 269-87; Zanovello 2014.

Also ist die newe Heinrichstädter
Kirche von der Septen anzu-
sehen.
Paul Franck. invenit.

54. Hauptkirche Beatae Mariae Virginis, Wolfenbüttel

Inga Mai Groote

Paul Francke, 1608–1624
Michael-Praetorius-Platz, Wolfenbüttel

Image: Paul Franke (architect) and Elias Holwein (engraver), *Eigendliche Contrafactur der newerbawten Kirchen in der Heinrichstadt*, 1625. Woodcut, 80 x 59.4 cm. Germanisches Nationalmuseum, Nuremberg. Photo courtesy of the Germanisches Nationalmuseum.

If a Calvinist church could easily be identified by its sober interior, at first sight a Lutheran church did not necessarily differ much from its Catholic counterparts, as can be seen in the Main Church (*Hauptkirche*) *Beatae Mariae Virginis* (BMV) in Wolfenbüttel, planned in the years immediately after 1600 as a new parish church for the Heinrichstadt district (Möller 1987, ill. 1). BMV, designed by Paul Francke and named after an earlier chapel of St Mary in the same location, has often been regarded as the first important, large-scale new Lutheran church project, and can probably claim to be the best-preserved example of a German Lutheran church space from the end of the Renaissance. Its architecture, furnishings and decoration, however, resemble those that could be found in contemporary Catholic churches. The architecture combines Gothic and Renaissance elements in the windows, façades, and pillars. The structure is that of a hall church, with a polygonal choir and a tower at the opposite end. Inside, the choir is dominated by a richly carved high altar (the only altar in the building, in contrast to exhibit 53), and a sculpted pulpit is located at the front on the right-hand side. In the back, an organ is located above the entrance, the original organ case still in situ today, built by Gottfried Fritzsche in 1620-24. On the walls are coloured stone epitaphs for members of the ducal family of Braunschweig-Wolfenbüttel, as well as epitaphs with painted portraits of other distinguished figures. The sides and back of the nave are surrounded by large galleries with paintings on the front sides: in line with Protestant principles, images and statues depicting Biblical stories or Christian figures were presented for contemplation, just like the examples cited in sermons, rather than as objects of devotion. The music heard by contemporary visitors to this church would have partially comprised repertory familiar from Catholic contexts, namely Latin chant and Latin polyphony. The clearly audible confessional difference lay principally in the German hymns sung by the congregation and the school choir.

The reason for the relative lack of radical change from the Catholic church paradigm lies in the rather pragmatic Lutheran approach to places of worship. After the establishment of the Reformation in German territories, Lutheran communities usually took over existing churches, so there was no immediate need for new buildings. The Protestant understanding of churches as places of worship, but not as consecrated spaces, did not, in principle, make older churches unusable (Isaiasz 2012). Iconoclastic movements in the earlier sixteenth century had, in some places, destroyed altars and artwork as possible objects of idolatry, and had left dismantled interiors, especially in the Southwest of Germany due to its proximity to Zwinglian and Calvinist influences; this, however, was by no means a generalised phenomenon. In wealthy cities and towns, especially in northern Germany, reformers often avoided destroying church interiors, considering that they had involved major investments by earlier generations (Heal 2017).

From a Lutheran point of view, church buildings are important for creating a public space devoted to worship, where the community performs religious practices. The architectural form of the hall church serves these purposes well, and the persistence of established architectural features and older styles of decoration can generally be observed in German-speaking regions well into the seventeenth century (Hipp 1979). Therefore, even the seemingly Gothic elements of BMV are not so much the product of intentional historicism, as a successful combination of common elements aimed at creating an impressive, richly decorated church. The project was initiated by the churchwardens of Heinrichstadt, but received major financial contributions from the duke, Heinrich Julius of Braunschweig-Wolfenbüttel (1564-1613), as part of a larger urban development project, with BMV as the burial place of the ducal family. BMV was also meant to become the central seat of the church of this territory, in which, from 1620 on, new pastors were ordained (Möller 1987, 35-36).

The first newly-built Lutheran churches were court chapels, which were not only venues for religious practice but also took on a role in representing the ruler. Earliest of all was the court chapel built in Neuburg in 1543 for Ottheinrich of Pfalz-Neuburg; but more influential was that completed the following year in Torgau for Johann Friedrich I of Saxony, inaugurated with a sermon by Luther himself, and the famous or notorious motet *Beati immaculati* by Johann Walter, which showcases canonic voices and an ostinato structure in the Bass as markers of sophisticated, stately polyphony. Torgau has a very sober interior, with virtually no decorations, and the prominent placement of the pulpit emphasises the importance of preaching; the organ is located above the altar. New parish churches, whose primary function was to serve the local congregations, were built in Joachimsthal (1534-40) and Marienberg (1564), but these have been either destroyed or extensively altered. The closest example to Wolfenbüttel is the Stadtkirche of Bückeburg, inaugurated in 1613 and built under similar circumstances: Count Ernst von Schaumburg wished to embellish the town when he moved his residency to Schloss Bückeburg (Albrecht 1999). In this case, the need was felt to mark a confessional stance: the inscription over the entrance reads "EXEMPLUM RELIGIONIS NON STRUCTURAE" (an example of faith, not of architecture), which is also an acrostic of Ernst's name. In Bückeburg we find once again a prominent altar, pulpit, and organ, the latter built by Esaias Compenius (Tiggemann 2012). For spatial reasons, the organ is located above the altar; there are galleries around the nave, and we know that some space in the gallery, on the left side close to the organ, was reserved for the choir (Albrecht 1999, 97).

The role played by music in BMV followed the by then well-established Lutheran tradition: music was sung by the choir of the school in Heinrichstadt under the direction of the school cantors (from 1600 Henning Schaper, from 1618 Heinrich Elsmann, then Erich Sötefleisch, Johannes Vilter, and David Leibius), and organists were also employed at BMV (during this period, Christophorus Sellius and Ludolph Schildt; Vogelsänger 2013, 267). The liturgy was determined by the relevant church orders, in this case those of Braunschweig (the oldest, authored by Johannes Bugenhagen, dates from 1528, the revised version from 1569). They provide examples of a Lutheran Mass—which omitted only the theologically contested portions of its Catholic model such as the Canon of the Mass, otherwise remaining close to the conventional formula—and of other kinds of services. The main services (Sunday Mass, Vespers, and Morning Sermon) included Latin chant in alternation with German hymns, and the school choir also had to sing a few polyphonic pieces (no more than two or three at once if the organ was also played; Sehling 1957, 141-44).

The school choir was trained through regular music lessons, as documented by the 1605 school order for Wolfenbüttel, which resembles those of other Lutheran centres (Koldewey 1890, 119-20, 123). The curriculum stipulates that music should be taught at noon, and the pupils should also perform sacred pieces on certain days in the streets and sing at funerals. For the latter, a school music book published by cantor Elsmann contains an appendix with the most common funeral hymns and chants complying with the church order (Elsmann 1619).

The musical repertory used in liturgy at the time BMV was built consisted of contemporary polyphony, motets, and concertos, as can be seen in the music inventories signed by the cantors (Groote, forthcoming): prints by Friedrich Weissensee (*Opus melicum*, 1602), Melchior Vulpius (*Canticum beatissimae Mariae*, 1605) and Hieronymus Praetorius (*Cantiones sacrae de praecipuis festis*, 1607) were part of the music collection. The local court chapelmasters, Michael Praetorius and (from 1621 onwards) Daniel Selichius, donated copies of their publications (*Musae Sioniae*, 1605 and ff., and *Opus novum*, 1624, respectively) to the church. Also a set of ten handwritten partbooks containing "motets by diverse outstanding authors" (as the contemporary description reads), copied by Franz Algermann (organist between 1598 and 1603) and donated to the church, obviously stayed in use for some time, and is still traceable as of 1668. An important portion of this repertory was written for large-scale performing forces, and probably intended for more formal events. We may therefore assume that hymns, Latin chant, and also elaborate polyphony were to be heard, the latter most likely with the participation of musicians from the court chapel, which still was of considerable size until it was disbanded in 1626 (Emans 2016).

As for the physical location of music in the church, it could usually be found in two places: for the purpose of singing responses and hymns and supporting the congregation in singing, the choir could be placed at the front, close to the ministers and the benches of the congregation; whereas for performing polyphonic and concerted repertory the ensemble was likely to gather close to the organ on a gallery. This spatial arrangement is described in one of the first theoretical treatises providing a model for Protestant church architecture, Joseph Furttenbach the Younger's *KirchenGebäw* (Furttenbach 1649). One of the few architectural traditions that can be regarded as relatively specific to Lutheran practice in the seventeenth century is indeed the building of prominent musicians' galleries (an example of which is the repurposing of a medieval rood screen in St Marien in Lübeck; see Range 2012). The use of a part of the gallery close to the organ for the choir is also attested in the Wolfenbüttel church: in the documents it is called "pupils' choir" (Schülerchor), and candle holders were bought for it in 1657, "to be used at the lecterns from which the pupils sing chant during the Morning Sermon" (*Rechnungen über Einnahme und Ausgabe bei der Kirche B.M.V.*, Niedersächsisches Landesarchiv Wolfenbüttel, 100 N, Nr. 720 II). The placement of musicians on the organ gallery (in this instance, a large group, including adult singers and instrumentalists) is also depicted in an engraving that shows the church interior on the occasion of a ducal entry in 1646 (fig. 54.1).

Figure 54.1: View of the interior (west side) of the Hauptkirche Beatae Mariae Virginis in Wolfenbüttel. Engraving by Sebastian Furck after Albert Freyse, in Martin Gosky, *Arbustum vel Arboretum Augustaeum* (Wolfenbüttel: Stern, ca. 1650). Wolfenbüttel, Herzog August Bibliothek, t-904-2f-helmst-1s. Photo courtesy of the Herzog August Bibliothek.

Those parts of a church interior where music takes place are sometimes depicted in the frontispieces of early seventeenth-century music prints, which often establish a symbolic parallel between church music and celestial music, with angels singing and playing instruments. On the frontispiece used for Michael Praetorius' *Musae Sioniae*, three choirs of musicians can be seen next to the organs, placed on galleries and at ground level (the latter probably to obtain a better image composition). The upper part of the page shows the heavens with choirs of angels making music, as a model to which church music could be compared (Praetorius 1607). The 1676 Dresden *Geistreiches Gesang-Buch* shows realistic elements including an organ in the gallery and the *Kantorei* (choir) in the foreground; here, an analogy between contemporary and Biblical music is established through the figure of King David playing the harp in front of the altar and hence inside the choir space, while the *Kantorei* is placed in a plausible position in front of the congregation, outside the choir screen (*Geistreiches Gesang-Buch* 1676). In both cases, the visual discourse clearly validates Lutheran church music practices as a reflection or foretaste of heavenly music, while at the same time evoking typical forms of music-making in church spaces. The role of music, therefore, although theologically regarded as accessory, is emphasised by the sumptuous organs and the prominent placement of the choirs, or other music ensembles, in Lutheran churches. Music may have been an accessory, but it was certainly a very powerful one—a prominent line of Lutheran thought. Thus the inner soundscape of BMV would have included the different types of music used in Lutheran liturgy, in addition to the spoken liturgy and sermons to be heard from the pulpit, so that the physical church building would have been an opportunity to realise the ideal formulated by theologians with the help of local structures and resources.

55. A Sow Playing the Organ

Mattias Lundberg

Albertus Pictor, Härnevi, ca. 1480
Mural
Church of Härnevi, Enköping (Sweden)

Albertus Pictor is unique among mural painters in late-medieval Sweden, as his work (and that of his workshop of apprentices) is so easily identified, with several distinct features, motifs, and stylistic peculiarities. His paintings are also uniquely well-preserved—some have never been painted over, while others have been carefully restored; in some instances in fact whitewashing has even acted as a preservative. In the vernacular Albertus was styled Albrecht Ymmenhausen, and on this basis it has been assumed that he hailed from the town of Immenhausen in Hessen, Germany. He and his workshop painted murals in 39 churches in Sweden, of which 37 have been partly or entirely preserved. Most of these are located throughout the region of the great Lake Mälaren, stretching westwards from Stockholm in southern Sweden.

Many of Albertus' paintings feature musicians or elements of music iconography. Some of the musical depictions have been interpreted as allegorical, while others appear to be intended as realistic scenes, often with moral and social connotations.

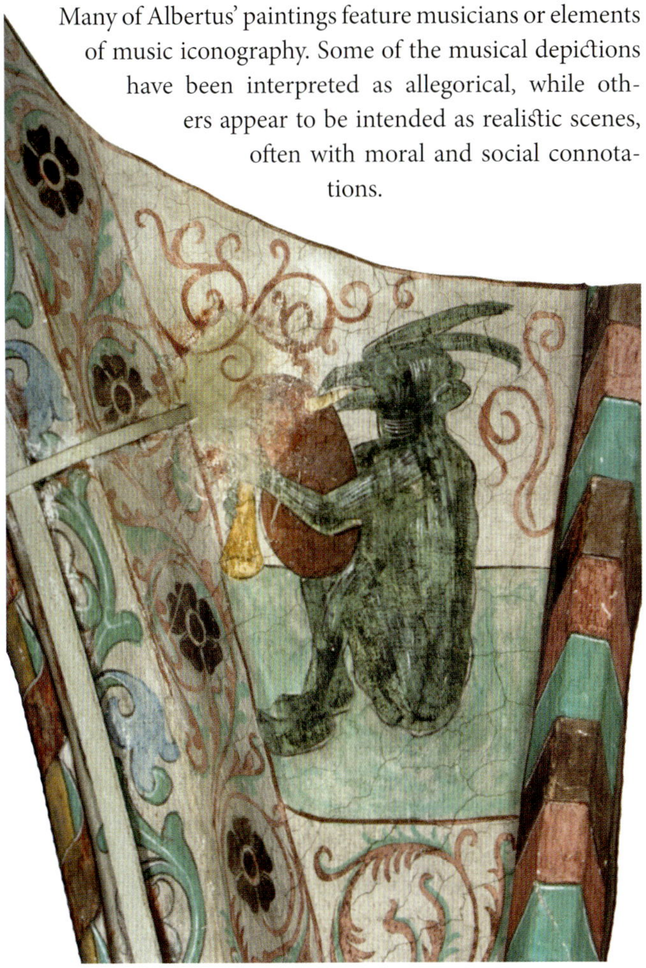

Among the most captivating and curious examples of Albertus' paintings are those in the Church of Härnevi, located about 11 km north of the city of Enköping. Here we find, in the eastern choir vault, a number of seemingly allegorical depictions of instruments being played by animals. In one bay is a sow playing a positive organ, and in the opposite bay a goat (or goat-devil) playing bagpipes (fig. 55.1). The red lead oxide pigments that produce the red tones and nuances of these paintings tend to turn black over time, but in the case of Härnevi they have been unusually well preserved under layers of soot from candles. As subject-matter the sow-musician is fantastical, or fable-like, but seemingly intended to be realistic in style. It is not, as in some other Albertus murals, a stylised or mannerist depiction of an animal, with anthropomorphic tendencies, but a pig just as any church visitor in Härnevi would have seen it in their daily life.

The little organ scene is particularly interesting in light of the fact that the last source to mention Albertus alive, dating from 1509, identifies him as a liturgical organist at the Guild of Corpus Christi in Stockholm (Collijn 1923, 11 June 1509). This testifies to his knowledge of instrument construction and performance practices, which can otherwise of course never be taken for granted with painters in this period. The painting is thus not only of artistic value for a modern observer, but also furnishes evidence for organology and the social history of instruments and musicians. Although the depiction is simplified, omitting the bellows, it can be fruitfully compared to a number of unusually well-preserved organs from late-medieval Sweden. These include the fourteenth-century Norrlanda and Sundre organs, and the fifteenth-century instrument from Knutby (fig. 55.2). The latter is a considerably larger instrument than that depicted in Härnevi, but one coeval with the painting, and which stood in a church within the same diocese (Uppsala), only 70 km from Härnevi. The comparison confirms that Albertus knew very well how such instruments were constructed and how they were played. While he certainly need not have identified with the sow, he knew

Figure 55.1: Albertus Pictor, *Devil Playing Bagpipes*, ca. 1480. Mural. Church of Härnevi, Enköping. Photo © Gabriel Hildebrand / Swedish National Heritage Board / CC-BY 4.0.

Figure 55.2: Remnants of the windchest from the late-medieval organ from the Church of Knutby in the diocese of Uppsala. Photo © Ola Myrin / The Swedish History Museum / CC-BY 4.0.

how she ought to be depicted when he planned out and executed this unusual scene. This type of technical understanding of the instrument is evident from the inverted perspective of the pipes, where the pipes are represented as being longer at the distant end of the perspective, and shorter at the proximate end. The top frame of the pipes follows this distinct contradiction of the expected proportions.

Even if the goat bagpiper and the porcine organist are depicted in separate bays, they belong to a context of the totality of the eastern vault murals in Härnevi (fig. 55.3). Typically

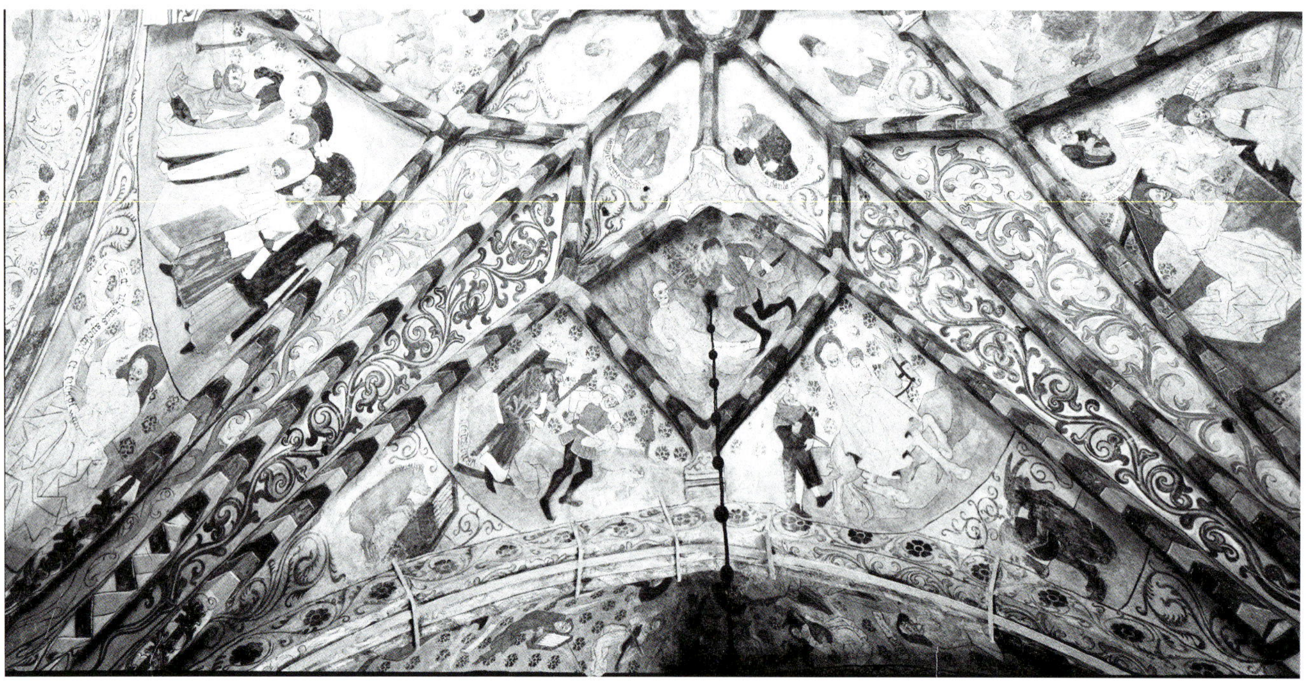

Figure 55.3: Albertus Pictor, general view of the western side of the eastern choir vault, c.1480. Murals. Church of Härnevi, Enköping. Photo © Nils Lagergren / Swedish National Heritage Board / Public Domain.

for Albertus, a Biblical narrative at the centre of the vault is "glossed," "commented," or simply ornamented, by scenes painted in a row below the biblical subject. Above the organ-playing sow we find as the main theme for this vault King Herod enthroned ordering the massacre of all infants in Judea, according to the Gospel of St Matthew, along with one of the king's lackeys slaughtering an infant with a dagger. Above the goat we can observe the Holy family fleeing to Egypt, as a consequence of the massacre. The four scenes are thus clearly related as a commented narrative disposed along two planes. In view of this we could perhaps interpret the sow as an anti-Semitic element, in its relation to the medieval Christian understanding of Herod's crime: in the tradition of the so-called "Judensau" Jews are shown suckling the teets of a sow (Fabre-Vassas 1997). The teets are indeed marked in the Härnevi sow, and such an interpretation also finds support from the presence of an equivalent scene in Albertus' murals in the Church of Husby-Sjutolft, depicting the medieval legend of a sow hiding under a brewer's tub, being exposed by Jesus. Attention has been drawn to one later anti-Semitic parallel depiction of organs in such a context, namely the frontispiece of Martin Luther's *Von der Juden und ihren Lügen* (Wittenberg: Lufft, 1543). Here it is the horned Moses who is depicted playing the organ (Bengtsson 2006, 32-33). The notion would be, according to such a contextual interpretation, that the organ in both cases provides baleful music to accompany shameful acts.

The two animal musicians below the scenes of Herod and the Holy family may also be seen as representations, fantastic though they are, of the earthly life, the world as observed by the lay parishioner in the 1480s. North-European mural painters often adorn the lowest panels of a vault with savage beasts and savage men, and below that the vegetation of the wild world, in keeping with the inclination to place the most celestial themes highest and more central, and the most mundane themes lowest and most peripheral. The two musicians moreover provide a common type of mirroring contrast between female (sow) and male (billy goat). Eva Helenius has interpreted the two animal musicians, along with other animal depictions by Albertus, as representing different deadly sins (Helenius 2007, 65-66). The pig raising its bristles, as our organist clearly does, recurs also in Albertus' paintings in the Church of Härkeberga, and appears to be connected to the deadly sin of wrath (*ira*). The wrath of the sow and the powerful instrument of the organ have thus been interpreted by some as the wrath *of* Herod, rather than *against* Herod (Kilström 1968, 51). Modern pigs do not raise their back hair to the same extent as do boars and the native breeds of the Swedish Middle Ages, but the enraged pig raising bristle is a common theme in medieval fables. The inflation of the bagpipe has similarly been linked in Albertus' paintings to the sin of pride (*superbia*).

While the vaults at Härnevi in general were left without whitewash for all to see over the generations since these paintings were executed, oddly the organ-playing sow alone was washed over in the eighteenth century. The reasons for hiding away this single motif from among the rich entirety of the murals are not obvious. It has been suggested that the subject appeared too "shameless" for the eighteenth-century clergy and parishioners (Melin 2006, 49). If that were so, why would it be considered more offensive than the goat with bagpipes facing it in the vault? The anti-Semitic connotations, so offensive to modern observers, are unlikely to have been considered problematic among the church's eighteenth-century occupants. A more plausible explanation, drawing on the social history of Swedish Lutheranism, would be to suggest that the perceived impropriety of this scene lay precisely in the conjunction of the lowly pig with the organ, an instrument that was in church use at the time—indeed, an instrument connected with the commendable and respectable offices of cantor and organist in Swedish Lutheran society at this later date. While the bagpiping of the goat-devil was to the early-modern observer unmistakably allegorical, in the case of the musical pig the liturgical presence and use of organs may have caused an undesired contamination between the realms of the allegorical and the real.

Interpretations of the striking manner with which the sow is depicted in this painting must take into account matters of organology, theological and homiletical currents, and social mores from the fifteenth century onwards. At the same time, however, it is important to recognise the playful character of this kind of image, fulfilling what seems to have been a desire on the part of late medieval artists and artisans to catch the viewer's interest practically as an end in itself. The fact that such a theologically and liturgically peripheral subject as a porcine organist could receive a central place in the choir nave of a church certainly invites such a reading, as Cornell and Wallin have observed:

> To some degree they represent humanity gone astray, her perversion and bestiality. But they have foremost been painted as an engaging, at times parodic and humorous, type of dissipation. [...] Several new combinations he [Albertus] has certainly made up himself and he has clearly taken pleasure in painting them, as they have also been much to the delight of laity and clergy alike (Cornell and Wallin 1972, 60-61).

Additional references: Lundberg 2017.

56. Ceiling with the Muses and Apollo

Tim Shephard

Alessandro Pampurino, Cremona, ca. 1500
Fresco on plaster, with gilt wood bosses, 427 (diameter) x 179 (depth) cm
Inscribed: CALLIOPE; APOLLO
Victoria and Albert Museum, London
Photo © Victoria and Albert Museum

In 1497 Francesca Maria Sforza, prioress of the large but relatively poor Cremonese Augustinian convent of Santa Monica, enlisted the help of her half-brother Ludovico Sforza detto il Moro, the duke of Milan, in a plan to improve the fortunes of her community. Together they persuaded Pope Alexander VI to force the Cistercian nuns of San Giovanni della Pipia, known colloquially as the convent "della Colomba," to merge with the nuns of Santa Monica, bringing with them the rich endowments of their eleventh-century monastery. On 25 September 1498 the Cistercian nuns entered their new home and became Augustinians; their former convent, now the property of Santa Monica, was assigned to a community of Benedictines (Merula 1627).

Unsurprisingly, some of the former nuns "della Colomba"—among whom were daughters, sisters, and aunts of the foremost families of Cremona—took a dim view of these developments. Forming a splinter group retaining the identity of their original community, they began litigation in Cremona and in Rome, and established a new cloister attached to the tiny church of San Marco, located on the opposite side of the city from Santa Monica. Although their legal action was ultimately unsuccessful, a small Cistercian community held fast to their new home up to the 1540s, when the antisocial behaviour of local youths forced the nuns to disperse to the houses of their respective families. Their cloister was quickly repurposed as a charitable hospice for poor women, many elements of its decoration remaining in situ up to the nineteenth century, when several paintings were detached and sold, among them this decorated ceiling (Merula 1627; Aglio 2005).

Pampurino's Muses were probably commissioned by the sisters as they built and occupied their new convent towards the end of 1498. Most likely the nine decorated the community's library, as they did in the Florentine Badia Fiesolana in frescoes completed around three decades earlier (Gombrich 1962). Apollo and the Muses, classical figures redolent of literature, learning, and the arts, are certainly an obvious choice for a space associated with reading and writing. They were also used in the decoration of study-rooms in contemporary secular palaces (Mottola-Molfino and Natali 1991)—for example, the Muses begun for Leonello d'Este's villa of Belfiore and completed under his successor Borso, and those in the so-called *Tempietto delle Muse* in Federico da Montefeltro's ducal palace in Urbino. Commenting on his choice of decorative scheme, Leonello's tutor Guarino da Verona noted that the name "Muses" means "seekers" in Greek, "because they seek after all things or because they are sought after by all men, desire for knowledge being innate in man" (Baxandall 1965, 186 and 202).

If the Muses were easy to justify in broad terms as occupants of a literary space, their meanings in such a context could be multiple and subtle. Guarino's etymological comment was borrowed from Isidore's *Etymologies*, an encyclopedic early medieval source that formed part of a whole battery of interpretations of the Muses cited repeatedly in commentaries on the works of Ovid and Virgil, and in mythographic guidebooks such as Giovanni Boccaccio's *Genealogy of the Pagan Gods*. Unlike their relatives the seven Liberal Arts, whose conventionalised personifications graced many medieval manuscripts, the iconography of the Muses was to a substantial extent a new task in the visual arts of the fifteenth century (Anderson 1991). Fortunately for Pampurino, the challenge of harnessing the Muses' rich mythography to a visual presentation had already been met, in a set of Ferrarese engravings from the 1460s known today, misleadingly, as the *Tarocchi di Mantegna* (Lippincott 1987, 1:58-67). Like several other artists of the later fifteenth and early sixteenth centuries, faced with painting Apollo and the Muses, Pampurino adopted the *Tarocchi* as his model (figs. 56.1-2).

The *Tarocchi* Muses and Apollo are indeed best seen as a visual encoding of the nine's written mythography, cuing exactly the range of readings found in—for example—Boccaccio's *Genealogy*. The order of the Muses in the set, a feature that varies greatly, derives from an etymological reading configuring them as an allegory of the acquisition of knowledge, found in Fulgentius' *Mythologies*. Their attributes and activities broadly follow those found in a short poem on the Muses, now usually ascribed to Ausonius, which circulated in the period within Virgil's oeuvre under the title "De musarum inventis," with a list appended assigning to the nine specific arts:

Figure 56.1: Ferrarese, *Euterpe*, ca. 1465. Engraving with gilding, 17.8 x 9.8 cm. National Gallery of Art, Washington. Photo courtesy of the National Gallery of Art, Washington.

Figure 56.2: Euterpe detail of Pampurino, *Ceiling with the Muses and Apollo*. Photo © Victoria and Albert Museum, London.

> Clio, singing of famous deeds, restores times past to life.
> Euterpe's breath fills the sweet-voiced flutes.
> Thalia rejoices in the loose speech of comedy.
> Melpomene cries aloud with the echoing voice of gloomy tragedy.
> Terpsichore with her lyre stirs, swells, and governs the emotions.
> Erato bearing the plectrum harmonises foot, song and voice in the dance.
> Urania examines the motions of the heavens and stars.
> Calliope commits heroic songs to writing.
> Polymnia expresses all things with her hands and speaks by gesture.
> The power of Apollo's will enlivens the whole circle of these Muses:
> Phoebus sits in their midst and in himself possesses all their gifts.
> (Ausonius 1921, 281)

> Clio invented history; Melpomene tragedy; Thalia comedy; Euterpe the pipe; Terpsichore the psaltery; Erato geometry; Calliope literature; Urania astrology; Polyhymnia rhetoric. (Virgil 1469, 382)

Accordingly, Euterpe plays pipes; Terpsichore plays a "lyre" (really a contemporary equivalent—a cetra); Erato is a dancer, based on a dancing maenad commonly found on late-antique Bacchic sarcophagi; Urania is the Liberal Art Astrology; and Calliope has a trumpet, commonly used in ancient and contemporary verse as a symbol for heroic themes in poetry. However, the artist of the *Tarocchi* was also aware that the words "Muses" and "music" shared a common etymology, an oft-repeated insight derived from Isidore's *Etymologies*. Thus, musical instruments are assigned even when pseudo-Virgil does not specifically mention one: Polyhymnia has a portative organ; Thalia plays a rebec; and Melpomene has a double pipe, probably modelled on the auloi-playing maenad found on several Bacchic sarcophagi.

The mysterious circles accompanying all of the Muses in the *Tarocchi* point to an interpretation found in Macrobius' widely-read commentary on Cicero's *Dream of Scipio*, and also in Martianus Capella's *The Marriage of Philology and Mercury*, according to which the Muses' singing gives voice to the heavenly spheres, a Muse assigned to each. This reading, which of course rests on the idea that all the Muses are musicians, was an adaptation of Plato, who had assigned the same role to the Sirens. Thalia, the only seated Muse and the only one in the *Tarocchi* to lack a circle, is surrounded by abundant foliage. Following Martianus, who gave specific designations for all the Muses, she is located on the immobile sphere of the Earth (Copernican heliocentrism is still some decades in the future). Apollo, meanwhile, addresses a starry sphere with a pedagogical pointer: he is, in Boccaccio's paraphrase of Macrobius, "the moderator and conductor of the celestial melody" (Boccaccio 2011, 638).

The Cremonese Muses follow the mythography implied in the *Tarocchi* in almost every important respect, producing a range of possible readings: as an allegory of knowledge, as patronesses of the arts, as musicians, and as the harmonious choir of the heavens. However, Pampurino replaces the *Tarocchi* Muses' landscape settings with elements of monumental architecture, an adaptation presumably designed to blend them with the fictive stonework of the vault. Thalia is given a colossal throne very similar to those in which Leonello d'Este's painted Muses sit, suggesting that Pampurino was aware of more than one Ferrarese model for his subject.

From among all the several contemporary sets of Muses that were modelled on those in the *Tarocchi*, Pampurino's is the only one to preserve the spheres, suggesting that the Macrobian interpretation of the Muses as purveyors of divine harmony had a particular importance to his patrons, the nuns della Colomba. By the second half of the fifteenth century their role in this respect had come to play a very particular part in poetics (Greenfield 1981), as explained for example in the university professor Cristoforo Landino's commentaries on Virgil's *Aeneid* and Dante's *Commedia*, which quickly won a place among the standard reference works of Italian literary culture. Here the Muses' identity with the harmonious spheres is combined with their traditional role as conveyers of divine inspiration to poets, turning poetry into an earthly echo of the divine order of the universe. Landino was well aware that this role had long been claimed for music, not poetry; but music, he explains, is of two kinds:

> There are some who delight themselves with the harmony of the voice and of musical instruments, and these are vulgar and shallow musicians; there are others who are of more profound judgement, who with measured verses express the intimate sentiments of their mind, and these are those who, spurred on by the divine spirit, can write the most profound and meaningful verses. And this is called "poetry" by Plato, which does not only delight the ears with the sweetness of the voice, as does that vulgar music, but as I say describes high and mysterious and divine insights, and on celestial ambrosia pastures the mind (Landino 2001, 1:260).

In a Christian context, the motive force animating the heavenly spheres, and thus directing them in their harmony, had long been identified with God himself. It was therefore a short step to identify the nine sphere-singing Muses with the nine orders of angels, a Christian correction that had already been applied to Plato's sphere-singing Sirens. In his *Book on the Nature of Love*, printed in 1525 but in drafting as Pampurino completed his work, Mario Equicola explains that:

> Platonists do not hesitate to say that by Apollo is meant God, by the Muses the spirits of the celestial spheres, called by some intelligences: Calliope represents all the voices and that which they believed to be on the Primo Mobile, Urania the starry sky, Polyhymnia to be in Saturn, Terpsichore in Jupiter, Clio Mars, Melpomene the sun, Erato Venus, Euterpe Mercury, Thalia the moon. These "muses," whose name the enemies of the Christian dare recklessly to affirm, are in fact none other than that which we call the nine orders of angels (Equicola 1525, fol. 60^{v}).

The angels, of course, made their music in constant celebration and praise of the Almighty God. As the nuns enjoyed the literary treasures and works of philosophy or theology stored in their library, they could feel comforted that even the most salacious verse, read with sensitivity and understanding, tantalised the mind of the reader with an echo of the harmony of the Christian heaven—a perspective strongly promoted by some of the literary personalities of the day, many of whom were also priests.

Equicola worked as secretary to the noblewoman Isabella d'Este, whose own study in Mantua was also adorned with a painting of Apollo and the Muses, completed shortly before Pampurino's by Andrea Mantegna (*Parnassus*, Louvre, Paris). Isabella's Muses cavort in a circle-dance beneath a fantastical arch of rock, atop which are the adulterous lovers Mars and Venus. Their salacious story was told in verse by Ovid and others, poets whose divine inspiration guaranteed a hidden imprint of heavenly truth, accessible to the reader capable of penetrating the veil of the poetic fiction. Isabella, an enthusiastic amateur musician who enjoyed singing contemporary love verse to the lute, was routinely compared to the Muses and even named a tenth muse. Although certainly a conventional compliment for a woman of literary or artistic inclinations, Isabella's muse-persona was also a strategy of literary self-fashioning, configuring her love songs as acts of divine revelation, and her broader literary interests as a commitment to sacred wisdom.

Figure 56.3: Oculus—detail of Pampurino, *Ceiling with the Muses and Apollo*. Photo © Victoria and Albert Museum, London.

Figure 56.4: North Italian, *Mirror frame*, ca. 1500. Carved walnut and partly gilt, 49 cm. Victoria and Albert Museum, London. Photo © Victoria and Albert Museum.

Pampurino's Muses offered an opportunity for the nuns similarly to project themselves into the resonant space of the spheres in their vault. At the apex of the ceiling is an oculus opening out onto a blue sky and a balcony where three figures are visible—probably inspired by a similar trompe l'oeil balcony painted by Mantegna for Isabella's husband Francesco Gonzaga. The three figures—an old man, a young woman, and a child—are quite distinctively disposed. The man stares down intently into the room below, whereas the woman's eyes are hooded, almost closed, and she cups a hand to her ear to listen attentively. The oculus with its circular stone framing is very similar in form to contemporary mirrors, usually small, round and encased in a frame of concentric circles (figs. 56.3-4).

Looking up at the figures looking down, the viewer is prompted to mirror herself in them, and especially in the woman, attending carefully to the divine harmony resounding across the concave space of the vault (fig. 56.5), in the hope of catching an echo of divine truth and a revelation of celestial bliss to come. In its vertical dimension the room places the viewer in the position occupied by St Cecilia in Raphael's famous altarpiece commissioned by the Bolognese noblewoman Elena Duglioli dall'Olio (Pinacoteca Nazionale, Bologna), turning away from earthly matters to direct the senses toward the harmony of angels above.

The mirror formed a visual counterpart to the sonic echo of divine harmony that found expression in inspired verse, and

Figure 56.5: Alternative view of Pampurino, *Ceiling with the Muses and Apollo*. Photo © Victoria and Albert Museum, London.

appears in that sense at the feet of Pampurino's Apollo (fig. 56.6). Another university professor, Angelo Poliziano, explains in his *Nutricia* that in the inspired mind gleams a reflection attesting "to the mystic Muse of heaven ... For as the image of a star is reflected in a mirror, as limpid water poured into a glass gleams in the sun's rays, so the celestial modulations fashion and enflame the luminous and purified spirits of poets" (Poliziano 2004, 120-23). In her 1468 treatise *Mirror of Illumination*, Sister Illuminata Bembo reported that during the worship of her Bolognese Clarissan community, "many angelic spirits descended from heaven and came together with us to praise the divine mercy" (Bembo 2001, 29). For the sisters della Colomba, such a mirroring of the divine in the earthly was not restricted to their audible celebration of the liturgy, but extended into their study and learning, in a library space prepared expressly to prompt such an interpretation.

Additional references: Christian et al. 2014; Fabianski 1988; Guidobaldi 1992; Haar 1974; Schröter 1977; Shephard 2014; Shephard et al. 2019; Ştefănescu 2020.

Acknowledgements: The research presented in this essay was completed within the project "Music in the Art of Renaissance Italy 1420-1540," funded by a Leverhulme Trust Research Project Grant. I gladly acknowledge the assistance and stimulating dialogue of my project colleagues, Patrick McMahon, Annabelle Page, Sanna Raninen, Serenella Sessini, and Laura Ştefănescu.

Figure 56.6: Apollo—detail of Pampurino, *Ceiling with the Muses and Apollo*. Photo © Victoria and Albert Museum, London.

D.H.

57. St Katherine's Convent Church, Augsburg

Barbara Eichner

Hans Hieber, 1516-1517
Katharinengasse, Augsburg
Image: Daniel Hopfer, *The Lesson of the Widow's Mite*, ca. 1525. Etching, 29 x 20.1 cm. Ailsa Mellon Bruce Fund, National Gallery of Art, Washington. Photo courtesy of the National Gallery of Art.

The architecture of the former convent church of St Katherine in Augsburg is very simple and yet sophisticated: it is a rare example of a hall church of two naves, which are divided by six slender pillars into seven bays, with no aisles or side chapels. The east end terminates in a polygonal three-eighth choir, and an elevated nuns' gallery was erected above the four western bays. As shown in an etching by Daniel Hopfer from the 1520s, a screen shielded the Dominican sisters from the view of the lay people who had access to the ground floor of the church and its altars. Above the gallery soars a lofty vaulted ceiling with round arches; the windows visible in the west wall (and those in the choir) are likewise rounded. These are not archaisms but self-consciously modern gestures, and an early example of Renaissance influences north of the Alps. The church belongs to the same intense period of building activity in Augsburg that resulted not only in the iconic Fugger chapel at St Anna, but also in newly built churches for the Dominican friars at St Magdalena (which also has two naves but slightly pointed vaults) as well as the Dominican convent churches St Margareth (1521) and St Ursula (1520) (Sölch 2010, 496 and 503).

The design of St Katherine's is commonly attributed to Hans Hieber, who is best known for the spectacular architecture of the Neupfarrkirche in Regensburg, surviving in a wooden model (Bischoff 1990). In the 1720s St Katharine's Church was embellished with Baroque stucco and frescoes, which were removed when the church was turned into a picture gallery following the convent's secularisation in 1802. Today it houses a branch of the Bayerische Staatsgemäldesammlungen, where South-German art from around 1500—much of it originating from Augsburg—is permanently displayed (Schawe 2001). It is difficult to form an impression of the church interior after the conversion of 1833-35 divided it into three separate rooms (roughly equivalent to the areas of choir, lay church, and nuns' gallery), blocked up the south and choir windows, and raised the floor so that the present gallery floor is above the floor level of the nuns' choir.

This church is of particular interest because it is one of a small number of religious buildings where we know that its design was motivated by its suitability for the sung liturgy performed by the Dominican sisters. The church was the last part of an extended construction project, begun by prioress Anna Walther in 1498 with the rebuilding of the convent buildings, led by Burkhardt Engelberg and Ulrich Glier. The new chapter house was adorned with a series of six spectacular paintings by leading Augsburg artists Hans Holbein the Elder, Hans Burgkmair the Elder and Master L.F. They show the seven principal churches of Rome and scenes from the lives of their patron saints, and commemorate a papal privilege for a virtual Rome pilgrimage granted to the convent in 1487 (Gärtner 2002). As exemplified by the building of convent and church, the Dominican sisters—most of whom came from patrician and upper-middle class merchant families (Roper 1989, 207-08)—invested the considerable private funds at their disposal in art and architecture to heighten and embellish their devotional work. Marie-Luise Ehrenschwendtner has argued that the commissioning of these paintings reacted to the tightening of monastic enclosure in the second half of the fifteenth century: they offered the community a way "spiritually to escape the walls of their convent" (Ehrenschwendtner 2009, 64). Indeed, when the old church had been demolished in 1516 under prioress Veronika Welser and the construction process started, the sisters literally "jumped the wall": they left their convent and went to St Magdalena, the church of the male Dominicans, in order to deliberate the design of their new church. This event is reported in three chronicles, which in their slightly different narration of the event illuminate decision-making processes as well as the reactions of contemporaries.

The first account is a contemporary chronicle by the merchant and entrepreneur Wilhelm Rem, whose recollections are probably based on notes made not long after the event:

Anno dni. 1516. a die primo majo am auffertag da was ain doctor prediger-minch zu den Bredigern, der fuort auff datum umb 3 ur vor tag all klosterfrauen von sant Katterina in sein kloster gen Predigern und lies sie sein zell sechen. und als es tag ward, da lies er sie die kirchen auch sechen, die was neu. und umb 5 ur da giengen die klosterfrauen wider haim, der waren bei 50 oder 60; es waren etlich alt darunder, die fuort man auff	In the year of our Lord 1516 on Ascension Day, 1 May, there was a Dominican doctor at the Preaching Friars [Johannes Fabri], who at 3 a.m. led all Dominican sisters from St Katherine's to his monastery and let them see his cell, and when day broke he let them see the church as well, which was new, and at 5 a.m. the sisters went home again. There were 50 or 60 of them, and several elderly ones among them who were conveyed on a little cart.

ainem wegelin und der burgermaister Jeronius Imhoff der gieng auch mit, der verhalf dem doctor zu ainem solichen gunckelhaus, und der Engelberg, der weber zunftmaister, und der Anthoni Artzt, Laux Grander und Matheus Langenmanttel die giengen auch darmit. (Rem 1896, 54)

And Mayor Hieronymus Imhoff went with them, who helped the doctor to arrange such a chattershop [gunckelhaus], and [Martin] Engelberg, the master of the weavers' guild, and Antonius Arzt, Laux Grander and Matheus Langenmantel came along as well.

According to Rem, it was Dr Johannes Fabri, the prior of the Augsburg Dominicans and confessor of the sisters, who had initiated the visit, but it was approved by the city authorities who joined the procession. The report is written from the perspective of a curious bystander—Rem mentions the carts for the elderly nuns and probably speculates about the sisters' visit to the prior's cell—and mirrors the sensation that the nocturnal excursion created. Throughout his chronicle he is very critical of the church and the funds lavished on architecture and display, as well as of the Augsburg city government (Kramer-Schlette 1970, 71-83), and in this instance he is clearly displeased that senior officials lent their authority to religious women leaving their cloister. The term *gunckelhaus* refers to a place where women came together in the winter months to spin, prepare textiles and gossip, and it also acquired the subsidiary meaning of a house for wanton women.

The second chronicler, scholar and mayor Marcus Welser, wrote in the last decades of the century and published his chronicle in 1595. However, he could possibly have drawn on family lore, since prioress Veronika Welser had been his great aunt. He writes:

Als auch diß Jar S. Catherine Closter allhie von newem zugericht ward / hatte sich ein grosser Streitt / zwischen der Priorin / so wol auch den fürnembsten Schwestern desselbigen Closters / vnd den verordneten Bawherrn deß Raths / als Burgermeister Hosern und Martin Angelbergern [!] der Weber Zunfftmeister / erhaben [!] / ob es besser were / daß das Tach darinnen gewelbt oder schlecht mit Zimmerhöltzer[n] beschlossen würde / vnnd welches Gebäw gesünder vnd helläuterer were. Solchen Stritt zuentscheiden / seynd alle dieselbe Nonnen zugleich bey eiteler Nacht / an der Auffarth Christi vmb zwey Uhr / auß jhrem Closter in die Prediger Kirchen gangen / zuprobieren / ob auch der Widerhall im gewelbten Chor / die reine WeiberStimm [!] etwas hinderte / haben als jre erste *horam* gesungen / vnd sich alsbald / demnach das Volck wegen deß newen vngewöhnlichen Singens zulieffe / widerumb in jhr Closter gemacht: da von stund an dieselbe Nonnen / nachdem sie in jhrem *refectorio* kniend / solch verbrechen bekandt hatten / *D. Iohann Fabri* der Dominicaner Prior / vnd dieser Nonnen Beichtvatter / wie bey jhn gebräuchlich / widerumb geweyhet / als die wider jhr Gelübd gethan hetten. (Welser 1595, 276)

When this year [1516] St Katherine's convent was built anew, there was a great dispute between the prioress and the senior sisters of the convent, and the official building inspectors of the city council (namely Mayor Hosern and Martin Angelberger[!], the master of the weaver's guild), whether it would be better to have a vaulted ceiling or one simply covered with wooden beams, and which type of building would be healthier and more resonant. In order to resolve the dispute all the nuns went at night, at 2 a.m. on Ascension Day, from their convent to the Dominican church, to determine whether the reverberations in the vaulted choir would impede the pure women's voices. So they sang their first office and then, as people flocked together because of the new, unusual singing, they went back to their convent. And after the nuns had—kneeling in their refectory—confessed this crime to Dr Johannes Fabri, the prior of the Dominicans and father confessor of the nuns, he consecrated them again, as is customary, because they had violated their vows.

Welser thus shifts the agency from the Dominican prior and the city officials to the nuns themselves, which clashes with Rem's assertion that Fabri had invited them. Welser does not mention the support of the city council, who accompanied the nuns, and his description of the act of penitence perhaps reflects attitudes from the later sixteenth century, after monastic enclosure had been reinforced in a visitation of the papal nuncio Felician Ninguarda. On the other hand Welser gives valuable information about the motivation of the sisters, namely their desire to make their church a space whose acoustics would be congenial to their higher voices.

The final chronicle was written by Maria Dominika Erhard, cantrix and main scribe of St Katherine's in the eighteenth century. Her somewhat random collection of materials dates from 1752/53 and is based on older sources. She writes:

Auch ist mehr zu wissen daß vnß gerathen wardt von vill weysen leithen gaistlich vnd weltlich wir sollten vnsern chor auch gewelben mit sambt vnser kirchen, da war etwaß ain wider werthigkeit vnder dem *Convent* etlich heten es gern gesehen vnd die andern nit, daß sye forchten daß singen würdt Ihnen wehe thuen in dem gewelb, daß ist als bestandten bis auff [?] den heillig auffahrt abent, da hett sich vnser Würdtiger Vatter *vicarj*, vnd der burger Maister Imhoff vnser bauherr bedacht, vnd redten mit vnß daß wir sollten gan, in der Prediger Kirchen, die auf die Zeit von neyem war gebauen [!] vnd gewelbt, da ist auf den H: auf fahrttag der ganz *convent* mit der *Process* gangen mit grosser Ersambkeit am Morgen frieh vor der firten Uhr gegangen in der Prediger Kirchen, vnd in Ihren chor, darin haben wir gesungen wohl bey ainer stundt, vnd haben versucht wie daß gesang in dem gewelb erhell, da hat es allen *Convent* sowohl gefallen

Furthermore one should know that we were advised by many wise people, religious and secular, that we should vault our choir and the church; there was some unpleasantness among the convent, because some were for it and others against as they were afraid that singing under the vault would hurt them. That was the situation until Ascension Day, when our reverend father and vicar [Fabri] and Mayor Imhoff, the building inspector, told us to go to the Dominican church, which at the time was newly built and vaulted. Thus on Ascension Day the entire convent processed most respectably before 4 a.m. in the morning to the choir of the Dominican church, and we sang there for about an hour, and tested how the singing resounded under the vault, and this pleased the entire convent so well that they all agreed afterwards to have our choir vaulted as well. And with us went our reverend father vicar, Mayor Hieronymus daß sye all darnach Ihren willen darzue geben hand daß man vnsern *chor* uch gewelben soll, vnd mit vnß ist gangen von der Vrsach wegen, vnser würdig Vatter *vicarj*, burgermaister *Hieronymus* Imhoff, zunfftmeister Engelberg vnsere Bauherrn, der *Antonj* argast [Arzt?], der Langem Mantl der grandra [Grander?] vnser Paumaister, vnd der yber Reitter, diser Erbar leith sind mitt außgangen, vnd haben vnd wider heimb gelait in vnser Closter, vnd vmb die fünfte stund sein wir widerumb herum kommen. Vnd darum wir so frieh auß sein gangen, daß ist geschehen daß nit ein grosser Zuefahl wird von den lithen[.] (Archiv des Bistums Augsburg, Handschrift 95 [Maria Dominika Erhard, OP, *Chronik des Klosters St. Katharina zu Augsburg*], fols. 49^{v}-50^{r})

Imhoff, guild master Engelberg (our building inspectors), Antonius Argast [Arzt?], Langenmantel, Grander, our master builder and the overseer. These respectable people went with us and led us back again to our convent, and we got back around 5 a.m. And we had gone out so early, so that there wouldn't be such a throng of people.

Maria Dominika Erhard—who, according to her own writing, had access to Marcus Welser's chronicle—thus clarifies that the conflict was not so much between the nuns and the authorities, but amongst the sisters themselves. She also stresses that both the father confessor and the mayor asked them to test the acoustics of the Dominican church, thus exculpating them from Welser's allegation that they had violated their vows. Twice she reinforces the message that this was a most respectable occasion and that the early hour had been chosen deliberately to avoid a scandal—not with much success, as Rem and Welser attest.

Once the decision to install a vaulted ceiling had been taken, construction progressed swiftly. Besides master mason and architect Hans Hieber, the building work was led by the carpenter master Mang, bricklayer master Leonhart Schmelcher and joiner master Hans Mußhardt (Bischoff 1990, 14). The new church and the high altar were dedicated on 16 November 1517, with three more altars consecrated on 17 November, the altar on the nuns' choir on 18 November, and finally the Holy Cross chapel on 19 November (Hörmann 1882, 369). The sisters moved into their new choir "with joy" and sang the day Offices and Matins on Christmas Eve in the new location (Archiv des Bistums Augsburg, Handschrift 95, fol. 51^{r}). The regular sung liturgy continued until the convent was forced to abandon their observances between 1534 and 1547 at the instigation of the now Protestant city council; additionally, the number of sisters dropped in mid-century, making extensive sung services unviable. By the 1580s, however, the liturgy was sung once more in full, and on feast days an organist and pupils from the collegiate church of St Moritz added to the solemnity of the occasion. The small (portable?) organ was replaced with a larger instrument in 1609, one year after the Dominicans of St Katherine's had introduced polyphonic music to their festive services (Eichner 2021, 124).

Through purchasing an organ and introducing polyphonic music, the Augsburg convent was in line with two larger developments: on the one hand, the cultural rejuvenation of Catholic religious houses in Augsburg—the Fugger family alone paid for new organs at St Ulrich and Afra, the new Jesuit church, and the male Dominican church, while they also supported music at the Franciscan tertiary house Maria Stern (Eichner 2011, 343-44); and on the other hand the spread of polyphonic practices among South-German nuns. As with the artwork commissioned for the chapter house of St Katherine, it was often the enforcement of enclosure that stimulated musical practices. Male musicians were more strictly separated from the nuns, as in the case of the Benedictine nunnery in Frauenchiemsee, where in 1630 the visitator demanded the separation of the nuns' choir from the gallery for singers and organist by means of a door (Weitlauff 2003, 325). At Nonnberg in Salzburg, the organist and music teacher were the only men who still had (carefully supervised) access to the nunnery. Their teaching enabled the nuns for the first time to take part musically in the Mass with a women-only ensemble on 1 January 1622. Manuela Kammerlander has even argued that the ceiling fresco completed in 1625 by Matthäus Ostendorfer, which shows a violin-playing nun among the angel musicians, allegorically commemorates this event (Kammerlander 2011, 82). Thus while the Dominicans of St Katherine rebuilt their convent church to suit their voices in the early sixteenth century (public opprobrium for their nocturnal excursion notwithstanding), a hundred years later the now strictly enclosed Benedictines of Nonnberg did not blush to immortalise their vocal and instrumental performances in the decoration of their church (Lawatsch Melton 2010, 269).

58. Misericord

Frédéric Billiet

Anon., Gaillon, ca. 1509
Oak, 39 x 27 cm
Basilica of Saint-Denis
Photo © Pascal Lemaitre / Bridgeman Images

This representation of a musical scene was carved around 1509 on a misericord in the choirstalls of the Chapel of the Château de Gaillon. These stalls are currently preserved in the Basilica of Saint-Denis, where they have been since the nineteenth century.

A misericord is a small console of wood fixed on the flap of a stall, on which the canons can lean for comfort while they sing the psalmody during services. As soon as choirstalls appeared in Europe, beginning in the thirteenth century following papal authorization, misericords were carved by *huchiers* (wood-carvers) to evoke scenes of everyday life or of the world turned upside-down, representing vices to combat with prayer and scenes with religious subjects. This medieval iconographic tradition persisted during the sixteenth century across Europe, in part driven by the circulation of the associated craftsmen, as can be seen in Elaine Block's digital collection of misericords available on the Princeton Index of Medieval Art (Billiet 2011, 285-94; Block 2003).

This particular misericord originated at the beginning of the sixteenth century, when Cardinal Georges d'Amboise—literato and promoter of Italian art—commissioned choirstalls for the chapel of his castle (Anterroches, 2014). D'Amboise gave specific instructions concerning the iconographic models: new Italian marquetry was to be used to represent the Sybils, and additionally he asked the *huchiers* to reproduce illustrations from recent books acquired for his library. Our misericord was among the latter, a carved reproduction of an illustration of *Ars Musica* (fig. 58.1) from the first encyclopedia of the Renaissance, entitled *Margarita Philosophica* (*The Philosophical Pearl*), published in 1503 at Freiburg-im-Breisgau by Gregor Reisch (Billiet 2011).

At first glance, the scene could represent a musical performance with, from left to right, a lutenist, a harpist, an organist (the pipes presented back-to-front in comparison to their usual arrangement), a woman holding an unfurled scroll, a musician playing a wind instrument, and two somewhat damaged figures. This disposition is not unusual for the period (further examples can be found in the Musiconis database of medieval music iconography, hosted by Sorbonne University), but questions arise concerning the presence of the figure on the right and the mutilated figure in the centre of the scene. Who are they and what are they doing here?

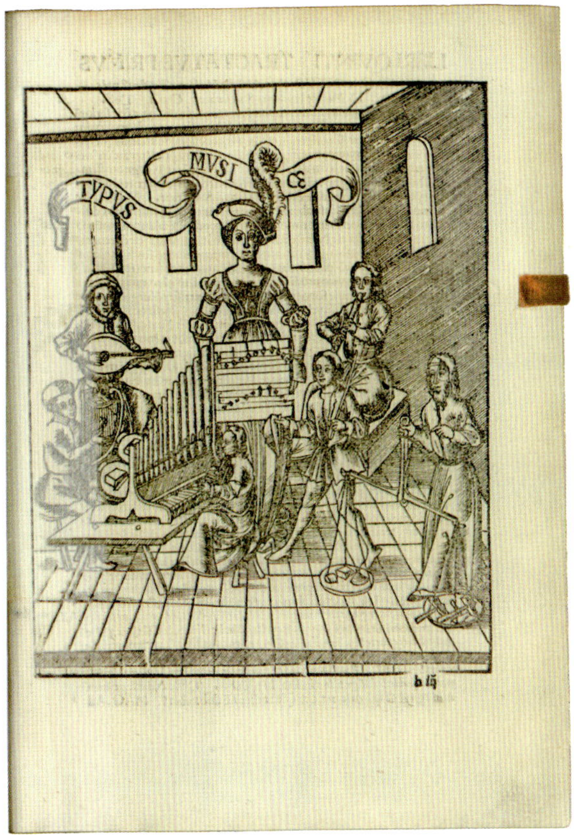

Figure 58.1: Gregor Reisch, *Margarita philosophica* (Freiburg: Johann Schott, 1503), fol. R126a. Munich, Bayerische Staatsbibliothek, Res/4 Ph.u. 114, urn:nbn:de:bvb:12-bsb00012346-8. Photo courtesy of the Bayerische Staatsbibliothek.

The answers to these questions are revealed through comparison with the model for this scene in the *Margarita Philosophica*. The engraving that inspired the craftsmen of Gaillon is an allegory of music that introduces the fifth chapter, "Musicae speculativae" (Speculative Music); it bears the title *Typus Musice* inscribed on the banner fluttering across the top of the scene.

Musica is personified by the woman in the centre holding the scroll, on which are two musical staves, now largely erased. Presumably there was an intention to paint musical notation on the staves—coats of arms, text, and musical notation were commonly added to choirstalls at this date (Billiet 1997).

The engraving enables us to reconstruct some of the details now missing from the misericord. Thus we can see that the figure on the right holds a balance, signalling the meaning of the scene as a whole: music appears here as a science related to weights and measures. This is the Music of the Quadrivium, one of the four mathematical Liberal Arts taught at European universities from medieval times. In this guise as an art-science, music was linked with the character of Pythagoras, the supposed founder of the science of music. In an anecdote repeated endlessly by Renaissance music theorists (indeed, told a few pages later in the *Margarita Philosophica*), he discovered the proportions that govern the consonant intervals by listening to the tones emitted as a blacksmith hammered at an anvil. Pythagoras extrapolated from this deduction a theory of the harmony of the universe as a whole (the so-called harmony of the spheres), and in a Christian context this notion was often linked with the Biblical assertion that God "ordered all things in measure, and number, and weight" (Wisdom 11:21). In its sacred setting, then, this scene could be understood to represent the harmony of God's creation in general, and the harmony of the heavens in particular—something that was also represented by the psalmody sung by the occupant of the choirstall, which was considered in the period to be an imitation of the singing of the angels.

On the other hand, it is still difficult to identify the badly damaged figure in the centre of the misericord, who is presented in the engraving in three-quarter profile, holding a hat in his right hand and a baton in his left. At the end of the Middle Ages, the baton was not used to direct musical performance; rather, it was used to follow the notes on the stave, or to give a beat for confused singers. Some scholars have seen these two props as a drumstick and drum (tabor); but a coloured version of the woodcut (fig. 58.2), in which the "drum" is given the same red hue as the majority of the clothing, suggests that at least one viewer saw it as indeed a hat. Perhaps this character is present to greet *Musica*.

Representations of musical subjects are not uncommon in late medieval choirstalls. Speculative music is depicted in choirstalls in Cologne through an image of a music theorist dictating notes to the sound of a set of bells, and angel musicians are particularly widespread on misericords, adding the sounds of real-world instruments to the concert of heaven. Indeed, the very architectural design of choirstalls engages at a fundamental practical level with the requirement to sing the liturgy. However, the particular representation of music found on our misericord is very unusual at the beginning of the sixteenth century.

Reisch's work was known to the patron of the choirstalls at Gaillon, who certainly prescribed this iconographic program with the specific intention of breaking with medieval modes of representation. Although the church furniture at Gaillon includes more conventional representations of religious scenes and episodes from contemporary daily life (such as one might find adorning the calendar at the beginning of a late medieval book of hours), sharing the same space are images conjuring another universe drawn from the classicising fashions of Italy: the Sibyls, scenes from ancient literature, and the Liberal Arts including Astronomy, Geometry, and Music. Among the other stalls preserved in the Basilica of Saint-Denis are further examples of the up-to-the-minute Italian taste of the Cardinal d'Amboise (Billiet, 2011), including a representation of Venus with a duo of instrumentalists playing lute and recorder, and the contest between Apollo and Marsyas as recounted in Ovid's *Metamorphoses* (a copy of which was in the cardinal's library; see Delisle 1868).

The influence of new Italian styles and subjects can be found in other choirstalls north of the Alps. It appears that decorative elements were particularly open to new ideas, as seen for example in the carving of medallions and portraits at Saint-Marcel (Indre) or at Saint-Geoire (Isère). But on the whole, French ecclesiastical communities and patrons were content to retain earlier iconographic traditions. A substantial change in the subjects represented on misericords outside Italy came later in the century, with the Tridentine reforms and the Counter-Reformation.

Additional references: Billiet 2002; Billiet 2019; Musiconis: http://musiconis.huma-num.fr.

Figure 58.2: Gregor Reisch, *Margarita philosophica*, 2nd edn. (Strasbourg: Johann Schott, 1504), fol. 103b. Universitätsbibliothek Freiburg, Ink. A 7315,d. Photo courtesy of the Universitätsbibliothek Freiburg.

BARTHOLO·FLORENTINO OPIFICE

59. The Chapel of King Sigismund, Wawel Cathedral, Krakow

Paweł Gancarczyk

Bartolomeo Berrecci et al., 1519-33
Wawel Hill, Krakow
Image: The dome of the Chapel of King Sigismund. Photo © Piotr Jamski.

When in January 1507 Sigismund I Jagiellon was crowned king of Poland, he was already 40 years old, mature and fully formed intellectually. He had witnessed the reigns of his three elder brothers: he took the crown of Poland after the deaths first of John Albert (1501), then of Alexander (1506), at a time when the senior member of the family, Vladislav, ruled as king of Bohemia, Hungary, and Croatia. Having spent some years at the Jagiellon court in Buda, Sigismund had become familiar with new artistic currents, acquired an artistic taste of his own, and consolidated his humanist education. He had a sense of royal sovereignty, resulting from a belief in the divine source of his power and its independence of the claims to supremacy of the emperor and the pope (Rutkowski 1996, 326). His numerous artistic foundations, established during the many decades of his reign, corresponded in their splendour to the praiseworthy qualities of he who commissioned them. In accordance with the virtue of *magnificentia*—possessed, according to humanist ideas, by outstanding individuals—these foundations were to ensure the admiration of his contemporaries as well as long-lasting fame. One of these foundations was a chapel in the cathedral on Wawel Hill in Krakow, known after its patron as the Sigismund Chapel.

Work on this royal mausoleum was begun in 1515 by Bartolomeo Berrecci, an architect brought from Florence. Once the king had approved the design, building began in 1519 in a campaign lasting more than a dozen years. The unusual construction of the chapel and its rich sculptural decoration required that a large group of specialists be brought to Poland; like Berrecci, they came from Tuscany. Combining grey sandstone with red-brown marble from Hungary produced an original interior, without close equivalents north of the Alps. References to the art of early sixteenth-century Tuscany and Rome can be found in individual elements of the composition and decoration of the chapel, as well as numerous antique inspirations, often drawn from original sources (Mossakowski 2012, 141-75). This very apparent love of Antiquity may have derived not only from contemporary artistic fashion, but also from the characteristic humanist myth of the origin of the Lithuanians, and thus the Jagiellonian dynasty from which King Sigismund came. According to Jan Długosz, Polish chronicler and the king's tutor, the Lithuanians were supposed to be descendants of those Romans who left the Italian peninsula during the wars between Julius Caesar and Pompey (Długosz 1985, 167-68). Persisting in the "error of paganism" until as late as the second half of the fourteenth century, they were supposed to have maintained the old gods and rituals which in other areas of Europe had been long forgotten.

The Sigismund Chapel was given a rich ideological programme, distinguished by three sets of content: glorificatory, ethical-religious, and eschatological. These themes are manifested through particular elements of the chapel's interior decoration: marble sculptures and sandstone reliefs. The chapel was built not only as a house of God, but also as a monument to the earthly glory of its founder, who is commemorated by a sumptuous tomb reminiscent of Roman sarcophagus sculpture. King Sigismund I is shown as a sleeping ruler-knight, and his heroization is enriched by military motifs in relief. There are tondos of Biblical kings, David and Solomon, ideal models to be followed by a religious monarch; images of the four evangelists and marble statues of patron saints of the kingdom. Grotesque decoration on the walls, full of mythological figures, fantastic beasts, animals, and plants, is divided into spheres corresponding to the four elements: earth, water, air, and fire, arranged in order from the floor up to the elliptical dome. The bowl of the dome is ornamented by coffers with rosettes—symbols of the stars—while the whole is crowned with a lantern, illuminated by windows, at its centre the head of a Seraph, a symbol of God, surrounded by nine little cherub heads. This is a reference to the journey of the soul through the four elements (following Virgil's *Aeneid*), leading from the earth to the sphere of the stars and divine heaven (Mossakowski 2012, 229-69). The ideological programme of the chapel is also explained by inscriptions carved at various locations, mainly paraphrases of verses from the book of Psalms. Of particular significance is the sentence which we read in the vault of the tomb, next to the marble head of the founder: "Si[gi]smu[n]di regis facies | est caetera longu[m] | dicere sed fama est | non moritura pete" (This is the face of King Sigismund, much could be said about the rest, try to ensure his fame does not die).

Such a splendid interior, built with great expenditure of effort and resources, its design worked out in the smallest detail, demanded to be filled with suitably chosen sounds to proclaim the king's fame after his death. Music was present in the chapel's decorations in the form of a depiction of King David with his attribute, the harp. The Biblical king was a model of a perfect monarch for the Jagiellonians (Boczkowska 1985, 71-87), and the presence of music was an essential element complementing the ideological programme of the chapel. Already in the year of its consecration (1533) the idea was mooted of establishing a special collegium of choristers at the chapel. This idea was put into practice ten years later, through the foundation act of 1543 (Czepiel 1996, 188-201), which established an ensemble of singer-priests to celebrate Mass at the king's tomb every day "in perpetuity." Since the Blessed Virgin—whose cult was of particular importance to the Jagiellons—became the patron of the chapel, this was a votive Mass to the Annunciation of the Blessed Virgin Mary, sung between morning Mass and Prime. As the Mass began with the introit *Rorate caeli*, the ensemble became known as the "collegium of Rorantists." Each month, the choristers also sang Matins in the presence of the king.

Unlike their colleagues engaged in providing music at other locations in Krakow cathedral, the Rorantists were specifically required to sing polyphonic music ("cantus figuratus"), thus creating a unique sound space, not known in other areas of the church. At the head of the ensemble was the prefect, appointed directly by the king. He employed nine choristers (called prebendaries), ordained priests, who were not allowed to obtain benefices other than those established in the foundation of the ensemble. Priests were accepted into the collegium after taking a special exam, selecting those "who were well versed in the art of singing and chanting, possessing good, sonorous voices." They were to be chosen only from among the Poles, although in the long history of the Rorantists we find at least a few cases of musicians originating from Italy. The number of prebendaries has sometime been seen as analogous to the nine angelic choirs symbolised by the nine angel heads in the chapel's lantern (fig. 59.1; Zwolińska 1987, 145-50). It seems that this is not a coincidence, since the ensemble could have been smaller in number and still fulfilled its basic functions, and in fact during its history it often had fewer members than the foundation postulated. Alongside the prefect and nine prebendaries, the collegium also included a cleric who assisted at the Mass who, when required, and if possessed of a good voice, could also be engaged to sing polyphonically.

We can learn about the music performed by the Rorantists in the sixteenth century from a number of sets of partbooks still preserved in Wawel cathedral library. The oldest of them reaches back to the 1540s, i.e. to the beginnings of the collegium's existence, at that time headed by prefect Mikołaj of Poznań, appointed by King Sigismund I. It contains votive Masses for four voices—ordinary and proper sections—mainly for the Annunciation of the Blessed Virgin Mary. These are not complex compositions; at some points one might even say they are dilettante works, in simple counterpoint, with long rhythmic values, and infrequent use of imitation. The Tenor parts are often notated in chant notation, since they had as their source melodies taken from the Gradual, and these were not noticeably changed (Czepiel 1996, 61-126). This type of simple polyphony, based on plainchant and consonant intervals, is referred to by the Italian term *falsobordone*—similar compositions could be heard in many churches across Europe at that time, although today they are overshadowed by the much more striking achievements of the Flemish and Italian polyphonists. Within the small space of the chapel, heard just before dawn, the singing of a few voices, uncomplicated and thus emphasising the meaning of individual words and musical harmonies, may have given the impression of unearthly euphony as well as ardent prayer. We do not know the authors of these compositions, although we may suppose that they were members of the collegium. We also know little about who listened to this music: due to the small dimensions of the chapel (approx. 6 x 6 m), votive Masses were inevitably attended by a small congregation and their artistic impact was limited. Consequently, they acquired an eschatological dimension, in harmony with the commemorative character of the chapel and the ideological programme of its sculpted decoration. The collegium not only sang to add to the splendor of the liturgy, for the pleasure of earthly listeners, but above all directed prayer toward heaven, to the Blessed Virgin, for the soul of the king.

After the death of Sigismund I in 1548 there were two occasions on which changes were made to the foundation of the Rorantists, adjusting the principles according to which the ensemble functioned, its obligations and the way it was financed. In 1552 the obligation was placed upon the collegium to provide polyphonic singing at the main altar of the cathedral during the most important feast days and ceremonies. The Rorantists still sang votive Masses in the archaic style every day, but on special occasions they reached for more ambitious and complex repertory, performed in front of a much larger congregation than could gather in the chapel. Surviving sources tell us that the singing at the main altar included works by Cristóbal de Morales, Jachet de Mantua, and Vincenzo Ruffo, copied from prints imported from Italy, Germany, and France. In the second half of the sixteenth century, among the Rorantists we find composers skilled in counterpoint and parody technique. Outstanding among them is Tomasz Szadek, the author of the *Missa "Pisneme,"* based on the chanson by Thomas Crecquillon, *Pis ne me peult venir.* In later periods composers who created works for the Rorantist ensemble included both native Poles and Italians active in Poland. However, their works were always conservative, looking to the past. Even at the beginning of the eighteenth century the Rorantists were still copying and performing works such as Josquin des Prez's *Stabat Mater* (Czajkowski 2000, 59-65).

Over successive decades of its activities, the Rorantist collegium had its highs and lows, to a large extent reflecting the history of Poland. However, it survived not only the death of its founder, but also the death of the last representative of the dynasty, Anna Jagiellon, in 1596. The Rorantists continued to carry out their duties after the king's seat was moved to Warsaw towards the end of the sixteenth century; they also did so during Poland's partitions towards the end of the eighteenth century, and after Krakow was incorporated into the Austrian monarchy. However, the foundation, even if established "in perpetuity," could not last forever: in 1872 the Austrian authorities suspended the financing of the collegium of Rorantists. It was still active at the start of the twentieth century, but its centuries-old tradition was inevitably coming to an end (Jochymczyk 2018, 35). Sigismund's chapel was deprived of the phonic representation which had been such an integral part of it, even though it still fascinates us today with the quality of its art and the richness of its symbolic references.

Figure 59.1: Detail showing the lantern of the chapel with nine angel heads symbolising nine angel choirs. Photo © Piotr Jamski.

60. The Bell Founder's Window, York Minster

Lisa Colton

Anon., York, ca. 1330
Stained glass
Inscribed: RICHARD TUNNOC
Deangate, York
Photo © Chapter of York: reproduced by kind permission

Pre-Reformation British churches remain some of the most visually arresting monuments of the five centuries post-Conquest. From the highest vaulted ceilings, decorated with colourful bosses, to the smallest statues and grotesques, cathedral churches in particular presented a wealth of opportunities for intricate and extravagant public display. During the Middle Ages and Renaissance it was common for parishioners to donate funds to support the fabric of their church, and the families most closely associated with the patronage of a building often included visual clues as to their input: funeral monuments, carved initials, memorial brasses, heraldry, and even portraiture in glass. The destruction of the English Reformation, of the English Civil War, and of more recent events such as the bombing of major towns and cities during World War II, had a profound effect on the quantity of early glass that still survives in situ. Within this context, the Bell Founder's Window of York Minster is especially remarkable.

Typically, the Gothic cathedrals of major towns and cities are a patchwork of building projects that took centuries to reach completion, with many phases of rebuilding and alteration. In some cases, the architecture is not only stunning to look at, but also hints at the many sounds associated with devotional life. Carvings of minstrelsy in Beverley Minster and angel musicians depicted on the ceiling of Tewkesbury Abbey give an impression of both secular life and the imagined sounds of celestial harmony. The Bell Founder's Window of York Minster, on the other hand, contains a more concrete representation of sounds familiar within churches of various sizes: that of the bells that sounded the hours and that marked many of the liturgical rituals that took place in and around religious buildings.

The Bell Founder's Window is located in the north aisle of the nave of York Minster, seat of the archbishop of York from the time of Ecgbert. The window's provenance is emphasised by its clear depiction of the man who commissioned it, Richard Tunnoc. Like most donors, Tunnoc was a prominent member of the local community. He lived on Stonegate, a road approaching the Minster, from 1311, and was active in the region as a goldsmith, bell founder, bailiff (1320-21), and Member of Parliament (1327) for the City of York; it is regularly, but inaccurately, reported that he served as York's mayor (Bayliss 2006, 82). It was not unusual during Tunnoc's lifetime for men and women to commission works reflecting their religious devotion to the church, whether the material object be a book, window, effigy, or altarpiece. However, Tunnoc is remarkable in that he was the first layman to endow a chantry in his and his wife Alice's memory in the Minster, in 1328, thus having a significant personal impact on the musical and liturgical space (Palliser 2014, 161).

The artistic choices made by patrons tended to emphasise elements of their personal piety, such as their devotion to particular saints. One thinks, for example, of the Wilton Diptych (1395-99; National Gallery, London), in which Richard II is shown, flanked by St Edmund King and Martyr, Edward the Confessor, and John the Baptist, in a panel facing the Virgin and Child. There, the king's special place as an anointed king of England was reaffirmed by the presence of his saintly royal predecessors, while the Baptist signalled Richard's humility and personal affection for his cult. Donor images were carefully crafted to indicate the individual's particular virtues and status, something we can see in Tunnoc's design. In the lowest part of the window, in the central panel, Tunnoc is shown offering a miniature version of the window to St William of York, whose shrine was once placed nearby in the Minster; a banner confirms Tunnoc's identity. St William served as archbishop of York in the 1140s, and was considered York's patron saint, even though the cathedral itself was dedicated to St Peter. He was an appropriate saint with whom Tunnoc might associate himself: William's canonisation was largely a result of his miraculous protection of the people of York who fell into the water on the collapse of Ouse Bridge, when they flocked to greet him there in 1153. In this way Tunnoc placed himself into York's permanent historical narrative, both in terms of its cult and through the archaeology of the city.

Arguably the most striking feature of the Bell Founder's Window is its depiction of gold and silver bells, framing the image and lending it a noisy, musical resonance. The designer and glazier used bells effectively as a motif or pattern. More impressively, however, the window shows a rare sight of bells being manufactured. In the left and right panels of the window, a small group of people work together to create new bells: to the left is the founding of a bell; to the right, an apprentice holds onto a ceiling pole in order to use his feet to work the bellows responsible for heating the metals to the necessary temperature, and the bell is created (fig. 60.1). The casting of the bell offered an opportunity to show the input that lay members of the community had on the spiritual life of the city. It is quite possible that Tunnoc donated actual bells to the church, though the surviving records do not document such a gift.

Figure 60.1: Bell manufacture. Detail of Anon., *Bell Founder's Window*. Photo © Chapter of York: reproduced by kind permission.

The process of bell making changed little through the Renaissance. It involved casting metals in a crucible heated to over one thousand degrees, before pouring the melted alloy into moulds. Although iron and copper alone were sometimes used, the vast majority of bells were cast from bronze, since the balance of copper and tin (in an approximate 4:1 ratio) was beneficial to the bell's durability and stability. Bronze bells were very beautiful, and the iridescence of medieval bells is well captured in Tunnoc's design. Bronze was also considered the best material on account of its sonic properties, and beyond the visual and practical aspects, it is clear that bronze was primarily the standard material because of its acoustic qualities (Debut et al. 2016, 545). The panels that flank the image of Tunnoc and St William show elements of this craft, including the creation of a wax mould on the left. Once the mould was ready, the founder melted the wax from it, which left a void to be filled by the molten metal in the final shape of the bell.

Although bells were a fundamental, daily part of religious experience, the way in which they were rung for specific occasions was perhaps so commonplace that records of the particular sounds of bells, or the ways in which they were to be struck, are rare. The late medieval church typically owned at least one bell, to be used at Mass, and from at least the Anglo-Saxon era, bell towers were used to call the community to prayer and for other diverse rituals. Small bells were regularly used in processions, especially for funerals, such as those depicted in the funeral procession for Edward the Confessor shown as part of the Bayeux Tapestry (eleventh century; Musée de la Tapisserie de Bayeux) as his body is taken to Westminster Abbey. Liturgical books indicated times at which bells should be rung, as well as instructions for ceremonies in which bells were blessed, named, and consecrated. In Bayliss' study of the 3390 bells that survive from pre-Reformation England, 1116 were found to contain some form of mark, such as a cross, a shield, or an inscription. In some cases, inscriptions comprise a short Latin prayer as one finds in the litany: "Sancte Petre ora pro nobis" (Saint Peter, pray for us) reads one example (Bayliss 2006, 578). Bells were thus a communication tool not only between priests and their communities, but between those that struck them and heaven. Perhaps, imaginatively, the potential sounding prayers of the bells in Tunnoc's window were part of his lasting memorial.

Medieval bells came in diverse sizes, and the loudest would have been clearly audible to those some distance from the internal rituals of the sacred space. In one early description, Bede recounts how the bell rung to mark the death of Hilda, founding abbess of Whitby, was audible 13 miles from the abbey church itself. The medieval bell thus had not only ritual but also community significance: it connected the secular world to the spiritual domain. Little wonder, then, that Richard Tunnoc chose to use the bell motif in his memorial window, illuminating the sacred building where he was buried. The presentation of bell founding served to unite the devotional and civic sides of Tunnoc's own life, as well as signalling the lavish generosity of his donation to York Minster.

The Bell Founder's Window belongs in a museum of Renaissance music for several reasons. First and foremost, it was designed not only as a backward-looking religious memorial, but as a permanent feature of the Minster, for people to view through the fourteenth, fifteenth, and sixteenth centuries, and beyond. Tunnoc's window was devised by craftsmen living in the early decades of the architectural "renaissance," a word that came to be associated with the music of the fifteenth and sixteenth centuries. Many of its visual signifiers of piety and civic identity are common to images found in devotional books of the early modern period. Although Tunnoc founded a chantry at the altar dedicated to St Thomas of Canterbury (Thomas Becket), and was buried there at his death in 1330 (Brown 1999, 42), it is the window that serves as his lasting commemoration. The window's construction assured its place in the Minster through some of the most dramatic episodes of the church's history, not least the English Reformation during which so much was lost. Perhaps Tunnoc's design, dominated by representations of his craft, went some way toward tempering the image of St William for those seeking to erase York's Catholic past, ensuring its preservation through the Renaissance and to the present day.

Additional references: Arnold and Goodson 2012.

COSME' TURA
1469

61. Organ Shutters from the Cathedral of Ferrara

Sophia D'Addio

St George and the Princess
Cosmè Tura, Ferrara, 1469
Tempera grassa on canvas, 363 x 170 cm (each).
Museo della Cattedrale, Ferrara
Photo © Alinari / Bridgeman Images

These twin canvases depicting the Annunciation originally constituted the exterior side of the organ shutters of Ferrara Cathedral. They were executed by Cosmè Tura, famed court artist to the Este rulers of the city, between July 1468 and June 1469, together with the canvases for the interior side of the shutters, which represent the *Annunciation* (fig. 61.1). This pairing of subjects reflects the dual dedication of the cathedral to the Virgin and to St George. The latter is also the patron saint of the city of Ferrara; his inclusion thus lends a tone of civic celebration to the exterior side of the shutters.

In their initial installation on the instrument, these two sets of canvases would have been stretched back-to-back on a shared support and attached to the carved wooden organ case with hinges. The new organ itself was commissioned from the celebrated organ builder Giovanni da Mercatello on 27 April 1465 by a committee of individuals representing the religious and civic powers of the city. The initiative was apparently led by the Bishop Lorenzo Roverella, in whose home the contract was drafted for "a good and beautiful organ, elegantly embellished, having all the perfections one could want from an organ, as much in beauty as in the harmony of its voices" (Campbell 1997, 131).

The instrument was installed at the centre of the choir by March 1468, where it remained for only three years; it was then moved to the eighth bay on the left-hand side of the nave, possibly for acoustic reasons (Cavicchi 1985, 108). This relocation of the instrument would have given Tura's massive shutters even greater prominence within the church interior, rendering them more easily visible to the laity.

Painted organ shutters were intended to serve a dual function, of both protection and adornment. When closed, in addition to being decorated with sacred images, the shutters shielded the pipes of the instrument from dust and vermin (and even theft—occasionally shutters were fastened with lock and key). When opened, they provided a visual accompaniment to the music of the Mass. Payment records of a few decades prior reveal that at Ferrara Cathedral the organ was played during the Masses of principal feast days, including Epiphany, the Purification of the Virgin, Easter, the Feast of St George, the anniversary of the consecration of the high altar (8 May), Ascension, Pentecost, Corpus Christi, the Feast of Saints Peter and Paul, the Assumption, the Nativity of the Virgin, All Saints' Day, and

Figure 61.1: Cosmè Tura, *Annunciation*, interior side of the organ shutters. Photo © Alinari / Bridgeman Images.

Christmas; several of these solemn celebrations also called for the engagement of professional singers. Occasionally the organ was played during Vespers as well (Peverada 1991, 34-36).

It is the interior images that painter and theorist Giovan Paolo Lomazzo focuses on in his *Trattato dell'arte della pittura, scoltura, et architettura* (Milan, 1584). Although written nearly a century after Tura's death, Lomazzo's is the only art treatise of the period to discuss organ shutters at length. Lomazzo stresses the importance of including musical subject matter on organ shutters, and gives particular emphasis to the interior:

> the pictures that truly belong to the organ should be in the interior part, which is seen when one observes the organ fully open and hears the melody and the voices of the pipes, and they should be such that they enhance the sweetness of the sight, and should be suitable to music (Lomazzo 1584).

Not only would the paintings on the interior side have been experienced in dialogue with the sound of the instrument and of the liturgy in performance, whether spoken or sung, but these images would also have been imbued with a musical dimension.

On the interior of Tura's shutters, the archangel Gabriel appears before the Virgin Mary to deliver the news to her that she has found favor with God and will bear the Christ Child. The sacred drama takes place within an *all'antica* architectural setting that is highly symmetrical. Both the archangel and the Virgin occupy rectangular modules, crowned with coffered barrel vaults filled with rosettes; these modules are open to the landscape that fills the background of the two canvases, thus suggesting a loggia-like space. Tura's architectural construction bears a striking similarity to that of Gentile Bellini's exterior shutters for the organ *in cornu epistolae* of the Basilica of San Marco in Venice, depicting *Saints Mark and Theodore* and completed only a few years prior in 1464-65, suggesting that Tura may have traveled to the Serenissima during these years, although no documentary evidence for such a visit survives (Molteni 1999, 90).

In their original configuration, these canvases hung on either side of the organ pipes; the interstitial space between the two interlocutors was therefore inhabited by the instrument. The perspectival construction that governs the architecture, arranged around a cluster of three vanishing points for each canvas, is more or less specular between the two shutters despite some instances of imprecision; to the naked eye, the effect is one of overall spatial coherence. The regularity of the architectural setting would thus have instantly united the two halves of the scene visually, creating a sense of continuity across the organ pipes, whereas elements of discontinuity in the background—particularly the rocky outcroppings and the variety in natural scenery—create the impression of a broader landscape for the beholder's gaze to traverse when passing from one shutter to the other. The expanse between the two interlocutors would nonetheless have appeared to emphasise the apparent paradox of the Incarnation, in which, as described in a celebrated sermon by San Bernardino da Siena, the incommensurable enters into measure, the invisible enters into the visible, and the inaudible enters into sound—just as the music of the organ gives voice to the archangel's silent salutation (Arasse 1999, 177-82).

On the left-hand shutter, Gabriel kneels as he utters the divine message that will imminently bring about the Incarnation. His lips part to show his teeth, rendering his enunciation visible, if not directly audible. His raised right hand delivers a gesture of blessing, and in his left hand, he delicately grasps the tall stem of a lily, the flower traditionally associated with the virginity of Mary due to the pristine whiteness of its petals. His head is crowned with a gold and ruby diadem, and his cloak is fastened with an equally opulent gold brooch bearing a darker, more opaque stone. His deep burgundy cloak, lined with blue, falls about him in heavy, elegant folds that betray the distinctively calligraphic impulse of Tura's hand.

The Virgin Mary, on the other hand, is dressed more modestly; the colors of her garments are the reverse of Gabriel's, for she wears a burgundy dress topped with her characteristic blue mantle, which is joined at her clavicle with a small but precious clasp, also bearing a ruby. The front of her dress is held together with a vibrant red thread, roughly stitched; it loosens and begins to unravel around her abdomen, underscoring the fecundity of her womb and its emblematic swelling at the moment of the Incarnation. She clasps her hands in prayer, and turns her gaze downward in gentle acquiescence to divine will.

Inserted into the niches in the walls behind both Gabriel and the Virgin Mary are eight monochrome figures in low relief, which represent the seven planetary deities and the Eighth Sphere. Their presence has been interpreted in light of contemporary astrological interests, particularly in regard to the horoscope of Christ, a highly contentious subject (Campbell 1997, 131-93). The twisting, dynamic poses of these figures suggest that they are dancing to the music of the organ, an earthly approximation of celestial harmony; it governs their steps, thereby asserting the power of divine providence, and the triumph of Christ over the pagan past.

There is a third principal actor present in the scene as well: this is the dove of the Holy Spirit, which hovers beside the left ear of the Virgin, its beak spread wide. This clearly recalls the early Christian doctrine of the *conceptio per aurem*, according to which Mary conceived the Christ child through the audible pronouncement of the Holy Word. The doctrine was espoused by Church Fathers and medieval theologians from St Augustine and St Zeno of Verona to St Bernard of Clairvaux, among others; it appears in the work of contemporary thinkers as well, such as that of the Carmelite reformer, humanist, and poet Baptista Mantuanus, who was active in Ferrara during the same decade in which Tura produced these canvases (Campbell 1997, 150).

The Annunciation is the single most common narrative subject chosen to decorate organ shutters throughout the flourishing of the genre, and among extant examples it appears slightly more often on the interior side. Patron saints, whether of the church, the city, or the patron, are also depicted frequently, whether through iconic representations or narrative scenes from their lives. Images with musical subject matter naturally abound as well, including angelic choirs, scenes from the life of King David, and St Cecilia as the patron saint of music, amongst others.

The earliest extant organ shutters, dating from the second quarter of the fifteenth century and all of Tuscan origin, were executed in tempera on panel; these include those by Francesco d'Antonio for Orsanmichele in Florence (1429). Such a solid support was made possible by the comparably modest dimensions of the instruments that these shutters adorned. Within a decade and a half, the first shutters on canvas began to appear, to fit the growing dimensions of monumental church organs: by 1465, Gentile Bellini had completed his shutters for the Basilica of San Marco in Venice, measuring 430 x 215 centimeters each and thus even larger than those for Ferrara Cathedral.

Simultaneously with the shift to canvas supports came a move toward an *all'antica* architectural language in the design of the wooden case, now conceived as a classicizing aedicule topped with a heavy and often intricately carved cornice. Although the San Marco organ case does not survive, subsequent examples in Spilimbergo (1515), Udine (1518-19), and Valvasone (1535-38) maintain a similar style, as does that of the church of San Salvador (1530) in Venice itself (Bisson 2012, 22). For the Ferrara Cathedral organ case, Adriano Cavicchi has proposed a reconstruction based upon surviving documentation, including a tripartite screen with two colonettes governing the distribution of the pipes; pilasters decorated with vegetal motifs; a tall entablature with a similarly decorated frieze; and a semicircular pediment (Cavicchi 1985, 113-17, figs. 10-14).

Cosmè Tura's shutters are all that survive of the fifteenth-century organ complex of the Cathedral of Ferrara, a powerful testimony to the precedent that they set, worthy of emulation: over the course of the following several decades, no fewer than 11 churches in the city would adorn their organs with painted shutters, including at least five that featured the Annunciation on one side. Only two of these survive, by Domenico Panetti (ca. 1505, for Sant'Andrea and now housed in the Pinacoteca Nazionale) and Gabriele Bonaccioli (1516, for Santa Maria in Vado); those by l'Ortolano (San Francesco), Venturini (Santa Maria degli Angeli), and Garofalo (San Silvestro) have unfortunately been lost (Degli Esposti 1985, 138-40). In any case, the importance of Cosmè Tura's shutters as a model for organ decoration is apparent, in Ferrara and beyond.

SIBENICHO
PARTE D'DALMACIA
Santo Dominico
S. Francesco

62. The Cathedral of St James, Šibenik

Ennio Stipčević

Juraj Dalmatinac et al. , early 15th - mid 16th centuries
Trg Republike Hrvatske, Šibenik

Image: Giovanni Francesco Camotio, *View of Sebenico*, 1571. Engraving, 15 x 21 cm. Published in Giuseppe Rosaccio, *Viaggio da Venetia a Costantinopoli Per Mare, e per Terra* [...] (Venice: Giacomo Franco, 1598; 76 fols.), fol. 13r. London, British Library, General Reference Collection, 571.b.21. Photo © The British Library Board; all rights reserved.

In Giuseppe Rosaccio's popular illustrated travelogue, *Viaggio da Venetia a Costantinopoli*, the author records his arrival in Šibenik, in modern-day Croatia: "All of a sudden the town of Šibenik appeared before us, not excessively affluent, not unlike other towns in Schiavonia. Surrounded by arid land and high, steep rocks, Šibenik is populated by common folk, inept in commerce and trade" (Rosaccio 1606, fol. 13^{v}).

Rosaccio's rather unflattering description is typical of contemporary travel literature concerning little-known "exotic regions." In truth, judging by several of the engravings and descriptions, it seems likely that our tour guide travelled on a map, never leaving the comfort of his Venetian home.

The relationship of Dalmatia to the wider narratives of European history in this period rests principally on its relationship with Venice. The coastal cities of Istria and Dalmatia formed part of the Serenissima's coastal empire, the *domini da mar*. Their economic development—resulting in developments in education, trades, and crafts to meet the requirements of an emerging mercantile middle class—was tied to Venetian policy. The *Riva degli Schiavoni*, the grand waterfront promenade stretching from the Basilica di San Marco to the Arsenal, today represents a memento of the centuries-long presence of a Croatian community in Venice. However, the very term *Schiavoni*, derived from *schiavo* (slave) and applied derogatively to Croatians working in the city, mirrors Rosaccio's colonial mentality.

In Camotio's engraving, the Cathedral of St James towers over the western side of the centre of Šibenik, just as it has towered over the historiography of Dalmatian architecture as a key masterpiece of the Renaissance period. The large three-nave church dominates the main town square, built entirely from white stone, carefully and skilfully carved and shipped to Šibenik from several Dalmatian quarries. The stone slabs were cut and dry-laid without any binding material, in keeping with the traditional building techniques of the region. This so-called "dry construction" had been used to erect simple shepherds' shelters in Dalmatia since ancient times, but Šibenik Cathedral represents its first and only use for such a complex and large-scale edifice.

The cathedral was built in several stages, from the early fifteenth to the mid-sixteenth century. Its chief architect, the Croatian sculptor and architect Juraj Dalmatinac (George the Dalmatian), was born in Zadar further up the coast. Most likely he was schooled in Venice, where he must have encountered the Flamboyant Gothic style, then at its zenith, but also elements of the new Tuscan Renaissance style. Active in his native Dalmatia and also in Italy (Venice, Florence, Ancona), he was the first and most distinctive representative of a mixed Gothic-Renaissance style, typical of Dalmatian regional art and architecture in the fifteenth and the sixteenth centuries. His long-term engagement on Šibenik Cathedral (1441-75) left an important legacy: the international workshop he established to complete the work continued successfully even after his death. His disciples included the Albanian Andrea Alessi and the Italian Nicolò di Giovanni Fiorentino, who brought the Brunelleschi-influenced dome of the cathedral to completion (Pelc 2007, 179-88).

Juraj Dalmatinac's distinctive art, and his investment in civic pride, are particularly reflected in a series of 72 life-size stone portrait heads, publicly displayed on the external cornice of the three apses of Šibenik Cathedral. Such carved portraits were not entirely novel in architecture within his cultural ambitus—for instance, several can be found on the column capitals in the western wing of the Doge's Palace in Venice. However, Juraj's portraits are not mere decorations; his gallery of tradesmen, women, children, and the elderly is located relatively low, almost within reach of passers-by, and realistically depicts the natural facial features of Šibenik's citizens, caught in a moment of candid, sincere expression (Ivančević 1994, 40; Pelc 2007, 187). Through this collective portrait, a secular element on a sacred monument, Juraj sought to immortalise his fellow townspeople; his signature—Georgius Mathei Dalmaticus—is carved nearby, on the inner side of the apses.

Although the Cathedral of Šibenik must have furnished a sonorous space for musicians throughout its existence, institutional documentation of its musical life before the tenure of the seventeenth-century chapelmaster Ivan Lukačić has not survived. Nonetheless, it is possible indirectly to connect the

CANTO

DI M. GIVLIO SCHIAVETTO,

LI MADRIGALI A QVATTO,

ET A CINQVE VOCI.

NVOVAMENTE COMPOSTI,

Datti in luce, & corretti.

In Vinegia appresso Girolamo Scotto.

M D LXIII.

Figure 62.1: Giulio Schiavetto, *Li madrigali a quattro et a cinque voci* (Venice: Gerolamo Scotto, 1563), title page. Verona, Biblioteca dell'Accademia Filarmonica, Fondo musicale antico b. 79.III. Photo courtesy of the Accademia Filarmonica di Verona / Maurizio Brenzoni.

sixteenth-century composer Julije Skjavetić (Giulio Schiavetto) with the cathedral, through his close association with the bishop of Šibenik, Girolamo Savorgnano (r. 1557-73).

Skjavetić came from a family of commoners in Šibenik; their family name was recorded in the civic register of deaths, marriages, and births during the sixteenth and seventeenth centuries as Schiauetich/Scauetich. We know very little about Julije's life, and what scant information we have comes from his surviving printed works, almost all of them issued by the major Venetian printing firm of Girolamo Scotto between 1562 and 1565. Two of Skjavetić's five-part madrigals are included in the anthology *I dolci et harmoniosi concetti fatti da diversi et eccellentissimi musici sopra vari soggetti. A cinque voci Libro secondo* (Venice, 1562); a year later he brought out his first and only sole-author madrigal collection "for four or five voices" (which unfortunately survives incomplete; fig. 62.1). In 1564 he published his first book of motets; a second book of motets issued in the following year does not survive, but is known from catalogues. In addition, two *greghesche* (songs in the dialect used by Venice's Greek community) by Skjavetić were included in the anthology *Il primo libro delle Greghesche* (Venice, 1564). After 1565 we hear nothing further of the composer.

Skjavetić dedicated both the madrigal book of 1563 and the motet collection of 1564 to Girolamo Savorgnano (Plamenac 1981). Born in Friuli into a family of Veneto aristocracy, Girolamo was a member of an ancient military dynasty: his father was a veteran of the Italian Wars, whilst his elder brother was commander of the Venetian garrison in Zadar. Girolamo was nominated bishop of Šibenik in 1557 soon after finishing his studies at the University of Padua, and remained in post until 1573; thereafter he returned to his native Friuli, where he administered his lands until his death in 1593. Girolamo was a prominent participant in the Council of Trent during its final years, arriving in Trento on 13 October 1561 (Sopta 2001, 237-49). Among his suite was Skjavetić himself, and the composer remained in service to the bishop until the conclusion of the council in 1563—thus, their direct association in Trento overlaps quite precisely with the period of Skjavetić's publishing activity in Venice.

Girolamo showed a notable commitment to Šibenik, and can be documented developing the cathedral's musical resources during exactly these years: he had the organ repaired during his absence, and hired Matteo Caputius (Cavazza) as organist in 1563 (Županović 2001, 971). Thus it seems very likely that his patronage of the Šibenik-born Skjavetić was also undertaken in relation to his duties as bishop of Šibenik, and that their association in Trento represents the visible portion of a musical relationship that also involved the cathedral in some way. Although the dedication of Skjavetić's 1564 collection of six-part motets specifically recalls performing the works in Girolamo's palace in Trento, these works are nonetheless also the best candidates from among his surviving oeuvre for performance in the cathedral. In these works Skjavetić shows an allegiance to a Netherlandish polyphonic style that in his day was rather old-fashioned, the dense texture of his music abounding in contrapuntal tricks. His motets are mostly built over fixed cantus firmi which are elaborated using various canonic techniques, in the manner of musicians of the post-Josquin generation such as Nicolas Gombert, Jacobus Clemens non Papa, and Adrian Willaert.

Skjavetić was not the only musician in sixteenth-century Croatia to attain a measure of fame. During the 1550s and 1560s, Andrea Patrizio (Andrija Patricij) from the North Dalmatian island of Cres, and the Frenchman Lambert Courtoys who served as *maestro di cappella* in the Doge's Palace in Dubrovnik, were also active in the region. Ironically, precisely because music printing did not develop in Dalmatia until centuries later, these musicians looked to Venice and Italy for publishing opportunities, and thus in spite of the derogatory attitudes recorded in Rosaccio's travelogue, their works entered into Europe-wide circulation (Stipčević 2016, 53-61). Together, these musicians reflect the considerable importance of the Dalmatian coast and its particular relationship with Venice in contemporary West-East musical exchange.

Additional references: Cavallini 2017; Skjavetić 1996 and 2004; Stipčević 1993.

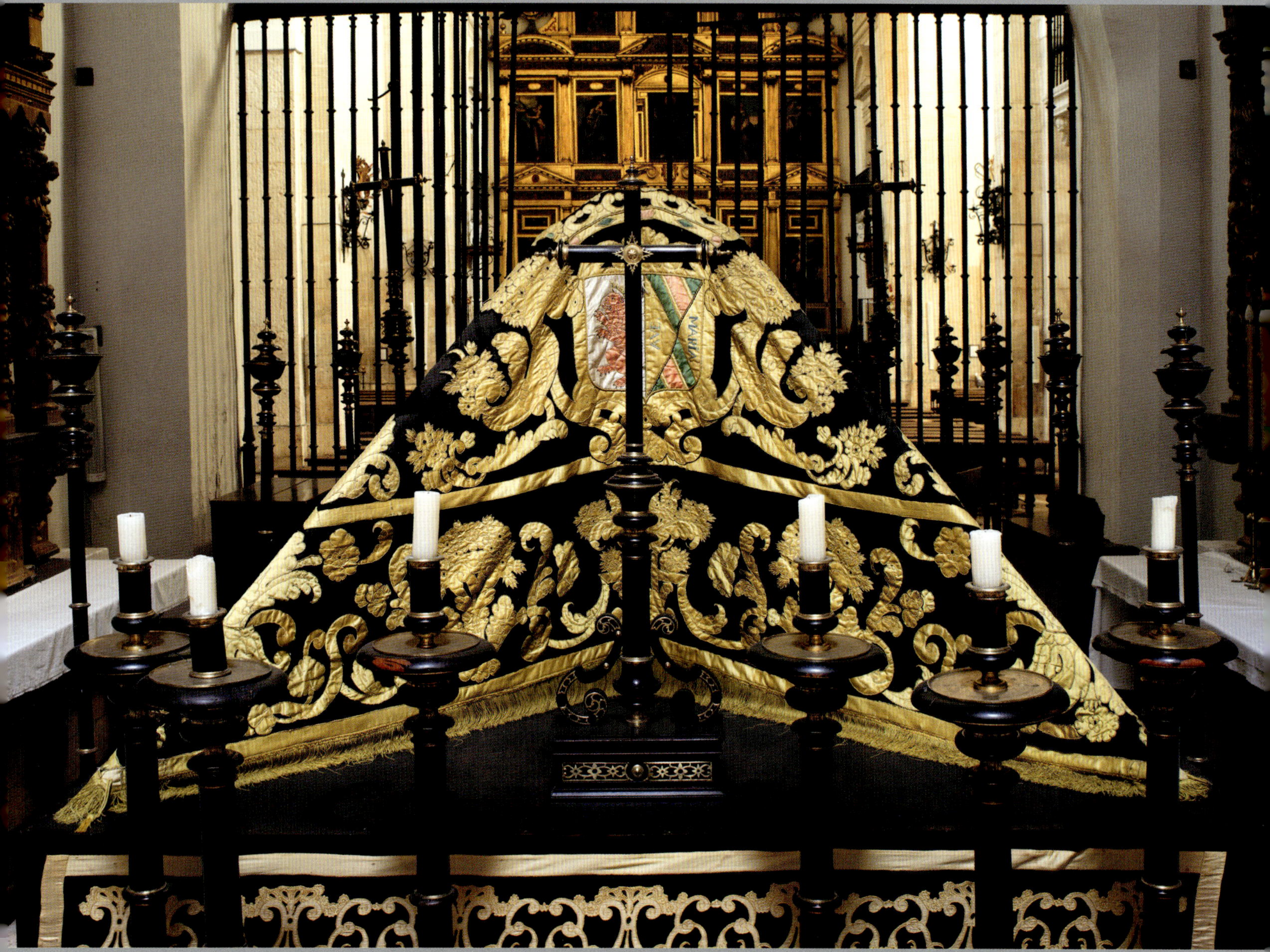

63. The Funeral Monument of the Princess of Éboli

Iain Fenlon

Anon., ca. 1630
Collegiate Church of Nuestra Señora de la Asunción, Calle Melchor Cano, Pastrana
Photo © Paul Maeyaert / Bridgeman Images

Ana de Mendoza y de la Cerda, Princess of Éboli, has numerous faces. For many she is the "proud, wilful, passionate" woman of compelling charm who appears in Giuseppe Verdi's five-act grand opera *Don Carlos* (1867), prominent above all in the popular Veil Song *Au palais des fees/Nel giardin del bello* which opens the second scene of Act I. Others may be familiar with Friedrich Schiller's historical drama *Don Carlos, Infant von Spanien* (1787), the source for Verdi's opera, which itself was based on the little-known pseudo-historical "nouvelle-historique" *Don Carlos* by César Vischard, L'Abbé de Saint-Real (1672). Cineastes may have come across her played by Olivia de Havilland in the historical romance *That Lady* (1955); there she appears as a swashbuckling beauty who had lost an eye defending the honour of Philip II (memorably played by the great Shakespearian actor Paul Scofield in his film debut). But the truth of the matter is more mundane. Depicted in a number of contemporary portraits with a patch over her left eye, her alleged blindness was probably the result of either a childhood accident or a natural defect. Nonetheless, armed with this romantic aid, her impetuous and disruptive personality runs like a thread through many later artistic and historical engagements with the culture and intrigues of Philip II's court.

Her biography is typical of someone of her class and social standing. The daughter of Diego Hurtado de Mendoza y de la Cerda, prince of Melito and duke of Francavilla and María Catalina de Silva y Álvarez de Toledo, Ana came from one of the most prominent Spanish aristocratic families. Her father's career (at various times he was president of the Council of Italy, and viceroy of Aragon and Catalonia), was typical of that of members of the most powerful dynasties and factions at the Spanish court. In 1552 Prince Philip sought Diego's agreement (Ana was only 12 years old at the time) for his daughter's marriage to Ruy Gómez de Silva, a Portuguese nobleman who had become the king's most trusted advisor and secretary (*privado*), and who was later granted the title of prince of Eboli (in the region of Campania, in Italy) as a reward for his services. The marriage itself finally took place in April 1553 (Boyden 1995, 24-38).

In 1569, Ana de Mendoza and her husband took up residence in the small Castilian town of Pastrana (Guadalajara), which had been bought from the military-religious Order of Calatrava by her grandmother, who had commissioned the architect Alonso de Covarrubias to build there an imposing if forbidding palace (Alegre 2003; Garcia López 2010). Designed on a square ground plan with four towers and a central courtyard, it is effectively the architect's first attempt to create an urban ensemble. Installed in this building, which resembles a fortress as much as anything, the new arrivals became active patrons of the local parish church of Santa María, which was subsequently elevated by a papal bull to the status of a collegiate church. Re-dedicated as the Colegiata de Nuestra Señora de la Asunción, it supported a number of prebends which provided funds for the master of ceremonies together with a succentor, chapelmaster, and organist. Four more posts were reserved for a *tiple* (soprano), contralto, tenor, and bass, together with chaplaincies for four more singers "so that the musical chapel shall be complete, and of doubled voices" (Martínez Gil 1994, vi; Freund Schwartz 2001, 441). The chapelmaster of the Colegiata was expected to give daily lessons in plainchant and polyphony to the members of the chapter, as well as to any of the ducal courtiers or others resident in the town. By the standards of the time this was a generous level of provision that elevated an unremarkable parish church to a position of prime importance in the musical and ceremonial life of Pastrana. The couple also founded both a convent and a monastery which were allocated to the new Carmelite order, and encouraged the local silk industry, which was mostly in the hands of the large *morisco* community (nominally Catholic descendants of the Spanish Muslim community), many of whom were refugees from the War of the Alpujarras (1568-71), which was concentrated in the newly-developed barrio of the Albaicín (Alegre Carvajal 2003, 131-41).

After the death of Gómez in 1573, the Princess of Éboli entered the Carmelite convent that she had founded, taking the name of Sor Ana de la Madre de Dios. There her insistence on being provided with both comfortable quarters and deference alienated the other members of the community. Now began the most intriguing period of her life, which in the space of 20 years was to see her return to prominence at the royal court, imprisonment, final expulsion from court, and effective house arrest in Pastrana. Following her departure from the convent after only a short period, she moved back to the ducal palace in Pastrana before returning to Madrid where she took up residence again at the royal court. Within a short time she attracted notoriety by forming an illicit relationship with Antonio Perez, one of Philip II's secretaries. Accused of betraying secrets, Ana was imprisoned in the Castillo de Pinto, 20 kilometres south of the city, for her supposed part in the death of Juan Escobedo, secretary to Don Juan of Austria (Philip II's half brother). Then, in 1581, she was finally exiled to Pastrana for the remaining years of her life, deprived of both the custody of her children and the administration of her property. Essentially a prisoner in her own palace, the princess died ostracised and in disgrace in 1592 (Kamen 1997, 284).

Following the death of the third duke of Pastrana in 1626, the Franciscan friar Pedro González de Mendoza, archbishop of Granada and Zaragoza, and the fifth son among Ruy Gomez de Silva and Ana de Mendoza's ten children, became a major patron of the ecclesiastical institutions founded by his mother in Pastrana, notwithstanding his appointment as bishop of Sigüenza in 1623. It was at his instigation that many modifications were made to the collegiate church; the Chapel of the Relics was founded, and Andres Extarja's *retablo* behind the High Altar, with its elaborate gilded structure which includes Pedro's coat-of-arms, was put in place. In 1628 González de Mendoza founded the Colegio de San Buenaventura in Pastrana with the express purpose of training musicians to serve the collegiate church. Eight of the approximately 30 places in the school were to be reserved for

> students who play instruments; six for *bajones* [dulcians], cornetts and shawms, and [of] the other two, one for organ and the other for stringed instruments: violins, vihuelas, theorbos, and harps; the rest of the students will be singers—*tiples*, contraltos, tenors and basses—and the students shall be divided among these voice parts equally, according to their numbers (Martínez Gil 1994, vi-vii; Freund Schwartz 2001, 447; Alegre Carvajal 2003, 164-65).

It would seem that these years witnessed the apogee of the musical life of Nuestra Señora de la Asunción.

It was also during these years that Pedro González de Mendoza put together the collection of books of music, some of which still survive at Pastrana. Although most were printed in the late sixteenth and early seventeenth centuries, there is one spectacular exception: a copy of the *Liber quindecim missarum*, the remarkable choirbook printed with woodblocks by the Istrian craftsman Andrea Antico in Rome in 1516 in an edition of more than 1000 copies (see also exhibit 39). Since González de Mendoza is known to have had a keen interest in the performance of music at the Colegiata, the acquisition of this iconic publication was clearly intended to lend authority and status to the provision of polyphony at the church on grand ceremonial occasions. Commonly referred to in archival documents as the "fifteen Masses by Josquin" ("quinze misas de Josquin"; see Fenlon 2001, 217-18), the *Liber quindecim missarum* is frequently cited in Spanish inventories such as those of the cathedrals of Plasencia (where a copy was bought as late as 1597), and La Seo in Zaragoza. Although it was widely distributed throughout the peninsula, many copies have been destroyed or lost, leaving the exemplar in Pastrana as the sole Spanish survivor (Fenlon 2016, 79-80); its sumptuous contemporary binding is decorated with the ducal coat-of-arms, thus associating the ducal house with the sound of the music of the most celebrated of all Renaissance composers. Copies of Lopez de Velasco's *Libro de missas* (1628), and Philippe Rogier's *Missae sex* (1598), published by the Typographia Regia in Madrid, are among the few books from the church library to have survived. Others known to have been in the library have been lost, while leaves from a number of sixteenth-century printed choirbooks, among them Cristóbal de Morales' *Missarum liber secundus* (Rome: Dorico, 1544), have been used to paper the wooden structure supporting the bellows of the organ, built in 1704 by Domingo Mendoza, chapelmaster of the royal chapel at the court of Philip V.

Many of the precious treasures from Pastrana's past are still kept in the Colegiata, among them a fine set of fifteenth-century Flemish tapestries (known as the Pastrana Tapestries) woven in the workshop of Paschier Grenier in Tournai showing a number of the military and naval victories secured by Alfonso V of Portugal; these were displayed in ceremonies held in the Colegiata. But the most remarkable and unusual of all is the catafalque ensemble of the dukes of Pastrana, ordered by Pedro González de Mendoza for his own obsequies and subsequently for those of other members of the extended ducal family (it is generally referred to as the Catafalque of the Dukes of Pastrana). The pall is worked from black velvet and silk ornamented with appliqué embroidery in gold and the coat-of-arms of the dukes, while the bier on which it sits is covered with four panels of similar style and design. Among the matching accoutrements are 12 large and 12 smaller candlesticks to surround the catafalque, as well as vestments, altar frontals, and other objects for use in the liturgy of the dead (fig. 63.1). These, which are made of ebony and bronze, include an aspersory, a thurible together with an incense boat, and a pair of cruets with its lavabo dish, all evidently brought from Portugal (Alegre Carvajal 2003, 164-67). The first of these was used to sprinkle holy water over the catafalque, the second to surround it with incense, and the last for use in the preparation by the officiant of the bread and wine for those who were to communicate.

As well as being used for the exequies of González de Mendoza, this equipment was probably also used for the obsequies of Ana de Mendoza when, on the orders of her son, her remains were translated from the monastery of San José to the Colegiata in compensation for the meagre funeral accorded to her at her death. Given the musical resources available at this period, and the size of the college of canons (48 at full strength), her exequies, and certainly those of González de Mendoza which were carried out according to his own testamentary instructions, would have been spectacular. The models for such were provided by a sequence of royal funeral rites beginning with those for Philip II and Philip III, both of which are described in detailed printed accounts which sometimes mention music alongside elaborate descriptions of the decorations, emblems ("hieroglyphs"), and at the centre of attention the *capilla ardente* with its many burning candles (Eire 1995, 283-99). Some of these compositions have survived. The six-voice motet *Quomodo sedet sola* by Luis de Aranda was composed for the exequies mounted for Philip II in Zaragoza in 1598 (Rees 2007), while the funeral of the Empress Maria at the Convent of the Descalzas in Madrid in March 1603 included Tomás Luis de Victoria's specially composed *Officium Defunctorum* and *Missa pro Defunctis*, which were probably repeated during the exequies held by the Jesuits one month later; both were published together in choirbook format as the *Officium defunctorum: in obitu et obsequiis sacrae imperatricis* (Madrid: Typographia Regia, 1605; see Rees 2019). It seems likely that the polyphony performed for the exequies of González de Mendoza (1639), and possibly for the translation of Ana de Mendoza two years earlier, was taken from Velasco's *Libro de misas*, which includes a setting of the requiem Mass and an associated motet by Francisco Dávila y Páez.

Together with Ruy Gomez de Silva, the Princess of Éboli was finally interred in a marble tomb in the family pantheon constructed in the crypt of the Colegiata under the high altar, again at the instigation of her son. There she remained undisturbed until Pastrana was sacked by the French in 1808 and her tomb desecrated, and the turbulence which had characterised her in life returned to besiege her in death.

Figure 63.1: Funeral accoutrements at the Iglesia Colegiata de Nuestra Señora de la Asunción, Pastrana. Photo © Paul Maeyaert.

VANITAS

VI

Public Sphere

Introduction: The Room of the Public Sphere

Robert L. Kendrick

RATHER THAN instantiations of the kind of "public sphere" classically described by Jurgen Habermas (Habermas 1962) for eighteenth-century northern Europe, the exhibits in this section reflect something of music's social face in fifteenth- and sixteenth-century Europe, Asia, and the Americas. Neither the exhibits' makers nor most of their publics were primarily musicians themselves, although the illustration of Milan's Cathedral (Filippi) in its choirbooks would have been seen largely by those singers memorising—or performing from—the Libroni, a simultaneously visual and sonic projection of civic tradition, local in its liturgy. On the other hand, Gumprecht's paraliturgical contrafacta for Jewish holidays (Matut) show one minority community's attempt to hold on to its internal musical practices in the face of persecution.

Other practices and genres evident in images, too many to be illustrated here, coalesced outside Europe in the sixteenth century: the first references to *kora* playing among the Mandinka of West Africa (Almada 1946 [1594], 24); *kunqu* opera in the late Ming dynasty at the hands of Wei Liangfu; or Garcilaso de la Vega Inca's description of indigenous suitors and their "talking flutes" in Cuzco (*Royal Commentaries of the Incas*, Book II, ch. 26). Another musical reference on an instrument itself is the depiction of scenes from *The Romance of the Western Chamber* on the bridge of a late Ming *pipa* now in the Metropolitan Museum in New York (see Ni 2014, 98). Among our images, Katz's commentary on the Mughal scene of Plato as organist resonates with other North Indian images, like the one (now in The Cleveland Museum of Art; Wade 1998, 118) showing the child prince of Isfahan hearing all possible instruments as a remedy for illness, while Mughal instruments even made it into a Christianised visual synopsis of the New Testament produced for the small Jesuit mission at the court (Carvalho 2012, 120). A different kind of Christian court is evident in the Kongo's royal musical ensemble (pictured in Fromont 2014: 42), as drawn by a seventeenth-century Capuchin missionary, with its tambourines, bells, nine-string harp, elephant horn, and balafon (locally "palaku"); all these were important given music's role in the foundational stories of this dynasty, and also were perhaps representative of the kingdom's extent.

In the territories actually seized by Europe, the direct counterposing of European and indigenous practices is most evident in Marín López's discussion of pre- and post-Cortesian musics on the *zócalo* of what would become Mexico City. Among European travelers in the Mediterranean, Belon's account (Zecher) shows uneven European comprehension when confronted with other traditions; it is telling that the two travelogues by practicing European composers—Francisco Guerrero and Giovanni Francesco Alcarotti—are largely unhelpful in describing other musical cultures. Beyond the high presence of sub-Saharan Africans in Lisbon, suggested as skilled in both European and African traditions on the Flemish panel discussed by Raimundo, Afro-Europeans also had confraternities in Seville, Valencia, Genoa, Naples, or Palermo, some of which may also have been musically active (e.g. Moreno Navarro 1997, 54). Although there was enormous music-making around the European journey of the four Japanese "princes" (Bosi), their musical work once back in the Japanese seminary must have been difficult, given the liturgical problems of the small Catholic community on the island (López Gay 1970).

Among communal musical practices, the ubiquity of dance, and its place between the secular and the sacred, are evident in the Bosnian *stele* (Blazekovic). How it worked in courtship rituals is evident in Daye's discussion of van Meckehem's print, and dancing's contested place in post-1559 England is clear from the social evidence (on its ambiguity, see Marsh 2014, 328-90). Despite episcopal strictures post-1550, dancing in Catholic churches continued throughout rural southern Europe and was even permitted (for women only, and at night) by the Dominican *lauda* collector Serafino Razzi (Razzi 1585, 173-76).

In part, our images testify to the classic division between court and urban musics. The public face of the former is evident in the 1585 Düsseldorf wedding music, which, as Pietschmann points out, differs from, and is more representative than, the 1539 and 1589 Medici celebrations in Florence or the 1568 Wittelsbach festivities starring Orlando di Lasso in Munich. Civic devotion in this latter city must have been sonically evident on occasions like Marian devotions (Fisher). For all that "urban soundscapes" have become an omnipresent heuristic in early modern studies over the last generation, the women and Moorish musicians of Granada (Mazuela Anguita), with its 70,000 inhabitants on the eve of the Morisco rebellion of 1568, show that much more is to be gained from the close study of music in its physical and architectonic settings.

Such issues include the role of ritual (not least religious) time as marked by recurrent chant and bells; the acoustics of urban waters and hills; or the aural chaos of streets (as in Knighton's example, and clear in the 1561 Milanese orders cited by Filippi; see also Rospocher 2017) filled with poetic singers, street instrumentalists, devotional processions, and tradespeople's calls. Peters' case of the Dijon trumpet shows how instruments (and their players) symbolised civic freedom from feudal lordship, embodied in a material object.

More hermetic court culture is on view in the *Apollo* related to Giraldi's pedagogical drama for the women of the Este dynasty (Stras). Similarly, the early modern fascination with automata is clear from the Habsburg fountain in Prague (Edwards; in the Room of Revivals), paralleled by similar machines in Tivoli, Pratolino, and Salzburg. Notably, none of our images contain notated music in themselves, traditionally a starting point for much work on music and painting. Memorised or orally transmitted, music-making in early modern Europe did not depend on the presence of writing, not least in the case of the practice of *falsobordone* or *faburdón* in and out of liturgy (Macchiarella 1995).

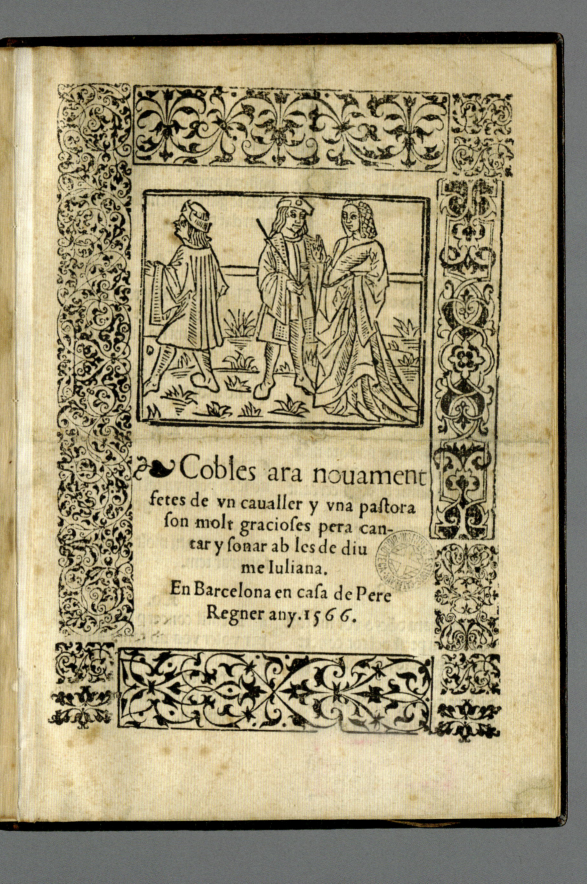

Cobles ara nouament fetes de vn caualler y vna pastora son molt gracioses pera cantar y sonar ab les de diume Iuliana.

En Barcelona en casa de Pere Regner any. 1566.

64. Street Music from Barcelona

Tess Knighton

Cobles ara nouamente fetes de vn caualler y vna pastora son molt gracioses pera cantar y sonar ab les de diu me Juliana
Barcelona: Pere Regnat, 1566
[4] pp., 20 cm (40)
Barcelona, Biblioteca de Catalunya, 1-IV-40
Image: Title page. Photo © Biblioteca de Catalunya.

Printed pamphlets and broadsheets, known in Spain as *pliegos sueltos*, were produced in large print-runs all over early modern Europe and were sold at the printing-shop or by street vendors for a small amount of money, making them one of the most widely accessible forms of printed material. They contain texts of many kinds, and are of particular interest as a reflection of the porosity between print and popular culture during the period, especially as a means of transmitting song texts. In general, only the words were printed; there are a few (generally later) examples with printed musical notation, but in most instances there is little or no indication as to the melody. Given the regularity of verse structure and metre in songs, such as Spanish villancicos and romances, this presented the potential performer with few problems: an existing melody could easily be adapted to fit the *coplas* (or strophes) as necessary. But in some cases, the printed text included a direct reference to the corresponding melody to which the song could be sung ("al tono de" or "al son de" in Spanish sources—Ros-Fábregas 2008; or "cantasi come" in Italian prints—Wilson 2009). A good example is the anonymous *Cobles ara nouamente fetes de vn caualler y vna pastora son molt gracioses pera cantar y sonar ab les de diu me Juliana* (*Newly devised and very entertaining verses about a knight and a shepherdess to be sung and played to "Diu me Juliana"* [*Tell me Juliana*]) in which the verses are to be sung and played to the tune of the otherwise unknown song *Diu me, Juliana* (Frenk 1987, 1:146). The performance of such popular songs (popular in the sense that they were widely disseminated and accessible) did not thus depend on a musical literacy that presupposed the ability to read mensural notation, but drew on a well-known musical repertory that circulated orally. The *pliego suelto* served as a mnemonic device, bringing to mind a familiar melody that enabled musical performance of the song, whether in the street or the domestic sphere.

The *pliego suelto* as material object was of little worth: a folded piece of paper that cost little and fell apart with use, a fragile, throw-away item. However, some bibliophiles, such as Ferdinand Columbus, collected them and preserved them by binding them together into volumes (Cátedra 2002, 146). Printers, ever anxious to keep their production costs to a minimum, nevertheless made some effort to make them attractive by using in-house woodcuts and embedding a sales patter into the text which could be read aloud by vendor and performer alike. The title-page of the *Cobles … de vn caualler y vna pastora*, a ditty on the popular pastoral theme of the knight "courting" the shepherdess, describes the song as "newly composed" and "very entertaining," while the selling-point at the start of the verses reads: "Those who wish to hear the fine love story of an elegant knight [and] a quite pretty and graceful shepherdess [will find] many words to give them much pleasure and a good laugh." The printer, Pierre Regnier, re-used a simple woodcut to suggest the theme of wooing (despite the fact that it appears to depict a noble lady rather than a shepherdess), and a decorative border to make the *pliego* more attractive. Regnier was active in Barcelona in the 1560s and early 1570s until his French origin made him a target for the Inquisition; tried for heretical beliefs, he was condemned to the galleys (Griffin 2005, 238).

Printing made such popular songs widely available for performance in public or private entertainments, but they were perhaps most commonly heard on the street. Street singers in early modern European cities had a major role as "crucial mediators in the dynamic continuum of learned and popular, oral and literate" (Degl'Innocenti & Rospocher 2016). They did not only sing songs but also, in many cases, acted as vendors of printed song sheets. In Spain, the practice became associated with a specific group in society: the blind *oracioneros*, who sang and recited prayers and songs of all kinds in return for alms (fig. 64.1; on the situation in Italy, see Carnelos 2016). By the seventeenth century, the *oracionero* was a stock figure in Spanish theatre and picaresque novels, often depicted as far from devout, scurrilous in behaviour—even to the extent of feigning blindness—and of negligeable musical ability. Yet even the eponymous prankster Lazarillo de Tormes, whose exploits first appeared in print in 1554, admired his blind master for his ability to memorise more than a hundred prayers which he sang or recited in a low, resonant tone to fill the acoustic of the church where he prayed for alms (Gomis Coloma 2010, 314). The repertory of prayers and songs was generally learnt

Figure 64.1: Georges de la Tour, *A Blind Hurdy-Gurdy Player*, 1620-30. Oil on canvas, 86 x 62.5 cm. Museo Nacional del Prado, Madrid. Photo © Photographic Archive Museo Nacional del Prado.

through apprenticeship to other blind musicians (Cátedra 2002, 136-45; Knighton 2018, 304-07), and, according to the *Recopilación en metro* (1554) by the playwright and poet Diego Sánchez de Badajoz (1479-1549), included the Penitential Psalms, prayers for souls in purgatory, that of St Gregory, Christian doctrine, the Rosary, and verses relating the main events of the life of Christ and the Virgin Mary, as well as the holy deeds of saints (Caro Baroja 1990, 54).

Memorization and oral tradition were clearly key to the transmission of the knowledge of blind *oracioneros*; as Vicente Espinel declared in his *Marcos de Obregón* (1618), they went "praising God and his saints with many devout prayers which they learn without knowing how to read" (Marcos Álvarez 2001, 225). Yet their mediation of written material and oral practice was more widespread than their disability might imply. For example, at the time of his death in 1591, Pere Caparo, a "sego [blind] orationer" who resided in Barcelona, owned not only the musical instruments of his trade—a five-course plucked *vihuela*, three bowed *vihuelas* and a rebec (probably to accompany dancing)—but also a handwritten collection of prayers ("libre de ma de orations") and a book of songs ("vn llibre llarch ab algunes cansons escrit") (Knighton 2018, 307). In his will, Caparo, like many of his blind colleagues, asked to be buried in the tomb of the Confraternity of the Holy Spirit, the organization founded in Barcelona in 1339 for the devotional purposes and social welfare of the blind, that increasingly regulated such matters as apprenticeships in the manner of a guild (Gomis Coloma 2010). By the mid-sixteenth century, the confraternity had built its own chapel and was active in the prohibition of blind beggars who were not members or who came from outside Barcelona from practising in the city. Music, notably the distinctive sound of plucked and bowed *vihuelas* so closely associated with the *oracioneros*, formed an integral part of their devotional festivities on their feast day—Whitsun—and other celebratory occasions, clearly identifying them as a discrete acoustic community within the soundscape of the city. At least by the early seventeenth century, a closely linked confraternity owned a basic printing press in order to produce *pliegos sueltos* relating to Marian devotion ("vna emprenta o mollo de emprentar papers de nostra señora"). Members of the confraternity would have sold these sheets (or "papers") at the street corners and church doorways where they customarily performed, thereby increasing their meagre earnings. This practice, widespread in sixteenth-century Italian cities (Carnelos 2016), was established in Spain at least by the mid-sixteenth century, when Sánchez de Badajoz wrote his *Farsa del Molino*, with its reference to a blind man selling printed verse and song texts (Cátedra 2002, 133-34).

Blind *oracioneros* varied in ability and expertise from the beggar who muttered a few prayers to the accomplished musician, able to sing and play a variety of stringed instruments. Music was acknowledged as a selling-point in Juan de Timoneda's *Entremes de un ciego y un moço y un pobre oracionero* (mid-sixteenth century) in which the "mozo" (guide or "lazarillo") declares that "Prayers are no longer / esteemed / unless they are sung and played / in the manner of a song" (Gomis Coloma 2010, 308). The reciting, singing, and playing of the *oracioneros* filled the streets of Spanish cities, contributing to a distinctive urban soundscape. According to the Swiss medical student Thomas Platter on his visit to Barcelona in 1599: "Among the blind are many who play very well the bowed or plucked vihuela, or other instruments. For a little money, they entertain the listening public in this way for some time. To try their luck, they sit outside the artisans' shops or in the whores' street" (Le Roy Ladurie 2000, 480). Platter's account reflects the *oracioneros*' ubiquitous presence in the city; far from being confined to church doorways and a repertory of devout prayers, their songs of all kinds—including ditties about knights and shepherdesses—would have filled a variety of urban spaces.

Early in the sixteenth century, the humanist Juan Luis Vives, in his treatise on the poor *De subventione pauperum* (1525), posited that the blind could avoid poverty by blowing the bellows in the smithy, treading grapes, or learning to sing and play a musical instrument (Cátedra 2002, 116). They thus had a status in society—even if a lowly one—that was given structure and urban presence by their confraternity and through the recognition of church and civic authorities. Yet their activities as street performers were often frowned upon by moralists such as Cristóbal Pérez de Herrera who, in his *Amparo de pobres* (1598), asked the king to legislate against the increasing numbers of blind *oracioneros* who "set up in the squares and main streets of large towns … to sing, to the accompaniment of guitars and other instruments, printed songs of apocryphal events, and to sell them on no authority" (Cátedra 2002, 161). Regulatory steps were taken: in a royal "instrucción" of 1597, the poor, even if they were blind or in some other way disabled, had to wear a rosary with the image of the Virgin Mary, and the arms of the city where they were registered, to show that they belonged to the city's recognised poor and were dedicated to seeking alms through prayer (Cátedra 2002, 164). Later in the seventeenth century, their virtual monopoly on the sale of *pliegos sueltos* was challenged in the courts by booksellers anxious to regain a relatively lucrative niche of the market (Botrel 1973, 431).

65. African Musicians at the King's Fountain in Lisbon

Nuno de Mendonça Raimundo

Chafariz d'el-Rei
Anon. (Netherlandish?), Lisbon(?), ca. 1570-1580
Oil on wood, 93 x 163 cm
The Berardo Collection, Lisbon
Photo © akg-images

THIS PAINTING, known as *Chafariz d'el-Rei* (*The King's Fountain*), depicts a busy riverfront street in Renaissance Lisbon. It displays the striking ethnic heterogeneity of the city's social fabric at the height of the Portuguese Empire, and the day-to-day presence of a great diversity of cultural manifestations, especially African music and dance, which ended up having a substantial influence on the Iberian music scene.

Since around 1420 the Portuguese had undertaken nautical voyages of exploration of the African west coast in search of new commercial opportunities. Through their expeditions, they established frequent, exclusive contacts with sub-Saharan African peoples, and secured a monopoly over the West African slave trade. Lisbon soon became Europe's largest hub of the black slave trade, exporting slaves to Spain, Italy, and Flanders.

At the time this painting was made, around 1570-80, Lisbon was a truly cosmopolitan city, the capital of a global commercial empire with trading posts from Brazil to West Africa to India to Japan, and a meeting point for people from all over the world: merchants, sailors, and artisans from all parts of Europe; and slaves from Asia, South America, and, mostly, Africa. The painting itself was probably made by a painter from the Low Countries, presumably astonished by the large number of black people in the city. It is estimated that slaves, the majority of whom were black Africans, accounted for about 10% of the total population of Lisbon in this period. This was the largest relative concentration of slaves in Renaissance Europe (Fonseca 2010, 100-04).

The painting shows a representative sample of the black population in Lisbon and its different occupations and social positions. Most slaves did unskilled work, mainly as domestic servants, errand boys, water-bearers, waste collectors, and street vendors—as shown in the background of the painting—but there were also those who had more specialised functions, such as artisans, entertainers, and soldiers. Some slaves were able to become free citizens, a small proportion of whom even enjoyed a degree of social mobility, as represented by the haughty black horseman to the right of the painting. Most probably, this figure depicts João de Sá Panasco, perhaps the first black African slave turned knight in modern Europe. A court jester for King John III of Portugal, Panasco gained the esteem of the monarch for his witty satire—to such an extent that, after manumitting him, the king made him a gentleman of the royal household and a member of the highly prestigious Order of Santiago, whose insignia is seen on the cape of the painted figure. Panasco became a famous figure in Lisbon, known to ride about the city on a mule, richly dressed, escorted by his own African servants (Caldeira 2017, 178).

As an entertainer, it is plausible that Panasco also sang and played instruments, as was the case for many African slaves who did not work as servants. In fact, musical and dance abilities were some of their most appreciated and valuable skills, so much so that these became commonly associated with black Africans as a kind of positive stereotype (Lowe 2005, 35). The black African performer is yet another typical character of the Lisbon social landscape that was registered in the painting. There we can find two black musicians, representing the two principal ways in which black Africans integrated into European musical culture—by playing European music and instruments, and by playing those from their own West African traditions.

One of the musicians is seen at the centre-top of the image, in the background, playing the lute, an instrument associated with court music. This man is probably a street performer, but many African musicians were employed in Portuguese and Spanish noble households, often organised into wind bands to play at festivities and solemn events. Ten of the 36 slaves owned by Teodósio, duke of Braganza, for instance, were shawm players (Sousa 1745, 186); and the well-known depiction of six black musicians playing shawms and sackbut in the painting *The Retable of Saint Auta* (ca. 1522-25; Lisbon, Museu Nacional de Arte Antiga, inv. 1462-A) certainly represents a wind ensemble of the royal court of John III, probably the one that played at his wedding with Catherine of Austria in 1525. John III's chapel also employed a black singer and composer (Figueiredo 1932, 25; Saunders 1982, 106; Jordan 2005, 158-59).

The other black musician is painted in the foreground of the painting, in the boat to the left, performing for a white, perhaps newly-wed couple during their romantic cruise down the river Tagus. The instrument he is playing is a tambourine, one of the most recognisable symbols of African musical culture, demonstrating that Africans in Europe were not limited to playing European instruments and music. In fact, the perceived exoticism of African cultural manifestations was greatly appreciated by the Portuguese—as early as 1451 there are descriptions of Moorish and black slaves performing dances from their own traditions at royal wedding festivities. At around the same time, black Africans also began to form brotherhoods that introduced their native music into religious processions, and they frequently held informal street dance parties during their leisure time. Other than the tambourine, the most commonly played instruments during these performances were flutes, horns, and percussion instruments like drums, cymbals, and rattles, their sound often labelled by the Portuguese as wild and thundering (Andrade 1972, 47-48; Saunders 1982, 106).

The black African community was thus able to not only preserve their musical traditions, but frequently showcase them to the white Portuguese. This was possible due to their relatively peaceful coexistence—black slaves and white commoners not only worked and conversed together, as we see in the painting's background, but they also shared leisure activities such as sports and gambling with no evidence of segregation. In fact, black slaves and white servants were often treated identically by their masters; this shared condition brought them closer together, to the point that black Africans eventually became fully integrated among the working classes (Saunders 1982, 89; Tinhorão 1988, 118).

Thus, every layer of society from the lowest to the highest ranks was in constant close contact with African musical manifestations. This created optimal circumstances for cross-cultural exchanges and influences, to which Iberian musicians—contrary to other Europeans—were particularly permeable, having already shown a keen interest in popular and "exotic" sounds before in the shape of rural folk tunes and Moorish dances. Thus, the fresh rhythms, forms, and sounds of the black African musical culture exerted much fascination on Portuguese and Spanish composers, who began to incorporate these foreign elements into established Iberian genres (Nery 2003, 18-20; Stevenson 1968, 483). This seemingly genuine interest in the slaves' musical culture and the "skilled African musician" trope, however, were also accompanied by negative stereotypes that quickly made their way into Iberian music and theatre, where black Africans were often portrayed as good-natured, but undisciplined, dim-witted big children. One of the essential features of the black African character as represented in Iberian music and theatre was speaking in a stereotyped corrupt form of Portuguese or Spanish, mimicking the pidginised manner in which slaves spoke these languages (then called *fala de negro* or *habla de negros*—literally, "black-speak"). Thus, the black African eventually became a comedic, sometimes even grotesque literary stock character.

The first known text to make use of a black character speaking in *fala de negro* (*Por breve de ũa mourisca ratorta* by Fernão da Silveira) can be dated to 1490 (Terra 1996, 521-23), but it is probably representative of a pre-established literary tradition in Portugal. It appears in the Portuguese literary collection *Cancioneiro Geral* (Resende 1516, 23), and was meant to be recited or sung as an introduction to a dance performance of African inspiration. Towards the beginning of the sixteenth century, perhaps inspired by the Portuguese tradition, we have the first examples of songs with black characters in Spanish literature (Rodrigo de Reinosa's "coplas a los negros"—literally, couplets of the blacks), one of them with an explicit instruction that it was to be sung to the tune of the *guineo*, a lively dance melody of West African origin (Russell 1978, 380-83). Throughout the same century, black characters associated with musical performance also appear in Portuguese theatre: in the play *Auto da Natural Invenção* (ca. 1545-54) by António Chiado, a black musician character sings a villancico while playing the guitar, and is praised for his skill and talent (Tinhorão 1988, 252-53).

Musical performances by black Africans in Lisbon may have also been an inspiration for the Spanish composer Mateo Flecha the Elder, author of the earliest known musical exemplar of an Iberian song with African-like characteristics. According to Maricarmen Gómez, it is possible that Flecha was in the Portuguese capital for the aforementioned wedding of John III (Gómez 2008, 55 and 77); there he would have listened to the royal black wind ensemble, and also to the traditional African songs and dances of the street performers. However, Flecha's contact with black African culture was surely not limited to this trip, for one year later he was working in one of the main export destinations for Lisbon's slaves, the Spanish city of Valencia (Villanueva 2009, 63-77). For some time, this city was also the workplace of Bartomeu Càrceres (documented 1546-59), to whom a similar African-inspired song is attributed. These two compositions, both titled *La Negrina*, are *ensaladas* (literally, salads), an Iberian song genre that mixed together several melodies and songs, many of which were of popular origin. Both are Christmas-themed, and their sections in African style are introduced by groups of black slave characters who come together to sing and dance for the infant Jesus, making it very plausible that they are musical renditions of performances given by black Africans at Christmas festivities, possibly even incorporating direct quotations thereof.

In fact, it is not difficult to detect elements drawn from black African culture in these songs, both in text and music. Besides the use of *habla de negros* (with Portuguese words in the mix, in the case of Flecha), their refrains reproduce words and sounds of West and Central African languages, such as "yamana yeya" (perhaps referring to the Yoruba mother goddess Yemanya, often syncretised with the Virgin Mary) or "gurumbé," also the name of a lively African dance of Guinean origin. Significantly, the music of these pieces is prominently dance-like, with a marked ternary rhythm interspersed with strong, percussive syncopations, and frequent repetition of melodic motives. Their main formal feature is a dialogic call-and-response structure, where a solo voice gives the motto and the choir responds, sometimes repeating the same text and music. This kind of responsorial structure, together with the use of hemiolas and syncopated rhythms, and of repetitive melodic patterns and ostinati, are defining characteristics of West-Central African traditional music (Brandel 1961, 51-92); perhaps not coincidentally, they also became standard musical features of the *villancicos de negros* (literally, villancicos of blacks) or simply *negros*, as hybrid Iberian-African villancicos would come to be known in the seventeenth century (Stevenson 1968, 496-97).

This anonymous Netherlandish portrait of Renaissance Lisbon as Europe's first multiracial capital of the modern era, demonstrating the sharp contrasts of an unequal society but also the peaceful cohabitation of blacks and whites—be it servants, artisans, or knights, in both groups—is a remarkably comprehensive illustration of the melting pot of constant cross-cultural interaction and exchange in Portuguese and Spanish urban centres that resulted in a miscegenation of African and Iberian music traditions. An important part of this process was undertaken by Iberian composers, who mixed African-inspired elements with local forms and idioms, following a long-standing curiosity towards foreign or "exotic" cultural expressions. To be sure, this practice was limited to imitation, accompanied by a considerable amount of socio-ethnic stereotyping. Nevertheless, it stands as a notable example of the earliest artistic products of intercontinental influences in the wake of European colonialism, one that eventually developed into one of the most unique genres in Western music history, the *villancico negro*, which for over a century was an integral part of the cultural scene of the Iberian Peninsula and Latin America.

Additional references: Earle 2005; Gschwend 2017; Rodrigues 2010; Spohr 2019; Vodovozova 1996.

גאט

דען השם [illegible] וויל איך לובן [illegible] זיין [illegible] וואונדר׳
ער האט דר [illegible] דיא דא וואורן דר הוך אויסגע[illegible]
[illegible] אז אויך [illegible] [illegible]
[illegible] וויל׳ זיין וואונדר [illegible] [illegible]׳ אונ
צו [illegible] האט ער אונש פון [illegible] דיזו מלאכים דיא
[illegible] [illegible] [illegible] צו ירושלים [illegible] [illegible]
אין אלן [illegible]׳

זייא [illegible] דאך האט השם [illegible] אודר האט ער
אין [illegible] [illegible] וואש [illegible] [illegible]
[illegible] [illegible] אז וועדר [illegible] דר [illegible] [illegible]׳
אין [illegible] [illegible] [illegible]׳ דער האט
[illegible] [illegible] זיין [illegible]׳ ער [illegible]
[illegible] [illegible] [illegible]׳ [illegible] דער
[illegible] [illegible] ער [illegible] [illegible]
אין וויל [illegible] ער [illegible]
[illegible] [illegible]

66. Songs for Hanukkah and Purim from Venice

Diana Matut

Budapest, Library of the Hungarian Academy of Sciences, Collection David Kaufmann, Ms A. 397
Venice, ca. 1553-1554
Manuscript on paper, 30 fols., 20.5 x 13.5 cm
Image: fol. 2r. Photo © Library of the Hungarian Academy of Sciences, Budapest.

In the mid-sixteenth century, a Jewish teacher named Gumprecht who presumably came from the Polish town of Szczebrzeszyn, wrote two songs in the now extinct Western Yiddish language. Western Yiddish was written in Hebrew characters and represents a fusion of Hebrew/Aramaic, Romance, and German dialects. It became the vernacular of Ashkenazic Jews, meaning those who lived in Central and Eastern Europe, but was brought by émigrés to places such as Italy too. Gumprecht of Szczebrzeszyn mentions that he was writing while living in Venice and at a difficult moment, when books were "taken from us" and remained "in the hands of the non-Jews," "the best ones already burned" (MS Kaufmann A. 397, fol. 1r) and "all lying in the garbage" (fol. 11r). What he refers to is very likely the confiscation and burning of Jewish books in Venice in October 1553, which offers a *terminus post quem* for dating his work.

Gumprecht's two songs were intended to be sung at the Jewish holidays of Hanukkah (no. 1), celebrating the victory of the Maccabees over the Seleucid occupying forces and Purim (no. 2), dedicated to the rescue of the Jewish people in their Persian exile by Queen Esther. The songs themselves retell the Biblical stories and historical background of the festivals, while at the same time enhancing and embellishing the stories proper with further legendary and narrative material.

The Hanukkah and Purim songs were part of a large body of para-liturgical songs, which were performed during the celebration of holidays, offering basic knowledge about these festivals, their origins as well as religious beliefs and practices surrounding them. Sometimes sung in synagogue, they were more commonly performed at home, during the festivities in public halls or private spaces. Thus, they are comparable to Christian hymns and songs intended for holidays such as Easter, Pentecost, Advent, or Christmas. Their functions were similar and could range from being educational, contemplative, or edifying , entertaining or diverting.

The Purim song of this manuscript is of special interest and importance for the history and development of the "Purim play." Not unlike lay theatre in the Christian world, Jewish non-professional actors, mainly the students of the Talmudic academies, called *yeshivot*, entertained the guests at Purim meals and festivities. They would enter several private houses, singing and performing their pieces, and were given wine, food, money or other goods as payment. Before fully-fledged Purim plays appeared, "poems, songs and monologues, either parodic or based on the book of Esther" (Baumgarten 2005, 367) were performed. It is most interesting that Gumprecht himself already calls his verses a "Purim play" (Stern 1922, 18):

> Well, who can tell it all?
> Only the best will I choose!
> In order to make people laugh
> I will make a Purim play.

As was common, the author dedicated his songs to "pious women" in general and in particular to a (probably unmarried) woman by the name of Tsorlayn. He also mentions her father, Simcha of Venice, but nothing else is known about them. In the manuscript, these two names were later crossed out and substituted respectively by Mestlayn and Kalman Azulay. It is possible that the manuscript changed hands and the new owner(s) wanted to be acknowledged in the text. Since the manuscript is not an autograph but a copy by an unknown scribe, it might also be that the original dedication was unintentionally copied and later corrected.

What is most fascinating in this manuscript version of the Hanukkah and Purim songs is the writers' choice of melodies, since both songs are contrafacta. While the Hanukkah song is based on the melody of the German *Ach Maidlein, was hat dir der Rocken getan* (*Oh maiden, what did the distaff do to you*, also known by other titles), the Purim song even offers not only one, but two possible melodies for its performance: *Von einem Kalb, das den Landsknecht auffraß* (*About a calf that has eaten the Landsknecht*) and *Aber heb ich an mein alte Weise* (*But now I will begin my old tune*).

Gumprecht explicitly states in the preface to the Hanukkah text:

> The melody is that of a song which begins:
> *Ach Maidlein, was hat dir der Rocken getan.*
> The melody is widespread in Germany,
> But unknown in Venice.
> Also, I made it in a hurry.
> Therefore, I did not think of another one. (fol. 1r)

An even more intensive involvement with the question of melody is apparent in the prologue to the Purim song, where he writes:

> Also, I made it using a nice chant
> So that time will not hang heavy on one's hands because of it.
> The melody has the same measure
> As *Von einem Kalb, das den Landsknecht auffraß*
> And to a song that is praiseworthy:
> *Aber heb ich an mein alte Weise.*
> Whoever knows the melody shall be glad.
> Whoever does not know it, shall nevertheless read it
> Or ask about the melody.
> Whoever does not want to do that can just give it a miss. (fol. 11[r])

All melodies mentioned by Gumprecht are indeed known from other sources of the period. *Von einem Kalb…*, for instance, refers to the song *Von einem Freyheit vnd von Cuntz zwergen ein hübsch lyedt ym Schyeler thon* (*About a certain Freyheit and Cuntz the Dwarf a nice song in the melody of Schyeler*) (Leipzig 1521), based, as the title states, on the *Ton* (melody) of master singer Jörg Schiller.

The freedom that Gumprecht allows the prospective singer—to use one melody or the other or leave it be and read the text—is not unusual for his time (Matut 2017). Other Jewish writers who came from the German-speaking lands but lived in Italy, such as Elia Levita Bakhur, were equally unperturbed about whether or not their suggested melodies were indeed used. In the preface to his famous *Bovo-Book* (finished 1507, printed 1541; Rosenzweig 2016, 205), he stated that he himself uses an Italian melody to sing the text, but since knowledge of music and solfège is so limited among his contemporaries, he cannot convey the melody. Thus, should someone invent "a better one," he has the author's thanks. As a side note, it must be said that this tradition of melodic freedom continues on far down into the eighteenth century within Yiddish song culture.

While the indication of a melody by giving the first line of a well-known song was commonplace, the apparent lack of knowledge of music theory within the Jewish community still becomes apparent—with Italy being, to some extent, the exception to the rule. Whereas Jewish cultural centres such as Mantua or Florence were home to several families that owned Latin works on music (Jütte 2015, 47), this stood in stark contrast to the situation in the predominantly Yiddish-speaking (transalpine) communities. Gumprecht, who came from Poland, in all probability never acquired knowledge of how to write musical notation. Thus, he resorted to the most common form of conveying a melody that he could think of and, moreover, to melodies he knew from his former home—unknown to most members of his new community in Italy.

The lack of music-theoretical knowledge, however, comes as no surprise, given how the contexts of place, institutions, social status, religious affiliation, and gender determined the degree of access to education in music theory (Murray et al. 2010). Furthermore, those publications on music that reached the Jewish community were in Latin or Hebrew, never in the vernacular Yiddish. Thus, access was only possible through a good teacher or excellent Hebrew skills, as well as copies of the relevant manuscripts and printed books. Latin treatises, however, were a great obstacle for Jews, who were in the main literate, but more rarely so in Latin.

The fact that a Jewish teacher from Poland, living in Venice, wrote his texts about Hanukkah and Purim as contrafacta of contemporary German songs, is as remarkable as it was commonplace. Multifarious sources are extant which bear witness to and offer a perspective on Jewish song culture in the Renaissance. They prove very clearly that the Jewish community used and cherished a multitude of melodies known from the Christian or secular worlds of the time. And some, such as the *Herzog Ernst* or *Dietrich von Bern*, were as popular and persistent among Jews as they were within the wider society. Melodies from the inner-Jewish tradition were used for contrafacta as well; but since the Jewish musical culture was predominantly an oral one, these melodies are, for the most part, lost to us.

Jewish music of the late Renaissance is, in public awareness, first and foremost connected with the name of Salamone Rossi, a contemporary and colleague of Monteverdi at the court of Mantua. His polyphonic compositions of Hebrew and Italian vocal music, as well as his instrumental works, are considered to be the greatest achievements of Jewish musicianship in the period. And although individuals like Rossi were indeed great composers, they were also rare exceptions within the Jewish world. Still, his name is where the description of Jewish Renaissance (and early Baroque) music often begins and ends. This is due to the emphasis that historical musicology put on what was considered "high culture"—the polyphonic/homophonic vs the monodic/unison or heterophonic. And while musicology has long since created an awareness of the permeability of the musical spheres within Renaissance culture and acknowledges the influence of European song cultures on composed (polyphonic) music—and vice versa—still, the supposed dichotomies of high and low, art vs folk, remain salient. It is all too easily forgotten that these categorizations are the result of a scientific and aesthetic discourse that began in the second half of the eighteenth century (Helms 2012, 127). It is legitimate to question whether or not these partly anachronistic categorizations are helpful at all in writing a history of Jewish music. Integral to this complex subject are also questions about space (ritual/representative or not), language (sacred/scholarly or vernacular), written and oral cultures, as well as the gender-specifics of the material and their performance. The few and exceptional polyphonic compositions by Jewish musicians that survive from the Renaissance do not represent the majority or bulk of music-making. It was liturgical music and song (as well as instrumental) culture in all its various aspects that was at the core of Jewish musical experience and practice.

Thus, to choose and present Yiddish songs in the *Museum of Renaissance Music* is to create an awareness of the tremendously rich and varied song culture of Jews in Europe, whose singing and music-making was as influenced by their contemporary co-territorial cultures as it was by internal Jewish traditions.

ADDITIONAL REFERENCES: Frakes 2004; Timm 1995.

67. A Tragedy from Ferrara

Laurie Stras

Statue of Seated Apollo after the Antique and Two Niches with Statues
Girolamo Sellari detto da Carpi, Ferrara, ca. 1531
Pen and brown ink on paper, 24 x 16.8 cm
Gift of János Scholz, The Morgan Library and Museum, New York
Photo courtesy of The Morgan Library and Museum

The Ferrarese artist Girolamo Sellari, detto da Carpi was a prominent portraitist, painter, architect, and theatrical set designer, who was engaged periodically throughout his life by various members of the Este family, the rulers of Ferrara. Carpi's output is typical of Renaissance artists, suffused with knowledge of and inspiration by classical sculpture. His sketches, now dispersed in collections in Europe and the United States, show dozens of studies of real and imagined classical bodies. The drawing now titled *Statue of Seated Apollo after the Antique and Two Niches with Statues* is based on a porphyry statue that was part of a celebrated collection belonging to the brothers Sassi. At the time it was believed to depict a female figure, either the Goddess Rome or Cleopatra (Dacos et al. 1995, 117). Carpi, according to contemporary practice, provided the statue with a head, lower arms, and hands in his sketch, accommodating the classical model to a modern view.

Carpi is best known to musicologists through multi-disciplinary collaborations with writers and musicians at the Ferrarese court. His *Venus on the Eridanus* (ca. 1546) was part of a tripartite tribute to Princess Anna d'Este, together with a poem by Girolamo Falletti and a secular motet by Cipriano de Rore (Lowinsky 1989a); and he designed the 1541 production of Giambattista Giraldi Cinzio's tragedy *Orbecche*, for which Alfonso Dalla Viola provided the music (Giraldi Cinzio 1543, fol. 3ᵛ), and the 1545 production of the poet's satire *Egle*, for which Antonio del Cornetto was the composer (Giraldi Cinzio 1545, 5). The nineteenth-century historian Giuseppe Campori claimed that Carpi also designed the 1548 production of *Gli Antivalomeni*, also by Giraldi Cinzio, and while he does not supply any documents to support the claim, it does not seem out of the question, for Carpi left Ferrara only in 1549, when he moved to Rome to serve Cardinal Ippolito II d'Este (Mezzetti 1977, 32).

The second half of the 1540s was a key period in the development of spectacle at the Ferrarese court: Duke Ercole II was heavily occupied in the process of identifying and then negotiating with potential marriage partners for his children, particularly his two eldest daughters, Anna and Lucrezia. Ercole gave permanent court appointments to Giraldi Cinzio and De Rore (secretary and *maestro di musica* respectively) in 1546, and it was clear that both were required to contribute to the cultural life of the court, including by creating entertainments for the French negotiators resident at the court throughout 1547 and 1548.

Already before arriving officially at court, Giraldi Cinzio had nurtured a reputation as an innovator in his quest to revitalise the genre of classical tragedy for his modern audiences. This he achieved—not wholly unlike Carpi's sketched recovery of body parts—by adjusting the form to contemporary taste. Tragedy, he maintained, should be didactic, but it should also be entertaining if it was to be effective. Although his earliest tragedy, *Orbecche*, retained the classical form with a chorus only at the end of the first and final (fifth) acts, thereafter he inserted choruses at the end of each act. He adopted this procedure from comedy, with the stated purpose of giving the audience some repose (Giraldi Cinzio 1864, 87).

Two other early tragedies, *Didone* and *Cleopatra*, both of which had been completed and staged by 1543, like *Orbecche* ended with the despair and death of the principal characters. These outcomes followed the classical narratives for the women, but they sat uncomfortably in the Christian moral context of Giraldi Cinzio's world. Eventually he lit upon the idea that tragedies could have a happy ending ("lieto fine"), in which misfortune befell the evil characters, and the heroes, after suffering both at the hands of the antagonists and through their own frailty, are finally rewarded. *Altile*, also completed by 1543, proceeds as a conventional tragedy until its climax, in which Altile turns away from the vial of poison she was about to consume, and pursues her husband on his way to execution, eventually securing his release and their reunion. The prologue to *Altile* makes the new design clear: "if it displeases you that it has the name *Tragedy*, then at your pleasure you may call it *Tragicomedy* (because our language allows it), [since] its end conforms to *Comedy*—after the travails, it is full of happiness" (Giraldi Cinzio 1583, fol. 9ʳ).

After *Altile*, Giraldi continued to work with classically-inspired narratives, but with less familiar stories that could bear reworking to fit his "lieto fine" paradigm. He also stuck to stories with regal female protagonists, almost certainly because they provided Duke Ercole with useful propaganda for instruction of his wife and daughters: the duchess, Renée of France, was Italy's most prominent Protestant and was openly raising her daughters outside the Catholic faith. Giraldi Cinzio's heroines invariably endure torments and lose status because of their own errors, but by the final scene they are rehabilitated through virtuous action that disrupts the slide towards a tragic end.

Gli Antivalomeni was the principal entertainment for the betrothal and proxy marriage celebrations for Anna d'Este in the late summer of 1548. It featured two princesses beset with obstacles that lie between them and happy-ever-after marriages. But the previous year, the court creatives collaborated on a more serious subject, the tragedy *Selene* (fig. 67.1), in which the widow queen of Egypt has been traduced by her wicked, but trusted, advisor into almost executing her estranged (second) husband, Rodobano, the king of Persia, and calamity is only avoided by the decisive actions of the queen's faithful servants.

The moral lesson of *Selene*—to be understood by the duchess, her daughters, and the negotiators who were to approve Anna's marriage to the future duke of Guise—is that faith alone was not enough to ensure that evil would be vanquished, and that action or good works were also necessary: a pointed rebuttal of the Protestant doctrine of *sola fide* (faith alone). Each of its five acts finishes with a chorus that expounds upon this central message. According to Giraldi Cinzio's plan, a musical interlude should occur between each act—in comedy, these intermedi would have little to do with the plot of the main play, but in the music for *Selene* that survives, it is plain that the interludes were essential to the delivery of the play's didactic purpose.

Four madrigals based on the play's choruses were published in Venice in 1548, in a collection of works by Ferrarese composers, the *Madrigali de la Fama* published in parallel (though slightly variant) editions by Girolamo Scotto and Antonio Gardano. Three are by Cipriano de Rore—*L'inconstantia seco han* (Act I), *Chi con eterne legge* (Act IV), and *La giustizia immortale* (Act V)—and the fourth, *Felice che dispensa* (Act II), is by Francesco Dalla Viola (Stras 2017). While the final work, *La giustizia immortale* (fig. 67.2), uses the chorus exactly as it is given in the printed text of the play, the other three madrigals lift portions of the spoken choruses, condensing the message and reiterating it in the context of sung polyphony. Each of these works is also composed with pauses or formal divisions that would allow for sectional repetition, enhancing even further the opportunities to get the point across.

The plot of Giraldi Cinzio's *Selene*, which he derived from one of his own novelle, has no direct precedent in classical literature, but the character of Selene could have been based on a real person from Antiquity: Cleopatra Selene, daughter of Cleopatra III and Ptolemy VIII, who was married multiple times to her brothers Ptolemy IX and Ptolemy X, kings of Egypt, and then to the Seleucid (Syrian) King Antiochus XIII, his brother Antiochus IX, and her stepson Antiochus X. (Queen Cleopatra VII, the consort of the Roman Marcus Antonius and the once supposed subject of Carpi's drawing, named their daughter Cleopatra Selene after her predecessor, but this second royal Selene was married only once, to Juba of Numidia and Mauretania.) Her first husband, Ptolemy IX, was banished from Egypt, leaving her and her children behind, as is Rodobano in the play. Just as Carpi completes the broken porphyry Cleopatra with his own invented limbs and head, Giraldi Cinzio's narrative breathes life into the classical Selene, with enough correspondence to historical events to give her story a human form.

SELENE
TRAGEDIA
DI M. GIO. BATTISTA
GIRALDI CINTHIO,
NOBILE FERRARESE.
CON PRIVILEGI.
IN VENETIA,
Appreſſo Giulio Ceſare Cagnacini.
M D LXXXIII.

QVINTO. 149
CHORO.
LA giuſtitia immortale
Di dar merto non manca
A chi ben'opra, e a chi è maluagio pena,
E s'anima talhor di uirtù piena
Doglia, o meſtitia aſſale,
E perche ſorga al ben'oprar piu franca,
E proui uita poi uia piu ſerena,
E pel contrario, chi'n operar male
Gioiſce, e'n quello inuecchia,
Proua, che tolerando gli apparecchia
Dio, nel piu bel gioir tormento tale,
Ch'à la colpa ſen va il ſopplicio uguale.
IL FINE.

Figure 67.1: Giambattista Giraldi Cinzio, Selene (Venice: Giulio Cesare Cagnacini, 1583), title page and 149 (chorus *La giustitia immortale*). Munich, Bayerische Staatsbibliothek, P.o.it. 426 d#Beibd.3 / urn:nbn:de:bvb:12-bsb10189833-9. Photo courtesy of the Bayerische Staatsbibliothek.

Figure 67.2: *Madrigali de la Fama* (Venice: Antonio Gardane, 1548), II (Cipriano de Rore, *La giustitia immortale*). Munich, Bayerische Staatsbibliothek, 4 Mus.pr. 96#Beibd.2 / urn:nbn:de:bvb:12-bsb00071900-6. Photo courtesy of the Bayerische Staatsbibliothek.

68. A Bosnian Gravestone

Zdravko Blažeković

Anon., Borje-Klobuk (western Herzegovina), 14th or 15th century

Image: Photograph by Tošo Dabac, ca. 1960. Muzej suvremene umjetnosti Zagreb, Arhiv Tošo Dabac, 11732. Photo courtesy of the Muzej suvremene umjetnosti Zagreb.

The distribution of the stone-carved grave markers called *stećci* (singular *stećak*) geographically overlaps with the widest boundaries of the medieval Bosnian state and the duchy of Hum (present-day Herzegovina and the Dalmatian coast from Pelješac to the river Cetina), also reaching to a wider region including the Dubrovnik Republic, western Serbia and Montenegro. *Stećci* emerged in the early thirteenth century and were produced until the early sixteenth century with the utmost consistency and stability in style and form. Considering the historical, social, political, and statistical indicators, it would appear that these grave markers belonged to social classes affiliated with all three religious practices in medieval Bosnia and Hum—the Orthodox, the Catholic, and the Bosnian churches—with the stone's shape, size, the extent of its decoration, artistic quality, and iconography reflecting the social significance and the wealth of the deceased. The amount of decoration varies a great deal because larger gravestones, with more intricate decorations, were more expensive. The more ornamented stones are located in the vicinity of fortified towns and courts which had wealthier populations than remote villages (Lovrenović 2011, 69).

Stećci are often preserved in inaccessible locations, and they have not been systematically photographed. The groundbreaking catalogue by Marian Wenzel is exhaustive but it includes only outline drawings of the motives (Wenzel 1965). Among the earliest systematic photographing of *stećci* was the campaign by the Croatian photographer Tošo Dabac during the 1950s. Although he worked in a variety of media, the most notable are his black-and-white photographs, which were exhibited in group shows at the Zemaljski muzej Bosne i Hercegovine in Sarajevo (1967), the Römisch-Germanisches Zentralmuseum in Mainz (1967), and the Národní galerie in Prague (1968), as well as represented in the international edition *Bogomil Sculpture* (Dabac 1963). Dabac's photographs and exhibitions contributed significantly to the international recognition of this medieval funeral art tradition, which in 2016 was included in the UNESCO World Heritage List.

A lack of written historical sources from medieval Bosnia and Hum, in addition to the anonymity and timelessness of these markers, complicates our contextualization of their iconography and our understanding of their symbolism and meaning in funeral ritual practices. As a group, seen against the broader context of European sepulchral monuments, the *stećci* represent a transformational form between the early medieval anonymity of unmarked graves to late medieval markers presenting a metaphorical portrait of the deceased. It is possible that precisely the illiteracy of individuals unable to self-represent with written epitaphs influenced the creation of the iconographic concepts carved into the stones, providing us with a rich visual legacy reflecting Bosnian social life, religious beliefs, and chivalric culture.

Stećci were carved by native stonecutters, usually in the vicinity of the cemetery itself. Considering their weight, sometimes reaching dozens of tons, their transportation across large distances in rocky and mountainous terrain would be extremely difficult. There are several main types of *stećci*: the slab, the coffin-like shape, the sarcophagus-like shape, the pillar stone, and the cross. The simplest decorations are architectural elements combined with vine, rope, or spiral ornament. More complex figurative elements included apples, grape clusters and vine branches, trees, a sword and shield, stars, a crescent moon, a hand or arm, and animals. These motifs are usually extremely stylised, and probably did not have a heraldic role.

The most complex representations are narratives concerning chivalry: hunting, tournaments, and riding. The hunter is shown mounted on a horse, holding a sword or launching a spear or arrow at a deer, a wild boar, or a bear. He is sometimes assisted by a dog or hawk. In the tournament scenes, knights fight with spears or swords. In the background an architectural detail sometimes appears, or noble ladies observing the fight. There are also scenes showing a knight on horseback led by his page, or a knight departing from a woman.

In interpreting these scenes, it is profoundly important to keep in mind their simultaneous realism and symbolism; it would be too easy to attribute realistic qualities to an image that may have an entirely symbolic meaning, and could perhaps even reflect a vision of the afterlife. The negotiation between realism and symbolism is particularly apparent in complex compositions where a perspective effect is achieved through the superimposition of different horizontal sections. A tournament scene with a line of dancers appears as if the scene is occurring in front of us, but such a reading of the image is potentially deceptive; the elements of the composition may be organised according to symbolic rather than spatial logic, particularly since the dancers appear to be wearing masks.

About 130 dance scenes shown on gravestones are the earliest representations of dance from the South Slavic areas. Dancers appear in different formations ranging from what may be a single dancer to line formations consisting of up to 12 dancers. They are shown as full-length figures, holding hands at shoulder height, with the leading and last dancers having their free hand placed at the waist. Women wear long bell-like dresses, and men short tunics with a belt at the waist. The direction of the dance movement is sometimes apparent from the placement of dancers' feet, the way they bend their knees, or from how the women's skirts are raised.

The dance iconography has here its quintessentially symbolic meaning. Some may be showing a courtly performance, others an exuberant dance associated with rural rituals, or even a heavenly *kolo* (traditional circle dance) reserved for the blessed. The circular form of the Slavic *kolo*—which could not have been shown as such in the reliefs, although the position of the dance leader may indicate the circular movement—may in this funerary context be read as a metaphor for the perpetual life cycle eternally repeating itself. However, interpretations such as this will remain hypothetical, since there are no medieval Bosnian texts or parallel artworks which could be used as points of reference in confirming them. The only possible clues are provided by rituals still practiced in the region, particularly in southern Serbia, although of course we should bear in mind that these rituals are separated from our gravestones by many hundreds of years (Blažeković 2013).

Dance is still today a part of commemorative ceremonies for the deceased among the Serbian and Vlach peoples. In southwestern Serbia, the region adjacent to Herzegovina, funeral celebrations include a dance called *sitan tanac* (small dance), the first part of which has the purpose of helping the soul of the deceased join with the other ancestral souls, whilst the second part protects the participants from evil forces. Through the dance, the relatives of the deceased establish a connection with the world of the dead. Its steps are simple; the dancers move in a double rhythm, and the line progresses in the direction contrary to the usual chain dance, giving the dance its alternative name *kolo naopako* (retrograde *kolo*). The dance is performed with vocal accompaniment known as counting (*brojanje*), rather than singing (*pjevanje*). It is possible that the *sitan tanac* originated from the ritual called *tužba* (grieving), also performed during funeral ceremonies in the area, in which the participants have an opportunity to grieve collectively. This ritual consists of a procession in which a flag-bearer is followed by women related to the deceased and then other relatives. The procession circles in slow steps several times around the grave, or alternatively around the deceased's hat, the socks he used to wear to market, his weapon, or in special circumstances around his horse. In more recent times it may also be performed around a photograph of the deceased, or even circulating around the female relatives as they perform a lament. In all of these performances, the fundamental principle of movement is circling (Vasić 2004).

For some social or religious groups, dance on the *stećci* might have meant mystic departure from the terrestrial life; for others it could be a snapshot of courtly pastimes favoured by the deceased. The more lavishly decorated stones were obviously commissioned by wealthier patrons, who preferred to have on their funeral monuments images in which their earthly life is transposed into a *memoria* left behind for family and friends. In the negotiation between the eschatological and the commemorative aspects of a life, both commonly reflected in sepulchral markers, in the case of *stećci* related to Bosnian chivalric culture the commemorative side has won. The dance does not have the memento mori qualities of the medieval dance of death (see exhibit 40). The knight is not shown in his eternal sleep awaiting resurrection at the day of judgement, but rather he is still present in action. Such sepulchral philosophy comes closer to ancient Roman markers picturing the deceased's biography, often showing his or her portrait and items identifying his or her occupation, than to Christian markers telling the eschatological story of resurrection and salvation.

Exhibiting a *stećak* in this *Museum of Renaissance Music* is interesting, then, precisely because of this surprising analogy with its antecedents of Antiquity—an analogy, however, that yields visual results so different from those of other European cultures of the time, where Roman Antiquity furnished a model to be emulated. This helps us to focus on two different relationships with the past and tradition in the same epoch. On the one side a (possible) continuous tradition since Antiquity in Bosnia, on the other side that more characteristic of Renaissance historiography, that is to say its modern reinvention, where (mostly iconographic) themes are derived from Roman Antiquity, but with a decidedly Christian reformulation.

In some representations, be they chivalric or otherwise, the dancers wear masks and hold flowers in their hands, a practice that may have parallels in more recent Carnival customs in southeastern Europe, in which participants wear costumes resembling animals. This phenomenon apparently has ancient religious and mythological roots. The ancient zoolatric cults believed that people after their death turn into their totem, and the animal costume and the mask in some circumstances symbolise ancestors. Such a relationship between the mask and the cult of ancestors has been documented in many archaeological excavations in the Mediterranean area, and also among the Celts and Germans. The ancestors may be masked to attract new inhabitants for their kingdom, to advance children into adults, or to transfer knowledge, power or skills to their descendants, which will give them social distinction. From this perspective, the zoomorphic masks in Carnival processions could be viewed as reflecting the dance and music of the afterworld (Lozica 2007, 205).

The cultural specificity of these funeral representations makes their interpretation difficult, originating as they do from a period and a location for which we have no written sources that might allow us to situate them specifically within the cosmological and religious beliefs of their creators. Also, contemporaneous architectural objects or artworks which would supplement their iconography with further examples are extremely rare. For the most part we have lost from our collective memory references to the symbolism these images bear, and without knowing how to place the boundaries between their symbolism, mythology, and cosmology, their relation to real musical practices can only ever be incompletely understood. Still, especially in the absence of written sources, these representations provide a valuable fund of evidence concerning individual and collective life and the daily activities of medieval Bosnians.

I·M

69. Morris Dancers from Germany

Anne Daye

Israhel van Meckenhem, Germany, ca. 1465-1503
Engraving in black on ivory laid paper, 17.2 x 17.2 cm
Inscribed: I. M.
Art Institute of Chicago
Photo courtesy of the Art Institute of Chicago

A single lady holding a ring in her right hand stands in a room. Three men and a fool in grotesque dancing poses form a semi-circle while a fifth man plays the pipe and tabor. Several onlookers perch on the sill or lean through the open window. This intriguing scene of dancing is found in several German and Dutch prints of the fifteenth and sixteenth centuries. Van Meckenhem himself worked the dance into vegetal ornament in an oblong engraving of similar date (*Ornamental Engraving with Morris Dancers*, Metropolitan Museum of Art). The lady stands in the crutch of a tree holding an apple, while encircled by the branches six men are found in dancing poses. At the foot of the tree stand a musician playing pipe and tabor and a fool, with a sleeping dog between them. An etching by Daniel Hopfer of the late fifteenth or early sixteenth centuries depicts six grotesque men dancing around an equally grotesque woman holding a jug of wine in one hand and six sausages on a spit in the other (*Morris Dancers*, Metropolitan Museum of Art). This time the musician appears to be playing a shawm and none of the dancers wears the regalia of a fool.

The scene is given an allegorical complexion in an anonymous engraving published by Johannes Baptista Vrints ca. 1600, the *Chorea Mundi* or The Dance of the World (fig. 69.1). As the lady holds a globe and wears an imperial orb on her head, she represents worldly power. A fool peeps out from under her skirt, implying that she has already chosen him as her partner. Six men from different ranks in life dance around her. A musician sits on a barrel playing a bladder pipe entwined with sausages, a fiddle poking out from his pocket. The artist points the viewer to this allegory of the shortcomings of the world with a bale of hay labelled "vanitas," an empty jug and a flaming torch referencing the destruction of war. The concept of the dance whirling around Lady World adds to the impression of the cycles of triumph and disaster in worldly affairs (Barlow 2012, 24-28).

These images relate to the *moresca*, a broad category of performance dance that was widespread across Europe in the fifteenth and sixteenth centuries (Nevile 2008, 324). Dancers might be noble or professional, the context royal and aristocratic or popular and crude, the themes constantly inventive. Acrobatic and gestural dances could be presented for simple choreographic entertainment or elaborated into mute narratives. Commedia dell'arte troupes were also exponents of this performative style of dancing. Origins in the Moorish culture of Spain are often proposed, based on etymology and the occurrence of black-face disguise in some types of *moresca*. The addition of bells on costume or ankles and wrists is often featured. The records are so widespread and varied, but also so sketchy, that the genre challenges dance-historical analysis. Similarly, any surviving music for the *moresca* evades classification, although simple tunes for playing on a pipe and tabor are found (Locke 2015, 117-25). The *moresca* was also known in the British Isles, and it was certainly a distant ancestor of the English morris dance, but to label this image "the morris dancers" is misleading. Spellings for the earliest English records of the dance genre vary considerably; for the purposes of this essay, "moresk" will serve as an English term used for a form of the morris dance relevant to this image of ca. 1500 (Forrest 1999).

The scene presents the mute choreographic expression of a common trope in dance-games, songs and European spoken drama: the competitive courting of rival wooers for the favour of one woman (Baskerville 1965, 247-88). Four men, each of a different social class, are vying for the affection of the lady, through hand-gestures, contorted body shapes, and, we assume, their dancing. This type of *moresk* has also been dubbed "the ring dance" (Lowe 1957, 65). Left from the musician, we see a peasant or farmer, a young man or apprentice, a fool, and a gentleman. The lady will give the ring, and with it her affections, to one of them—conventionally to the fool. The fool can be identified by his marotte (stick with a fool's head), hood, motley (parti-coloured tunic), and the bell on his sleeve. Moral lessons derived from the outcome may refer cynically to the way of the world, or to the traditional sexually-charged nature of the fool, or the fool's reputation as the best dancer of a company.

The text of a late sixteenth-century dramatic jig entitled *The Wooing of Nan* provides an important literary source for this genre of dance in England. Art prints from northern Europe were the height of fashion in late sixteenth-century

England, and scholars have discussed this text alongside images of the ring *moresk* since the early twentieth century. Nan is not a lady but a village girl who is courted in turn by four men: first, Rowland her lover and Pierce his rival (two young countrymen), then a gentleman, and finally a fool. Each is put to the test by dancing with Nan, who in the end deserts her first love Rowland for the fool (Clegg and Skeaping 2014, 70-85). The performance of the jig requires at least one musician, although none is mentioned in the text: a pipe and tabor player would suit the context.

Also connected with engravings representing the ring *moresk* is a text entitled *An Epithalamium upon the Marques of Huntlies mariage*, written by King James VI of Scotland and I of England in 1588 and surviving in two manuscript copies (Daye 2008, 78-81; Dunlap 1926, 249-56; Craigie 1955-58, 134-44). The piece provides the spoken part of a martial contest and an indoor entertainment for the wedding of the marquis of Huntly to Henrietta Stewart, daughter of the king's deceased French favourite Esmé Stewart, lord of Aubigny and duke of Lennox. With no stage directions or information on the setting and performers, the short and pithy speeches for the indoor event indicate that the performance was probably a *moresk* of the ring dance type.

In the text, a woman appeals to the king for guidance as to who she should choose. Her five suitors are a scholar, a virtuous man, a country gentleman, a soldier, and a *zanie* (fool). King James gives each a code of language and style of discourse to match their status, exemplifying his own rules for composition as stated in his 1584 *Ruelis and Cautelis for Scottis Poesie* (Craigie 1958, 245-47). His use of the term "zanie" suggests that he had in mind a character from the commedia dell'arte. Considered incomplete by literary scholars, the speeches are very likely the preface to a dance of courtship. The *zanie* has a mere two lines, being very confident in claiming the lady and dismissing the rest. The country gentleman has a final remark probably spoken after the dance, suggesting that the *zanie* has indeed usurped his place: "What a villain is this?"

One manuscript copy of the entertainment is in the king's own hand; the other was anthologised by his son Charles ca. 1616-18 in a manuscript entitled *All the kings short poesis that are not printed* (London, British Library, Add MS 24195). King James' *moresk* probably furnished the inspiration for the opening antimasque of *Love's Triumph through Callipolis*, the first masque of King Charles' reign, staged in 1631. Although Ben Jonson composed the libretto, the antimasque entry was entirely mute, strikingly novel in lacking any spoken context. Twelve depraved lovers led by a mistress "leap forth below ... with antic gesticulation and action ... dance over a distracted comedy of love ... expressing their confused affections," and complete the entry by dancing in a circle (Orgel 1969, 455-56). Each lover presents a different temperament, such as boasting, whining, quarrelling, or despairing. The costume designs by Inigo Jones present the mistress and the men as figures from the commedia dell'arte, such as Scaramuccia and Il Capitano, based on the French printmaker Jacques Callot's popular series *Balli di Sfessania* (Orgel and Strong 1973, 409-15). This characterisation suggests that Charles was aware of the commedia inspiration of his father's entertainment of 1588. As an antimasque, these grotesque lovers made a vivid contrast with the main masque, danced by the king as the Heroical Lover supported by 14 noblemen as perfect lovers, symbolising qualities such as modesty, courtesy, valiance, and wit. His French Queen Henrietta Maria was, of course, the perfect mistress, already committed to her lover, in parallel with the French bride of 1588.

Van Meckenhem's image is inspired by a European-wide theme, of lovers competing for the heart of one woman, the outcome being unexpected yet revelatory of the way of the world. Here it is expressed in art, evoking for viewers typical performances in dance and music, but also in drama and song. It is testament to the ability of *moresk* dancers to express character and emotion through bodily posture, hand gestures, and footwork.

Figure 69.1: Anon. (Peeter Baltens?), *Chorea mundi*, ca. 1600. Engraving on paper, 32.9 x 41.4 cm. Rijksmuseum, Amsterdam. Photo courtesy of the Rijksmuseum.

6 *Als aber nun verrichtet war*
Mitt großer Eher vnd ſthad verwar
Das hochzeitliches banckettieren,
Mitt ſeher luſtigem muſiciren
Mit Furſtlicher Eher, ſtaht vnd pracht
Vnd Gott dem Hern danck geſacht
Nach altem brauch mitt jubiliren
Mitt Eher vnd lieblichem houirn
Vnd mitt vill freudē, dantzen ſie
Nach ſeußem ſpill vnd melodie.
16. Junij 1585.

70. A Princely Wedding in Düsseldorf

Klaus Pietschmann

Franz Hogenberg, scene showing dancing after the wedding banquet in the great parlour
Engraving from Dietrich Graminaeus, *Beschreibung derer Fürstlicher Güligscher etc. Hochzeit [...]*
Cologne: [Gras], 1587
142 fols., 15.17 x 26.15 cm
Vienna, Österreichische Nationalbibliothek, *48.C.32 ALT PRUNK

In his description of the ducal Jülich wedding the court historiographer (*Landschreiber*) Dietrich Graminaeus gives a detailed report on the elaborate wedding celebrations for Johann Wilhelm von Jülich-Kleve-Berg and Jakobe von Baden, which were held in Düsseldorf in June 1585. The festival book is written in German and includes 37 engravings by Franz Hogenberg, which illustrate in detail some of the stages of the eight-day celebration that are described in the text. Some of these images had already been published immediately after the wedding in 1585, in versions differing slightly from those in the later publication. The somewhat shorter *Descriptio Pompae Nuptialis exhibitae Dusseldorpii mense iunio Anni 1585* (*Description of the Wedding Festivities staged in Düsseldorf in the month of June 1585*) by Albert Lithocomus, and the *Historicum pro principis Joannis Guilhelmi Juliae [...] Ducis necnon dominae Jacobae a. 1585 celebratis nuptiis tapetum* (*Record of the Wedding Celebrations of Prince Johann Wilhelm von Jülich [...] Duke, and Lady Jakobe in the year 1585*) by Bernhard Moller, were also published as early as 1585 in Düsseldorf in order to inform an educated, courtly public promptly about the events. Graminaeus' German description, aimed at a wider public, pays more attention than these to the musical elements of the festival, even though specific compositions are not mentioned.

The wedding was celebrated with great effort and documented in detail because of its political importance. The Duchy of Jülich-Kleve-Berg was created in 1521 as a result of several mergers of different dominions and territories. It formed an important power factor in the northwest of the Holy Roman Empire, and saw several wars as well as Reformation turmoil during the second half of the sixteenth century. Duke Wilhelm V ruled from 1539 to 1592, although after 1566 with limited capacity because of a stroke. Following the unexpected death of his heir Prince Karl Friedrich in 1575, all hopes rested on the only other son, Johann Wilhelm, who then broke off his ecclesiastical career. The Jülich marriage in 1585 significantly strengthened the duchy's ties to the Wittelsbach dynasty of Munich, at whose court the bride Jakobe of Baden had grown up following the death of her parents. The marriage contributed significantly to the cementing of Wittelsbach influence in the region, notwithstanding the physical distance of these areas in the northwest of the empire from the Wittelsbach territories in the south: Ernst of Bavaria, son of Albrecht V of Bavaria and bishop of Freising, had become prince-bishop of Liège in 1581, archbishop and elector of Cologne in 1583, and in 1584 also took over the prince-bishopric of Münster (previously assigned to Johann Wilhelm). The wedding added to this list indirect Wittelsbach control over the strategically important duchy of Jülich-Kleve-Berg, and additionally made a significant contribution to strengthening Catholic forces in a region where confessional conflicts played a key role at the time.

Graminaeus' description begins with the extensive preparations that preceded the actual feast, in particular the arrival of the guests in procession on 15 June, led by the groom and followed by the bride. The celebration itself began the day after, with the afternoon wedding ceremony in the castle chapel. This was followed by a wedding banquet in the large banqueting hall of the Düsseldorf Palace and dancing in the neighbouring great parlour (*Große Stube*). On the following morning the bridal gifts were handed over; then in the evening a rich dinner was followed by a naval battle staged on the Rhine with fireworks. On the third day a first tournament took place in the nearby estate of Pempelfort where the court had hunting grounds and gardens, preceded by a musical-theatrical performance on the theme of the power of music. The dinner was followed by the honouring of the tournament winners, and another fireworks display on the Rhine, dedicated to the deeds of Hercules. The hunting excursion planned for the morning of the fourth day had to be cancelled due to bad weather, and in the afternoon a public fencing school (*Fechtschule*) was held in the courtyard of the castle. After another tournament on the fifth day, on the sixth day the guests were invited to the princely garden to engage in conversation and amusements aimed at the ladies. The seventh day was dedicated to another tournament in Pempelfort, followed by fireworks and dinner, then dancing, and the award ceremony. At the end of the evening yet another firework display took place on the Rhine, which represented the combat of a dragon with a whale. The eighth and last day began with a foot tournament in the Düsseldorf market square, the winners of which were awarded after the evening meal. At the dance that followed, a symbolic theatrical play (*Mummerey*) was performed. At a late hour there was a spectacle with knights, horses, and soldiers in the castle courtyard, followed by a final fireworks display. This varied festive sequence, in which tournaments, banquets, dancing, and theatrical performances alternated, is typical of courtly wedding ceremonies of the early modern period.

Sonic and musical elements play an important role in Graminaeus' description. In the case of the ceremonial entry, the increasing number of trumpeters is specified meticulously: three at the beginning, four in the second group, eight in the third, and finally eight trumpeters and two kettle-drummers accompanied the bride. The number of trumpeters in the entourage of the guests is also precisely outlined, as it corresponds to their rank: Margrave Philipp of Baden, for example, was accompanied by nine trumpeters, Margrave Jacob of Baden by five, and Landgrave Georg Ludwig zu Leuchtenberg by two and one assistant ("Trummeters Jung"). The drummers and trumpeters functioned as sounding symbols of the princes, and also referred to the rulers through the coats of arms on the pennants of the instruments, as Hogenberg's engravings show.

In most cases, however, the focus is on the place and character of the sonic-musical components. For the wedding ceremony, a "wonderful music ensemble with all kinds of instruments" (herrliche Musica mit allerhandt Instrumenten) was prepared, which "after the wedding ceremony and sermon [...] began to sing the *Te Deum laudamus* with artistic and delicate music with great glory, prayer and devotion" (nach der Trauung und Predigt [...] mit kuenstreicher und zierlicher Musick das Te Deum laudamus mit großer herrligkeit, andacht und devotion zusingen angefangen). Before and after the ceremony, the trumpeters and timpanists also played "most magnificently as a sign of joy" (auffs herrligst angeblasen und zum freudenzeichen geschlagen worden). It is also expressly pointed out that a temporary gallery was erected in the courtyard of the castle for the trumpeters and timpanists, from which they announced dinner.

The meal itself was accompanied by a mixed ensemble of hired and court musicians, which also performed on other occasions. The ensuing dance, however, was accompanied by the trumpeters and timpanists. This remarkable juxtaposition of the musical forces is also documented in one of the illustrations, serving here as the main image, which shows on the right an ensemble consisting of two viole da braccio, a viola da gamba, a lute, a harpsichord, a cornet, and four singers, while separated from them, close to the audience, four trumpeters can be seen. However, it is clear from the text that these ensembles did not play together, as the illustration implies.

Of particular interest are the references to musical-theatrical elements within the festive event. For example, the staged naval battle on the Rhine was musically underscored by numerous trumpets and kettle-drums. Graminaeus emphasises that all four fireworks displays were considered as theatrical performances, "two as tragedies, the other two as comedies" (zwey in gestalt und art der Tragedien / die andern zwey nach art der Comedien). However, the most striking feature is undoubtedly an artificial mountain that was driven through the arena before the first tournament (fig. 70.1). From the illustration and description it can be seen that on the two peaks two singers playing the lyra embodied Amphion and Orpheus, interacting with various animals, Pan, the nine Muses (not visible) and the personifications of Justitia, Fortuna, and Aequitas. In addition, a motet was apparently performed by musicians both on the mountain and inside of it ("alsolche Musica auß und inwendig gebraucht"). Although Graminaeus reproduces in the left top corner of the engraving the six-line text of the motet ("Harmoniam coelo venientem amplectra Princeps" etc.), he does not mention the composer. Obviously this scenography evoked Mount Parnassus with its two peaks, Helikon and Citheron, on the one hand, but at the same time it alluded to the name of the duchy, "Berg" (meaning "mountain"), which together with Jülich and Cleves formed the bridegroom's domain. Also of interest is the *Mummerey*, which opened the dances on the last evening of the festivities (fig. 70.2). At the beginning of the procession, which embodied good rule with Christian and pagan allusions, four musicians dressed in antique costumes walked along, playing a viola, a "cyter" (cittern), a lute, and a harp.

The musical highlight was obviously the performance in connection with the artificial mountain. Graminaeus takes this as an opportunity to list a number of the musicians involved in the celebrations by name. First and foremost, there is the chapelmaster of Duke Wilhelm V, Martin Peudargent, who certainly was the overall director and probably also wrote the compositions. The aforementioned motet is not among his surviving works, but there is a *Te Deum*, which may well have been played after the wedding ceremony. The English lutenist Gregory Howet, who was working in Antwerp at the time, is mentioned in second place. Most of the musicians listed below came from Cologne and Liège, including the composers Adamus de Ponta and Felix Nevolun (who was born in Mantua). Apart from the short distance, the main reason for these recruitments was probably the close proximity of

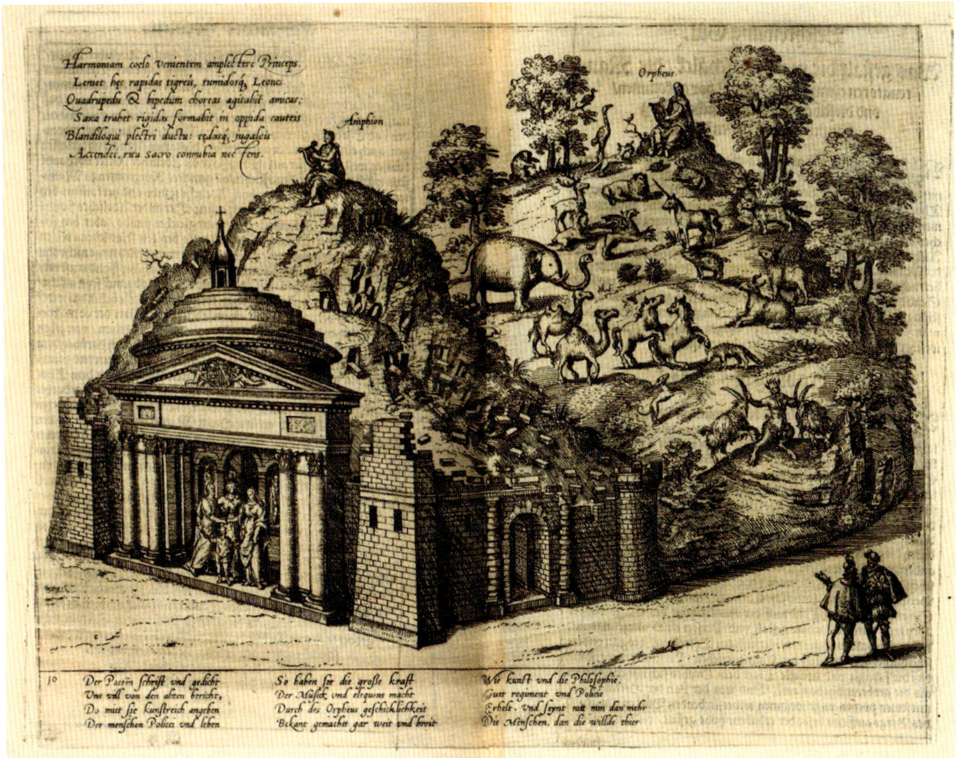

Figure 70.1: Engraving showing an artificial mountain for the music performance before the tournament, from Graminaeus, *Beschreibung derer Fürstlicher Güligscher etc. Hochzeit.* Sig. Miiv-[Miiir]. Vienna, Österreichische Nationalbibliothek, *48.C.32 ALT PRUNK. Photo © CC BY-NC 1.0.

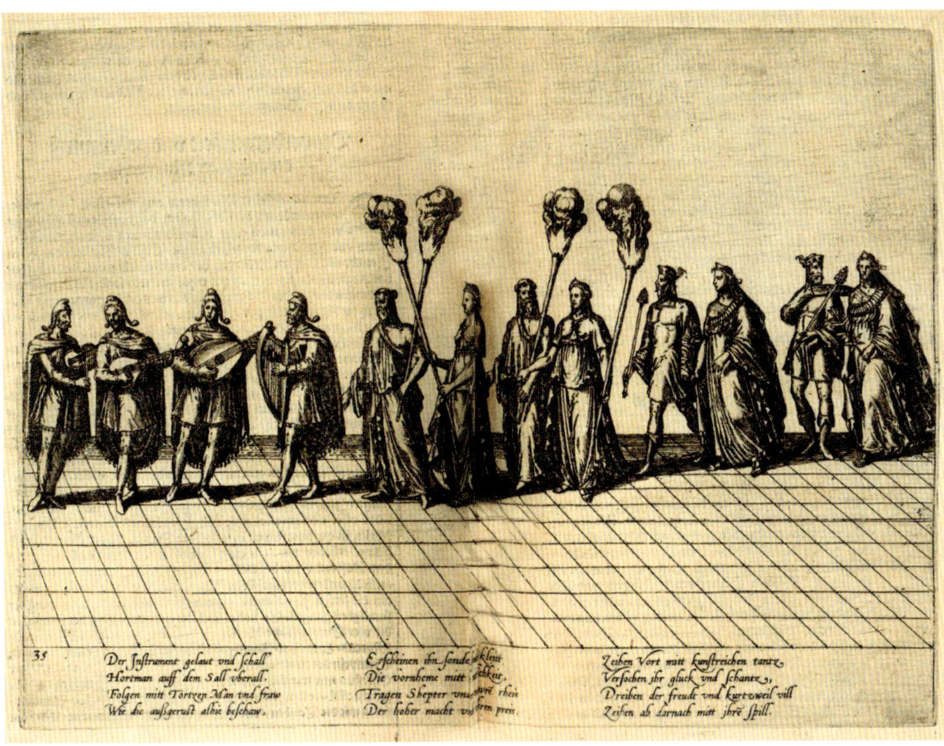

Figure 70.2: Engraving showing a group of theatrical dancers, from Graminaeus, *Beschreibung derer Fürstlicher Güligscher etc. Hochzeit.* Sig. Xxv-[Yir]. Vienna, Österreichische Nationalbibliothek, *48.C.32 ALT PRUNK. Photo © CC BY-NC 1.0.

the event to the Liège ruler Ernst von Bayern, even though he himself did not attend the wedding festivities. Two other composers who we might expect to find among the musicians are not mentioned in the list. Jean de Castro, then living in Cologne, composed his chanson *Vien vien doux Hymenée* for the wedding, as he mentioned in the foreword of his *Livre de chansons à cinq parties* (Antwerp 1586), dedicated to Johann Wilhelm. The other, Konrad Hagius, became a court musician to Johann Wilhelm only in the year after the wedding, as he mentioned in the print of his setting of the Ulenberg Psalter (Düsseldorf 1589).

Graminaeus' *Beschreibung* stands in a long series of similar commemorative descriptions and illustrated festival books whose relevance to music history is well known. The phenomenon has been discussed above all in connection with the Munich princely wedding of 1568, described in the *Dialoghi* of Massimo Troiano (Troiano 1569), and with the wedding of Ferdinando de' Medici and Christine de Lorraine in Florence in 1589, documented in the *Descrizione dell'apparato e degl'intermedi fatti per la commedia rappresentata* by Bastiano de' Rossi (Rossi 1589). The main audience for such festive descriptions were, besides the participants themselves, especially other courts and a more general public, who were to be impressed by the efforts and the magnificence of the event as well as by the presence of foreign dignitaries. By consequence these descriptions have to be considered as intentional texts, and they were an essential component of courtly representation and "marketing." Their main concern was less the objective description of actual procedures and events than the idealised depiction of the magnificent and ceremonially correct course of the festivities. At the same time, they often have the intention of introducing the reader to an inner logic of the events and their underlying symbolic levels. Thus Graminaeus also endeavours to explain allegories and reveal their significance. It is, of course, not always clear to what extent a writer records the meanings intended by the inventors or ascribes their own interpretation to the events. In contrast to the descriptions of festivities at financially strong courts with a large musical apparatus, the description of the "Jülich Wedding" bears witness to the efforts that a middle-ranking court such as that of Jülich-Kleve-Berg had to go to in order to give such an elaborate festivity a musically adequate form. It is therefore more representative of the musical festive culture of the Renaissance than the previously mentioned examples from Munich and Florence, and at the same time makes the exceptional character of those more celebrated examples all the more evident.

Additional references: Early Modern Festival Books Database: https://festivals.mml.ox.ac.uk; Lubenow 2006; Mulryne et al. 2004; Pietschmann 2008; Pietzsch 1962; Rahn 2006; Rümmler 1983; von Büren 2010.

VI

Public Sphere

Cities

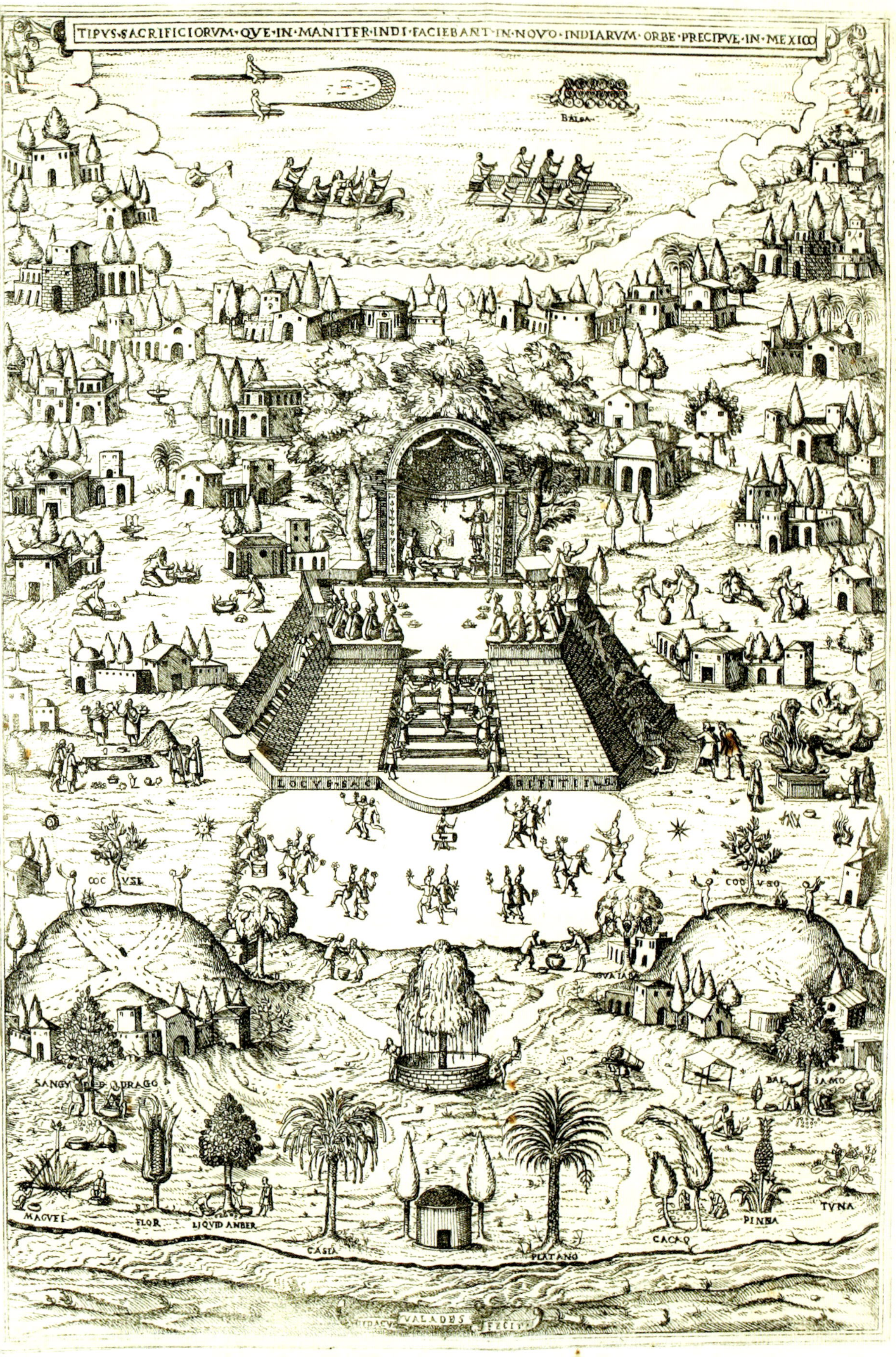
TIPVS·SACRIFICIORVM·QVE·IN·MANITER·INDI·FACIEBANT·IN·NOVO·INDIARVM·ORBE·PRECIPVE·IN·MEXICO
BALSA
COC VSE
COC VSO
MAGVEI
FLOR
LIQVID ANBER
CASIA
PLATANO
CACAO
PINEA
TVNA
BAL SAMO
VALADES
FECIT

71. Mexico City - Tenochtitlan

Javier Marín-López

Didacus (Diego) Valadés, *Bird's-eye view of Mexico City - Tenochtitlan*
Engraving from Valadés, *Rhetorica Christiana*
Perugia: Pietro Giacomo Petrucci, 1579
378 pp., 31 x 21.6 cm
Inscribed: Tipvs sacrificiorvm qve in maniter Indi faciebant in Novo Indiarvm orbe precipve in Mexico
Los Angeles, The Getty Research Institute Research Library, BV4217 .V34 1579, folded plate between pp. 168 and 169
Photo courtesy of the Getty's Open Content Program

ALTHOUGH HE WAS CONSIDERED for decades a *mestizo*, the son of a Spanish soldier and an indigenous woman from Tlaxcala, recent scholarship shows that Diego Valadés was born in Villanueva de Barcarrota (today Barcarrota, Badajoz, Spain) and that he moved to Mexico in 1537 when he was only four years old (Chaparro Gómez 2015, 29). He was trained there, under the renowned Flemish friar Pedro de Gante (Pieter van der Moere), at the Hospital of San José de los Naturales and the Colegio de Santa Cruz of Tlatelolco, and developed an intense evangelising activity among the Chichimecas, a group of nomadic tribes who inhabited the north of what is now Mexico. In addition to Castilian and Latin, he was able to speak Nahuatl (the missionaries' auxiliary language and a major lingua franca in Mesoamerica), Otomi, and Tarasco.

After 30 years of evangelizing activity in New Spain, Valadés went back to Europe, where he was appointed General Procurator of the Franciscan Order in Rome and published his *Rhetorica christiana* (fig. 71.1), a singular theology treatise written in Latin, dedicated to Pope Gregory XIII and devoted to the training of preachers. In this book he combines the ideals of the rhetorical tradition of Christian Humanism with his own experience as a missionary in the New World. In fact, two of the most original elements of this volume—until then unusual in books on rhetoric—are related to the methods of conversion used in his missionary activity: the art of memorising (to which he devotes a chapter explaining the types of memory, mnemonic rules, etc.), and the use of illustrations (as a complement to the preacher's words, as a memory aid and, ultimately, as effective strategy to ensure the new trainees' understanding and memorising of the Gospel's dogmas) (Báez Rubí 2005, 126-29). The book contains 27 copper engravings (including that on the title page), created by Valadés himself from 1575. These engravings are suited to European technical conventions and iconographic traditions, although the contents and activities that are depicted feature indiginous communities. Valadés's aim, therefore, is not to reproduce the reality of America, but to approach it in an idealized manner, by means of a selective series of illustrations which are in the service of the rhetorical and pedagogical ideals of the treatise, and which efficiently combine a view taken from St Augustine and St Thomas Aquinas (typical of the medieval Franciscan imaginary) with the new components of Renaissance Humanism (Branley 2008).

The engraving entitled "Tipus sacrificiorum que in maniter indi faciebant in novo indiarum orbe precipue in Mexico" (Type of sacrifices which the Indians barbarously performed in the New Word, mainly in Mexico) offers an original, symbolic, and encyclopaedic perspective on the indigenous world of the Mexica (known historically as the Aztecs), in the light of the Western model of the polis. The image is printed on a folio which is folded because it is larger than the regular pages of the book. This demonstrates its importance among the other engravings. The main scene depicts the stages of a human sacrifice. In the centre, there is an impressive *teocalli* or pyramid crowned by a chapel-temple where a sacrifice in honour of Huitzilopochtli, Mexica god of sun and war, is being celebrated. A human heart, which has just been removed from a condemned victim, is offered to him. Those who are to be sacrificed are sitting, waiting their turn, while those who have already been sacrificed are pushed down the steps and then burned on a pyre. In order to find an easier correspondence with European mentalities, the composition is symmetrical and well-organised, the so-called Indians are wearing classical clothes and the chapel-temple, under a lush grove of *ahuehuetls* (also known as trees of paradise), is of typical Renaissance design, including a semi-circular archway with panelled vault and Italian grotto motifs on the jambs and keystones. Huitzilopochtli appears as a Roman god (Maza 1945, 39), wearing hummingbird feathers on his head, holding the attributes of the turquoise snake or fire in his right hand, and with an emblem featuring five feather ornaments in his left hand.

At a large esplanade, opposite to the *teocalli*, a *macehualiztli* is taking place. This is a ritual dance with a circular choreography in which four mixed couples of dancers participate (referring to the four elements of nature). They are wearing crests, flowers, branches, pumpkin shakers (*ayacachtli*), shell

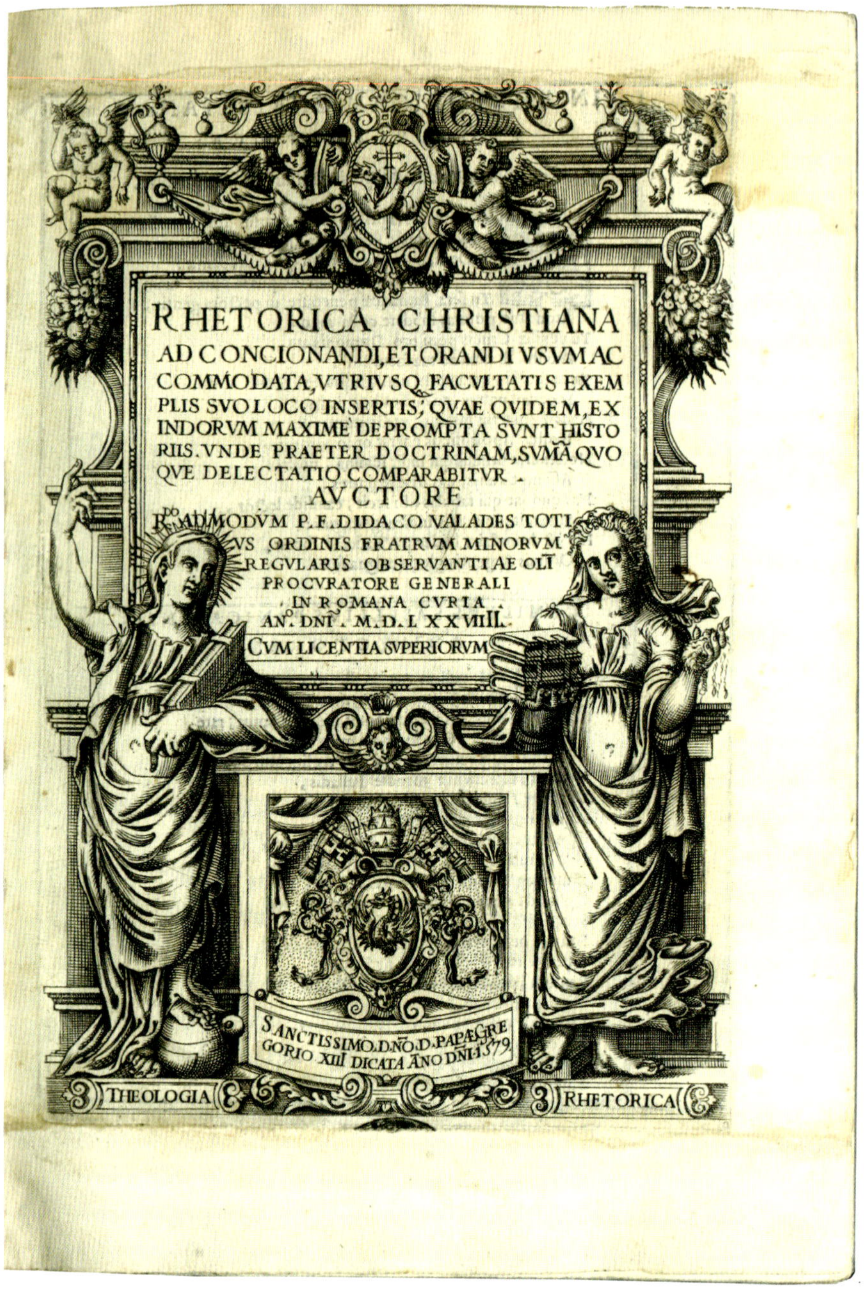
RHETORICA CHRISTIANA
AD CONCIONANDI, ET ORANDI VSVM AC
COMMODATA, VTRIVSQ. FACVLTATIS EXEM
PLIS SVO LOCO INSERTIS; QVAE QVIDEM, EX
INDORVM MAXIME DEPROMPTA SVNT HISTO
RIIS. VNDE PRAETER DOCTRINAM, SVMÃ QVO
QVE DELECTATIO COMPARABITVR.
AVCTORE
R.do ADMODVM P. F. DIDACO VALADES TOTI
VS ORDINIS FRATRVM MINORVM
REGVLARIS OBSERVANTIAE OLĨ
PROCVRATORE GENERALI
IN ROMANA CVRIA.
AN.o DNĨ. M. D. LXXVIIII.
CVM LICENTIA SVPERIORVM
SANCTISSIMO D. NÕ. D. PAPAE GRE
GORIO XIII DICATA ÃNO DNI 1579
THEOLOGIA
RHETORICA

Figure 71.1: Valadés, *Rhetorica Christiana*, title page. Los Angeles, The Getty Research Institute, BV4217 .V34 1579. Photo courtesy of the Getty's Open Content Program.

bells tied to the ankles (*ayoyotl*), and sticks (or what might be a wind instrument with a thin and straight tube held by a dancer on the right). According to the evidence provided by some Mexica codices and chroniclers, the dancers sang and performed with accurate steps, gestures, and movements, deploying a complicated symbolism which they learned at the *cuicacalli* (singing and dance house); Valadés himself refers to a demonstration of Mexica dances before Emperor Charles V in Valladolid. In the centre, a musician plays a *teponaztli*, a horizontal idiophone with slits cut to form an H, which is percussed using two sticks with rubber ends named *olmaitl*. On the left there is another *teponaztli* accompanied by a *huehuetl*, a vertical membranophone which was percussed using the hands or else (as in the image) with two sticks; both of the cylindrical instruments, generically named *atambor* and/or *atabal* by the Spanish chroniclers, were played at the same time. Each of them produced two pitches, forming intervals of a third and a fifth respectively. Moreover, they bore carved or painted figures or mottos, and they were highly regarded from a ritual point of view. These pantomimic ritual dances with collective singing were named *areítos*, a Taino term from the Caribe which was very popular among the Mesoamerican chroniclers in the sixteenth century (Scolieri 2013, 24-43). The scene provides us with evidence on the close relationship between music and dance, and their unbreakable link with the great Mexica ceremonies.

In the landscape surroundings depicted in the engraving, one can find a variety of trees, hills, paths, fountains, and indigenous buildings with Renaissance design features (some of them have circular forms, similar to the classical rotondas known by Valadés in Rome), and outdoor scenes of Mexica daily life which would have been familiar to any preacher active in the region: the five types of fishing at Texcoco lake; different types of rafts and boats; corn milling; the preparation of the dough and the cooking of tortillas—tasks which belonged to women; a burial; the collection of liquids (on both sides of the *teocalli*); and four priests on two hills carrying out astrological tasks. Below, other farming activities are depicted, such as the collection of fruits and resins, the bleeding of the dragon tree, the extraction of pulque, the exudation of liquidambar, and the preparation of cocoa; also included here is a detailed taxonomical description of the indigenous flora, using more or less Latinised names for trees and endemic plants including the coconut tree, drago, maguey, liquidambar, casia, banana tree, cocoa, pineapple, tuna or *higo indio*, balsamo, and guava.

Another picturesque engraving of musical interest which forms part of Valadés' book is eloquently entitled "Tipus eorum que fratres faciunt in novo indiarum orbe qua dictum est: dilataberis ad orientem, occidententem, septentrionem ac meridianem et ero custos tuus et tuorum" (Type of activities carried out by the Brothers in the New World, according to what was written down: you will extend towards East and West, towards South and North, and I will take care of you and your endeavours; fig. 71.2). This offers an, again, idealised, symbolic and encyclopedic view of Franciscan pastoral activities in the New World, particularly pertinent to the first decades of colonialization (Bermúdez 2017). The engraving consists of a large rectangular patio closed by four "capillas posas" or open chapels at the corners (they are typical of the atriums of sixteenth-century Mexican monastery-churches); the trees framing the atrium resemble the Garden of Eden or Earthly Paradise. In the centre are the so-called 12 apostles of New Spain, a group of 12 Franciscan missionaries who arrived in Mexico in 1524 with the purpose of launching evangelisation, who are allegorically carrying the Church on their shoulders. The Church is represented as the dove of the Holy Spirit inside a Renaissance-style building reminiscent of Bramante's design for the Basilica of Saint Peter in Rome, crowned by the representation of the Trinity with Christ crucified. The procession is led by St Francis (the founder of the order) and concluded by Fray Martín de Valencia, the superior of the first Franciscan province in Mexico and leader of the 12 apostles of New Spain. Nine beams radiate from the Holy Spirit, pointing at other scenes which remind the prospective missionary and priest of their obligations concerning systematic education in Christian doctrine and the administering of the sacraments, as if in a kind of outdoor classroom; in this way, the indigenous people (represented using autochthonous customs, including their clothing and manner of sitting) are trained and led through the full cycle of their conversion.

Each scene is accompanied by both a letter (which refers to a detailed explanation included in the treatise itself) and a caption in Latin. At the very top is a Christian funeral accompanied by a group of indigenous singers dressed in the European manner, who symbolise the importance of music in the catechising process; one of the singers holds a book, while a Franciscan is conducting with a stick. It is difficult to assess if they are singing plainchant or polyphony; Valadés himself wrote that the Indians sang and played musical instruments at the Mass and the Office in such a solemn way that "none of the Spanish cathedrals can achieve this magnificence" (Valadés 1579, 226). Moving clockwise to the next scene, a friar is pointing at a drawing with a stick and explaining the story of the Creation of the world; below, we can find a representation of the examination before marriage (symbolised by a flourishing tree); then learning how to write one's name; then the ceremonies of marriage, baptism at the font, and confession; and the teaching of penitence and doctrine. At the top left corner, Fray Pedro de Gante is depicted teaching, through pictograms, the tools of the mechanical arts. Rectangles indicated with dotted lines separate the scenes and represent tombs. In the centre of the lower frieze, under a majestic arch, is a scene showing the administration of justice; in the lateral cells we find, on the left, daily-life scenes of indigenous confessing and, on the right, a Mass surrounded by two sacramental practices, communion and extreme unction. In the gardens surrounding the patio, the friars carry the sick (three on stretchers and other on a friar's back) and, in the four "capillas posas" at the corners of the atrium, girls, boys, women, and men are receiving their training separately. With this comprehensive program of catechising, Valadés aims to restore the ideal of the Franciscan friars who arrived in New Spain in 1524 at a moment (the 1570s) when what Franciscans recalled as the foundational utopia of their first missions to the region was undermined by political and doctrinal conflicts among the religious orders, the secular clergy and the Crown (Serés 2017, 276).

Both images, which are of considerable historical value, constitute eloquent testimonies of the meeting between cultures viewed from a European perspective, and have their correlate in the several textual and visual references to music included in Valadés' treatise itself. There, Valadés highlighted the skill of indigenous musicians in choral singing (but not in solo singing), which resulted in "an extremely pleasant harmony"; he also mentioned the variety of musical instruments that they skilfully played, including horns (cornets?), trumpets, shawms, flutes, lyres (harps?), organs, and drums ("cornua, tubae, tibiae, fistulae, lyresides, organa et timpana"), and also the common practice of playing these instruments from bell towers, blending their sound with that of the bells, from first Vespers to dawn the following day (Valadés 1579, 226-27). Music appears in a further engraving which depicts the seven Liberal Arts, in the form of a maid wearing classical attire who plays a portative organ, a commonplace representation in contemporary European art which blends with the iconography of St Cecilia. Valadés' explanatory text following this image invokes Boethius and defines music—according to the long-established cosmological tradition of *musica mundana*—as the numerically proportioned merging of voices into a harmony and consonance of sounds (Valadés 1579, 17-18).

Moreover, the two main images analysed above are in dialogue: the first presents the violence of the "idolatry" of the indigenous people in order, later, to justify their conversion and integration in the universal Christian republic, and legitimise the spiritual conquest. Although these illustrations are allegorical in nature, both may be linked to particular locations: the first to the great Tenochtitlan (the capital of the Mexica empire) and its Templo Mayor during the feast of the Toxcatl, just before the European arrival; and the second to the patio of the school of San José de los Naturales, founded by Gante and attached to the convent of San Francisco in Mexico City, the main Franciscan house in New Spain, where Valadés himself was trained and, later, served in the 1560s. Valadés' engravings and their new symbolic Indo-Christian order, highly ritualised, acquired an iconic status and went on to furnish the starting point for more than 50 representations of Mexico-Tenochtitlan in European books (the first, including copies of both engravings, Jerónimo de Mendieta's *Historia eclesiástica indiana* of 1595). In these books, the Mexican past is identified with dance spectacles and human sacrifices, and the Spanish colonisation with the missional practices of the friars. Ultimately, the aim was to represent visually a long-lasting tradition of juridical-ecclesiastical and theological thinking of Biblical origin, with the purpose of legitimising both the incorporation of the pagan world into Catholicism and the change imposed upon indigenous spiritual identities, by invoking the need to remove their "idolatrous" traditions, which to Catholics constituted a symbol of demonic sin. This was achieved by means of the educational project of the religious orders. The ideological construction of the Christianised and redeemed "Indian," accompanied by its iconographical representation, has had a huge impact on Mexican cultural and religious history to this day.

TRANSLATION: Ascensión Mazuela-Anguita

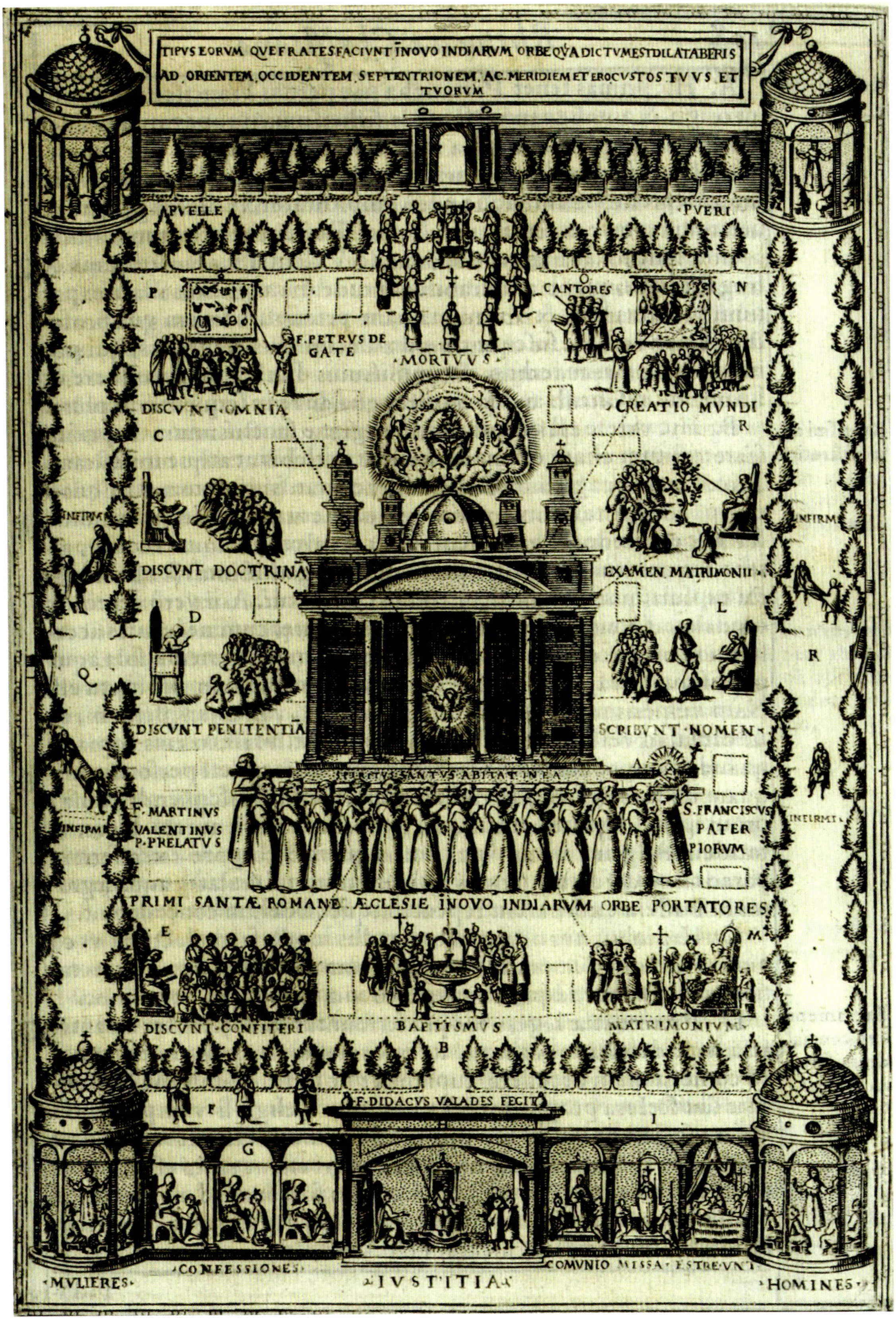

Figure 71.2: Engraving showing the Franciscan organisation of Mexico's evangelization, from Valadés, *Rhetorica Christiana*, p.[107]. Los Angeles, The Getty Research Institute, BV4217 .V34 1579. Photo courtesy of the Getty's Open Content Program.

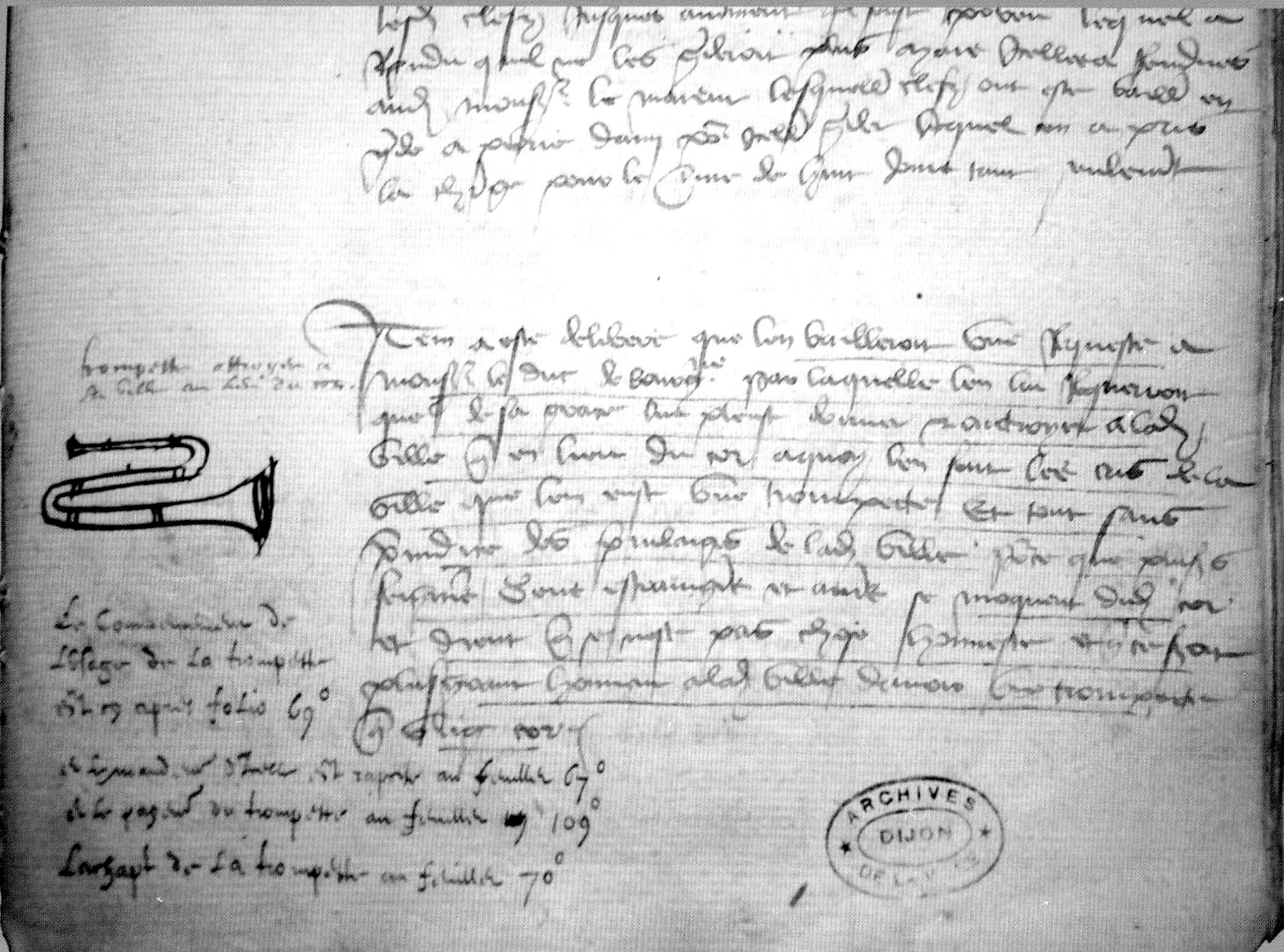

ARCHIVES
DIJON
et le serment [illegible] est rapporte au feuillet 67°
et les gages du trompette au feuillet 109°
Lachapt de la trompette au feuillet 70°

72. Dijon

Gretchen Peters

Request from the City of Dijon to the Duke of Burgundy
Dijon, 9 Oct 1433
Archives Municipales de Dijon, B154, fol. 13r
Photo courtesy of the Archives Municipales de Dijon

Music organised and gave meaning to life in French towns during the Renaissance. In towns throughout France, music was used for the opening and closing of town gates, official proclamations, processions, weddings, celebrations, and more, though the nature of these sounds varied significantly from town to town and were embedded with the histories of each region (Peters 2012; Charles-Dominique 1994; fig. 72.1). The significance of these differences, both overt and subtle, was understood by the townspeople. The sound of the trumpet, more so than that of any other instrument, reflected on a city's image, and the features of the trumpet were fundamental to the message it created. While references to trumpets are ubiquitous in archival documents of French cities, a formal request by the city of Dijon dating from 1433 is unusual in its careful and detailed depiction of one such instrument. It provides the physical details of a trumpet the city of Dijon desperately sought, as the city claimed that in contrast to trumpets in other "good cities" in France, the "harsh sound" of the instrument in use by the public crier was a source of ridicule.

Throughout France, cities commonly hired trumpeters to serve as public criers to draw attention to official decrees, to provide announcements and warnings from central bell-towers, and to contribute to the solemnity of processions, but the details surrounding the instrument depended upon the city's political structure and specifically the extent to which the civic government had autonomy from external authority. Cities with long histories of independent city councils created prominent rituals involving the trumpet to reflect their power. For example, Montpellier, a large, wealthy, and independent city in France in the fifteenth century, hired multiple musicians, including trumpeters for various functions (Peters 2012, 34). Donning official livery, trumpeters served as official criers and performed in processions, situated near the city council, for local ceremony or visiting royalty. Trumpeters also performed the "watch" morning and night from the bell-tower of Notre Dame-des-Tables, the location for civic ritual, for which they were provided a candle, a wool mat, and a feather pillow for the long nights (Archives Municipales de Montpellier, BB 49, fol. 16v). Details are lacking concerning the specifications of these trumpets, though one member of the "watch" had to promise not to make a trumpet while in the bell-tower, as well as not to entertain others or teach the trumpet (A.M.Mo., BB 36, fol. 55r). In contrast, cities with more limited civic authority employed the trumpet less in civic ritual, while symbols of royal power tended to figure more prominently. In Tours, for example, civic-employed trumpeters were heard from the towers of the royal collegiate church of St. Martin, though civic ritual was marked by morality plays which glorified nobility, processions steeped in themes of the rise and recovery of the French crown, and performances by the choir of St Martin (Peters 2012, 101).

The city of Albi was dramatically denied the right to the sound of the trumpet and its embodiment of political power by the city's overlord, the bishop. In the fifteenth century in Albi, a crier, wearing a coat embroidered with the coat of arms of the city, published announcements in the name of the bishop and city council to the sound of a silver trumpet. In 1491, a revolt against the bishop was summoned by the crier with his trumpet. In retaliation, according to the deliberations of the city council, the bishop had the trumpet "nailed to the pillory" in the middle of town and forced the crier to use a horn of an animal (Vidal 1903, 46).

Instruments used in these capacities ranged from animal horns, to simple instruments made while serving watch on the bell-tower, to expensive silver instruments made by specialists. Up until the late fourteenth century, trumpets were constructed with a straight tube of a fixed length. Instruments with shorter tubes had limited, higher ranges, while those with longer tubes, often five feet in length and more unwieldy, offered a more desirable extended range (Montagu 1976; Duffin 1989). This problem was solved in the late fourteenth century when trumpet-makers acquired the technology to bend the tube without distortion. The material (and subsequent value) for the instruments varied significantly from animal horns to brass, bronze, and the more prestigious silver.

The records of Dijon during the fifteenth century reveal great civic concern over the instrument of the public crier. By at least 1393, and probably much earlier, the city hired a sergeant/crier to sound his horn ("le cor") and announce "the edicts of grape-gathering … and many other decrees" at street corners and other accustomed places within the city (A.M.D., M50, fol. 18v). The exact nature of the horn is not clear, though a payment in 1400 to repair and to resolder ("ressoudre") the horn indicates that it was made from metal and not an animal horn (A.M.D., M49, fol. 109r). As the capital of the Duchy of Burgundy since the tenth century and the seat of its administration, the city of Dijon made a formal request to the duke of Burgundy in 1433, the document with which this essay began. The request was

> to give and to grant to the city, in place of the horn on which are made the decrees of the city, a trumpet. And all without detriment to the privileges of the city because many seigneurs, foreign people and others mock the said horn and that is not a respectable thing and that it would be a most grand honor to the city to have a trumpet rather than a horn.

Over a year after the request was made, on 12 November 1434 the city was granted the right to have its first trumpet. In a document with a large green wax seal and tied in green and red silk string, the city was granted the right to make its proclamations to the sound of the trumpet in place of the horn, which was described as having "a harsh sound" (un rude son) (Langeron 1851, 92). The city was also allowed to attach a banner with the coat of arms of the city to the trumpet, as was the custom in "other good cities." Confirming this right bestowed upon the city, a document from 4 March 1434 reads,

> the mandate is given to the city, that in place of the horn on which it has been the custom to make the decrees and other announcements for the city, that the city promises to make the said decrees to the sound of the trumpet. And also that the "grant Guille," who had been the crier, will not sound the said trumpet. And that a man Joffroy de Vauthigny from the duchy of Normandy will serve in this function (A.M.D., B154, fols. 69v-70r).

Joffroy received, along with the official livery of the city and lodging, a salary substantially higher than that of his predecessors, without an apparent increase in duties.

Within this broader practice in France, clearly, the practice of making official proclamations on a harsh-sounding horn in Dijon, a city with many foreign visitors, was degrading, and the new instrument was perceived as a "most grand honor to the city." In the margins of the formal request for the trumpet is a drawing of the desired instrument, and this depiction is consistent with a description in a payment receipt for the trumpet which was acquired by the city four years later. A goldsmith made an S-shaped trumpet in multiple sections out of silver, for an incomparable sum for a city trumpet in France. It consisted of three large straight pieces, two curved pieces, six connecting pieces, and the mouthpiece, as well as elaborate decoration that clearly connects the instrument to the city of Dijon. The receipt reads,

> and for the fashion of this which is thirteen pieces with horn-like curves where there are many new gildings and certain letters around the buisine of the trumpet, also gilded. And in each horn are the arms of the city… and on the said buisine the said arms are enameled (A.M.D., M 63, fol. 80r).

Not surprisingly, the instrument required frequent maintenance. For example, not long after its purchase, repairs to the metalwork were required as the trumpet was making a "crude sound," and 30 years later, a goldsmith "rebuilt all to new the silver trumpet of this city" for a substantial sum (A.M.D., M 63, fol. 125v; B58). An elaborate banner was attached to the instrument, which was made from multi-colored pieces of silk and was decorated with silk tassels, buttons, and a painting of the coat of arms of Dijon.

The duties attached to this position remained consistent throughout the century, with the obligations to make pronouncements and to participate in special events, such as an archery contest for the crossbowmen or a royal entry of the king and queen of France. Despite having acquired a prestigious instrument, the crier in the early sixteenth century was formally reprimanded for bringing ridicule on the city. In 1516, he was admonished for knowing "nothing on how to play the trumpet, that he has neither the words nor the eloquence to proclaim the announcements and that people mock him and the city" (Langeron 1851, 88-89). He was also charged at times with not willingly participating with the sergeants during the celebrations of Christmas and failing to provide the necessary announcements, resulting in serious confusion.

The sound of the trumpet, in some form, was commonly heard throughout French cities during the Renaissance, and references to it can be found throughout archival records. Visual images of the trumpet, or of any musical instrument, however, are extremely rare in these records. This uncommon drawing reflects the importance to the city of Dijon of accurately capturing the details of this musical instrument. The townspeople of Dijon, as in other cities in France, understood the significance of the sound and image of this elaborate silver trumpet.

Figure 72.1: Miniature from the "Harley Froissart" (Jean Froissart, *Chroniques*) showing the entry of Isabella of Bavaria into Paris (ca. 1385) with trumpeters atop the city gatehouse, Bruges, ca. 1470-72. London, Britsh Library, Harley MS 4379, fol. 3r. Photo © The British Library Board.

73. Milan

Daniele V. Filippi

Anon., illuminated initial "S" with Madonna, angels and the façade of the Cathedral of Santa Maria Maggiore
From Milan, Archivio della Veneranda Fabbrica del Duomo, Sez. Musicale, Librone 1, fol. 2v (detail)
Milan, ca. 1490
Manuscript on paper, [3] + [1] + 188 + [3] fols., 64 x 45.5 cm
Photo © Veneranda Fabbrica del Duomo di Milano

The picture chosen to represent the city of Milan in our museum reproduces a detail of a page from the manuscript Librone 1, copied ca. 1490. This large choirbook-format manuscript is part of a set of four Libroni (literally, big books) copied for the musical chapel of the Duomo during Franchinus Gaffurius' tenure as chapelmaster (1484-1522). It is in many ways emblematic of musical life in the city. On the one hand, the Libroni were the first substantial collection of polyphonic music gathered for the cathedral, probably marking the transition from a musical practice dominated by semi-improvised polyphony to the reception of a composed repertory by Franco-Flemish masters and by Gaffurius himself. On the other hand, the presence of works by members of the Sforza ducal chapel, notably Loyset Compère and Gaspar van Weerbeke, attests to a link and a transfer of music between the two institutions. Especially in the last third of the fifteenth century, under Dukes Galeazzo, Gian Galeazzo, and Ludovico Sforza, the axis between the Duomo and the Castle of Porta Giovia (now Castello Sforzesco) was pivotal in the soundscape of the city, both metaphorically and literally, on the occasion

of solemn processions for dynastic weddings and other public celebrations. Furthermore, the Libroni are the only extant sources that indirectly reflect the repertory of what was then, especially in the 1470s under of Duke Galeazzo (d. 1476), one of the most prestigious polyphonic chapels in Europe.

The picture on display here reproduces a detail from the first full opening of the manuscript, with the cantus voice of a polyphonic setting of the hymn *Mysterium ecclesiae*. The historiated initial "S" (for the second stanza of the hymn, "Sola in sexu foemina"; the first and the remaining odd-numbered stanzas were sung in plainchant according to the practice of *alternatim*) is decorated with the emblem of the Veneranda Fabbrica (literally, Venerable Works), the vestry board of the Duomo established to supervise its construction and maintenance, which had a strong civic identity and enjoyed a certain independence from both ducal and archiepiscopal power. The Virgin Mary, with her arms open wide and her mantle lifted by two angels, protects the façade of the old Cathedral of Santa Maria Maggiore—the new Duomo was to remain under construction for centuries. This illuminated initial—the only one in the Librone—is associated with the music of the hymn sung at Vespers on the main Marian feasts of the liturgical year according to the Ambrosian rite, specific to the diocese of Milan. The illumination thus highlights the role of polyphonic music in manifesting the identity of the Duomo as a Marian shrine, as the mother church of the Ambrosian rite—rooted in a venerable tradition reaching back to St Ambrose himself—and as home to a religious community devoted to the cultivation of liturgy and sacred song for the spiritual benefit and honor of the entire civic and ecclesiastical body.

Because of its position in the middle of the Po Valley, its strategic importance for the control of Italy and of the commercial and military routes between the Peninsula and the rest of Europe, the fertile agricultural lands surrounding it, its numerous manufacturing and commercial enterprises, and its rich cultural and spiritual heritage, Milan was one of the foremost European cities in the early modern period. Thanks especially to the presence of a ducal (and later gubernatorial) court, of a metropolitan cathedral, and of numerous churches, monasteries, and noble houses, schools, and confraternities, Milan was a place where plentiful and noteworthy music-related activities took place. New music was composed in and for the city (though chiefly for its élites), both vocal and instrumental—Milan had, for instance, a rich tradition of lute music (Bollini 1986). But Milan was also a place where foreign and "international" music was introduced: the Sforza chapel in the last decades of the fifteenth century, with its largely Franco-Flemish roster of singers and composers, is the best-known example, even though the connections with ultramontane musical cultures were older and more ramified. It is remarkable that Duke Galeazzo tried to tie his foreign singers to Milan by granting them citizenship, giving them houses in the city, and even bestowing mining concessions, besides obtaining for them ecclesiastical benefices (Merkley and Merkley 1999). In a later phase, Milan, thanks to its music printing firms, was a hub for the circulation of different musics: as for example when a repertory in the process of becoming canonic, the sacred polyphony of such Roman composers as Palestrina and Victoria, had numerous Milanese editions in the 1580-90s (Filippi 2019, 236-39). New music reached Milan in many ways, including via the gifts its leaders received from abroad, as is the case with Pietro Giovanelli's collection of motets *Novus thesaurus musicus* of 1568, a specially customised copy of which was sent to Archbishop Carlo Borromeo and is currently preserved at the Biblioteca Trivulziana (MS E 371; Filippi 2019, 230-31).

Both locally or internationally renowned virtuosi, including women (Blackburn 2012) and Milanese dilettanti, performed music, and musical skills were taught at different levels, from the systematic schooling of *pueri cantores* at the Duomo to the private musical education of the scions of noble and wealthy families. Famous is the case of Cicco Simonetta, the learned and cunning chancellor of Duke Galeazzo: in a letter of the early 1470s Simonetta requested from Venice an adolescent singer and lute player "able to sing with and without lute accompaniment" (che sappia sonare bene de liuto, et cantare con dicto liuto et senza liuto), who "should also master the theory" (havesse [...] fondamento et raxone del chanto), in order to teach his children (Motta 1887, 554-55). In 1551 the then 13-year-old Carlo Borromeo had a teacher who taught him how to sing and play the *violone*, and his tutor described this "ability to sing and play" (virtù di sonare et cantare) as an important asset (Filippi 2013, 666).

On a much more elementary level, but with a wider social impact, the basics of singing were taught at the Schools of Christian Doctrine, the free popular education programme started in Milan by Castellino da Castello in 1536 and later disseminated across Italy. As was customary in the curricula of many such schools in the early modern era (even across the confessional divides), singing formed a triad with a rudimentary alphabetization and the teaching of the catechism (Filippi 2017b). As we read in contemporary documents and printed booklets, the teachers made sure that the children were able to answer to the litanies and sing simple devotional songs in Italian (*laude*), notably in order to participate actively in public processions. At the opposite end of the spectrum of music education, Gaffurius cultivated in Milan ambitious studies in music theory and published the results in an epoch-making trilogy: *Theorica musicae* (1492), *Practica musicae* (1496), and *De harmonia musicorum instrumentorum* (1518). Gaffurius' writings had a wide and enduring impact for the unprecedented coverage of ancient theory (facilitated by recent humanistic translations of Greek treatises) and for the remarkable balance between theoretical speculation and attention to practical musical matters.

Milan was a place where music and sound were used purposely and intensely to mark the ordinary rhythms and extraordinary events of civic and religious life, to define community, to enhance the symbolic meanings of topography (for example during processions or solemn entries), and to accompany and characterise the many forms of sociability. Three days of bonfires, processions, and pealing of bells were the standard "signs of merriment" ordered by dukes and governors to celebrate victories, alliances, dynastic events, and good news in general (Santoro 1961). Cesare Negri's *Le gratie d'amore* of 1602 retrospectively illuminates the most refined accomplishments of dance culture in Milan in the second half of the sixteenth century, whereas Simon Boyleau's *Madrigali* of 1564, with their multiple dedications to (mostly) Milanese noble men and women, exemplify the city's "collective culture of secular song" (Getz 2005).

Ambrosian chant was a distinctive element of Milan's sacred soundscape, and its cultivation was actively promoted by church authorities and considered an important part of priestly education: the document instituting a chantry at the

Duomo in 1528 required the candidates to be "Good singers … and able to read and celebrate Mass properly" (Boni cantores … et sciant competenter legere et missas celebrare; AVFDMi, A.S., cart. 58, XIX, 7, n. 1). The vocal praise and intercession of Milan's many religious communities was valued for its objective worth: Duke Galeazzo wrote in 1475 to a monastic community that was, so to speak, on strike, that "we deeply regret that the divine worship in the Abbey of Chiaravalle is silent!" (molto ne dispiace che in quella Abbatia de Chiaravalle el culto divino stia in silentio; ASMi, Registri delle missive, 120, fol. 301^{r}). But it also progressively became a kind of attraction for citizens and tourists avant la lettre, especially in the case of singing nuns: in 1624, visiting Milan on his way to Rome, Prince Ladislaus Wasa of Poland went to hear the sung Vespers at the female monastery of San Paolo, where he admired the "marvellous voice of one of those virgins" (mirifica virginis cuiuspiam vox notata; Kendrick 1996, 115).

Religious houses, however, sometimes hosted musical performances of a quite different character: as some witnesses declared at Carlo Borromeo's canonization process, "when I was young, I went to public parties organised in certain parsonages, with viols and violins, where people danced openly," "and in some female monasteries during Carnival there were public parties and dances to the sound of viols and violoni" (in alcune canoniche essendo giovane andai alle feste pubbliche, che si facevano con viole et violini, ballandosi pubblicamente; et in alcuni monasterii de monache al tempo del Carnevale si facevano publiche feste et balli sonandosi viole et violoni; Marcora 1962, 305, 295).

Again, Milan was a place where a variety of musical experiences was accessible, and where musicians of different provenance crossed paths among themselves and with other artists, artisans, and intellectuals: Enrico Boscano's *Isola beata* describes meetings (ca. 1490) gathering, among others, Leonardo, Bramante, the poet Bernardo Bellincioni, and Lancino Curti, and such musicians as Gaspar van Weerbeke and the German lutenist Giovanni Maria "Giudeo" (Bizzarini 2014; Rossetti 2019).

Finally, Milan was a place which required regulations against noise and other sonic abuses. Civic and religious authorities, for instance, emanated edicts urging all sort of "street artists" ("masters and players of comedies, herb-sellers, charlatans, jesters, zanies, and mountebanks,"—Maestri et Recitatori di Comedie, Herborarii, Zarlatani, Buffoni, Zanni, Canta in banchi) to abstain from practicing their professions on the Duomo square during the celebration of the divine Offices (gubernatorial *grida*—public announcement—of 1561, ASDMi, Visite pastorali, Metropolitana, LIV), and the dukes and governors repeatedly legislated against blasphemies.

Milan was clearly the theatre of battles between different agencies and their sonic apparatuses. Emblematic is the case of Archbishop Carlo Borromeo as described by one of his biographers: "During the revelries [of Carnival] he found a splendid way to make the people desist from their follies, for hymns were sung in the Duomo on feast days, and all the people were refreshed by music" (Et baccanalibus diebus praeclarissimam invenerat rationem, qua populus desineret insanire. Nam diebus festis hymni in Ecclesia canebantur. Musica tota plebs recreabatur; Valier 1586, 30). Carlo aimed, thus, to make real the ideal epitomised in our exhibit: the people of Milan, gathered in the Duomo under the mantle of the Blessed Virgin and enveloped by the strains of sacred polyphony, could experience a foretaste of the celestial harmony. A sonic bridge was established between the earthly city and the City of God (Filippi 2017b).

Abbreviations: ASDMi - Archivio Storico Diocesano di Milano; ASMi - Archivio di Stato di Milano; AVFDMi - Archivio della Veneranda Fabbrica del Duomo di Milano

Additional references: Daolmi 2017; Gamberini 2014; Getz 2015; Kendrick 2002; Strohm 1993. Gaffurius Codices Online, https://www.gaffurius-codices.ch

DEO OPT: MAX
BENIGNISS:
PROTECTRICI
POTENTISS:
OB PATRIAM
ET SPES SVAS
SERVATA
MDCXXXIIX

74. Munich

Alexander J. Fisher

Devotions before the Mariensäule, Munich
Bartholomäus Kilian, Augsburg, ca. 1660
Engraving, 16.9 x 21.2 cm
Historischer Verein von Oberbayern, Stadtarchiv München

With a population of only around 15,000, the city of Munich might have seemed an unpromising representative of a vital urban soundscape in the early sixteenth century. But the consolidation of the duchy of Bavaria following the War of Landshut Succession (1503-05), and its subsequent leadership by a series of powerful dukes—Wilhelm IV (1508-50), Albrecht V (1550-79), and Wilhelm V (1579-97)—led to a waxing in the city's political fortunes as the centre of an ambitious Wittelsbach dynasty, whose aspirations to the imperial college of electors would finally be realised in 1623 under Maximilian I (1597-1651). Maximilian's election was the political culmination of Bavaria's alignment with the Roman Church, a process that gathered steam after the mid-sixteenth century and led to the emergence of Munich as the northern bastion of Counter-Reformation Catholicism. At the same time, the Wittelsbach dukes promoted an increasingly opulent musical culture at their court, led by Europe's arguably most famous musician, Orlando di Lasso. The intense piety of the court meant that the urban soundscape was profoundly shaped by religious and moral considerations. Civic and ecclesiastical elites deployed sound and music—and, conversely, imposed silence—to shape the experience of an idealised, sacral, Catholic space. Yet this space was not identical to that produced by visual perception. Closely bound up with temporality and motion, sound could produce alternative senses of urban space, and its ambivalent nature meant that the control of the soundscape could easily be contested. The present essay explores aspects of Munich's soundscape in the sixteenth century, especially in the context of the religious and social discipline that was increasingly applied in the service of confessional politics. The conclusion will offer some broader considerations about the term "soundscape" and its deployment in early modern urban history.

From a purely visual perspective, Munich increasingly featured an architectural programme that represented the city as a nexus of Catholic devotion and Wittelsbach dynastic culture. In the expanding ducal residence (*Neuveste*) the court chapel of St George (1434) was enlarged by 1540 and redecorated in a Renaissance style around 1560. A further wave of expansion would unfold under Maximilian I, whose new court chapel dedicated to the Immaculate Conception (dedicated 1603) was joined by Hans Krumper's sculpture of the Apocalyptic Virgin as Patroness of Bavaria, placed prominently on the residence's façade in 1616. Maximilian would also instigate the construction of one of Munich's most visible monuments to Marian devotion, the great *Mariensäule* (1638) that still today marks the geographical centre of the city. The most spectacular monument to Counter-Reformation Catholicism, however, was the Jesuit church of St Michael, consecrated in 1597 after a lengthy building programme financed by Duke Wilhelm V. Its façade, featuring the archangel slaying the dragon of heresy, crowned by rows of dukes and saints who defended the Bavarian Church, makes plain the spiritual priorities of the Jesuits and the ducal house.

These structures formed a part of the spatial code of the city (Lefebvre 1991, 46-53), but sounding and moving bodies enacted sacral space as well. Accounts of the opulent consecration of St Michael in July 1597 fit into an intersensorial history in which sound plays a prominent role. Pompous processions, polychoral and militaristic music, bell ringing, cannon fire, a great feast, and a climactic open-air drama entitled *The Triumph of St Michael* exemplify the multisensory character of Jesuit worship and ritual. To this counterpoint of the visual, aural, and gustatory, we can add the olfactory, in the form of incense routinely deployed during the divine service, and even the haptic in the form of rosary beads, amulets, and holy water. Beyond such sumptuous occasions, parishes and confraternities routinely mounted processions that traced networks of sacral space through the city streets, while the daily ringing of the *Angelus* bell commanded all residents to conspicuously drop to their knees and pray to the Virgin. More generally, cycles of bell ringing from Munich's churches—principally, Unsere Liebe Frau, St Peter, Heiliger Geist, and St Michael—structured experiences of sacral space and time; during thunderstorms in particular the ringing of one or more "storm bells" from church towers was thought to dispel the airborne demons that were the proximate causes of these tempests (Fisher 2014, 192-205).

Few of Munich's residents would have heard the increasingly opulent sounds of the court chapel, where systematic cycles of polyphonic liturgical music were copied into still-extant choirbooks from the time of Ludwig Senfl (chapelmaster 1523-43) to Orlando di Lasso (chapelmaster 1563-94). The music of the prolific and famous Lasso was likely heard elsewhere in the city, and is represented in inventories and sources from St Michael and for the principal parish church of Unsere Liebe Frau. Direct reports of performances of Lasso's music in a public context are rare, but we are told that a performance of Lasso's motet *Gustate et videte quam suavis sit Dominus* (*Taste and see how good is the Lord*) dispelled storm clouds that threatened the procession in 1584. The association of Lasso's gustatory motet with the celebration of the transsubstantiated Eucharist served the confessional interests of his Wittelsbach masters, but court music more generally reflected a culture of assertive Counter-Reformation: we might mention here Lasso's burgeoning number of new Magnificat and Marian litany settings copied into court manuscripts (Crook 1994), the Catholic psalm versifications by Kaspar Ulenberg (themselves intended as a riposte to "falsified" Protestant translations), set into three-voice polyphony by Lasso and his son Rudolph (1588), or the elderly master's swansong, the great cycle of spiritual madrigals *Lagrime di San Pietro* (1594), which bears the hallmarks of Jesuit-inspired devotion and penitence (Fisher 2007). While it is difficult to locate specific performances in space and time, musical sources like these represent carefully planned prescriptions for the organization of sound that testify to an idealised or intended soundscape shaped in the spirit of Catholic reform.

Sonic practices both augmented and came into conflict with existing regimes of visual space. The great Corpus Christi processions, for example, were embellished by musical ensembles, while the report of hundreds of cannon and muskets met the procession as it made its stations around the city. In the built environment of Munich with its narrow streets and restricted sightlines, militaristic sound expanded the procession's acoustic horizon to encompass the entire city, creating an acousmatic effect whereby the aural was sundered from visual perception. In this way sound not only conveyed a more ample sense of sacral space, but also allowed people to "see the unseen" (Ihde 2007). Moreover, the "acoustic regime" (Atkinson 2016) created by regular cycles of bell-ringing projected overlapping senses of jurisdictional space and time: the geographical divisions between the main parish churches, the distinction between secular and church authority, and cycles of liturgical, profane, and astronomical time.

Even in Munich, however, it initially proved difficult to stamp out temporal spaces for Protestant identity created through sound. Most dramatic, perhaps, was the irruption of defiant Lutheran chorale-singing in the Augustinian church in June 1558 (Fisher 2014, 1-2 and 34-35). The 11 men arrested by the authorities were released by the city council with a stern warning, but the episode may have helped convince Duke Albrecht V that a general visitation of Bavarian churches was now warranted. Unfolding over a period of two years, this visitation revealed that congregations, wittingly or unwittingly, often sang illicit vernacular songs in the divine service. Even in Munich, German schoolmasters were widely suspected of teaching vernacular psalms to children, sometimes under pressure from local burghers; secret Protestant conventicles involving the sounds of prayer, reading, and singing allowed the unseen to reveal itself to nosy neighbours and hostile officials (Fisher 2014, 174-75). Maintaining a sense of Catholic auditory space led to outright attempts to suppress illicit singing and to offer orthodox alternatives. For example, the *Gesang- und Psalmenbuch* printed at Munich in 1586 promotes the spiritual benefits of song in its preface, but also calls for the uprooting of "all manner of false, sectarian songbooks that have been brought into the noble Catholic land of Bavaria, through which the impressionable have been seduced." Songs for the liturgical cycle are augmented by those honouring the Virgin Mary, regional pilgrimage shrines, and the traditional sacraments; in addition we find psalm paraphrases from Kaspar Ulenberg's psalter. Whether songs such as these represent an organic development stemming from lay initiative is unclear, at best. Arguably they participate in a broader agenda of official propaganda, a programmatic effort to shape public behavior in the spirit of Catholic reform.

In this context of religious reform and surveillance, the sounds of secular or profane life occupied a contingent and liminal position. There was indeed a tradition of civic music provided by Munich's *Stadtpfeifer* for all manner of social rituals, but they fell under the same regime of surveillance and discipline that had strongly religious overtones. A court trumpeter, the so-called *Spielgraf*, was tasked with maintaining decorum among the musicians, and by 1613 officials moved to ban performances in taverns entirely. Inebriated patrons, stimulated by music, represented a general immorality that risked God's collective punishment. The same is true for unauthorised music by children, vagrants, and beggars, which was regulated or banned on similar grounds. Further research is needed, moreover, to clarify the role of rumour and gossip as tactics used by commoners to navigate the city and to circumvent official communication strategies. In an age of limited popular literacy, modes of face-to-face communication through the media of speech and song persisted as a primary means of circulating information, and posed challenges for a regime intent on monopolising the control of sound.

The advent of sound studies has provided new opportunities and challenges for understanding the sonic environment of early modern cities like Munich. One might explore surviving acoustic spaces using empirical tools: of special interest might be the vast interior of St Michael, featuring the world's largest barrel vault outside of St Peter's in Rome. The architectural plan of the nave, with uninterrupted sightlines to the altar and relatively shallow side chapels, would have allowed for an unimpeded visual experience of the liturgy. The immense nave, shallow chapels and transepts, and stucco decorations likely would have made for a highly reverberant but an evenly diffused sound, without significant delayed reflections. A more accurate profile might follow models by scholars such as Deborah Howard and Laura Moretti (Howard and Moretti 2009), John Wall (Wall 2014), and a team from Stanford University exploring the acoustics of the Hagia Sophia (Serinus 2016). Similarly, analyses of sound propagation might show how sounds like speech, music, bells, and gunfire resonated in the built environment of the city, dependent on variables like intensity, reflective surfaces, temperature, and humidity.

There are many historical variables that remain unknown, however, and a nominally "accurate" acoustic profile of a building or an outdoor environment would tell us little about phenomenological experiences of sound. Documenting the acoustic environment remains a critical task, but one must recall that most definitions of soundscape require attention to sound as perceived or understood (ISO 2014; Kelman 2010; Ingold 2007). Therefore, the notion of an objective, unitary soundscape that can be accurately reconstructed and analysed is something of a chimera. Court and church officials in Munich aimed for a representation of urban space as a bastion of Catholic practice and symbolism; moreover, a significant part of the musical production seems to represent an idealised soundscape in a similar vein. Sensation and perception are radically subjective, but it is possible to understand how collectivities might have understood the meaning of spaces and their transformations, and how they reacted when experiences of space changed. This is precisely the significance of sonic disruptions like that at Munich's Augustinian church in 1558, the great Corpus Christi processions of the late sixteenth century, or the consecration of St Michael in 1597: they are collective acts of reshaping space through sound, and leave traces in the archives that complement the insights of acoustic modelling.

فتادند
ازخویش رفتند پاک

VI

Public Sphere

Travels

Dubrovnik (Raguse)
Plovdiv
Durrës
Sidirókastro
Sérres
Kavála
Komotini
Lagos
Tekirdağ
Istanbul (Constantinople)
Izmit
Vlorë
Thessaloníki (Salonique)
Mount Athos
Bursa
Hissarlik (Troie)
LEMNOS
Ankara
CORFU
Kütahya
LESBOS
Afyonkarahisar (Afyon)
Akşehir
CHIOS
Izmir (Smyrne)
Konya
MOREA
Ereğli
Adana
Antākyā
Allepo (Al
RHODES
Maarrat al-Nu'm
Hamāh
CRETE
Homs
Damascus (Damas)
Sea of Galilee (Lake Tibériade)
Ramala
Rosetta (Rashîd)
Damietta (Dumyât)
Jerusalem
Gaza City
Fuwah
Al-Maṭarīya
Alexandria
El Ballah
Bilbeis
Cairo (Le Caire)
El-Suweis (Suez)
Mount Sinai
El Tor (Al-Tur)
N
Kilometers
0
125
250
500

75. The Travels of Pierre Belon du Mans

Carla Zecher

Pierre Belon du Mans
Les observations de plusieurs singularitez et choses memorables trouvées en Grèce, Asie, Judée, Egypte, Arabie et autres pays estranges
Paris: Guillaume Cavellat and Gilles Corrozet, 1553
[12] + 212 fols., 4°
Image: Map showing the locations visited by Pierre Belon. Image © Emily Kelley.

One day in the late 1540s, pirates seized a crate containing botanical and zoological specimens that the French naturalist Pierre Belon du Mans had gathered while traveling in the Middle East. Belon's accumulated treasures included the skins of serpents, birds, and animals; samples of plants and seeds; and dried sea creatures. He entrusted the crate to a Genoese ship bound for England, but the objects ended up for sale in Algiers instead. Fortunately Belon, a self-styled "man of curiosity," still had the copious daily notes he had taken during his nearly three-year journey (Belon du Mans 2001, 60). After he returned to France he produced several important works of natural history and a 400-page travelogue, his *Observations on many singularities and memorable things found in Greece, Asia, Judea, Egypt, Arabia, and other foreign countries* (see fig. 75.1). Reading Belon's book is like wandering through a Renaissance cabinet of curiosities and the great bazaar of Istanbul all at once (Beuchat 2009, 140-41 and 149). In addition to weightier topics like religious belief, marriage practices, and slavery, he reports on everything from trees to costume to food, pets, chewing gum, hair dye, games—and music (his book is translated into English as Belon 2012).

The lost crate probably contained materials that served in the Middle East to craft musical instruments. According to Belon, the Turks extracted a gum taken from the root of a plant of the daisy family to make a glue for constructing lutes and other objects of marquetry (Belon du Mans 2001, 128 and 396). Perhaps the crate also contained the skin of the Nile catfish, which the Egyptians used to fashion the bridges of viols, instead of wood. The skin held the strings elevated (Belon 2001, 321). The Turks made the sounding boards of their small lutes from juniper wood, and when the wood was whorled these lutes sold for more than six ducats, but Belon says they found a market among sailors even at that price because juniper "never cracks." Belon seems himself to have been an amateur lutenist, which may account for his particular interest in music. He explains that having tuned a mid-sized, four-course Turkish lute like a Renaissance guitar and added frets, he was able to play it like a guitar. In his judgment, the Turkish *chanterelles* (treble strings) were not as "silvery" sounding as the European ones, because they were triple wound, but he found that lacking any others it was possible to use them on a Venetian lute. Belon was surprised to find that many people in Turkey knew how to play one or another kind of lute, even villagers—which was unlike France and Italy, where the lute was an instrument of the upper classes. But as he points out, the smallest type of Turkish lute had only three strings, so it was easy to play (Belon du Mans 2001, 520-22).

Belon's travelogue gives us the musical equivalents of rare picture postcards: glimpses of things he heard as he traversed Greece, Turkey, Egypt, Syria, and the Holy Land. For Belon and his readers musical expression took place within a fundamentally oral environment. In this respect the culture he came from resembled the ones he was observing. Pieces of music, composed and notated, existed in Europe at the time, but they did not regulate musical practice (Burstyn 1997, 697). The increasing circulation of music in written form in the fifteenth century, linked to the advent of music printing on a commercial scale, had not erased the improvisatory nature of much of the musical activity of the Renaissance. According to Walter Ong, orally-based thought and expression tend to be additive rather than subordinative in nature, aggregative rather than analytic, and situational rather than abstract (Burstyn 1997, 699). These characteristics are evident in Belon's manner of treating music as a "singularity" worthy of attention in his book.

In the Greek isles (by then under Ottoman control) Belon watched village women confront death through ritual lamentation. He found this spectacle very moving, as the women wailed, scratching their cheeks and yanking on their hair. He noted that the custom was to hire a woman with a good voice and have her sing loudly, to set the pauses and accents for the others (Belon du Mans 2001, 71).

In the ports of the Ottoman capital of Constantinople (Istanbul), Belon heard the singing of bands of slaves as they loaded and unloaded cargo from the ships. He also listened to the *ney*, the reed-flute associated with the dervish orders. He was interested in its manner of playing, commenting that the embouchure is quite different from that of European flutes and requires the player to sing into it rather more than to blow (Belon du Mans 2001, 520-21).

Belon did not think much of the sound quality of the *ney*, but was captivated by the *miskal* (panpipes). On one occasion, he was upstairs in the lodging of the French ambassador in Constantinople, and through an open window he overheard a musician playing beautiful music in the street below. He assumed it was a "German flute" (transverse flute), until he looked out the window and realised it was a set of 24 pipes bundled together: "Anyone who has not heard this would have trouble believing that such a sweet music can proceed from an instrument which for us is simple" (Belon du Mans 2001, 225). Sixteenth-century Frenchmen knew the panpipes as a rustic instrument, played by peasants in the field and by street vendors, not an instrument of art.

In both Turkey and Egypt Belon had occasion to hear the *çeng*, the small square harp that was then its heyday, before it fell out of use in the late seventeenth century. He liked the sound of the *çeng* well enough, saying that although it did not make a "great music," still, it was pleasant to hear, especially when used to accompany singing rather than played solo (Belon du Mans 2001, 304). He states that the "wives" of Egyptian men played these harps, but it is more likely that he was watching performances of the *çengi*: non-Muslim women, professionals hired to dance, mime, sing, and play the tambourine and the harp to entertain local dignitaries and their European guests.

Traveling up the Nile, Belon heard a sound coming from the Egyptian villages that he found very puzzling, until finally, on the outskirts of Cairo, he discovered that it was made by women greeting each other in the streets with joyful tongue trills (ululation). This kind of vocalization reminded him of the cry sounded by the milkmaids in Paris. He also remarked that in Cairo the women, girls, and little children did not go out in the streets much. There were no women buying and selling, as they did in Europe, and the city therefore seemed less populated (Belon du Mans 2001, 293 and 301). In this soundscape largely devoid of high voices, the women's vocal salutations must have especially stood out.

No doubt this is also why the sound of the Islamic call to prayer carried so far, even without the amplification used today. As he traveled through Ottoman lands, the rhythm of Belon's day was structured by the voices of muezzins proclaiming the call to prayer, rather than the ringing of bells to which he was accustomed. Belon marveled at the fact that the voices of the muezzins could be heard from as far as half a league away. He says it would be impossible for anyone who has never heard such a cry to believe that a man's voice can carry such a distance. He also jokes that the prayer call sounds like the wail of a vendor of little cakes who has lost his basket. But then he goes on to say that it reminded him of the manner of singing pastorales in the Maine region of France in the Christmas season, because the muezzins recite in falsetto (Belon du Mans 2001, 498-99). In this period, to speak of a male style of singing in a high voice did not yet carry the sense of effeminacy that it would later acquire. While poking fun at the muezzins Belon also appears to have been searching for musical universals.

Overall, Belon listened to the great variety of liturgical music practices in the Middle East with equanimity. While traveling in the countryside he sometimes lodged in Greek Orthodox monasteries. He reports that the Caloyers (Basilian monks) had the custom that those among them with a better knowledge of classical Greek were called upon to read aloud what the others would then chant, since the others knew only modern Greek. In Egyptian villages he heard antiphonal Qur'anic recitation sounding from the mosques, and it brought to mind the voices of Catholic priests chanting the psalms in Latin. In El Tor he attended Mass in a Maronite church and commented on the multilingualism of the liturgy, noting that the priests sang "honorably" in Arabic, Armenian, and Greek (Belon du Mans 2001, 289 and 350).

However, Belon's capacity to find a kind of musical universality in this diversity of devotional practices did not translate into greater tolerance for alternative forms of Christianity and Christian music making back in France. Variety was acceptable (or at least could be managed) in foreign lands, but a threat at home (Beuchat 2009, 157). Whereas in the years prior to Belon's great journey questions of religious identity were still being negotiated in France, after his return the negotiations broke down. When the first French civil war broke out in 1562, Belon expressed fiercely anti-Huguenot sentiments, publicly. Then he set about writing an autobiographical narrative addressed to King Charles IX, which comprised a lengthy diatribe against the Huguenots. His Levantine experience features prominently in this text (which was destined to remain unfinished), but he uses that material to authenticate his vituperative observations about the dangers he believed the Huguenots posed to France. With regard to music, he scoffs that apart from the settings by Claude Goudimel of Clément Marot's French translations of the psalms, the Huguenots have no ability to sing at all, and are even obliged to print their music clandestinely (Belon 2001, 116-17). One night, in the month of April 1565, when Belon was walking home through the Bois de Boulogne to his lodging in the king's Palace of Madrid, he was murdered—supposedly by prowlers. But his death was probably an assassination, motivated by religious discord.

Belon was not an ethnomusicologist. He did not travel to listen. His mission was to document the flora and fauna of the Middle East. But sound is invasive. It carries around corners and even through walls, and Belon seems to have been enough of a musician himself that he could not help but acquire a cosmopolitan ear: an ear that was nowhere a stranger.

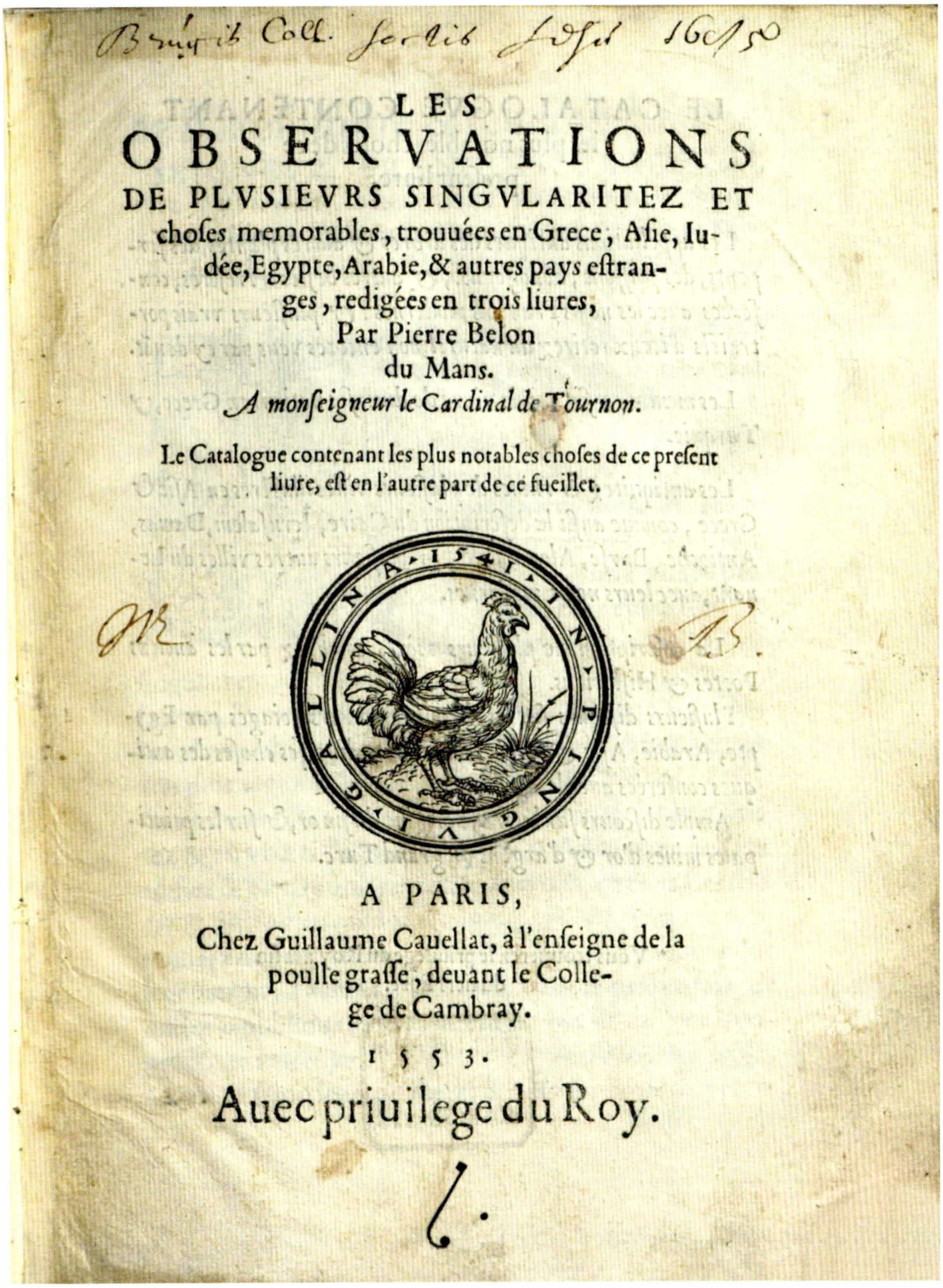
LES
OBSERVATIONS
DE PLVSIEVRS SINGVLARITEZ ET
choſes memorables, trouuées en Grece, Aſie, Iudée, Egypte, Arabie, & autres pays eſtranges, redigées en trois liures,
Par Pierre Belon
du Mans.
A monſeigneur le Cardinal de Tournon.

Le Catalogue contenant les plus notables choſes de ce preſent liure, eſt en l'autre part de ce fueillet.

A PARIS,
Chez Guillaume Cauellat, à l'enſeigne de la poulle graſſe, deuant le College de Cambray.
1553.
Auec priuilege du Roy.

Figure 75.1: Pierre Belon, *Les Observations de plusieurs Singularitez et choses memorables* (Paris: Guillaume Cavellat, 1553), title page. Munich, Bayerische Staatsbibliothek, Res/4 H.nat. 17 / urn:nbn:de:bvb:12-bsb10201127-7. Photo courtesy of the Bayerische Staatsbibliothek.

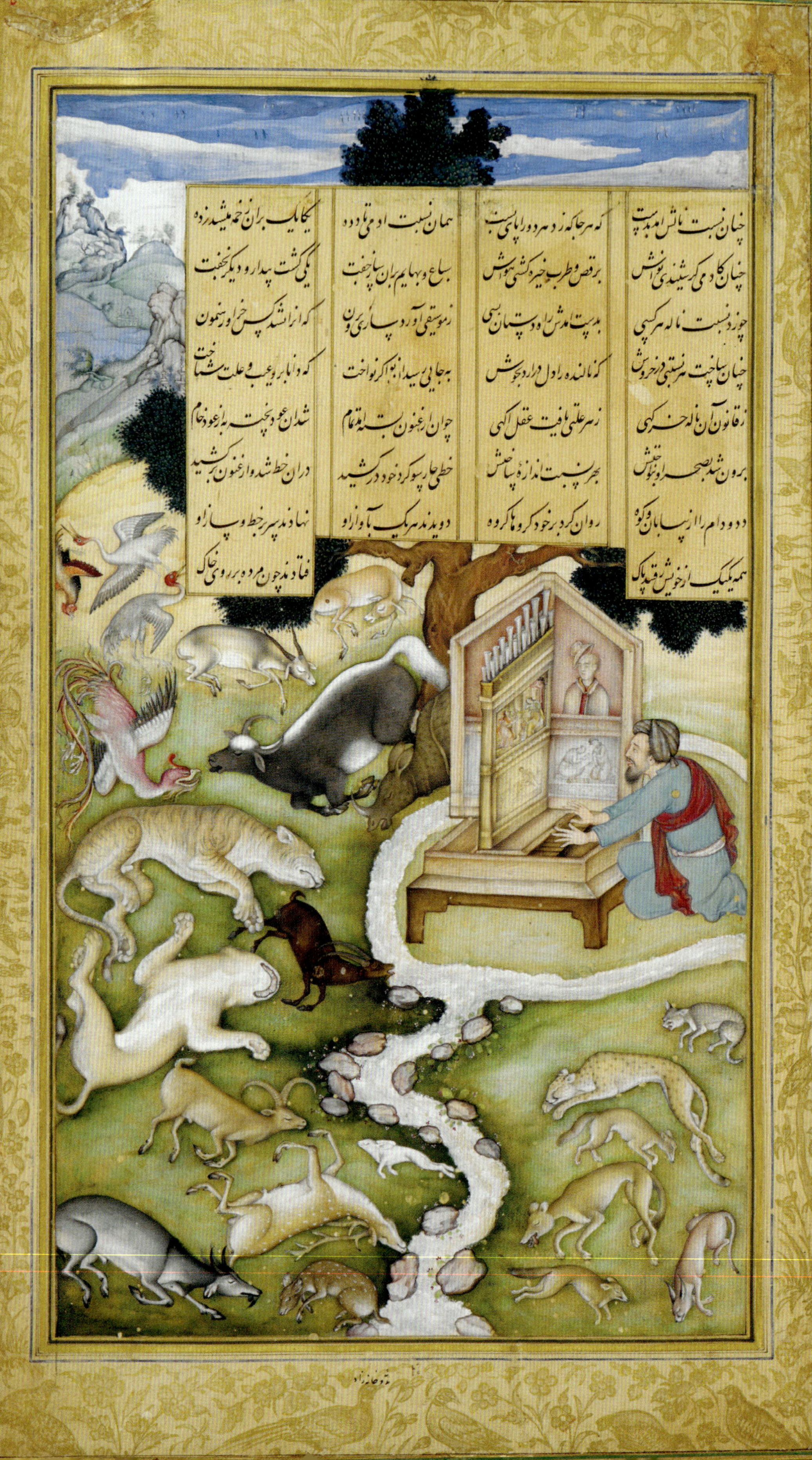

چنان نسبت نالش آمد بدست
که هر جا که زد هر دو را پای بست
چنان کادمی کز شنیدی نوایش
برقص و طرب خیره گشتی هوایش
چو زد نسبت ناله هر کسی
بدست آمدش راه دستان بسی
چنان ساخت هر نسبتی در خروش
که ماننده را دل در آرد بجوش
ز قانون آن ناله خرگهی
ز سر علتی یافت عقل آگهی
برون شد بصحرا و بنواختش
بهر نسبت اندازه بشناختش
دد و دام را از بیابان و کوه
روان کرد بر خود گروها گروه
همه یکیک از خویش رفتند پاک
همان نسبت آدمی تا دده
یکایک بران نغمه میشد زده
سباع و بهایم بران سان جفت
یکی گشت بیدار و دیگر بخفت
ز موسیقی آورد بسیاری فنون
که از انشد کس خر او رهنمون
به جایی رسید از نوا کز نواخت
که دانا بر عیب و علت شناخت
چو آن ارغنون بسته آمد تمام
شد آن عود پخته بآن عود خام
خطی چار سو گرد خود در کشید
در آن خط شد و ارغنون بر کشید
دویدند هر یک با آواز او
نهادند سر بر خط و پای او
فتادند چون مرده بر روی خاک

76. Aflatun Charms the Wild Animals with the Music of the *Arghanun*

Jonathan Katz

Maddu Khanazad
Miniature from *Khamsa of Nizami*, London, British Library, Or 12208, fol. 298r
Lahore, 1595
Manuscript on paper, 325 fols., 31.8 x 19.6 cm

The *Khamsa* (literally, *Quintet*) is a collection of five epic verse narrative tales by the great Persian poet Nizami Ganjavi. Among other Persian classics, Nizami's poems were much prized over the centuries by the educated élite of Mughal India (Parrello 2010). The British Library houses an illustrated manuscript of the *Khamsa* made for the Emperor Akbar in the capital Lahore in the mid-1590s, a work of exceptionally fine calligraphy and accompanied by paintings of superb quality judged even by the highest standards of Mughal book production (Brend 1995). The last of the five stories is a version of the *Iskandarnama*, legends of Iskandar (Alexander the Great) from among the Eastern traditions (Stoneman et al. 2012). Among the illustrations is a depiction of an apparently inspired Mughal scholar-musician playing an organ on a small island surrounded by a stream, beyond which a number of animals, all real except for one mythical *simurgh* raptor, repose in deep, even comatose slumber. The painting has attracted the attention and curiosity of art historians and musicologists (Losty and Roy 2013; Latif 2018, 135-51; Wade 1997 and 1998), and is offered here as a sample of cross-cultural imagery and fantasy in the early modern world.

In this episode of the Persian Alexander story, the king has sought the company and wisdom of distinguished sages, among whom are, anachronistically from the strictly historical Western standpoint, Aflatun (Plato) and Aristu (Aristotle). The two philosophers are rivals in prowess and learning, and in order to demonstrate his superiority Aflatun constructs and plays upon a wondrous musical instrument, an *arghanun*, described as having a gourd resonator, a skin membrane and strings. In proving the power of his music, Aflatun beguiles the wild animals, sending them at one point to sleep, and reviving their spirits and joie de vivre at another. Aristu is unable to do more on his own than put the animals to sleep, and is thus shown as Aflatun's inferior.

Clearly Nizami's text uses the word *arghanun* to mean a chordophone, but in the miniature of the British Library manuscript, painted by one Madhu or Maddu Khanazad (Losty and Roy 2013, 55), our now distinctly Mughal-looking Aflatun plays upon a Western-style portative pipe organ. As far as we can tell, the musical practices and lores of India and Europe enjoyed very limited mutual appreciation, even after Western missionaries and other settlers began to observe and record their impressions in the seventeenth century. The composer and music theorist Pietro della Valle visited both Persia and India. In his account of his travels he published, in the middle of that century, an early technical description of the double-gourd stringed *vina*, an instrument already known a little earlier, but less directly, by Marin Mersenne. Della Valle, perhaps rather untypically for his time, praised the music, observing that it was more pleasing than the "ordinary [music] of the vulgar Indians" (Bor 1988, 52ff.). More serious European engagement with Indian music came later, and the first of a number of English treatises on the subject was written by the scholar Sir William Jones in the 1780s.

Western music was hardly more familiar to most Indian listeners before the rise of the European presence in the eighteenth century, but in the longer term left its mark in the Indian adoption of certain instruments, notably from band music the violin, now a standard member in the instrumentarium particularly of South Indian (Carnatic) classical music, and from missionary use in Christian religious singing the harmonium, now used routinely in North Indian (Hindustani) classical music as well as many types of devotional and popular and folk traditions. While it can be well argued that the fixed intonation of a keyboard is inimical to the subtly flexible tuning needed in Indian music, remarkable illusions of flexibility can be achieved by skilled players, especially while accompanying singers. But it seems that the first encounters with the ancestor of the harmonium, the organ, impressed equally through the power and brilliance of the sound it could produce and the visual aesthetic appeal of the instrument.

The pneumatic organ is, indeed, not only a Western instrument in its early history, and even its origins, though most commonly held to be Greek, or more precisely Hellenistic Alexandrian, may have arisen in Egypt or Mesopotamia. In any case from the time of the earliest Muslim dynasties Greek scientific writings were sought out and translated into Arabic, and these included works on both musical theory and organology. Furthermore, actual instruments appear to have been known and used by Arabs at least as early as the first quarter of the ninth century, most likely as a result of contact with Byzantine Greek practice.

Usage was reflected in literature, both technical and lay (Farmer 1931, 21 and 54ff.). Medieval Arabic texts refer to a technical treatise by one Muristus or Murtus, a work which was probably derived from Greek sources and may in fact have been written originally much earlier by a Greek author (Owen and Williams 2014, 691). Muristus is quoted as a source not only for the construction of organs but for the beauty and force of the sound the instrument could make; among the many affective states it could induce, it could make you hear a sound "compelling sleep, for he who hears it sleeps where he stands" (Farmer 1931; Natif 2018, 141). Persian and Indian poetic sources evocatively use similar ideas, which indeed have Western classical antecedents, sometimes for the power of music in general but also specifically for what is referred to as a particular instrument. The second part of the Persian text *Akbarnama*, composed by the emperor's official court biographer Abul Fazl, is a year-by-year account of Akbar's reign. The fourth year opens with a poetic evocation of the spring season, in which "on every branch a bird made melody; with every tune the rosebud bent its head" (so translates Wheeler M. Thackston in a recent edition of the text: Abū al-Fazl ibn Mubārak 2014-18, 3:249). The Persian text does in fact refer in the first line to an instrument named as *arghanun*. There is evidence that the word was used now at least in Persian precisely for a musical instrument in which the sound was produced by the blowing of air through pipes. The Arabic word is, of course, ultimately derived from the Greek *organon* (originally no more than a contrivance or implement for "doing" something), which in earlier sources could refer to a wind-blown but also to a stringed instrument, and appears to be so used, for instance, by Plato in discussing musical modes in Book 3 (399.c.) of his *Republic*.

In Britain the Puritan reforms of the later sixteenth century led to the first of two great removals, and often the destruction, of many church organs. Before a temporary revival in the early seventeenth century, a few instruments appear to have been constructed in the 1590s (Bicknell 1996, 45ff.), and mechanical instruments including organs were sometimes included as desirable items among diplomatic gifts to foreign rulers, especially in the hope of creating or furthering trade agreements. Perhaps the most celebrated such gift was the presentation by the prominent organ-builder Thomas Dallam, on behalf of the Levant Company, of a mechanical (clockwork) instrument to the Ottoman Sultan Mehmet in 1599. To the Sultan's delight the organ was lavishly adorned with special visual and tonal effects. Dallam himself recorded these, noting for example that "[i]n the top of the organ, being 16 foot high, did stand a holly bush full of black birds and thrushes, which at the end of the music did sing and shake their wings. Divers other motions there was which the Grand Signor wondered at" (Mayes 1956; Woodfield 1990, 39-46).

Organs were already present by this time in India not only through diplomatic and other gifts but in secular musical settings and, what is less surprising, Catholic churches, with which there is evidence that Mughal dignitaries became acquainted (Natif 2018, 142ff.; Wade 1998, 154). We may therefore reasonably accept Wade's bolder translation of Abul Fazl's verse: "On every branch the birds were organists."

Returning to our painting, the iconography is striking in many ways. First, although at least one other Mughal painting of a pipe organ, and also a slightly earlier vivid contemporary Mughal description of such an instrument and its playing (Wade 1998, 153), show awareness of bellows as an integral part of the organ, and of assistants working them, the present image features the keyboard player alone, and no bellows, as is sometimes the case in European images of portative organs which may have been known to Indian scholars and artists. The focus is clearly on Plato himself and his wonder-working, but Mika Natif (Natif 2018, 141) invites us to see a little more here. Without the pumping air through the pipes there can be no sound. Rather than a "failure of verisimilitude," this organ may be "a unique article with universal powers" requiring "specific knowledge ... to make it work. Only Plato can produce music out of this 'silent' instrument, a creation that requires 'divine skill.'"

Here, anyway, is an updating, a contemporary Mughal view of Nizami's instrument and player under the combined influences of the Graeco-Arabic-Persian and the European traditions. The ecstatic pose of Aflatun is balanced by one of the images shown as painted in a panel, a European figure with a hat curiously floating above his head. There is further balancing of East and West in the other painted panels of the organ and perhaps also in the arrangement and philosophical implications of the whole main scene, which is reminiscent of depictions of Orpheus charming nature and surrounded by animals in European painting and, more directly, of Orphic-type themes originating in Greek, Jewish, and Christian sources and surviving in Islamic tradition (Losty and Roy 2013, 55; Koch 2001, 112-16).

Above the keyboard, below a Christian Annunciation, is a recognizable scene from the famous Arabic and Persian story of the lovers Layla and Majnun, here showing a standard image of Majnun, alone and emaciated, in the desert. The story is told in full by Nizami in an earlier part of the *Khamsa*, also illustrated in this manuscript by another court artist. To the right of Plato, below the man and his hat, is a painting of a European probably dictating to an Indian scribe (Natif 2018, 144; Brend 1995, 58). Is the hat perhaps raised in astounded admiration of the musician? Natif ingeniously proposes, on the other hand, that this may be a three-dimensional figure of an automaton, of a kind known from mechanical contrivances attached to instruments like the Dallam gift, in which the hat was indeed raised and lowered pneumatically with certain keyboard actions. Wade (Wade 1997, 1483) tentatively suggests a different interpretation, namely that the man and hat form a deliberately humorous image of a European.

Different critical eyes have reacted differently to the appearance of the animals in the painting; some see here a state of blissful sleep (Losty and Roy 2013; Natif 2018), others believing that for some reason they are actually dead or moribund (Wade 1997, 1484, who detects a possible element of humour), or that the images were based on dead models (Titley 1983, 205, who finds the painting "rather grim"). It would be consistent with the manner of illustration throughout the manuscript that the painting fairly, and without irony, represents Nizami's story, but the European presence in the instrument and its adornment gives an engaging sense of cosmopolitan sensitivity and sophistication.

GR
A. GRANADA.
B. ALVEISIN.
C. ALHAMBRE.
D. ANTIQVERVELA.
1. S.t Hieronymo.
2. Hospital S.t Juan.
3. Yglesia maior.
4. S.t Christoual.
5. Castillo Atobin.
6. Castillo Maior.
7. S.t Francesco
8. Palatio Real nueuo.
9. Sancta Maria.
10. Sanct Genes.
11. Puerta serrada.
12. Sancta Helena.
13. Masmoros.
14. Los martires.
15. Gannos antigos.
16. Sierra neuada.
17. Sierra del Sol.
B
A
Occidens

T A
Oriens
16
17
15
12
14
13
11
9
8
C
10
D
s Houfnaglius
LXV.

77. Granada in Georg Braun's *Civitates Orbis Terrarum*

Ascensión Mazuela-Anguita

Joris Hoefnagel, Netherlands, 1565
Engraving from Georg Braun, *Urbium praecipuarum mundi theatrum quintum*
Cologne: Peter von Brachel, n.d. [orig. 1598]
[8] + 69 (maps) + [6] fols.; 20
Washington DC, The Library of Congress, G1028 .B7 1612, vol. 5 between pp. 13 and 14
Photo © Library of Congress, Geography and Map Division

Civitates Orbis Terrarum (Cologne, 1572-1617), a six-volume world atlas that contains over 500 depictions of cities, includes a panoramic view of Granada created by the Flemish artist Joris Hoefnagel in 1565. In the foreground of the image, three women are represented making music: one plays a square frame drum, another a tambourine, while the third dances and clicks her fingers; two of them are holding rosaries. An anonymous illustration of Seville included in the same work also contains a musical scene with women dancing and playing the same percussion instruments, and a similar dance performance forms part of one of the representations of Cádiz (fig. 77.1). Hoefnagel's view of the city of San Juan de Aznalfarache, in the province of Seville, meanwhile, includes a man playing a *vihuela* for a woman equipped with a square frame drum.

Among all the hundreds of engravings that form part of Georg Braun's atlas, it is striking that the musical scenes are concentrated exclusively in Andalusian towns, and that they all include women playing small percussion instruments and dancing. In contrast, women are largely invisible in the written records that document the history of sixteenth-century Spanish music. As well as allowing musicologists to imagine the music that sounded in these scenes, of a kind generally not recorded in music notation, Hoefnagel's engravings may shed light on the role of women as transmitters of secular Spanish music—a role necessarily shaped by the moral restrictions imposed upon them in the period, related to the coexistence of different cultural traditions in Spain.

Hoefnagel, a diamond dealer, sojourned in Spain between 1564 and 1567 with the purpose of developing his commercial activities, his stay following on from a period travelling in France and concluding with a move to England. He had benefited from a humanist education and was able to play several musical instruments. The accuracy with which he illustrates musical instruments in other works, such as his illuminations in the second part of Georg Bocskay's *Mira Calligraphiae Monumenta* (Los Angeles, J. Paul Getty Museum, MS 20) or in a Roman missal in the Österreichische Nationalbibliothek (Cod. 1784), reflects his training and interest in music (Hendrix and Vignau-Wilberg 1992). Two of his three years in Spain were spent in Andalusia, as Seville was, in commercial terms, the gateway to the New World. Anton van den Wyngaerde, another celebrated topographical artist, was working in Spain at the same time under the patronage of Philip II; of the two, Hoefnagel has generally been thought the less accurate, but the more concerned with foreground scenes such as those featuring our musicians (Kagan 1986; Gil and Sánchez 1996; García Arranz 2008).

The precise circumstances of the Granada scene are not unambiguous, and several conflicting descriptions have been published in modern scholarship. According to Gámiz, a young man contemplates the dance lesson of two maidens, who dance to the sound of a tambourine played by a gypsy woman, utilising "her ancestral skills in rhythm and singing" (Gámiz 2008, 111). Mauricio Molina, meanwhile, argues that these women were members of one of the "sisterhoods of the rosary," a type of female lay association dating back to the end of the fifteenth century, dedicated to the worship of the Virgin as Mother of Christ, in which frame drums were used to accompany songs and dances (Molina 2006, 155). One wonders whether these sisterhoods and their orally transmitted musical tradition were so well-known and characteristic of Andalusia that they could have caught the attention of travellers. Scholars have also pointed to correspondences between Hoefnagel's scene and some representations of Morisco female dancers. A graffito discovered in a Morisco house in Granada depicts a woman dancing, and it has been argued that the position of her arms is similar to that of the woman illustrated by Hoefnagel (Barrera 2007). Dances of Morisco origin have usually been connected to flamenco, and it has also been argued that Hoefnagel's musical scene may represent a proto-flamenco practice (Cruces 2003, 98-99).

Indeed it is far from certain that Hoefnagel represented a real-life scene, for there is an established iconographical tradition of similar musical ensembles in the region, images which propose several further possible readings of the Granada scene. A Catalan manuscript dated ca. 1320 contains a miniature representing Miriam and the Israelite women celebrating the Exodus from Egypt; they are dancing and playing decorated square and round frame drums, cymbals, clapper, and

Figure 77.1: Anonymous depictions of Seville and Cádiz from Georg Braun, *Civitates Orbis Terrarum [liber primus]* (Cologne: Peter von Brachel, 1612; orig. 1572), fols. 2v-3r. Washington DC, Library of Congress, G1028 .B7 1612. Photo: © Library of Congress, Geography and Map Division.

lute (fig. 77.2). There is evidence of a Sephardic tradition of drum-dance leaders, named *tanyaderes*, who generally performed in an ensemble of three and were invited to play at ceremonies and celebratory occasions such as weddings (Sautter 2010, 48). In 1529 a German traveller depicted a similar scene in the nearby region of Narbonne, in the south of France, including a decorated square frame drum and a dancer clicking her fingers (fig. 77.3), their positions strikingly similar to those of Hoefnagel's Granada musicians. The trio also bear comparison to descriptions and depictions of witches: women accused of being witches by the Spanish Inquisition were said to play small percussion instruments linked to dance, and were usually represented in groups of three (Mazuela-Anguita 2015).

The attire of Hoefnagel's female dancers is also noteworthy. The women in the Granada scene wear *chapines*, a type of shoe with thick cork soles, which are emphasised in Hoefnagel's picture: the shoes of the woman on the left are exhibited in the foreground, while the dress of the woman on the right is slightly lifted so that her shoes can be clearly seen. The *chapín*, characteristic of the dress code of sixteenth-century Spanish women and exerting also a broader influence on European fashion, came from the medieval *alcorque*, a shoe design of Muslim origin (Bernis 1962, 19, 22, and 87). While Morisco women covered their heads and faces with large veils and wore wide trousers (Bass and Wunder 2009), the dress of the trio matches that of the Spanish peasants illustrated in costume books.

Another German codex, containing illustrations of European costumes and dated to the first half of the sixteenth century, presents Spanish women in the same attire, representing a strikingly similar musical trio (fig. 77.4). This scene appears alongside another showing a woman playing a square frame drum and a couple dancing, under the caption "Der Spanichs Dantz." The relationship is so close that it seems quite likely Hoefnagel modelled his Granada scene on this very codex. Although it is difficult to evaluate whether the artist had witnessed a scene similar to that he depicted or if he adopted it as a customary representation of Spanish women, the concentration of music and dance in depictions of Andalusian cities in the atlas suggests not only that this region was thought to offer the most representative example of the so-called "Spanishs Dantz," but also that women played a defining role in these oral musical practices.

Füssel has observed that Georg Braun's atlas "maintains a constant awareness of the impact of religion on urban culture" (Braun and Hogenberg 2008, 7), a concern exemplified by the prominent inclusion of rosaries in Hoefnagel's Granada dance scene. European travellers must have identified Spanish culture with the distinctive combination of Muslim and

Figure 77.2: Detail from *Golden Haggadah*, Catalonia, ca. 1320. London, British Library, Add MS 27210, fol. 15r. Photo © British Library Board - All Rights Reserved / Bridgeman Images.

Figure 77.3: Illustration from Christoph Weiditz, *Trachtenbuch*, ca. 1530-40. Nürnberg, Germanisches Nationalmuseum, Hs. 22474, p. 92. Photo courtesy of the Germanisches Nationalmuseum.

Figure 77.4: *In Spania die Medlach* from [*Costume Codex*], 16th c. Madrid, Biblioteca Nacional de España, MS Res/285, fol. 3v. Photo © Biblioteca Nacional de España / CC BY 4.0.

Christian elements. The widely-attested link between square frame drums and women in medieval Spain is found across Christian, Muslim, and Jewish communities (Doubleday 1999; Cohen 2008). It might be that the manner of dance and musical performance used by these Andalusian women was presumed by contemporaries to be of Muslim origin. If that is the case, we could conclude that dance scenes were attached to Andalusian cities in *Civitates Orbis Terrarum* as emblems of the region's Muslim heritage, as it was understood by cosmopolitan European travellers.

The dance music of the Moriscos in the Kingdom of Granada was known as *zambra*, and female dancers played an important role in its practice (Carrasco and Vicent 1987, 69). Over the course of the first half of the sixteenth century, through to the expulsion of the Moriscos in 1568 following their revolution against the Christian government, the mingled Christian, Muslim, and Jewish Andalusian culture underwent a re-orientation towards the culture of Christian Castile. Islamic musical traditions preserved in Granada were transformed into Christian ones, although simultaneously some aspects of a continuing Muslim musical culture were tolerated (Fernández 2012, 232-33; Castillo 2016, 318-22; Ruiz 2019). Hoefnagel's drawing of Granada coincides with the end of that period of transition. In 1567 Morisco music was officially prohibited in Granada, only two years after Hoefnagel drew his depiction. Drumming and dancing performed by women was also a part of the Sephardic heritage of the region, but in contrast with court dance and the Morisco *zambra*, Jewish women's dancing was associated with the celebration of religious events and thus presumably carried spiritual meaning (Sautter 2010, 49). It is difficult to establish whether the Granada scene represents a dance in the Morisco manner, or a tradition of ritual celebrations related to Sephardic history.

The European fondness for the Moorish as an exotic Other is demonstrated by the popularity of the *morisca*, a court dance with a choreography widely disseminated in Europe (Arbeau 1588; Aranda 1978; Reyna 1981; Nocilli 2007, 598-99; see also exhibit 69). At the same time, numerous travel accounts report memorable encounters with a distinctive Morisco dance tradition in Iberia. Almost a quarter of Hieronymus Münzer's account of his travels through Spain and Portugal is devoted to his visit to Granada in 1494 (Münzer 1987, 12); he commented extensively on the Morisco culture and, in addition to this, he describes in particular an entertainment of music and dance "in the Morisco manner" arranged for him by a group of German merchants in Barcelona (García Mercadal 1952-62, 332). Johannes Lange, meanwhile, wrote of his visit to the Alhambra gardens in 1526 in the suite of Charles V in order to attend a dance performed by Morisco women. According to his account, the women danced "in the manner of their country" to the sound of lutes and drums played by other women, who were approximately 50 years old; a 40-year-old woman sang with an unpleasant and rough voice and clicked her fingers (Fernández 2012, 232-33). In 1603, Bartolomé Joly described another dance performance in the Morisco manner: Moorish men dressed in rich jewellery danced to the sound of a large guitar; then three or four men and six women joined them dancing, clicking their fingers and playing castanets (Navarro 1993, 14-15). Such accounts, emphasising the Otherness born of viewing Andalusia's Muslim heritage from a Christian perspective, can be seen as written equivalents to the repetition of foreground musical scenes in the Andalusian cityscapes of Georg Braun's atlas.

The association of dance music and festive occasions with female percussion players and the Muslim or Sephardic heritage made these female musical practices problematic as regards religious orthodoxy and moral rectitude, from the perspective of the Christian authorities (Ramos 2015, 419). The fact that the women in the drawings are holding or wearing rosaries is striking, as if their honesty and their Christianity both required visual clarification. In comparable earlier drawings—such as the German costume books mentioned above—rosaries do not appear, suggesting that the expulsion of the Moriscos from Granada in 1568 necessitated an unambiguous Christianisation of this musical practice.

It seems clear that the so-called "Spanish dance" and its music was particularly practised by women, and grew out of the melting pot of cultures which still persists in Spanish folk music. A close reading of the Granada scene allows us to assess the importance attributed to female musical activities in sixteenth-century Spain, by European travellers such as Hoefnagel, and also by the authors of the German costume albums. The weight of evidence provided by images and anecdotal accounts provides compelling witness to the importance of oral traditions in establishing women's place on the map of music history. While the musical historiography of Renaissance Spain has focused on grandiose polyphony created by male composers, this iconography administers to us much-needed "doses of cultural shock" (Darnton 1984, 4), a corrective that may help point music historians down new paths.

ADDITIONAL REFERENCES: Bouza 1995; Casado et al. 2016; Cortés 2018; Fernández 1985; Forney 1989; Gil and Sánchez 2003; Goss 1992; Miller 2003; Molina 2010; Vignau-Wilberg 2017.

Newe Zeyttung/auß der Insel Japonien.

Retract vnd Contrafähung der vier Jüngling vnd Königklichen Gesandten auß Japon/wie sie zu Mayland den 25. Julij ankommen/vnd den 3. Augusti von dannen wider verruckt.

COntrafähung der vier Jüngling vnd Gesandten auß Japon/mit namen Mancius/Julianus/Martinus/vnd Michael/so den 23. Martij des 1585. Jars/im Namen vnd an stat Francisci Königs in Bungen/Prothasij Königs in Arimania/vnnd Bartholomei Hertzogs zu Omura zu Rom sich Bäpstlicher Hayligkeit/beneben der heyligen Kirchen Gottes vnderworffen. Vnd nach dem sie Neaples/Venedig/vnd Mayland besucht/durch Hispanien wider haimbwartz gezogen sein/sampt einem Priester der Societet IESV, P. N. Meschita genañt/der sie im Christlichen Glauben vnderwisen/vnd die drey Jar/so sie auß Japon biß gehn Rom/auff Wasser vnd Landt jhr Raiß zugebracht/das gelayt geben. Deren die zwen ersten auß Fürstlichem Geschlecht von Omura/die andern zwen sonst von hohem vnd sehr Altem Adel geborn. Alle vier aber von Natur/wie es jr Lands art mit bringt/gar Siñreiche/Hochuerstendige/vnd vber die maß wolkündige Leüt/Wie an mehr ortten von jrer Nation in gemein/vnd von disen vier sonderbar geschriben wirdt.

Getruckt zu Augspurg/durch
Michael Manger.

Anno, M. D. LXXXVI.

天正遣欧使節肖像画

昭和二七年十二月十一日
濱田稔氏寄贈

78. News from the Island of Japan

Kathryn Bosi

Newe Zeyttung aus der Insel Japonien. Retract und Contrafähung der vier Jüngling und Königklichen Gesandten aus Japon wie sie zu Mayland den 25. Julij ankommen und den 3. Augusti von dannen wider verruckt
Augsburg: Michael Manger, 1586
Broadsheet, 31 x 38 cm
University of Kyôto Library, 5-6 N 18*
Photo courtesy of the Main Library, University of Kyôto

This print, entitled *News from the island of Japan. Portrait and description of four young princely ambassadors who arrived in Milan on 25 July and departed on 3 August* and issued in Augsburg by Michael Manger in 1586, shows four Japanese youths of noble birth—Mancio Itō, Michele Chijiwa, Martino Hara, and Giuliano Nakaura—with their Jesuit tutor and guardian, Diego de Mesquita, who in August 1584 disembarked from the ship *Santiago* in the port of Lisbon, after a voyage from Japan which had lasted some two years and six months. Converted to Christianity, along with their families, by Jesuit missionaries in Japan, and students of the Jesuit seminary of Arima, they had been sent as an embassy to bring the pope in Rome the homage of three Christian *daimyō* (warlords) of Japan, but also to witness in person the power and splendour of the Christian church in Europe, in order to be able to take back first-hand accounts to their homeland. The Jesuit missionary Alessandro Valignano, who conceived this remarkable diplomatic manoeuvre, chose boys of a tender age, because their youth would enable them to better stand the hardships of a long, tedious, and dangerous journey, while at the same time they would be particularly susceptible to the "wonders of Europe," and would be long-living testimonies to those marvels once returned. Valignano hoped that the "ambasceria" would also raise financial support for the Jesuit missions in Japan, which were under-staffed, and under-financed. This aim was realised: both ecclesiastical and temporal authorities showered the boys with gifts, and the pope, along with others, pledged generous financial support for the missions (Gualtieri 1586).

Fortunately for posterity, a detailed account of their European tour was published by Guido Gualtieri in 1586: the *Relationi della venuta degli ambasciatori giaponesi* [sic] *a Roma fino alla partita di Lisbona* (*Report of the arrival of the Japanese ambassadors in Rome up to their departure to Lisbon*). Other significant sources of information can be found in Valignano's *De missione* ([Valignano] 1590), based on the youths' diaries and translated into Latin by Eduardo de Sande, and a manuscript *Tratado* compiled by the Jesuit Father Luís Fróis, again based on the notes of the voyagers ([Fróis] 1942). These three sources contain a vast amount of information about the triumphal progress of the four youths from Portugal to Spain and Italy, then back to Portugal, whence they departed for Japan. Some of the documentation regarding musical events raises questions for the attentive reader. We are told by Fróis, for example, that in the city of Évora, on their way to Spain, two of the delegates—Mancio and Michele—played the splendid organ of the cathedral for a large audience, to the wonder and satisfaction of the archbishop and all those present ([Fróis] 1942, 42-44). A report on their arrival in Italy published in Venice in 1585 informs us that "they know how to play the harpsichord, the guitar and the lira, and they keep these instruments in their rooms" (*Relatione degli honori* 1585).

We know from documents that the Japanese youths had learned to play the organ and a variety of other European instruments, and also that they showed a close interest in an innovative European keyboard instrument they encountered during their visit, of which they left a very detailed description ([Fróis]1942, 139; *De missione* 1590, 230). Annual letters from Jesuit missionaries in Japan to their superiors in Rome have left a great deal of information about the teaching of European music to Japanese youths within Jesuit seminaries in Japan in the second half of the sixteenth century. European music was appreciated by the Japanese, and was regarded by the Jesuit missionaries as a valuable tool for conversion to the Christian faith (see also exhibit 45). One such missionary, Padre Organtino, writes in a letter dated 29 September 1577 from Japan, to Padre Magliano, "Preposito Generale della Compagnia di Giesu" in Rome, that

> we know from our experience ... that with the ceremonies ... of the divine cult as carried out in our church, millions of them will be converted. And if we use organs and other musical instruments with singers ... without doubt all this Miaco [Kyoto] and Sacai [Osaka] will be converted within a year, and these are the two principal cities of Japan (Rome, Archivum Romanum Societatis Iesu, Ital. K.8 I, 178-79).

The boys reached Macau on 9 March 1582, where they were delayed by unfavourable winds for ten months. Michele, in one of the dialogues of the *De Missione*, tells us that "what with the various proper things to do, reading, writing, playing musical instruments, and so on, our time was not wasted" (*Japanese travellers* 2012, 57). Similarly, the boys were delayed for another eight months in Cochin while again waiting for favourable winds, and here, Gualtieri recounts, they put their time to good use in studying Latin, and European instrumental and vocal music "as a pleasant way of passing the time, but also because European music is greatly esteemed in Japan" (Gualtieri 1586, 43). The boys finally reached their European destination in August 1584.

In published descriptions of the embassy's travels in Europe there are constant references to "buonissima musica" welcoming them throughout Portugal, Spain, and Italy, and it is clear from accounts of their reception in the various towns and cities of Europe that music always played an important part in the celebrations. Their arrival in towns and cities was heralded by the sounds of trumpets, drums, church bells, and artillery fire, and on many an occasion, a solemn *Te Deum* in the local cathedral (Gualteri 1586). Visits to abbeys and cathedrals called for "suono d'organo" and "soavissima musica." There is one outstanding report which confirms the boys' keen interest in European music. In Florence ([Fróis] 1942, 137-81), or in Cardinal Gambara's villa at Bagnaia (*De missione* 1586, 230-31)—reports differ, but most probably the latter—they heard an ingenious keyboard instrument called a "clavicymbalum," made by a Venetian, which could reproduce the sound of a variety of instruments. It was clearly a *claviorgano*, since it is documented that "the covers for the holes" for taking in the air were so disposed that with a slight shift of the same, the sounds and voices of different instruments could be heard: "the cithera, the lyra, the organ, the pipes ... trumpets ... harp, lute, mandolin, psalterium or any other instrument you may like ... whether you want to hear many sounds at the same time, or this or that single sound, you can obtain it with a minimum of effort." There was a second entity: a central water tank, with receptacles attached to its sides, which opened up if one called up the "bellicose sound" by action of the air, and triremes came out to do battle, trumpets sounded, and catapults were released (*Japanese travellers* 2012, 270-71). The use of such elaborate mechanical instruments to prompt wonder in international diplomatic contexts is quite widely documented in the period (see exhibit 76).

After the embassy's reception in Rome, and the prolonged festivities for their reception in that city, the long trip north which the boys undertook was enlivened by celebrations in the numerous cities that they passed through: bells, organs, and trumpets heralded their arrival, banquets accompanied by music were given in their honour, a motet was specifically written for their arrival in Perugia, a splendid Mass for three choirs performed in Venice (thought to be by Andrea Gabrieli; much later, Sansovino [Sansovino 1663] would even increase its magnificence, referring—certainly wrongly—to a Mass for four choirs) followed by an extraordinary procession in their honour (*Relazione degli honori* 1585), chamber concerts performed in their honour in Ferrara (Ianello 2012), Vicenza, Verona, and Mantua (Bosi 2016), and solemn Masses heard everywhere (Gualtieri 1586). The boys at last set sail for Spain from the port of Genoa on 9 August 1585, to the valedictory sound of trumpets and artillery fire, "taking with them the affection and universal applause of the whole of Italy and leaving behind perpetual memory of their virtue and nobility of spirit," as Gualtieri tells us (Gualtieri 1586, 150).

During their return journey through Spain, the boys were received in Alcalà by Ascanio Colonna, who presented them with a harpsichord decorated with mother of pearl which he had imported from Rome: an object of great value, which indicates that the youths' ability to play the harpsichord was already well known to him (*Japanese travellers* 2012, 303-04). Moreover, Fróis says ([Fróis] 1942, 53) that when the boys were staying in Vila Vicosa shortly afterwards, the duke of Bragança sent harpsichords and "viole da gamba" to their rooms, and everyone admired their performance on these instruments ([Fróis] 1942, 53). And we are told that the boys put their long journey home to good use by practising on the harp, lute, clavier, and rebec (Waterhouse 1997, 336). While delayed in Macau for almost a year by unfavourable winds, and a newly unfavourable climate for Christianity in Japan, they are said to have continued their studies and practiced assiduously on their musical instruments. The "ambasceria" played in a church in Macau on the evening of the Circumcision (6 January) to a receptive public (Cooper 2005, 158).

The four boys returned to their homes after all of eight years and five months of travel. They brought back with them experiences and acquired abilities which their tutors certainly hoped would impress and amaze those at home. Their tutors were eager to report how their ability to play European instruments in consort caused wonder and admiration. In a Jesuit letter sent back to Rome shortly after their arrival home, we can read that:

> The Japanese take great pleasure in seeing and hearing such a variety of musical instruments that these Lords have brought back from Europe, and they remain enchanted by their melody, and amazed by the harmony and consonance of so many instruments tuned together. And they confess that our music is much more sweet and pleasing than they had previously supposed (*Copia di due lettere* 1593, 56).

This purposefully optimistic assessment of the appreciation of European music among the Japanese is nuanced by other accounts, including one discussed below. Alessandro Valignano had joined the boys in Goa and accompanied them back to Japan: with caution, since the country was now practically unified under the ruler Hideyoshi, known to be unfavourable towards the Christian religion. Wishing to present the four youths to the ruler, Valignano requested a meeting in his role of ambassador of the Governor General of the Portuguese Indies and was granted an audience. They were received with ceremony and kindness, and we read that after a banquet,

> The tables were removed, and returning to the place where the Padre had remained, they called the four Japanese youths so as to hear the music which they had learnt in Europe, and a gravi cembalo [harpsichord], a harpeleuto [almost certainly an error for a harp and lute] and a ribeca being immediately brought forth, they began to play with such grace that Quabacondono, having heard the sweetness of this music, made them repeat it three times. Then, taking up the instruments into his own hands, he asked questions about each of them. And he said, in conclusion, that he was most proud that they were Japanese (Fróis 1595, 46).

On their return to Japan, the boys entered the Jesuit novitiate in July 1591. They seem to have immediately assumed the role of music teachers—and exceedingly efficient ones at that, for we can read later in the same publication, where the author, speaking of one of the seminaries, writes:

> I here send word to Your Paternity of the great expectations and hopes that the pupils of the Seminary bring us ... With the arrival of these four Japanese lords, who are now our Brothers, they have immediately understood and learnt how to play, with great facility, a number of instruments, so that soon they have played in consort a music as fine and consonant as do those who have studied in Europe. And moreover, since our music seems to them dissonant in comparison to their own, as in fact their own seems to us, they apply themselves nonetheless to playing harpsichords and similar instruments with great gusto, and they warmly appreciate the use of organs within the rites of our church. (Fróis 1595, 148).

Although he evidently favours European music and instruments, Valignano here offers an interesting—and modern—comparison of the mutual difficulties of Japanese and European cultures in appreciating each other's music.

With the turn against Christianity in Japan, the teaching of European music ceased, and this chapter of Japan's musical history drew to a close. Of the four youthful ambassadors, Mancio died young, Martino went into exile in Macau, where he lived out his life as a priest, Michele abandoned his Christian faith, and Giuliano, who remained Christian, was executed for this reason in 1633 (Cooper 2005, 185-92).

Manger's print is based on a manuscript containing portraits and descriptions of the four youths and their tutor produced in Milan by Urbano Monte while they were resident there in late July 1585. Manger's version, issued in Augsburg one year later, is just one of some 80 surviving publications regarding the legation issued during or shortly after their European visit. All of 49 were issued in 1585 alone (Boscaro 1973), indicating the enormous interest that the visit of the *ambasaceria* aroused in Europe.

Additional references: Boscaro 1965; Boscaro 1973; Boscaro 1987; Bosi 2021; Brown 1994; Gutierrez 1938; Guzmán 1601; Harich-Schneider 1973; Lach 1965; Massarella 2013; Moran 2001; Morena 2012; Ng 2015/16; Pasio 1604; Pinto 1943; *Relatione degli honori* 1585; *Relatione del viaggio* 1585; Schütte 1980-85; Valignano 1946.

VII

Experts

Introduction: The Room of Experts

Jessie Ann Owens

Going into the Room of Experts takes us into a complicated nexus of lives lived, of craft learned, and of music seen and heard.

Whose lives do we encounter in this room? For one, a certain John Dunstaple (Colton). Or rather, a plethora of John Dunstaples, including one who was an esquire and one a gentleman. One died in 1459, and one just disappeared from sight. But what about the John Dunstaple known to us as the great English composer and thought to have died in 1453? Maybe more excerpts from wills used for tracing ownership of property will someday sort out these John Dunstaples.

For another, a German singer and composer, Ludwig Senfl (Lodes). Just when *Komponist* was becoming a title and an identity and a profession, we find our musician commissioning no fewer than four portrait medals of himself. A composer with a face, and with the visual trappings with which he wanted to be remembered.

And an Italian musician working at the court of Ferrara (Blackburn). Another legal document, this one from a pay register, takes us into the complicated bureaucracy of court finances. Cloth given to a musician for livery needed for a trip to Hungary accompanying the duke's second son turned out to be not a provision but a debt. Zampolo dalla Viola's supplication speaks volumes about the life of this musician and expert mask-maker.

But how do we know what we know about music? We turn to experts, like the anonymous author of the Muburak Shah Commentary, written about 1450, and preserved in a seventeenth-century copy (Levenberg). Admire the ingenious triangle that can explain the relationship between any two numbers. Did this diagram from a treatise written in Arabic find its way into European music theory?

Marvel at the accomplishment of an expert who could define an entire canon of writing about music. Humanist Cardinal Bessarion, whose library became the foundation of the Biblioteca Marciana in Venice, commissioned the copying of an elegant parchment manuscript that preserves virtually the entire corpus of Greek musical thought (Rocconi).

Notice the stark binary between the clothed and naked women in Titian's allegory, *Sacred and Profane Love*. Just as it was far harder, presumably, to paint a nude, so too it was far harder to compose good polyphony for just two voices than for four or five voices. Or, as two Italian experts, Vicentino and Tigrini, put it, compositions for two voices were naked (Cascelli).

And how sweet to find an expert—university professor and scholar of ancient Greek Martin Crusius—who treasured a music theory book from his own years as a student, writing in it, and eventually using it to teach his own nephew (Groote).

But now, as you look around the rest of the room, focus on the music itself, as embodied in printed and manuscript sources, and imagine the gaze of the viewer. This Room of Experts demands expertise and appreciation from those who read and perform. How else could you negotiate a six-voice composition using three texts in two languages notated on a single large sheet of paper? Imagine Johannes Gryll a Gryllova, newly appointed mayor in Rakovnik (Czeckia), commissioning a composition based on the crab (in Czeck, *Rak*, and thus an emblem for the city): it took an expert (or an expert and five expert friends) to make sense of the complex imagery and to appreciate the message of a world going backwards (Schiltz).

You could get overwhelmed by the Cancionero Musical de Palacio with its 458 compositions. But zoom in on Juan del Encina's *Gasajémonos de huzia* (ignore the later addition, *Vida y alma*). Step into the world in which this piece lived, as part of an *égloga*, a pastoral play, presented before the duke and duchess of Alba in their Alba de Tormes palace in Salamanca in 1496 in a room just like the one you see. How odd that the message of this text, performed by the composer and three other singers—"Let's enjoy with confidence, that sorrow comes without looking for it"—should be just as pessimistic in its way as Gryll's crab canon (Ros-Fábregas).

Or imagine the pleasure and pride Philip, king of Castile, took at seeing and hearing his name in a Mass by Josquin, found in a luxurious choirbook (Borghetti). No matter that this is a second-hand Mass, dedicated originally to "Hercules dux Ferrarie." Who cares if the vowels in the new name "Philippus rex Castilie" no longer match the notes: a king needs to be celebrated in the sounds of the Mass, his name trumpeted in the Tenor, and given in red letters for all to admire.

Sounds. Everything in this room is about sound but everything is silent. How does a singer make a sound? Explore a treatise from 1601, *Anatomical History of the Organs of Voice and Hearing*, and know that in that very year the renowned singer and composer, Jacopo Peri, published his setting of

Rinuccini's libretto about Orpheus and Euridice (Wistreich). This "play in music," arguably the first opera, attempts to capture the sound of the human voice in notation. Alas, "an image of the dissected human larynx is no more able to shed much light on how any of this may have manifested in sound than is a page of notation."

Omnibus Christi fidelibus etc Philippus Straye de Com Hertf salutem etc. Cum
Philippus Tyrell de Com Essex ar per cartam suam feoffamenti cuius
dat est apud le Herne ultimo die Januarii anno R Henrici Sexti
post conquestum Quarto dederit etc Humfrido comiti Stafford Philippo Hotoft
Ledbite Philippo et Thome Horne Manerium de Bradfeld etc habendum etc
ipsis heredibus et assignatis suis imperpetuum et nominavit me prefat
Philippum Straye in eadem carta feoffamenti prout etc. Quod vero
Manerium etc Philippus Clerk senior civis et grocerus London et Thomas
Clerk filius eius die confeccionis presencium eis heredibus et assignatis suis
imperpetuum in eorum plena et pacifica possessione ex dono et
feoffamento Philippi Clerk sen et Ludeley et Elizabeth uxoris eius
et Philippi Hyngleston de ch Nevell prout per quandam cartam eis
inde confect liquet manifeste. Noveritis me prefat Philippum Straye
nunquam aliquid in Manerio predicto etc clamasse sed omnino disclamasse
aliquid habuisse in manerio predicto etc virtute seu colore predicte carte
feoffamenti predicti Philippi Tyrell sic prefat comiti Stafford et
aliis fact. in qua quidem carta etc. predictus nominatus fui.
Excepto et reservato michi dicto Philippo Straye heredibus et assignatis
meis imperpetuum iure meo de et in omnibus redditibus et serviciis ab
antiquo debitis de terra vocata Symondescroft et terra vocata
Kyngesgate ad dominium manerii de Cattes pertinentibus. Necnon de et in
omnibus redditibus et serviciis ab antiquo provenientibus de tenementis
prati vocati Creyesmede ad dominium manerii de Ins... pertinentibus
Et etiam excepto et reservato imperpetuum iure meo quod habeo in predictis
Symondescroft et terra vocata Kyngesgate ac in predicto
prato vocato Creyesmede unde predictus redditus etc. Et ulterius noveritis
quidem Symondescroft etc sunt parcelle predicti Manerii de Bradfeld
noveritis me prefat Philippum Straye statum et possessionem
predictis Philippo Clerk seniori et Thome Clerk de et in predicto manerio
de Bradfeld etc excepto preexcepto approbasse ratificasse et
tenore presencium in omnibus confirmasse. Preterea remisisse etc
prefat Philippo Clerk seniori et Thome Clerk heredibus et eorum assignatis
imperpetuum totum statum meum ius clameum possessionem et
demandam que unquam habui etc. Excepto superius excepto etc
In cuius rei testimonium etc. Dat xxvj die mensis Julii
anno R Henrici Sexti post conquestum quinto.

Hec est ultima voluntas mei Philippi Dunstaple ad presentes facta apud
Bradfeld in Com Hertf xxvj die mensis Julii anno domini Millesimo
quadringentesimo quinquagesimo nono et anno R Henrici
Sexti post conquestum xxxvij. Quoad disposicionem omnium et singulorum
maneriorum terrarum et tenementorum meorum cum pertinentiis ubicumque infra regnum
Anglie existencium in quibus diversi persone ad usum meum ex mandato
feoffati existunt. videlicet
In primis volo quod dicti feoffati mei incontinenter post decessum

meum permittant et faciant Margaretam uxorem meam percipere et
habere ad totam vitam suam absque impeticione calumpnia seu
implacitacione vasti ... reddituum et proficuorum provenientium
de omnibus illis maneriis terris et tenementis meis cum pertinentiis que habeo tam
in Com Hertf quam Essex Que quidem vero maneria terre et
tenementa predicta cum pertinentiis predicta Margareta tenet ad terminum vite
sue coniunctim cum aliis personis ad meam denominacionem. Et insuper
volo quod eadem Margareta uxor mea incontinenter post decessum
meum si per eam ad hoc faciendum dicti feoffati requisiti fuerint
habeat solam seisinam et possessionem omnium et singulorum predictorum
maneriorum terrarum et tenementorum meorum cum pertinentiis in predictis Com
Hertf et Essex Tenendum eadem Margarete et assignatis suis
ad totam vitam suam et executoribus suis per unum annum integrum
ultra absque impeticione calumpnia seu implacitacione vasti
Ita quod post decessum eiusdem Margarete et post dictum annum ultra
volo quod feoffati mei predicti inde per cartam indentatam faciant statum
Margarete filie mee habendum et tenendum sibi et heredibus de
corpore suo per Ricardum Hatfeld ad virum suum legitime procreatis
Et si contingat prefat Margaretam filiam meam sine heredibus
de corpore suo per predictum Ricardum virum suum legitime procreatis
obire tunc omnia predicta maneria terre et tenementa cum pertinentiis integre
remaneant eidem Margarete filie mee et heredibus de corpore
suo legitime procreatis. Et si contingat ipsam Margaretam filiam
meam sine heredibus de corpore suo legitime procreatis obire tunc
volo quod omnia tenementa que habeo in Com Essex per executores et feoffatos
meos vendantur. Et quod pecunia ex huiusmodi vendicione percepta
inter Abbatem Monasterii de Stratford Langthorne et Priorissam
Prioratus de Stratford atte Bowe per discrecionem executorum
meorum equaliter participetur et distribuatur etc.

Hec est finalis concordia facta in curia domini Regis apud Westmonasterium
a die sancti Johannis Baptiste in xv dies anno regnorum Henrici Regis
Anglie et Francie Septimi a conquestu quinto etc inter Henricum
Gmarre? civem et pannarium London et Magdalenam uxorem
eius querentes et Thomam Hatfeld gen et Elizabeth uxorem
eius deforciantes de Manerio de Bradfeld etc unde placitum etc
Scilicet quod predicti Thomas et Elizabeth recognoverunt predictum Manerium etc
esse ius ipsius Henrici et illa remiserunt etc de ipsis Thoma
et Elizabeth et heredibus ipsius Thome predictis Henrico et Magdalene
et heredibus ipsius Henrici imperpetuum. Et etc.

Omnibus Christi fidelibus etc Philippus Stayrtwart de Mylenale in Com
Suff ... Husbondman etc Senior Ricardus Wolaplede vicarius ecclesie
de Stepilmordon et Philippus Enterty per quandam cartam suam
cuius dat est apud Bradfeld xxvj die Marcii anno R Henrici
Sexti post conquestum xxxvij dimiserunt etc Philippo Dunstaple armigero
et Margarete uxori eius Ricardo Orty et predicto Henrico Wellis
Manerium de Bradfeld etc habendum et tenendum predictum Manerium
etc prefat Philippo Dunstaple et Margarete uxori eius Ricardo et

79. Will of John Dunstaple, Esquire

Lisa Colton

16th-century copies of deeds relating to manor of Broadfield, Hertfordshire
Will dated 1 July 1459
Hertford, Hertfordshire Archives and Local Studies, MS DE / Z120 / 44505

English music from before the Tudor period largely lacks attribution to named composers in surviving choirbooks, and, with very few exceptions, the biographies of those who wrote and performed such music are poorly documented. A significant opportunity therefore lies in the preservation of a series of extracts copied from deeds that include relevant parts of the will of John Dunstaple (d. 1459), compiled during the reign of Henry VII. A composer of this name is well known from diverse manuscripts containing sacred choral music, and from music-related writings of the fifteenth century, and so the Hertfordshire will may provide information about a successful English composer at the end of his life.

The sixteenth-century manuscript, containing copies of deeds associated with land and property in Hertfordshire, was not noticed by music historians until recently (Colton 2017). The document contains items that name Dunstaple, his wife, and their associates, as joint owners of a large manor; Dunstaple's part of Broadfield manor was granted to him by Richard Whaplode, vicar of the parish church at Steeple Morden in Cambridgeshire, on 16 March 1449. Dunstaple had been made tenant-in-chief of the manor of Brewis, Steeple Morden, by the Crown in 1435, and this is probably how he came to know Whaplode. The College of Arms preserves a late fifteenth-century record of John Dunstaple of Cambridgeshire's official arms, "sable chevron ermine between three staples argent," effectively a chevron surrounded by three distinctive "staples" that offer a pun on his surname (MS 10, fol. 113r).

John Dunstaple, his wife Margaret, priest Henry Wells, and Ralph Grey jointly held the manor at Broadfield, and the Dunstaples' portion of the estate remained in their family for two generations, eventually passing to John Dunstaple's grandson Thomas Hatfield (Colton 2017, 101). Grey's stepson, Richard Hatfield, was the first husband of John and Margaret's eldest daughter, Margaret. Wells was employed as the private chaplain to John Dunstaple and prominent London mercers (including London mayor and his wife, Sir Hugh and Dame Alice Wiche). Wells spent his later years in London as a well-paid chantry priest at the church of St Dionis, Backchurch. The joint ownership of Broadfield manor reflected the on-going personal and professional relationships of Whaplode, John and Margaret Dunstaple, Grey, and Wells.

The most significant aspect of the will and other documents recorded in the sixteenth-century source is the opportunity to connect their contents to the biography of well-known English composer John Dunstaple. The composer was active in the first half of the fifteenth century, producing a large body of devotional music (Bent 1981). Composer John Dunstaple's music was widely championed in the 1400s by international writers, who credited him as a propagator of heavenly polyphonic English song, a *contenance angloise* that apparently inspired continental musicians such as Guillaume Du Fay and Gilles Binchois.

Before the discovery of the will of this land-owning John Dunstaple (d. 1459), archival work by Judith Stell and Andrew Wathey had suggested that the composer was identified with an eponymous John Dunstaple of Cambridgeshire (Stell and Wathey 1981; Wathey 1985), certainly the same individual. The answer cannot be so simple, however. One piece of evidence presents what may be an insurmountable stumbling block. The gazetteer of London wards made by John Stow in 1598 recorded a posthumous monument to the composer in the church of St Stephen, Walbrook. In Anthony Munday's expanded edition (1618), the epitaph to John Dunstaple was recorded, albeit with some minor inaccuracies, as he read it from two inscriptions in the chancel of the church. The Latin lines present a florid paean of praise for the composer's astrological and musical skills, and explicitly name 24 December 1453 as his date of death. The authenticity of Munday's account is confirmed by a second, well-known epitaph in memory of the composer, as penned by John Whethamstede. Whethamstede's epitaph alludes to Dunstaple's motet *Preco preheminencie*, suggesting that he knew this work in addition to Dunstaple's *Albanus roseo rutilat*, a motet in honour of the Abbey's patron saint. The authors of the epitaphs were familiar with John Dunstaple's musical and astrological expertise.

We have, then, John Dunstaple the composer, who died in 1453, and John Dunstaple the landowner, who died in 1459. Why might the dates disagree? The most obvious reason for such a contradiction would be that the composer was not the same man as the landowner with whom he shared his name.

After all, nothing in the remaining portions of the will mentions music, and the name John Dunstaple was not uncommon, comprising a place-based surname and one of the most common forenames. It seems impossible to reconcile the specific details of the epitaph's date with any other reading than 1453, albeit we have this record only from Stow and Munday's edition, one that sometimes made basic factual errors as to the placement or date of monuments (Stow and Munday 1618). To add a further complication, two John Dunstaples are found side-by-side in property records from London in 1445: one is demonstrably the landowner, since he is styled "John Dunstaple, esquire, of Steeple Morden, Cambridgeshire" with his wife Margaret Dunstaple, but a second man is styled "John Dunstaple, gentleman." Although John Dunstaple "gentleman" thereafter disappears from the historical record, his title suggests that he was a younger or less wealthy relative of the same family. Could this other man be the composer? Or might one of the other men of that name, which crop up in various locations, be the musician (Colton 2017, 153-62)?

Arguably, one of the men in the London documents is likely to be the musician, a proposition considerably strengthened by the third male owner named on the London property records. He is William Trukyll (or Trokyll), clerk and then rector of St Stephen's, Walbrook from 1440 until his death in 1474. Trukyll was a member of the Fraternity of St Nicholas, the guild of London parish clerks, from at least 1449; he co-owned further properties in the Walbrook ward with Robert Whittingham, who had presented him to the post as rector and who served as alderman of the same ward from 1422. Whittingham's positions as receiver-general of the Duchy of Cornwall in the 1430s and manager of the English estates of John, Duke of Bedford placed him simultaneously in the immediate context of the composer's final resting place in Walbrook's parish church of St Stephen, and in the company of the musician's most reliably documented musical patron. An inscription within the book now conserved as Cambridge, St John's College, MS 162, claims that it is "libellus pertinebat Iohanne Dunstaple cum Iohanni duce Bedfordie musico" (a book belonging to John Dunstaple, musician with John Duke of Bedford). The shared ownership of London properties—among John Dunstaple esquire, Margaret Dunstaple his wife, John Dunstaple gentleman, and William Trukyll clerk—reliably connects the personal and business interests of all four individuals in the mid-1440s, but the disappearance of the second Dunstaple from later sources relating to the properties suggests that the gentleman predeceased the esquire.

Other information in John Dunstaple's will provides only circumstantial evidence to connect the man with London, either directly or through his wider family, some of whom lived or were buried in the Walbrook ward. His charitable donations are missing from the Broadfield document, but in the event of him or his daughter dying without legitimate heirs Dunstaple's landholdings were to pass to the benefit of monastic institutions in London and Essex: the Benedictine nunnery of St Leonard, Stratford-at-Bow, and the Cistercian Abbey of St Mary, Stratford Langthorne. John Dunstaple's son-in-law, Richard Hatfield, designed an elaborate tomb as part of his memorial in the church of St Mary Woolchurch, Walbrook, even though he also maintained separate patronage at Steeple Morden as tenant-in-chief. In sum, it seems highly likely that the will of John Dunstaple of Steeple Morden, Cambridgeshire, is that of a man intimately connected to the composer, but it remains possible that they were not one and the same individual.

Evidence suggests that churches in Walbrook were capable of supporting the sort of complex polyphonic music that the composer John Dunstaple wrote, and with which a wealthy and well-connected man like John Dunstaple (d. 1459) will have been familiar. Many churches in neighbouring parishes owned or had the facilities for the performance of polyphonic vocal or organ music from at least the end of the fifteenth century. Records include payments for new music to be copied and for boys to be taught, old choir books listed in inventories, and provision for special services (Williamson 2005). The churchwarden accounts of St Stephen, Walbrook confirm payments during the fifteenth century for the repair of a wooden case for their church organ, as well as to singers for performances on Palm Sunday—in the latter case, payment in kind, in the form of wine. Between 1526 and 1558, St Stephen's welcomed skilled singers for various special feasts and celebrations, including the clerks of the Hospital of St Anthony (parish of St Benet Fink) for a Corpus Christi Mass for a whole year and for the *Salve* or polyphonic antiphon that followed the service; an inventory of 1558 lists "one old prycke songe booke," a book of choral polyphony likely used in such liturgical rites (Williamson 2005, 34). The phrase "for a whole year" suggests that, unlike standard annual celebrations of Corpus Christi—which took place on the Thursday after Trinity Sunday and were often marked by elaborate processions—St Stephen's, Walbrook had developed a tradition of some form of weekly votive Mass, at which St Anthony's Master of the song school and his seven lay clerks were required to sing. Overall, musical activities at St Stephen's and its environs can be traced within the century leading to the English Reformation.

The will of John Dunstaple survives only in a very imperfect copy. Its scribe was not interested in providing details of the artistic or intellectual preoccupations of the testator. In this way, the scribe had much in common with the clerk of Dunstaple's original document—of the wills that survive from the fifteenth century, even those by high-status figures rarely give much impression of the possessions, professional skills, or creative interests of their subjects. It is relatively rare, even, for books to be named, and music books tend to be restricted to those used in liturgy, such as missals. It is unlikely that the composer's original will had much more to say about his work as a musician. However, a full copy would provide the triangulation needed either to disambiguate the two men, or to prove that the 1453 date of the composer's death has been mistakenly recorded. What the Hertfordshire will does, at least, is to raise questions about the identity of John Dunstaple. Was he a wealthy landowner, with connections to religious and political figures in London and at court? Or was he more isolated, a man whose status as "gentleman" is but a fleeting presence in the historical record? Perhaps we are left with a musician almost exclusively known from musical sources and those appreciative of his artistic innovation. It is possible that further archival research will uncover more evidence about the life of the composer. Having examined and followed through the implications of the Hertfordshire will, the most illuminating sources will likely prove to be those at some distance from the choirbooks of the period.

PSALLAM DEO MEO QVAMDIV
ANNO
SALVTI.
H.
XXVI

VE
RA . IMAGO .
LVDOVVICI
SENNFL

80. Portrait Medal of Ludwig Senfl

Birgit Lodes

Friedrich Hagenauer, Augsburg, 1526
Lead, 6.4 cm
Inscribed: obverse: PSALLAM • DEO • MEO • QVAMDIV • FVERO • ANNO • ; SALVTI. XXVI; FH.; reverse: VERA. IMAGO. LVDOVVICI SENNFL.
Samuel H. Kress Collection, National Gallery of Art, Washington
Photo courtesy of the National Gallery of Art

When it comes to faces, the majority of composers only really gained one from the second half of the sixteenth century. That we have a good picture of composers such as Adrian Willaert, Orlando di Lasso, Giovanni Pierluigi da Palestrina, and many later composerly types comes from the tendency towards the authorization of musical compositions. This tendency results from the rise in status of composers alongside a general proliferation of portraiture in paint and print as well as, finally, the political endeavors to give a face to important personalities in cabinets of curiosities. This was not always the case: even up to the fifteenth century composers appear visually—if at all—more often in groups of musical performers and, here, mostly in miniatures (like Johannes Ockeghem), on funerary monuments (like Guillaume Du Fay) or, exceptionally and at best, in representational projects like the *Triumphal Procession* of Emperor Maximilian—where Heinrich Isaac probably appears alongside numerous musicians of the imperial court chapel. At least, two genuine portraits per se of musicians have survived from the environs of the Burgundian court chapel: the singer Gilles Joye and the singer/composer Jacob Obrecht. For other important composers like Pierre de la Rue or Josquin des Prez we are obliged—as so often—to rely on the fantasies of later times.

Against this background, it seems surprising that a group of sources produced in Germany from the 1520s onwards by extremely sought-after and high-quality artists has only received marginal attention in the historiography or biography of musicians. Portrait medals offer a precious opportunity to give a face to at least a few musicians and composers of the period. Perhaps this neglect relates to the aesthetics of medals leaving us twentieth and twenty-first century viewers indifferent. Another reason could be the lack of recognition accorded up to now to studies by numismatists within the context of cultural history, despite the "material turn" that has swept the humanities in general over recent decades—of which this *Museum* is one of the best examples.

The emergence of the portrait medal came about in German-speaking regions—notably later than in Italy—with the rise of Humanism and is generally linked with the Diet of Augsburg in 1518 and the corresponding need for self-promotion by the attendees. These early modern medals make use of certain characteristics from the medals of Roman Antiquity depicting the powerful: a profile view, majuscule inscription, "heroic" nudity, and attributes such as laurels. These medals were, of course, known in Augsburg from the famous collection of Konrad Peutinger (Kranz 2004, 304-06).

Ludwig Senfl is the only composer for whom as many as four different medals were minted over a period of ten years (plates and references in Hirsch 2013). The earliest of these medals probably dates from 1520 (Kastenholz 2006, 213) and was produced by the Augsburg medalist Hans Schwarz. The largest and most representational—reproduced here with obverse and reverse—was made by Friedrich Hagenauer in 1526: in this medal Senfl is presented typically in profile, revealed through his clothing, chain, and hat to be a man of means. Obviously, Senfl had many takers for this medal since it exists still today, according to the latest research, in three exemplars (Tröster 2019a, 321; Tröster 2019b, 314) with minimally diverging details and sizes: diameter ca. 6.3 cm for the exemplars in the Maximilianmuseum, Augsburg, and in the National Gallery of Art, Washington (displayed here), diameter 6.7 cm in the longer-known exemplar at the Staatliche Münzsammlung, Munich. Several years later (1529 and around 1528/30) Hagenauer produced two further medals of Senfl which were somewhat smaller. These reveal a starker individuality and appear more intimate through the setting aside of outward attributes in favor of pure physiognomy. What, then, can be learned from the existence of these medals?

Portrait medals of the Renaissance are generally known—irrespective of their artistic quality—for seeking to capture a likeness that resembles the subject as closely as possible. This is often emphasised by the impression of the year of production and, more often, by the numerical age of the person portrayed. The overarching goal of these popular medals was, therefore, to provide an image as close as possible to reality which had in no way been artistically altered. In this way, the lifelike image was perfectly suited for the repeated awakening of memories of the individual (Pfisterer 2013, 18).

The method of production always required a detailed, live sketch of the subject which could subsequently be worked, if not into a painting or print, then into a medal (although portraits across the different media were often reliant on each other; Smith 2004). Following the drawing phase, a model (most often of wood) would be produced which led, in turn, to a finished product in bronze or lead. Erasmus of Rotterdam is known as having ordered a medal portrait from the Antwerp painter Quinten Massys. Indeed, he had launched from 1519 a "portrait publicity campaign not with print but with metal" at exactly the time in which his singularly important works were being printed in the university city of Leuven (Silver 2003, 6). Nevertheless, he was bitterly disappointed several years later with Albrecht Dürer's likeness of him, that did not seem to him to bear a good resemblance.

When we want to know what Senfl looked like, we are able to get a good impression from the four medals which neither idealize nor allegorize, but present a portrait firmly grounded in reality. The focus of all four medals of Senfl—and, in particular, the two later, smaller ones—falls typically on the facial features; attributes typical of his profession (manuscript paper, quill, or similar) are missing. (Note also that all other drawings, engravings, or pictures known today that apparently depict Senfl are not of him, but are of another individual, or else present an imagined construction of a later time—Gasch and Tröster 2014.)

In general, scholars have proceeded on the basis that Senfl himself commissioned the medals, especially since they do not display his position at court, at least explicitly. Of particular note is that the first medal of Senfl (ca. 1520) was produced at a time when the musician had lost his fixed position, after the death of Emperor Maximilian I in January 1519, having been officially made redundant on 12 September 1520. During this period he worked in Augsburg as editor of a representational print in choirbook format, the *Liber selectarum cantionum*, that includes 24 motets from the repertory of the former court chapel of Emperor Maximilian, a point specifically emphasised in the printed afterword written by the humanist Konrad Peutinger (see exhibit 37). In this expensive print, Senfl appears not only as an editor schooled in humanist thought, but he also self-confidently places at the end of each block of motets for a given group of voices one of his own motets which enters thereby into dialogue with the classical or exemplary models of Josquin or other international masters like Heinrich Isaac, Pierre de la Rue, or Jacob Obrecht.

Senfl appears to follow a similar strategy concerning the medium of the medals. By commissioning Hans Schwarz to produce a medal, he positioned himself as the leading force in the field of music, just like other leading individuals who, in their turn, had commissioned medals in Augsburg from Schwarz (for plates and descriptions, see Scher 1994; Cupperi 2013; and Lange-Krach 2019): for example, the humanist and collector of Roman medals, Konrad Peutinger "Iuris Consulti" (1517); Jakob Fugger, in his time most probably the richest man in the world (1518, the year of the Diet of Augsburg, with a crowning Apollo on the reverse); or the painter Hans Burgkmair the Elder ("S[acrae] Caes[arae] Maiestat[is] A[vlici] Pictvris" 1518 and again 1519 with a reference to the imperial granting of heraldic arms in 1516); or Albrecht Dürer as the leading German painter ("Pictorts [sic] Germanicus" 1520; see the diary entry where Dürer had the Fuggers send Schwarz two guilders for the model—Scher 1994, 218). Hopes were thereby justified, as Frederick the Wise duke of Saxony once opined, "to obtain honor, praise and memorialization" by such coinage (Ludolphy 2006, 25).

When Friedrich Hagenauer finished the three later medals for him, the composer had since 1523 been once again in fixed employment and, more precisely, at the court of the Bavarian duke; Hagenauer resided in Munich between 1525 and 1527 where he finished different medals mostly for various individuals connected to the court (Habich 1907, 195)—including Senfl's musician colleagues Caspar Birker and Lucas Wagenrieder.

The fashionable medals of the Renaissance undoubtedly served a variety of purposes and were ultimately perceived in different circles of individuals in different ways. In addition to self-fashioning, they also naturally functioned as a form of gift exchange between (humanist) friends. The medal was offered primarily as a medium of recollection. The recipients could, of course, do with the comparatively intimate medium what they wished: hold it in their hand, wear it on a chain round their neck, caress it, moisten it with tears, deride it, or even mistreat it—personal reactions of these kinds are reported relatively often in the sources (Pfisterer 2013, 18-19). In any case, a portrait medal generated a wistful relationship between giver and recipient. The two principal functions—of self-fashioning and humanist gift exchange between friends—thereby flowed into each other, as the following examples should demonstrate.

A plaster cast of the Hagenauer 1529 medal of Senfl found its way to the Baltic (today University of Tartu Art Museum; Schwindt 2018, 9-10). Senfl had probably sent an exemplar of this medal along with one of the other numerous consignments of his own compositions to the court of Duke Albrecht of Prussia-Brandenburg which, following the marriage of the duke with Dorothea of Denmark in summer 1526, were documented over many years (Gasch 2012, 404). This leads to the suggestion that in this case—similarly to 1520—professional self-fashioning and amicable recognition in a humanist sense went hand in hand. Indeed, the reverse of the Erasmus medal by Massys mentioned above contains a (Greek) inscription that "the better image will his writing show" which clearly illustrates how, amongst humanists, it was usual to send portraits (painted, printed, or as medals) together with the products of one's own intellectual endeavors (texts or—as in the current case—compositions). And a letter from Erasmus to the humanist and enthusiastic medal collector, Willibald Pirckheimer in Nuremberg, in which he thanks the latter in 1524 for the delivery of two portraits, may illuminate how meaningful such likenesses were for contemporary humanists:

> I have the medal of you on the right-hand wall of my bedroom, the painting on the left; whether writing or walking up or down, I have Willibald before my eyes ... There is another very pleasant thing—the portraits often occasion a talk about you when my friends come to visit me (Silver 2003, 7).

Three of the four medals (those from ca. 1520, 1526, 1529) cite Senfl's motto, Psalm 145:2: "Psallam deo meo quamdiu fuero" (I will sing praises unto my God while I have any being). If one compares German medals around this time, it is noteworthy that the printed mottos are rarely taken from the book of Psalms or from the Bible at all. Thus Senfl's motto is something of an exception. Since the Psalms, in general, played an important role in the Catholic as well as the Protestant traditions, this should not be read as any sign of a decidedly Protestant mentality (Lodes 2012; Horz 2013)—in any case, the chronology of the earliest medal would be too early. More characteristic, in fact, is that this maxim perfectly fits both a singer (Senfl performed as an alto in the court chapel of Emperor Maximilian as well as in the court chapel of Duke Wilhelm IV of Bavaria) and a composer: singing God's praises was the central motivation for the art music of the time—for composing just as much as for performing within the liturgy. With this motto, therefore, Senfl explicitly placed himself within the tradition of Christian worship and, moreover, took up the cudgels for the art of polyphonic composition itself whose cultivation during his lifetime was anything other than self-evident thanks to different Reform movements (above all Johannes Oekolampad in Basel, Martin Bucer in Strasbourg, and Huldrych Zwingli in Zurich; Lodes 2018). Senfl, who from the 1520s onwards composed for both his Catholic employers as well as for Protestant clients, including Martin Luther, presented himself with this motto imprinted on his medal as the self-confident defender of polyphonic church music par excellence.

Additional references: Groote 2013a; Maué 2003; Salmen 1982.

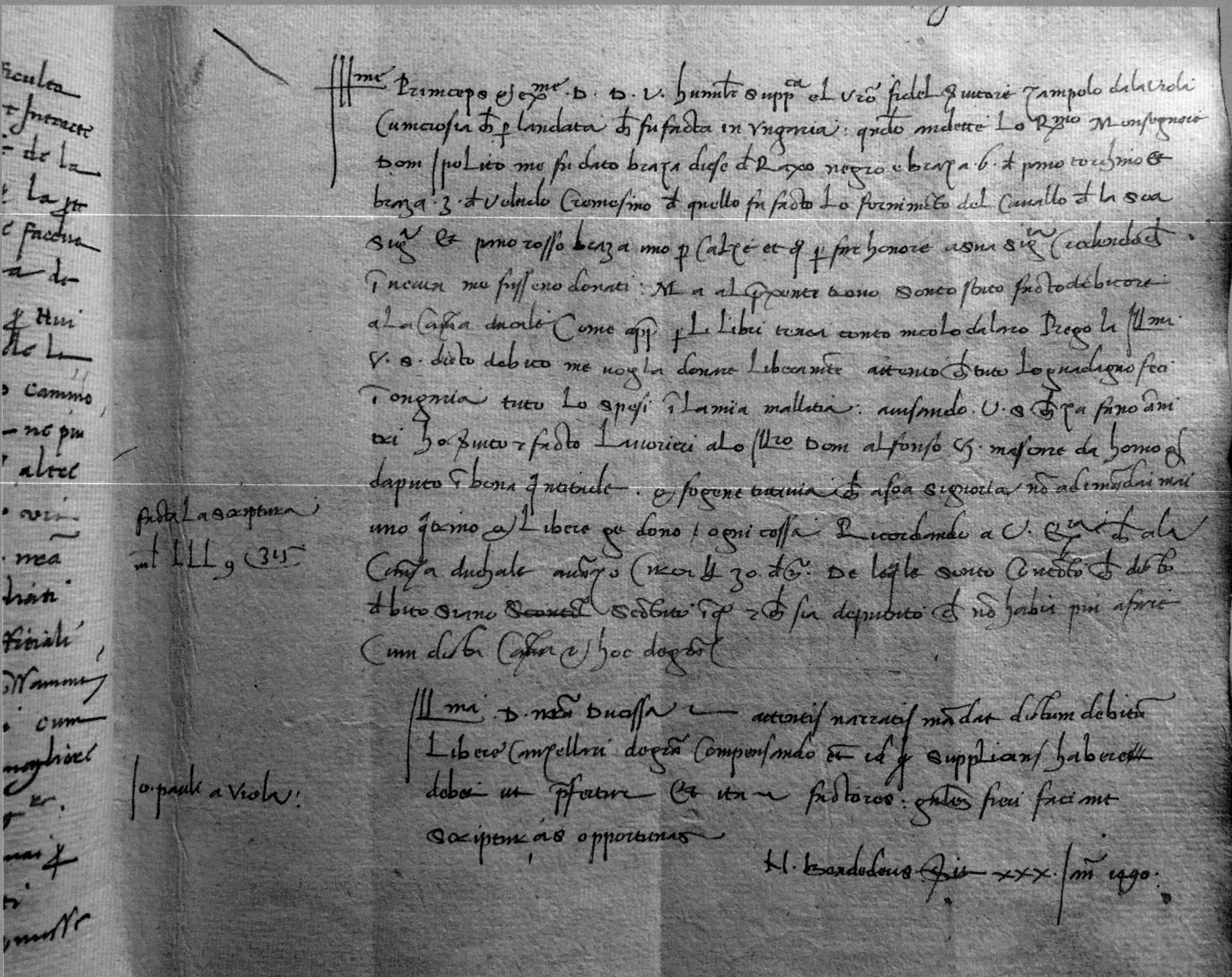
Ill.me Principe et Ex.me D. D. V. humile supp.ca el v.ro fidel servitore Zampolo dali Croli
Cum ciò sia che per l'andata che fu facta in Ungaria: quando andette lo R.mo Monsignore
Dom Ipolito me fu dato braza diese de raxo negro e braza 6 de panno turchino et
braza 3 de veluto cremesino de quello fu facto lo fornimento del cavallo de la soa
sig.ria et panno rosso braza uno per calze et questo per fare honore a soa sig.ria credendo che
in recompensa me fussero donati: Ma al presente sono sento stato facto debitore
a la Camera ducale come appare per li libri tenuti conto Nicolo dal Aro. Prego la Ill.ma
V. S. dicto debito me voglia donare liberamente attento che tuto lo guadagno feci
in Ongaria tuto lo spesi in la mia malatia: avisando V. S. che za sono anni
dei ho servito e facto servicii alo Ill.mo Dom Alfonso che mesone da homo che
da puto in bona quantità. E sogene tra mia che a soa signoria non adimandai mai
uno quatrino che libere per dono in ogni cossa. Ricomandome a V. ... ale
Camera duchale avanzo circa lire 30 de ... De le quale sono Nicolo che dicto
debito ... Scoluto ... sia depenato che non habii più a fare
cum dicta Camera e hoc de gratia.

Ill.mi D. n.ri Ducis ... attentis narratis mandat dictum debitum
libere cancellari de gratia compensando etiam id quod supplicans haberet
debere ut prefertur. Et ita ... factores generales fieri facient
scripturas opportunas.

H. Bardelonus ... xxx ... 1490.

facta la scriptura
ut ... (31)

Io. paulo a Viola.

81. Zampolo dalla Viola Petitions Duke Ercole I d'Este

Bonnie J. Blackburn

Zampolo to Ercole I d'Este, Duke of Ferrara
Ferrara, 30 January 1490
Modena, Archivio di Stato, Camera ducale, Computisteria, Mandati in volume 29 (1490), fol. 20r
Photo by permission of the Ministero della Cultura – Archivio di Stato di Modena, 14 September 2021, prot. N° 2298

Court musicians constantly complain that payments due to them are late, even by years. Mostly they have to wait patiently till they are paid, but this petition, by a fifteenth-century player of the viola at the court of Ercole I d'Este, duke of Ferrara, reveals surprising details about what he was owed and why.

Archival documents are not straightforward. First they must be transcribed accurately, and one always hopes that they are legible. Then a decision needs to be made about how to present the document: diplomatically, with no emendations to spelling or punctuation and no corrections of errors, or in an edited form? If the latter is decided, how modernised should the language be? In the following transcription I have retained the fifteenth-century spellings of the original, though modernising the use of *u* and *v*, silently resolved the abbreviated words, separated words joined together, normalised capitalization, and added punctuation.

[in margin: facta la scriptura ml. [memoriale] LLL_9 315 / Jo.pauli a viola]

Illustrissime Princeps et Excellentissime Domine. Dominationi Vestre humiliter supplica el vostro fidel servitore Zampolo da la viola cumciosia che per l'andata che fu facta in Ungaria, quando andette lo Reverendissimo Monsignore Dom Ipolito, me fu dato braza diese de raxo negro e braza 6 de pano torchino et braza 3 de veludo cremesino de quello fu facto lo fornimento del cavallo de la soa Signoria et pano rosso braza uno per calze, et questo per far honore a sua Signoria credendo che in verun [= vero] me fusseno donati. Ma al prexente trovo sonto [*sic*] stato facto debitore a la camera ducale come appare per li libri tenea conto Nicolo da Laro. Prego la Illustrissima Vostra Signoria dicto debito me vogla donare liberamente attento che tuto lo guadagno feci in Ongaria tuto lo spesi in la mia mallatia, avisando Vostra Signoria che za fano anni tri ho servito et facto lavorieri alo Illustrissimo Dom Alfonso, videlicet mascare da homo et da puto in bona quantitade. Et fogene tutavia che a Soa Signoria non adimandai mai uno quatrino et libere ge dono ogni cossa. Ricordando a Vostra Excellentia che ala camera duchale avanzo circa L. 30 de marchesane. De le quale sonto contento che dicto debito siano [*sic*] scontato in questo et che sia deputato che non habia piu a fare cum dicta camera et hoc de gratia.

Illustrissima Domina nostra Ducissa etc. actentis narratis mandat dictum debitum libere canzellari de gratia, compensando etiam id quod supplicans habere debet ut prefertur. Et ita vos factores generales fieri faciant scripturas opportunas.

N. Bendedeus scripsit xxx Januarii 1490

[in margin: the contract has been entered in Memoriale LLL_9 on fol. 315 / For Jo. Paolo da la viola]

Most Illustrious Prince and Excellent Lord. Your faithful servant Zampolo da la viola humbly supplicates Your Lordship for the reason that for the journey that was made to Hungary, when the Most Reverend Monsignor Ippolito went, I was given ten braccia [a Ferrarese braccio of cloth = 0.673607 m] of black satin and six braccia of dark blue cloth and three braccia of crimson velvet, of that made for the trappings of His Lordship's horse, and one braccio of red cloth for hose, and this to honor His Lordship, truly believing that they were given to me. But as of now I find that I have been made a debtor of the ducal chamber, as appears on the account books kept by Nicolò da Laro. I beg Your Illustrious Lordship to [for]give me the debt freely since all that I earned in Hungary I spent on my illness, informing Your Lordship that it is now three years that I have served and undertaken work for the illustrious Lord Alfonso, that is, a good quantity of masks for men and children. And I make them even though I never demanded a penny from His Lordship, and I freely gave him everything. Reminding Your Excellency that I am owed about LM 30 [Lire Marchesane, the local currency unit] by the ducal chamber, out of which I am content that the said debt be deducted, and that it be ordered that I no longer have anything to do with the said chamber, and this by grace.

The most illustrious Lady our Duchess, etc. according to the matter described orders that the said debt be freely cancelled by grace, also compensating that which the said supplicant ought to have, as described. And thus let you Factors General have the opportune contract made.

N. Benedidio wrote this on 30 January 1490.

The petition is addressed to the duke of Ferrara, Ercole d'Este, and while it incorporates (after the initial salutation in Latin) Zampolo's original Italian wording, it has been entered into the register of supplications by the secretary Nicolò Bendidio. The register of mandates includes only successful petitions, and following the supplication, Duchess Eleonora, in the absence of the duke, orders the administrative office, the Factors General, to relieve Zampolo of the debt. Zampolo's reference to the LM 30 credit he has with the ducal chamber is not clear: it was probably for back salary, but if so, he would end up having to pay for the clothing, the cost of which is not specified.

Ferrarese account books have been surprisingly well preserved for the fifteenth century, unlike, say, those from the duchy of Milan. The accounting system was very complex; as recorded in the margin of the petition, the payment ordered in this register was subsequently entered into a Memoriale with the number LLL_9 on fol. 315 (Memoriale della Camera 39). Following up on this mandate, it appears that Zampolo was compensated for the clothing in the amount of LM 103.12.2 on 17 March 1490 (Conto Generale 27, fol. 267 left). Yet another account lists the exact details of the clothing Zampolo and his companions received on 7 May 1487; for Zampolo the cost of the cloth amounted to LM 124.16.0 (Memoriale del Soldo 8, fol. 16 right). This account claims that the expenses were to be offset against the musicians' salary ("per conto de loro page"); hence it is not surprising that Zampolo was being chased for what he owed the ducal chamber. I give a few of the references to this case to show how complicated the accounting system was at the court. Debts incurred by court employees could be in arrears by as much as 13 years: Rainaldo dal Chitarino complained in 1492 that he could not possibly verify that he owed the ducal chamber LM 10.17.0 for one *castellata* of wine from 1479; he would have to search through 13 years of two types of ducal registers and his salary payments (Mandati 31, 23 July 1492, fol. 125^v). Fortunately, his debt was forgiven.

The trip to Hungary for which Zampolo's clothing was made had enormous significance for the court. Duchess Eleonora's younger sister, Beatrice d'Aragona, had married Matthias Corvinus, king of Hungary, in 1476, thus creating a family alliance between the kingdoms of Naples and Hungary and the duchy of Ferrara. Beatrice had no children, much to her chagrin. In March 1486 she proposed to Eleonora that her son, Ippolito, who as the second son was destined for the church, be named archbishop of Esztergom, a post previously held by Beatrice's late brother Giovanni d'Aragona (Guerra 2010, 14). At that point Ippolito was all of seven years old. This disconcerting proposal was eventually accepted, even by the pope, though reluctantly, and in June 1487 Ippolito, then aged eight, set out for Hungary with a delegation that included six musicians: the singer and composer Johannes Martini, the renowned lutenist Pietrobono dal Chitarino with his *tenorista* Francesco dalla Gatta, and the two viola players, Zampolo and his brother Andrea, with their *tenorista*, the lutenist Rainaldo dal Chitarino. The archbishopric enjoyed a huge income of 50,000 ducats annually, but unlike with many benefices, residence was a requirement. One can imagine how this child felt, uprooted from his family and thrust into a country where they spoke a strange language. The journey, by sea across the Adriatic and land over mountains, was arduous, some of it only feasible on foot. Pirates infested the coast, and Turkish troops endangered the route between the seaport and Vienna, which Mathias Corvinus had conquered in 1485. It must have been a relief for Zampolo and his companions to return safe and sound to Ferrara at the end of October; each was rewarded by Matthias with 50 ducats and by Ippolito with a horse (Cancelleria ducale, Carteggi ambasciatori, Ungheria 2, busta 1, undated). Pietrobono, at Beatrice's insistence, remained in Hungary for another year.

In the second half of his petition Zampolo mentions the masks he had made for Alfonso, the eldest son of Ercole and Eleonora, then aged 14. Mask-making, as we can see from multiple entries in the ducal registers, was a very lucrative sideline for him. On the same day, 30 January 1490, the duchess signed an order to the Factors General to pay Zampolo LM 12 "for the price of six masks with beards bought from him for the ambassadors who are going to the marchese" (Francesco Gonzaga, marquess of Mantua, whom her daughter Isabella was to marry in the following month; Mandati 29, fol. 25^r). Most of the payments, dating from 1486 to 1490, come from Eleonora's personal accounts. Eighteen masks were given to the Neapolitan ambassador in 1486, 35 sent to Ippolito in Hungary in June 1488, and a further 56 in December (Amministrazione dei Principi 633, fols. 31 left and 164 left; Amministrazione dei Principi 639, fols. 40 left and 69 right; Amministrazione dei Principi 639, fol. 40 left).

Masks were used during Carnival, as mentioned by various chroniclers. Carnival celebrations were cancelled in Ferrara in 1483 and 1484, owing to the war with Venice, but there was great happiness on 6 January 1485, when "today we began to go about in masks in the city" (Zambotti 1934, 162). Masks were also used for dancing, when it might be politic (say, if one were a cleric) to conceal one's identity, or to allow closer contact than might be warranted in a social situation.

One of the most interesting uses of masks is in the comedies by Plautus that Duke Ercole had performed at court. On 25 January 1486, before an audience of a thousand in the ducal courtyard, "was performed the comedy of Menegin and Domenegin [*Menaechmi*], of which, with the ship and the city and in general, all the things contained in Plautus were recited word for word" (Caleffini 2006, 668). The performance took four to five hours, during which men in masks, also dressed as women ("travestiti"), "sang in vernacular verse all the lines of the said comedy, with fireworks and a thousand delightful things" (Caleffini 2006, 668). Another chronicler, Bernardino Zambotti, remarks on the performance of Plautus' *Amphitruo* in February 1487 that "one heard singing and playing with the most perfect singers, and Jove came down from the sky" (Zambotti 1934, 180). Zampolo would have been one of those performers. The comedies of Plautus were so successful that they continued to be performed in succeeding years, and masks were requested from Zampolo. In December 1488 he was paid LM 27.18 for making masks for *Amphitruo* and again for *Menaechmi* (Memoriale del Soldo 8, fol. 66 left; Memoriale del Soldo 9, fols. 30 right and 83 left).

Both Zampolo and his brother Andrea, who came to the Este court from Parma at the end of 1466, were very highly paid musicians, with an annual salary of LM 200, just slightly under that of the virtuoso Pietrobono (Lockwood 1984, 183). Zampolo died before 1498, but Andrea lived on to become the progenitor of an illustrious family of musicians: by the sixteenth century the instruments the brothers were associated with had become a family name, Dalla Viola, of whom the most renowned were the instrumentalists, singers, and composers Alfonso and Francesco Dalla Viola, still serving at the court of Ferrara into the 1570s.

ACKNOWLEDGEMENT: I am grateful to Evan MacCarthy, who has shared with me his new findings on Pietrobono.

فضلة
بقية
بعد بقية
اخرى
ايضا
البعد المسمى
متمم
تتمة
مدة
تتمة وبقية
مدة وبقية
مدة وفضلة
مدة ومتمم
مدة وتتمة
مدتان
ذو الاربع
ذو الاربع وبقية
ذو الاربع وفضلة
ذو الاربع وتتمة
ذو الاربع ومتمم
ذو الخمس
ذو الخمس وبقية
ذو الخمس وتتمة
ذو الخمس ومتمم
ذو الخمس ومدة
ضعف ذو الاربع
ذو الكل الا متمم
ذو الكل متمم
الضعف ذو الكل

82. A Diagram from the Mubarak Shah Commentary

Jeffrey Levenberg

From the Mubarak Shah Commentary, London, British Library, MS Or. 2361, treatise at fols. 68v-153r, diagram at fols. 80v, 163r-164v
Treatise: ca. 1370; this copy: Mughal Empire, 1662
Manuscript on laid paper, 85 fols. (whole manuscript: [1] + 269 + [4] fols.), 24.5 x 13.5 cm
Photo © British Library / Bridgeman Images

Labyrinthine in appearance yet simple in its construction, this geometrical diagram is exemplary of Islamic music theory in the period after the fall of Baghdad in 1258. As the reader opens these pages, all possible combinations of musical pitches unfold before their eyes. In awe of its revelatory power, the author of this treatise believed the diagram was "blessed" (*mubārak*; d'Erlanger 1938, 576).

This diagram was likely first envisioned by the preeminent music theorist Safi al-Din al-Urmawi, musician-servant to the new Mongol court in Baghdad, whose treatises set a paradigm for Islamic music theory (Arabic/Persian) for some five centuries. Safi al-Din's treatises are especially vivid in their geometrizations of music theory and therefore they are often exhibited to represent the heritage of Islamic musical scholarship (Arslan 2007). This diagram, however, is first recorded in the most substantial entry in music theory to follow Safi al-Din in the Muzaffarid dynasty of the fourteenth century. Known among devoted students of Arabic-Persian music history as the Mubarak Shah Commentary on Safi al-Din's theories, this treatise (hereafter MSC) was dedicated to Shah Shuja (r. 1358-84) by an anonymous author. The one clue to the author's identity is his self-identification as a physician studying music for medicinal ends (Shiloah 1979, 420). Given the association between music and healing in Islamic science (although not a physician himself, Safi al-Din famously lured the frenzied Mongol ruler to sleep through his music—plus a glass of wine—Gelder 2012), some potent antidotes could be concocted using this diagram.

Two copies of the MSC are known: one dated 1426 in the Topkapi Palace Museum (Istanbul), the other (shown here) dated 1662 in the British Library. Bundled with several monuments of Islamic musical literature, including treatises by (in chronological order) al-Kindi, al-Munajjim, al-Farabi, al-Khudjandi, Ibn Zayla, Safi al-Din, and al-Shirwani, the British Library MSC is part of one of the most extensive sources on Arabic-Persian music kept in Europe (Shiloah 1979). Pioneering scholars consulted this collection to write the first large-scale histories of Arabic music in the West. Henry George Farmer (1930) combed through it in his quest for Arabian influences upon European music. At the same time, Rodolphe d'Erlanger (1938) translated some of its treatises (including the MSC) for inclusion in his voluminous *La Musique arabe*.

Since d'Erlanger's translation, the MSC has remained rather neglected in scholarship. In fact, it would not be an exaggeration to say that much Arabic-Persian music history between the fourteenth and seventeenth centuries, whether in and of itself or in its relationship to that of the West, is still uncharted territory, on both sides of the Mediterranean. The current state of this field in the historiography of Western music is in part a product of previous tendencies in scholarship now commonly charged with Orientalism. By some prior assessments, the value of Arabic-Persian treatises presumably depreciated if they were written while Europe was undergoing its Renaissance. Only in recent decades have many important Muslim scholars of the period begun to emerge from the shadows of a so-called Islamic Golden Age in the eighth to thirteenth centuries minted by the West. This exhibit offers a glimpse of the work of one such under-recognised scholar of music (for others see Wright 2014; Schofield 2010).

This diagram is also a window, as it were, through which we may peer into the scriptorium and observe the scribal process to preserve the MSC. Behind this one formidable diagram, there is (as the viewer can imagine) a small trail of triangles pointing towards (and away from) musical understanding. Tellingly, some of those triangles are void. The scribe of this copy of the MSC underestimated the dimensions of the diagram and tried to squeeze it onto just one leaf. Upon recognising that he had not left himself enough space inside to write, he simply moved on (fol. 80^{v}). Therefore, the image seen here is taken from a brief treatise (one still unclassified) following the commentary. Again the scribe misgauged the diagram (fol. 162^{r}), but this time he committed himself to getting it right, even drawing it three times. He not only presented the music theory legibly, he also projected it through coloration. When the reader homes in upon a segment of the diagram, the lattice's red lines recede and bring the black text into focus.

One need not be versed in music theory or even the Arabic language to understand the principle of this diagram. The more modest triangle in fig. 82.1 sums up in familiar terms how to read it. On this basic multiplication table, the product of any two numbers listed at the base may be found by tracing from the multiplicand diagonally upwards, over, and back down to the multiplier; the diamond midway between the two numbers has the product (e.g. 2 x 5 = 10, fourth row from the base, second entry). The music theory diagram works in much the same way, owing to a peculiar phenomenon that musical pitches accumulate through the mathematical operation of multiplication.

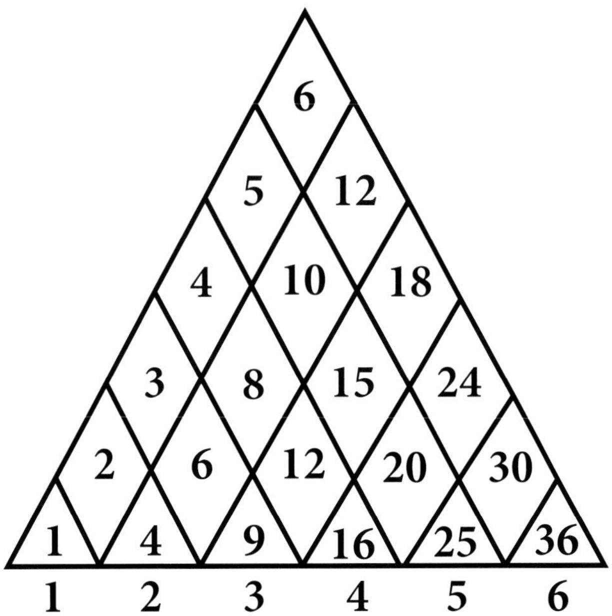

Figure 82.1: A simple multiplication table. The exhibit is read likewise, but with musical pitches in place of the numbers at the base and their proportions in place of the products. Arabic and Latin diagrams were flipped in orientation.

The MSC thus demonstrates the relationship between any two musical pitches, expressed as a mathematical proportion. Viewed from outside of both the culture and the discipline, one might wonder: What would the necessity of such a diagram have been for music? Underlying such a question, however, would be commonly held assumptions about the nature of music in the modern West. Indeed, the musical scales then in currency in Arabic-Persian music are more intricate than those made up of the seven white keys and five black keys on the modern (and common Renaissance) keyboard. Unlike Europe, the pre-colonial Middle East was not home to a procession of music theorists striving towards the elusive goal of equal-tempered tuning. Instead of a knotty keyboard, Safi al-Din conceptualised music upon the flexibly tuned oud (lute). His oud tunings had descended from a long-necked string instrument most unfamiliar to Renaissance Europe, the *tunbur* (not to be confused with the tambourine), as practiced in the region of Khorasan (present-day northeastern Iran). The microtonal nuances on these Arabic-Persian string instruments are not immediately obvious to the mind, eye, and the ear; they are moreover most cumbersome calculations for the hand. They practically defy expression in conventional Western music notation, but, to illustrate the point, Safi al-Din's complete scale can be represented as in ex. 82.1. Although Arabic-Persian and European music both inherited Greek harmonics, this sequence of 17 pitches (in so-called Pythagorean tuning) is not yet documented with certainty in medieval and Renaissance music theory or practice (cf. Berger 1987).

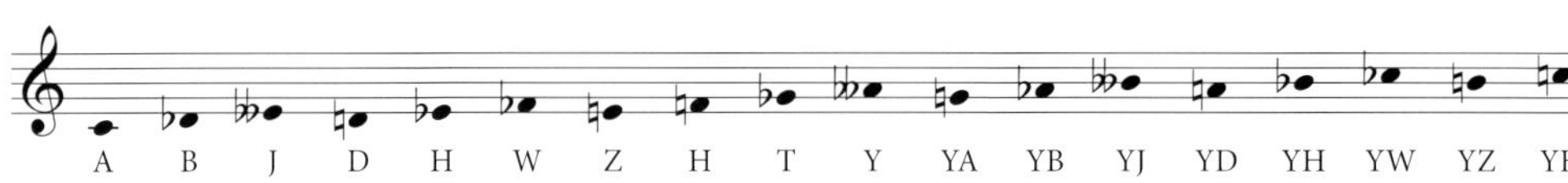

Example 82.1: Safi al-Din's complete scale (division of the octave) represented in Western notation. The letters beneath the staff are those assigned to the pitches at the base of the MSC diagram (in red; some of the letters were sliced off during re-binding).

Confronted by all of the possible relationships among these pitches, theorists inevitably turned to combinatorics to sort them all out. For this reason, music historians have characterised Safi al-Din and his successors as "The Systematist School" (Wright 1978), albeit perhaps with a nod to the modern Western discipline of systematic musicology, meaning the scientific study of musical acoustics. The MSC diagram is the summation of that work. Upon closer inspection of this diagram, however, the viewer might intuit that the task was not quite finished. While legible, the diagram is neither polished nor necessarily complete. Some erasures and blanks may be spotted on it. For example, the scribe had to erase and then rubricate the first and third boxes (upper right), in order to define in numbers the two basic musical intervals that generate the entire scale. Looking closely, one can make out the complex superpartient ratios 1 13/243 in the first box, the interval AB, and 1 7153/524288 in the third, JD. Elsewhere, in the rows of diamonds, it appears that some combinations of pitches still escaped theoretical explanation (or perhaps did not warrant it according to practice). For instance, the interval between D and Y (pitches D and Gbb), seventh row / fourth diamond, was left blank. In other instances, it was the scribe (not the theorist) who drew a blank errantly. The empty diamond between YA and YZ (pitches G and B) was misplaced: it should be one row above, between Y and YZ (pitches Abb and B). While musicologists will continue to untangle this diagram, let us for now just sympathise with the cross-eyed scribe!

Perhaps this exhibit is out of place in a museum of mostly European Renaissance music. Then again, the diagram may look vaguely familiar: these triangles appear throughout European treatises to demonstrate (as in Arabic-Persian treatises) both melodic and rhythmic relationships. A prime example would be Thomas Morley's *Plain and Easy Introduction to Music*, in which a triangular diagram is offered to those "curious" readers willing to take an extra step (Morley 1597, 33). Moreover, music theorists have noted a similarity between the musical scales of Safi al-Din and one of the early reformers of European tuning in the Renaissance, Bartolomeo Ramos de Pareja. Considering that the latter was a native of Andalusia, where Islamic musical ideas and practices must have been more widely familiar than in most other European regions (see exhibit 77), this comparison may seem hardly coincidental (Isacoff 2009, 112). Such circumstances raise a question long puzzled over by Renaissance historiographers of all disciplines: Were there Arabic influences or not? While historians of mathematics, astronomy, and medicine have many sources pointing toward the positive, musicologists working on the transmission of music theory have as yet come up comparatively empty-handed. To be sure, isolated instances are well-documented, especially in the Middle Ages: some European writers on music theory quoted al-Farabi's *Classification of the Sciences* (but not his *Great Book of Music*—Randel 1976). And, even if not a treatise, there is a world of musical thought to be gleaned from the *Cantigas de Santa Maria* of Alfonso X, the celebrated miniatures which depict Muslim and Christian musicians playing together (Ferreira 2015). But rarely has European music theory betrayed indebtedness to Arabic music theory, least of all in pre-seventeenth-century Renaissance humanist theories—so it stands now. As one scholar wittily put it after conducting an optimistic corpus study: "Not only did the Latins not translate Arabic works dedicated to music, but also they left out portions of Arabic works which dealt with music" (Burnett 1993, 12).

Until found otherwise, one can say that the theories Safi al-Din, no matter their continued importance in the Middle East, had no bearing on Renaissance European music. While triangular diagrams spread throughout Renaissance music theory, the contents of ones written in Arabic did not. Only a vestige of the Islamic "Golden Age" remained in the outlines of Renaissance European music theory. The knowledge that such geometrical diagrams as this were originally Arabic at point of introduction was probably lost upon Renaissance music theorists, if not suppressed elsewhere in the curriculum (Hasse 2016). Renaissance theorists adhered firstly to Boethius and then later divided to side with either Ptolemy or Aristoxenus (Palisca 1985).

But why perpetuate that history unchecked? Perhaps by reframing the instigating question of "influence" in more open-ended and, indeed, post-colonialist terms—say, in the exchange of "glances" (Blickwechsel) from one culture to the other advocated by art historian Hans Belting (Belting 2011)—musicologists might find more compelling points of convergence or divergence between these two music-theoretical cultures. That additional hall to the *Museum of Renaissance Music*, where European theories are hung on the walls face to face with Arabic and Persian theories (and why not with those from even further afield too?—Tonietti 2014), with viewers in between glancing back and forth, is still under construction. While the MSC diagram can stand out on its own and call attention to the state of scholarship on Islamic music theory at the time of the European Renaissance, its exhibition here is temporary.

Additional references: al-Din al-Urmawi 1984; Joseph 2011; Ramos de Pareja 1482; Reynolds 2013; Wright 2004; Ghrab 2009.

Ἐν τούτῳ τῷ βιβλίῳ περιέχονται, Ἀριστείδου Κοϊντιλιανοῦ περὶ μουσικῆς, λόγοι τρεῖς.
Ἔτι Μανουὴλ Βρυεννίου, ἁρμονικῶν βιβλία τρία.
Ἔτι, Πλουτάρχου περὶ μουσικῆς· λόγος εἷς.
Ἔτι, Εὐκλείδου, εἰσαγωγὴ ἁρμονική· περὶ τοῦ αὐτοῦ, κατατομὴ τοῦ κανόνος.
Ἔτι, Ἀριστοξένου ἁρμονικῶν στοιχείων, τρία.
Ἔτι, Ἀλυπίου, εἰσαγωγὴ μουσική.
Ἔτι, Γαυδεντίου, ἁρμονικὴ εἰσαγωγή.
Ἔτι, Νικομάχου, ἁρμονικὸν ἐγχειρίδιον.
τὸ ἕτερον. Ἔτι, τοῦ αὐτοῦ ἁρμονικὸν ἐγχειρίδιον.
Ἔτι, Πτολεμαίου ἁρμονικῶν, βιβλία τρία· αὐτὸ δηλονότι τὸ κείμενον τοῦ μουσικοῦ.
Ἔτι, Πορφυρίου ἐξήγησις εἰς τὸ α΄ τῆς μουσικῆς Πτολεμαίου. καὶ μέρος τοῦ δευτέρου. βιβλίον ἄριστον καὶ δυσεύρετον.

Κτῆμα Βησσαρίωνος καρδιναλίου τοῦ Νικαίας· ἐπισκόπου Σαβίνων.

In hoc libro continentur Aristidis Quintiliani de Musica libri tres.
Item Manuelis Bryennii, de Musica libri tres.
Item Plutarchi de Musica liber unus.
Item Euclidis introductio in Musicā: & eiusdē partitio instrumenti.
Item Aristoxenis de elementis musicæ libri tres.
Item Alypii introductio in Musicam.
Item Gaudentii introductio in Musicam.
Item Nicomachi enchiridium in Musicam.
Item eiusdem aliud enchiridium.
Item Ptolemæi Musica, in libris tribus: videlicet ipse textus.
Item Porphyrii expositio ī pmū librū Musicorū Ptolemæi, et partē secūdi.
Liber optimus, et qui raro reperitur.
Liber. B. cardinalis Niceni, episcopi Sabini.

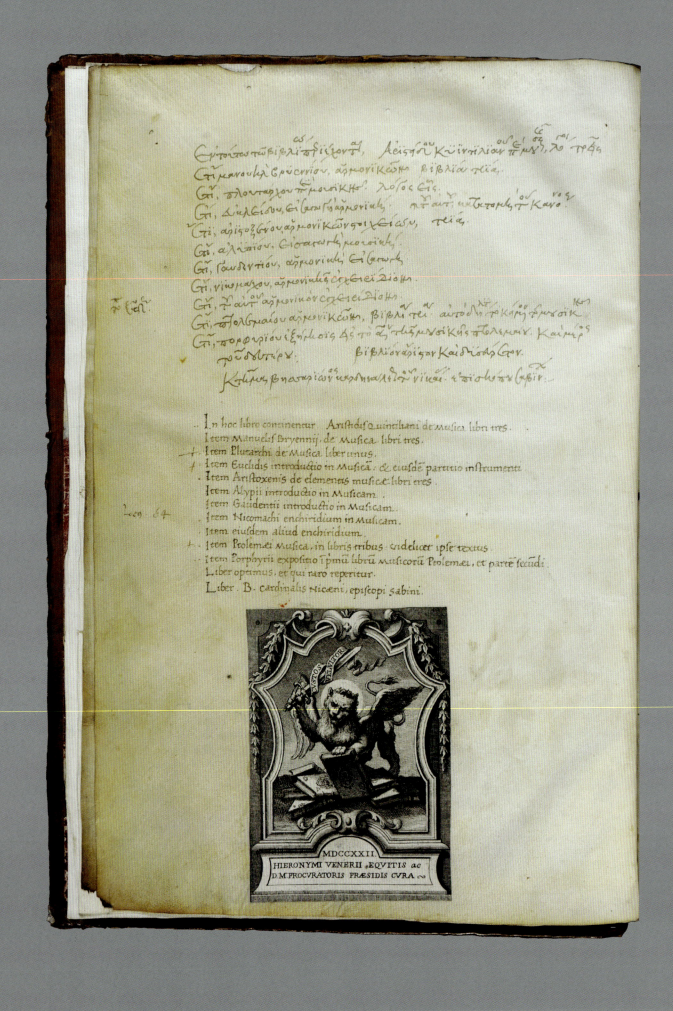

MDCCXXII.
HIERONYMI VENERII EQVITIS ac
D.M. PROCVRATORIS PRÆSIDIS CVRA

83. Cardinal Bessarion's Manuscript of Ancient Greek Music Theory

Eleonora Rocconi

Venice, Biblioteca Nazionale Marciana, Ms Gr. Z. 322 (=711)
Ioannes Rhosos, Rome, ca. 1450-1475
Manuscript on parchment; [3] + 241 (an unnumbered fol. follows fol. 74) + [2] fols.; 33.5 x 23.2 cm

This document is one of the most important manuscripts containing treatises on ancient Greek music theory. It is listed among the 750 books that Cardinal Bessarion, the Byzantine humanist and theologian who was a central figure in the revival of Classical Antiquity in Renaissance Italy, donated to the city of Venice in 1468, becoming the original nucleus of what developed into the Biblioteca Marciana. Copied by the Greek scribe Ioannes Rhosos, associated with Bessarion since 1447, the codex was probably commissioned by the cardinal in the third quarter of the fifteenth century for his famous personal library located in Rome. Indeed, after the fall of Costantinople in 1453, Bessarion's passion for books (begun, as he himself states, in his early youth) had grown exponentially, leading him to increase his collection not only for personal needs but with the more ambitious purpose to preserve the whole intellectual heritage of Greek Antiquity. This scope was pursued by acquiring—with the help of other scholars and booksellers—all the Greek works still absent from his library, as well as by having emendated and "beautifully written manuscripts" (codices ... pulcherrimi—as he himself describes them in his Act of Donation) copied in his house or commissioned from booksellers.

The books owned by Bessarion and donated to the city of Venice were all inscribed by him with a shelfmark, an indication of their contents, and his ex-libris, elements which may still provide valuable clues for tracing their origins and routes. The ex-libris of Marc. Gr. Z. 322 (=711), here reproduced, suggests that this document was not included in the first set of boxes sent to Venice by the cardinal, but it arrived after 1468: in fact, Bessarion is styled "Episcopus Sabinensis," a dignity conferred upon him in October 1468 and usually reported in codices acquired (or prepared for delivery) only after this date. Moreover, the manuscript is not mentioned in the first inventory (*A*) accompanying the Act of Donation of 1468, addressed to Cristoforo Moro and the Venetian Senate, rather appearing in the second inventory (*B*) compiled in 1474. So, even had the codex been completed before 1468, it was most probably among those kept by Bessarion for his own use after that date, and sent to Venice only in 1474, two years after his death. In the inventory *B*, the book is described as a "new book on music ... a great book, on parchment, and difficult to find" (inv. *B* no. 571; Labowsky 1979, 222: Liber musicae novus ... liber optimus, in pergameno, et difficilis inventu). This suggests that, unlike other documents on ancient music theory packed in the same box (as no. 570 and 572, both "in papyro"—on paper), it had been commissioned by the cardinal himself, probably to combine in a single anthology a richer selection of particularly significant content on the same topic. Certainly none of the earlier anthology manuscripts on music owned by Bessarion and delivered to Venice with the first installment of his gift (listed in Palisca 1985, 27-28) displays such a great variety of musical theoretical texts. See, for example, inventory *A* n. 232 = *B* n. 572 (Item musica Ptolemei, cum expositione Aristidis Quintiliani ei Brienii, in papyro), which includes only three of the authors we find in Marc. Gr. Z. 322 (=711): Ptolemy, Aristides Quintilianus, and Bryennius.

Fol. [3]^{v} lists the entire content of the codex mentioning the Greek and Latin titles of all the treatises (see fig. 83.1), which span a period running from late classical to Byzantine times (here listed in chronological order): Aristoxenus' *Harmonic Elements* (fourth century BCE), [Pseudo] Plutarch's *On Music* (second century CE), Cleonides' *Introduction to Harmonics* (second century CE, erroneously ascribed to Euclides in this codex), Nicomachus' *Introduction to Harmonics* (second century CE) followed by what modern scholars consider extracts from another lost work of Nicomachus on harmonics (the so-called *Excerpta Nicomachi*, here described as "another introduction"—alium enchiridium), Ptolemy's *Harmonics* (second century CE), Porphyrius' *Commentary on Ptolemy's Harmonics* (third century CE), Gaudentius' *Introduction to Harmonics* (third/fourth century CE), Aristides Quintilianus' *On Music* (late third/fourth century CE), Alypius' *Introduction to Music* (fourth/fifth century CE), and Manuel Bryennius' *Harmonics* (fl. 1300).

The materials here collected include the most important works on harmonic science, the main ancient theoretical discipline concerned with music, which identified, classified, and described the regular and repeated patterns underlying melodic sequences in musical compositions (Barker 2007). The two major traditions of thought in Greek harmonics were the

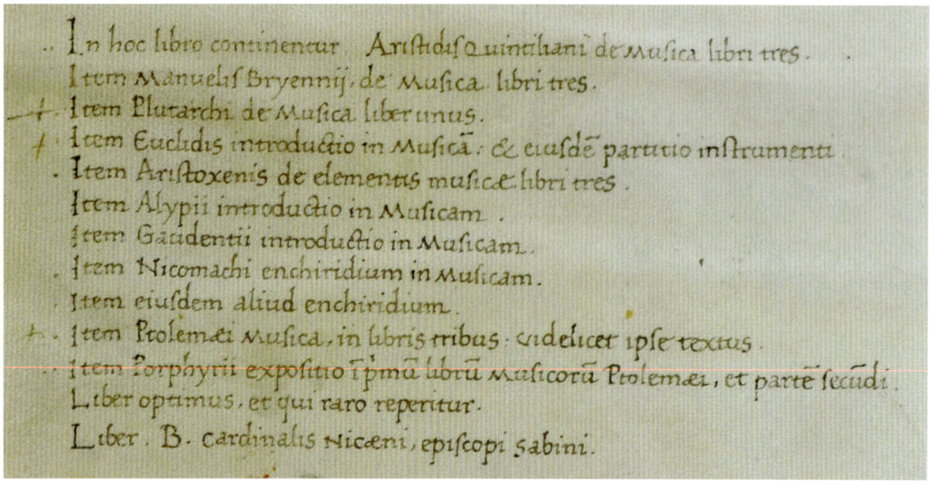
In hoc libro continentur Aristidis Quintiliani de Musica libri tres.
Item Manuelis Bryennii de Musica libri tres.
Item Plutarchi de Musica liber unus.
Item Euclidis introductio in Musicā: & eiusdē partitio instrumenti.
Item Aristoxenis de elementis musicae libri tres.
Item Alypii introductio in Musicam.
Item Gaudentii introductio in Musicam.
Item Nicomachi enchiridium in Musicam.
Item eiusdem aliud enchiridium.
Item Ptolemaei Musica, in libris tribus videlicet ipse textus.
Item Porphyrii expositio ī pmū librū Musicorū Ptolemaei, et partē secūdi.
Liber optimus, et qui raro reperitur.
Liber B. cardinalis Niceni, episcopi Sabini.

Figure 83.1: Detail from main image showing the Latin contents list. Photo © Biblioteca Nazionale Marciana / Shylock e-solutions.

Pythagorean and the Aristoxenian: the former, highly influential throughout the Middle Ages and the early Renaissance, gave a mathematical representation of musical intervals, conceiving them as relations between quantitative pitches; the latter—firmly established by Aristoxenus of Tarentum but with a significant pre-history—investigated melodic items as they appeared in the perceptual realm, with the aim to discover, by means of reason, the principles governing their combination in music. All scientific literature on harmonics was developed within one of these two main traditions, or a mixture of both, including both synoptic handbooks (Cleonides, Gaudentius, Nicomachus, Alypius) and texts of greater intellectual depth (such as Ptolemy), sometimes heavily influenced by Platonic and Neoplatonic philosophy (as Aristides Quintilianus), and in turn exerting a profound cultural influence on scholars of various kinds over nearly two millennia thanks to the logical rigour of their scientific approach. Moreover, the cardinal's anthology includes a commentary on other texts (Porphyry), a historical work in dialogue form (Pseudo Plutarch), and a very late compilation (Bryennius) demonstrating the persistence of ancient Greek musical culture through the centuries as an intellectual model.

The juxtaposition of different authors displayed in this document, quite common in ancient manuscripts organised along thematic lines, may be found in earlier revival manuscripts too, such as Biblioteca Apostolica Vaticana, Vat. Gr. 2338 (twelfth century). The relevance of Marc. Gr. Z. 322 (=711) lies especially in the fact that the texts here included soon converged as a kind of canon of ancient treatises on music, including nearly all of what has been preserved in the field (Mathiesen 1992, 14). Indeed, the codex shows a close relationship with several later manuscripts, copied in the sixteenth-century Venetian area, which are clearly based upon it (directly or via lost copies) in whole or in part. Thus we should conclude that the books donated by Bessarion, despite being stacked in boxes for many decades before the full establishment of the library that he hoped to furnish "for the benefit of all," were in some way accessible to scholars and copyists after their arrival in Venice. As further evidence of this, we may note that the lending records of the Biblioteca Marciana in the years around 1550 explicitly allude to texts on music theory, although without mentioning this specific item (see, for example, Marc. Lat. XIV, 22 =4482).

To sum up, this manuscript is of fundamental importance for the modern reception of ancient Greek music theory, and not only because it is placed at the end of the long and complex process of textual transmission (begun in Byzantine times), which helped to establish a composite archetype of Greek musical writings. It also stands at the head of their circulation in the modern era. From the early fifteenth century, in a cultural climate that looked to the classics for models across multiple domains of cultural production, there was a growing demand for the most authoritative evidence on ancient music theory, known until then only through Boethius' mediation. The first mention in the West of a manuscript containing ancient musical treatises is in a letter of Ambrogio Traversari, who in 1433 reported that he had seen books on Greek music theory in the library of Ca' Gioiosa in Mantua, during his visit to Vittorino da Feltre (Palisca 1985, 25-26; Meriani 2016). During the fifteenth and especially the sixteenth century, a great number of texts gradually became available thanks to the activities of large scriptoria, where many copies of the same work could be produced in a great variety of anthology combinations. In this way, the circulation of Greek books on music theory became increasingly widespread, arousing interest not only among scholars.

It is precisely through the authority of ancient Greek evidence, finally available, that practical musicians of the late Renaissance were able to find intellectual justification and validation of new trends in contemporary music. Among the phenomena involved, we should certainly remember the rise of monody, which was inspired by the ancient ideal of song because of its power to move the affections, as we are told by Girolamo Mei, the Italian humanist who provided the intellectual impetus to the Florentine Camerata: "The music of the ancients was considered a valuable means for moving the soul" (la Musica delli Antichi era tenuta si valoroso mezo à commouere gl'affetti; Mei 1602, 2). But the authority of the classics also gave support to new harmonic theories, such as equal temperament, a system of musical intonation that could solve some of the practical problems of the Pythagorean and natural scale: relying on the authority of Aristoxenus and his empirical tuning system, Vincenzo Galilei felt encouraged to dismiss the long-established Pythagorean approach, whose legacy was still prevalent among the intellectuals of his time (Litchfield 1988; Palisca 1993). Hence we can reasonably affirm that the importance of this manuscript goes far beyond the object itself: the history of its composition, dissemination, and reception was part of a broader process in which the revival of Classical Antiquity influenced to a great extent the cultural life of late Renaissance and early modern Italy.

84. The Analogy of the Nude

Antonio Cascelli

Sacred and Profane Love
Titian, Venice, 1514
Oil on canvas, 118 x 279 cm
Galleria Borghese, Rome
Photo © 2021 Photo Scala, Florence

Sacred and Profane Love, probably commissioned by Nicolò Aurelio, grand chancellor of Venice, on the occasion of his marriage in May 1514 to the widow Laura Bagarotto, is undoubtedly one of Titian's most famous paintings. Described in 1613 as "Beauty adorned and beauty unadorned" (Barolsky 1998), only in a 1693 inventory of the Borghese collection is the painting given its now-familiar title *Sacred and profane love*, a moniker that has nonetheless shaped the modern literature on the painting as scholars debate which figure is sacred and which profane (see Howard 2013). Among the various interpretations, Erwin Panofsky's reading of the painting as a representation of the celestial Venus (the nude) and the earthly Venus (the clothed figure) mentioned by the fifteenth-century philosopher Marsilio Ficino has been particularly influential (Panofsky 1969).

Here, however, I am less interested in the history of the interpretation of the painting than in a trajectory that connects it to music. Among Titian's works the two versions of *Venus with an Organist and a Dog* seem the most obvious choices for an exhibit in a Museum of Renaissance Music (McIver 2014). Nevertheless, even though *Sacred and Profane Love* is not an explicitly musical painting, the invitation it offers to consider the contrast between nude and clothed female figures is one also evoked in sixteenth-century music treatises by Nicola Vicentino and Orazio Tigrini.

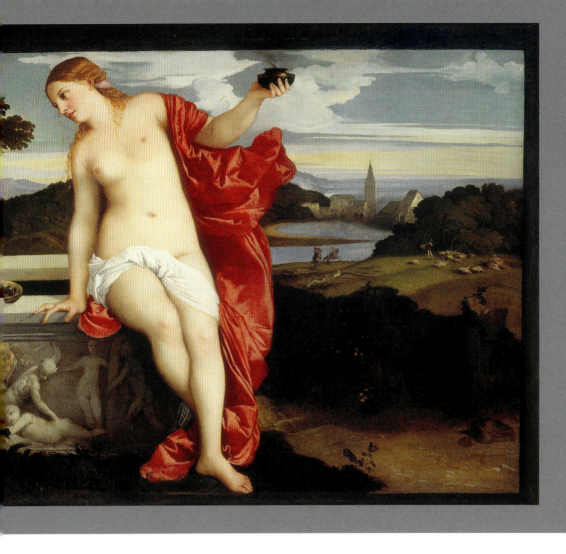

In Chapter 23 of his 1555 *L'antica musica ridotta alla moderna prattica* (*Ancient music accommodated to modern practice*), entitled "How to compose for two voices, with examples," Vicentino writes:

> With respect to compositions for three, four, and five voices, the duo is comparable to the difference between the nude and the clothed figure in painting. Every painter depicts a completely clothed figure quite well, whereas not all painters can do the same with a nude. The same is true of composers of music. Many write works for four or more voices, but few possess the refined manner required to combine the steps and consonances in a duo (Vicentino 1996, 263-64).

The comparison is repeated by Tigrini, who in the equivalent chapter of his 1588 *Il compendio della musica* (*Compendium on music*) writes:

> Some say that the duo, compared to compositions for three, four, five and more voices, is similar to the difference that one finds between the nude and the clothed figure in painting: because every painter will do a fully clothed figure well; but not all painters will do a naked figure well. It happens likewise in compositions: that is, that many will compose cantilenas for four, five, and more voices; but few will be those who have a good way of proceeding, and know well and in an orderly manner how to accompany the steps and the consonances in a duo (Tigrini 1588, 35).

The three texts—by Titian, Vicentino, and Tigrini—belong to a complex mosaic of meanings attached to the nude in this period. As Thomas Martin reminds us, in Renaissance Europe and Italy the nude figure became, together with the geometry of pictorial perspective, an increasingly distinguishing element between Renaissance and medieval art (Martin 2012, 402). During the Renaissance, artists began to paint the human body with growing attention to detail: the use of perspective enabled them to present the body effectively in its three-dimensional shape, capturing all the elements that contribute to a real-life impression (Burke 2018a, 187-90). The human body and its representations were central in conceptions of selfhood and community, and the way human subjectivity relates to God. At the same time, the body became the object of scientific investigation in medicine and anatomy (Burke et al. 2018, 7).

Two Renaissance writers on the arts who placed the nude at the centre of their critical perspectives were Giorgio Vasari and Ludovico Dolce. In his *Le vite de' più eccellenti pittori, scultori, e architettori* (*Lives of the Most Excellent Painters, Sculptors, and Architects*: first edition 1550, second edition 1568), in accordance with his broad view of the sweep of art history and of value in the visual arts, Vasari considers Michelangelo's nudes as absolute beauty, exemplifying the predominance of invention and drawing. Raphael's paintings and nudes, in contrast, are considered to be only relative beauty, because of their prominent use of colour, which he deemed of secondary importance in comparison to drawing (Lazzarini 2010, 42). In opposition to Vasari's view, Dolce inverts the terms of evaluation in his *Dialogo della pittura* (*Dialogue on painting*, 1557). He favours graceful bodies, their softness best exemplified in the nudes of Raphael and Titian (in that order), which in Dolce's view achieve a pictorial supremacy over the angularity of Michelangelo's nude figures (Lazzarini 2010, 108). For both Vasari and Dolce, painting a nude is difficult, but they treat the rhetoric of difficulty in different ways: in Michelangelo, the difficulty is visible; in Raphael, difficulty is present as facility, sign of the greatest perfection (Lazzarini 2010, 110).

In the context of Renaissance Italy, where the nude figure in its pervasiveness was central to critical debates, the use of an analogy with nude and clothed figures in a music treatise, bringing together discourses of polyphonic composition and the representation of the body and its subjectivity, demands careful consideration. The analogy carries over to the sphere of musical ambiguities present, and sometimes thematised and discussed, in the visual field—ambiguities whose implications for the changing musical practices of the late sixteenth century may be quite profound.

Vicentino and Tigrini propose that polyphony for three or more voices be associated with the clothed figure, whereas two-part counterpoint is the same figure exposed in its nudity. A few lines earlier in *L'antica musica*, Vicentino has mentioned that the duo is often placed in the middle of a motet, surrounded by sections using a richer polyphonic texture. The notion of a "nude" duo in the midst of "clothed" polyphony, in the context of a composition setting a sacred text, invites comparison with the use of the naked body in sacred art. Nudes in paintings of sacred subjects served to emphasise the human nature of the saints, Christ, and the Virgin Mary. Yet they sit on a threshold between the sacred and the secular; it was not uncommon for these vivid representations of human flesh to cause sensual tensions in the viewer, a difficulty exemplified in the contemporary polemics surrounding Michelangelo's *Last Judgement* (Burke et al. 2018, 3).

Similar interchangeabilities between sacred and profane characterised contemporary musical culture, not infrequently centred on the female form, producing similar debates. The long-standing practice of building Mass settings upon the music of secular songs is a case in point, its threshold difficulties neatly exemplified in Orlando di Lasso's *Missa Entre Vous Filles* (1581) based on an erotic song describing the bodies of 15-year-old girls. Another musical practice exploring exchange between sacred and profane is the tradition of contrafacta, where music initially created for secular texts was reused for sacred texts (or vice versa)—for example, Claudio Monteverdi's *Il pianto della Madonna* set to the music of his *Lamento di Arianna*.

More fundamentally, the analogy proposed by Vicentino and Tigrini prompts us to reflect on the nature of two-part counterpoint as a musical practice. The positioning of the analogy, and of the subject of the duo, in these authors' organisation of musical topics and musical knowledge is significant here. The passage in *L'antica musica* is found in Book IV, Chapter 24, on Music Practice; in the Proem Vicentino explains that he will write about "the clefs and show how they are notated in plainchant and polyphony for two or more voices…; different manners of composing various ideas for playing and for singing on plainchants or measured polyphony with various canons" (Vicentino 1996, 229). Chapter 24, which is specifically about "How to Compose for Two Voices," follows on immediately from a chapter on "How to Improvise on Plainchants," which begins:

> It is good to hear improvised singing on a plainchant in church, if the members of the group are well-coordinated and if all the parts keep to their ranges—that is, if the sopranos, contraltos, and tenors make their *passaggi* over the bass, which is the plainchant. Indeed, every part must observe its own patterns. But it is difficult to avoid the incidence of errors, and not just a few of them (Vicentino 1996, 258).

The analogy of the nude and the topic of the duo thus arise in the context of—or at least follow straight on from—a discussion of improvised singing above a plainchant cantus firmus ("cantare alla mente"). Tigrini, meanwhile, places the analogy in Book 2, where he treats the contrapuntal rules of consonance and dissonance; he does not connect it with improvisation directly, but he follows a similar pattern of ideas in that the analogy launches off from a discussion of composition over a cantus firmus.

The ramifications of all this are very rich; improvisation and its relationship with notated composition in the Middle Ages and the Renaissance is a complex subject (McGee 2003). As Elena Abramov-van Rijk has shown, reflections on the contrast between improvised and notated composition go back at least as far as Eustache Deschamps's *L'art de dictier ed de fere chançons* (*The art of making poetry and songs*, 1392). Deschamps distinguishes between *musica artificialis* (music made through artifice—that is, notated composition) and *musica naturalis*.

Even "the most uncivilized men on earth," he notes, can "learn to sing, harmonise, and double at the octave, fifth, and third, as well as sing the tenor or the descant, following the notation, clefs and staff lines," and thus produce music through artifice. In contrast, spontaneous *musica naturalis*

> is called natural because it cannot be learned at all, except for conjuring up a sound-image springing from the heart upon delivery of versified texts, often in the shape of *laiz*, or *balades*, simple and double *roundeaux*, and *chanson-balladées* of three double verses… which some today call *virelay* (Abramov-van Rijk 2009, 42-43).

Written composition and improvisation are almost incompatible activities; or at least, whereas anyone can learn facility with *musica artificialis*, skill in *musica naturalis* must emerge fully formed from within.

Whilst Deschamps, a poet, favours improvised monody governed by the structure of a poetic text, his contemporary Johannes Ciconia, a church musician, develops the comparison in the opposite direction in his early fifteenth-century *Nova Musica*:

> Even though this natural music by far precedes the artificial, nevertheless no one can acknowledge the power of natural music except through the artificial. Natural music has been given to everyone; artificial, however, to few. But indeed the natural occurred first, then the artificial. The natural is experienced by the ear; the artificial, however, by the ear, the heart, pitch, consonances, species, modes of the tones, songs, proportions of numbers, accidents, declensions, and many other similar arguments (Abramov-van Rijk 2009, 45).

With Ciconia, *musica artificialis* becomes the more difficult practice, its difficulties elevating it into the sphere of liberal studies, and rendering it more exclusive.

This debate contrasting the natural spontaneity of poetic monody with the expert artifice of polyphonic composition intersects with a broader discourse in Renaissance poetics, and one that brings us back into the presence of the nude. In poetry by Dante, Francesco Landini, Francesco di Vannozzo, and others we find the opposition of *nudo/ignudo* and *vesta/vestita* used to characterise the relationship of text to music: poetry without music is *nuda*, bare, whereas poetry set to music is *vesta*, dressed. Once Aristotle's *Poetics* had entered general circulation around 1500, his term *psilometria* was also used to indicate "bare" poetry, for example by Francesco Patrizi in his *Della Poetica* (*On Poetics*) of 1587 (Abramov-van Rijk 2009, 59-61).

Psilometria denotes verse that lacks harmony because it is not set to music. Counterintuitively, Vicentino comments that two-part counterpoint is also "devoid of harmony and ensemble," and indeed it is because it lacks harmony that "every poorly ordered and maladroit consonance is obvious." Thus the nudity of music and the nudity of poetry share a similar quality, affording the practitioner no opportunity to hide errors in a colourful thicket of notes, just as a nude figure affords the painter no opportunity to hide poor *disegno* behind flowing folds of colourful fabric.

Although Vicentino is writing about two-part counterpoint, ostensibly a practice of *musica artificialis*, his discussion destabilises the value system proposed by Ciconia. Vicentino's duo is more difficult than polyphony in three or more parts precisely because it contains less artifice; it is more "bare." At the same time, by aligning two-part counterpoint with vocal improvisation above plainchant, Vicentino implies that the duo could be seen as a kind of disrobed *musica naturalis*. Indeed, the kind of chanson "springing from the heart" proposed by Deschamps as a form of spontaneous and "natural" expressive performance of a poetic text is "solo" song only in a special sense; in such song practices the voice is usually joined by accompanying instrument/s. Improvised solo song is thus a form of two-part counterpoint, and in turn two-part counterpoint can furnish a framework for solo song.

In establishing the difficulty of writing down two-part counterpoint, Vicentino is capturing, albeit briefly, the moment when oral traditions (improvisations) become the foundation of monodic music, leading then to the development of fully written solo song. In saying that two-part composition is more difficult than writing for three and more voices, there is the idea that two-part composition, initially "improvvisata alla mente," is put down in writing where mistakes, if present, are more evident. In contrast, even though mistakes might still be recognised, in improvisations they are somehow transitory; once they are performed, the composition is over.

Associating this moment with the difficulty of the nude figure, in the midst of the Renaissance fascination with the naked human figure, suggests for two-part counterpoint a multi-layered and interconnected nakedness. Technically, two-part counterpoint is simply the smallest combination of voices. From the performance point of view, whether appearing in the middle of a polyphonic motet or functioning as the basis for solo accompanied song, two parts appear and sound "naked." This performative nakedness, like the nude figure in a sacred context, creates tension with the text, and highlights how solo song might emphasise aspects of eroticism and nakedness expressed in the text. Ultimately, Vicentino and Tigrini add a small but significant piece in the mosaic from which opera will emerge, where the solo song is the musical embodiment of the human figure, exposed in its nudity to the audience.

COMPENDIVM MVSICES, TAM

figurati quàm plani cantus ad formam Dialogi, in usum ingenuæ pubis ex eruditis Musicorum scriptis accurate congestum, quale ante hac nunq̃ uisum, & iam recens publicatum. Adiectis etiam regulis de Concordantiarum & componendi Cantus artificio, summatim omnia Musices præcepta pulcherrimis exemplis illustrata, succincte & simpliciter complectens.

PRÆTEREA ADDITÆ SVNT FORMVLAE INTONANDI

Psalmos, & ratio accentus Ecclesiatici, legendorum quoque Euangeliorum & Epistolarum.

Martini Crusij

AB AVCTORE LAMPADIO Luneburgensi elaborata.

1541

85. The Music Book of Martin Crusius

Inga Mai Groote

Auctor Lampadius
Compendium musices
Bern: Apiarius, 1541
61 fols., 11 x 16 cm
Manuscript additions by Martin Crusius (Memmingen/Tübingen, 1542-1594)
Tübingen, Universitätsbibliothek, De4
Image: Title page with handwritten annotations by Martin Crusius. Photo: Public Domain.

This copy of the music theory schoolbook *Compendium musices* by Auctor Lampadius accompanied its owner over more than 50 years. That owner was Martin Crusius, who made his name as a professor at the university of Tübingen and as an eminent scholar of ancient Greek (Wilhelmi 2011), and left an impressive manuscript diary which gives detailed insights into his everyday life (Crusius 1927-61; Mährle 2019). He bought the book in 1542 in Ulm, when still a student at the Latin school of that city, and added manuscript parts to the volume later on. His annotations to the printed text also show that he worked intensively with the book.

Similar books could be found in many sixteenth-century Lutheran households, and many of them were personalised by their owners: we have annotated copies, copies with ownership entries, sometimes several of them (from which we can infer that they were handed down between siblings), and such books are often mentioned in post-mortem inventories. Nearly every pupil of a Latin school in Lutheran Germany had regular music lessons, as the school curriculum usually prescribed several hours of "musica" per week, usually at noon, in order to also profit from the relaxing qualities of musical activities (Niemöller 1969; see also Küster 2016). In these settings, "musica" comprised (at least the rudiments of) theoretical knowledge, but also musical practice, which was usually related to the repertoire that the school choirs were expected to perform during services: they supported the congregation in singing German hymns, performed Latin chant and, in many instances, polyphonic pieces as well. In theory, the pupils thus had to learn about the system of music, intervals, and solmisation, they had to understand the modes, and—if polyphony was performed—also the rules of mensural notation. Consequently, teaching supports were needed in great quantities, which motivated many school teachers, even in small towns, to publish their own music textbooks.

Lampadius' book is one of them: the *Compendium* emanated from Lampadius' occupation as a cantor at the Johannischule in Lüneberg in Lower Saxony during the 1530s. The book addresses plainchant and mensural notation in the first parts, as well as basic compositional rules (Owens and Ruhnke 2001). Crusius' reading of Lampadius is documented by his annotations. For many paragraphs, he added a neatly written cue or headword for the content and marked key terms: these are typical traces of readers who aim at familiarising themselves with the content (Weiss 2010; Groote 2013b). There are also some marginalia containing additional information and references to other texts, written in the more fluent handwriting Crusius used in his working manuscripts later on: he gave a cross-reference to the Pseudo-Aristotelian *Problemata* and added more rules for reading ligatures (that is, combined notational signs). Furthermore, he copied some items into the print: two tables for proportion signs and for the values of notes under different mensurations, and the definition of "canon" with the two-voice example associated, all obviously taken from Andreas Ornithoparchus' *Musice active micrologus* of 1517 (Fi^{r-v}, Fij^{v}, and Fiij^{r}), a widely circulating introduction to music at the time. Crusius' book also contains manuscript pages bound after the print with an overview of consonances (dated 1551). Crusius added, as another separate item, another set of rules for ligatures in Latin mnemonic verses, which enjoyed vast dissemination in sixteenth-century schoolbooks. By adding these materials, Crusius enhanced his printed textbook—a practice that is often observed in the case of books used by teachers (Groote 2018).

Crusius also used his music book at later stages in his career (at some point he even jotted down some Greek vocabulary on the title page and the back): after continuing his studies in Strasbourg and teaching for some time at the local Gymnasium, in 1554 he became rector of the Latin school in Memmingen, where he had the task of re-organising the school (Reichenhart 1880). In the same year, he wrote down a small question-and-answer music primer, which was used in Memmingen (the title reads *Compendium musices per quæstiones explicatum pro incipientibus. 1554, in Aprili. Memmingæ—Musical Compendium for Beginners, Explained in Questions. 1554, in April, Memmingen*), and forms the third item of his music book. It was not necessarily the rector's duty to teach music, as the music lessons were usually given by the cantor (a teacher in charge of singing and musical instruction along with other subjects) or one of the lower-ranking teachers. Crusius probably had such a strong interest in music that he wished to have the local textbook at hand, or devised it himself, or even chose to give music lessons himself.

The Memmingen *Compendium* covers the usual elementary topics. It opens with a very short definition of music: music is the "science of singing artfully" (artificiose cantandi scientia). This formulation already openly and clearly states that the aim is not competence in speculative theory ("judging the relationships between high and low sounds," according to the Boethian definitions), but competence in practical music. Only three chapters follow: the "scala" as the representation of the tonal system; signs for notes and rests (in order to learn how to decipher mensural notation); and solmisation (the use of syllables for memorising the tone system). This complies with Crusius' Memmingen school order of 1554, which stipulates the following: the teacher of the fourth, and lowest, class "has to come to the school together with the other teachers on Saturdays at noon, where he and the teacher of the third class have to exercise German psalms [that is, German hymns based on psalm texts] for half an hour"; meanwhile, the two other teachers have to instruct the second and first class, as well as those pupils who are more inclined towards "Latin music," and they will do this "with short rules (*praecepta*) recorded for this purpose" in the other half hour, until one o'clock (Reichenhart 1880, 407). That the more advanced pupils also learned "Latin music" may relate both to relevant repertoire and to basic theory, and the "short rules" mentioned in the school order can with all probability be identified with the handwritten *Compendium*. The fact that in Memmingen music is taught only on Saturdays—while other schools, under the influence of Philip Melanchthon's Saxon school order, scheduled music on three or four days per week—is due to the influence of Johannes Sturm's curriculum for the Strasbourg Gymnasium.

In 1559 Crusius left Memmingen and became Professor at the University of Tübingen. He published grammars, editions of and commentaries on Greek authors, and a three-volume history of the region of Swabia, as well as writings on the situation of the Orthodox Church in his time. Notwithstanding his professorial duties and his scholarly work, he continued to practice music: he sang regularly, performed together with students and professional musicians, and commissioned settings of Latin poetic texts that he himself had written for academic festivities in Tübingen (Reichert 1953). In 1595, he compiled a list of over 70 pieces (hymns as well as polyphonic motets), which he knew and had sung by heart for many years, "particularly after the morning prayer, between dressing and combing"—even if some students mocked his singing by nicknaming him "Bumble-bee" (Reichert 1953, 188-89). Motivated by his interest in the Greek world, he also recorded some information concerning late Byzantine notation (Tübingen, Universitätsbibliothek, MS Mb37).

At the very end of his music book is a little biographical entry, which connects the volume to Crusius' musical activities in his later years (fig. 85.1). After the ligature rules, Crusius notates a short exercise: it begins with the hexachord, followed by a simple melody, with little strokes to help the student count correctly. The inscription above reads "On 1 August 1594, for Johann Jacob Maier, my grandson." The boy was a son of Crusius' daughter Maria Magdalena, who had married a pastor named Johann Jacob Maier in Berg, near Donauwörth. The melody is notated in the descant clef, suitable for a young boy's voice, and the hexachord even has the names of the syllables written next to every tone. Crusius' note may be a piece of family memorabilia, perhaps recording the time when the boy, who had lived in Crusius' house since 1592 (Crusius 1927-61, 3:804), began to learn music. In July 1595 Crusius' grandson probably took music lessons from a student, Andreas Gundelfinger (Reichert 1953, 190), when he attended the third class (Tübingen, Universitätsbibliothek, MS Mh466-5, 424); so he may have been aged five or six years the year before. In 1599, it is recorded that Johann Jacob also learnt to play the clavichord (Crusius 1927-61, 2:365).

Crusius' music book, with its typical combination of printed and manuscript material that can be found in many contemporary volumes (see exhibit 14), remained in use at different stages of his life, from his own school days until his old age. It perfectly epitomises the role of music in the life of a Protestant scholar, who learned, and probably also taught, music at school and continued to practice it as an amateur throughout his adult life. In Crusius' case, the hope regularly expressed by Lutheran educators that music should become an honest pastime, both recreation and spiritual exercise, seems to have been fulfilled.

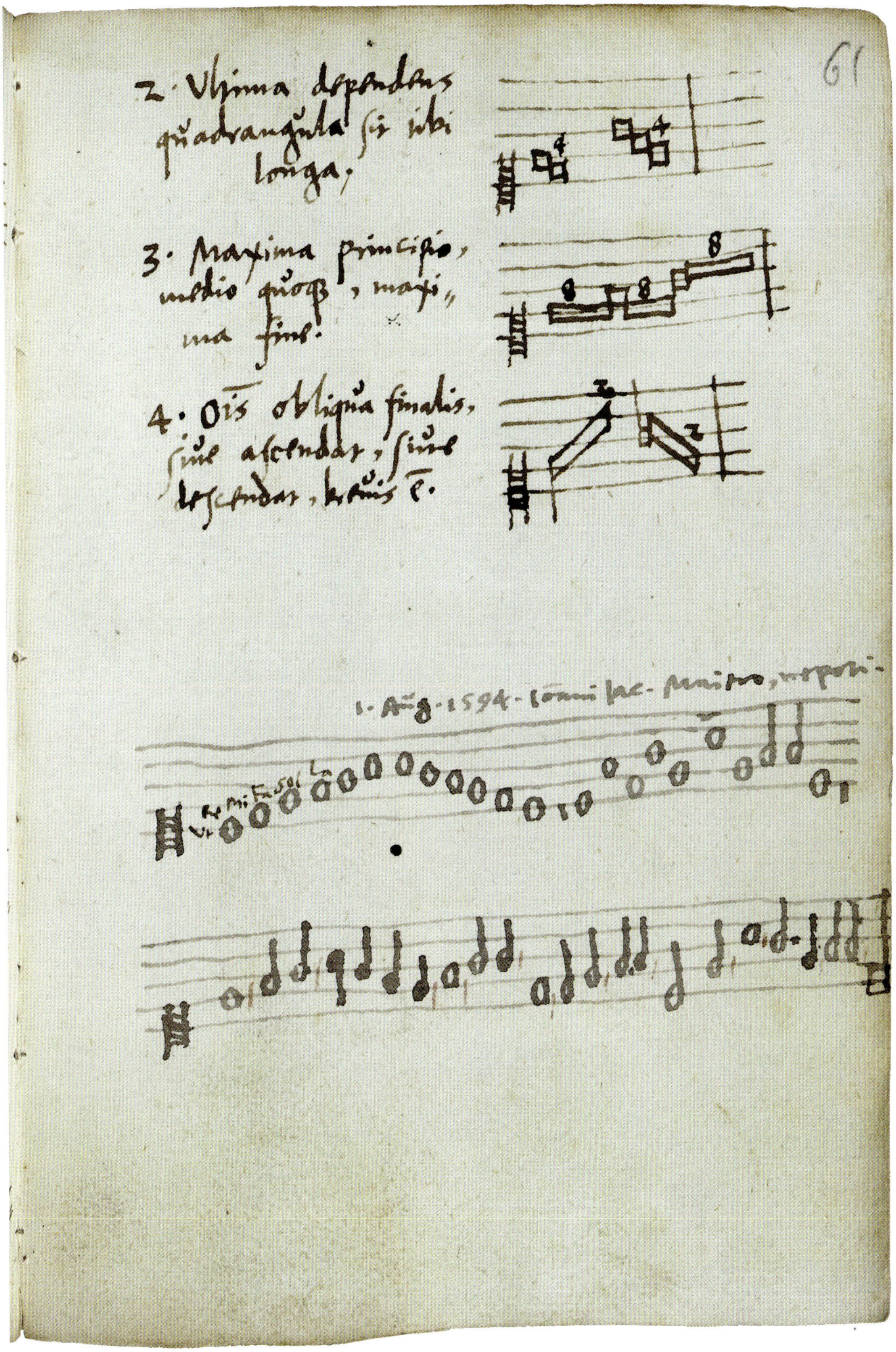

Figure 85.1: *Compendium musices* (1541) with annotations by Martin Crusius. Universitätsbibliothek, Tübingen (De4), fol. 61r. Photo: Public Domain.

Excusum Pragæ, apud Georgium Nigrinum,
Impensis Joannis Grilli Senioris à Grillovva.

ANNO M. D. LXXXIX.

86. The World on a Crab's Back

Katelijne Schiltz

Anon., Prague, 1589
Broadsheet, 37 x 28.8 cm
Prague, Královská kanonie premonstrátů na Strahově (Strahov Monastery Library), DR I 21, fol. 92r (p. 307)
Photo courtesy of the Královská kanonie premonstrátů na Strahově

THE COLLECTIONS of Strahov monastery library include a lavish broadside by an anonymous composer, printed in Prague by Georgius Nigrinus in 1589. Framed by a decorative border are four voices, laid out in such a way that the two pairs face each other. They sing the following, somewhat enigmatic text: "Miraris mundum dorso consistere cancri? Desine, sic hodie vertitur orbis iter" (Are you surprised to see the world on the crab's back? Refrain! This is the way of the world nowadays).

The distich is repeated in the centre of the broadside, which is the part that immediately attracts the viewer's attention. Above the distich is a crab (or rather a crayfish, but let us stick with the crab for the sake of simplicity) which carries a globe on its back—the vista includes a landscape with a man in a boat, a town's silhouette and a starry sky with a waning moon. Upon the body of the animal is a short five-note palindromic sequence *g-a-b-a-g*, under which the words "Cancer cancrisat" (The crab goes backwards) are printed backwards. A c4-clef and three breves' rest on either side not only produce a symmetrical layout, but also suggest that the pattern forms a "soggetto ostinato," that is, the motif is repeated throughout the piece. This ensemble is surrounded by a circle presenting another passage of music, underlaid with a text that is also written backwards. In a macaronic mixture, Czech verses alternate with Latin:

Svět se točí rovně jako kolo,
Protož přítele hleď míť dobrého,
Multa vadunt cum feria sexta,
Neb mnohé věci jdou v světě zpátkem,
retro cedunt in deteriora & non meliora.

The world is turning straight like a wheel
Therefore make sure to have a good friend,
Many things go on Friday,
Because many things in the world go backwards,
They go backwards to the worse and not to the better.

Translation: Leofranc Holford-Strevens

Both the text underlay and the reversed mensuration sign indicate that the music is to be sung anti-clockwise. The music turns out to produce a second ostinato, which starts alternately on *d'* and *g'*—most of the Czech verses have one syllable more than those in Latin, but this is solved by splitting the second minim into two semiminims for the Czech text. The result is a six-voice bilingual work for four free voices plus the two ostinato voices (Schiltz 2015, 296-98).

The anonymous composer was neither the first nor the last to use the distich "Miraris mundum…" (or parts of it) accompanied by a crab with the globe on its back. On the contrary, it turns out to be well known in the late sixteenth and early seventeenth centuries, where it occurs in a variety of contexts and media. I have traced its usage in the *album amicorum* of the Augsburg organist Abel Prasch (Munich, Bayerisches Nationalmuseum, MS 245, fol. 130[r]); in the lepers' chapel of St Michael's church in Zwolle, where it is part of a commemorative plaque from 1584; on a medal from the Altdorf Academy (Stopp 1974, 168-69); and as part of the emblematic ensemble in the Golden Hall of the Nuremberg town hall, to name just a few examples. The Nuremberg town hall was bombed during World War II, but a reconstruction of the emblems in the Golden Hall was partly possible by way of the drawings in Peter Isselburg's *Emblemata politica* from 1617; additionally, colour transparencies were made during the years 1943-45 at the command of the Nazi regime, which sought to document significant works of arts in the territory of the German Reich in view of the impending bombing.

What is it that the phrase and the image want to tell us? Only a few years before the publication of this broadside from Prague, the humanist Joachim Camerarius introduced these verses in his manuscript treatise *Symbola et emblemata* from 1587 (Stadtbibliothek Mainz, shelfmark Hs. II.366; see Harms and Heß 2009, 196-97 and 514-15). The central idea of Camerarius' work is to capture the natural world and to decrypt its components as elements in the history of salvation. In other words, plants and animals are not only interpreted in a scientific sense, but they also form part of a complex "mundus symbolicus." The distich "Miraris mundum" serves as the emblem's *subscriptio* (epigram) that conceptually connects the *pictura* (showing a crab with the globe on his back) and the motto "Sic vertitur orbis iter" (This is the way of the world). Camerarius goes on to explain that the backward movement of the crab symbolises a regressive world, a world that is desperate and losing its purpose. The negative connotations of the crab in fact go back to Classical Antiquity and the Middle Ages, and were further developed in the Renaissance. For example, in Sebastian Brant's famous satire *The Ship of Fools* (*Das Narren Schyff*) from 1494, one page shows a fool with his dunce's cap sitting on a crab (fig. 86.1). The accompanying text stresses the animal's instability, hence it is a bad foundation for the world to rest upon.

Camerarius supports his view with a quote from Virgil's *Georgicon* 1:200, where it is said that all things tend "in peius ruere ac retro sublapsa referri" (to speed to the worse, and backward borne glide from us). In the multi-volume printed version of his treatise (Camerarius 1604, fols. 54^{v}-54^{r}), he considerably expands his commentary and adds further sources to support the pessimistic image of the retrogressive movement of the world. He especially brings in antique authorities (Aristophanes, Euripides, Horace, and Seneca), as well as humanist scholars such as Piero Valeriano and Erasmus.

What could have inspired the anonymous composer to set this text? I believe the person who is mentioned at the bottom of the broadside—and apparently paid for it—played a central role: Johannes Gryll a Gryllova was a legal counsel and writer from Rakonitz (Rakovník). He wrote poems in Greek and translated several books of the Bible into Czech. In 1571 Emperor Rudolf II made him a *vladyka* (a member of the lower nobility), and in 1588, a year before the publication of the broadside, Gryll not only became mayor of his native town, but Rakonitz was also named a royal city. It may well have been the connection of these events that prompted Gryll to commission the broadside. What is more, since 1482 Rakonitz has carried a crab in its coat of arms—the central place of the animal in the city's heraldry has an etymological explanation: the Czech word for crab is "Rak." At first sight, if we accept the hypothesis of Gryll's mayoral appointment as the main impetus for the broadside, the festive occasion is strangely at odds with the inherently pessimistic tone of the text and the negative connotations of the crab carrying the world (Schiltz 2015, 299-300). However, if we take into account the difficult political and religious situation in the late sixteenth century, it looks as if the broadside reflects the city's (and Gryll's) consciousness of the ongoing perils, and offers its viewers (and listeners) something to meditate and reflect upon. Moreover, the polyphony could be said to symbolise and strengthen the communal feeling of the citizens.

The 1589 page exhibits a high degree of self-referentiality. Music, text, and image are strongly interdependent, and each medium intensifies the effect of the others. The underlying idea of the regressive world in particular is expressed by all possible means. Apart from the text "Miraris mundum," which serves as the verbal commentary to the image of the crab with the world on its back, several visual details, such as the retrograde notation of the Czech and Latin verses on the one hand, and the retrograde typography of "Cancer cancrisat" for the short palindromic ostinato on the other, reinforce the central message of the broadside. One could also argue that the layout of the four free voices serves the work's central purpose: as the performers see each other's parts upside down, this could also be a reference to a "mundus inversus," which is conceptually related with the idea of the retrogressive world.

This six-voice *Miraris mundum* not only offers its recipient a rich musical, visual, and textual programme to reflect upon, but it also seeks to integrate music in a wider emblematic context. To the emblem's traditional combination of text and image, music has been added as a third medium that underlines the moral message with its own means. The music in the circle, which literally encapsulates the emblem (i.e. the epigrammatic *inscriptio* "Cancer cancrisat," the *pictura* of the crab with the globe on its back, and the *subscriptio* in the form of a Latin distich), is a compressed form of the emblem's tripartite structure. It summarises and illustrates the three aspects in a condensed form: the circle revisits the image of the world—it is an abstract reproduction of the globe on the back of the crab; the text, with its mixture of Czech and Latin verses, reformulates the contents of the Latin distich about the world developing in a negative sense; and finally, the retrograde reading of the music visualises the backward movement of the world that is criticised in the emblem. As a whole, this broadside both conceals and reveals its intention: it demands active recipients, offering them interpretive clues and forcing them to decipher both the notation and the meaning of the work at the same time.

Figure 86.1: Sebastian Brant, *Das Narrenschiff* (Basel: Johann Bergmann, 1494), [146]. Universitätsbibliothek Basel, UBH Ai II 22. Photo: Public Domain.

J. del encina
Tenor.
Cont.
viene se sin le buscar
los placeres

87. Juan del Encina's *Gasajémonos de huzía*

Emilio Ros-Fábregas

Madrid, Real Biblioteca de Palacio, Patrimonio Nacional, II-1335 (Cancionero Musical de Palacio), fols. ci^{v}-$ciii^{r}$ (104^{v}-106^{r})
Several scribes, Court of Castile, ca. 1498-1520
Manuscript on paper, 261 fols., 21 x 15 cm
Image: fols. ci^{v}-cii^{r} (104^{v}-105^{r}). Photo courtesy of the Real Biblioteca de Palacio, Madrid.

A CONCERT WITH Spanish secular vocal music of the early Renaissance usually includes works from the manuscript known as Cancionero Musical de Palacio (henceforth CMP), dated ca. 1498-1520. This small-format book (21 x 15 cm), which nonetheless contains 458 pieces, constitutes the largest source of Spanish music from any era, and the two editions of its repertory (Barbieri 1890; Anglés 1947 and 1951) are used as an enormous repository by performers everywhere. Since the book was compiled in different stages, in a process of accretion taking place for the most part during the time of the Catholic monarchs, Isabel of Castile and Ferdinand of Aragon, it has usually been associated with their peripatetic courts in general. However, the origin of the CMP has been controversial—although we know that in the early seventeenth century the manuscript belonged to the bibliophile Diego Sarmiento de Acuña, first count of Gondomar. In 1785 his extraordinary library was donated to King Carlos III of Spain, and thus today the manuscript is found in the Real Biblioteca at the Royal Palace in Madrid, from which derived the name Cancionero Musical de Palacio.

In a typical concert featuring Spanish music of the Renaissance, short pieces from the CMP follow one another according to performers' diverse criteria, such as the special popularity of some works (as a result of modern recordings), particular genres such as the villancico and romance, common themes of the texts, and preference for a composer, particularly Juan del Encina, traditionally considered the best among those represented in the manuscript. It is well known that many villancicos and romances by Encina were composed as part of *églogas* (eclogues), short theatrical performances, but since in modern editions of these compositions the connections between pieces and *églogas* are not obvious, and the original manuscript has not been available online until recently, it has been difficult for performers and public alike to approach the overwhelming CMP repertoire in what historical research considers its own terms. This *Museum of Renaissance Music* provides an opportunity to re-think this extraordinary manuscript in a broader perspective, not only as a huge collection of music, but also, at least for some of its pieces, as part of musical-literary-theatrical performances that a fresh analysis of its content allows us to reconstruct.

How can we use the CMP to afford a glimpse of the literary-theatrical-musical life of late fifteenth-century Spain? What do we know about the context in which these pieces by Encina were performed? Let us examine two openings in the oldest section of the CMP to enter the world of a ducal court in Renaissance Castile. The upper image at the head of this essay shows the opening at fols. ci^{v}-cii^{r} of the CMP, bearing two works: according to the numbering in Anglés's edition, no. 165 *Gasajémonos de huzía* by Encina (for four voices, three on the left-hand page and one at the top of the right-hand page); and, a later addition in a different hand, no. 166 *Ya murieron los plaseres* by García Muñoz (for three voices, squeezed in the middle of the right-hand page). Recent codicological findings (Ros-Fábregas 2017) indicate that the earliest section of the manuscript is found in the middle of the codex (where these two works are located), coinciding with paper gatherings carrying a special watermark dated in the late 1490s; those gatherings contain precisely musical works by Encina found in *églogas* performed before the duke and duchess of Alba in their Alba de Tormes castle-palace in Salamanca in the 1490s.

In the following opening (lower main image), fols. cii^{v}-$ciii^{r}$, in similar disposition, we find two other works: no. 167 *Ninguno çierre las puertas* (*Nobody should close the doors*; 4vv) by Juan del Encina; and, again a later addition, no. 168 *Vida y alma el que os mirare* (*The one who looks at you does not value his own life and soul*; 3vv) by Gabriel Mena/de Texerana. Interestingly, the two pieces by Encina (nos. 165 and 167) in the oldest section of the manuscript, originally copied by the same scribe one after another, are the only two villancicos sung in one of the *églogas* performed before the duke and duchess of Alba in their Alba de Tormes palace in 1496. It would seem appropriate, then, to connect these two works in modern performances, to better understand their purpose and context.

The long title of the pastoral play in which the two villancicos by Encina were performed runs: *Égloga representada por las mesmas personas que en la de arriba van introduzidas, que son: un pastor que de antes era escudero, llamado Gil, y Pascuala, y Mingo y su esposa Menga* (*Eclogue performed by the same people who are introduced in the one above, who are: a shepherd who used to be a squire, named Gil, and Pascuala, and Mingo and his wife Menga*; *Égloga representada* 1496; Encina 1496; Pérez Priego 1991). Gil, a former squire who has been a shepherd for a year, introduces Mingo (played by Encina), who presents his works—most likely the 1496 printed edition of his literary *Cancionero* (Encina 1496)—as an offering to the duke and duchess. Gil praises them and commends Mingo to serve them and to make "cantilenas" for them and also for his own wife, the shepherdess Pascuala. Mingo, recalling that Pascuala had left him a year before, is not in the mood to sing. However, in memory of love ("en memoria del amor"), they decide to call their respective wifes, Pascuala and Menga, to enjoy a celebration, singing and dancing Encina's villancico no. 165: "Gasajémonos de huzía / qu'el pesar / viénese sin le buscar" (Let's enjoy with confidence, that sorrow comes without looking for it). The literary context provides interesting performance practice information, since it seems clear that when presenting the work before the duke and duchess they sang one to a part, two men and two women, and they also danced while singing. It should be pointed out that the CMP has only two strophes of the text, but in Encina's Égloga published in his 1496 literary *Cancionero* this villancico has two additional strophes that, as we will see later, are particularly significant to understand the context surrounding this piece.

After *Gasajémonos de huzía* has been sung, Mingo is ready to go back to his village with Gil, but the latter has decided to abandon the shepherd's life and to remain at court. Pascuala, Gil's wife, will follow him, since a year earlier, he had followed her, becoming a shepherd, and now she wants to show her love in return. After very amusing exchanges about how all four would help each other to adapt their external appearances and manners to courtly life, they all end up deciding to live at the court; they are convinced that love has been responsible for such a change in their lives. Thus, the play concludes with Encina's no. 167: "Ninguno çierre las puertas / si Amor viniere a llamar, que no le ha de aprovechar" (Nobody should close the doors if Love is calling, it will be to no avail). As with the other villancico, the CMP transmits one strophe only, but Encina's literary *Cancionero* provides five more strophes for the conclusion of this *Égloga*.

We know exactly where these pieces were originally performed, something very unusual for secular repertory of the time. Fadrique Álvarez de Toledo Enríquez, second duke of Alba, and his wife Isabel de Zúñiga played host to Encina's *Égloga* in their magnificent castle-palace in Alba de Tormes, of which only the restored Tower of Homage is extant. Inside the tower, the Sala de los Frescos (Room of the Frescos; see the images in the video at the following link: https://www.youtube.com/watch?v=goHzeue-OCY&t=4s) is the one used at that time for theatrical performances—including those involving Encina—and other courtly activities. It should be pointed out that in 1476 the Franco-Flemish composer Johannes Wreede, known as Urreda in Spain, had been singer and chapelmaster to the first duke of Alba, García Álvarez de Toledo, author of the text of Wreede's *Nunca fue pena mayor* (*Never was there a greater pain*), one of the most widely circulating secular pieces of the time, also found in the CMP. The second duke, Fadrique, was responsible for major reforms in the castle-palace and entertained an active literary court. The Sala's frescoes, discovered in the 1950s, are from a later period and represent three scenes from the Battle of Mühlberg (1547), a victory of the third duke during the reign of Charles V; they were painted by Cristóbal Passini between 1567 and 1571 (Subirá, 1927; González Zymla, 2013).

The different layers of compound manuscripts, such as the CMP, are sometimes studied only from the chronological point of view with respect to the original copying of the source, and have sometimes been perceived by modern scholars as unrelated intrusions or deviations from the original purpose and context of the manuscript; this perception can be visually reinforced if the added handwriting appears to be aesthetically less pleasing than the original. However, further investigation may reveal unexpected findings. Later additions to the CMP have been treated simply as works copied into available spaces left empty by previous scribes, but a closer look at the evidence reveals the dialogues of other poet-musicians with this source. Let us examine, for instance, the later addition no. 166, mentioned above, *Ya murieron los plaseres* (*Pleasures died already*) for three voices by García Muñoz, squeezed between the two villancicos of Encina's *Égloga*. Was this composition added in that particular place just by chance, or is it in any way related to the work by Encina found alongside it? The missing strophes of Encina's no. 165 *Gasajémonos de huzía* transmitted in his 1496 *Cancionero* contain verses such as "andemos tras los plazeres" (let's go after pleasures), "Tras los plazeres corramos" (let's run after pleasures), and this villancico ends with "Busquemos siempre el plazer, / qu'el pesar / viénese sin le buscar" (Let's look always for pleasure, that sorrow comes without looking for it). Thus, even though the text of Encina's *Gasajémonos* copied in the CMP does not contain the word "pleasure" (a case of censorship?), it is very possible that García Muñoz's inserted villancico "Ya murieron los plaseres / del alma y del coraçon, / que ya, triste, muertos son" (Pleasures of the soul and heart have died, and, sadly, they are dead) is a direct response to the

Figure 87.1: Madrid, Real Biblioteca de Palacio, Patrimonio Nacional, II-1335 (Cancionero Musical de Palacio), fols. cii^{v}-ciii^{r} (105^{v}-106^{r}). Photo courtesy of the Real Biblioteca de Palacio, Madrid.

"plazeres" sought after by Gil, Mingo, Pascuala, and Menga in the complete text of Encina's *Gasajémonos*; moreover, some short musical motifs also seem to connect both pieces, even though they were copied by different scribes, at different times, and reflecting different contexts.

The comparison between musical and literary sources, the exploration of original venues for performances, and the discovery of previously unnoticed literary and musical relationships between seemingly unrelated works, are just a few examples of the kinds of active dialogue that we could establish with the CMP. Just as contemporary museums now offer alternative narrations of modern history, new forms of intermediation, and consider the spectator not as a consumer, but as an active agent (Borja-Villel 2020), the *Museum of Renaissance Music* presents the CMP as an open source to foster those objectives. Indeed, this music book contains many compositions, but it is not a presentation manuscript: in contrast with so many others surviving from the period, it does not have those decorative elements that help modern scholars to describe its relation to its readers and to the contexts of its use. I hope, however, that this short essay will show how useful it is to study such a book and its contents with a focus wider than just "the music itself" (and/or perhaps "the literary texts themselves"). The Cancionero Musical de Palacio, like all music books (actually like all books), is an archive in which many stories are preserved, which can be extracted and told in order to generate new narratives and aesthetic experiences, in order to apprehend more vividly a historical moment.

Additional references: Link to the digital reproduction of the manuscript – https://rbdigital.realbiblioteca.es/s/realbiblioteca/item/2396

Josquin
Philippus rex castilie
Kyrie
eleison
Christe
eleison
Kyrie
eleison
Kyrie
eleisonn
Tenor
Philippus rex castilie
Philippus rex
castilie
Philippus rex
castilie
eleison

Kyrie
eleison
Christe
eleison
Kyrie
elei son
Kyrie
eleison
Christe
eleison
Kyrie

88. Josquin des Prez's *Missa Philippus Rex Castilie*

Vincenzo Borghetti

Brussels, Bibliothèque Royale de Belgique Albert 1er/Koninklijke Bibliotheek Albert I, MS 9126, fols. 72^{v}-82^{r}
Scribe B, Habsburg-Burgundian court of the Low Countries, ca. 1504-1506
Manuscript on parchment, 182 fols., 38.2 x 27 cm

Image: fols. 72^{v}-73^{r}.

Manuscript 9126 (henceforth 9126) of the Royal Library of Belgium is a luxury parchment music book containing polyphonic Masses and motets by different composers. It was made ca. 1504-06 for Philip the Fair and his wife Juana of Castile, whose portraits and coat of arms, together with Philip's mottos and devices, can be found on the first two pages (fols. 1^{v}-2^{r}). On fols. 72^{v}-82^{r} is the Mass *Philippus Rex Castilie* (*Philip King of Castile*) by Josquin des Prez: the image given here shows the first opening of this Mass in the manuscript. The name of the dedicatee of the composition and his royal title appear in the rubric at the beginning of the highest voice (fol. 72^{v} at the top on the left), and are repeated further down the page beneath the Tenor. The king of Castille who is placed at the centre of this Mass is the same Philip who was the recipient of the manuscript. Son of Mary of Burgundy and Maximilian I, husband of Juana (who was daughter of Isabel of Castile and Ferdinand of Aragon), after many dynastic vicissitudes Philip ascended the throne of Castile following the death of his mother-in-law in 1505 (Cauchies 2003, 159-217). He would die shortly thereafter, in 1506.

At the centre of the upper margin of fol. 72^{v}, the manuscript names "Josquin" as the author of the composition. Josquin, however, did not compose his Mass in the form in which it is transmitted by this book. The *Missa Philippus Rex Castilie* originally had a different name and a different dedicatee: Ercole I d'Este, duke of Ferrara. That he, and not Philip, was the sovereign at the centre of the composition is revealed by the music itself. Josquin had obtained the cantus firmus on which the Mass is composed (i.e. the melody functioning as the cornerstone of the entire composition) with the artifice of a "soggetto cavato dalle parole" (subject carved from the words; Zarlino 1558, 66), by matching the vowels of a short acclamation directed to Ercole as duke of Ferrara (*Hercules Dux Ferrarie*) to the corresponding vowels of the traditional Guidonian solmization syllables (*ut re mi fa sol la*) (Lockwood 2001):

Her-cu-les Dux Fer-ra-ri- e
re ut re ut re fa mi re
d c d c d f e d

The new *Philippus* text of the cantus firmus has the same number of syllables as the *Hercules* text, and therefore could easily be set to the eight notes "carved from" the original text; however, by changing the words, the *Philippus* text destroys the correspondence between notes and vowels.

This Mass is not the only known adaptation of Josquin's *Hercules* Mass. Around 1518-20 the same scriptorium in the Low Countries created another version, contained in another luxury choirbook—this time for Frederick the Wise, duke of Saxony (Jena, Universitätsbiblithek, MS 3, fols. 43^{v}-58^{r}; fig. 88.1)—and equipped with another new text for the cantus firmus, cut to the size of the new dedicatee: *Fridericus Dux Saxonie* (Kellman 1999, 87; Ammendola 2013, 248-49). Nor is this the only adaptation made for Philip known from the manuscript 9126, given that Agricola's motet known in other sources as *Ergo sancti martyres* appears here as *Sancte Philippe Appostole* (Fitch 1999, 6).

As the two Masses for Philip and Frederick demonstrate, the rupture of the intimate correspondence between the text of the cantus firmus and its music did not constitute a problem for the appropriation of the Mass on the part of sovereigns other than Ercole. We can in fact immagine that Philip (like Frederick after him) took an interest in qualities of the composition beyond those arising from its ingenious construction upon a *soggetto cavato*, and which concern the Mass as a sounding artifact (Long 2014, 36).

As a matter of fact, beyond the *soggetto cavato* Josquin's Mass employs a compositional style which over the course of the fifteenth century served Western European ruling classes as a musical symbol of their own power (Borghetti 2008). By the privilege of his caste, and by the specific attention reserved for music in the traditions of his family, Philip knew well that the musical style appropriate for celebrating the power of sovereigns entails, as in the *Hercules* Mass, a radical separation between the cantus firmus, invariably placed in the Tenor and usually in long notes, and the other voices composed around it. These voices move differently from the cantus firmus, generally unconcerned with its melodic material, with more rapid and varied figurations, demonstrating the author's inventiveness in composing all five movements of a Mass on the basis of the same given melody, but without thereby obscuring the pre-eminence of the musical cornerstone of the composition, which remains always clearly perceptible precisely because it

Figure 88.1: Josquin des Prez, *Missa Fridericus dux saxonie*, Kyrie, beginning of the Superius and Tenor parts. Jena, Thüringer Universitäts- und Landesbibliothek, Bibliotheca Electoralis, Chorbuch 3, fol. 15v. Photo: Public Domain.

is rhythmically and melodically distinct from the rest of the polyphonic complex.

In the *Hercules* Mass, therefore, Philip found one of the most recent instantiations of this type of composition, where these particular celebratory characteristics were exhibited even more explicitly than in earlier pieces. Firstly, the cantus firmus is not derived from liturgical repertory, but intones a new text created ad hoc and addressing directly a specific sovereign—no matter that now as *Philippus Rex Castilie* it was not carved from Philip's own name. Secondly, Josquin availed himself of a cantus firmus technique that he used in ways simultaneously archaic and modern: archaic was the separation of the Tenor from the free voices; whereas modern, and unprecedented in the Mass repertory of the time, was the rigidity and formal clarity of its application (Fallows 2009, 256-62). Thus Josquin, through this fusion of old and new, creates a style that "attempts to blur the perception of the work's temporality, placing it beyond history, together with the prince and his ideology of princely power, both objects of the celebration." (Borghetti 2019, 70).

Nevertheless, Philip's enjoyment of Josquin's Mass—recognising it as a polyphonic Mass which celebrates him as king by putting him at the heart of the composition—was not due only to its characteristics as a sounding artifact. In this respect its inclusion in a book like 9126 is significant. We are dealing with a presentation manuscript, a luxury book not conceived exclusively for music-making, but also intended for readers of the ruling class. As a sign of social distinction, these readers were familiar with polyphonic music, but were not necessarily musically literate—at least not in a professional sense. Their reading of the music contained in their luxury books—whatever the circumstances under which it took place—had to be encouraged, guided, sustained in various ways. The exuberant decorative apparatuses typical of such books, their layout, and the graphic and material characteristics of their texts and paratexts served not only to render these books beautiful or precious; they served also and perhaps primarily to enrich the sensory experience of their musical content for an audience of wealthy and powerful amateurs, to afford them insights in compositional features and symbolic meanings even when "merely" looked at (Borghetti 2015).

As an example of what one might call this enriched, deepened experience of the music made possible by a presentation manuscript, let us try to imagine Philip finding himself before his precious codex 9126, contemplating the opening of fols. 72^{v}-73^{r} during Mass whilst his chapel sings the *Missa Philippus Rex Castilie*. Or else, let us imagine him recalling the celebration whilst occupied simply in reading his book in his rooms.

Opening the manuscript at fol. 72^{v}, we can imagine his gaze going straight to the point from which one always begins to read a book—at the top on the left—where the highest voice of the composition is to be found, the Superius. There, after the large calligraphic initial "K" (it is the Kyrie, the beginning of the Mass), Philip lingers upon the rubric, which acclaims him as king of Castile, and then on the notes which accompany this text, all written in arresting red, for he will not see notes in this color again over the course of the entire Mass. The notes are all equal (*breves*), and for Philip they recall visually no less than aurally the quotation of a liturgical chant, performed in notes all of the same duration (and for this reason called "cantus planus"), which in music books like 9126 could appear at the beginning of compositions, but kept distinct from the polyphonic elaboration.

In this moment, the high voices of the chapel may indeed be singing "Philippus Rex Castilie" under those equal red notes, or perhaps instead they substitute "Kyrie eleison," the text of the Mass ordinary. Whichever text the sopranos sing (or whatever performance he recalls in his memory), Philip, who reads from 9126, knows that this music celebrates him as "Rex Castilie." He is reminded of the fact that he is the dedicatee of the music that splendidly enriches the Eucharistic celebration, thanks to the art of one of the foremost composers of the age.

Moving his gaze further down the page, Philip notes that the same text, "Philippus Rex Castilie," appears (in red) at the Tenor, accompanied by the same music that he heard at the beginning, which now enters in this voice, as the Superius finishes its phrase and unites with the Contratenor and Bass in fast musical figurations. From this moment on the melody of equal notes which hails him as king of Castile will appear almost exclusively in the Tenor. Philip now understands that this is the cantus firmus of the Mass. He was expecting it, because he knows that the Tenor is the most important part of the composition (the "fundamentum relationis" as defined in a musical dictionary of the period; Tinctoris 2004, 48), and it is here that the cantus firmus usually goes—called "firmus" precisely because it has longer notes, contrasting with the faster movement of the other voices. The Superius has only introduced it, making it heard at the beginning of the Mass and in the highest voice, and serving so-to-speak as a red carpet to prepare its entrance in the Tenor, its proper seat. It is perhaps for this reason that its notes are red in the highest part: to signal their importance as the first thing heard of this Mass right at the beginning and in the acoustically most prominent voice, and at the same time to indicate that this is an announcement of the music belonging to the Tenor, the cornerstone of the whole composition.

Reading from 9126 whilst he listens to a performance, or reading and recalling or imagining one, Philip thus understands that his acclamation is the pivot of the composition. He sees it and hears it repeated in equal notes, for the most part in long note values, which enter and exit from the musical edifice at regular intervals; he sees and he hears it beginning and ending always with the same notes (on *d*, on *a*, on *d* an octave higher—or backwards), which are the fundamental tones in the scale of the first mode (the mode in which the Mass is composed); he sees and he hears it presented in its standard form, then from the middle of the Credo also in retrograde motion, and he thus comprehends a compositional artifice that could easily escape his notice just listening to this Mass without his precious book before him.

At every page turn, Philip sees his cantus firmus always in the same position, always isolated visually from the rest of the voices, and connects this graphic device with its aural counterpart, each as the metaphor of the other. Therefore, he understands himself to be not only the patron of the Mass as a composition—like one of those little figures at the sides of a sacred scene, found in the altarpieces and devotional images whose appearance and use were familiar to him—but the centre of it. The text "Philippus Rex Castilie" thus becomes for him an expansion of the text of the Mass (a trope, technically speaking), which makes of him another "Kyrie," "Dominus," "Pater," "Agnus": the "Rex Castilie" of whom the Mass celebrates the (divine) power and to whom the Mass calls for aid. The music, whose structural characteristics are made evident in the pages of 9126, makes his authority at once both visible and audible: Philip, placed in the cantus firmus, is seen and heard as the centre and origin of a (musical) world which rotates around him; he who literally resounds on the fundamental tones of the musical scale, and always those; and who in this way marks the beginning, the middle, and the end of this world, its alpha and omega.

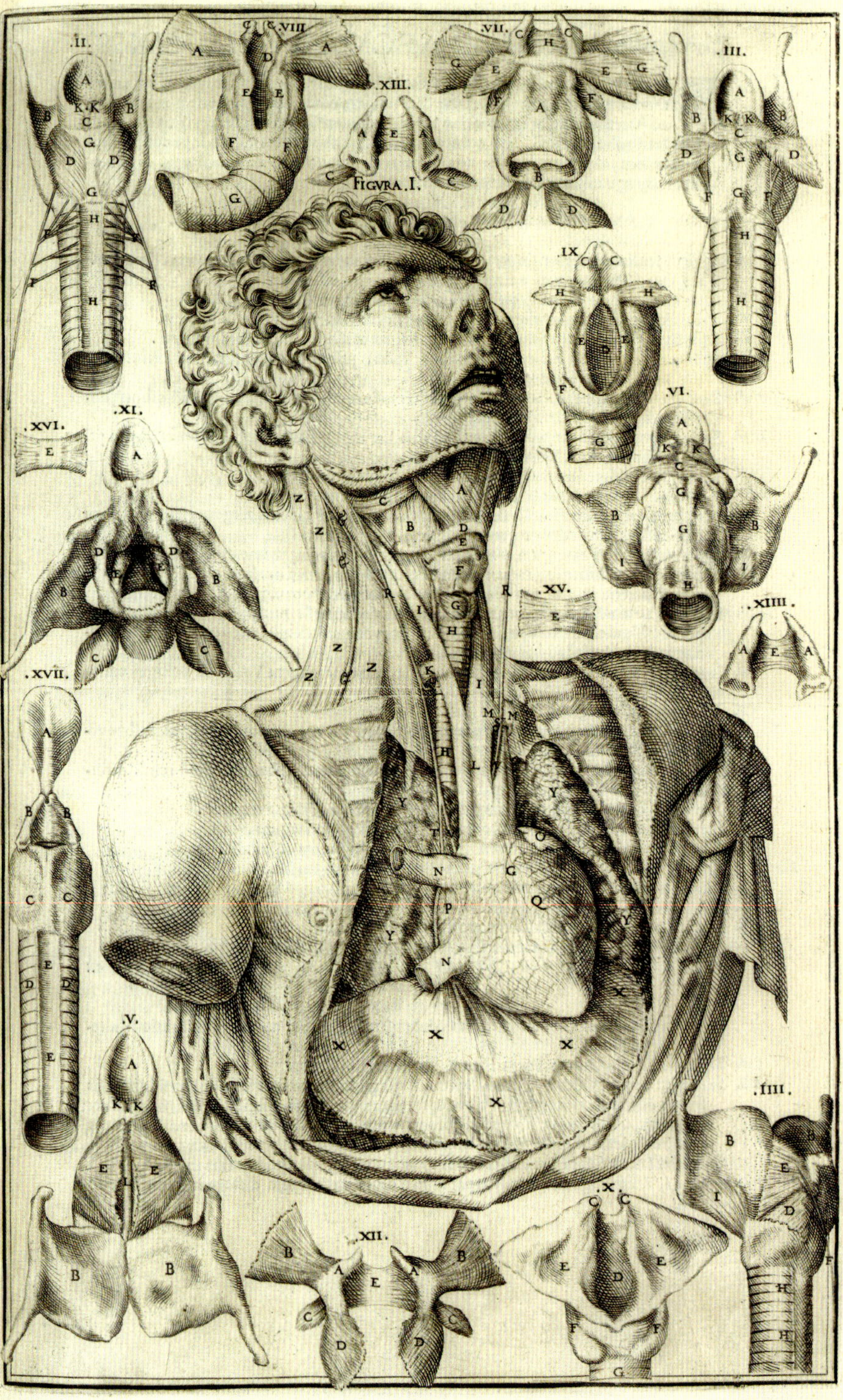
.II.
.VIII
.XIII.
.VII.
.III.
FIGVRA I.
.IX
.XVI.
.XI.
.VI.
.XV.
.XIIII.
.XVII.
.V.
.IIII.
.X.
.XII.

89. The Elite Singing Voice

Richard Wiſtreich

Francesco Valesio
Engraving from Giulio Casserio, *De vocis auditusque organis hiſtoria*
Ferrara: Vittorio Baldini, 1600-1601
2 parts in 1 vol. ([58]-191-[1]-126 pp.), fols., 37 x 24 cm
Paris, Bibliothèque nationale de France, FOL-S-923 (2), tabula XIII, p. 69

Of all the exhibits in the *Museum of Renaissance Music*, this one is diſtinguished by a glaring absence. In 1600, Vittorio Baldini published a sumptuous folio book in Ferrara, the *De vocis auditusque organis hiſtoria anatomica* (*Anatomical Hiſtory of the Organs of Voice and Hearing*) by the great Paduan anatomiſt, Giulio Cesare Casserio. One of the book's moſt celebrated features is its series of extraordinarily precise copperplate engravings by Francesco Valesio that accompany the section of the book describing the parts of the larynx, explicated with a level of detail never before seen in print, of which this is one. Meanwhile, in the same year, the Florentine printer Giorgio Marescotti issued an equally impressive folio-sized book, *Le mvsiche di Iacopo Peri ... sopra l'Euridice del sig. Ottavio Rinvccini*, presenting in print the "play in music" *Euridice* (fig. 89.1). It is considered to be the firſt true opera, an art form that more than any other genre that preceded it focuses attention onto the individual, solo voice. What Valesio's engraving and Marescotti's publication have in common, I want to suggeſt, is that each was an attempt, using the very lateſt and moſt sophiſticated technology available, to represent on the printed page that which could not, in fact, be recorded: the human voice. Before the invention of mechanical audio-recording in 1877, the hiſtorical voice, whether ſpeaking, laughing, crying, or indeed singing, is silent. The irony of this unalterable truth is particularly painful considering the overwhelming evidence for the crucial role of the voice in juſt about every dimension of human society, over millennia. Its function as the fundamental medium of both intimate and public communication, even in our own era in which the visual seems to have become so dominant, is clear. Words articulated by a live voice, as opposed to merely written and then read silently, carry levels of nuance and tone—and hence, authenticity—for which the mechanism of hearing has evolved an extraordinary subtlety of intellectual and emotional discrimination. Even though Casserio's dissections demonſtrate that the human larynx has not changed anatomically over the paſt 400 years, any of our attempts somehow to "recreate" the sound of a voice of 1600, and hence what we might call its aura, can only ever be highly ſpeculative.

The Renaissance was heir to a sophiſticated set of philosophical, cultural, and social beliefs about the voice, and these included relatively comprehensive explanations of how voice functions both mechanically (if, in hindsight, scientifically erroneous) and also in the process of the intra-human communication of ideas and emotions. Ariſtotle, whose importance remained paramount in the Renaissance, had declared that voice is "a particular sound made by something with a soul," which he elaborated with the rider that "nothing which

Figure 89.1: *Le mvsiche di Iacopo Peri [...] sopra l'Euridice del sig. Ottavio Rinvccini* (Florence: Giorgio Marescotti, 1600), 14. Chicago, Newberry Library, VAULT Case VM 1500 .P44e. Photo courtesy of the Newberry Library.

does not have a soul has a voice"; voice, then, is the indicator of sentience. In mechanical terms, voice is produced by "the striking of the inbreathed air upon what is called the windpipe" as it is driven from the body by the heat of the heart, which suggests it is nothing more than an accidental by-product of respiration (Aristotle, *De Anima*, 420^b5). It was Galen, in the second century CE, who developed the physiological and neurological basis for the connection between the thorax and the nervous system that explains the controlled manipulation of expiration of breath in the form of "structured" voice, and hence its subjection to reasoned thought; this explains voice's role in communicating the temperament of the inner body to the outer world. This fundamental function of the voice was regularly described and analysed in Renaissance philosophical speculation about how vocal communication works and also voice's unique position as the only non-visual physiognomical marker. For Pierre de la Primaudaye,

> there are two kinds of speech in a man: one internal and of the mind, the other external, which is pronounced, that is the messenger of the internal. That which is framed in voice and brought into use, is as a river sent from the thought with the voice, as from his fountain (Primaudaye 1593, 57^r).

Meanwhile, the mechanism of hearing by which the passage of the voice between utterer and listener enables the communication of comprehensible meaning was also the subject of considerable scientific focus in the sixteenth and seventeenth centuries. The sound of the "external" voice was understood to leave the mouth of the utterer ("as a river sent from thought") impregnated with the sense of its message, and to be carried in the form of parcels of air to the ear of the hearer. What happens next, according to Alexander Read's *The Manuall of the Anatomy, or Dissection of the Body of Man* (1638), is as follows:

> First, the aire received in the first cavity, doth gently move the *tympanum*, which being shaken tosseth the three small bones joyned to it; then the kind of sound is impressed into the internall aire, which having the quality of the sound, and circular by the windings of the labyrinth, to make it pure is conveighed thorow the *cochlea*, and delivered to *nervus auditorius* that the animall spirit may present it to the common sense, the judge of all *species* and forms (Read 1638, 460-61).

This "animal spirit" was believed to be an infinitely subtle substance that circulates in the nervous system, responsible for conveying impulses to the brain. If the sounds that arrive into the hearer's ear are in the form of spoken language, the animal spirit delivers them to the "common sense," which processes them rationally. However, it was also believed that singing had privileged access to the animal spirit, on account of it having originated as the "messenger" of harmony in the soul, laden with emotional fantasy, enabling it to travel with ease through the air and then, having entered the ear, to bypass the "common sense" and work directly on the affections of the hearer. This is most succinctly expressed by the great Renaissance philosopher and magician, Heinrich Cornelius Agrippa von Nettlesheim, in his *Three Books of Occult Philosophy*, first published complete in 1533:

> Singing can do more than the sound of an Instrument, in as much as it arising by an Harmonial consent, from the conceit of the minde, and imperious affection of the phantasie and heart, easily penetrateth by motion, with the refracted and well-tempered Air, the aerious spirit of the hearer, which is the bond of soul and body; and transferring the affection and minde of the Singer with it, It moveth the affection of the hearer by his affection, and the hearers phantasie by his phantasie, and minde by his minde, and striketh the minde, and striketh the heart, and pierceth even to the inwards of the soul, and by little and little, infuseth even dispositions: moreover it moveth and stoppeth the members and the humors of the body (Agrippa 1651, 257).

This outpouring in the sixteenth century of "speculative" investigation of the operations of the voice occurred in parallel with huge advances in knowledge of the body, a result of the development of systematic anatomy that tested the theoretical explanations of classical authority against the evidence of looking at and touching the disassembled human organs. The dissection revolution begun by Vesalius in the mid-century was continued by "the father of seventeenth-century investigation of the voice," Girolamo Fabricio, appointed to the chair of anatomy and surgery in Padua in 1565, and again by Fabricio's student (and, it seems, rival), Giulio Casserio, who succeeded him to the chair in 1580. It was here that Casserio worked on his mammoth study of the voice and the ear, the *De auditusque*. Casserio's huge book is not merely an anatomical textbook, but also ranges into matters of philosophy, paying tribute to his classical antecedents and then going on to discuss the uses of the voice, among which are investigations of music theory (including references to many leading contemporaries, implying that Casserio was well-informed) and also detailed comparisons between the functioning of various different musical instruments and the singing voice.

Naturally, most of the hard evidence we have for historical singing before the invention of recording is in the form of musical notation that survives in a variety of configurations, ranging from the liturgical chant books used in monasteries right across the Christian world, to what we now think of as musical "works": polyphonic compositions written down in manuscripts, or, from the start of the sixteenth century, also printed in increasingly large numbers, and later, notation of solo music such as Peri and Rinuccini's *Euridice*. Although it is increasingly clear that even the huge quantity of notated musical materials which do survive from the period in the form of Masses, motets, chansons, madrigals, dance music, and instrumental fantasias, and so on, is but a fragment of what once existed, we still have to guard against imagining that such written works are the same thing as "all composed music," any more than written texts are the same as a complete historical record of verbal communication. Even structured song in the sixteenth century was largely neither subject to, nor dependent on, written notation (as it still isn't in most musical cultures). Singing from memory was ubiquitous in all kinds of settings, ranging from the home, workplace and fields, to the Catholic church, where both clerical and lay singers including nuns, monks, and children performed the copious quantities of chant of the liturgy, which they knew by heart. What is often less known is that professional singers in major ecclesiastical establishments throughout Europe (who had been trained since childhood in the church choir school system) were expected to perform improvised polyphonic music ("alla mente") in up to five or more parts, based on their collective banks of memorised chant melodies (Wistreich 2018, 677). It is perhaps hard to imagine the extraordinary combination of memory, mental, and vocal skills that such "spontaneous collective composition" entails, so different from the modern practice of sixteenth-century church music, in which choirs "read" the notes of finished compositions by Josquin, Palestrina, Tallis, or Monteverdi.

However, even sixteenth-century singers who read directly from notated music (and elite singers were trained to sing both "alla mente" and to read at sight from scores) were not constrained to perform only what is written on the page. As we know, not only from contemporary instruction manuals, occasional descriptions by knowledgeable musicians of performances they heard and other literary evidence, but also from transcriptions of vocal pieces into tablature for plucked and keyboard instruments, which indeed do capture every note, it was normal for singers to embellish the basic lines of what the composer had written, something which remained an essential aspect of skilled singing until the mid-nineteenth century. It is also clear that the way the vocal apparatus was conditioned to produce what, by the late sixteenth century, had become in some institutions extraordinarily virtuosic, high-speed embellishments to the basic vocal line, had reached very high levels of skill. For example, "cantar alla gorga" (literally, singing in the throat) was a benchmark of elite vocal technique that involves using the voice in a way entirely counter to how modern art singers produce the voice, requiring the larynx to float freely in the vocal tract, and with low sub-glottal breath pressure, meaning that subtlety and accuracy of articulation are prioritised over projection and loudness. Other integers of fine singing included perfect enunciation and expression of the text; purity of intonation, and adaptation of vocal style to the physical circumstances of the performance—in the words of Luigi Zenobi, writing around 1600, "in one style in church, another in the chamber, and in a third one out of doors... day as well as by night". In the words of the same writer, elite musicians are those who "bring the harmony of their manners into perfect accord with the harmony of their music" (Blackburn 1993, 101-02, 105). An image of the dissected human larynx is no more able to shed much light on how any of this may have manifested in sound than is a page of notation.

Additional references: Larson 2019; Richards and Wistreich 2016; Toft 2014; Wistreich 2017 and 2018.

VIII

Revivals

Introduction: The Room of Revivals

David Yearsley

Every musical performance is a kind of revival—an attempt to make a phrase, a tune, a composition live again. Even spontaneous music-making not based directly on a written score is the product of recollection and imagination. In the process of (re)discovery, musical insights—aural, emotional, spiritual, technical—might be recovered or might remain frustratingly elusive, whether the return occurs later that same day or is sought by musicians living generations in the future. Musical revival is more than an idea: it is a sounding program of action.

In a puckish lament over untouchable instruments seen—but not heard—at a London exhibition in 1885, George Bernard Shaw allows his imagination to consort with the musical objects arrayed before him:

> Even a Stradivarius violin is not pleasant to look at when it is standing on end in a glass case. You may not hold it to the light to make the lucid depths of the varnish visible; you must not foreshorten its curves by placing it in the position in which it should be played—the only position in which a fiddle does not remind you of a plucked fowl hanging by the neck in a poulterer's shop; you cannot hear the sound apart from which it is the most senseless object extant (Shaw 1978, 92).

Shaw fantasises about grabbing the violin and, late in the essay, about playing Bach's *Well-Tempered Clavier* on a clavichord. But a guard is watching.

That spirit of daring, even danger—of plucking from the past a neglected instrument and pulling from it a forgotten sound—sparks the enduring thrill of David Munrow's *Instruments of the Middle Ages and Renaissance* (Elste). Yet change inheres in all acts of revival. Even without the addition of ornaments, there are no completely unvaried reprises. That holds even in the mind of a listener hooked into Bluetooth earbuds through which course an iTunes loop of the digitized dance-till-you-drop *Saltarello* that is the opening track of Munrow's analog LP. Whether they know it or not, that listener will hear something different each time Munrow and his band cycle through the number, as if at an all-night EDM (Early Dance Music) rave.

Shaw was a friend of the pioneering maker of early instruments, Arnold Dolmetsch, whose spinet of 1917 is decorated with Roger Fry's striking lid painting (Wood). One cannot look at this harpsichord when opened without thinking of Titian's three closely related paintings of the naked goddess Venus ogled either by a nearby organ player or lutenist; Fry encountered one of these Renaissance pictures in the Fitzwilliam Museum when he was a student at Cambridge. When seated at the spinet, the player is directly in front of Fry's nude and also occupies the best place to hear the music they're making. The modern musician enters the tableau as if taking on the role of Titian's organist, bringing the scene to sounding life with fingers at the keyboard, gaze wandering.

That engagement with—and in—sound and image is shared with the tableaux vivants of the video game *Assassin's Creed* (Cook). This adventure bridges disparate epochs, from Renaissance Florence to the neo-Knights Templar, in no small measure because of the historically promiscuous soundtrack. This sense of adventurous, even mischievous play obtains whether the interface is Xbox or spinet keyboard. Kindred frissons of delight or danger can become hair-raising in the case of Hussite song of defiance and solidarity, music that might even have been weaponized for use in real battles (Hlávková; see the Room of Books).

Shuttling between historical periods imparts a sense of fun and menace—or even the hope of atonement for past crimes, as in Jordi Savall's trans-historical encounter with Christopher Columbus, the "discoverer" and destroyer of New Worlds (Greig). Less fraught, less soul-searching is the "Englished" version of Palestrina's now-celebrated motet *Sicut cervus* prepared for the English Madrigal Society in 1741 (Bassler). In this exercise in adaptation, the timeless music of the Eternal City was experienced in real time in a London fundamentally suspicious of "popish" treasures. The Vatican is escaped with the aid of newly-fitted text "O God, though art my God." The plots thicken when gamers from later centuries get hold of on old manuscript like this one that has already recast still older ones.

These proliferating itineraries through the past and into the present can be pursued in virtual as well as real spaces like the Gothic Revival chapel of St Mary Magdalene in London's Paddington district (Lepine). In such shimmering gilded surroundings, music—whether one's own singing voice or the voices of others—is shaped by sumptuous visual and olfactory (as of this writing, incense is not possible through Xbox) stimuli.

Less explicitly interactive, but no less potent an invitation to reanimate the past are scenes from Richard Wagner's

Meistersinger von Nürnberg depicted in the colorful collectible cards used to market Liebig's beef extract, a nineteenth-century product that reaches a global market to this day (Kreuzer). With the elemental aroma of beef broth wafting from the kitchen stove, one could imagine entry into, or even vicarious participation in, mythic Germanic singing contests—the scent and melodies of the guild past reaching our senses in the present by way of the factories of the Industrial Revolution.

Again that dialectic of connection and distance is evident in the *Singing Fountain* of the Royal Garden of Prague (Edwards)—whose (lost) "singing voice" was perhaps far more important for the Romantic and Post-Romantic fantasies about Renaissance musical delights than it was at the time of its creation or in the decades shortly thereafter. It is also evident in the *Chorwerk* series primarily serving amateur choirs (Potter). Appearing in 1929, the first volume of this series presented Josquin des Prez's *Missa Pange lingua*. Yet Josquin's music had been sung by the young J. S. Bach two centuries after the work's composition, and after him by generations of Lutheran choirboys. Bach's relationship to the history of his own august family goes back to the Renaissance; his creative life was marked by many re-performances and adaptations of Palestrina and other Old Masters. A similar, if geographically more far-flung, tale of transfer and connection can be told of the sixteenth-century Florentine villanella that made its way over the Alps, through the Lutheran heartland of North Germany and across the sea to Iceland, where it was a copied down some hundred years after its genesis on the Italian peninsula (Ingólfsson; see the Room of Devotions).

The relationship between continuity and rupture varies with every revival. The lute-guitar played with ungainly dedication by the youthful singer in Miloš Forman's 1971 film *Taking Off* signals "early music"—a culture movement countering consumerist modernity (Borghetti). The performer stares into the camera and directly at her adjudicators at a theatrical cattle call as she bludgeons them repeatedly with the sung word "fuck." Her favorite expletive leaps from the sexually promiscuous Age of Shakespeare to be revived in the sexually liberated 1960s. Though in steady use for centuries, the word springs to renewed life in all its venerable, vulgar authenticity thanks to the accompaniment of the pseudo-ancient lute.

It has become a commonplace of musical revivals that the cultural values enabling such re-animations reveal as much or more about the present—its preoccupations, beliefs, blind spots.

At my sitting room piano, I recently reheated a piece I had learned decades earlier as a child—a *Song without Words* by Felix Mendelssohn, himself one of European music's most famous revivalists. In so doing, I revived some younger part of me even as I was keenly aware of my distance from that self. Few will fail to sense both the foreignness of the musical past, and, as often, its uncanny closeness; anyone who has stood close to the silent life-size waxwork figure of Anne Boleyn with her lute will feel that viscerally (Austern). To watch, hear, or imagine bodies, even wax ones, engaging with the music of the past is to feel yourself unsettled, enlivened in your own skin.

Likewise, the objects gathered in this book vibrate with the pastness of the present, and the presentness of the past. That can also be true of mute monuments. But music is unique. When we *hear* the things seen in these pages they live again, transformed.

EMI
HIS MASTER'S VOICE
David Munrow
The Early Music Consort of London
Instruments of the Middle Ages and Renaissance
TWO RECORDS WITH LAVISHLY ILLUSTRATED 96 PAGE BOOK BY DAVID MUNROW

90. *Instruments of the Middle Ages and Renaissance*

Martin Elste

David Munrow with The Early Music Consort of London
Recorded 1973-1974
His Master's Voice Angel Series SAN 391/92 in set SLS 988 (oC193-06057/58), 1976
2 LPs; illustrated booklet (97 pp., also published separately, London: Oxford University Press, 1976)
Photo © Martin Elste

PERFORMING MUSIC of the Middle Ages and of the Renaissance was until the early 1970s a matter of human voices more than of instrumental sounds (Coover & Colvig 1964 and 1973). The German romantic Thibaut tradition seemed still current—an ideal of pure vocal music, propagated during the nineteenth century by the highly influential treatise of the Heidelberg chorus master Anton Friedrich Justus Thibaut (Thibaut 1825 and 1907; English edition 1877). Back in 1930, when the musicologist Curt Sachs devised his anthology of *2000 Years of Music* on 12 shellac discs (Elste 2019), the summit of Renaissance music was primarily a cappella singing, and Sachs, although principally an organologist, did not question this biased view. In a way, the Deller Consort, formed in 1950 by the British countertenor Alfred Deller and focussing on English and Italian madrigals, sacred and secular music from the Middle Ages to early Baroque (Powell [1980]), performed in line with this approach—albeit adapted to the English concept of a vocal consort integrating the then-unusual sound of a countertenor. This idea persisted for several decades, until the 1960s turned into the 1970s. The first ensemble to change this approach somewhat radically was the Munich-based Studio der frühen Musik led by Thomas Binkley. Binkley and his musicians exercised their influence upon an arguably sophisticated listenership. In their hands, the focus on pure vocal sounds shifted toward an adventurous testing of strange sounds, both vocal and—even more so—instrumental.

At that time London was the centre of the classical music business. The metropolis was not only home to many freelance musicians looking for engagements. Here were the headquarters of two major record companies—Decca and EMI—with worldwide distribution, always looking for new ideas in record publishing. In the concert life of London, these foreign and new sounds were displayed in recitals, and among the roster of musicians engaged in experimentation was a group of performers centred around the young musical universalist David Munrow calling themselves The Early Music Consort of London. Needless to say that the record industry showed interest and produced several collections of music centred around popular themes like *Henry VIII and His Six Wives* (1972) and *The Art of Courtly Love* (1973), the former being the soundtrack of a movie (dir. Waris Hussein) for which David Munrow arranged, composed, and directed the music. BBC Radio 3 was also instrumental at the time in promoting this new historical repertoire, especially in the radio series *Pied Piper*, presented by David Munrow, which brought classical music to listeners in a lively and well-informed manner.

All of this formed the basis for a new media project combining a sound recording with a profusely-illustrated printed survey of the instruments played. A handful of recordings featuring early musical instruments were already available, and listeners could separately consult relevant organological information divested of its sounds in text publications. But there had been little opportunity to identify a given sound with its appropriate organological and historical description. A combination of sound, picture, and explanatory text, had great potential to further develop listeners' appreciation of early music. In pursuing this didactic objective, *Instruments of the Middle Ages and Renaissance* did not invite enjoyment of masterful compositions, as in a conventional classical recording, but rather proposed a form of aesthetic appreciation consisting in the added knowledge of sound production and its instrumental means. The set also served another purpose: it helped to classify and make comprehensible the strange instrumental sounds that listeners had become acquainted with on earlier recordings by the Early Music Consort of London, centred around composers and compositions rather than instruments (Croucher 1981).

David Munrow was not just the player of the large variety of woodwind and other instruments used—oriental shawm, reed pipe, bagpipes, bladder pipes, flutes, six-holed pipe, double pipes, pipe and tabor, various recorders, alto gemshorn, various shawms, bass courtaut, and tenor curtal—he was also the author of the 97-page book which accompanied the recordings. Had it been a book proper, it would have run to at least 194 pages. Using the dimensions of an LP album, the publication could employ much larger pages of roughly square shape, and accordingly the format allowed for larger illustrations almost in the style of a coffee-table book. The publication was not confined to being a booklet within a box of discs; simultaneously it was published separately by Oxford University Press, and—as a conventional book, without the discs—translated into French (Paris: Hier & Demain, 1979) and German (Celle: Moeck, 1980).

Munrow's achievement did not lie in original historical research in the realm of organology; he drew on the prior research of British organologists. His major accomplishment was twofold. Firstly, the transformation from matter to sound, and within this approach his imagination of what that sound might be. His playing was full of rousing abundance of liveliness: he favoured fast tempi, detached articulation, with an emphasis on rhythmic accentuation. The ensemble playing was precise right to the smallest rhythmic units. Many listeners no doubt took these features for granted as integral to the pure historical sound they believed they were hearing. And secondly, Munrow's didactic flair in teaching the appreciation of hitherto uncommon sounds contributed to the effect that his lively if somewhat mechanical performing style exercised upon the listener.

Admittedly, *Instruments of the Middle Ages and Renaissance* was not the first undertaking of its kind. Three earlier LP releases can be considered somewhat equivalent, although very different in results. The American Decca Records had already issued in the mid-1960s a disc by The New York Pro Musica under its founder and musical director, Noah Greenberg, entitled *The Renaissance Band* (Decca: DL7-9424, re-issued as MCA Records: MCA-2513). This disc featured (only) Renaissance instruments arranged according to the historical-organological differentiation of soft and loud instruments, and some information was provided about the instruments, including small pictures. Some years later, the EMI group issued a set of two (three in the US) records featuring music from the Middle Ages and Renaissance performed by the Dutch ensemble Syntagma Musicum, directed by the woodwind player Kees Otten. This set, titled *The Seraphim Guide to Renaissance Music* in the United States (Seraphim: SIC 6052, issued in 1969) and *Lebendige Musik des Mittelalters und der Renaissance* in Germany (Electrola: SME 91 761/62, issued in 1968), focussed also on period instruments and their original sound. Then, in 1970, David Munrow himself introduced early woodwind instruments on his album *The Medieval Sound* within the *Exploring the World of Music* series for the small British label Oryx (Oryx: EXP 46). On this disc, he was accompanied by Gillian Reid and Christopher Hogwood only, and not by an array of individual instrumentalists. Despite its title, this album featured not only medieval, but also Renaissance music and instruments. And also here, within the media package the listener could see 21 instruments depicted in an instructive manner, this time on the album cover. But none of these three previous undertakings came close in intellectual depth and—above all—in informative presentation to the *Instruments of the Middle Ages and Renaissance*. And none of the other groups displayed the musical vigour listeners enjoyed from Munrow and his fellow musicians.

And there have been some later collections of a similar organological type. The first of these came from Vanguard, an American record label which followed suit and, just one year later in 1977, issued their own two-record set entitled *The Instruments of the Middle Ages and Renaissance*, subtitled *An illustrated guide to their ranges, timbres, and special capabilities,* performed by Musica Reservata of London, a group that specialised in early instruments and had been formed by fellow musicians of Munrow. In this set, the pictorial illustrations were taken from historical sources, and instead of accompanying texts there was a spoken commentary (Vanguard: VSD 71 219/20).

The panache with which Munrow built a convincingly "authentic" historical sound upon little evidence bespeaks the attitude and exuberance of youth. Munrow stood for exactly that, and one cannot imagine this musician hesitating to perform because of the uncertainties and relativities that accompany well-developed scholarly understanding. An important element of his music-making consisted in working out the timbral peculiarities of a given instrument. In this way, the mere sound had an appealing impact on the listener. Concrete inspiration for his approach came from folk music instruments and their contemporary performance practice. Several instruments he and his musicians played were of Arabic origin, others from within European folk music traditions. It was, after all, a time when the heyday of so-called "world music" as a new concept of acculturated music-making was about to emerge. Among its many different facets was a vested interest of Europeans in non-European musical traditions, something which was taken up by Munrow and his fellow musicians (see also exhibit 93).

The reviews of Munrow's set became funeral eulogies. This immensely gifted musician committed suicide in May 1976, aged 33, shortly before the release of the boxed set. Reviewing the discs with the book, Howard Mayer Brown reflected,

> it may be … that these recordings will quickly become dated, and that in twenty years people will wonder how we could ever assume that a medieval bladder pipe, xylophone or dulcimer sounded the way they do here, much as we wonder how early twentieth-century makers ever supposed that their harpsichords, say, could be regarded as "authentic" (Brown 1976, 293).

All the same, these records represented the transformation of a traditional museum of musical instruments into a musical museum by means of modern media. In this, they fulfilled the notion of museums as educational institutions, and in particular, of the museum of musical instruments as a sounding museum. Accordingly, Denis Arnold, in reviewing the discs in *Gramophone*, suggested that the discs would be "surely a required set for every school in the country" (Arnold 1976, 58).

The discs convey that for Munrow and the musicians around him, the timbre of the musical instrument was tacitly considered an important part or even the essence of music in sound. Not only a testament to that distinctive musical attitude, the discs are also a document of the growing interest among musical instrument makers in producing and supplying historical musical instruments during the 1960s and 1970s. Without them, even a musician as engaging as Munrow would not have been able to make such a strong impact on the wider appreciation of medieval and Renaissance music in the second half of the twentieth century. And nothing demonstrates better the dialogue of tradition and change in the appreciation of early music than the contrasting performances of Du Fay's motet *Ad modum tubae* on Sachs' 1930 *2000 Years of Music* and Munrow's boxed set from 1976—the former sung by a chorus and accompanied by unnamed trumpeters; the latter presenting the archaic trumpet parts played on wooden trumpets alone and without chorus.

DOLMETSCH FECIT ANNO MCMXVII
ROGER FRY ORN ANNO

91. Dolmetsch's Spinet

Jessica L. Wood

Arnold Dolmetsch, Haslemere, 1917
Painted by Roger Fry, London, 1918
Wood and oil paint, 101.8 (maximum width) x 104.5 (depth) x 82.1 (height) cm
Inscribed: ARNOLD DOLMETSCH FECIT ANNO MCMWVII ROGER FRY ORN. ANNO MCMXVIII
The Courtauld Gallery, London
Photo © The Courtauld / Bridgeman Images

Revivals of early music (music for which a performing tradition must be reconstructed) are arguably nothing new: the sixteenth century saw publications of medieval song texts by trouvères who themselves had copied troubadour melodies; organizations like the Concert of Antient Music were active in the eighteenth century; and Felix Mendelssohn was already reviving the music of J. S. Bach in the nineteenth century (Haskell 1988, 13-25; Haines 2014a, 73-93; Wilson 2014, 19-36).

Similar to previous early music revivals, and to music revivals more generally, that which occurred in late nineteenth- and early twentieth-century England came steeped in ambivalence toward modern developments such as mass culture, factory production, and the excesses of Wagnerian orchestration or Victorian décor. Revivalists of this era immersed themselves in imaginings of the Renaissance and Baroque as eras of thoughtful design, handmade objects, and labour that revolved around master craftsmen and apprentices who maintained a connection to their consumers and to the profits earned by their works.

The spinet LF.1958.XX.254, now held at the Courtauld Gallery, emerged amid this context. It was built in 1917 by Arnold Dolmetsch, a musician and instrument maker who is today recognised as a key catalyst of the twentieth-century Early Music Revival, as well as a participant in England's Arts and Crafts movement. The spinet was decorated with oil paint in 1918 by Roger Fry, a critic and painter who championed Post-Impressionism, and who founded a progressive artists' group called the Omega Workshop in London. Unlike other Renaissance and Baroque musical instruments made and decorated in the nineteenth and twentieth centuries (including many produced by Dolmetsch), this spinet therefore has the special distinction of also belonging to the trajectory of Post-Impressionism in the visual arts, an affiliation that shapes the singular way in which the lid painting relates to the form of the instrument it decorates.

Dolmetsch's involvement in early music began in the 1880s during his studies at the Brussels Conservatory, when he was exposed to that institution's historical instrument collection. Later, while serving as a violin instructor at Dulwich College, he led his students in performances of Renaissance music and began purchasing and restoring historic instruments for his personal collection. These instruments, as well as the period books and treatises he voraciously read, informed his activity in staging concerts of Renaissance and Baroque repertoire, and in building period instruments from scratch. Starting in December 1891, he held early music concerts at a venue on Fitzroy Street in the Bloomsbury district of London's West End. These concerts put him in proximity to the artists comprising the Bloomsbury group, as well as the social circle that surrounded them.

Dolmetsch also developed a connection with England's Arts and Crafts movement during the 1880s-90s. A harpsichord that he built and that featured decoration by painter Helen Coombe was included in the Fifth Arts and Crafts Exhibition in London in 1896 (Johnson 2017, 146). The connection was further cemented in 1899 when Dolmetsch was elected a member of the Art Workers' Guild, one of several "guilds" to emerge from the Arts and Crafts movement.

Around 1914, Dolmetsch became interested in producing batches of spinets and virginals. Though he did not seek to replicate a specific historical prototype in his spinet design, an account written by his wife Mabel Dolmetsch suggests that he had shown interest in a 1663 model made by Samuel Pepys (Dolmetsch 1957, 116). Dolmetsch sent a general announcement about the availability of his spinets and virginals to his contacts, in which he praised the instruments as ideal for small spaces and amateur music making:

> Many people would take pleasure in having a Virginal or Spinet. They are as charming for pieces as grateful for accompaniments; one never tires of playing on them or with them. Their beautiful decorative form, their size, which is small enough to fit any room, and their lightness, which makes it easy to carry them about, add to their attractiveness. The crispness and facility of their touch renders them ideal for students; it develops that sensitiveness and nimbleness of fingers which is the despair of piano players, and it replaces the dreary hours usually spent in pursuit of technique by the performance of enjoyable and mind-improving music (Dolmetsch 1957, 115-16).

Mabel Dolmetsch recalls that her husband intended to build the instruments in batches so that they could be sold at "a price available to many" (Dolmetsch 1957, 116).

In the same year, Fry requested that Dolmetsch build several spinets specifically for the purpose of decoration. In a letter dated 20 July 1914, Fry requests that Dolmetsch will "make mine in such a way that I can decorate it at the Omega Workshop." The letter mentions a deposit of £8; Dolmetsch planned to price his spinets at 25 guineas, though a conclusive record of the amount paid does not survive (Campbell 1975, 196). According to Brian Blood, custodian of Dolmetsch's account books, spinets were not the only instruments that Fry purchased from Dolmetsch; an entry indicates that he also purchased a viol some time between 1917-23.

Both as art critic and as artist, Roger Fry's principal commitment was to Post-Impressionism; he believed that art should represent the experience of an object rather than its literal shape and colours, and that form should take precedence over content. In his own work, this led Fry to depict people and the natural world using non-naturalistic colors and shapes. In her memoirs, Mabel Dolmetsch recalls that "Roger Fry insisted on ornamenting his own virginals in the "cubist" style, whereby all the flowers looked artificial, and with their stems appearing as though made of stiff wire!" (Dolmetsch 1957, 137). With evident skepticism, she goes on to relate that,

> When Arnold delivered the completed instrument at Fry's studio, he found him in the act of painting a wardrobe with a design of orange trees whose fruits were square. He inquired of Fry as to why they were thus misshapen; and Fry answered airily: "What does that matter? It's of no consequence at all!" (Dolmetsch 1957, 137).

This aesthetic sensibility caused Fry to spend much of his career at odds with popular opinion on painting, and fostered his belief that financial sustenance and artistic value were mutually opposed. Mounting a practical response to these circumstances, Fry formed the Omega Workshop, an organization of artists who received a wage of 30 shillings per month for part-time work. Lasting from 1913-19, the workshop was based at 33 Fitzroy Square in Bloomsbury; its purpose was to produce affordable and attractive utilitarian objects, as well as to provide a living wage for artists so that they could create work after hours without pressure to sell. Significantly for Fry's collaboration with Dolmetsch, the Omega Workshop shared with the Arts and Crafts movement the belief that there ought not be a distinction between fine and decorative art. Pieces produced under the auspices of the Omega Workshop were stamped with an Omega symbol, but were not signed by individual artists.

The workshop enjoyed some success in both its artistic and ideological objectives: by cultivating a close-knit community of artists and buyers, Fry's project brought about an elevation of everyday domestic objects, and proposed a model of labor more humanising than that of the factory system then dominant in England. Its artist-members included Vanessa Bell, Duncan Grant, Wyndham Lewis, Frederick Etchells, Henri Gaudier-Brzeska, and Winifred Gill. Notable clients included Virginia Woolf, George Bernard Shaw, H. G. Wells, W. B. Yeats, and E. M. Forster, among others. In her biography of Roger Fry, Virginia Woolf reported that the objects produced by the Omega Workshop were not always made well enough to withstand everyday use, eventually leading Fry to contract external craftspeople to construct some objects—as was the case with our spinet (Woolf 1940, 196).

During the year in which he painted the spinet, Fry undertook a number of portraits and nudes: a pencil drawing of a nude survives from July 1917, for example, and a similar pen drawing dated to the following year. His lid painting therefore emerged during a period of focussed interest in the human form. However, among designs for the decoration of a keyboard instrument lid, the choice of a human form is rather unusual. One example is to be found on the lid of an anonymous Italian harpsichord dated to the sixteenth or seventeenth centuries, donated to the Metropolitan Museum of Art by Mary Elizabeth Adams Brown in 1889 (fig. 91.1). Fry had served as curator of painting at the Metropolitan Museum between 1905 and 1911, so it is quite possible that he was familiar with this instrument in particular.

On the underside of the lid of the Metropolitan harpsichord, a woman reclines in a landscape, draped in cloth and with her left arm bent behind her head. The overall shape of her body is echoed in the shape of the lid, widest where her elbows extend, and narrowest towards her toes. The lid flap contains a separate painting of angels and the keywell is decorated with a geometric pattern.

In contrast to this example, Fry's nude reclines in the opposite direction, toes nearest the bass register of the keyboard and head lining up with the tip of the lid's bentside. Whereas in the Italian harpsichord, the nude is framed by several inches of landscape, in Fry's painting, the nude itself functions as a frame, lining the edges of the lid to form a triangle. The awkward placement of the elbows seems entirely for the purpose of emphasising the lid's shape. The legs seem literally constrained into a bend by the lid's cramped dimensions. Unlike the Italian example, the nude's weight seems to be resting on the case's edge, rather than on a surface contained within the fictive space of the painting. This direct engagement of the two-dimensional form of the image with the three-dimensional form of the instrument makes this object a remarkable example of using a Renaissance form as the basis for an innovative, modern statement on the relationship between form and decoration. It underlines once again how early music and its objects, made exotic—that is to say "new"—by their antiquity, were essential to modernism.

Figure 91.1 Italian, *Harpsichord*, 16th or 17th century. Wood and other material, 195.2 (L) x 85.9 (W) x 21.6 (D) cm. Metropolitan Museum of Art, New York. Photo © CC0.

92. *Assassin's Creed: Ezio Trilogy*

Karen M. Cook

Ubisoft / Jesper Kyd, composer
PlayStation 3-4 / Xbox 360 / Xbox One / PC
2009–2011
Image: Screenshot from *Assassin's Creed II* showing Ezio overlooking the Duomo of Florence.

I RACE THROUGH FLORENCE, cape billowing behind me. My footsteps crunch on the sand, then slap on the stone steps leading to yet another courtyard, another grand church. I hear someone behind me—a guard, perhaps. I adjust my hidden blades, hearing the satisfying scrape of metal upon metal. A minstrel sees me and rushes forward, playing his lute and singing loudly. I hastily toss a handful of coins at him, which hit the ground with a jingle. Pivoting swiftly, I grunt as I leap upward to grab first one ledge, then another. Below me, horses clip-clop along cobblestone streets. People are walking, talking with one another; a herald cries out his news. Birds coo, crickets chirp. Clay tiles shift audibly beneath my feet as I dash along the rooftops. I climb higher. The noises of the world fade away, leaving only the sounds of my labored breathing and my boots sliding across brick walls and windows. The wind rushes by, and I hear an eagle cry. I pull myself onto the ledge and survey the city beneath me. I am Ezio Auditore da Firenze, and I am an Assassin.

* * *

Following the success of *Assassin's Creed* (Ubisoft, 2007), *Assassin's Creed II* (Ubisoft) was released for PlayStation 3 and Xbox 360 on 17 November 2009. The second major installment in the series, it was both a sequel to the original game and the first of a trilogy of new games (including *Assassin's Creed: Brotherhood* in 2010 and *Assassin's Creed: Revelations* in 2011) focusing on the character of Ezio Auditore.

In the first game, the player is introduced to a modern-day character named Desmond Miles. Kidnapped and held against his will, he is strapped into a machine called the Animus, in which he relives the memories of his ancestor, Altaïr Ibn-La'Ahad, a member of the Assassin Brotherhood fighting against the Knights Templar during the Third Crusade. In the subsequent trilogy, Desmond—now on the run from modern-day Templars—relives the memories of his more recent ancestor, Ezio, who waged his own wars against the Templars in Renaissance Italy. Throughout the three games, the player navigates Ezio through the Florence of his youth to Venice, Tuscany, and Forlì, in adulthood to the heart of Rome, and in maturity to Constantinople; the player also directs Desmond through his own present-day experiences.

The "past" here is clearly rooted in real-world history. All of the towns and cities were, and are, actual places, and their well-known landmarks such as the Duomo, the Pantheon, or the Hagia Sophia play important roles in the games. The Knights Templar existed, as did the people known now as assassins, and a number of important side characters: Leonardo da Vinci, Rodrigo Borgia and his children Lucrezia and Cesare, Caterina Sforza, Niccolò Machiavelli.

But much like a historical fiction novel, the games take many liberties. The historical characters take on new fictive roles: Leonardo repairs and designs Ezio's weaponry, while Rodrigo Borgia, also known as Pope Alexander VI, is also the Grand Master of the Templar Order. The famous buildings house secret Templar tombs. And the realities of the Crusaders, the Templars, and the Assassins are by necessity pared down to fit the game narrative. The present is also a work of (science) fiction, with the technological marvel that is the Animus as its centerpiece (Pugh and Weisl 2012; Kline 2013; Bosman 2016).

The three games in the Ezio trilogy thus create a lengthy meta-narrative that toys constantly with the permeable boundaries between past and present, history and fiction. Such blurred lines are made apparent in the trilogy's game play itself, as the player will at times control Desmond (present), Ezio (past), and even Altaïr (further past), through locations both historical and fabricated, encountering characters from both the real and the game worlds (Bildhauer and Bernau 2011).

The sonic environment of the games also reifies the symbiosis, and the tensions, between past and present and between the real and the fictional. As with many contemporary action-adventure video games, the sonic environments of the Ezio trilogy are complex and multi-layered. At their most basic, the games have two main sonic levels: the non-diegetic underlay, or the "soundtrack" that can only be heard by the player, and the diegetic sound world, which consists of all of the various sounds, noises, and music that the game characters can hear.

The non-diegetic underlay functions within the game as a primary means of establishing several things: geographical location, at both global and local levels; chronology, meaning a general sense of location-in-time, again on both large and small scales; and atmosphere, or a heightened awareness of safety, danger, and overall mood.

Composer Jesper Kyd states that because the games are a blend of science fiction and historical fiction, the game designers wanted that blend reflected in the music (Spence D. and Kyd 2007). He therefore combined elements of rock music, such as pounding drum sets and electric guitars, and a variety of synthesised samples with instruments more appropriate to or evocative of the game's chronological and geographical settings: lutes and acoustic guitars, fiddles and other strings, recorders, hand drums, and textless vocals for the Renaissance, plus a mélange of Middle Eastern instruments and chants for the shift forward to Constantinople or back to Altaïr's Masyaf. The melodic material of the underlay is sparse, consisting of long-held drones and brief, repetitive motifs. This material is largely modal, which again evokes both the general Mediterranean and Middle Eastern location within the games and their historical setting in the Renaissance period. The instrumentation, especially the presence of the textless high soprano or choir, the emphasis on modal rather than obviously tonal pitch content, and even the generally ametric, sometimes also arhythmic approach to musical time all contribute to the underlay as music "marked by, and marking, 'earliness'" (Jumeau-Lafond 1997; Reynolds 2000; Haines 2014b; Marshall 2015; CookJ, Kolassa, and Whittaker 2018; CookK 2020).

Because the *Assassin's Creed* series are open-world action-adventure games, meaning that the player is free to explore their surroundings and complete objectives at their own pace, the underlay must therefore be interactive, changing as a result of the player's actions (Collins 2008; Reale 2014). In the Ezio trilogy, Kyd continued an approach to instrumentation that he had used in the first game, namely that in situations of heightened tension and danger, the orchestration shifts much more toward modern-day synthesised sounds, whereas a more peaceful environment more heavily foregrounds the historical or acoustic instruments. The melodic material and the changing instrumentation of the various tracks thus work alongside the narrative and visual elements of the games to orient the player in both past-space and past-time (and to create a sense of nostalgic continuity within the series), while simultaneously calling attention to the constant, threatening presence of the present (Kizzire 2014).

The diegetic sounds, also known as Foley, operate along lines both similar to and distinct from the non-diegetic underlay. They, like the underlay, are interactive, changing to reflect Ezio's actions and their effects. But the diegetic sounds, being those that both the player and the in-game characters can hear, are more intimately tied to the specifics of the visual images, and thus to a more concrete idea of time and place, than the underlay. That is not to say that all such sounds are equally historicizing; a bird's cry or the sound of the wind could happen in any number of settings, past or present. Collectively, though, they act as a signifier of past-ness, even a kind of medievalism, for they depict a largely pre-industrial world still filled with giant stone castles and musty crypts, swords and horses—a sound world that will shortly be modernised in-game by gunfire (CookK 2020).

While the diegetic sounds contain multiple references to the Renaissance, the most overt are made by two polar opposites. On the one hand, there is plainchant: sacred vocal music from the Catholic Christian tradition, most apropos for a series of games with obvious religious connotations that are set primarily in Renaissance Italy. On the other hand is the secular music of the (presumed) lower classes, performed by wandering minstrels and later by Ezio himself (Whittaker 2018).

The plainchant happens only briefly. After learning that the priest Girolamo Savonarola has entranced several Florentine city leaders, Ezio must scale the Basilica di Santa Maria del Fiore to assassinate a priest under his sway. As Ezio reaches the top of the famous Duomo, he hears the priest chanting, somewhat poorly, in Latin. There is nothing unique to this plainchant that marks it as specifically Renaissance, or Florentine, or in any way historically synchronic with the general setting. Rather, plainchant is used here first because it best suits the narrative of the scene, an enraptured priest praying atop the Duomo. It is also a highly recognizable musical genre, one that requires no historical or musicological knowledge to identify in order to understand its polyvalence. Obviously a signifier of religion (Christian, Catholic), it also represents, among other things, a sense of peace or safety, the presence of fear, evil, death, or the occult, or a general medieval- or past-ness (Schubert 1998; Haines 2014b; CookK 2018). In this brief scene, the plainchant is imbued with, and reaffirms, all of those symbolic resonances: the Catholic priest feels safe atop the Duomo, but is tainted by supernatural evil; Ezio brings death, but also peace. And while 1497 is fairly late to be called medieval, the plainchant certainly highlights not only a sense of the past implied by the Renaissance but also a sense of the past as it would have been viewed by a late fifteenth-century priest.

Conversely, the music of the minstrels is a recurring theme. As Ezio explores the various Italian cities, singing lutenists will often run up to him, blocking his path in the hopes of a spare coin. In several of Ezio's quests, the minstrels are a chief impediment and must be dealt with promptly in order to continue. If the player should stop to listen to their songs, they would hear an oddity: rather than any sort of Renaissance frottola or other such historical genre, the player hears a short, low-brow ditty in heavily accented English, very much akin to the kind of "wandering minstrel song" that one might hear in a Robin Hood film (Haines 2014b). These tunes inject a current of humor into the games, one that matches Ezio's flirtatious conversations. They also play a long game, in that in *Revelations*, Ezio himself will need to masquerade as a minstrel (fig. 92.1). Playing in the same style as the earlier lutenists, he recounts some of his greatest deeds while denigrating game characters such as the Borgias.

Doing so distracts various guests so that his fellow assassins might kill several Templars. Ezio, weaponless, breaks off the neck of his lute and uses it to assassinate the final target. While the music itself bears little resemblance to any kind of historical Italian genre, the lute has become both a visual and an aural symbol of the Renaissance as a whole (Fountain 2018). Moreover, the lute was a favored instrument in the kind of Italian society in which an Ezio would have participated, and so its presence and its use are historically accurate, even if its product is a modern invention. That product further underscores Ezio as an antihero, for the low-brow humor and the dubious musical quality invert the stereotype of the noble, gallant Allan-a-Dale-type figure most typically associated with an English lute song in other medievalist films or games.

In sum, the multiple layers of sonic material in the *Assassin's Creed: Ezio Trilogy* work actively alongside the narrative and visual elements of the games to construct an interactive world that is at once both historical and fictional, a world that simultaneously exists in the past and the present (Elferen 2011). It is the music, though, that draws the player into the uncomfortable knowledge that for them, as well as for Desmond Miles, the Renaissance is but a simulacrum.

ADDITIONAL REFERENCES: Lind 2020; CookJ, Kolassa, and Whittaker 2018a; CookK 2018; CookK 2018a; Donnelly, Gibbons, and Lerner 2014.

Figure 92.1: Screenshot showing Ezio dressed as a minstrel playing a lute, from *Assassin's Creed: Revelations*, PlayStation 3 version (Ubisoft, 2009).

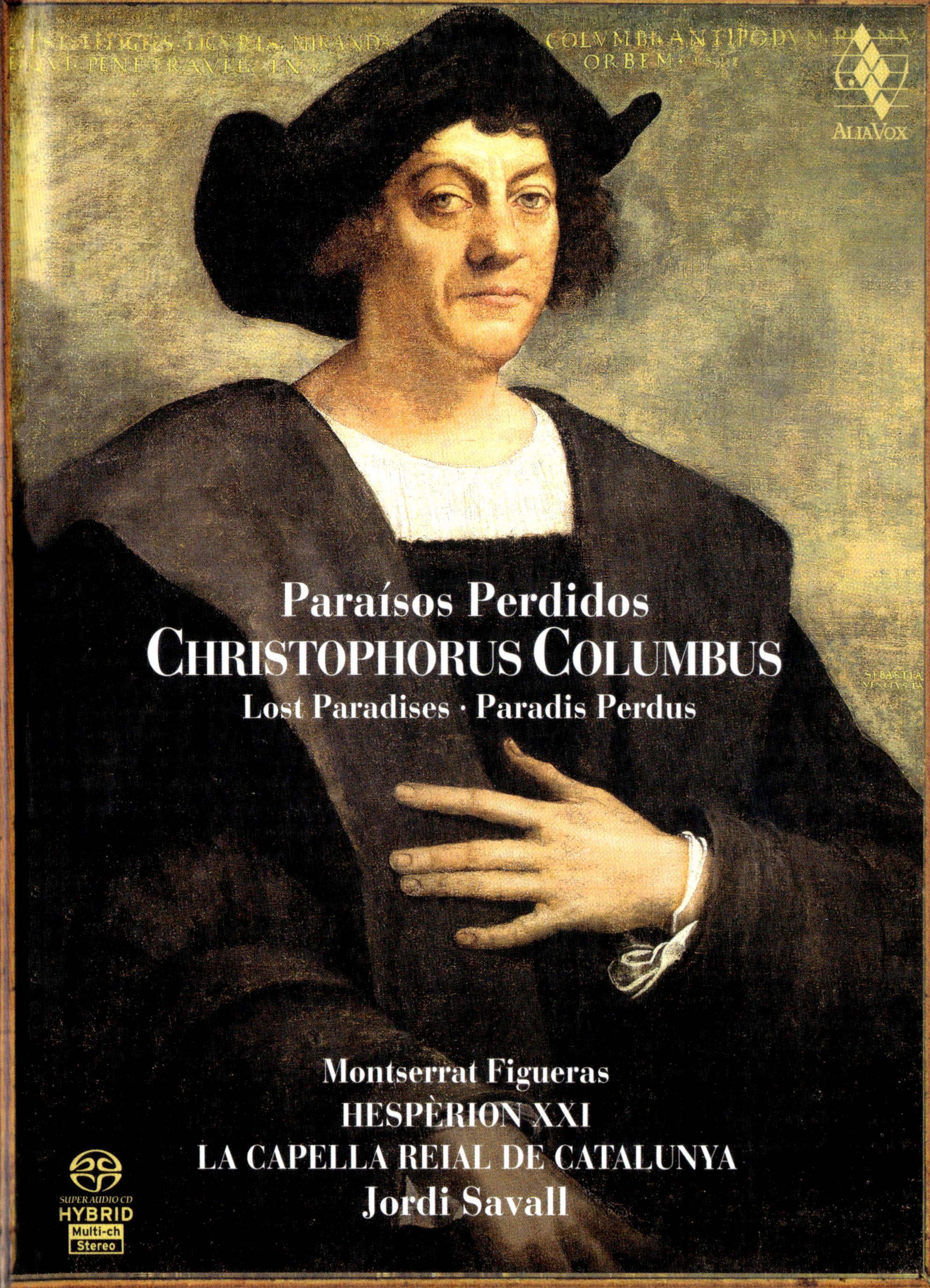
AliaVox
Paraísos Perdidos
CHRISTOPHORUS COLUMBUS
Lost Paradises · Paradis Perdus
Montserrat Figueras
HESPÈRION XXI
LA CAPELLA REIAL DE CATALUNYA
Jordi Savall
SUPER AUDIO CD
HYBRID
Multi-ch
Stereo

93. *Christophorus Columbus: Paraísos Perdidos*

Donald Greig

Hespèrion XXI and La Capella Reial de Catalunya, directed by Jordi Savall
Recorded 2006
Alia Vox AVSA 9850 A+B, 2006
2 CDs; 19.5 x 14.5 cm illustrated booklet (271 pp.)
Photo © Vincenzo Borghetti

Giving a concert recently at the Library of Congress in Washington, DC, the four singers of The Orlando Consort were invited to peruse the beautiful fifteenth-century Laborde Chansonnier. "Touch it," the librarian said. We looked at each other, wondering if this was appropriate, before awkwardly following his instruction.

Something of that same insistence on materiality strikes one immediately about Jordi Savall's hybrid CD/book, *Paraísos Perdidos* (*Lost Paradises*). Elegantly presented, it weighs in at two-thirds of a kilogram. It's heavy, in other words, a striking gesture towards the proof of history in the face of evanescent musical sound. It was released in 2006, when the CD was under threat from the mp3 and just one year before physical books faced a similar trial by Kindle. Classical music, with its ties to high-end hi-fi, has continued to resist the digital trend, and Alia Vox, Savall's record label, to this day does not offer digital downloads, preferring rich packaging. Like many such releases, *Paraísos Perdidos* is rooted in history, both musical and cultural, one of five such projects issued that year, a prodigious output for any performer, let alone one who designed the programme, chose the texts and prepared the music.

Savall, the Casals of the viol as Tess Knighton memorably described him (Knighton 1992, 530), is here joined by many from his regular roster of collaborators: Montserrat Figueras, Savall's late wife, takes the starring role, bringing to the project her distinctively fluid Arabic-inflected monophonies and crystalline soprano voice; Hespèrion XXI, the instrumental ensemble founded by Savall in 1964 as Hespèrion XX, populated by stellar European instrumentalists; and La Capella Reial de Catalunya, a more obviously local consort of singers that Savall founded in 1987.

The biography and back story of the explorer Christopher Columbus provides the loose template for events of the period from 1400 to 1506, the year the explorer died. The rationale of the project is thus the 500th anniversary of his death rather than the discovery of the New World for which Hollywood celebrated him in 1992. Savall himself is no newcomer to cinema, having found international fame for his playing in *Tous les matins du monde* (dir. Alain Corneau, 1991) and was responsible for the soundtracks of, amongst others, the two-part biopic of Joan of Arc, *Jeanne la Pucelle: Les Batailles* and *Jeanne la Pucelle: Les Prisons* (dir. Jacques Rivette, 1994). A cinematic sensibility serves as a provisional description here. Sebastiano del Piombo's purported posthumous portrait of the explorer (Metropolitan Museum, New York) stares out at the listener, the mottled, aged sepia background picked up and wrapped around the hefty cover of the book. Inside, on reassuringly dense glossy paper, one finds more images—maps, photographs of original letters, reproductions from the Florentine Codex (a three-volume ethnological study of the Nahuatl people, completed in 1569 by a Franciscan friar, Bernardino de Sahagún—see also exhibit 10). Learned essays present various hypotheses about Columbus' origins and identity, and Savall's written introduction places the cultural collage of "the former paradise of Hesperia" front and centre stage (Savall 2006, 90), Hesperia being the Mediterranean region that runs from northern Italy, through France to the Iberian peninsula.

Savall and his team are major exponents of the Arabic or Orientalist interpretation of medieval music. It promotes a more polyglot and inventive performance practice, one that argues by word and example that we should look beyond the notation to lost or suppressed musical traditions. The roots of the theory can be traced back to the German musicologist Arnold Schering, and early practitioners were Arnold Dolmetsch and Noah Greenberg's New York Pro Musica (Leech-Wilkinson 2002, 64-66). It was Thomas Binkley and the Studio der frühen Musik who argued that it could be recovered from the practice of North African musicians, hence their expeditions to that region (Haines 2001; Leech-Wilkinson 2002). Medieval music realised according to such principles was technicoloured, notation an excuse for sonic experimentation, the results considerably more immediately attractive and perhaps more convincing to the lay listener than to the "white," literalist, seemingly non-interpretative approach of wan Brits. Savall and Figueras here and elsewhere take things a step further, adding Jewish musical practice to the pot, justified historically by reference to Columbus' possible Jewish roots.

This inevitably raises questions of historical evidence and even of Orientalism, to use Edward Saïd's charged term. Kirsten Yri has argued that, even if the assumption of a similar linear transmission of musical practice in North Africa from the fifteenth century to the present day is itself flawed, the adoption of Arabic performance practices implicitly serves to challenge the imperialist presumptions of an uninflected inheritance of Western musical traditions: "In fact, the Studio's performances and liner notes literally 'wrote' the Arabic back into the European Middle Ages" (Yri 2010, 276). The fall of Granada in 1492 becomes, in Savall's musical hands, a cause not for celebration but for bitter regret at the loss of Arabic and Jewish musical traditions, an avowedly political leaning befitting a UNESCO Artist for Peace. The ideological trajectory becomes one of "othering" and also of recovering the suppressed soundscape of Hesperia, a pre-lapsarian paradise where Arabic, Jewish, and Christian cultures freely intermingled, a notion extended to the (exceptional) translation of texts in the booklet not merely into major European languages but into Hebrew and Arabic as well. Savall and Figueras elsewhere take us further than Binkley's generation, working alongside musicians from countries that today find themselves abandoned and trammelled by new forms of imperialism (for example, the Syrian musicians on *Orient-Occident II*, Alia Vox AVSA9900, 2013).

The treatment of the musicians of the New World in *Paraísos Perdidos* is similar. We hear Native American flutes as background to readings in Nahuatl, a considerably less integrated approach than that manifested by instruments from the Old World. This is not an attempt to reconstruct what Columbus heard nor an echo of the invitation to natives of foreign lands to add their instruments to Christian ceremony, such as happened in Goa in the early sixteenth century (Coelho 2008, 100). Rather, the sound of the Amerindian flute is to be understood as an act of cultural and musical atonement for imperialist aggression: "In a symbolic, but deeply sincere gesture, we wish to make amends to the countless men and women to whom we failed to show understanding and respect, simply because their culture and beliefs were different from our own" (Savall 2006, 91).

The music and texts proceed broadly diachronically. We begin with a passage from Seneca's *Medea*, a Roman play of the first century CE that Columbus quoted in *El Libro de las Profecías*, his revisionist account of the discovery of the New World in Christian apocalyptic terms. Du Fay's polyphonic setting of the sequence for Pentecost, *Veni Sancte Spiritus*, provides the musical material, the cantus part the basis for Figueras' improvisation, the text transplanted in accordance with the medieval practice of contrafactum. Other events that prefigure Columbus' discoveries follow—Prince Ferdinand's conquest of Antequera and Alfonso V's triumphal entry into Naples in 1443—with conjectural and sometimes contradictory links to such events provided by musical and textual means. Josquin's *In te, Domine, speravi*, for example, which probably postdates Columbus' presentation to Ferdinand and Isabella in 1486, expresses not the vaunting hope of an ambitious explorer but that of an anguished penitent (Fallows 2009, 208). Similarly, the anonymous *O tempo bono* that heralds Columbus' birth actually bemoans the loss of good news rather than its arrival.

Much of the courtly music comes from three main manuscripts, the Cancionero de Palacio (Madrid, Palacio Real, Biblioteca, MS 1335—see exhibit 87), the Cancionero Musical de Montecassino (Montecassino, Biblioteca dell'Abbazia, MS 871), and the Cancionero de la Colombina (Seville, Catedral Metropolitana, Biblioteca del Coro, MS 7-1-28), the last specifically tied to Columbus in so far as his second son, Ferdinand, bought it in 1534. Surprisingly, this fact is nowhere mentioned, nor is there any acknowledgement of the adaptation of Du Fay's *Veni Sancte Spiritus* or his *Vexilla regis* (track 22, CD 2) despite Savall's assertion that the disc adheres to "appropriate historical accuracy in vocal and instrumental performance" (Savall 2006, 91). But quite what this means in the context of historical fantasy is not immediately apparent. Are we to take the opening tracks, say, that set Columbus' journal to music as an example of how they might have been treated ca. 1500? If so, we are still talking about a very private event, one that existed in Columbus' imagination.

This all reminds us of Umberto Eco's observation about the rekindling of interest in the medieval world as "a curious oscillation between fantastic neomedievalism and responsible philological examination" (Eco 1986, 63). But musicological exactness is not the point, or at least not the entire point. What is at stake here is also "the corresponding creative imagination for which the vocalists and instrumentalists of the ensembles … as well as the soloists … are justly famous" (Savall 2006, 91). And, in addition to the obvious musical and rhetorical craft, there is certainly plenty of imagination at work. A montage of oppositions obtains—between *haut* and *bas* instruments, solo and ensemble voices, monophony and polyphony, spoken and sung texts, a cappella and instrumental arrangements—that produces a satisfying alternation of moods and textures in the service of a musical drama. Many of the pieces are set *alternatim*, plainchant expanding paraphonically to cover three octaves, contrasting arrangements of voices and instruments providing textural variety, voices doubled at a lower octave, even in polyphony. Readings in Arabic, Latin, Hebrew,

I: P: A: Prenestini

Aramaic, Nahuatl, and Spanish with misty instrumental interpolations intersperse the main musical performances, a macaronic presentation matched by a similarly cosmopolitan melange of Native American flute, North African oud and rebab, and medieval European instruments. Some of the tracks come from earlier releases, perhaps the only way that Alia Vox's impressive turnover of releases could be achieved.

The strangely absent figure in this rich tapestry, though, is Christopher Columbus himself. "Myth always feeds on the information gaps that scholarly research has not been able to fill in," read the liner notes (Nery 2006, 92), and Manuel Forcano's essay on the explorer similarly embraces speculation rather than evidence. Columbus, rather than being the object of an imaginary camera's gaze, is the camera itself, viewing his life—or lives—and his pre-history. All of which suggests that the project is not so much a cinematic biopic or even a musico-historical reconstruction as it is a concept album, specifically one by a Prog Rock band in the 1970s. It shares with them a sense of mystery (Alan Parsons Project's *Tales of Mystery and Imagination*), a broad musical palette (the "symphonic rock" of Rick Wakeman), a narrative, often of a single individual (Genesis' *The Lamb Lies Down On Broadway*), a dollop of medievalism (Gryphon's *Red Queen to Gryphon Three* and Jethro Tull's medieval folk rock), fantastical worlds (one might imagine Roger Dean, responsible for *Yes*' album covers, providing a painting of Hesperia), high production values (a double album more often than not, or at least a doublefold album), a narrator (Viv Stanshall on Mike Oldfield's *Tubular Bells*, Richard Burton on *Jeff Wayne's War of the Worlds*), virtuosity (one of the defining features of Prog Rock), and earnest nationalist history (Rick Wakeman's *Six Wives of Henry VIII* and *The Myths and Legends of King Arthur and the Knights of the Round Table*).

It's heavy, man.

94. A Palestrina Contrafactum

Samantha Bassler

O God thou art my God
Giovanni Pierluigi da Palestrina, arranged by Henry Aldrich (1647-1710)
London, British Library, Mad.Soc.J82. f. 68r
Manuscript on paper, 172 fols., 33 x 20 cm

This exhibit is from the London Madrigal Society library, donated to the British Library's collections in 1954. Founded in the eighteenth century—according to music historian John Hawkins, an early member, in 1741—and still active today, the London Madrigal Society is an institution with performance traditions that originated in the domestic sphere, but later evolved, with the changing tastes of London audiences, to include public performances and music competitions. The Society is an antiquarian society for "ancient music," connected not only to the contemporaneous eighteenth-century London club culture, but also to a long history of English antiquarianism. The Madrigal Society was founded to further early music at a time when "ancient" music was not popular with the wider London concert-going public, originally conducting the majority of their business in closed, members-only meetings at public houses. The earliest gatherings featured performances of Italian and English madrigals, and English contrafacta of Italian madrigals and motets; later, English catches and glees gained popularity. The manuscript image featured here is the opening of a contrafactum of Palestrina's *Sicut cervus* motet (first published 1584), entitled *O God thou art my God* in English. John Hawkins names Henry Aldrich as the person responsible for recomposing the motet; Aldrich valued Palestrina greatly and wrote many "recompositions" of his works (Shay 1996, 368-400).

While musical antiquarianism in England is most often discussed as a late nineteenth- and early twentieth-century phenomenon, closer inspection of the holdings of the Madrigal Society reveals a tradition that is rooted in early modern English culture, and connects antiquarianism with museum culture. Despite its name, the growing number of catch and glee publications purchased, and named in the Society's performance lists, demonstrate members' interests in many genres, and also a connection to other eighteenth- and nineteenth-century singing clubs (Robins 2006, 16-17 and 24). The Society's nineteenth-century tradition of madrigal competitions eventually led to more public performances (Robins 2006, 16-17). In the eighteenth century, the prominence of Palestrina and other revered masters connects the Madrigal Society to antiquarian activities of the seventeenth century.

The popular view of antiquarians in the early modern period was not always positive. Already in the seventeenth century, antiquarians in England were caricatured for their obsession with the past. John Earle wrote in 1660 that antiquarians are

> [men] strangely thrifty of Time past, and enemies indeed to this maw, whence he fetches out many things when they are now all rotten and stinking. Hee is one that hath unnaturall disease to bee enamour'd of old age and wrinckles, and loves all things (as Dutchmen doe Cheese) the better for being mouldy and worme-eaten (Sweet 2008).

Earle was not alone in his contempt for, or at least suspicion of, antiquarians' work. A seventeenth-century commonplace book in the Pierpont Morgan Library contains another, similar caricature of antiquarians, as moth-eaten, ancient, and dusty:

> Hee loues no Libraries but where are more spiders volumes, then Authors: and lookes with great admiration on the Antiq[u]e worke of Cobbwebs. Printed bookes hee contemns as a noualtie of this latter age, but a manuscript hee pores on euerlastingly especially if the couer bee moath eaten & the dust make a parenthesis betweene euery sillable. Hee will giue all the bookes in his studdie (which are rarities) for one of the Romane bindinge or six lines of Tully in his owne hand (Hackel 2005, 33).

The author describes the antiquarian as so focused on relics from the past, in this case manuscripts, that the antiquarian cannot appreciate the new technology available, namely the printed book. The antiquarian is not only missing out, but even worse, is not contributing to furthering the advancement of new technologies. The antiquarian, in their obsession to hold onto the past, is in danger of losing cultural relevance in the present.

The alternative viewpoint was that antiquarians were integral to preserving past artifacts for future prosperity. In a 1693 letter to the Yorkshire antiquarian Ralph Thorseby, the cleric and historian William Nicolson states,

> I wish we had in this kingdom, as they have in Sweden, a society for the collecting and preserving [of] antiquities. This would do something for us. But as long as particular men engage in burdens beyond their strength we have millions of great matters attempted, and nothing performed to any purpose (Sweet 2004, 81).

Again, in 1694, Nicolson writes of his desire for a society which cultivates history and antiquities, giving examples of such organizations elsewhere on the continent in France, Italy, and Sweden: "And why should not we have the like in England?

… We have the best stock of true remains of antiquity of any nation, perhaps, in Europe; and yet our histories hitherto have been most lazily written" (Sweet 2004, 81). Nicolson values the work of antiquarians and views their work in a nationalistic light: England has great antiquities, and deserves a society to preserve them.

Richard Taruskin has connected the sense of musical tradition emerging in the eighteenth century in the wake of Mozart and Haydn with contemporary museum culture. He asserts that musicians felt a sense "of obligation to illustrious forebears and their great works," which in the nineteenth century "becomes… a stronger force… than ever before" because of a "growing sense of *canon*, of an accumulating body of permanent masterworks that never go out of style but form the bedrock of an everlasting and immutable repertory that alone can validate contemporary composers with its authority" (Taruskin 2005, 637-38). Taruskin argues specifically that the city of London and the public concert series of the Academy of Ancient Music were instrumental in the "erecting" of this musical museum culture. He further declares that the invention of "classical music" in this period directly influenced the present-day familiar "'classical' curatorial function" of concert music, characterised by "faultless reproduction, heavy sense of obligation to texts, radical differentiation of creative and performing roles, the elevation of the literate tradition and the denigration of the oral one" (Taruskin 2005, 639).

The musical antiquarians involved in organisations such as the London Madrigal Society were certainly contributors to this canonisation of past musical monuments. Not only did the Madrigal Society amass great collections of music from the past and copy it into scores and partbooks for their archive, as this exhibit exemplifies, but they also sought to integrate early music into the present day. As John Hawkins put it, their activities pursued the objective of "naturalizing as it were the compositions of the old Italian masters, and accommodating them to an English ear" (Shay 1996, 371).

An analysis of the programmes and meeting records in the Madrigal Society collection at the British Library demonstrates that certain works were performed more frequently than others. Five such favoured works in the eighteenth century are the madrigal *Dissi l'amata mia lucida stella* by Luca Marenzio; the canon *Non nobis*, originally attributed to William Byrd but now removed from his oeuvre by Philip Brett (Brett 1972); *This sweet and merry month of May* by Byrd; a contrafactum of Thomas Tallis's *O sacrum convivium*, refashioned as the English anthem *I call and cry*; and the contrafactum of Palestrina that forms this exhibit.

Similar programming was in vogue at the closely related Academy of Ancient Music, founded in London as the Academy of Vocal Music in 1726. The two societies shared repertoire and members, including the founder of the Madrigal Society John Immyns, and strongly influenced one another's selection of repertoire (Hobson 2015, 57). A performance programme dated 24 April 1746, entitled "Motets, Madrigals, and Other Pieces, Performed by the Academy of Ancient Music," includes Palestrina's *Angelus Domini*, an excerpt from Henry Purcell's *The Indian Queen*, Alonso Lobo's *Kyrie* for four voices, Thomas Morley's madrigal *Say, Gentle Nymphs*, Tomás Luis de Victoria's *Quam pulchri sunt*, Byrd's madrigal *The Eagle's Force*, the pseudo-Byrd canon *Non nobis*, and George Frideric Handel's *Te Deum* (Hobson 2015, 40-42).

Although the repertoire choices at the two societies were notably similar, differences emerged in the ways they interpreted their historical remits. There was unrest at the Academy of Ancient Music for its lackadaisical approach to defining ancient music as more than 20 years old. John Wesley recounts a 1748 meeting with co-founder of the Academy, the German-born composer Johann Christoph Pepusch:

> I spent an hour or two with Dr Pepusch. He asserted that the art of music is lost: that the ancients only understood it in its perfection; that it was revived a little in the reign of Queen Elizabeth, who was a judge and a patroness of it; that after her reign it sunk for sixty or seventy years, till Purcell made some attempts to restore it; but that ever since, the true, ancient art, depending on nature and mathematical principles, had gained no ground, the present masters having no fixed principles at all (Wesley 1827, 61).

Although the Madrigal Society did feature some contemporary works, there is evidence that Pepusch influenced the Madrigal Society's stricter guidelines and codes regarding early music, and that the younger Society was meant to rectify issues within the Academy.

Palestrina was widely revered in the eighteenth century, and not only by antiquarians. In the 1770s, the widely-travelled music historian Charles Burney demonstrated tolerance towards the music of earlier composers, and esteem for Palestrina's music, naming him "the Home of the most Ancient Music," which "merits all the reverence and attention which it is in a musical historian's power to bestow" (Lovell 1979, 401). However, Palestrina's prominent role in the activities of the Madrigal Society arose not only from their appreciation for the composer's musical style and reputation, but also because his ecclesiastical *stile antico* fitted well with the ideological position of their antiquarian project. On the whole, antiquarians shared Pepusch's displeasure with the state of contemporary music, and looked to monuments of musical history as a more morally and technically robust alternative to debased and insubstantial modern efforts. In a sermon delivered on 8 July 1784, the bishop of Oxford, George Horne, stated that: "Great care should be taken to keep the style of [church music] chaste and pure, suitable to holy places, and divine subjects … The light movements of the theatre, with the effeminate and frittered music of modern ITALY, should be excluded" (Day 1971, 575). Horne goes on to cite Tallis, Byrd, Orlando Gibbons, and Handel, among others, as "English classics in this sacred science." Such attitudes were certainly not unique to England: interest in Palestrina's Counter-Reformation style played a similar role in E. T. A. Hoffmann's critique of Enlightenment culture, as an ancient style preserving moral and religious values lost in the musical culture of the present day (Garratt 2002).

Contrafacta of Palestrina's music were not new in the hands of the Madrigal Society, however; English antiquarians were already copying his compositions into manuscripts in the seventeenth century, and it is in this earlier layer of revivalist reception that the contrafactum *O God thou art my God* finds its origin. Henry Aldrich, fellow and later dean of Christ Church, Oxford, hosted a weekly music club at least from the 1680s, for which he had copied works by Marenzio, Byrd, and Palestrina alongside music by contemporary composers. Among the Palestrina motets are several re-worked with English words: *Doctor bonus* becomes *We have heard with our ears*, for example, and of course *Sicut cervus* becomes our *O God thou art my God* (Day 1971, 579-80). Aldrich's recompositions were highlighted by Hawkins as admirable efforts to "naturalize" the Italian masters. For modern scholars, his activities were among the principal forces propelling the aesthetic movement that supported and cultivated ancient music, leading ultimately to the "museum" of revered musical works that characterises classical music culture today (Weber 1994).

95. St Sepulchre Chapel, St Mary Magdalene, London

Ayla Lepine

John Ninian Comper, 1895
Rowington Close, London
Photo © Ayla Lepine

In 1895, the architect and ecclesiastical designer John Ninian Comper completed a memorial chapel dedicated to St Sepulchre in the crypt of St Mary Magdalene in Paddington, London. The chapel, which served as a memorial to the parish's first vicar as well as a place of reservation of the Blessed Sacrament, combined imagery of Christ's tomb and resurrection with imagery celebrating both Mary Magdalene and the Virgin Mary. It represented the culmination of a new and experimental form of Gothic Revival design, in which intensive layers of iconographically rich sculptures, painting, and gilding expressed the immersive multi-sensory world of the fin de siècle church. This space is simultaneously guided by the pivot-point between death and new life in the Incarnation, and by the women closest to Christ in his ministry, namely Mary Magdalene and the Blessed Virgin Mary.

With its stained glass windows inspired by Rogier van der Weyden and Hans Memling's Northern Renaissance visions of heaven and hell, fifteenth-century-inspired painted organ case, inscribed and highly decorative patterned walls, glinting lead stars with their mirrors and gilding, and rows of golden saints, this is a museum in itself as well as a holy place of sacred sacrament and liturgy—and, indeed, music. Additionally, in the centre of this chapel there is a narrative in which the Bible, Renaissance art, and Victorian art circles intersect. The chapel as a whole is not only a site within a site, but also a resonating instrument, a music-box, and a singular whole within which word and image combine forces with notation and sacred song. Its walls include a series of unusual canvases pressed directly onto the walls that contain fragments of plainsong (fig. 95.1). Circumambulating the chapel engages visitors in a different kind of liturgical activity from gathering for prayer or for Mass: it becomes possible to sing a prayer as the perimeter is marked out in song and footsteps, the body of the worshipper resonating as the body of the chapel resonates with the voice of the singer.

This concept, developed in earlier Gothic Revival interiors by Comper's mentors G. F. Bodley and Thomas Garner, working with William Morris and others, unites music, prayer,

Figure 95.1: Plainchant appearing in the decoration of St Sepulchre Chapel. Photo © Ayla Lepine.

movement, and aesthetics in a unique and quasi-liturgical way (Lepine 2017, 81). The plainsong notation that Comper deployed in fragments of canvas/manuscript, with visual allusions in scale and colouring to Renaissance monastic large missals and psalters, is the Latin hymn by Venantius Fortunatus, bishop of Poitiers, written in the seventh century as a celebration of the Easter Resurrection. It is a hymn designed to be used in procession, and begins "Salve, Festa Dies!" (Hail thee, Festival Day!), concluding with "Darkness and chaos and death flee from the face of the light" (Messenger 1953, 112).

St Sepulchre's chapel was one of Comper's most important projects, although the architect himself was embarrassed by it in later years. Many recognised the particular appeal of this small, glowing sacred space, and none more than the poet and architectural writer John Betjeman. Betjeman championed Comper's work from the 1930s onwards, despite having an ambiguous and sometimes barbed professional relationship with him (Symondson and Bucknall 2006, 220). In the early 1940s Betjeman wrote to Comper:

> I saw for the first time the other day your crypt at St Mary Mag, Paddington. My! It is a gleaming vision of perp [Perpendicular Gothic] resplendence. I have already taken the following people to see it: H. de C. Hastings, Editor of the Architectural Review, Dr N. Pevsner, John Piper, Osbert Lancaster, T. D. Kendrick, Keeper of Brit and Medieval Antiquities at the BM and I have recommended it to Sir Kenneth Clark. All are stupefied to silence by its magnificence (Symdonson and Bucknall 2006, 220).

He later wrote regarding the dominance of Modernist architecture that Comper's multi-faceted architectural historicism could be a kind of architectural tonic: "I am continually demolishing high-brow functionalists by giving them my London course on Comper" (Symondson and Bucknall 2006, 234).

Comper pursued a particular kind of beauty. Its features—a great deal of gold, heroic, and indeed homoerotic images of triumphant saints and figures of Christ, and the preference for painted decoration over structural polychromy—are all subordinated to one deceptively simple theme in their arrangement within architectural interiors: the Eucharist. In a 1951 account of Comper's characteristics, a writer for the *Times Literary Supplement* stated that "In all of his works the altar is his chief concern—how best to show the altar, how to lead the eye to it through colour and light, how to bend the knee to it through scale, how to humble the heart to it" (Anson 1960, 280-81).

In 1882, Comper was introduced to Alfred Gurney, parish priest of St Barnabas, Pimlico. He offered Comper one of his earliest commissions, to insert a rood and produce interior decoration for the crypt chapel (Symondson and Bucknall 2006, 196). Gurney was well-connected in artistic circles and in 1893 reviewed Edward Burne-Jones' retrospective exhibition for the *Newberry House Magazine* (Crossman 2015). Through Gurney and his connections, Comper's world as an emergent architect and designer was shaped by Aesthetic encounter, in which the "cult of beauty" was a core theme in shaping a new medievalist and devout Anglican beauty of holiness (Hall 2014, 129-51). Reflecting on his early career in the offices of Bodley and Garner, Ninian Comper believed that "In the writings of Bodley and still more in his work there is trace of slight preciousness, an affinity perhaps with Pater, or a more delicate expression of the Aesthetic side of William Morris" (Hall 2014, 275).

Comper would very likely have known Pater's essay on William Morris' poetry, first published in *The Renaissance* and re-issued in 1889 as "Aesthetic Poetry." Here, Pater traces the intertwining relationships between Greek and Gothic influence in relation to a new flowering in late Victorian poetics. In 1895, the same year that Comper devised his designs for the St Sepulchre chapel at St Mary Magdalene, Pater's *Greek Studies* was published (Østermark-Johansen 2015). This collection of essays traversed the Hellenic arts, and did so through characteristically sophisticated cultural references. When it came to church architecture, Pater was an active critic. Indeed, in 1894 he wrote to the incumbent at Holy Redeemer, Clerkenwell, a classical building recently completed by the architect John Dando Sedding. While remarking on its successful and appealing design, Pater admitted, "I am one of those who think that when Gothic may perhaps have fallen into disuse again everywhere else, it will still continue to be our sacred style of architecture" (Evans 1970, 141). Pater's investment in poetic beauty, Aestheticism, and religion, would have made him a key figure for the young Anglo-Catholic London-based Comper.

In 1894, the same year he visited Clerkenwell to comment on the architecture and in the same span of time Comper was building his London reputation as an Anglican Aesthete, Pater wrote "The Age of Athletic Prizemen: A Chapter in Greek Art." In its conclusion, Pater turns to scripture to account for Greek ideal masculine beauty in athletic action, writing:

> He had been faithful, we cannot help saying, as we pass from that youthful company, in what comparatively is perhaps little—in the culture, the administration, of the visible world; and he merited, so we might go on to say—he merited Revelation, something which should solace his heart in the inevitable fading of that.

Moving swiftly forward from the notion of Revelation, Pater seizes on the vitalising force of the Logos:

> We are reminded of those strange prophetic words of the Wisdom, the Logos, by whom God made the world, in one of the sapiential, half-Platonic books of the Hebrew Scriptures:—"I was by him, as one

brought up with him; rejoicing in the habitable parts of the earth. My delights were with the sons of men" (Pater 1894, 87).

Pater ends his essay on Greek ideal beauty with Proverbs 8:31, the same inscription that Comper chose—as a revised idea in 1895—for the canopy over the altar within which the True Body of Christ, perfect man, was reserved for the worship of all.

In the St Sepulchre chapel, dedicated to the holy tomb of Christ itself with reference to the Church of the Holy Sepulchre in Jerusalem, Comper combined multiple references to the Gothic Revival and the European Renaissance to create an interior where music, sculpture, painting, glass, and glinting surfaces combine in a subterranean jewel. Opening the door to the crypt at St Mary Magdalene, the church within which Comper's chapel is situated, opens the door to a revivalist multi-dimensional music box, resonant with Christian prayer and scripture that encircles the walls and proclaims the resurrection and God's presence, whether anyone is present to sing and worship or not, and whether they sing in dialects of northern or southern Renaissance or medievalism. Occupying multiple territories at once, the plainsong ribbon around the chapel interior ties these strands of history together in unison notation, without rests or bar lines, as endless as the praises surrounding the throne of God following the resurrection from the tomb.

95. St Sepulchre Chapel, St Mary Magdalene, London

96. The Singing Fountain in Prague

Scott Lee Edwards

Tomáš Jaroš and Francesco Terzio, 1564-68
Bronze fountain, 405 cm (height); 220 cm (diameter, lower basin); 157 cm (diameter, upper basin)
Royal Garden of Prague Castle, Prague, Czechia
Photo © Paul Seheult / Eye Ubiquitous

Since its installation in 1573 in the gardens of Prague Castle, the Singing Fountain has enjoyed pride of place in front of the Summer Palace of Queen Anne, a monument of Renaissance architecture commissioned by Ferdinand II, archduke of Austria, and completed in 1563. Designed by the court painter Francesco Terzio, the fountain was cast from bronze in the years 1564-68 by Tomáš Jaroš—a founder who also made the so-called Zikmund bell in the Cathedral of St Vitus—with the collaboration of Antonio Brocco, Wolf Hofprugger, Vavřinec Křička z Bitýšky, and Hans Peißer (Diemer 1995, 19-25). Its pastoral iconography reflects its garden setting: four grotesques support the lower, wider basin, decorated with mascarons and palmetto fronds, in the middle of which rises a central pillar surrounded by atlases, deer-bearing fauns, ram's heads, and festoons. This column serves as a pedestal for the upper basin, ornamented with putti, masks, and garlands, and at the top of which rises a curly-haired putto riding a sea-dragon and playing the bagpipe. Water jets from the bagpipe, the dragon, the masks, and putti of the upper basin, as well as the ram's heads and deer of the central pillar.

The name Singing Fountain suggests that it produces a kind of music, but the only audible sound today is simply the sound of water falling into pools. As an object exposed to almost 450 years of weather, regime change, and military conflict, the fountain has undergone numerous modifications since it was made. Its evocative name and royal perch above the city, along with the changing ways the fountain has either sung or been silent since its creation, inform its status as an evolving national symbol rich in associative possibilities.

Two documents provide clues to the fountain's original sonic design. A drawing by one of its founders, Vavřinec Křička, survives in a manuscript of bronze casting techniques in the National Library of the Czech Republic (*Mathesis bohemica*, sign. XVII. B. 17., Křička ca. 1550-1625, fol. 29^{r}). Křička depicts the fountain with striking precision, including details in the stand, basins, and pillar that closely match the fountain's present form. The bagpiper, however, is considerably different, most noticeably in the fact that atop his head sits a larger crowned imperial double-headed eagle. Křička's version appears more human than putto, playing a bagpipe with a drone curved over the shoulder in contrast to the present fountain's droneless bagpipe, which features an elongated chanter capped by a goat's head. In the drawing, water jets emanate from the two mouths of the eagle, the chanter, and the drone, whereas today they spurt from the horns of the goat's head. Křička does not describe the sound produced by the fountain, but a second manuscript in the Bibliothèque nationale de France (*Voyages de Bergeron en France, Italie, Allemagne et Espagne, de 1601 à 1612*, sign. Français 5560) provides evidence that the fountain had also been designed to "sing." On a walk through the gardens in June 1603, the French courtier Pierre Bergeron describes an orchard of orange and fig trees leading to a bronze fountain, from which "water that jets from the top falls so proportionately into the basin that it imitates through a harmonious sound that of a bagpipe" (fols. 162^{v}-163^{r}).

Bergeron's account is unfortunately the only known document prior to the nineteenth century with information about the fountain's sound. Early visitors to the royal gardens, such as Jacques Esprinchard and Paul Hentzner, were often more taken by the flora imported from Italy, Spain, and Asia, the hitherto unfamiliar tulips from Turkey, and the lions housed in the so-called Löwenhof. The view over the city impresses Hentzner, while the artworks in Rudolf II's Kunstkammer, displayed in the Summer Palace, are highlighted by Esprinchard, who mentions only the presence of a bronze fountain in a small garden surrounded by green iron bars (Hentzner 1612, 414; Esprinchard 1989, 33).

After the start of the Thirty Years War, the garden suffered damage, and it is possible that by this time, the fountain's imperial eagle had been removed. In 1632, Martin Zeiller insists that a visit to the royal gardens is necessary due to the many "splendid native and foreign plants," including pomegranates, found there, and a "beautiful stone house with a pretty view and adorned with beautiful pictures" (Zeiller 1632, 170-71). Zeiller notes that earlier visitors had once been entertained by foreign animals, but does not mention the fountain. According to the nineteenth-century historian Anton Schwarz, it may no longer have been a highlight, for the advance of Saxon troops in Prague in 1631 caused damage to the garden and especially to the fountain, which was not repaired until 1651 (Schwarz 1845, 256).

In 1681, the Jesuit historian Bohuslav Balbín laments the fallen state of the garden since its former glory during the time of Rudolf II, when it was a wonder to visiting foreigners. To Balbín, the Summer Palace is known as the Mathematical House in honour of the scientific activities carried out there by Tycho de Brahe (Balbín 1681, 126-27). Carl Redel's 1710 travelogue, *Das Sehens-würdige Prag* (*Prague Worth Seeing*), is informed by his reading of Balbín combined with first-hand experience. He mentions the Mathematical House and the deterioration of the garden, but also marvels at the fountain's visual beauty, which he describes as changing according to perspective, located on a pathway decked by trees and hemmed by bushes, and worthy of regard as "a beautiful and large machine" (Redel 1710, 75-77).

The fountain was again damaged in 1742, when French regiments fighting the War of Austrian Succession made the palace their encampment, and in 1757, when Prussian troops in the Third Silesian War disfigured the garden's statuary (Schwarz 1845, 256 and 259). Later, under Emperor Joseph II, the Summer Palace was handed over to the imperial military administration for long-term use as an artillery laboratory (Mihulka 1934, 79-80).

For the coronation of Leopold II in 1791, the production of gunpowder in the garden was temporarily suspended, the water mains repaired, flora replanted, and new terraces were created with statuary by Ignatz Platzer (Schwarz 1845, 259). The fountain, too, was renovated. As the inscription still visible on the central shaft indicates, erroneously following Křička's dating, "this machine" was constructed in 1554 and repaired by a certain W. Frank in honour of Leopold's coronation.

This renewal of the garden is described by Jaroslaus Schaller, who writes in 1794 that at the end of a leafy corridor stands the metal fountain, preserved since the time of Rudolph II (Schaller 1794, 456). Although apparently accessible to the public, the garden nevertheless remained in military hands until after the coronation of Ferdinand V in 1836, when Karel Chotek, the supreme burgrave of the Bohemian Kingdom, oversaw the evacuation of soldiers and acquired permission to undertake repair work (Mihulka 1934, 80). The summer palace was assigned to the Society of Patriotic Friends of Art for the purpose of a museum, and in 1844 a plan of repair was approved.

Part of this repair seems to have included taking apart the fountain, since Schwarz provides the weights of its separate parts and a summary of its metallic make-up in his 1845 history of the garden (Schwarz 1845, 251). In addition to renovation, an important part of reopening the garden and palace to the public was a rebranding of the complex, and thus we find in Karel Zap's 1848 *Průwodce po Praze* (*A Guide Around Prague*) a new name for the palace: "Belvedere" (Zap 1848, 220).

It was not, however, until the arrival of Rudolf, crown prince of Austria, in Prague in 1878 to serve in the 36th Infantry Regiment, that the long-lost "song" of the fountain was restored. An article in the newspaper *Prager Tagblatt* from 17 May 1878 documents the many preparations in advance of the prince's arrival, including renewal of the royal gardens and 18 fountains within the castle complex. According to the article, all of the fountains had been long out of service, mainly due to murky water in the water mains. Therefore, new conduits were created connecting the fountains to ponds near Liboc and Veleslavín by way of a large filter near the Strahov gate. The mechanical engineer František Božek, famed as a creator of musical automata, was appointed to assess whether the bronze fountain, "which had been dormant since time immemorial," could be revived. The bagpiper, "which stood on 2 dolphins," had been stolen, but the thief was identified and the figure recovered by the castellan. In the vault below the fountain, Božek found only a pair of broken sixteenth-century pipes. During research in the imperial library, he discovered a letter with documentation of a "singing fountain in the imperial garden," while physical inspection of the fountain revealed that the lower basin had been shaped at various thicknesses most likely for this purpose. Božek then recast missing parts of the fountain, using an oxide to create an artificially aged patina, and constructed a new apparatus with two pipes pushing water upward to fill the nozzles of the bagpiper and dolphins. Once the upper basin filled, holes in the basin wall poured streams into the lower basin, while water jets fell symmetrically from the central pillar but in an opposing direction. By calibrating their curvatures, Božek was able to produce rhythmic, harmonious tones when the jets hit the basin, similar to a bell ringing in the distance. The contact of water and metal yielded "two minor thirds in a minor key," but only as long as the lower basin remained empty of water ("Vom Tage" 1878, 3).

Thus was the Singing Fountain reborn, but such a carefully calibrated outdoor mechanism would inevitably deteriorate, especially following the departure of the crown prince in 1884 and the death of Božek in 1886. Eduard Herold's 1884 *Malerische Wanderungen durch Prag* (*Picturesque Walks Through Prague*) speaks of the fountain's melodic tones (Herold 1884, 443), and Josef Svátek's 1899 *Ze staré Prahy* (*From Old Prague*) still acclaims its bell-like metallic reverberations, while pointing out the sixteenth-century origins of the fountain's name (Svátek

1899, 141; see also Herain 1905). But after the turn of the century, writers increasingly struggle to account for the fountain's singing. By 1917, the art historian Karel Chytil can only assume that the fountain must once have been musical, since a bellcaster like Jaroš was by necessity also a musician (Chytil 1917, 27), and the youth magazine *Naše Praha* (*Our Prague*) informs its readership, "it has been said that a playing mechanism, concealed in the bagpipes, accompanied the streams of water falling from basin to basin with subtle music" (Gebauerová 1925, 121).

Despite questions about how this fountain was supposed to sing, the name posed an opportunity for musicians to revitalise the fountain through newly composed songs. One of the first was Leoš Janáček, who composed *Plačící fontána* (*The Weeping Fountain*) in February 1916 to a text by František Procházka, in which the "unrung, already unsung" fountain weeps over a dying fairy tale. The dramatist and songwriter Karel Hašler contrasts the "strange songs" of the fountain heard by the silent (Bohemian) lion in the song *Zpívající fontána* (*The Singing Fountain*), performed with guitar and celesta in the 1932 film *Písničkář* (*The Ballad-Singer*) to incite anti-Austrian resistance in World War I. Straddling the Velvet Revolution is the Eben Brothers' *Praha 1581*, a song first performed in the 1980s but only later released in 1996, with lyrics and music, including a fountain-imitating Orff metallophone, that tries to capture for a modern audience the lost sixteenth-century voice of the fountain.

The garden was reconstructed in 1956 into the form in which it appears today, the dense foliage that once surrounded the fountain replaced with symmetrical grass beds divided by gravel lanes. In 1966, new restoration work led by the sculptor Lumír Klas removed sediments from the fountain's surface, replaced corroded bolts, installed new copper pipes, restored lead seals, and strengthened the inner surface of the upper basin with a copper plate (Ramdan 2016, 31-33). Due to its weakened material and excessive pressure in the inner pipe, the figure of the bagpipe-player was replaced with a copy. The original is today part of a permanent exhibition in the Old Royal Palace titled *The Story of Prague Castle*.

Die Meistersinger von Nürnberg. Oper von Richard Wagner. (1.)
Liebig's
Fleisch-
Extract.
1. Aufzug. Walter: „Verweilt! – Ein Wort! Ein einzig Wort."
Nachdruck verboten.
Siehe Rückseite.

Die Meistersinger von Nürnberg. Oper von Richard Wagner. (2.)
Liebig's
Fleisch-
Extract.
1. Aufzug. Walter: „Auf da steigt, ob Meister-Krahn ihm ungeneigt,
Das stolze Minnelied. – Ade! Ihr Meister hinied!"
Nachdruck verboten.
Siehe Rückseite.

Die Meistersinger von Nürnberg. Oper von Richard Wagner. (3.)
Liebig's
Fleisch-
Extract.
2. Aufzug. Beckmessers Ständchen.
Nachdruck verboten.
Siehe Rückseite.

Die Meistersinger von Nürnberg. Oper von Richard Wagner. (4.)
Liebig's
Fleisch-
Extract.
3. Aufzug. Hans Sachs: „Wahn! Wahn! Ueberall Wahn!"
Nachdruck verboten.
Siehe Rückseite.

Die Meistersinger von Nürnberg. Oper von Richard Wagner. (5.)
Liebig's
Fleisch-
Extract.
3. Aufzug. Hans Sachs: „Aha, hier sitzt's! Nun begreif ich den Fall!"
Nachdruck verboten.
Siehe Rückseite.

Die Meistersinger von Nürnberg. Oper von Richard Wagner. (6.)
Liebig's
Fleisch-
Extract.
Schluss-Szene: Walter Stolzings Krönung zum Meistersinger.
Nachdruck verboten.
Siehe Rückseite.

97. Liebig Images of *Die Meistersinger von Nürnberg*

Gundula Kreuzer

Liebigbild series number 855
Liebich & Kuntze: Leipzig, 1912
6 chromolithographs, each 11 x 7.1 cm
Private collection
Photos © Gundula Kreuzer

Something of an early twentieth-century equivalent to a TV period drama, this series of industrial collector's images from 1912 offers a triply mediated perspective on music-making in sixteenth-century Germany: it presents a popularised account of Richard Wagner's 1868 opera *Die Meistersinger von Nürnberg*, which itself refashioned Romantic ideas of late medieval culture. Issued by a Leipzig art print shop, the highly stylised chromolithographs circulated in Germany, Belgium, Holland, France, and Italy as tie-ins for Justus Liebig's famous meat extract. Such so-called Liebig images had been boosting sales of the pioneering beef stock since 1872, eight years after it first hit the market (Abbate 2021). With topics ranging from zoology, geography, and ethnography to history, fairy tales, and music, they were organised in sets of six with short educational texts on their flipsides. By 1900, the trading cards stood as the most trendy European tie-in product, printed in several languages and by the millions: upper-middle-class families who could afford the bouillon avidly collected them in special scrapbooks, while teachers employed them as pedagogical aids (Böcher 2006; Lorenz 1992).

Following a number of series on nineteenth-century composers and operas, this set presents six scenes from Wagner's only mature comic opera, which built on the gradual revaluation of late-medieval German guild culture since the late eighteenth century. Geographically, the locus classicus of this revival was the Franconian town of Nuremberg, formerly a free imperial city and one of the most prosperous mercantile centres of the German Middle Ages, due to its advantageous position on major European trading routes. Its importance was buttressed by the Golden Bull's stipulation, in 1356, that each emperor was to hold his first diet in Nuremberg. Between 1424 and 1797, moreover, Nuremberg hosted the imperial insignia of the Holy Roman Empire of the German Nation (Brockmann 2006). The city's renaissance in the nineteenth-century imagination was thus seminally tied to an awakening nationalism, which anachronistically construed Nuremberg (since 1808 part of the Bavarian kingdom and, by then, an industrial town) as the heart of a cohesive German Reich. Nostalgic and Romantic, this medievalism bolstered abstract political desires for a unified German nation-state. But it also manifested concretely in the touristic discovery of Nuremberg, whose medieval city centre had largely survived intact, following the city's sudden economic slump after the Thirty Years' War and conservative municipal building policies (Groos 1992; Spencer 1992). Previously considered oppressive and backward, Nuremberg's "narrow crooked streets" with their "ancestral houses and churches" were first revalued in the influential 1797 *Herzensergießungen eines kunstliebenden Klosterbruders* (*Outpourings of an Art-Loving Friar*) by the avowed Romantic writer Wilhelm Heinrich Wackenroder: he celebrated these traditional structures as carriers of "the imprint of our fatherland's ancient art" (Wackenroder 1797, 109; Spencer 1992; Smith 2017). Similarly, Wagner in 1866 extolled Nuremberg as "the old, true seat of German art, German uniqueness and splendor, the powerful old free city, well-preserved like a precious jewel" (Spencer 1992, 36).

Indeed, Nuremberg's wealth had fostered an extraordinarily rich cultural life during the fifteenth and sixteenth centuries, epitomised for posterity by the continuing esteem for the local painter and printmaker Albrecht Dürer. Musically, Nuremberg had been home, since the fifteenth century, to an influential guild of Meistersinger, which cultivated a tradition of strictly rule-based poetry and monodic singing that flourished primarily in southern German imperial cities during the late fourteenth through seventeenth centuries (Brunner 2001). The Romantic rediscovery of this tradition was driven by idealised visions of such guilds' alleged unity of art and life as well as of its perceived democratization of culture and the latter's purported roots in the folk—aspects contrasted, on the one hand, with the feudal vernacular song tradition of the troubadours and trouvères that had preceded Meistergesang and, on the other, with coeval polyphony, associated with aristocratic or ecclesiastical patronage. At the centre of this reassessment stood the cobbler and poet Hans Sachs, a prolific Nuremberg Meistersinger who left upwards of 4000 poems to be sung and 13 different *Töne* (sanctioned melodies with a particular metric and rhyme scheme), among other moralising writings and plays (Brunner 1997). Nearly forgotten in the wake of the Thirty Years' War,

Sachs re-entered German cultural consciousness after Johann Wolfgang von Goethe in 1776 dedicated an admiring poem to the master (*Hans Sachsens poetische Sendung—Hans Sachs' Poetical Mission*), whom he likened to Dürer's genius. Sachs became all the more useful to the budding national project of German intellectuals as he had supported the Reformation: the poet exemplified a particularly German art of the late Middle Ages that could be harnessed for a protestant Teutonic counter-narrative to the dominant influence of the Italian (and Catholic) Renaissance (on this counternarrative see Ruehl 2015).

Richard Wagner furthered such idealising trends in *Die Meistersinger*, his only mature work based on a concrete historical figure. Accordingly, he took great pains to include supposedly accurate details when drafting a scenario in 1845 and (as was his habit) writing his own libretto, beginning in 1861. Among other sources, he used Georg Gottfried Gervinus' then-recent history of German poetry and included rituals, terms, and individual singers' names from the 1697 *Buch von der Meister-Singer holdseligen Kunst* (*Book of the Master-Singers' Blessed Art*) by the Nuremberg historian and lawyer Johann Christoph Wagenseil. For what would become the opera's most celebrated chorus—the people's "Wach auf" chorale greeting Sachs in Act 3—Wagner even cited words from Sachs' famous poem dedicated to Martin Luther (Minor 2013). Musically, however, Wagner revealed his Romanticizing take when rendering the mastersingers' world not through late-medieval song but through stentorian diatonic polyphony, which nevertheless contrasts with Wagner's lyrical chromaticism elsewhere.

To be sure, Wagner was not the first to dramatise the figure of Sachs. Instead, he adapted seminal plot elements of Albert Lortzing's 1840 comic opera *Hans Sachs*, which in turn was based on the popular eponymous "dramatic poem" by Johann Ludwig Deinhardstein of 1827 (Brockmann 2006). All three works centre on a singing competition whose prize is the hand of the well-to-do goldsmith's beautiful daughter. In Lortzing and Deinhardstein, Sachs himself wins the contest and, eventually, his beloved, if only after the emperor intervenes to affirm Sachs' poetic preeminence over his socially superior but artistically dubious rival. Wagner, however, moved the plot from 1517 to the mid-sixteenth century and has the mature Sachs renounce his love for the sake of Walther von Stolzing, an (albeit haughty) young out-of-town aristocrat who is both fancied by the maiden Eva and brings much-needed creative rejuvenation to the Meistersinger guild. Realising all this, Sachs teaches Walther the basics of Meistergesang before orchestrating things such that Walther may outperform the elderly and archconservative town clerk Beckmesser. Not only is no emperor needed in this scenario; but Sachs' artistry even garners him a position of social leadership, which he utilises to proclaim his aesthetic standards as socio-political ideals: his notorious final speech, rewritten on the eve of the Franco-Prussian War (1870-71), advocates for a moderately innovative yet deeply patriotic art that respects tradition, preserves Germanic essence, and steers clear of foreign infiltration—Wagner's evident blow against both the dominance (above all) of Italian opera and Germany's political arch-enemy, France. Consequently, Wagner brazenly re-routed the tribute of the "Volk" from the emperor to Sachs himself: *Die Meistersinger* collapses social, political, and artistic conflicts into the seemingly holistic vision of a community following its most revered artist.

Wagner thus fashioned "the blueprint for a pristine bourgeois world" (Adorno 2005, 85)—a utopian vision his music dramas were meant to help bring about. Yet his entwinement of art and life, symbolised in the linking of song contest and marriage, is not without frictions: Act 2 ends with a brawl that engulfs even Sachs; and Beckmesser (whose portrayal has since been associated with anti-Semitic traits) is inexorably booed off the contest's stage-upon-the-stage: Wagner's society has no place for a stickler for tradition. Even Walther fits uneasily into this small-town world: Sachs needs to convince him of the value of regulated mastery and art in the first place. In the end, the opera steers a complex path between tradition and renewal, music and politics, historicism and activism, with both Sachs and Walther bearing traits of Wagner himself, the self-declared redeemer of German culture.

The Liebig images remove much of this complexity and social strife, pushing their vision of late-medieval guild culture further towards a clichéd holism: they (literally) distill for bourgeois consumption the opera's medievalism into a picturesque background. Neither the scuffle nor Beckmesser's artistic humiliation appear. Instead, the chromolithographs predominantly trace Eva's and Walther's bourgeoning relationship, beginning with their furtive exchange after church at the opening of Act 1 (image 1) and Walther's subsequent musical education, crystallised into his first appearance before the mastersinger guild—with Beckmesser "marking" his mistakes on a tablet—in Act 1, scene 2 (image 2). The explanatory texts on the reverse of the cards leave no doubt about this streamlined bourgeoisification. Eva is dubbed an affluent "middle-class daughter" (*Bürgerstochter*); Beckmesser's failure to win her—represented through his nocturnal serenade of Act 2 (image 3), which is hampered by Sachs' outdoor cobbling and the lovers' attempted elopement—is attributed simply to amorous, not artistic, grounds; and Walther alone is linked to Wagner's musical mission: note the shafts of sunlight glorifying his entrance into Sachs' workshop in Act 3, scene 1 (image 5). This focus on the love triangle awkwardly sidelines Sachs into a mere accomplice of Walther's pursuit; even the rendition of the opera's triumphal finale (image 6) places Eva's adorning of Walther centre stage, while Sachs (shown from behind) merely blesses the couple: there is no trace here of his rousing patriotic speech. To make up for this imbalance, image 4 depicts Sachs on the morning after the fight (Act 3, scene 1), with his amanuensis David entering to honor him on his name day. Albeit gratuitous within the series' abridged storyline, this card allowed for a condensed biography of Sachs on its flipside.

Visually, the lithographs reflect some widespread conventions in the staging history of *Die Meistersinger*. Due to Wagner's involvement in the opera's 1868 Munich premiere, subsequent productions tended to display common features (Bauer 2016), such as Eva's blue dress, the layout and color scheme for Walther's trial singing (image 2), or the design of the nocturnal scene (image 3) with its central lilac tree, Sachs' bench towards the left, and, in the background, a narrow alleyway with gable roofs and *Chörlein*—rectangular oriel windows characteristic of Nuremberg. Just like the trading cards' storyline, though, the images zoom in on the protagonists, leaving less space for evocative Nuremberg settings or the final massive crowd. One exception is once more Sachs' home. As did the influential 1888 Bayreuth production by the composer's widow Cosima Wagner, images 4 and 5 feature *Butzenscheiben*, bull's-eye panes typical of the fifteenth and sixteenth centuries that became icons of nineteenth-century architectural historicism. In addition, the tile stove in image 5 resembles one in Sachs' historical house, which had been reconstructed in 1910 (Schmidt 1995) to cater precisely to the late-Romantic fad for late-medieval German culture that had given rise to the rediscovery of Sachs in the first place. Thus did the Liebig images pursue an updated "authenticity" of Wagner's settings—an approach entirely befitting the composer's own aesthetic agenda.

If, however, this series downplayed the political dimensions of the nineteenth-century Nuremberg cult and Wagner's opera, Adolf Hitler would soon harness both. An ardent admirer of Wagner and, no doubt, inspired by *Die Meistersinger*, the leader of the Nazi party in 1923 chose the former imperial city to host his party rallies. Between 1933 and 1938, during the pre-war years of the so-called Third Reich, the annual pageants even took place on the putative site (a meadow outside the old city) of the Wagnerian song contest, patently linking Hitler's dictatorship with German cultural heritage and history. Stagings and reality, Wagner's celebratory finale and Nazi party rallies increasingly resembled one another (Reichard et al. 2018). It was surely not coincidental, then, that the Liebig company in 1938 devoted a second series to *Die Meistersinger*, the only opera thus honoured (Böcher 2006). This time, monumentalized settings in predominantly brown hues dwarf the protagonists. Moreover, the card dedicated to Sachs is replaced with the scene of Beckmesser stealing Walther's song, while the final image focuses less on the loving couple than on the people hailing a barely visible Sachs with outstretched right arms. Tellingly, the new series was limited to German distribution. At the eve of World War II, the nationalized and Romanticized reception of Hans Sachs and his late-medieval Nuremberg Meistergesang came to a bitter climax.

JOSQUIN DES PRÉS

MISSA PANGE LINGUA

AUSGABE KALLMEYER NR. 12

DAS CHORWERK · HEFT 1

98. Das Chorwerk

Pamela M. Potter

Wolfenbüttel: Kallmeyer Verlag and Möseler Verlag, 1929-2006
144 vols., 27 cm

Image: Josquin des Pres, *Missa Pange Lingua*, edited by Friedrich Blume, Das Chorwerk 1 (Wolfenbüttel: Möseler Verlag, 1929), front cover. Photo © Michele Calella.

Das Chorwerk is a series of performance editions of predominantly Renaissance choral music, consisting of 144 issues published between 1929 and 2006 and spanning repertoire up to the eighteenth century. The purpose of the series was to make early music accessible to amateur choral groups and to bring recognition to otherwise neglected works, with an emphasis on Franco-Flemish and German composers in its Renaissance offerings. The first 52 issues came out between 1929 and 1938, followed by a publication gap that lasted from the outbreak of World War II until 1956.

The format of Das Chorwerk drew on the skills of musicologists trained in the science of producing critical editions, but strove to make the series affordable, useable, and unintimidating to a broader public. Each issue consists of one larger work, such as a Mass or motet, or a small number of pieces, such as five to ten settings of secular songs. An issue typically opens with an introductory text no more than five pages in length that offers a thoughtful but readable overview discussing the composer, his place in music history, and sometimes a description of the sources, concluding with a brief but thoroughly researched synopsis of the editorial decisions made in producing the edition that addressed such issues as the use of accidentals, clefs, meters, and text. Most significantly, the vast majority of the editions also provide a carefully underlaid German translation of the text, offering amateur groups the opportunity to perform the works in German. In later issues, however, the series might tend to take on a more scholarly and less user-friendly aura, indulging in lengthy and technical introductions and no longer appearing in affordable editions geared toward everyday use by choral groups. Latter issues from the 1950s on also expanded the geographical scope of the project, with more works of French, English, and Spanish origin.

A noteworthy feature of the first series of volumes that came out prior to World War II was the engagement of a host of well-qualified musicologists. Under the general editorship of Friedrich Blume, the series drew on the expertise of German and Austrian scholars, with the participation of other Europeans and Americans beginning only in the late 1950s (Simon Wallon in 1957, Albert Seay in 1958). Over the course of this initial run, there is also an increasingly pronounced emphasis on rediscovering German contributions to Renaissance choral music and, in some of the introductory remarks, to speculate on the explicitly German characteristics of these composers' styles. The publications were affordable and effectively presented in a usable format, leading to their successful sales and their appearance in multiple reissues.

Das Chorwerk is significant not only for its longevity but also for the role it played in popularising the otherwise esoteric preoccupation of German musicologists with editing early music. Das Chorwerk was, in fact, one of several projects initiated in the 1920s to fulfill a dual mission: to provide repertoire to the burgeoning field of amateur choral groups, and to legitimise the massive investment musicology had made in the editing of early music. The emergence of amateur performance organizations in the 1920s in all socio-economic groups comprised a powerful reaction against the nineteenth-century soloist cult. Amateur groups were springing up all over Germany in the form of male choirs, mixed choirs, amateur orchestras, and chamber groups, and the workers' choral groups alone doubled their membership between 1920 and 1928 to account for over half a million participants. The music activities of the growing Youth Movement (*Jugendmusikbewegung*) not only attracted the attention of musicologists as a market for editions but also invited their direct involvement, as the movement as a whole was keen on promoting early music.

With the increase in amateurs' participation came a demand for repertoire that was within their technical reach, a burden that fell not only on the shoulders of composers, but also publishers and editors. German musicologists had already invested much of their energy over the preceding decades into the rediscovery of early music, and the vast amount of material already accumulated yielded a rich source of "new" and less challenging repertoire that could be prepared for performance editions. Scholars drew attention to newly-discovered works of long-forgotten German masters, exposed the community to the fruits of their labours by facilitating performances, and secured government funding for the continuation of such large editing projects as the Denkmäler deutscher Tonkunst. (Monuments of German Musical Art; hereafter DDT)

The demand for performance repertoire in the post-war period provided an opportunity for German musicology to turn its scholarly activities into a practical enterprise as well as to avert the potential crisis of budget cuts for editing projects and musicology departments. Some series had already been initiated at the turn of the century, such as Collegium musicum (edited by Hugo Riemann from 1903 to 1911), and the period following the hyperinflation of 1921-23 saw the emergence of important new multi-volume performance editions that included Das Chorwerk alongside Nägels Musik-Archiv (1927), Kammersonaten (1928), Organum, edited by Max Seiffert (1924), Das Chorbuch des Musikanten, edited by Fritz Jöde (1927), and Musikalische Formen in historischen Reihen, edited by Heinrich Martens (1930).

In many ways, the precarious fate of large-scale scholarly editions served as a warning to the field to turn its attention to the needs of the marketplace. There was a growing perception that musicology, having found its home in the university rather than the conservatory, allowed scholars to retreat from community service and become alienated from musical life. The field's intense preoccupation with critical editions of early music had been inspired by classical philology, and large-scale government-funded projects to underwrite the activity allowed for the production of heavily notated scores with archaic clefs and hefty critical reports.

But the postwar economy could no longer support such luxury enterprises, as the uncertain fate of the DDT illustrates. DDT had been in operation since 1889, when publishers appealed to the kaiser by presenting an edition of Frederick the Great's compositions for flute. They thus drew attention to the need for preserving musical "treasures" in published editions while fulfilling a "patriotic and artistic goal." DDT was forced to suspend its publication in 1919, facing competition from an increased number of editions of early music intended for performance. DDT could resume publication only after undergoing significant changes that clearly reflected a desire to justify the project to the government and to meet the needs of performers. At a meeting attended by both Prussian ministry representatives and musicologists in the fall of 1924, participants agreed forthwith to remove the critical commentary from the edition and publish it in a separate volume and to render editions of older works that would be "performance-ready." Thus the DDT revived its suspended activities but adopted a new design that would make its volumes more practical and less intimidating.

By 1936, the renamed Erbe deutscher Musik (Heritage of German Music) signaled an even more radical break with the old tradition: the new series would produce musical editions not for the purpose of exhibiting them as museum pieces but for the purpose of reviving the music of the past in editions that lent themselves well to practical use for live performances. Heinrich Besseler explained this change in title and emphasised the new task of German musicology to preserve the German musical heritage as a "living acquisition." The goal of the new series was to reach the "people's community" (Volksgemeinschaft) by standardising the format of the editions to meet both scholarly requirements and the needs of amateur musicians. Forthcoming editions would eliminate archaic clefs, provide translations for Latin and Italian texts and full realizations of figured basses, and—perhaps an unforeseen sacrifice on the side of scholarship—shorten the introductions and critical commentaries. Clearly, successful undertakings such as Das Chorwerk had added to the pressure on lavishly-funded editions projects to justify their existence in an atmosphere of shrinking resources during the lean years of the Weimar Republic and to the ideological pressure to serve the greater good of the German "people's community" during the Nazi era.

Das Chorwerk was undoubtedly a pioneering venture in transforming the scholarly edition into something useful and marketable. Das Chorwerk came into existence under very specific economic, social, and political circumstances: a pressing need for amateur repertoire, a reduction of financial resources to support critical editions of early music, and an increasing pressure to instill pride in the German musical legacy by educating the population at large. In the second half of its lifetime, as it resumed its postwar activities in 1956, Das Chorwerk found itself in good company as the result of an upsurge of performance editions from the 1950s on that included Diletto Musicale (1955), the Recent Researches in Music series (1964), Le Pupitre (1967), Musica da Camera (1973), and Early Music Library (1987). Yet throughout its lifespan of more than 75 years, it largely preserved a commitment to its founding principles of enlisting the expertise of musicologists to produce affordable performance editions of early music, with a special focus on Germanic masters of the Renaissance.

Additional references: Charles et al. 2001; Potter 1994.

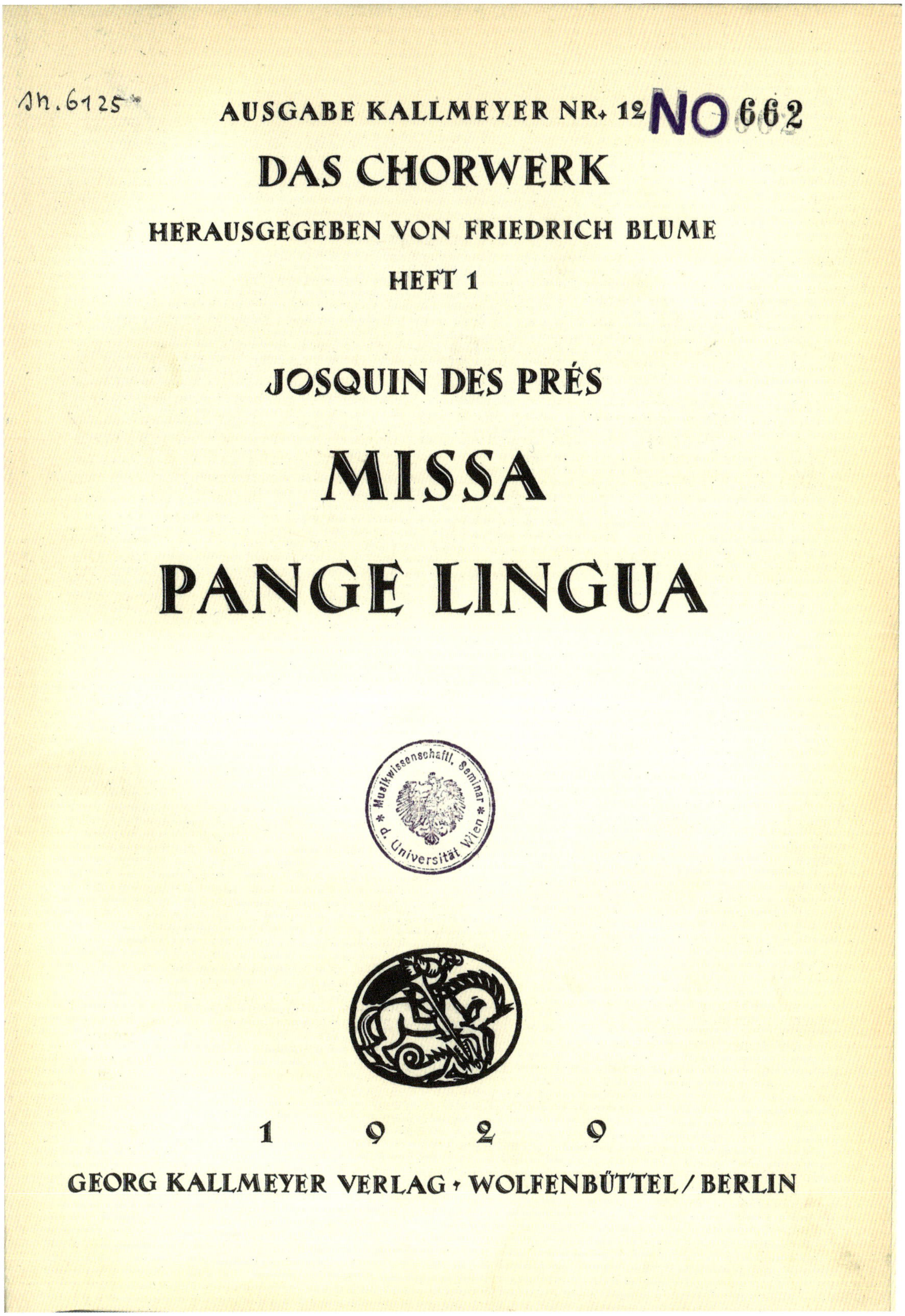

AUSGABE KALLMEYER NR. 12

DAS CHORWERK

HERAUSGEGEBEN VON FRIEDRICH BLUME

HEFT 1

JOSQUIN DES PRÉS

MISSA

PANGE LINGUA

1 9 2 9

GEORG KALLMEYER VERLAG · WOLFENBÜTTEL / BERLIN

Figure 98.1: Josquin des Pres, *Missa Pange Lingua*, ed. Blume, title page.

99. *Ode to a Screw*

Vincenzo Borghetti

Tom Eyen (lyrics); Peter Cornell (music); Mary Mitchell (performer)
From *Taking off*, directed by Miloš Forman
Written by Miloš Forman, John Guare, Jean-Claude Carrière, and John Klein
Universal Pictures, 1971

Image: Screenshot showing Mary Mitchell performing *Ode to a Screw*.

This image is taken from *Taking off*, the first American film of Czech director Miloš Forman, released in 1971. The film is a caustic comedy set in the America of the early 1970s that puts the bourgeois family under the spotlight. Forman targets this institution, lampooning its ineffectiveness in meeting the emotional needs of its members, and making fun of its inadequacy when confronted with the generational conflicts exploding in the era of youth protest. Like the parents of its fictional family, however, *Taking off* does not spare the young "revolutionaries" from criticism, showing the contradictions, the naivety but also the opportunism of countercultural movements, by that time already a mass phenomenon (Martini 2017, 52). The film tells the story of the Tynes, a typical middle-class family living in the well-to-do suburbs of New York. When their 15-year-old daughter Jeannie runs away from home, the parents, searching for her, embark on a voyage of discovery into contemporary youth culture. Their attempt to understand the incomprehensible modern world of their daughter is as grotesque as it is pathetic: it leads them to enroll in the SPFC, the Society for Parents of Fugitive Children, and to learn about drugs, the pleasures of sexual liberation, and all the other fetishes and rituals of rebellion. Jeannie's first flight is only temporary, though: the teenager skips school to participate in an audition for young singers, where, when her turn comes, she lacks the courage to perform. The long sequence of the audition frames and counterpoints the story of the Tynes throughout the film. It is in this sequence that we find the scene from which this image is taken.

In the screenshot we see Mary Mitchell, one of the many wannabe artists—more or less talented—taking part in the audition. Although they cannot be seen in the image, she is surrounded by many young people attracted by the audition. Mitchell performs before a panel of men and women in their twenties, that is to say, approximately her age. From the clothes, the length and style of the hair, the beards and the attitudes, both of the members of the panel and of many of the hopefuls, we understand that the event is dominated by hippies, a characteristic group in large metropolitan centres at the beginning of the 1970s, not only in the United States. In this case we are in Manhattan, in the East Village, which at the time was among the most prominent locations of hippy culture.

As it did in the reality of contemporary youth movements, music plays a central role in the film. The audition offers a sample of the music cultivated by hippies, and in particular several variations on the theme of the singer-songwriter. Following its conventions (think of Joan Baez, Bob Dylan, or Pete Seeger), most of the contestants accompany themselves on a plucked stringed instrument, including Mary Mitchell. Her instrument, her song and her performance style, however, are clearly different from those that precede and follow.

Mitchell does accompany herself on a plucked instrument, but not the guitar, like the others at the audition. Rather she uses a so-called lute-guitar, an instrument which combines features of the guitar with those of the Renaissance lute. From the guitar it takes its six single strings (a lute would have five double and one single string), the fixed metal frets (on the lute the gut frets are moveable), and the long, thin neck. The position of the left hand on the neck is also guitar-like. From the lute come the teardrop-shaped soundboard and the vaulted body. Although the pegbox is not exactly that of a lute (which is usually at right-angles to the neck), its design contributes to the instrument's antique aspect.

Like her instrument, from the outset Mitchell's performance seems to have little in common with the others. Her light and graceful voice, accompanied in a hesitant manner on the lute-guitar, contrasts with the forthright and even aggressive vocality and performance manner adopted by the other contestants, typical of "true" singer-songwriters in the making. At the same time, though, none of the others dare to sing what Mitchell sings. The title of the song, given in the end credits, is revealing in this respect: *Ode to a Screw*. The text is as follows:

> You can fuck the lilies and the roses too.
> You can fuck the maidens who swear they've never been screwed.
> You can fuck the Russians and the English too.
> You can fuck the Germans and every pushy Jew.
> Fuck the Queens.
> Fuck the Kings.
> Fuck the boys with the very small dings.
> Fuck the birds, fuck the pigs, fuck every Guinea with a thorny twig.
> You can fuck the Astros and all nurses in white.

You should fuck the uglies just to be kind and polite.
You can fuck the moon and June and the sea,
But before you fuck them first you must fuck me.

The text, then, celebrates in a very direct manner one of the themes dearest to the youth movements of the Sixties and Seventies, namely the disruption of bourgeois sexual propriety. In setting it to music, however, its composer Peter Cornell does not draw inspiration from rock, or from rhythm and blues, as would be expected, and as he does in *Long term physical effects*, the song about smoking hashish presented earlier in the audition. Instead, Cornell draws inspiration from late Renaissance music. Thus, the antique flavour of the *Ode* comes not only from the lute-guitar. This song is a clear imitation of a lutesong by John Dowland or some other English composer of the Elizabethan period, from which Cornell borrows both the harmonic style and aspects of melodic design, as is particularly evident, for example, in the setting of lines 5-7.

Before analysing the music and its meaning in more detail, it is worth taking a moment to note some aspects of the staging of this scene. Forman lingers on Mary Mitchell's performance to an unusual extent compared with other songs; more significant still, this is the only audition piece that does not also become the soundtrack to a different scene. Mitchell's song is one of the few to which the audition panel listens attentively, and the only one to produce in them an evident reaction—one of them is visibly speechless at 20:32. It is also the only performance that Forman presents always from the front. Beginning as a medium shot and slowly becoming a close-up, the camera never leaves the singer, except for a quick sequence of cuts showing the faces of the panel, synchronised with the rhythm of the music—thus emphasising the centrality of the *Ode* in the film.

So what is music à la Dowland doing at a hippy gathering in the East Village in the early 1970s, setting a text like that of the *Ode*? And why does Forman give it such prominence?

From its origins as a fringe phenomenon, during the 1960s and 1970s so-called Early Music became much more widespread, in terms of both performances—which became more frequent and moved to higher-profile venues—and recordings—major record companies inaugurated labels or series specifically devoted to medieval and Renaissance music. What is more, forgotten music from the past was performed in styles radically different from those used for standard classical music. Many of the leading early music performers put into practice what they had read in the studies of influential musicologists such as Thurston Dart and Arnold Schering, drawing inspiration for "authentically ancient" performance practices in folk and traditional music, thus distancing the Middle Ages and Renaissance from the conventional rhetoric of classical performance and its established pedagogy. The remit of these musicians was not only to recover the historical performance practices most appropriate to medieval and Renaissance music, but to narrate through their radical performances a counter-history of Western music, now considered from the perspective of the poor and the illiterate, to whose culture they intended to give back its own voice, silenced over centuries of oppression by hegemonic cultures (Dreyfus 1983, 306; Borghetti 2011, 42-45).

The Middle Ages and the Renaissance of the 1960s and 1970s thus sounded "popular," sharing ideological and discursive spaces with the alternative culture characteristic of contemporary youth movements. Indeed, reviews often censured elements judged outrageous if measured against the performance conventions of classical music, but they also showed awareness of the proximity between early music and some contemporary popular music, for example the Beatles (Leech-Wilkinson 2002, 97-98). It is because of this proximity that, like popular music (whether of the Beatles or of singer-songwriters), Renaissance music could become an instrument of protest against the mainstream—not only "classical" and not only musical. This was also possible because like popular music—but emphatically *unlike* standard classical music—early music was within the reach of everyone, as the example of the fake-Dowland performed by Mitchell demonstrates, thus it was easily transportable and performable in informal contexts (Borghetti 2011, 44).

In this *Ode*, then, the protest against the mainstream is contained not only in the text sung and in the style of the music, but also in the performance of the song, an instance and at the same time a parody of a "historically informed" performance of its day. With her youthful voice and her simple chords, Mitchell is (or impersonates) a spontaneous musician because she is evidently not "properly" trained. Thus, she conforms to the ideals associated with the performance of early music in the 1960s and 1970s. By that time these ideals already had a long pedigree, reaching back to the very roots of the Early Music Movement, which at least since the turn of the twentieth century had preferred "natural" musicians and voices, not "corrupted" by the education provided by the conservatoires. As Gabriele D'Annunzio recalled in his notebooks and later in his 1916 novel *Notturno*, one of the most influential pioneers of the movement, Arnold Dolmetsch, would praise his wife Elodie Désirée whilst accompanying her on the lute with the words: "She doesn't know how to sing. It is her greatest quality" (Meucci 2017, 154; Panti 2011, 31; Borghetti 2011, 42-45).

But there is more to this. Mary Mitchell, in contrast to her colleagues in the audition, does not sound like a professional (or a wannabe professional) musician. At the same time, she is not presented as a "radical" hippie, as are most of the others. As her soft voice, her hairstyle, her perfect white teeth and her discrete jewellery indicate, Mitchell resembles one of the many middle-class daughters who, like Jeannie Tynes, have escaped to the East Village from a well-to-do home in the suburbs. The *Ode* that she sings, to which Forman calls the close attention of both the audience for the film and the audience in the film, is not only representative of the musical landscape of the youth movements: it is also the symbol chosen by the director to highlight the inanity and decadence of these movements. With its mixture of cultivation (the Renaissance) and spontaneity (the amateurish manner of performance), of vulgarity (the text) and propriety (the voice and the outfit), the *Ode* is for Forman an example of "playing" at rebellion, nothing more than a bourgeois experiment in the exotic world of the hippies, analogous to those—simultaneously hilarious and pathetic—of Jeannie Tynes' parents at the meetings of the SPFC, as they sample the frisson of transgression without really calling into question the values and privileges of their social class.

100. Wax Figure of Anne Boleyn

Linda Phyllis Austern

Madame Tussauds, London, ca. 1984
Waxwork, life-size
Warwick Castle, Warwick, a subsidiary of Merlin Entertainments Group, Ltd
Image: Juliet Simpkin, with photography by Kenneth Griffiths and Ric Gemmell, *Illustrated Guide to Madame Tussaud's* (London: Madame Tussaud's, 1985), 16 (Anne Boleyn, Catherine Parr, and Jane Seymour).

It seems especially fitting that an historical figure from whose life no portraits survive and whose persona has proved infinitely malleable for nearly half a millennium should be modelled in wax for a popular tourist destination. In fact, this is only the latest replica Anne Boleyn to be displayed at Madame Tussauds since 1861, if the first given a musical signifier. Like its predecessors, the image was created for a display of Henry VIII and his six wives, among the museum's "most enduring and popular" groupings for the last century and a half (Pilbeam 2003, 158).

In common with its companion pieces and all such effigies, this Anne Boleyn is formed from the sculptural substance that most nearly simulates human flesh, associated in earlier eras and perhaps the modern subconscious with magic and dissolution of the boundaries between absence and presence, life and death. However, the aesthetic qualities and moribund material of wax have more often suggested a corpse than an animate body, historically used for anatomical studies and funerary rites. Wax figures are further individuated and their eerie liminality enhanced by the addition of realistic hair, clothing, and accessories associated in memory or imagination with the person represented (Bloom 2003, 1-3; Bryson 2000, 61; Freedberg 1989, 230-31; Pilbeam 2003, 102; Roach 2007, 54-55). The modern wax museum, of which the epitome remains Madame Tussauds, deliberately juxtaposes history with fantasy, truth with falsehood, the authentic with the counterfeit, life with death, the famous with the infamous, and the real with the imaginary (Bloom 2003, 159-61; Freedberg 1989, 230; Kornmeier 2004, 152-54; Panzanelli 2008, 2-3; Pilbeam 2003, 222-24). These are the same paradoxes that have haunted successive portrayals of Anne Boleyn across media since the mid-sixteenth century.

The second wife of Henry VIII seems an especially appropriate subject for the kind of presentation enabled by wax museums, in which visitors engage in asynchronous, face-to-face encounters with a carefully researched pantheon of lifelike celebrities and favorite fictitious characters past and present. Anne Boleyn, queen of England from 1533-36 and star of countless novels, plays, songs, films, comic books, and television shows, among other imaginative media, is a bit of each. She remains an easy object for the intersection between historical speculation and frank fantasy encouraged by wax portraiture, because, in spite of five centuries of never-ending fascination, surviving information about her life is surprisingly scant. What does remain is so fragmented that it must be patched together and its gaps filled by a blend of deduction and story-telling, even by academic historians.

Scholars disagree about how to interpret extant evidence and how to order it into a coherent narrative—let alone, in some cases, what is spurious and what authentic (Bernard 2010, ix and 4-18; Bordo 2013, 4-6; Norton 2011, 7; Warnicke 1985, 939-44). Was Anne a cold-hearted temptress or helpless victim of circumstance? Where and when was she born? Was she a heroine of the English Reformation, a proto-feminist, a sixteenth-century Salomé? What were her actual relationships with King Henry and the other two of his wives she certainly knew, who join her in evident amicability in the Tussauds display? Even Anne's appearance is largely a matter of conjecture, since contemporary descriptions come from notoriously biased sources and her earliest surviving portraits date from after her demise (Bernard 2010, 19-20 and 196-200). That wax museums deliberately blur the boundaries between history and fiction, wax effigies the distinction between the subject represented and qualities spectators project onto them from previous encounters with their other avatars, makes the medium an especially effective way to present such an elusive if malleable personage (Bloom 2003, 172-74; Roach 2007, 55).

A 1993 illustrated guide to the Tussauds exhibit grounds Anne and her companion effigies in historical verisimilitude. "Each of the figures in this group," it begins, "has been carefully researched from contemporary paintings and descriptions: the likeness of Henry VIII, for example, is based on Holbein portraits of the monarch. Every costume is made by historical costume specialists using authentic materials such as silk velvet and antique lace" (Madame Tussauds 1993). Anne is immediately recognizable by the accoutrements that define her in countless replicas of her earliest surviving likeness (fig. 100.1), equally familiar from stage and screen costuming: center-part-

Figure 100.1: Anon. English, *Anne Boleyn*, late 16th century, based on a work of ca. 1533-1536. Oil on panel, 54.3 cm x 41.6 cm. National Portrait Gallery, London. Photo © Mondadori Portfolio / Bridgeman Images.

ed hair smoothed under the French hood with pearl edging, velvety black gown trimmed with pearls and gilt discs, lush fur sleeves, and, above all, that signature pearl necklace with its gold "B" pendant at her throat.

And then there is the lute that enables Anne to be further individuated and differentiated from the other wives, as well as to guide the viewer's projection onto her character. The figure holds, fingers, and plucks the lute in a spurious position, perhaps most advantageously to display the detailed bodice, sleeves, and instrument itself. Yet it is evident that Anne is to be seen—and heard in imagination—as playing. Her right ear is turned toward the instrument, in line with her plucking fingers. With beringed left hand bridging a chord, right poised as if in motion between individual notes, she is the one of her grouping that stimulates an echo of the sense of hearing as well as sight and touch. These fine-motor actions enliven the effigy, bringing it closer to the realm of life than death. The illustrated guide implies inspiration from "contemporary descriptions," as not even a copy of a copy of a contemporary portrait presents her with the instrument. In this space where documentary history merges with individual experience, each wax figure brought to life by realistic accessories, might this Anne converge in imagination with such dark-haired, black-clad guitar-playing rock rebels from the era of its construction as Chrissie Hynde or Joan Jett?

The extent to which music, and the lute in particular, has contributed to the legend of Anne Boleyn remains to be fully explored. As with other aspects of Anne's biography, details about her musicianship remain speculative, supported by myth, supposition, story-telling and a small number of almost-talismanic objects about which scholars and other authenticators have debated furiously for decades: just the right blend for a modern wax portrait. The elusive historical Anne belonged to a time, place, and social class in which young women as well as men were starting to be trained in music to enhance their capacities as courtiers—and for women, perhaps to have a chance to make advantageous marriages (Austern 2008, 130 and 135-37; Warnicke 1985, 943-44). The young Anne almost certainly developed musical interests and was exposed to current Franco-Flemish repertory at the courts of Brabant and France where she served as a child. She likely sang among girls and women at both, and may have been gifted at the latter with the music book that currently stands as the sole extant musical object with which she plausibly came into contact (London, Royal College of Music, MS 1070—see Skinner 2017, 2 and 11; Warnicke 1985, 943; Urkevich 2011, 105-06).

It was after death that Anne was recalled as having played the lute, making it all the more appropriate for a waxwork display. The instrument became widely recognizable as her attribute with the 1545 publication of Lancelot de Carle's 1536 poetic account of her life, trial, and execution. The relevant passage simply states that the late queen knew well how to play the lute and other instruments to chase away sad thoughts (Carle 1545, 5). Around the same time as Carle, Jean de Laval, comte de Châteaubriant, claimed to recall a youthful Anne who sang like a siren to the same instrument, among other musical skills praised with no less hyperbole (Strickland 1842, 158-59).

It is thus the lute that most often stands synecdochically for the polite accomplishments and musical skill of semi-legendary and frankly fictitious Annes, most often as a lure for King Henry or other vulnerable men, or for eloquent self-expression at her death. Which does this waxwork, alone in private reverie but surrounded by the king, his other wives, and the viewer who is guided to recognise the subject? Perhaps that depends on previous acquaintance with her character. At least three novelizations of Anne's life present an accomplished lutenist whom Henry commands to play and sing for his pleasure (Anthony 1957; Drew 1912; Hackett 1939), not so distant from Edward Lowinsky's academic reverie of her doing the same with one of the few secular songs in the music book she may have owned (Lowinsky 1989b, 500). Rosemary Anne Sisson's teleplay *Catherine of Aragon* for the 1970 BBC Television series *The Six Wives of Henry VIII* introduces a smug and knowing Anne smiling at the sound of Henry singing to his lute before she grabs a similar instrument from an unnamed young man who "gazes at her adoringly" as she plays "an intricate little tune" on it (Sisson 1972, 51-53). Depictions of Anne's music-fuelled indiscretion have a long, ongoing history, generally based on her presumed interactions with the historical musician Mark Smeaton. In Donizetti's opera *Anna Bolena* (1830) the frisson between Anna and singer-lutenist Smeton is crucial to the plot, his musical entertainments part of the diegesis. The same is true in Nick McCarty's screenplay "Anne Boleyn" for the 1970 BBC series *Six Wives of Henry VIII*. Popular historian Norah Lofts explains that Anne was a particularly accomplished lutenist who composed, sang, and played her own songs in a century when all young ladies "of good birth" played the instrument (Lofts 1979, 67, 164-65). She reiterates the now-debunked claim that Anne composed a swansong and sang it to her lute while awaiting death in the Tower of London, replete with a photograph of her purported instrument, then in the collection at Anne's childhood home of Hever Castle and later recognised as having been made around 1900 (fig. 100.2; Austern 2008, 137-38; Lofts 1979, 164-66; Sotheby Parke Bernet 1983, 126).

In the realm of wax encounters, shifting facts or origins at the intersection between history and fiction matter less than the impact of the finished work. Perhaps the ultimate expression of this—and image of Anne Boleyn—is in Hiroshi Sugimoto's haunting photograph of this figure for his series *Portraits* (https://www.guggenheim.org/artwork/10924), which, by the nature of the photographic medium, further blurs the line between life and death, documentation and fantasy. With it, the artist has not only revivified the corpse-like object, but claims to be the first to photograph not an image but Anne herself (Adams 2006, 96; Spector 2000, 18). And he has captured her likeness from an angle that foregrounds her lute-playing.

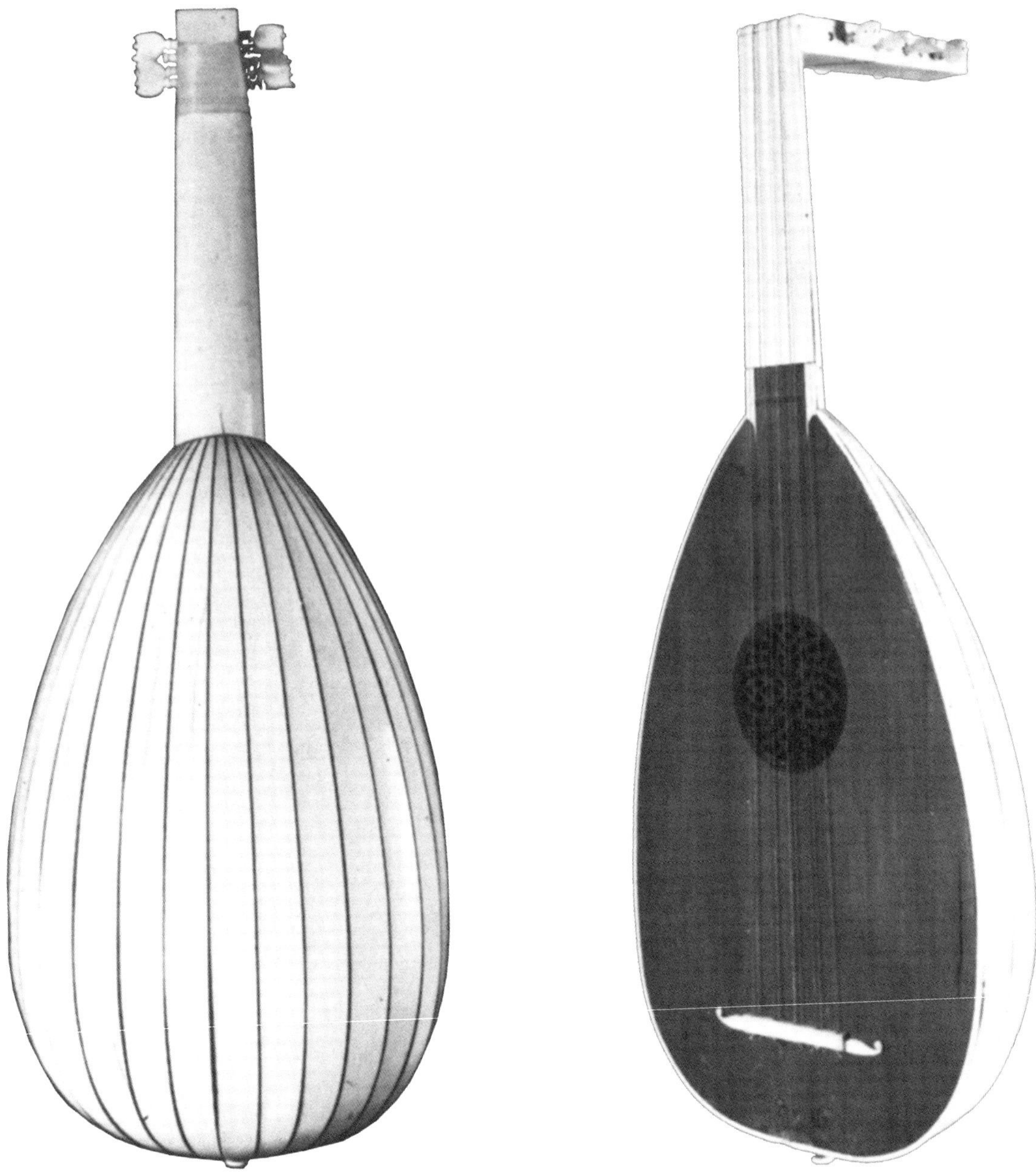

Figure 100.2: Anon., lute (once thought to have belonged to Anne Boleyn), ca. 1900. Ivory and ebony, 47.6 cm (length). Private collection (formerly Hever Castle). Photo © Sotheby's.

Notes on Contributors

Jane Alden is Professor of Music and Medieval Studies at Wesleyan University. She researches notational innovations and the sociability of music in the medieval and modern eras. Currently writing a book on the ancestry of notations for the Scratch Orchestra, her past publications include *Songs, Scribes, and Society: The History and Reception of the Loire Valley Chansonniers* (OUP, 2010). Alden is active as a singer and directs the Vocal Constructivists.

Linda Phyllis Austern is Professor of Musicology at Northwestern University. A specialist in Western European, and especially English, music of the sixteenth, seventeenth, and early eighteenth centuries, she is the author of *Both from the Ears and Mind: Thinking About Music in Early Modern England* (2020), and co-editor of *Beyond Boundaries: Re-Thinking Music Circulation in Early Modern England* (2017), among many other publications.

Barbara Baert is Professor of Art History at the University of Leuven. Her research concerns medieval iconology, with interdisciplinary interests spanning sacred topography, visual anthropology, relics and devotion, and medieval gender. The director of several international research programmes, her articles have appeared in a wide range of journals, including *Artibus et Historiae, Cahiers de civilisation médiévale, Critica d'arte, Gesta*, and many others.

Geoffrey Baker was formerly a professor at Royal Holloway, University of London. He now works for the music charity Agrigento. He specialises in music in Latin America, and he has published extensively on colonial Peru. His book *Imposing Harmony: Music and Society in Colonial Cuzco* (Duke University Press, 2008) won the American Musicological Society's Robert Stevenson Award in 2010. He co-edited *Music and Urban Society in Colonial Latin America* (Cambridge University Press, 2011) with Tess Knighton, and he has contributed essays to several journals and collected volumes.

Katie Bank is a Leverhulme Early Career Fellow in History at the University of Birmingham and Honorary Research Fellow in Music at the University of Sheffield. She researches musical-visual culture in early modern England. Her recent book, *Knowledge Building in Early Modern English Music* (Routledge, 2020), considers historiography, musical-textual relationships, and ideas surrounding sense perception and the formation of knowledge in early seventeenth-century English recreational vocal music.

Samantha Bassler is music history coordinator, administrator, and Adjunct Assistant Professor of Music History and Theory at New York University's Steinhardt School Department of Music and Performing Arts Professions. Her research interests are in music, disability, theatre, and gender in early modern England, and the reception history of early English music during the long eighteenth century.

Frédéric Billiet is Professor of Medieval Music at Sorbonne University, and co-director of the Organology/Iconography program at IReMUS (www.iremus.cnrs.fr). His major fields of research are medieval musical iconography and the soundscapes of the Middle Ages. He is responsible for the MUSICONIS research programme on medieval musical iconography supported by the ANR and by IReMUS (musiconis.huma-num.fr) and coordinates the initiative on medieval choirstalls with Misericordia International.

Bonnie J. Blackburn is a member of the Faculty of Music at Oxford University. She has edited the music of Johannes Lupi, two volumes for the New Josquin Edition, and with Edward E. Lowinsky and Clement A. Miller *A Correspondence of Renaissance Musicians* (1991). She is also the author, together with Leofranc Holford-Strevens, of *The Oxford Companion to the Year* (1999). Her contribution stems from her long-term investigation of music and musicians at the court of Ferrara in the fifteenth century.

Zdravko Blažeković is Director of the Research Center for Music Iconography at the CUNY Graduate Center and executive editor of Répertoire International de Littérature Musicale. He is the founder and editor of the journal *Music in Art*, and the monograph series Music in Visual Cultures (Brepols). His research concerns eighteenth- and nineteenth-century music of Southeast and Central Europe, music iconography, organology, historiography of music, and reception of Greek and Roman organology in modern times.

M. Jennifer Bloxam is the Herbert H. Lehman Professor of Music at Williams College. Her projects focus on the ritual context of sacred polyphony, the interactions between plainsong and polyphony in Mass and motet, and strategies of narrative and exegesis in sacred music and the arts. She especially values her ongoing collaboration in concert, recording, and film projects with the Dutch vocal ensemble Cappella Pratensis directed by Stratton Bull.

Vincenzo Borghetti is Associate Professor of Music History at the University of Verona. He holds a doctorate in musicology from the University of Pavia-Cremona, and in 2007-08 was a fellow of Villa I Tatti, The Harvard University Center for Renaissance Italian Studies in Florence. His research interests are centred on Renaissance polyphony and opera. His essays and articles have appeared in *Early Music History*, *Acta musicologica*, *Journal of the Alamire Foundation*, and *Imago Musicae*, among other journals, and in several edited collections. In 2019 he was elected to the Academia Europaea.

Kathryn Bosi Monteath was born in Oamaru, New Zealand, and studied piano and musicology at the University of Otago, obtaining her PhD in Musicology in 1982. From 1973 to 2016 she served as Morrill Music Librarian at the Biblioteca Berenson of Villa I Tatti, the Harvard University Center for Italian Renaissance Studies in Florence. Her research interests focus around the court of Mantua in the late sixteenth century, and encompass dance, commedia dell'arte, and music iconography, as well as the madrigal.

Katherine Butler is Senior Lecturer in Music at Northumbria University. Her research focuses on the musical culture of sixteenth- and seventeenth-century England, encompassing genres ranging from court music to ballads and popular song, and spanning themes such as politics, gender, death, mythology, science and medicine, manuscript studies, and early music printing. She is the author of *Music in Elizabethan Court Politics* (Boydell, 2015), and co-editor of *Music, Myth and Story in Medieval and Early Modern England* (Boydell, 2019).

Lorenzo Candelaria, a native of El Paso, Texas, is a first-generation, Mexican American college graduate. He is currently Dean of the Blair School of Music of the Vanderbilt University. He received his PhD in Musicology from Yale University, specializing in Renaissance music, while pursuing a performance career with groups that included Walt Disney World's Mariachi Cobre and the Grammy-nominated Mariachi Sol de México. He has published extensively on Catholic plainchant and liturgy in Spain and Mexico.

Antonio Cascelli is Associate Professor at Maynooth University, Ireland. His research interests are in arts and music in sixteenth- and seventeenth-century Italy, nineteenth-century piano music, and music analysis. His article "Place, Performance and Identity in Monteverdi's Combattimento di Tancredi e Clorinda" appeared in *Cambridge Opera Journal* (2017), and his "L'Orfeo: memory, recollection and the tragedy of choosing between seeing and hearing" is published in *Philomusica on-line* (2019).

Camilla Cavicchi is Research Fellow at the University of Padua. Previously she was a CNRS musicologist at the Centre d'études supérieures de la Renaissance, Tours; Berenson Fellow at Villa I Tatti; and Research Scholar at Columbia University. She takes a multidisciplinary approach to the history of music in Renaissance Europe and the Mediterranean, drawing from archives, prosopography, music iconography, organology, and ethnomusicology. She has published on musical iconography, organology, history of music, and orally transmitted repertoires.

Lisa Colton is Professor of Musicology at the University of Liverpool. Her publications, which include the book *Angel Song: Medieval English Music in History* (2017), largely focus on music from medieval Britain and France. She has also published on medievalism in the work of British composers Judith Weir and James MacMillan, and on gender and performance in the music of Lady Gaga and Beyoncé.

James Cook is Senior Lecturer in Early Music at the University of Edinburgh. He works on medieval and Renaissance music, as well as popular medievalism in the present day. He is co-editor of *Recomposing the Past: Representations of Early Music on Stage and Screen* (Routledge, 2018), and author of *The Mass Cycle in England and the English Mass Cycle Abroad* (Routledge, 2020), as well as numerous journal articles.

Karen M. Cook is Associate Professor of Music History at the University of Hartford. She specializes in theory and notation of the fourteenth and fifteenth centuries, and also in medievalism in contemporary music and media, especially video games. Recent works have appeared in the *Medieval Disability Sourcebook*, *The Oxford Handbook of Music and Medievalism*, and the new *Journal of Sound & Music in Games*, for which she is on the editorial board.

Sophia D'Addio received her PhD in Art History from Columbia University. She also holds Master's degrees in Art

History, Music Performance, and Italian. Her research has been supported by a Mellon Humanities International Travel Fellowship, a Gladys Krieble Delmas Foundation Grant, a Rudolf Wittkower Dissertation Grant, an RSA-Kress Centro Branca Research Fellowship, a Rosand Library & Study Center Research Fellowship, and a Casa Muraro Fellowship, among others. She is currently an Editorial Fellow at Save Venice, Inc. and a Lecturer in Art History at Columbia University.

Anne Daye is a teacher, researcher, and writer on historical dance, primarily of social and theatre dance of England within the European Renaissance. Her doctoral thesis of 2008 broke new ground by discussing the performance and dance of the Jacobean masque. Investigating the vernacular forms of morris and country dance is central to her studies. Anne publishes widely, most recently an article on Shakespeare's use of masque for *The Oxford Handbook of Shakespeare and the Dance* (2019).

Flora Dennis is Senior Lecturer in Art History at the University of Sussex. Following a PhD on music printing in sixteenth-century Ferrara, she spent several years as a Research Fellow at the V&A, co-curating the major exhibition *At Home in Renaissance Italy* (2006). She has held fellowships at Villa I Tatti and The Italian Academy, Columbia University, and is preparing a monograph entitled *Music, Art and Objects in the Italian Renaissance Home*.

Scott Lee Edwards received his PhD in the History and Literature of Music at the University of California, Berkeley, with a dissertation on music in the lands of the Bohemian Crown at the turn of the seventeenth century. He subsequently served a two-year appointment as College Fellow in the Department of Music at Harvard University and is currently employed at the University of Music and the Performing Arts, Vienna, as co-editor of the New Senfl Edition. His research and publications focus on sixteenth- and seventeenth-century music in Central Europe and its conjunctions with book culture, linguistics, and migration and diaspora studies.

Barbara Eichner is Reader in Music at Oxford Brookes University. Her research falls into two strands: one concerned with music and identity in nineteenth-century Germany; the other with sixteenth-century sacred music, especially that of Orlando di Lasso, and musical life in German convents.

Martin Elste was Research Curator in the Museum of Musical Instruments, National Institute for Music Research, Berlin, until 2018. His research centres on the relationship of music and media in the areas of discology, organology, and performance research. He has written 15 monographs and some 230 articles, and serves as Editorial Advisor for Die Musik in Geschichte und Gegenwart. From 2000 to 2008 he was President of the German Record Critics' Award, having served as a jury member since 1983.

Iain Fenlon was until September 2017 Professor of Historical Musicology at the Faculty of Music of the University of Cambridge. He is a Fellow of King's College. An RMA Dent Medallist (1984), his principal area of research is music in Italy 1450-1650, with a particular focus on Mantua and Venice. Among his many publications are *The Ceremonial City: History, Memory and Myth in Renaissance Venice* (Yale, 2007), and *Piazza San Marco: Theatre of the Senses, Market Place of the World* (Harvard, 2012).

David Fiala is Lecturer in Musicology at the Centre d'études supérieures de la Renaissance in Tours (University of Tours), the holder of a joint CNRS / University of Tours Chair. His research themes include music, musical institutions, and musicians at the end of the Middle Ages and in the Renaissance.

Daniele V. Filippi is Assistant Professor of Music History at the University of Turin. Among his recent publications are the book *Motet Cycles between Devotion and Liturgy* (Basel, 2019), co-edited with Agnese Pavanello, and the chapter "Roma Sonora: An Atlas of Roman Sounds and Musics" in Brill's *Companion to Early Modern Rome: 1492-1692* (Leiden, 2019).

Alexander J. Fisher is Professor of Early Music at the University of British Columbia. His interests include German music of the sixteenth and seventeenth centuries, ritual contexts for sacred music in the early modern era, sound studies, and aspects of music, soundscape, and religious identity in the Reformation and Counter-Reformation. Among numerous publications, he is the author of *Music, Piety, and Propaganda: The Soundscapes of Counter-Reformation Bavaria* (OUP, 2014).

Paweł Gancarczyk is Associate Professor in the Institute of Art of the Polish Academy of Sciences, where he is Head of the Department of Musicology, and Editor-in-Chief of the quarterly Muzyka. In 2020 he was elected to the Academia Europaea. His main areas of research are the musical culture of late-medieval Central Europe, manuscript studies, and early music printing. Recently he published *La musique et la révolution de l'imprimerie* (Lyon, 2015; recipient of the 2016 Prix des Muses).

Giuseppe Gerbino is Professor of Historical Musicology at Columbia University, New York. He is the author of *Canoni ed Enigmi: Pier Francesco Valentini e l'artificio canonico nella prima metà del Seicento* (1995), and *Music and the Myth of Arcadia in Renaissance Italy* (2009), which won the 2010 Lewis Lockwood Award of the American Musicological Society. He is currently at work on a book on music and mind in the Renaissance.

Marianne C.E. Gillion is a Marie Skłodowska-Curie Postdoctoral Research Fellow at Uppsala Universitet. She previously held postdoctoral positions at the Universität Salzburg and KU Leuven. Her research interests include book history, Reformation and Counter-Reformation liturgies, and the musical and devotional lives of beguines.

Ortensia Giovannini is an ethnomusicologist and a folk musician. Her research interests include Armenian folk music, culture, and diaspora studies. Giovannini received her PhD in Music and Performance Studies from the University of Rome "La Sapienza" focusing on the diasporic Armenian communities' musical practices and their relationships with the homeland.

Elisabeth Giselbrecht researches the music of the early modern period, in particular questions surrounding the dissemination of music in central Europe. Following undergraduate and Master's studies in Vienna and New York, Elisabeth completed a PhD at the University of Cambridge. She then held a postdoctoral position at the University of Salzburg and since 2015 has been a Leverhulme Early Career Fellow at King's College London, with a project entitled "Owners and Users of Early Music Books."

Donald Greig is a professional singer and an independent scholar, noted for his work with The Tallis Scholars and Gothic Voices. He is also a founder member of The Orlando Consort. He received his doctorate in Music from the University of Nottingham where he is an Honorary Research Fellow. He has written extensively on historical and modern performance practice, on medievalism, and on film music, and is currently writing a book on the intersections of early music and cinema.

John Griffiths is a musician and musicologist specialised in music for guitar and early plucked instruments, especially the vihuela and lute. He has researched aspects of the sixteenth-century Spanish vihuela, its history and its music. He has also had an international career as a solo lutenist, vihuelist, and guitarist, and as a member of the pioneer Australian early music group La Romanesca. After a 30-year career at the University of Melbourne (1980-2011), he now works as a freelance scholar and performer.

Inga Mai Groote is Professor and Director of the Institute of Musicology at the University of Zürich. She has led projects on the transmission and materiality of early modern music theory texts, and tradition-building in Lutheran contexts (as part of the HERA project "Sound Memories"). Her current research examines the history of early modern music theory and its book culture, the impacts of confessional differentiation in sixteenth/seventeenth-century German-speaking musical culture, and French music history around 1900.

Eleazar Gutwirth is Professor (retired) in the Department of Jewish History, University of Tel Aviv. Interested in the history and culture of Iberian Jews, his recent publications include "Judeo-Mudéjar?: Identities, Letters and Numbers in Toledan Synagogues," *Cadernos de Estudos Sefarditas* 20 (2019); "Cultura material Hispano-Judía: Entre la norma y la práctica," in ¿Una sefarad inventada? (2014); and "Opera Digitorum Tuorum: Zacut and the Salamancan Heavens," *Hispania judaica bulletin* (2017).

Alexandros Maria Hatzikiriakos holds a PhD in Musicology from the University of Rome La Sapienza. Following postodoctoral positions at the University of Verona (2017-2020) and at Villa I Tatti, The Harvard University Center for Italian Renaissance Studies in Florence (2020-2021), he is currently a BE-FOR-ERC Fellow at Sapienza, working on a project entitled "Sounds, Spaces, and Identities in Early Modern Crete." His research focuses on the relationship between music and literature, and on musical materialities, from the medieval to the early modern period.

Lenka Hlávková is a Deputy Director of the Institute of Musicology at the Charles University in Prague. In her research, she focuses on the musical culture of Central Europe in the fifteenth and early sixteenth centuries, source studies, polyphonic repertories, cantus fractus and cantio. Currently, she is a member of the project "Old Myths, New Facts" (www.smnf.cz) and a CELSA scholarly collaboration between KU Leuven and CU Prague.

Louisa Hunter-Bradley obtained her doctorate from Royal Holloway, University of London. She has worked as a fellow at Harvard University and KU Leuven and served on the academic staff at the University of Melbourne, Australia. Louisa's main area of academic study concerns Christopher Plantin, his business practices in relation to music printing and publishing, and the European market for printed music in the latter half of the sixteenth century. She is also active as a singer and a recorder-player specialising in Renaissance and Baroque repertories.

Sylvia Huot is Professor Emerita of Medieval French Literature at the University of Cambridge and fellow of Pembroke College. She is the author of *From Song to Book* (Cornell University Press, 1987); *The Romance of the Rose and its Medieval Readers* (CUP, 1993); *Allegorical Play in the Old French Motet* (Stanford University Press, 1997); *Madness in Medieval French Literature* (OUP, 2003); *Postcolonial Fictions in the Roman de Perceforest* (D.S. Brewer, 2007); and *Dreams of Lovers and Lies of Poets: Poetry, Knowledge and Desire in the Roman de la Rose* (Legenda, 2010). She is also the co-editor of *Rethinking the Romance of the Rose* (University of Pennsylvania Press, 1992). She was elected a Fellow of the British Academy in 2011.

Árni Heimir Ingólfsson is a musicologist, pianist, and music educator. He is Visiting Professor at the Iceland University of the Arts and was Artistic Advisor to the Iceland Symphony Orchestra from 2014-2022. His research focuses on the transmission of music to and within Iceland during the sixteenth and seventeenth centuries, and Icelandic music and nation-building in the twentieth century. His most recent book is *Jón Leifs and the Musical Invention of Iceland* (Indiana University Press, 2019).

David R. M. Irving is an ICREA Research Professor in Musicology at the Institució Milà i Fontanals de Recerca en Humanitats (IMF), CSIC, Barcelona; Corresponding Fellow of the Australian Academy of the Humanities; and Honorary Senior Fellow at the Melbourne Conservatorium of Music, University of Melbourne. He holds a PhD in Musicology from the University of Cambridge. He is the author of *Colonial Counterpoint: Music in Early Modern Manila* (Oxford, 2010), and co-editor of *Eighteenth-Century Music*.

Jonathan Katz is Lecturer in Classics at Brasenose College, Oxford, and St Anne's College, Oxford, and a Fellow of All Souls College. His research interests are Indian music theory and history, and Plato and Greek philosophy. He has published books, articles, and reviews on Greek, Latin, and Sanskrit literary subjects, as well as translations from German and Italian.

Moritz Kelber is a Researcher and Lecturer at the University of Bern. Between 2016 and 2018 he was Forschungsassistent at the University of Salzburg where he worked in the FWF research project on "Music printing in German-speaking lands: From the 1470s to the mid-16th century." In 2016 he finished his doctoral dissertation on "Music in the Context of the Augsburg Imperial Diets in the 16th century" at the University of Augsburg.

Robert L. Kendrick is Robert O. Anderson Distinguished Service Professor in Music at the University of Chicago. He works in early modern music and culture, with additional interests in Latin America, historical anthropology, traditional Mediterranean polyphony, laments, and the visual arts. His most recent book is *Fruits of the Cross: Passiontide Music Theater in Habsburg Vienna* (University of California Press, 2018).

Andrew Kirkman is Peyton and Barber Professor of Music in the University of Birmingham; from 1997-2012 he was a professor in the Music Department at Rutgers, The State University of New Jersey. He has published three monographs, including two books for CUP, *The Cultural Life of the Early Polyphonic Mass* (2010) and *Music and Musicians at the Collegiate Church of St Omer* (2020), as well as numerous articles, and 13 CDs with Hyperion Records with The Binchois Consort.

Martin Kirnbauer is Head of Research and Member of the Board of the Schola Cantorum Basiliensis / FHNW. After being trained as a musical instrument maker he was conservator for historical musical instruments at the Germanisches Nationalmuseum in Nuremberg. He studied musicology in Erlangen and Basel, obtaining his PhD in 1998, followed by a Habilitation in 2007. From 2004 to 2017 he was Director of the Musicmuseum of the Historical Museum Basel and curator of its collection of musical instruments.

Tess Knighton has been an ICREA Research Professor since 2011, first at the Institució Milà i Fontanals (CSIC), and subsequently at the Universitat Autònoma de Barcelona. Her research interests embrace music and culture in the Iberian world from the fifteenth to the seventeenth centuries, and she has published widely in this field. She is Series Editor of the Studies in Medieval and Renaissance Music series for The Boydell Press, and forms part of several editorial and advisory committees in Spain and in Europe.

Franz Körndle is Professor of Musicology at the University of Augsburg. His 1990 dissertation was published in 1993 as *Das zweistimmige Notre-Dame-Organum Crucifixum in carne und sein Weiterleben in Erfurt* (Hans Schneider Verlag), and his Habilitationsschrift concerned liturgical music at the Munich court in the sixteenth century. Körndle is a specialist in church music and currently researches historical organs and town musicians of the Renaissance and Baroque. He has published many articles in Germany, the UK, Italy, the USA, and Spain on keyboards and their music, Orlando di Lasso, and Jesuit Drama.

Gundula Kreuzer is Professor of Music at Yale University and author of the award-winning *Verdi and the Germans: From Unification to the Third Reich* (CUP, 2010) as well as *Curtain, Gong, Steam: Wagnerian Technologies of Nineteenth-Century Opera* (University of California Press, 2018). In 2019 she launched the annual YOST (Y | Opera | Studies Today) symposium to explore contemporary experimental opera and received the Dent Medal of the Royal Musical Association.

Matthew Laube is Assistant Professor of Music at Baylor University in Waco, Texas. His work focuses on the social and cultural history of music in early modern Germany and the Low Countries. His research has appeared in *Past & Present*, and a monograph on music in Reformation Heidelberg is in preparation. After completing his PhD at Royal Holloway, University of London in 2014, Matthew was a Wiener-Anspach Postdoctoral Fellow at the University of Cambridge and the Université Libre de Bruxelles, and a Leverhulme Early Career Fellow at Birkbeck College, University of London.

Ayla Lepine is an art and architectural historian specialising in the intersections of theology and the arts, especially in modern Britain. Recent publications include articles on gender, Christianity and sculpture in the *Journal of Victorian Studies* and the *Journal of Theology and Sexuality.* She has held fellowships at Yale, the Courtauld, and the National Gallery and was Lecturer in Art History at the University of Essex. She is also a priest and is the Associate Rector at St James's Piccadilly.

Jeffrey Levenberg served as an Assistant Professor of Music at the Chinese University of Hong Kong from 2015-21. His research centers on Carlo Gesualdo's reception history while broadly engaging global music history. Among other honors and contributions, Levenberg hosted an international conference in 2018 at CUHK on "Music between China and the West in the Age of Discovery."

Birgit Lodes is Professor of Historical Musicology at the University of Vienna. Her research focuses on music in German-speaking lands both ca. 1500 and in the nineteenth century. She was a collaborator on the Ludwig Senfl Catalog Raisonné, and edits the series Wiener Forum für ältere Musikgeschichte (Hollitzer Verlag).

Mattias Lundberg is Professor of Musicology at Uppsala University. His research mainly concerns music and music theory of the late Middle Ages and the sixteenth century. Between 2006-15 he was Head of Rare Collections at the Swedish National Collections of Music. His current research project addresses Early Modern Lutheran ecclesiastical music, funded by the Swedish Research Council.

Javier Marín-López is Professor of Music at the Universidad de Jaén. He researches musics of the sixteenth-eighteenth centuries in Latin America and Iberia within the wider European context. His first book, *Los libros de polifonía de la Catedral de México* (2012), considers the most important collection of polyphonic choirbooks in the Americas. He is Editor-in-Chief of *Revista de Musicología* (since 2013) and General Director of the Festival de Música Antigua Úbeda y Baeza (since 2007).

Diana Matut is Lecturer in Jewish Studies at the University of Halle-Wittenberg and teaches Jewish music at the Oxford Centre for Hebrew and Jewish Studies. Her 2011 doctoral dissertation was entitled "Poetry and Music in the Early Modern Aschkenas." In addition to her academic career, Diana is a singer and leader of the group Simkhat Hanefesh (Joy of the Soul) which performs Jewish music and Yiddish songs from the Renaissance and Baroque periods.

Ascensión Mazuela-Anguita is Associate Professor of Music at the University of Granada. She received the 2012 J. M. Thomson Prize from the journal *Early Music*, the Spanish Musicological Society 2012 Research Prize, and the Jon B. Lovelace Fellowship for the Study of the Alan Lomax Collection (2016) at the John W. Kluge Center, Library of Congress, Washington, DC.

Laura Moretti is Professor of Art History at the University of St Andrews. She is the author of *In the House of the Muses: Collection, Display, and Performance in the Veronese Palace of Mario Bevilacqua (1536-93)* (2020) and co-author (with Deborah Howard) of *Sound and Space in Renaissance Venice* (2009). Her specific field of interest is the relationship between art, architecture, and music in sixteenth-century Italy.

Zuleika Murat is Associate Professor of the History of Medieval Art at the University of Padua. She obtained her PhD in the History of Art at the University of Padua in 2013, and has been a Postdoctoral Research Fellow at the University of Warwick (2013-2014), a Research Fellow at the University of Padua (2014-2016), and Principal Investigator of a two-year multidisciplinary project also based at the University of Padua (2018-2020). She is the PI of the ERC Starting Grant project "The Sensuous Appeal of the Holy: Sensory Agency of Sacred Art and Somatised Spiritual Experiences in Medieval Europe (12th-15th century)" (2021-2026). Her main research interests concern the visual, material and devotional culture of medieval Europe.

Bernadette Nelson is a Senior Researcher at CESEM-FCSH (Centre for the Study of Sociology and Aesthetics of Music) at the Universidade Nova, Lisbon, and is also affiliated with Wolfson College, Oxford. She has published widely on topics in Iberian and Franco-Flemish sacred polyphonic and instrumental music, institutional and contextual studies, musico-liturgical practice, sources studies, and the music of Morales and Noel Bauldeweyn. She has participated in several research projects in music and the history of art financed by the Foundation of Science and Technology (FCT), Lisbon, including most recently "The Anatomy of Late 15th- and Early 16th-Century Iberian Polyphonic Music" (2017-20).

Marina Nordera is a dancer and cultural historian. She is Professor and member of the Centre transdisciplinaire d'épistémologie de la littérature et des arts vivants at Université Côte d'Azur, where she is Head of the Arts Departement and leads the PhD programme in Dance Studies. She has published on dance historiography and on the history of dance transmission, the body, and gender in early modern Europe.

Jessie Ann Owens is Distinguished Professor (emeritus) at the University of California, Davis, where she previously served as Dean of Humanities, Arts and Cultural Studies and Professor of Music. The author of numerous books and articles, Owens has pursued a number of research interests within the field of Renaissance studies, focussing in particular on the music of Cipriano de Rore, and the Italian madrigal. She edited the 30-volume series *The Sixteenth-Century Madrigal* with Garland Publishing, the first modern edition of a number of madrigal books.

Emily Peppers is a musicologist and cultural heritage professional, working with the University of Edinburgh, Museums Galleries Scotland, and Creative Scotland. Her PhD research explored the introduction of the viol into sixteenth-century France. In 2021 she joined the University of Warsaw as a Marie-Skłodowska Curie Fellow to lead the project "Musical Materialities and Conduits of Culture: revealing the hidden histories of music during Poland's 'Golden Age' (ca. 1475-1600)."

Gretchen Peters has a PhD in Musicology from the University of Illinois and is a Professor of Music at the University of Wisconsin-Eau Claire where she teaches in the Music and Theatre Arts Department. She has published extensively on urban musical culture in late medieval France, including a book entitled *The Musical Sounds of Medieval French Cities: Players, Patrons and Politics* (CUP, 2012).

Klaus Pietschmann is Professor of Musicology at the Johannes Gutenberg-University of Mainz. His principal research interests are the social, institutional, and theological aspects of sacred music in late-medieval and early modern Italy and Germany, in particular the papal chapel in the sixteenth century; iconography; and eighteenth- and nineteenth-century opera. Recent publications include the article "(Re-)Constructing Renaissance Music: Perspectives from the Digital Humanities and Music Theory."

Pamela M. Potter is Professor of German and Musicology at the University of Wisconsin-Madison. She is author of *Most German of the Arts: Musicology and Society from the Weimar Republic to the End of Hitler's Reich* (1998; trans. German, Portuguese) and *Art of Suppression: Confronting the Nazi Past in Histories of the Visual and Performing Arts* (2016); and she is co-editor of *Music and German National Identity* (2002) and *Music in World War II: Coping with Wartime in Europe and the United States* (2020).

Massimo Privitera is a Professor of Musicology at the University of Palermo. His research is chiefly focused on the sixteenth- to seventeenth-century Italian madrigal. He has edited Frescobaldi's madrigals (with Lorenzo Bianconi), Orazio Vecchi's six-voice canzonette (with Rossana Dalmonte), and the madrigals of Achille Falcone. He has published articles on Marenzio, Monteverdi, Vecchi, and a monograph on Arcangelo Corelli. He also works on song on the cinema screen.

Nuno de Mendonça Raimundo is a Researcher in Historical Musicology at the Centre for Research in Sociology and Aesthetics of Music (CESEM) based at the Universidade Nova, Lisbon, where he is also a Lecturer. His main area of research is fifteenth- to seventeenth-century Iberian polyphonic music. He is currently completing his doctorate on seventeenth-century Portuguese vocal music in the vernacular.

Sanna Raninen is a postdoctoral researcher specialising in early modern material and visual cultures of music. Her current research focuses on the cultural history of music books in post-Reformation Sweden, and her other research interests include visual arts of Renaissance Italy as well as music printing in Europe.

Eugenio Refini is Associate Professor of Italian at New York University. His research focuses on reception, translation, and forms of adaptation, which he explores through the intersections of rhetoric, poetics, drama, music, and voice studies. He is the author of the monographs *Per via d'annotationi: le glosse inedite di Alessandro Piccolomini all'Ars poetica di Orazio* (Pacini Fazzi, 2009), and *The Vernacular Aristotle: Translation as Reception in Medieval and Renaissance Italy* (CUP, 2020).

Eleonora Rocconi is Associate Professor of Greek Language and Literature at the Department of Musicology and Cultural Heritage of the University of Pavia (Cremona). She is Editor-in-Chief of the journal *Greek and Roman Musical Studies* (Brill), the first specialist periodical in the fields of ancient Greek and Roman music, and co-editor of the *Companion to Ancient Greek and Roman Music* (Wiley-Blackwell).

Emilio Ros-Fábregas, a native of Barcelona, is a tenured researcher ("Investigador Científico") in Musicology at the Consejo Superior de Investigaciones Científicas (CSIC), Institución Milá y Fontanals (IMF) in Barcelona. His research focuses on Spanish music of the Renaissance, the historiography of Spanish music in an international context, and the recent developments of digital musicology. As PI of a national R+D Project (HAR2012-33604; 2013-16), he has created the website / database Books of Hispanic Polyphony (https://hispanicpolyphony.eu ISSN: 2565-1579) to catalogue books of polyphony in Spain and books with Hispanic polyphony elsewhere.

Katelijne Schiltz is Chair of the Musicology Department at the University of Regensburg. She studied musicology at the University of Leuven and early vocal music at the Conservatory of Tilburg. Her dissertation on the motets of Adrian Willaert appeared in 2003 with Leuven University Press. Her monograph *Music and Riddle Culture in the Renaissance* (CUP, 2015) was awarded the Roland H. Bainton Prize from the Sixteenth Century Society and Conference.

Paul Schleuse is Associate Professor of Musicology at Binghamton University, State University of New York. His work on early-modern music engages themes of sociability, print culture, recreational singing, sexuality, and class. He is the author of *Singing Games in Early Modern Italy: The Music Books of Orazio Vecchi* (Indiana University Press), the editor of Vecchi's *Selva di varia ricreatione* (A-R Editions), and a member of the editorial board of the Tasso in Music Project (tassomusic.org).

Serenella Sessini (PhD, University of Sheffield) is an art historian specialising in Italian Renaissance domestic and ecclesiastical art with a focus on the use of images in education and devotion. She has co-authored the book *Music in the Art of Renaissance Italy 1420-1540* and written articles and essays focusing on portraiture and miniatures. She currently works in collection management at the V&A and is co-editing a volume entitled *Music and Art in the Italian Church Interior*.

Tim Shephard is Professor of Musicology at the University of Sheffield. He is the co-author of *Music in the Art of Renaissance Italy* (Harvey Miller, 2020), as well as numerous other books and essays on Italian musical culture in the fifteenth and sixteenth centuries. He currently leads the project "Sounding the Bookshelf 1501: Musical Knowledge in a Year of Italian Printed Books," funded by the Leverhulme Trust.

Laura Ştefanescu is an art historian interested in Italian Renaissance art and the interplay between theatre, religion, and music. She is Research Associate for the project "Sounding the Bookshelf 1501," at the University of Sheffield. Her dissertation was focused on the representation of heavenly music in Italian Renaissance art, and her publications include the co-authored book *Music in the Art of Renaissance Italy 1420-1540* (Harvey Miller), and a co-authored article on musical images in *Renaissance Quarterly*.

Ennio Stipčević has served since 1984 as a researcher, now a senior scholar, at the Institute for the History of Croatian Music at the Croatian Academy of Sciences and Arts, and from 1994 he has also taught at the Zagreb Academy of Music. He spent 1996/97 as a Fulbright Visiting Scholar at Yale University. His publications, mostly on Croatian Renaissance and Baroque music, include monographs on Ivan Lukačić (2007) and Francesco Usper (2008), together with a dozen music editions.

Laurie Stras is Research Professor of Music at the University of Huddersfield and Professor Emerita of Music at the University of Southampton. She co-directs the early music ensemble

Musica Secreta and has published widely on sixteenth-century Italian music, with a particular focus on women musicians.

Jane H. M. Taylor is Emeritus Professor of Medieval French at Durham University. Her research focuses first on late medieval French lyric—most notably with books on François Villon and on late-medieval lyric anthologies, and second on the transition from manuscript to print in the Renaissance, most recently with a book on Arthurian romance. She has also translated into English two chivalric biographies, Boucicaut and Le Jouvencel, as well as a chivalric romance, Jean de Saintré.

John J. Thompson is Professor Emeritus at Queen's University, Belfast. He has written widely on literary and codicological aspects of late medieval and early modern English book history and characterises his research as a series of "cultural mapping" exercises. His most recent work includes a number of large-scale collaborative scholarly projects focusing on important transitional moments in pre- and post-Reformation English textual cultures.

Emanuela Vai is the Scott Opler Research Fellow and Lecturer at Worcester College and an Associate Lecturer in Renaissance History of Art and Music, both University of Oxford. She has recently been appointed as Visiting Professor at the Centre d'études supérieures de la Renaissance, Tours. Previously she held positions at the University of Cambridge, at the Centre for Renaissance and Early Modern Studies at the University of York, and at Villa I Tatti, The Harvard University Centre for Italian Renaissance Studies in Florence. Her research is located at the interdisciplinary intersection of art history, architectural history and musicology, and her publications focus on musical instruments, soundscapes, space and the senses in Renaissance social life.

Kate van Orden is a cultural historian and the Dwight P. Robinson Jr. Professor of Music at Harvard University. Her prize-winning books include *Music, Discipline, and Arms in Early Modern France* (2005) and, most recently, *Materialities: Books, Readers, and the Chanson in Sixteenth-Century Europe* (2015). Among her recent awards are a Medaille d'Honneur for her contributions to Renaissance studies and a Stanford Humanities Center Senior Fellowship (2017-18).

Laura S. Ventura Nieto completed her PhD at Royal Holloway in 2017 under Professor Stephen Rose with a thesis that explores how theatricality, performativity, and gender construction can inform our readings of depictions of female musicians produced in Italy between 1520 and 1650. Her current research interests include the representation and construction of the image of Italian courtesans in early modern sources. She has also taught in the Music Department at Royal Holloway.

Philip Weller (1958-2018) studied at the Universities of Cambridge, Heidelberg, Paris, and London. He was a Yates Fellow at the Warburg Institute, and more recently Visiting Research Fellow at the University of Tours. His interests included the field of research where language, image, and music converge (multimedia stage genres, Renaissance, Enlightenment). He taught at the Universities of Liverpool and Nottingham.

Beth Williamson is Professor of Medieval Culture at the University of Bristol. She works principally on the culture of western European Christianity, with a particular focus on the forms and functions of religious imagery, visual and aural culture, sensory and bodily experience, and on religious belief and behaviour. She is currently working on an interdisciplinary project, funded by the Leverhulme Trust, on English late medieval devotional culture, entitled "Describing Devotion."

Magnus Williamson is Professor of Early Music at Newcastle University. His research focuses on musical sources and contexts, improvisation, voices, and keyboards from the fourteenth to the seventeenth centuries. His facsimile edition of the Eton Choirbook (2010) was awarded the American Musicological Society's Palisca Prize. He has been principal investigator of numerous projects including "Tudor Partbooks" (AHRC, 2014-17), and is chairman of the British Academy series, Early English Church Music.

Jonathan Willis is Senior Lecturer in Early Modern History and Director of the Centre for Reformation and Early Modern Studies at the University of Birmingham. He is the author of *Church Music and Protestantism in Post-Reformation England* (2010) and *The Reformation of the Decalogue* (2017); editor of *Sin and Salvation in Reformation England* (2015); and co-editor of *Dying, Death, Burial and Commemoration in Reformation Europe* (2015) and *Understanding Early Modern Primary Sources* (2016).

Richard Wistreich is Research Professor at the Royal College of Music in London and a historian of early modern vocality. His publications include two edited collections about Claudio Monteverdi, and articles on the cultural and technical history of singing. He is co-editor with Iain Fenlon of *The Cambridge History of Sixteenth-Century Music* (2019). He also had a long career as a professional singer specialising in sixteenth- and seventeenth-century solo and ensemble music.

Jessica Lee Wood is Assistant Curator in the Music Division of the New York Public Library of the Performing Arts. Her research focuses on twentieth century US topics related to consumer culture, masculinity, and social class, with particular interest in the Early Music revival, DIY instrument building, the social life of the Canon, and the gender politics of J. S. Bach reception.

David Yearsley was educated at Harvard College and Stanford University, where he received his PhD in Musicology in 1994. At Cornell University he continues to pursue his interests in the teaching, history, literature, and performance of music. His musicological work investigates literary, social, and theological contexts for music and music-making, and while he focuses on J. S. Bach, he has written on topics ranging from music and death to musical invention, from organology and performance to musical representations of public spaces in film, from musical travelers to the joys of the keyboard duet.

Giovanni Zanovello is Associate Professor of Music at Indiana University. He specializes in fifteenth-century music and institutions. He has received research grants and awards from various institutions, including the University of Padua, the CNRS, Villa I Tatti, the Swiss Society of Musicology, and Indiana University. Zanovello regularly participates in international conferences and has published in specialized venues, including the *Journal of the American Musicological Society*, the *Journal of Musicology*, and *MusikKonzepte*.

Carla Zecher is Executive Director of the Renaissance Society of America. She is the author of *Sounding Objects: Musical Instruments, Poetry, and Art in Renaissance France* (University of Toronto Press, 2007) and a co-editor, with Gordon Sayre and Shannon Dawdy, of *Jean-François-Benjamin Dumont de Montigny, Regards sur le monde atlantique* (Septentrion, 2008) and *The Memoir of Lieutenant Dumont, 1715-1747: A Sojourner in the French Atlantic* (Omohundro Institute and University of North Carolina Press, 2012).

Bibliography

Abbate, Carolyn. 2021. "Certain Loves for Opera." *Representations* 154: 47-68.

Abramov-van Rijk, Elena. 2009. *Parlar Cantando: The Practice of Reciting Verses in Italy from 1300 to 1600*. Bern: Peter Lang.

Abū al-Faẓl ibn Mubārak. 2014-18. *The History of Akbar*. 4 vols. Edited and translated by Wheeler M. Thackston. Cambridge, MA: Harvard University Press.

Adams, Parveen. 2006. "Out of Sight, Out of Body: The Sugimoto/Demand Effect." *Grey Room* 22: 86-104.

Adorno, Theodor. 2005. *In Search of Wagner, with a foreword by Slavoj Žižek*. Translated by Rodney Livingstone. London: Verso.

Aercke, Kristiaan. 1994. *Gods of Play: Baroque Festive Performances as Rhetorical Discourse*. Albany: State University of New York Press.

Aglio, Roberta. 2005. "Le tavolette da soffitto del monastero della Colomba a Cremona." *Arte Lombarda* n.s. 145: 56-61.

Agrippa, Henry Cornelius. (1533) 1651. *Three Books of Occult Philosophy*. Translated by John French. London: Gregory Moule.

Ajmar-Wollheim, Marta, and Flora Dennis, eds. 2006. *At Home in Renaissance Italy*. London: V&A Publications.

Ajmar-Wollheim, Marta, Flora Dennis, and Ann Matchette, eds. 2007. *Approaching the Italian Renaissance Interior: Sources, Methodologies, Debates*. Oxford: Blackwell.

Alberti, Leon Battista. 1988. *On the Art of Building in Ten Books*. Translated by Joseph Rykwert, Neil Leach, and Robert Tavernor. Cambridge, MA: MIT Press.

Alberti, Leon Battista. 1996. *De re aedificatoria*. Edited by Giovanni Orlandi and Paolo Portoghesi. Milan: Il Polifilo.

Albrecht, Thorsten. 1999. *Die Bückeburger Stadtkirche: Ein bedeutendes Beispiel der deutschen Spätrenaissance*. Petersberg: Imhof.

Alden, Jane. 2010. *Songs, Scribes, and Society: The History and Reception of the Loire Valley Chansonniers*. New York: Oxford University Press.

al-Din al-Urmawi, Safi. 1984. *Book on the Cyclic Forms of Musical Modes and Treatise Dedicated to Sharaf al-Din on Proportions in Musical Composition*. Frankfurt: Institute for the History of Arabic-Islamic Science.

Alegre Carvajal, Esther. 2003. *La villa ducal de Pastrana*. Guadalajara: AACHE.

Alexiou, Stylianos. 1985. *I Kritiki logotechnia kie i epochi tu. Meletì filologikì kie istorikì* [Αλεξίου, Στυλιανός. Η Κρητική λογοτεχνία και η εποχή του. Μελέτη φιλολογική και ιστορική]. Athens: Stigmi.

Alfonso XI, King of Castile and Leon. 1991. *Poema de Alfonso Onceno*. Edited by Juan Victorío. Madrid: Cátedra.

Alison, Richard. 1599. *The Psalmes of Dauid in Meter the Plaine Song* [...]. London: William Barley.

Allen, Christopher. 2002. "Ovid and Art." In *The Cambridge Companion to Ovid*, edited by Philip R. Hardie, 336-67. Cambridge: Cambridge University Press.

Allen, Joanne. 2009. "Choir Stalls in Venice and Northern Italy: Furniture, Ritual and Space in the Renaissance Church Interior." PhD diss., University of Warwick.

Almada, André Álvares d'. (1594) 1946. *Tratado breve dos rios de Guiné*. Edited by Luís Silveira. Lisbon: Oficina Gráfica.

Ames-Lewis, Francis. 1993. "Art in the Service of the Family: The Taste and Patronage of Piero di Cosimo de' Medici." In *Piero de' Medici, "il Gottoso" (1416-1469): Kunst im Dienste der Mediceer / Art in the Service of the Medici*, edited by Andreas Beyer and Bruce Boucher, 207-20. Berlin: Akademie Verlag.

Ammendola, Andrea. 2013. *Polyphone Herrschermessen (1500-1650): Kontext und Symbolizität*. Göttingen: V&R.

Anderson, Jaynie. 1991. "Il risveglio dell'interesse per le Muse nella Ferrara del Quattrocento." In *Le Muse e il Principe: Arte di corte nel Rinascimento padano*, 2 vols., edited by Alessandra Mottola-Molfino and Mauro Natali, 2:165-85. Modena: Franco Cosimo Panini.

Andrade, Sérgio Guimarães. 1972. "Os músicos negros do retábulo de Santa Auta." In *Retábulo de Santa Auta: Estudo de investigação*, 47-48. Lisbon: Ministério da Educação Nacional, Instituto de Alta Cultura, Centro de Estudos de Arte e Museologia.

Anglés, Higinio. 1947, 1951. *La música en la corte de los Reyes Católicos*. Vols. 2-3: *Cancionero Musical de Palacio*. Monumentos de la Música Española 5 and 10. Barcelona: Consejo Superior de Investigaciones Científicas, Instituto Español de Musicología.

Anson, Peter. 1960. *Fashions in Church Furnishings*. London: Faith Press.

Anthony, Evelyn. 1957. *Anne Boleyn*. New York: Thomas Y. Crowell.

Anthony, James R. 1997. *French Baroque Music from Beaujoyeulx to Rameau, revised and extended edition*. Portland OR: Amadeus Press.

Aranda Donce, Juan. 1978. "Las danzas de las Fiestas del Corpus en Córdoba, durante los siglos XVI y XVII: Aspectos folklóricos, económicos y sociales." *Boletín de la Real Academia de Córdoba* 47, no. 98: 173-94.

Arasse, Daniel. 1999. *L'Annonciation italienne: Une histoire de perspective*. Paris: Hazan.

Arbeau, Thoinot (Jehan Tabourot). 1588. *Orchesographie Et traicte en forme de dialogve, par leqvel tovtes personnes pevvent facilement apprendre & practiquer l'honneste exercice des dances*. Lengres: Iehan des Preyz.

Arcangeli, Alessandro. 2003. *Recreation in the Renaissance: Attitudes towards Leisure and Pastimes in European Culture, 1350-1700*. Basingstoke: Palgrave Macmillan.

Ariès, Philippe. 1985. *Images of Man and Death*. Translated by Janet Lloyd. Cambridge, MA: Harvard University Press.

Aristotle. 1993. *De Anima: Books II and III (With Passages from Book I)*. Translated by D. W. Hamlyn. Oxford: Clarendon Press.

Arnold, Denis. 1976. Review of *Instruments of the Middle Ages and Renaissance*. *Gramophone*, July, 1976.

Arnold, John H. 2005. *Belief and Unbelief in the Middle Ages*. London: Bloomsbury.

Arnold, John H., and Caroline Goodson. 2012. "Resounding Community: The History and Meaning of Medieval Church Bells." *Viator* 43, no. 1: 99-130.

Arslan, Fazli. 2007. "Safi al-Din al-Urmawi and the Theory of Music." http://muslimheritage.com/article/safi-al-din-al-urmawi-and-theory-music.

Artusi, Giovanni Maria. 1600. *L'Artusi, overo Delle imperfettioni della moderna musica*. Venice: Vincenti.

Aslanian, Sebouh D. 2012. "Wings on their Feet and on their Heads: Reflections on Port Armenians and Five Centuries of Global Print Culture." *The Armenian Weekly*, September 1. https://armenianweekly.com/2012/08/28/wings-on-their-feet-and-on-their-heads/.

Atkinson, Niall. 2016. *The Noisy Renaissance: Sound, Architecture, and Florentine Urban Life*. University Park: Penn State University Press.

Atlas, Allan. 1998. *Renaissance Music: Music in Western Europe 1400-1600*. New York: Norton.

Ausonius, Paulinus Pellaeus. 1921. *Volume II: Books 18-20. Paulinus Pellaeus: Eucharisticus*. Translated by Hugh G. Evelyn-White. Loeb Classical Library 115. Cambridge, MA: Harvard University Press.

Austern, Linda Phyllis. 1989. "'Sing Again Siren': The Female Musician and Sexual Enchantment in Elizabethan Life and Literature." *Renaissance Quarterly* 42: 420-48.

Austern, Linda Phyllis. 2003. "'All Things in this World is but the Musick of Inconstancie': Music, Sensuality and the Sublime in Seventeenth-Century Vanitas Imagery." In *Art and Music in the Early Modern Period: Essays in Honor of Franca Trinchieri Camiz*, edited by Katherine A. McIver, 287-332. Aldershot: Ashgate.

Austern, Linda Phyllis. 2005. "Portrait of the Artist as (Female) Musician." In *Musical Voices of Early Modern Women: Many-Headed Melodies*, edited by Thomasin LaMay, 15-59. Aldershot: Ashgate.

Austern, Linda Phyllis. 2008. "Women's Musical Voices in Sixteenth-Century England." *Early Modern Women* 3: 127-52.

Ayres, Lewis, and Medi Ann Volpe. 2019. "*Lectio Divina*: Resting in the Silence of Scripture." In *The Oxford Handbook of Catholic Theology*, edited by Lewis Ayres and Medi Ann Volpe, 353-54. Oxford: Oxford University Press.

Azzaiolo, Filippo. 1557. *Villotte del Fiore alla Padoana*. Venice: Gardano.

Babbi, Anna Maria, ed. 1985. *Paris e Vienna: Romanzo cavalleresco*. Padua: Marsilio.

Bachelin, Léo. 1898. *Tableaux anciens de la Galerie Charles Ier: Catalogue raisonné*. Paris: Braun, Clément et Cie.

Bacon, Francis. 1862. "The Second Counsellor Advising the Study of Philosophy." In *The Works of Francis Bacon*, 14 vols., edited by James Spedding et al., 8:334-35. London: Longmans & Co.

Badiali, Federica. 2011. "Paesaggi del cibo: Scritti ed immagini dal XIV al XVI secolo." In *I paesaggi del vino: Il paesaggio tra reale e virtuale*, edited by Lucilia Gregori, 39-48. Città di Castello: Nuova Phromos.

Baert, Barbara. 2012. *Caput Joannis in Disco: {Essay on a Man's Head}*. Visualising the Middle Ages 8. Leiden: Brill.

Baert, Barbara. 2015. "Vox Clamantis in Deserto. The Johannesschüssel: Senses and Silence." *Open Arts Journal* 4: 143-56.

Baert, Barbara, and Sophia Rochmes, eds. 2017. *Decapitation and Sacrifice: St. John's Head in Interdisciplinary Perspectives: Text, Object, Medium*. Art & Religion 6. Leuven: Peeters.

Báez Rubí, Linda. 2005. *Mnemosine novohispánica: Retórica e imágenes en el siglo XVI*. Mexico City: Instituto de Investigaciones Estéticas, Universidad Nacional Autónoma de México.

Bagnall Yardley, Anne. 2006. *Performing Piety: Musical Culture in Medieval English Nunneries*. New York: Palgrave MacMillan.

Bagnoli, Martina, ed. 2016. *A Feast for the Senses: Art and Experience in Medieval Europe*. New Haven: Yale University Press.

Bain, Susan E. 1974. "Music Printing in the Low Countries in the Sixteenth Century." PhD diss., Cambridge University.

Baker, Geoffrey. 2008. *Imposing Harmony: Music and Society in Colonial Cuzco*. Durham: Duke University Press.

Balbín, Bohuslav. 1681. *Liber III. Decadis I. Miscellaneorum historicorum regni Bohemiae, topographicus et chorographicus, qui fines et terminos totius Bohemiae*. Prague: Typis Georgij Czernoch.

Ball, Patrick. 2021. "The Playing Cards and Gaming Boards." In *Music and Instruments of the Elizabethan Age: The Eglantine Table*, edited by Michael Fleming and Christopher Page, 47-57. Woodbridge: Boydell and Brewer.

Bank, Katie. 2020. "(Re)Creating the Eglantine Table." *Early Music* 48, no. 3: 359–376.

Barbaro, Francesco. 1915. *De re uxoria liber in partes duas*. Edited by Attilio Gnesotto. Padua: Randi.

Barbaro, Francesco. 2015. *The Wealth of Wives: A Fifteenth-Century Marriage Manual*. Edited and translated by Margaret L. King. Toronto: Iter Academic Press.

Barbieri, Francisco A. 1890. *Cancionero musical de los siglos XV y XVI*. Madrid: Huérfanos.

Barker, Andrew. 2007. *The Science of Harmonics in Classical Greece*. Cambridge: Cambridge University Press.

Barlow, Jeremy. 2012. *A Dance through Time*. Oxford: The Bodleian Library.

Barnett, Rod. 2009. "Serpent of Pleasure: Emergence and Difference in the Medieval Garden of Love." *Landscape Journal* 28: 137-50.

Barolsky, Paul. 1998. "Sacred and Profane Love." *Source: Notes in the History of Art* 17: 25-28.

Barrera Maturana, José Ignacio. 2007. "Representación de una mujer morisca en un graffiti del Albayzín (Granada)." *Anaquel de Estudios Árabes* 18: 65-91.

Barreto Xavier, Ângela, and Ines G. Županov. 2015. *Catholic Orientalism: Portuguese Empire, Indian Knowledge*. New Delhi: Oxford University Press.

Bartrum, Giulia. 1995. *German Renaissance Prints: 1490-1550*. London: British Museum.

Baskerville, Charles. (1929) 1965. *The Elizabethan Jig*. New York: Dover Publications.

Bass, Laura R., and Amanda Wunder. 2009. "The Veiled Ladies of the Early Modern Spanish World: Seduction and Scandal in Seville, Madrid, and Lima." *Hispanic Review* 77, no. 1: 97-144.

Bator, Angelika. 2004. "Der Chorbuchdruck 'Liber selectarum cantionum' (Augsburg 1520): Ein drucktechnischer Vergleich der Exemplare aus Augsburg, München und Stuttgart." *Musik in Bayern* 67: 5-38.

Batov, Alexander. 2006-17. "The Vihuela and Guitar Crossroads: Looking for Evidence." http://www.vihuelademano.com/vgcrossroads.htm.

Bätschmann, Oskar, and Pascal Griener. 2014. *Hans Holbein*. 2nd edn. London: Reaktion Books.

Bauer, Oswald Georg. 2016. *Die Geschichte der Bayreuther Festspiele*. 2 vols. Berlin: Deutscher Kunstverlag.

Bauer-Eberhardt, Ursula. 1999. "I Trionfi di Petrarca per Andrea della Valle." *Rivista di storia della miniatura* 4: 161-68.

Baumgarten, Jean. 2005. *Introduction to Old Yiddish Literature*. Translated by Jerold C. Frakes. Oxford: Oxford University Press.

Baumgartner, Emmanuèle. 1992. "The Play of Temporalities; or, the Reported Dream of Guillaume de Lorris." In *Rethinking the* Romance of the Rose*: Text, Image, Reception*, edited by Kevin Brownlee, and Sylvia Huot, 22-38. Philadelphia: University of Pennsylvania Press.

Baxandall, Michael. 1965. "Guarino, Pisanello and Manuel Chrysoloras." *Journal of the Warburg and Courtauld Institutes* 28: 183-204.

Bayer, Andrea, ed. 2008. *Art and Love in Renaissance Italy*. New York: Metropolitan Museum.

Bayliss, Alexandra Louise. 2006. "Validating Classical Multivariate Models in Archaeology: English Medieval Bellfounding as a Case Study." PhD diss., University of London.

Becon, Thomas. 1550. *The Iewel of Ioye*. London: J. Daye and W. Seres.

Bell, Audrey F. G. 1920. *Four Plays of Gil Vicente*. Edited with translation by Audrey Bell. Cambridge: Cambridge University Press.

Bell, David. 1995. *What Nuns Read: Books and Libraries in Medieval English Nunneries*. Kalamazoo: Cistercian Publications.

Bellettini, Pierangelo, Rosario Campioni, and Zita Zanardi. 2000. *Una città in piazza: Comunicazione e vita quotidiana a Bologna tra Cinque e Seicento*. Bologna: Editrice compositori.

Belon, Pierre. 2001. *L'énigme de la chronique de Pierre Belon: Avec édition critique du manuscrit Arsenal 4651*. Edited by Monica Barsi. Milan: LED Edizioni Universitarie di Lettere Economia Diritto.

Belon, Pierre. 2012. *Travels in the Levant: The Observations of Pierre Belon of Le Mans on Many Singularities and Memorable Things found in Greece, Turkey, Judaea, Egypt, Arabia and Other Foreign Countries (1553)*. Translated by James Hogarth. Edinburgh: Hardinge Simpole.

Belon du Mans, Pierre. 2001. *Voyage au Levant: Les observations de Pierre Belon du Mans de plusieurs singularités et choses mémorables, trouvées en Grèce, Asie, Judée, Égypte, Arabie et autres pays étranges (1553)*. Edited by Alexandra Merle. Paris: Éditions Chandeigne.

Belting, Hans. 2011. *Florence and Baghdad: Renaissance Art and Arab Science*. Cambridge, MA: Harvard University Press.

Bembo, Illuminata. 2001. *Specchio di illuminazione*. Edited by Silvia Mostaccio. Florence: SISMEL.

Bembo, Pietro. 1961. *Opere in volgare*. Edited by Mario Marti. Florence: Sansoni.

Benassi, Vincenzo, Odir J. Dias, and Faustino M. Faustini. 1987. *A Short History of the Servite Order*. Rome: General Secretariat for the Servite Missions.

Benediktsson, Bogi. 1909-15. *Sýslumannaæfir*. Vol. 4. Reykjavík: n.p.

Bengtsson, Herman. 2006. "Samtida mode eller antisemitism? Demonisering och rasistiska tendenser i medeltidens bildkonst." *Nordic Review of Iconography* 3-4: 4-41.

Benham, Hugh. 1993. "'Stroke' and 'Strene' Notation in Fifteenth- and Sixteenth-Century Equal-Note Cantus Firmi." *Plainsong and Medieval Music* 2: 15-68.

Bent, Margaret. 1968. "New and Little-Known Fragments of Early Medieval Polyphony." *Journal of the American Musicological Society* 21: 137-156.

Bent, Margaret. 1981. *Dunstaple*. London: Oxford University Press.

Bent, Margaret, and Roger Bowers. 1981. "The Saxilby Fragment." *Early Music History* 1: 1-27.

Bente, Martin, Marie Louise Göllner, Helmut Hell, and Bettina Wackernagel, eds. 1989. *Bayerische Staatsbibliothek. Katalog der Musikhandschriften: 1. Chorbücher und Handschriften in chorbuchartiger Notation*. Kataloge Bayerischer Musiksammlungen 1. Munich: Henle.

Berger, Karol. 1987. *Musica Ficta: Theories of Accidental Inflections in Vocal Polyphony from Marchetto Da Padova to Gioseffo Zarlino*. Cambridge: Cambridge University Press.

Berger, Teresa. 2011. *Gender Differences and the Making of Liturgical History: Lifting a Veil on Liturgy's Past*. Farnham: Ashgate.

Bermúdez, Egberto. 2017. "Sounds from Fortresses of Faith and Ideal Cities: Society, Politics, and Music in Missionary Activities in the Americas, 1525-1575." In *Listening to Early Modern Catholicism: Perspectives from Musicology*, edited by Daniele V. Filippi and Michael J. Noone, 301-25. Leiden: Brill.

Bermudo, Juan. 1555. *Comiença el libro llamado declaracion de instrumentos musicales*. Ossuna: Juan de León.

Bernard, G. W. 2010. *Anne Boleyn: Fatal Attractions*. New Haven: Yale University Press.

Bernau, Anke, and Bettina Bildhauer, eds. 2011. *Medieval Film*. Manchester: Manchester University Press.

Bernis Madrazo, Carmen. 1962. *Indumentaria española de tiempos de Carlos V*. Madrid: CSIC, Instituto Diego Velázquez.

Berthier, Joachim Joseph. 1910. *L'église de la Minerve à Rome*. Rome: Cooperativa tipografica Manuzio.

Berti, Luciano. 1991. "Ricordo di Filippino." In Luciano Berti and Umberto Baldini, *Filippino Lippi*, 25-118. Florence: Edizioni d'arte Il Fiorino.

Bertoni, Giulio. 1925. *Il maggior miniatore della Bibbia di Borso d'Este "Taddeo Crivelli"*. Modena: Orlandini.

Bertoni, Giulio. 1926. "La Biblioteca di Borso d'Este." *Atti della Reale Accademia delle Scienze di Torino* 41: 705-28.

Beuchat, Robin. 2009. "Formes diverses de la *varietas mundi*: Les *Observations* de Pierre Belon (1553)." *Versants: Revue suisse des littératures romanes* 56: 139-58.

Bicknell, Stephell. 1996. *The History of the English Organ*. Cambridge: Cambridge University Press.

Bierhorst, John, ed. and trans. 1985. *Cantares Mexicanos: Songs of the Aztecs*. Stanford, CA: Stanford University Press.

Bierhorst, John. 2009. *Ballads of the Lords of New Spain: The Codex* Romances de los señores de la Nueva España. Austin: University of Texas Press.

Billiet, Frédéric. 1997. "Témoignages insolites dans le chœur des églises européennes (XVe-XVIe)." In *Histoire, humanisme et hymnologie: Mélanges offerts au professeur Edith Weber*, edited by Pierre Guillot and Louis Jambou, 47-56. Paris: Presses de l'Université Paris-Sorbonne.

Billiet, Frédéric. 2002. "Un mobilier pour le chant: La vie musicale dans les stalles de la cathédrale d'Amiens." In *Actes du colloque de l'Université d'Amiens et de Rouen*, 21-36. Amiens: Encrage.

Billiet, Frédéric. 2011. "Choir-Stall Carvings: A Major Source for the Study of Medieval Musical Iconography." In *From Minor to Major: The Minor Arts in Medieval Art History*, edited by Colum Hourihane, 285-94. Princeton: Pennsylvania State University Press.

Billiet, Frédéric. 2019. "La modernité des scènes musicales dans les stalles de Gaillon au début du XVIe siècle." In *Musiques-Images-Instruments: Mélanges en l'honneur de Florence Gétreau*, edited by Fabien Guilloux, Catherine Massip, Alban Framboisier, and Yves Balmer, 197-211. Turnhout: Brepols.

Bindman, David, et al. 2010. *The Image of the Black in Western Art*. Vol. 3/1: *From the "Age of Discovery" to the Age of Abolition: Artists of the Renaissance and Baroque*. Cambridge, MA: Belknap Press.

Bischoff, Franz. 1990. "'Hans Engelberg': Der angebliche Sohn des Burkhard. Ein Beitrag zur Planungsgeschichte St. Katharina und zu Hans Hieber." *Zeitschrift des Historischen Vereins für Schwaben* 83: 7-29.

Biskup, Marian, and Roman Czaja, eds. 2008. *Państwo zakonu krzyżackiego w Prusach: Władza i społeczeństwo* [*The Teutonic State in Prussia: Government and Society*]. Warszawa: PWN.

Bisson, Massimo. 2012. *Meravigliose macchine di giubilo: L'arte e l'architettura degli organi a Venezia nel Rinascimento*. Venice: Fondazione Giorgio Cini.

Bizzarini, Marco. 2014. "Gli enigmi del Musico di Leonardo e dei cantori oltremontani alla corte sforzesca." In *Cultura oltremontana in Lombardia al tempo degli Sforza (1450-1535)*, edited by Frédéric Elsig and Claudia Gaggetta, 261-79. Rome: Viella.

Blackburn, Bonnie J. 1997. "For Whom Do the Singers Sing?" *Early Music* 25: 593-600, 602-06, 609.

Blackburn, Bonnie J. 2012. "Anna Inglese and Other Women Singers in the Fifteenth Century: Gleanings from the Sforza Archives." In *Sleuthing the Muse: Essays in Honor of William F. Prizer*, edited by Kristine K. Forney and Jeremy L. Smith, 237-52. Hillsdale, NY: Pendragon Press.

Blackburn, Bonnie J. 2015. "'Notes Secretly Fitted Together': Theorists on Enigmatic Canons – and on Josquin's Hercules Mass?" In *Qui Musicam in Se Habet: Studies in Honor of Alejandro Enrique Planchart*, edited by Anna Zayaruznaya, Bonnie J. Blackburn and Stanley Boorman, 743-60. Middleton: American Institute of Musicology.

Blackburn, Bonnie J., and Edward Lowinsky. 1993. "Luigi Zenobi and His Letter on the Perfect Musician." *Studi musicali* 22: 61-114.

Blair, Ann M. 1989. "Lectures on Ovid's 'Metamorphoses': The Class Notes of a 16th-Century Paris Schoolboy." *The Princeton University Library Chronicle* 50: 117-44.

Blair, Claude. 1974. *Arms, Armour and Base-Metalwork: The James A. de Rothschild Collection at Waddesdon Manor.* Fribourg: Office du Livre.

Blažeković, Zdravko. 2003. "Variations on the Theme of the Planets' Children, or Medieval Musical Life According to the Housebook's Astrological Imagery." In *Art and Music in the Early Modern Period*, edited by Katherine A. McIver, 241-86. Aldershot: Ashgate.

Blažeković, Zdravko. 2013. "Representations of Dance on Late-Medieval Bosnian Gravestones." In *Music & Ritual: Bridging Material & Living Cultures*, edited by Raquel Riménez, Rupert Till, and Mark Howell, 327-44. Berlin: ēchō Verlag.

Block, Elaine. 1998. "La chapelle et les stalles du château de Gaillon: Leurs secrets." In *Château et société castrale au Moyen Âge*, edited by Jean-Marc Pastré, 107-14. Rouen: Publications de l'Université de Rouen.

Block, Elaine. 1999. "L'influence italienne sur les stalles de chœur du château de Gaillon." In *Léonard de Vinci entre France et Italie*, edited by Silvia Fabrizio-Costa, 117-28. Caen: Presses universitaires de Caen.

Block, Elaine. 2003. *Corpus of Medieval Misericords*. Turnhout: Brepols.

Bloechl, Olivia A. 2019. "Case Study 2: The Catholic Mission to Japan, 1549-1614." In *The Cambridge History of Sixteenth-Century Music*, edited by Iain Fenlon and Richard Wistreich, 163-75. Cambridge: Cambridge University Press.

Bloom, Michelle E. 2003. *Waxworks: A Cultural Obsession*. Minneapolis: University of Minnesota Press.

Bloxam, M. Jennifer. 1992. "Sacred Polyphony and Local Traditions of Liturgy and Plainsong: Reflections on Music by Jacob Obrecht." In *Plainsong in the Age of Polyphony*, edited by Thomas Forrest Kelly, 140-77. Cambridge: Cambridge University Press.

Blume, Dieter. 2004. "Children of the Planets: The Popularisation of Astrology in the 15th Century." *Micrologus* 12: 549-63.

Boccaccio, Giovanni. 2011. *Genealogy of the Pagan Gods, Volume I: Books I-V*. Edited and translated by Jon Solomon. Cambridge, MA: Harvard University Press.

Böcher, Friederike. 2005. "'Bildung und Bildchen–Heinrich Schütz, die Musik und das Liebig-Bild': Liebig-Sammelbilder als Quelle für die Musikwissenschaft." In *Beiträge zur musikalischen Quellenforschung*. Vol. 6: *Beiträge der Kolloquien 2002 - 2003*, 71-126. Bad Köstritz: Forschungs- und Gedenkstätte im Geburtshaus des Komponisten, Heinrich-Schütz-Haus.

Bochi, Giulia, ed. 1961. *L'educazione femminile dall'Umanesimo alla Controriforma*. Bologna: Malipiero.

Boczkowska, Anna. 1985. "The King of Poland as David: The Idea of *Regnum Davidicum* in the Contents of the Tomb of Casimir Jagellon by Wit Stwosz." *Polish Art Studies* 6: 71-87.

Boeheim, Wendelin. 1888. "Urkunden und Regesten aus der k. k. Hofbibliothek." *Jahrbuch der Sammlungen des Allerhöchsten Kaiserhauses* 7: xci-cccxiii.

Bohatcová, Mirjam. 1982. "Farbige Figuralacrostichen aus der Offizin des Prager Druckers Georgius Nigrinus (1574/1581)." *Gutenberg-Jahrbuch* 57: 246-62.

Böhme, Hartmut. 1995. "Die Enthauptung von Johannes dem Täufer." In *Glaube, Hoffnung, Liebe, Tod*, edited by Christoph Geismar and Eleonora Louis, 379-84. Vienna-Klagenfurt: Kunsthalle-Ritter.

Bolens, Guillemette. 2012. *The Style of Gestures: Embodiment and Cognition in Literary Narrative*. Baltimore: John Hopkins University Press.

Bollini, Alessandra. 1986. "L'attività liutistica a Milano dal 1450 al 1550: Nuovi documenti." *Rivista Italiana di Musicologia* 21: 31-60.

Bonatti, Guido. 1506. *Decem continens tractatus astronomie*. Venice: Jacobus Pentius.

Böninger, Lorenz. 2006. *Die deutsche Einwanderung nach Florenz im Spätmittelalter*. Medieval Mediterranean 60. Leiden: Brill.

Boorman, Stanley. 2006. *Ottaviano Petrucci: A Catalogue Raisonné*. Oxford: University Press.

Bor, Joep. 1988. "The Rise of Ethnomusicology: Sources on Indian Music c.1780-c.1890." *Yearbook for Traditional Music* 20: 51-73.

Bordo, Susan. 2013. *The Creation of Anne Boleyn: A New Look at England's Most Notorious Queen*. Boston: Houghton Mifflin Harcourt.

Borghetti, Vincenzo. 2009. "Music and Representation of Princely Power in Late Medieval and Early Modern Europe." *Acta Musicologica* 80: 179-214.

Borghetti, Vincenzo. 2011. "Purezza e trasgressione: Il suono del medioevo dagli anni Cinquanta ad oggi." *Semicerchio* 44: 37-54.

Borghetti, Vincenzo. 2015. "The Listening Gaze: Alamire's Presentation Manuscripts and the Courtly Reader." *Journal of the Alamire Foundation* 7: 47-66 and 132-35.

Borghetti, Vincenzo. 2018. "La sovrana lettrice: Margherita d'Austria e il suo chansonnier (Bruxelles, Bibliothèque royale de Belgique, Ms 228)." In *Cara scientia mia, musica: Studi per Maria Caraci Vela*, 2 vols., edited by Angela Romagnoli, Daniele Sabaino, et al. 1:43-63. Pisa: ETS.

Borghetti, Vincenzo. 2019. "Matthaeus Pipelare, *Missa Fors seullement*." In *The Mechelen Choirbook: Study / Het Mechels Koorboek: Studie*, edited by David Burn, and Honey Meconi, 65-76, 162, 186, 197-202. Antwerp: Standaard/Davidsfonds.

Borja-Villel, Manuel. 2020. *Campos magnéticos: Escritos de arte y política*. Barcelona: Arcadia.

Bos, Agnès, and Jacques Dubois, 2007. "Les boiseries de la chapelle du château de Gaillon." In *L'art des frères d'Amboise: Les chapelles de l'hôtel de Cluny et du château de Gaillon. Exposition presentée du 3 octobre 2007 au 14 janvier 2008 au Musée national du Moyen âge-Thermes et Hôtel de Cluny 2007/2008*, 83-97. Paris: Réunion des musées nationaux.

Boscaro, Adriana. 1965. "La visita a Venezia della prima ambasceria giapponesi in Europa." *Giappone: Rivista trimestrale a cura del Centro di studi di cultura giapponese* 5: 19-32.

Boscaro, Adriana. 1973. *Sixteenth-Century European Printed Works of the First Japanese Mission to Europe: A Descriptive Bibliography*. Leiden: Brill.

Boscaro, Adriana. 1987. "Giapponesi a Venezia nel 1585." In *Venezia e l'Oriente*, edited by Lionello Lanciotti, 409-29. Florence: Olschki.

Bosi, Kathryn. 2016. "Tenshō Shōnen Shisetsu: The Reception of a Japanese at the Court of Mantua in 1585." In *Maestranze, artisti e apparatori per la scena dei Gonzaga (1480-1630)*, edited by Simona Brunetti, 230-43. Bari: Edizioni di Pagina.

Bosi, Kathryn. 2021. "European Music as Taught in Jesuit Seminaries in 16th Century Japan: The Case of Four Noble Youths who Visited the Pope in 1585." In *Interactions between Rivals: The Christian Mission and Buddhist Sects in Japan during the Portuguese Presence (c. 1549-c. 1647)*, edited by Alexandra Curvelo and Angelo Cattaneo, 211-38. Berlin: Peter Lang.

Bosman, Frank G. 2016. "'Nothing Is True, Everything Is Permitted': The Portrayal of the Nizari Isma'ilis in the Assassin's Creed Game Series." *Online - Heidelberg Journal of Religions on the Internet* 10. https://doi.org/10.17885/heiup.rel.23546.

Boström, Hans-Olof. 1994. "Philipp Hainhofer: Seine Kunstkammer und seine Kunstschränke." In *Macrocosmos in Microcosmo: Die Welt in der Stube: Zur Geschichte des Sammelns 1450 bis 1800*, edited by Andreas Grote, 555-80. Wiesbaden: Springer.

Botrel, Jean-François. 1973. "Les aveugles colporteurs d'imprimés en Espagne." *Mélanges de la Casa de Velázquez* 9: 417-82.

Boubín, Jaroslav. 2014. "Jan Čapek a Ktož jsú boží bojovníci" ["Jan Čapek and You Who Are the Warriors of God"]. In *Husitské století* [*The Hussite Century*], edited by Pavlína Cermanová, Robert Novotný, and Pavel Soukup, 508-09. Prague: Lidové noviny.

Bouvet, Sébastien. 2003. "Les couteaux de bénédicité conservés au musée national de la Renaissance." *Musique–Images–Instruments* 5: 138-47.

Bouza Álvarez, Fernando. 1995. "Joris Hoefnagel." In *De Mercator a Blaeu: España y la Edad de Oro de la cartografía en las diecisiete provincias de los Países Bajos*, edited by Fernando Bouza Álvarez, 141-43. Madrid: Fundación Carlos de Amberes.

Bowen, Karen L., and Dirk Imhof. 2008. *Christopher Plantin and Engraved Book Illustrations in Sixteenth-Century Europe*. Cambridge: Cambridge University Press.

Bowers, Roger. 1983. "The Performing Ensemble for English Church Polyphony, c.1320-c.1390." In *Studies in the Performance of Late Medieval Music*, edited by Stanley Boorman, 161-92. Cambridge: Cambridge University Press.

Bowers, Roger. 1987. "The Vocal Scoring, Choral Balance and Performing Pitch of Latin Church Polyphony in England, c.1500-58." *Journal of the Royal Musical Association* 112: 38-76.

Bowers, Roger. 1999. *English Church Polyphony: Singers and Sources from the 14th to the 17th Century*. Aldershot: Ashgate.

Boxer, C. R. 1951. *The Christian Century in Japan: 1549-1650*. Berkeley: University of California Press.

Boyden, James M. 1995. *The Courtier and the King: Ruy Gómez de Silva, Philip II and the Court of Spain*. Berkeley: University of California Press.

Brandel, Rose. 1961. *The Music of Central Africa: An Ethnomusicological Study*. The Hague: Martinus Nijhoff.

Branley, Brendan R. 2008. "Visual Rhetoric in Transcultural Communication in Sixteenth Century New Spain: The Engravings of Fray Diego Valadés." PhD diss., University of New Mexico, Albuquerque.

Brant, Sebastian. 1494. *Das Narren Schyff*. Basel: Johann Bergmann.

Braun, Georg, and Franz Hogenberg. 2008. *Civitates orbis terrarum = Cities of the world: 363 engravings revolutionize the view of the world: complete edition of the colour plates of 1572-1617*. Edited by Stephan Füssel. New York: Taschen.

Braun, Reiner, ed. 1991. *Die bayerischen Teile des Erzbistums Salzburg und des Bistums Chiemsee in der Visitation des Jahres 1558*. St Ottilien: EOS.

Brend, Barbara. 1995. *The Emperor Akbar's "Khamsa" of Nizami*. London: British Library.

Brett, Philip. 1972. "Did Byrd Write 'Non Nobis, Domine'?" *The Musical Times* 113: 855-57.

Brockmann, Stephen. 2006. *Nuremberg: The Imaginary Capital*. Rochester, NY: Camden House.

Brotzman, Ellis R. 1988. "Man and the Meaning of Nefes." *Bibliotheca Sacra* 145: 400-09.

Brown, Beverly Louise. 1981. "The Patronage and Building History of the Tribuna of SS. Annunziata in Florence: A Reappraisal in Light of New Documentation." *Mitteilungen des Kunsthistorischen Institutes in Florenz* 25: 59-146.

Brown, Christopher Boyd. 2005. *Singing the Gospel: Lutheran Hymns and the Success of the Reformation*. Cambridge, MA: Harvard University Press.

Brown, Clifford M. 2002. *"Per dare qualche splendore a la gloriosa cità di Mantua": Documents for the Antiquarian Collection of Isabella d'Este*. Rome: Bulzoni Editore.

Brown Clifford M., and Anna Maria Lorenzoni. 1999. "The 'studio del clarissimo Cavaliero Mozzanico in Venezia': Documents for the Antiquarian Ambitions of Francesco I de' Medici, Mario Bevilacqua, Alessandro Farnese, and Fulvio Orsini." *Jahrbuch der Berliner Museen* 41: 55-76.

Brown, Howard Mayer. 1975. "A Cook's Tour of Ferrara in 1529." *Rivista italiana di musicologia* 10: 216-41.

Brown, Howard Mayer. 1976. Review of *Instruments of the Middle Ages and Renaissance*. *Early Music* 4: 288-93.

Brown, Howard Mayer, and Louise K. Stein. 1999. *Music in the Renaissance*. 2nd edn. Upper Saddle River: Prentice Hall.

Brown, Judith. 1994. "Courtiers and Christians: The First Japanese Emissaries to Europe." *Renaissance Quarterly* 47: 872-906.

Brown, Sarah. 1999. *Stained Glass at York Minster*. London: Scala.

Brundin, Abigail, Deborah Howard, and Mary Laven. 2018. *The Sacred Home in Renaissance Italy*. Oxford: Oxford University Press.

Brunini, Marcello, et al. 2008. *Ecce Ancilla Domini: L'iconografia della Vergine Annunziata in Matteo Civitali scultore*. Pisa: Pacini.

Brunner, Horst. 1997. "Meistergesang." In *Die Musik in Geschichte und Gegenwart. Zweite, neubearbeitete Ausgabe* [MGG], edited by Ludwig Finscher, vol. 6 (Sachteil), 5-16. Kassel-Stuttgart-Weimar: Bärenreiter-Metzler.

Brunner, Horst. 2001. "Meistergesang." *Grove Music Online*.

Bruto, Giovanni Michele. 1598. *The Necessarie, Fit, and Couenient Education of a Yong Gentlewoman* [...]. London: Adam Islip.

Bryson, Norman. 2000. "Everything We Look at Is a Kind of Troy." In *Sugimoto: Portraits*, edited by Tracey Bashkoff and Nancy Spector, 54-65. New York: Guggenheim Museum Publications and Harry N. Abrams.

Buccheri, Alessandra. 2014. *The Spectacle of Clouds, 1439-1650: Italian Art and Theatre*. Farnham: Ashgate.

Buckley, Ann. 1998. "Music Iconography and the Semiotics of Visual Representation." *Music in Art* 23: 5-10.

Bugini, Elena. 2008. "Un 'testimonium' liutario del pensiero ficiniano: La lira da braccio androgina del Kunsthistorisches Museum di Vienna." *Journal de la Renaissance* 6: 239-48.

Bulman, Louisa M. 1971. "Artistic Patronage at Santissima Annunziata 1440-c.1520." PhD diss., Courtauld Institute, University of London.

Burgess, Clive. 2004. *The Pre-Reformation Records of All Saints' Bristol. Part III: Wills, the Halleway Chantry Records and Deeds*. Bristol: Bristol Record Society.

Burke, Jill. 2018a. "The Body in Artistic Theory and Practice." In *The Renaissance Nude*, edited by Thomas Kren with Jill Burke and Stephen J. Campbell, 183-246. Los Angeles: J. Paul Getty Museum.

Burke, Jill. 2018b. *The Italian Renaissance Nude*. New Haven: Yale University Press.

Burke, Jill, Stephen J. Campbell, and Thomas Kren. 2018. "Introduction: The Renaissance Nude, 1400-1530." In *The Renaissance Nude*, edited by Thomas Kren with Jill Burke, and Stephen J. Campbell, 1-13. Los Angeles: J. Paul Getty Museum.

Burke, Peter. 2000. "Repräsentation und Re-Präsentation: Die Inszenierung des Kaisers." In *Karl V. und seine Zeit: 1500-1558*, edited by Hugo Soly, Wim Blockmans and Peter Burke, 393-477. Cologne: DuMont.

Burn, David J. 2017. "The Leuven Chansonnier: A New Source for Late Fifteenth-Century Franco-Flemish Polyphonic Song." *Journal of the Alamire Foundation* 9: 135-58.

Burnett, Charles. 1993. "European Knowledge of Arabic Texts Referring to Music: Some New Material." *Early Music History* 12: 1-17.

Buron, Emmanuel. 2011. "'Faire en personnages': De la théorie de l'*Instructif* à la pratique du *Jardin de Plaisance*." *Cahiers de recherches médiévales et humanistes* 21: 205-23.

Burstyn, Shai. 1997. "In Quest of the Period Ear." *Early Music* 25: 692-701.

Busch, Karl. 1960. "Die Residenz der Wittelsbacher in München." In *Der Mönch im Wappen: Aus Geschichte und Gegenwart des katholischen München*, 259-83. Munich: Schnell & Steiner.

Busch-Salmen, Gabriele. 2000. "Die Frau am Tasteninstrument: Thesen zur Interpretation eines Bildtopos." In *Frauen- und Männerbilder in der Musik: Festschrift für*

Eva Rieger zum 60. Geburtstag, edited by Freia Hoffmann and Eva Rieger, 41-46. Oldenburg: Bibliotheks- und Informationssystem der Universität Oldenburg.

Busuioceanu, Alexandru. 1937. "Dipinti sconosciuti di Ercole Roberti e della sua scuola." *L'arte* 40: 161-82.

Busuioceanu, Alexandru. 1939. *La galerie de peintures de Sa Majesté le roi Carol II de Roumanie*. Paris: Edition d'études et de documents.

Buszin, Walter E. 1946. "Luther on Music." *Musical Quarterly* 32: 80-97.

Butler, Charles. 1636. *The Principles of Musik in Singing and Setting: With the Two-Fold Use Therof, Ecclesiasticall and Civil*. London: J. Haviland.

Butler, Katherine. 2015. *Music in Elizabethan Court Politics*. Woodbridge: Boydell and Brewer.

Butt, John. 2002. *Playing with History: The Historical Approach to Musical Performance*. Cambridge: Cambridge University Press.

Butterfield, Ardis. 2002. *Poetry and Music in Medieval France: From Jean de Renart to Guillaume de Machaut*. Cambridge: Cambridge University Press.

Bynum, Caroline Walker. 2006. *Wonderful Blood: Theology and Practice in Late Medieval Northern Germany and Beyond*. Philadelphia: University of Pennsylvania Press.

Cabrera de Córdoba, Luis. 1998. *Historia de Felipe II, rey de España*. 3 vols. Edited by José Martínez Millán and Carlos Morales. [Valladolid]: Junta de Castilla y León, Consejería de Educación y Cultura.

Caglioti, Francesco. 2004. "Su Matteo Civitali scultore." In *Matteo Civitali e il suo tempo: Pittori, scultori e orafi a Lucca nel tardo Quattrocento*, edited by Maria Teresa Filieri, 28-77. Cinisello Balsamo: Silvana.

Caglioti, Francesco. 2017. "'Falsi' veri e 'falsi' falsi nella scultura italiana del Rinascimento." In *Il falso, specchio della realtà*, edited by Anna Ottani Cavina and Mauro Natale, 105-56. Bologna and Turin: Fondazione Federico Zeri and Università di Bologna-Allemandi.

Calame-Levert, Florence, Maxence Hermant, and Gennaro Toscabo, eds. 2017. *Une Renaissance en Normandie: Le cardinal Georges d'Amboise, bibliophile et mécène*. Montreuil: Gourcuff-Gradenigo.

Caldeira, Arlindo Manuel. 2017. *Escravos em Portugal: Das Origens ao Século XX*. Lisbon: A Esfera dos Livros.

Caleffini, Ugo. 2006. *Croniche 1471-1494*. Serie Monumenti vol. 18. Ferrara: Deputazione Provinciale Ferrarese di Storia Patria.

Calmeta, Vincenzo. 1959. *Prose e Lettere Edite e Inedite*. Edited by Cecil Grayson. Bologna: Commissione per i Testi di Lingua.

Calogero, Elena Laura. 2006. "'Sweet aluring harmony': Heavenly and Earthly Sirens in Sixteenth and Seventeenth Century Literary and Visual Culture." In *Music of the Sirens*, edited by Linda Austern and Inna Naroditskaya, 140-75. Bloomington: Indiana University Press.

Calvesi, Maurizio. 1996. *La "Pugna d'amore in sogno" di Francesco Colonna romano*. Rome: Lithos.

Camerarius, Joachim. 1604. *Symbolorum et emblematum ex aquatilibus et reptilibus desumptorum centuria quarta*. Nuremberg: Vögelin.

Camille, Michael. 1985. "Seeing and Reading: Some Visual Implications of Medieval Literacy and Illiteracy." *Art History* 8: 26-49.

Camille, Michael. 1992. *Image on the Edge: The Margins of Medieval Art*. London: Reaktion Books.

Camille, Michael. 1998. *Mirror in Parchment: The Luttrell Psalter and the Making of Medieval England*. London: Reaktion Books.

Campbell, Margaret. 1975. *Dolmetsch: The Man and his Work*. London: Hamilton.

Campbell, Stephen J. 1997. *Cosmè Tura of Ferrara: Style, Politics, and the Renaissance City, 1450-1495*. New Haven: Yale University Press.

Canali, Ferruccio. 2006. "Il tondo del marchese Lodovico." In *L'uomo del Rinascimento: Leon Battista Alberti e le arti a Firenze tra ragione e bellezza*, edited by Cristina Acidini and Gabriele Morolli, 261-63. Florence: Mandragora.

Candelaria, Lorenzo. 2014. "Bernardino de Sahagún's *Psalmodia Christiana*: A Catholic Songbook from Sixteenth-Century New Spain." *Journal of the American Musicological Society* 67: 619-84.

Cantaro, Maria Teresa. 1989. *Lavinia Fontana Bolognese "pittora singolare" 1552-1614*. Milan: Jandi Sapi.

Cardamone, Donna G., ed. 1978. *Canzone Villanesche alla Napolitana and Villotte*. Recent Researches in the Music of the Renaissance 30. Madison: A-R Editions.

Carle, Lancelot de. 1545. *Épistre Contenant le Procès Criminel Faict à l'Encontre de la Royne Anne Boullant d'Angleterre*. Lyon: n.p.

Carnelos, Laura. 2016. "The Role of Blind Performers in Early Modern Italy." *Italian Studies* 71: 184-96.

Caroli, Flavio. 1987. *Sofonisba Anguissola e le sue sorelle*. Milan: Mondadori.

Carpitella, Diego. 1996. "L'esorcismo coreutico musicale del tarantismo." In Ernesto De Martino, *La terra del rimorso: Contributo fra cultura medica e terapia popolare*, 335-72. Milan: Il Saggiatore.

Carrasco, Rafael, and Bernard Vicent. 1987. "Amor y matrimonio entre los moriscos." In *Minorías y marginados en la España del siglo XVI*, edited by Bernard Vicent, 47-71. Granada: Diputación Provincial de Granada.

Carvalho, Pedro Moura. 2012. *Mir 'āt al-quds (Mirror of Holiness): A Life of Christ for Emperor Akbar*. Leiden: Brill.

Cary, Phillip. 2000. *Augustine's Invention of the Inner Self: The Legacy of a Christian Platonist*. Oxford: Oxford University Press.

Casado Soto, José Luis, and Agustín Hernando Rica. 2016. *Civitates orbis terrarum*. Salamanca: CM Editores.

Casalini, Eugenio M. 1995. *Michelozzo di Bartolommeo e l'Annunziata di Firenze*. Biblioteca della provincia toscana dei Servi di Maria 6. Florence: Convento della SS. Annunziata.

Casalini, Eugenio M., et al., eds. 1987. *Tesori d'arte dell'Annunziata di Firenze*. Florence: Alinari.

Casella, Maria Teresa, and Giovanni Pozzi. 1959. *Francesco Colonna: Biografia e opere*. 2 vols. Padua: Antenore.

Castellani, Marcello. 1973. "A 1593 Veronese Inventory." *Galpin Society Journal* 26: 15-24.

Castiglione, Baldassare. 1544. *Il cortegiano del conte Baldessar Castiglione* [...]. Venice: Gabriel Giolito.

Castiglione, Baldassare. 1561. *The Courtyer of Count Baldessar Castilio*. Translated by Thomas Hoby. London: Wyllyam Seres.

Castiglione, Baldassare. 1967. *The Book of the Courtier*. Translated by George Bull. London: Penguin.

Castillo Ferreira, Mercedes. 2016. "Chant, Liturgy and Reform." In *A Companion to Music in the Age of the Catholic Monarchs*, edited by Tess Knighton, 282-322. Leiden: Brill.

Catalogue. 1912. *Catalogue of Books Printed in the XVth Century Now in the British Museum, Part II Germany Eltvil-Trier*. London: British Museum.

Cátedra, Pedro M. 2002. *Invención, difusión y recepción de la literatura popular impresa (siglo XVI)*. Mérida: Junta de Extremadura.

Cauchies, Jean-Marie. 2003. *Philippe le Beau: Le dernier duc de Bourgogne*. Turnhout: Brepols.

Cavallini, Ivano. 2017. "The 'Other' Coastal Areas of Venice: Musical Ties with Istria and Dalmatia." In *A Companion to Music in Sixteenth-Century Venice*, edited by Katelijne Schiltz, 493-527. Leiden: Brill.

Cavicchi, Adriano. 1985. "L'organo della Cattedrale nella tradizione musicale e organaria ferrarese: Una proposta di ricostruzione ideale." In *San Giorgio e la Principessa di Cosmè Tura: Dipinti restaurati per l'officina ferrarese*, edited by Jadranka Bentini, 95-122. Bologna: Nuova Alfa Editoriale.

Cavicchi, Camilla. 2006. "Maistre Jhan alla corte degli Este (1512-1538)." PhD diss., University of Bologna.

Cavicchi, Camilla. 2013. "La scena di iatromusica nella *Phonurgia Nova* di Athanasius Kircher." *Medicina & storia: Rivista di Storia della Medicina e della Sanità* 11: 75-88.

Cavicchi, Camilla. 2015. "Pietrobono Burzelli detto dal Chitarino." *Dizionario Biografico degli Italiani*. Vol. 83. Rome: Treccani. http://www.treccani.it/enciclopedia/pietrobono-burzelli-detto-dal-chitarino_%28Dizionario-Biografico%29/.

Cecchi, Paolo. 2002. "'Ov'è condotto il mio amoroso stile?' Poetica e committenza nei madrigali di Marenzio dedicati a Mario Bevilacqua." *Musica e Storia* 10: 439-49.

Cermanová, Pavlína, Robert Novotný, and Pavel Soukup, eds. 2014. *Husitské století* [*The Hussite Century*]. Prague: Lidové noviny.

Černý, Jaromír, et al., eds. 2005. *Historická antologie hudby v českých zemích (do ca 1530) / Historical Anthology of Music in the Bohemian Lands (up to ca 1530)*. Prague: Koniasch Latin Press.

Cervio, Vincenzio. 1581. *Il trinciante*. Venice: Tramezini.

Chailley, Jacques. 1969. "La danse religieuse au moyen âge." In *Arts libéraux et philosophie au moyen âge: Actes du IVe Congrès international de Philosophie médiévale (Université de Montréal, 27 août-2 septembre 1967)*, 357-80. Montréal and Paris: Institut d'études médiévales.

Chamberlain, David S. 1970. "Philosophy of Music in the *Consolatio* of Boethius." *Speculum* 45: 80-97.

Champion, Matthew S. 2017. *The Fullness of Time: Temporalities of the Fifteenth-Century Low Countries*. Chicago: University of Chicago Press.

Chan, Eleanor. 2020. "What we mean when we talk about style: The 'Redolent' Eglantine Table (c.1568)." *Word & Image* 36, no. 3: 248-260.

Chaparro Gómez, César. 2015. *Fray Diego Valadés: Evangelizador franciscano en Nueva España*. Badajoz: CEXECI.

Charles-Dominique, Luc. 1994. *Les ménétriers français sous l'ancien régime*. Toulouse: Klincksieck.

Chater, James. 1997. "'Un pasticcio di madrigaletti?' The Early Musical Fortune of *Il pastor fido*." In *Guarini, la musica, i musicisti*, edited by Angelo Pompilio, 139-55. Lucca: Libreria Musicale Italiana.

Cheetham, Francis. 1984. *English Medieval Alabasters: With a Catalogue of the Collection in the Victoria and Albert Museum*. Oxford: Phaidon.

Cheetham, Francis. 2003. *Alabaster Images of Medieval England*. Woodbridge: Boydell / Association for Cultural Exchange.

Chevalier, Jean, and Alain Gheerbaert. 1996. *Dictionnaire des symboles: Mythes, rêves, coutumes, gestes, formes, figures, couleurs, nombres*. Paris: Robert Laffont / Jupiter.

Chevalier, Tracy. 2004. *The Lady and the Unicorn*. London: Penguin.

Christian, Kathleen W., Clare E. L. Guest, and Claudia Wedepohl, eds. 2014. *The Muses and Their Afterlife in Post-Classical Europe*. London: Warburg Institute.

Christie's. 2006. "Lot 3, Sale 5013. Follower of Pieter Coecke van Aelst. *An Allegory of the Transience of Earthly Beauty*." www.christies.com/lotfinder/Lot/follower-of-pieter-coecke-van-aelst-an-4697233-details.aspx.

Christie's. 2007. "Lot 33, Sale 7530. The Master of the Female Half-Lengths. *A Vanitas with a Lady Playing a Lute and a Man Holding a Skull and a Mirror*." www.christies.com/lotfinder/Lot/the-master-of-the-female-half-lengths-active-4942856-details.aspx.

Chytil, Karel. 1918. "Mistr Tomáš Jaroš z Brna" ["Master Tomáš Jaroš of Brno"]. In *Ročenka Kruhu pro pěstování dějin umění za rok 1917* [*Yearbook of the Circle for the Cultivation of Art History for 1917*], edited by František Xaver Harlas and Ješek Hofman, 20-28. Prague: Kruh pro pěstování dějin umění [Circle for the cultivation of art history].

Clegg, Roger, and Lucie Skeaping. 2014. *Singing Simpkin and Other Bawdy Jigs*. Exeter: University of Exeter Press.

Coelho, Victor Anand. 2008. "Music in New Worlds." In *The Cambridge History of Seventeenth-Century Music*, edited by Tim Carter and John Butt, 88-110. Cambridge: Cambridge University Press.

Cohen, Evelyn M. 1992. "L'artista della 'Haggadah di Prato': Tradizionalista ed innovatore." In *Il Codice Miniato: Rapporti tra codice, testo e figurazione. Atti del III Congresso di Storia della Miniatura. Cortona, 20-23 ottobre 1988*, edited by Melania Ceccanti and Maria Cristina Castelli, 439-84. Florence: Olschki.

Collijn, Isak. 1932-33. *Sveriges bibliografi intil år 1600*. Vol. 3: *1583-1599*. Uppsala: Svenska Litteratursällskapet.

Collijn, Isak, ed. 1923. *Handlingar rörande Helga Lekamens Gille i Stockholm*. Uppsala: Almqvist & Wiksell.

Collins, David. 1976. "A 16th Century Manuscript in Wood: The Eglantine Table at Hardwick Hall." *Early Music* 4: 275-80.

Collins, Karen. 2008. *Game Sound: An Introduction to the History, Theory, and Practice of Video Game Music and Sound Design*. Cambridge, MA: MIT Press.

Collinson, Francis. 1975. *The Bagpipe: The History of a Musical Instrument*. London: Routledge & Kegan Paul.

[Colonna, Francesco]. 1499. *Hypnerotomachia Poliphili: Ubi humana omnia non nisi somnium esse docet atque obiter plurima scitu sane quam digna commemorat*. Venice: Manuzio.

Colonna, Francesco. 1980. *Hypnerotomachia Poliphili*. Edited and commented by Giovanni Pozzi and Lucia A. Ciapponi. Padua: Antenore.

Colonna, Francesco. 1999. *Hypnerotomachia Poliphili: The Strife of Love in a Dream*. Translated by Joscelyn Godwin. New York: Thames & Hudson.

Colonna, Francesco. (1998) 2004. *Hypnerotomachia Poliphili*. 2 vols. Edited by Marco Ariani and Mino Gabriele. Milan: Adelphi.

Colonna, Stefano. 2009. *La fortuna critica dell'"Hypnerotomachia Poliphili"*. Rome: CAM.

Colton, Lisa. 2017. *Angel Song: Medieval English Music in History*. Abingdon: Routledge.

Coluzzi, Seth. 2013. "'Se vedesti qui dentro': Monteverdi's 'O, Mirtillo, Mirtillo anima mia' and Artusi's Offence." *Music & Letters* 94: 1-37.

Coluzzi, Seth. 2014. "Tirsi mio, caro Tirsi: *Il pastor fido* and the Roman Madrigal." In *Perspectives in Luca Marenzio's Secular Music*, edited by Mauro Calcagno, 51-73. Turnhout: Brepols.

Cook, James. 2019. *The Cyclic Mass: Anglo-Continental Exchange in the Fifteenth-Century*. New York: Routledge.

Cook, James, Alexander Kolassa, and Adam Whittaker. 2018. "Introduction: Understanding the Present through the Past and the Past through the Present." In *Recomposing the Past: Representations of Early Music on Stage and Screen*, edited by James Cook, Alexander Kolassa, and Adam Whittaker, 1-14. New York: Routledge.

Cook, James, Alexander Kolassa, and Adam Whittaker, eds. 2018a. *Recomposing the Past: Representations of Early Music on Stage and Screen*. New York: Routledge.

Cook, Karen M. 2018. "Beyond (the) Halo: Plainchant in Video Games." In *Studies in Medievalism, XXVII: Authenticity, Medievalism, Music*, edited by Karl Fugelso, 183-200. Woodbridge: Boydell & Brewer.

Cook, Karen M. 2020. "Gaming the Medievalist World in *Harry Potter*." In *The Oxford Handbook of Medievalism in Music*, edited by Stephen C. Meyer and Kirsten Yri, 750-63. Oxford: Oxford University Press.

Cooper, Michael. 2005. *The Japanese Mission to Europe, 1582-1590: The Journey of Four Samurai Boys Through Portugal, Spain and Italy*. Folkestone: Global Oriental.

Coover, James, and Richard Colvig. 1964. *Medieval and Renaissance Music on Long-Playing Records*. Detroit: Information Service.

Coover, James, and Richard Colvig. 1973. *Medieval and Renaissance Music on Long-Playing Records: Supplement, 1962-1971*. Detroit: Information Service.

Copia di due lettere. 1593. *Copia di due lettere annue scritte dal Giapone del 1589. & 1590. L'vna dal p. viceprouinciale al p. Alessandro Valignano, l'altra dal p. Luigi Frois al p. Generale della Compagnia di Giesu. Et dalla spagnuola nella italiana lingua tradotte dal p. Gasparo Spitilli della Compagnia medesima*. Rome: Zannetti.

Corbin, Solange. 1951. "Les textes musicaux de l'Auto da Alma." In *Mélanges d'Histoire du moyen âge dédiés à la mémoire de Louis Haplhen*, 137-43. Paris: Presses Universitaires de France.

Corbin, Alain. 1995. *Time, Desire, and Horror: Towards a History of the Senses*. Translated by Jean Birrell. Cambridge, MA: Polity.

Córdova Salinas, Diego de. (1651) 1957. *Crónica Franciscana de las provincias del Perú*. Washington, DC: Academy of American Franciscan History.

Čornej, Petr. 2000. *Velké dějiny zemí Koruny české* [*The Great History of the Lands of the Bohemian Crown*]. Vol. 5: *1402-1437*. Prague-Litomyšl: Paseka.

Cornell, Henrik, and Sigurd Wallin. 1972. *Albertus Pictor: Sten Stures och Jacob Ulvssons målare*. Stockholm: Bonnier.

Corradi, Giulio Cesare. 1698. *Il gran Tamerlano, drama per musica*. Venice: Per i Nicolini.

Corry, Maya, Deborah Howard, and Mary Laven, eds. 2017. *Madonnas and Miracles: The Holy Home in Renaissance Italy*. London: Philip Wilson Publishers.

Cortés García, Manuela. 2018. *La música árabe y andalusí de las dos orillas en los estudios musicológicos: ss. XVII-XXI*. Granada: Ediciones del Genal.

Costello, Bonnie. 1992. "Jorie Graham: Art and Erosion." *Contemporary Literature* 33, "American Poetry of the 1980s": 373-95.

Covarrubias Orozco, Sebastián de. (1611) 1984. *Tesoro de la lengua castellana o española*. Madrid: Turner.

Craigie, James. 1955-58. *The Poems of James VI of Scotland*. Edinburgh: Scottish Text Society.

Craig-McFeely, Julia. 2002. "The Signifying Serpent: Seduction by Culture Stereotype in Seventeenth-Century England." In *Music, Sensation and Sensuality*, edited by Linda Phyllis Austern, 299-317. New York: Routledge.

Croce, Giulio Cesare. 1599. *I parenti godevoli*. Bologna: Giovanni Rossi.

Croce, Giulio Cesare. 1601. *Gioco della sposa*. Ferrara: Vittorio Baldini.

Croce, Giulio Cesare. 1604. *Mascherate piacevolissime*. Bologna: Heredi di Giovanni Rossi.

Croce, Giulio Cesare. 1639. *Barceletta piacevolissima sopra i fanciulli, che vanno vendendo le ventarole per la città, & un capitolo, e lode sopra la bella ventarola*. Bologna: Eredi del Cochi.

Crociani, Lamberto. 1987. "La liturgia." In *Tesori d'arte dell'Annunziata di Firenze*, edited by Eugenio Casalini et al., 137-60. Florence: Alinari.

Crook, David. 1994. *Orlando di Lasso's Imitation Magnificats for Counter-Reformation Munich*. Princeton: Princeton University Press.

Crosby, Brian. 1992. "The Choral Foundation of Durham Cathedral c.1350-c.1650." 2 vols. PhD diss., University of Durham.

Crosby, C. Russell, ed. 1967. *Die Flötnerschen Spielkarten und andere Curiosa der Musiküberlieferung des 16. Jahrhunderts in Franken*. Denkmäler der Tonkunst in Bayern. Neue Folge. Sonderband 1. Wiesbaden: Breitkopf & Härtel.

Crossman, Colette. 2015. "Seeing the Sacred: Burne-Jones's Reception as a 'Great Religious Painter.'" *19th Century Art Worldwide*, Summer. http://www.19thc-artworldwide.org/summer15/crossman-on-burne-jones-s-reception-as-a-great-religious-painter.

Croucher, Trevor. 1981. *Early Music Discography: From Plainsong to the Sons of Bach. 1981 Edition*. London: The Library Association.

Cruces Roldán, Cristina. 2003. *El flamenco y la música andalusí: Argumentos para un encuentro*. Barcelona: Carena.

Crusius, Martin. 1927-61. *Diarium Martini Crusii* [1596-1605]. 4 vols. Edited by Wilhelm Göz et al. Tübingen: Laupp.

Cullington, J. Donald, ed. and trans., with Reinhard Strohm. 2001. *'That Liberal and Virtuous Art': Three Humanist Treatises on Music*. Newtownabbey: University of Ulster.

Cupperi, Walter, Martin Hirsch, Annette Kranz, and Ulrich Pfisterer, eds. 2013. *Wettstreit in Erz: Porträtmedaillen der deutschen Renaissance*. Berlin: Deutscher Kunstverlag.

Curry, Robert. 2011. "Music East of the Rhine." In *The Cambridge Companion to Medieval Music*, edited by Mark Everist, 171-82. Cambridge: Cambridge University Press.

Czajkowski, Stanisław. 2000. "*Stabat mater* Josquina des Prés w nieznanej kopii wawelskiej z początku XVIII wieku" ["Josquin des Prés's *Stabat Mater* in an Unknown Copy from Wawel Cathedral in Kraków from the Beginning of the Eighteenth Century"]. *Muzyka* 45: 59-65.

Czepiel, Tomasz M. M. 1996. *Music at the Royal Court and Chapel in Poland, c. 1543-1600*. New York: Garland.

D'Accone, Frank A. 1961. "The Singers of San Giovanni in Florence during the 15th Century." *Journal of the American Musicological Society* 14: 307-58.

D'Accone, Frank A. 2001. "Sacred Music in Florence in Savonarola's Time." In *Una città e il suo profeta: Firenze di fronte al Savonarola*, edited by Gian Carlo Garfagnini, 311-54. Florence: SISMEL Edizioni del Galluzzo.

d'Alvarenga, João Pedro. 2019. "Juan de Anchieta and the Iberian Motet around 1500." *Acta Musicologica* 91: 1-27.

d'Anterroches, Cécile Meneau. 2014. "Autour des stalles du château de Gaillon, l'art, les artistes et les commanditaires en France dans les années 1500." MA diss., Université de Grenoble.

d'Erlanger, Rodolphe. 1938. *La musique arabe*. 6 vols. Vol. 3. Paris: Librairie Orientaliste Paul Geuthner.

Dabac, Tošo. 1963. *Bogomil Sculpture*. Preface by Oto Bihalji-Merin and Alojz Benac. New York: Harcourt, Brace & World. [Also published as: *Stećci*. Belgrad: Jugoslavija, 1962; *L'art des Bogomiles*. Paris: Arthaud, 1963; and *Steine der Bogomilen*. Vienna: A. Schroll, 1964].

Dacos, Nicole, Bert W. Meijer, and Chris Billen. 1995. *Fiamminghi a Roma: 1508-1608. Artisti dei Paesi Bassi e del Principato di Liegi a Roma durante il Rinascimento*. Milan: Skira.

Dal Pino, Andrea M. 1953. "Il 'De Reverentiis Beatae Mariae Virginis' nelle Costituzioni dei Servi di Maria." *Studi Storici dell'Ordine dei Servi di Maria* 5: 202-53.

Dal Pino, Franco Andrea, et al., eds. 2002. *Fonti storico-spirituali dei servi di Santa Maria*. Vol. 2: *Dal 1349 al 1495*. Gorle: Servitium.

Damiani, Giovanna. 1992. "La Madonna dell'Umiltà e cinque angeli." In *Una scuola per Piero: Luce, colore e prospettiva nella formazione Fiorentina di Piero della Francesca*, edited by Luciano Bellosi, 59-63. Venice: Marsilio.

Daolmi, Davide, ed. 2017. *Ritratto di Gaffurio*. Lucca: Libreria Musicale Italiana.

Darnton, Robert. 1984. *The Great Cat Massacre*. London: Penguin.

Dati, Gregorio. ca. 1475. *La sfera*. Venice: Gabriele di Pietro.

Davidsson, Åke. 1957. *Studier rörande svenskt musiktryck före år 1750*. Uppsala: Almqvist & Wiksells Boktryckeri AB.

Davies, Glyn, and Kirstin Kennedy, eds. 2009. *Medieval and Renaissance Art: People and Possessions*. London: V&A Publications.

Davies, Paul, and David Hemsoll. 1991. "Palazzo Bevilacqua e la tipologia del palazzo veronese." *Annali di Architettura* 3: 58-69.

Davis, Natalie Zemon. 1975. *Society and Culture in Early Modern France*. Stanford: Stanford University Press.

Day, Thomas. 1971. "A Renaissance Revival in Eighteenth-Century England." *The Musical Quarterly* 57: 575-92.

Daye, Anne. 2008. "The Jacobean Antimasque Within the Masque Context: A Dance Perspective." PhD diss., Roehampton University and University of Surrey.

Daza, Esteban. 1576. *Libro de Musica en cifras para Vihuela intitulado el Parnasso*. Valladolid: Diego Fernández de Córdoba.

de Boer, Wietse, and Christine Göttler, eds. 2013. *Religion and the Senses in Early Modern Europe*. Intersections 26. Leiden: Brill.

De Fraine, Jean. 1959. "Le démon du midi (Ps. 91 (6))." *Biblica* 40: 372-83.

De Labriolle, Pierre. 1934. "Le démon de midi." *Bulletin du Cange: Archivum Latinitatis Medii Aevi* 9: 46-54.

De Martino, Ernesto. 1996. *La terra del rimorso: Contributo fra cultura medica e terapia popolare*. Milan: Il Saggiatore.

De Morgan, Jaques. 1981. *Histoire du peuple Arménien*. Île de Saint-Lazare: Imprimérie des Pères Mechitaristes.

De Oré, Fray Luis Jerónimo. (1598) 1992. *Symbolo catholico indiano*. Lima: Australis.

De Souzenelle, Annick. 1991. *Le symbolisme du corps humain*. Paris: Albin Michel.

Dean, Jeffrey J. 2017. "The Polyphonic Vesperal Manuscript Type, Du Faÿ's Hymns, and Institutional Identity in the Papal Chapel." In *Sources of Identity: Makers, Owners and Users of Music Sources Before 1600*, edited by Lisa Colton and Tim Shephard, 133-68. Turnhout: Brepols.

Debae, Marguerite. 1995. *La bibliothèque de Marguerite d'Autriche: Essai de reconstitution d'après l'inventaire de 1523-1524*. Leuven: Peeters.

Debut, Vincent, Miguel Carvalho, Elin Figueiredoc, José Antunes, and Rui Silva. 2016. "The Sound of Bronze: Virtual Resurrection of a Broken Medieval Bell." *Journal of Cultural Heritage* 19: 544-54.

Decor puellarum. 1471. Venice: Nicolaus Jenson.

Degl'Innocenti, Luca, and Massimo Rospocher. 2016. "Street Singers: An Interdisciplinary Perspective." *Italian Studies* 71: 149-53.

Degl'Innocenti, Luca, and Massimo Rospocher. 2019. "Urban Voices: The Hybrid Figure of the Street Singer in Renaissance Italy." *Renaissance Studies* 33: 17-41.

Degli Esposti, Giovanna. 1985. "Le portelle d'organo." In *San Giorgio e la Principessa di Cosmè Tura: Dipinti restaurati per l'officina ferrarese*, edited by Jadranka Bentini, 123-40. Bologna: Nuova Alfa Editoriale.

Delgado Morales, Manuel. 2014. "The Quest for Spiritual Transcendence in the Theater of Gil Vicente." In *A Companion to Early Modern Hispanic Theater*, edited by Hilaire Kallendorf, 217-77. Leiden: Brill.

Delisle, Léopold Victor. 1868. *Le Cabinet des manuscrits de la Bibliothèque impériale, Tome I*. Paris: Imprimerie impériale.

Dennis, Flora. 2006. "Music." In *At Home in Renaissance Italy*, edited by Marta Ajmar-Wollheim and Flora Dennis, 228-43. London: V&A Publications.

Dennis, Flora. 2010a. "Scattered Knives and Dismembered Song: Cutlery, Music and the Rituals of Dining." *Renaissance Studies* 24: 156-84.

Dennis, Flora. 2010b. "Resurrecting Forgotten Sound: Fans and Handbells in Early Modern Italy." In *Everyday Objects: Medieval and Early Modern Material Culture and Its Meanings*, edited by Catherine Richardson and Tara Hamling, 191-209. Aldershot: Ashgate.

Dennis, Flora. 2010c. "Unlocking the Gates of Chastity: Music and the Erotic in the Domestic Sphere in Fifteenth- and Sixteenth-Century Italy." In *The Erotic Cultures of Early Modern Italy*, edited by Sara Matthews-Grieco, 223-45. Aldershot: Ashgate.

Dennis, Flora. 2017. "Musical Sound and Material Culture." In *The Routledge Handbook of Material Culture in Early Modern Europe*, edited by Catherine Richardson, Tara Hamling, and David Gaimster, 371-82. New York: Routledge.

Denores, Giason. 1586. *Discorso [...] intorno a que' principii, cause, et accrescimenti, che la comedia, la tragedia, et il poema heroico ricevono dalla philosophia morale, et civile, et da' governatori delle Repubbliche*. Padua: Meietti.

Denores, Giason. 1590. *Apologia contra l'auttor del Verato [...] di quanto ha egli detto in un suo discorso delle tragicomedie, et delle pastorali*. Padua: Meietti.

Di Bacco, Giuliano, and Yolanda Plumley, eds. 2013. *Citation, Intertextuality and Memory in the Middle Ages and Renaissance*. Vol. 1. Exeter: The University of Exeter Press, 2011. Vol. 2. Liverpool: Liverpool University Press.

di Lasso, Orlando. 2019. *The Complete Motets*. Vol. 20. Edited by David Crook. Recent Researches in the Music of the Renaissance 147. Madison: A-R Editions.

Dickey, Timothy J. 2008. "An Undiscovered Sienese *Lauda*, *Adoramus te, Christe*, and the Provenance of Domenico di Bartolo's *Madonna of Humility* (1433)." *Explorations in Renaissance Culture* 34: 91-123.

Didi-Huberman, Georges. 2000. *Être crâne: Lieu, contact, pensée, sculpture*. Paris: Les Éditions de Minuit.

Diemer, Dorothea. 1995. "Antonio Brocco und der 'Singende Brunnen' in Prag." *Jahrbuch der kunsthistorischen Sammlungen* 91: 18-36.

Dillon, Emma. 2002. *Medieval Music-Making and the "Roman de Fauvel"*. Cambridge: Cambridge University Press.

Dillon, Emma. 2012. *The Sense of Sound: Musical Meaning in France 1260-1330*. Oxford: Oxford University Press.

Dillon, Emma. 2018. "Song and the Soundscape of Old French Romance." In *Thinking Medieval Romance*, edited by Katherine C. Little and Nicola McDonald, 155-69. Oxford: Oxford University Press.

Długosz, Jan. 1985. *Annales seu cronicae inditi Regni Poloniae. Liber decimus 1370-1405*. Warsaw: PWN.

Dobbins, Frank. 1992. *Music in Renaissance Lyons*. Oxford: Clarendon Press.

Dodgson, Campbell. 1903. *Catalogue of Early German and Flemish Woodcuts Preserved in the Department of Prints and Drawings in the British Museum*. London: British Museum.

Dolce, Ludovico. 1557. *Dialogo della pittura*. Florence: Nestenus and Moücke.

Dolmetsch, Mabel. 1957. *Personal Recollections of Arnold Dolmetsch*. London: Routledge & Kegan Paul.

Donnelly, K. J., William Gibbons, and Neil Lerner, eds. 2014. *Music in Video Games: Studying Play*. New York: Routledge.

Dooley, Brendon, ed. 2014. *A Companion to Astrology in the Renaissance*. Leiden: Brill.

Doutrepont, Georges, and Omer Jodogne, eds. 1935-37. *Chroniques de Jean Molinet*. 3 vols. Brussels: Palais des Académies.

Drew, Reginald. 1912. *Anne Boleyn*. Boston: Sherman, French & Company.

Dreyfus, Laurence. 1983. "Early Music Defended against Its Devotees: A Theory of Historical Performance in the Twentieth Century." *The Musical Quarterly* 69: 297-322.

Duffin, Ross. 1989. "The *trompette des menestrels* in the 15th-Century *alta capella*." *Early Music* 17: 397-402.

Duggan, Mary Kay. 1992. *Italian Music Incunabula: Printers and Type*. Berkeley: University of California Press.

Duggan, Mary Kay. 2010. "Fifteenth-Century Music Printing: Reform, Uniformitas, and Local Tradition." In *NiveauNischeNimbus: Die Anfänge des Musikdrucks Nördlich der Alpen*, edited by Birgit Lodes, 17-31. Tutzing: Schneider.

Duggan, Mary Kay. 2018. "Early Music Printing and Ecclesiastic Patronage." In *Early Music Printing in German-Speaking Lands*, edited by Andrea Lindmayr-Brandl, Elisabeth Giselbrecht, and Grantley McDonald, 21-45. Abingdon: Routledge.

Duguid, Timothy. 2014. *Metrical Psalmody in Print and Practice: English* Singing Psalms *and Scottish* Psalm Buiks, *c. 1547-1640*. Farnham: Ashgate.

Dunlap, Rhodes. 1926. "King James' Own Masque." *Philological Quarterly* 41: 249-56.

Earle, Tom F., and Kate J. P. Lowe, eds. 2005. *Black Africans in Renaissance Europe*. Cambridge: Cambridge University Press.

Eco, Umberto. 1986. "Dreaming of the Middle Ages." In *Travels in Hyperreality*, translated by Harcourt Brace Jovanovich, translation revised by William Weaver, 61-72. New York: Harcourt.

Edinger, Dora. 1948. "Rilke and the Tapestries of the Lady with the Unicorn." *The Metropolitan Museum of Art Bulletin*, New Series 6: 166-68.

Edwards, Richard. 1576. *The Paradyse of Daynty Deuises Aptly Furnished, with Sundry Pithie and Learned Inuentions*. London: Henry Disle.

Égloga representada. 1496. *Égloga representada por las mesmas personas que en la de arriba van introduzidas, que son: un pastor que de antes era escudero, llamado Gil, y Pascuala, y Mingo y su esposa Menga* [...]. In Juan del Encina, *Cancionero*. Salamanca: s.n. http://www.cervantesvirtual.com/obra-visor/egloga-de-mingo-gil-y-pascuala--0/html/ff978b36-82b1-11df-acc7-002185ce6064_2.html.

Ehrenschwendtner, Marie-Luise. 2009. "Virtual Pilgrimages? Enclosure and the Practice of Piety at St Katherine's Convent, Augsburg." *Journal of Ecclesiastical History* 60: 45-73.

Eichberger, Dagmar. 2002. *Leben mit Kunst, Wirken durch Kunst: Sammelwesen und Hofkunst unter Margarete von Österreich, Regentin der Niederlande*. Turnhout: Brepols.

Eichberger, Dagmar. 2005a. "Margaret of Austria 1480-1530: *Fortune infortune fort une*." In *Women of Distinction: Margaret of York, Margaret of Austria*, edited by Dagmar Eichberger, 26-27. Leuven: Brepols-Davidsfonds.

Eichberger, Dagmar. 2005b. "Margareta of Austria: A Princess with Ambition and Political Insight." In *Women of Distinction: Margaret of York, Margaret of Austria*, edited by Dagmar Eichberger, 49-55. Leuven: Brepols-Davidsfonds.

Eichner, Barbara. 2011. "Sweet Singing in Three Voices: A Musical Source from a South German Convent?" *Early Music* 39: 335-47.

Eichner, Barbara. 2021. "Dominikanerinnenkloster St. Katharina." In *Stiften gehen! Wie man aus Not eine Tugend macht*, edited by Heidrun Lange-Krach, 122-25. Regensburg: Schnell & Steiner.

Eire, Carlos M. N. 1995. *From Madrid to Purgatory: The Art of Dying in Sixteenth-Century Spain*. Cambridge: Cambridge University Press.

Elders, Willem. 1994. *Symbolic Scores: Studies in the Music of the Renaissance*. Leiden: Brill.

Elferen, Isabella van. 2011. "¡Un Forastero! Issues of Virtuality and Diegesis in Videogame Music." *Music and the Moving Image* 4: 30-39.

Elizabeth I. 1559. *Iniunctions Geven by the Quenes Maiestie Anno Domini MD.LIX., the Fyrstyeare of the Raigne of Our Soueraigne Lady Quene Elizabeth*. London: Richard Jugge and John Cawood.

Elsmann, Heinrich. 1619. *Compendiolum artis musicae latino-germanicum, cum brevi tractatu de modis*. Wolfenbüttel: Holwein.

Elste, Martin. 2019. *2000 Jahre Musik auf der Schallplatte / Two Thousand Years of Music. Alte Musik anno 1930: Eine diskologische Dokumentation zur Interpretationsgeschichte. Herausgegeben von Martin Elste und Carsten Schmidt*. 2nd edn. Vienna: Gesellschaft für Historische Tonträger.

Emans, Reinmar. 2016. "Musiker in Wolfenbüttel/Braunschweig: Ein prosopografischer Versuch." *Hamburger Jahrbuch für Musikwissenschaft* 31: 9-53.

Emsheimer, Ernst. 1969. "Zur Typologie der schwedischen Holztrompete." In *Studia instrumentorum popularis I. Bericht über die 2. Internationale Arbeitstagung der Study Group of Folk Musical Instruments des International Folk Music Council in Brno 1967*, edited by Erich Stockmann, 87-97. Stockholm: Musikhistoriska museet.

Encina, Juan del. 1496. *Cancionero*. Salamanca: s.n. http://www.cervantesvirtual.com/obra-visor/cancionero-de-juan-del-encina-primera-edicion-1496--0/html/ffadf59c-82b1-11df-acc7-002185ce6064_232.html.

Equicola, Mario. 1525. *Libro de natura de amore di Mario Equicola*. Venice: Lorenzo Lorio.

Ernst, Josef. 1989. *Johannes der Täufer: Interpretation Geschichte Wirkungsgeschichte*. Berlin: De Gruyter.

Esprinchard, Jacques, Pierre Bergeron, and François de Bassompierre. 1989. *Tři francouzští kavalíři v rudolfínské Praze* [*Three French Courtiers in Rudolfine Prague*]. Edited by Eliška Fučíková. Translated by Rudolf Chadraba and Eva Špinková. Commentary by Josef Janáček. Prague: Panorama.

Essling, Prince d'. 1874-1914. *Les livres à figures vénitiens de la fin du XVe siècle et du commencement du XVIe*. 4 vols. Florence: Olschki. Paris: Leclerc.

Evans, Lawrence. 1970. *The Letters of Walter Pater*. Oxford: Clarendon Press.

Evitascandolo, Cesare. 1598. *Dialogo del Maestro di casa*. Rome: Martinelli.

Evliyā Çelebi. 2012. *Narrative of Travels in Europe, Asia and Africa: In the Seventeenth Century*. Translated by Joseph von Hammer-Purgstall. 2 vols. Cambridge: Cambridge University Press.

Ewington, Julie. 2018. "'The Lady and the Unicorn' at the Art Gallery of New South Wales: Six exquisite tapestries form one of the great works of medieval art." *The Monthly*, June. https://www.themonthly.com.au/issue/2018/june/1527775200/julie-ewington/lady-and-unicorn-art-gallery-new-south-wales.

Fabianski, Marcin. 1988. "The Cremonese Ceiling Examined in Its Original Studiolo Setting." *Artibus et Historiae* 17: 189-212.

Fabre-Vassas, Claudine. 1997. *The Singular Beast: Jews, Christians, and Pigs*. New York: Columbia University Press.

Fallows, David. 2008. *Chansonnier de Jean de Montchenu (ca. 1475): Commentary to the Facsimile of the Manuscript Rothschild 2973 (I.5.13) in the Bibliothèque Nationale de France*. Valencia: Vicent García Editores.

Fallows, David. 2009. *Josquin*. Turnhout: Brepols.

Fantoni, Marcello. 1989. "Il culto dell'Annunziata e la sacralità del potere mediceo." *Archivio Storico Italiano* 167: 771-93.

Farmer, Henry George. 1930. *Historical Facts for the Arabian Musical Influence*. London: W. Reeves.

Farmer, Henry George. 1931. *The Organ of the Ancients: From Eastern Sources (Hebrew, Syriac, and Arabic)*. London: W. Reeves.

Farmer, Henry George. 1933. "Maimonides on Listening to Music." *The Journal of the Royal Asiatic Society of Great Britain and Ireland* 4: 867-84.

Fastenrath Vinattieri, Wiebke, and Johannes Schaefer. 2011. *Pietro Perugino: Die hl. Margarethe von Antiochia und der sel. Franziskus von Siena. Die Dokumentation der Restaurierung der beiden Gemälde sowie der Forschungen zur Geschichte und Rekonstruktion des Altars, zu dem sie gehören*. Altenburg: Lindenau-Museum.

Fava, Domenico, and Mario Salmi. 1950. *I manoscritti miniati della Biblioteca Estense di Modena*. Vol. 1. Florence: Electa.

Federmann, Maria. 1932. *Musik und Musikpflege zur Zeit Herzog Albrechts: Zur Geschichte der Königsberger Hofkapelle in den Jahren 1525-1578*. Kassel: Bärenreiter.

Feldman, Walter. 2012. "Mehter." *Encyclopedia of Islam*. 2nd edn. http://dx.doi.org.ezp-prod1.hul.harvard.edu/10.1163/1573-3912_islam_SIM_5149.

Fenlon, Iain. 1980. *Music and Patronage in Sixteenth-Century Mantua*. Cambridge: Cambridge University Press.

Fenlon, Iain. 1995. *Music, Print and Culture in Early Sixteenth-Century Italy*. London: British Library.

Fenlon, Iain. 2001. *Musica e stampa nell'Italia del Rinascimento*. Milan: S. Bonnard.

Fenlon, Iain. 2005. "The Claims of Choreography: Women Courtiers and Danced Spectacle in Late Sixteenth-Century Paris and Ferrara." In *Frauen und Musik im Europa des 16. Jahrhunderts: Infrastrukturen – Aktivitäten – Motivationen*. Trossinger Jahrbuch für Renaissancemusik 4, edited by Nicole Schwindt, 75-90. Kassel: Bärenreiter.

Fenlon, Iain. 2008. *The Ceremonial City: History, Memory and Myth in Renaissance Venice*. New Haven: Yale University Press.

Fenlon, Iain. 2015. "Printed Polyphonic Choirbooks for the Spanish Market." In *Specialist Markets in the Early Modern Book World*, edited by Richard Kirwan and Sophie Mullins, 199-222. Leiden: Brill.

Fenlon, Iain. 2016. "Lost Books of Polyphony from Renaissance Spain." In *Reconstructing the Print World of Pre-Industrial Europe*, edited by Flavia Bruni and Andrew Pettegree, 75-100. Leiden: Brill.

Fernández Manzano, Reynaldo. 1985. *De las melodías del reino nazarí de Granada a las estructuras musicales cristianas: La transformación de las tradiciones musicales hispano-árabes en la Península Ibérica*. Granada: Diputación Provincial de Granada.

Fernández Manzano, Reynaldo. 2012. "La música de al-Andalus en la cultura medieval, imágenes en el tiempo." PhD diss., Universidad de Granada.

Ferreira, Manuel Pedro. 2015. "Rhythmic Paradigms in the Cantigas de Santa Maria: French versus Arabic Precedent." *Plainsong & Medieval Music* 24: 1-24.

Ficino, Marsilio. 1989. *Three Books on Life*. Edited by Carol V. Kaske and John R. Clark. Binghamton, NY: The Renaissance Society of America.

Figueiredo, José de. 1932. *Catálogo e guia de algumas obras de arte temporariamente agrupadas neste Museu, representativas de diversos aspectos artísticos derivados do Descobrimento do caminho marítimo da Índia*. Lisboa: Museu Nacional de Arte Antiga.

Filippi, Daniele V. 2013. "Carlo Borromeo e la musica, 'a lui naturalmente grata'." In *Atti del Congresso Internazionale di Musica Sacra (Roma, 26 maggio - 1 giugno 2011)*, 2 vols, edited by Francesco Luisi and Antonio Addamiano, 2:665-76. Vatican City: Libreria Editrice Vaticana.

Filippi, Daniele V. 2017a. "'Catechismum Modulans Docebat': Teaching the Doctrine through Singing in Early Modern Catholicism." In *Listening to Early Modern Catholicism: Perspectives from Musicology*, edited by Daniele V. Filippi and Michael Noone, 129-48. Intersections: Interdisciplinary Studies in Early Modern Culture 49. Leiden: Brill.

Filippi, Daniele V. 2017b. "Sonic Afterworld: Mapping the Soundscape of Heaven and Hell in Early Modern Cities." In *Cultural Histories of Noise, Sound and Listening in Europe, 1300-1918*, edited by I. D. Biddle and Kirsten Gibson, 186-204. London: Routledge.

Filippi, Daniele V. 2019. "The Soundtrack for a Miracle and Other Stories of the Motet from Post-Tridentine Milan." In *Mapping the Motet in the Post-Tridentine Era*, edited by Esperanza Rodríguez-García and Daniele V. Filippi, 228-49. Abingdon: Routledge.

Filippi, Daniele V., and Agnese Pavanello, eds. 2019. *Codici per cantare: I Libroni del Duomo nella Milano sforzesca*. Lucca: Libreria Musicale Italiana.

Findikyan, Michael Daniel. 2006. "Eastern Liturgy in the West: The Case of the Armenian Church." *Colloquium: Music, Worship, Arts* 3: 56-65. https://ism.yale.edu/sites/default/files/files/Eastern%20Liturgy%20in%20the%20West.pdf.

Finiello Zervas, Diane. 1988. "'Quos volent et eo modo quo volent': Piero de' Medici and the *Operai* of SS. Annunziata, 1445-55." In *Florence and Italy: Renaissance Studies in Honour of Nicolai Rubinstein*, edited by Peter Denley and Caroline Elam, 465-79. London: University of London, Westfield College, Committee for Medieval Studies.

Fischer, Kurt von. 1992. "The Biographies." In *Il Codice Squarcialupi, MS. Mediceo Palatino 87, Biblioteca Medicea Laurenziana di Firenze*, edited by F. Alberto Gallo, 127-43. Florence and Lucca: Giunti Bàrbera and Libreria Musicale Italiana.

Fisher, Alexander J. 2007. "'Per mia particolare devotione': Orlando di Lasso's *Lagrime di San Pietro* and Catholic Spirituality in Counter-Reformation Munich." *Journal of the Royal Musical Association* 132: 167-220.

Fisher, Alexander J. 2014. *Music, Piety, and Propaganda: The Soundscapes of Counter-Reformation Bavaria*. New York: Oxford University Press.

Fisher, Alexander J. 2015. "*Thesaurus Litaniarum*: The Symbolism and Practice of Musical Litanies in Counter-Reformation Germany." *Early Music History* 34: 45-95.

Fitch, Fabrice, ed. 2000. *Choirbook for Philip the Fair and Juana of Castile, c. 1504-6: Brussel, Koninkijke Biblioteek MS. 9126*. Peer: Alamire.

Fleming, Michael, and Christopher Page, eds. 2021. *Music and Instruments of the Elizabethan Age: The Eglantine Table*. Woodbridge: Boydell and Brewer.

Fonseca, Jorge. 2010. *Escravos e Senhores na Lisboa Quinhentista*. Lisbon: Colibri.

Forcano, Manuel. 2006. "The Mystery of Christopher Columbus." Liner notes to *Paraísos Perdidos*, Alia Vox AVSA9850A+B, 99-104.

Forman, Benno. 1971. *Continental Furniture Craftsmen in London, 1511-1625*. London: Furniture History Society.

Forney, Kristine K. 1987. "Music, Ritual and Patronage at the Church of Our Lady, Antwerp." *Early Music History* 7: 1-57.

Forney, Kristine K. 1989. "16th Century Antwerp." In *The Renaissance: From the 1470s to the End of the 16th Century*, edited by Iain Fenlon, 361-79. London: Macmillan.

Forney, Kristine K. 1995. "'Nymphes gayes en abry du Laurier': Music Instruction for the Bourgeois Woman." *Musica Disciplina* 49: 151-87.

Forrest, John. 1999. *The History of Morris Dancing 1458-1750*. Cambridge: James Clark & Co.

Forrester, Peter. 1994. "An Elizabethan Allegory and Some Hypotheses." *The Lute* 34: 11-14.

Fortini Brown, Patricia. 2004. *Private Lives in Renaissance Venice*. New Haven: Yale University Press.

Fountain, Danielle. 2018. "'Frame not my lute': The Musical Tudor Court on the Big Screen." In *Recomposing the Past: Representations of Early Music on Stage and Screen*, edited by James Cook, Alexander Kolassa, and Adam Whittaker, 51-63. New York: Routledge.

Frakes, Jerold C. 2004. *Early Yiddish Texts, 1100-1750*. Oxford: Oxford University Press.

France, James. 2007. *Medieval Images of Saint Bernard of Clairvaux*. Kalamazoo: Cistercian Publications.

Franzoni, Lanfranco. 1970. *Per una storia del collezionismo. Verona: La galleria Bevilacqua*. Milan: Edizioni di Comunità.

Freedberg, David. 1989. *The Power of Images: Studies in the History and Theory of Response*. Chicago: University of Chicago Press.

Freedman, Richard. 2013. *Music in the Renaissance*. New York: Norton.

Frenk, Margit. 1987. *Nuevo corpus de la antigua lírica popular hispánica (siglos XV a XVII)*. 2 vols. Mexico: Universidad Nacional Autónoma de México / El Colegio de México-F.C.E.

Freund Schwartz, Roberta. 2001. "*En busca de liberalidad*: Music and Musicians in the Courts of the Spanish Nobility, 1470-1640." PhD diss., University of Illinois at Urbana-Champaign.

Frick, Carole Collier. 1989. "The Downcast Eyes of the Women of the Upper Class in Francesco Barbaro's 'De re uxoria.'" *UCLA Historical Journal* 9: 9-31.

Fróis, Luís. 1595. *Lettera del Giapone degli anni 1591 et 1592*. Mantua: Osanna. Rome: Zanetti. Milan: Pontio. Venice: Ciotti. Köln: Falckenburg.

[Fróis, Luís]. 1942. *La première ambassade du Japon en Europe, 1582-1592. Première partie: Le traité du Père Frois*. Edited and annotated by F. A. Abranches Pinto, Yoshitomo Okamoto and Henri Bernard, S. J. Tokyo: Sophia University.

Fróis, Luís, and Josef Franz Schütte, SJ. 1955. *Kulturgegensätze Europa-Japan (1585): Tratado em que se contem muito susinta e abreviadamente algumas contradições e diferenças de custumes antre a gente de Europa e esta provincia de Japão*. Tokyo: Sophia Universität.

Fromont, Céline. 2014. *The Art of Conversion: Christian Visual Culture in the Kingdom of Kongo*. Chapel Hill: University of North Carolina Press.

Frye, Susan. 2011. *Pens and Needles: Women's Textualities in Early Modern England*. Pennsylvania: University of Pennsylvania Press.

Fuenllana, Miguel de. 1554. *Libro de Musica de Vihuela, intitulado Orphenica lyra*. Seville: Martin de Montesdoca.

Furttenbach, Joseph (the Younger). 1649. *Tractate über Baukunst*. Vol. 4: *KirchenGebäw*. Augsburg: Schultes.

Gabriele, Mino. 2007. "Armonie ineffabili nell'*Hypnerotomachia Polihili*." *Musica e Storia* 15: 57-66.

Gaignebet, Claude. 1986. *À plus hault sens*. Vol. 1. Paris: Maisonneuve et Larose.

Gallo, F. Alberto. 1987. "La 'chorea o vero ballo' dell'*Hypnerotomachia Poliphili*." In *La letteratura, la rappresentazione, la musica al tempo e nei luoghi di Giorgione*, edited by Michelangelo Muraro, 239-44. Rome: Jouvence.

Gallo, F. Alberto. 1995. *Music in the Castle: Troubadours, Books, and Orators in Italian Courts of the Thirteenth, Fourteenth, and Fifteenth Centuries*. Translated by Anna Herklotz. Chicago: University of Chicago Press (orig. *Musica nel castello: Trovatori, libri e oratori nelle corti italiane dal XIII al XV secolo*. Bologna: Il Mulino, 1992).

Gamberini, Andrea. 2014. *A Companion to Late Medieval and Early Modern Milan: The Distinctive Features of an Italian State*. Brill's Companions to European History 7. Leiden: Brill.

Gámiz Gordo, Antonio. 2008. *Alhambra: Imágenes de ciudad y paisaje (hasta 1800)*. Granada: Fundación El legado andalusí.

Gancarczyk, Paweł. 2012. "The Musical Culture of the Teutonic Order in Prussia Reflected in the Marienburger Tresslerbuch (1399-1409)." In *The Musical Heritage of the Jagiellonian Era*, edited by Paweł Gancarczyk and Agnieszka Leszczyńska, 191-200. Warszawa: Instytut Sztuki PAN.

Gancarczyk, Paweł. 2015. *La musique et la révolution de l'imprimerie: Les mutations de la culture musicale au XVIe siècle*. Lyon: Symétrie.

García Arranz, José Julio. 2008-09. "El castigo del 'cornudo paciente': Un detalle iconográfico en la *Vista de Sevilla* de Joris Hoefnagel (1593)." *Norba-Arte* 28-29: 69-79.

Garcia López, Aurelio. 2010. *El palacio ducal de Pastrana: Una obra desconocida de Alonso de Covarrubias*. Guadalajara: AACHE.

García Mercadal, José. 1952-62. *Viajes de extranjeros por España y Portugal: Desde los tiempos más remotos hasta comienzos del siglo XX*. Madrid: Aguilar.

Gardner von Teuffel, Christa. 2005. *From Duccio's Maestà to Raphael's Transfiguration: Italian Altarpieces and Their Settings*. London: Pindar Press.

Garnett, Jane, and Gervase Rosser. 2013. *Spectacular Miracles: Transforming Images in Italy from the Renaissance to the Present*. London: Reaktion Books.

Garratt, James. 2002. *Palestrina and the German Romantic Imagination: Interpreting Historicism in Nineteenth-Century Music*. Cambridge: Cambridge University Press.

Garside Jr., Charles. 1951. "Calvin's Preface to the Psalter: A Re-Appraisal." *Musical Quarterly* 37: 566-77.

Gärtner, Magdalene. 2002. *Römische Basiliken in Augsburg: Nonnenfrömmigkeit und Malerei um 1500*. Augsburg: Wißner.

Gasch, Stefan. 2012. "Ludwig Senfl, Herzog Albrecht und der Kelch des Heils." In *Senfl-Studien 1*, edited by Stefan Gasch, Birgit Lodes, and Sonja Tröster, 389-442. Tutzing: Hans Schneider.

Gasch, Stefan. 2013. *Proprienvertonungen der Münchner Hofkapelle im 16. Jahrhundert: Tradition und Entwicklungsschichten eines Repertoires*. Tutzing: Hans Schneider.

Gasch, Stefan, and Sonja Tröster. 2014. "Senfl, Ludwig." *Grove Music Online*.

Gasch, Stefan, and Sonja Tröster, in collaboration with Birgit Lodes. 2019. *Ludwig Senfl (c.1490-1543): A Catalogue Raisonné of the Works and Sources*. 2 vols. Turnhout: Brepols.

Gauthier, Claudine. 2012. *La décapitation de saint Jean en marge des évangiles: Essai d'anthropologie historique et sociale*. Paris: Publications de la Sorbonne.

Gaze, Delia, ed. 1997. *Dictionary of Women Artists*. 2 vols. London: Fitzroy Dearborn.

Gebauerová, Marie. 1925. "O hradě Pražském" ["About Prague Castle"]. *Naše Praha, vlastivědný časopis pro mládež* [*Our Prague, National History Magazine for Youth*] 1: 121-24.

Geiger, Gail L. 1981. "Filippino Lippi's Carafa 'Annunciation': Theology, Artistic Conventions and Patronage." *The Art Bulletin* 63: 62-75.

Geiger, Gail L. 1986. *Filippino Lippi's Carafa Chapel: Renaissance Art in Rome*. Kirksville: Sixteenth Century Journal Publishers.

Geistreiches Gesang-Buch. 1676. *Geistreiches Gesang-Buch, An D. Cornelii Beckers Psalmen und Lutherischen Kirchen-Liedern: Mit ihren Melodeyen unter Discant und Basso, sammt einem Kirchen-Gebeth-Buche* [...]. Dresden: Hamann.

Gelder, Geert Jan van. 2012. "Sing Me to Sleep: Ṣafī al-Dīn al-Urmawī, Hülegü, and the Power of Music." *Quaderni di studi arabi, nuova serie* 7: 1-9.

Gell, Alfred. 1998. *Art and Agency: An Anthropological Theory*. Oxford: Oxford University Press.

Gerbino, Giuseppe. 2009. *Music and the Myth of Arcadia in Renaissance Italy*. Cambridge: Cambridge University Press.

Gertsman, Elina. 2010. *The Dance of Death in the Middle Ages: Image, Text, Performance*. Turnhout: Brepols.

Getz, Christine Suzanne. 2005. *Music in the Collective Experience in Sixteenth-Century Milan*. Aldershot: Ashgate.

Getz, Christine Suzanne. 2015. "Music in the 16th and 17th Centuries." In *A Companion to Late Medieval and Early Modern Milan: The Distinctive Features of an Italian State*, edited by Andrea Gamberini, 306-29. Brill's Companions to European History 7. Leiden: Brill.

Ghrab, Anas. 2009. "Commentaire anonyme du Kitāb al-adwār: édition critique, traduction et présentation des lectures arabes de l'œuvre de Ṣafī al-Dīn al-Urmawī." PhD diss., Université Paris-Sorbonne.

Giegher, Mattia. 1639. *Li tre trattati*. Padua: Frambotto.

Gil Sanjuán, Joaquín, and Juan Antonio Sánchez López. 1996. "Iconografía y visión histórico-literaria de Granada a mediados del Quinientos." *Chronica Nova* 23: 73-133.

Gil Sanjuán, Joaquín, and Juan Antonio Sánchez López. 2003. "El flamenco Joris Hoefnagel pintor de las capitales andaluzas del Quinientos." In *Los extranjeros en la España moderna: Actas del I Coloquio Internacional celebrado en Málaga del 28 al 30 de noviembre de 2002*, edited by M. B. Villar García, and P. Pezzi Cristóbal, 2:341-58. Málaga: the authors.

Gillion, Marianne C. E. 2015. "'Diligentissime emendatum, atque correctum'? The Transmission and Revision of Plainchant in Italian Printed Graduals, 1499-1653." PhD diss., University of Manchester.

Gillion, Marianne C. E. 2019. "Retrofitting Plainchant: The Incorporation and Adaptation of 'Tridentine' Liturgical Changes in Italian Printed Graduals, 1572-1653." *The Journal of Musicology* 36: 331-69.

Gillion, Marianne C. E. 2017; published 2021. "Archiepiscopal Archetypes, Printed Books, and Parish Practices: Musical Notation in Editions of the Missale Salisburgense (1492-1515)." *Florilegium* 34: 119-46.

Giovannini, Ortensia. 2016. "One Nation, But One Culture? This Is a Question. Espressioni musicali e costruzione identitaria degli armeni della diaspora." PhD diss., Università di Roma "La Sapienza."

Giraldi Cinzio, Giambattista. 1543. *Orbecche: Tragedia*. Venice: Aldo.

Giraldi Cinzio, Giambattista. 1545. *Egle satira di M. Giovan Battista Giraldi Cinthio da Ferrara*. S.l.: s.n.

Giraldi Cinzio, Giambattista. 1583. *Altile: Tragedia*. Venice: Cagnacini.

Giraldi Cinzio, Giambattista. 1864. *De' romanzi, delle comedie e delle tragedie: Ragionamenti*. Edited by Eugenio Camerini. Milan: G. Daelli.

Girouard, Mark. 2006. *Hardwick Hall*. Rev. ed. London: National Trust.

Giselbrecht, Elisabeth. 2017. "To Have and to Hold: Music Books as Collectables." In *Sources of Identity: Makers, Owners and Users of Music Sources Before 1600*, edited by Lisa Colton and Tim Shephard, 239-59. Turnhout: Brepols.

Giselbrecht, Elisabeth, and Elizabeth Upper. 2012. "Glittering Woodcuts and Moveable Music: Decoding the Elaborate Printing Techniques, Purpose and Patronage of the 'Liber selectarum cantionum'." In *Senfl-Studien 1*, edited by Stefan Gasch, Birgit Lodes, and Sonja Tröster, 17-67. Tutzing: Schneider.

Głuszcz-Zwolińska, Elżbieta. 1988. *Muzyka nadworna ostatnich Jagiellonów* [*Music at the Court of the Last Jagiellons*]. Kraków: Polskie Wydawnictwo Muzyczne.

Godden, Rumer. 1937. *The Lady and the Unicorn*. London: n.p.

Goette, Alexander. 1897. *Holbeins Totentanz und seine Vorbilder*. Strassburg: Verlag von Karl J. Trübner.

Gombrich, Ernst H. 1962. "Alberto Avogadro's Descriptions of the Badia of Fiesole and of the Villa of Careggi." *Italia medioevale e umanistica* 5: 217-29.

Gómez Muntané, Maricarmen, ed. 2008. *Las Ensaladas (Praga, 1581): Con un Suplemento de obras del género*. 3 vols. Valencia: Institut Valencià de la Música, Generalitat Valenciana.

Gomis Coloma, Juan. 2010. "Intermediarios entre el texto y su público: La Cofradía de Pobres Ciegos Oracioneros en Valencia." In *Opinión pública y espacio urbano en la Edad Moderna*, edited by James S. Amelang, Antonio Castillo Gómez, and Carmen Serrano Sánchez, 301-18. Gijón: Ediciones Trea.

González, Carlos, ed. 2007. *Estudios sobre la vihuela*. Madrid: Sociedad de la Vihuela.

González Zymla, Herbert. 2013. "El Castillo Palacio de los Álvarez de Toledo en Alba de Tormes." *Anales de Historia del Arte* 23: 455-68.

Goodwin, Godfrey. 1994. *The Janissaries*. London: Saqi.

Gori, Valente. 1981. "La musica alla SS. Annunziata di Firenze dall'origine alla fondazione della cappella musicale (I-II)." *Accademia Musicale Valdarnese. Bollettino d'Informazioni* 18-19: 9-22, 4-23.

Goss, John. 1992. *Ciudades de Europa y España*. Madrid: LIBSA.

Gottron, Adam. 1959. "Die Kanones Erbachs im Pommerschen Kunstschrank 1617." *Die Musikforschung* 12: 466-67.

Gozzi, Marco. 2013. *Il Graduale Giunta Venezia 1572*. Lucca: Libreria Musicale Italiana.

Grande Qujigo, Francisco Javier. 2003. "La representación de la liturgia de la Pasión y Resurrección en el teatro de Gil Vicente." *Anuario de Estudios Filológicos* 26: 171-88.

Green, Ian. 2000. *Print and Protestantism in Early Modern England*. Oxford: Oxford University Press.

Greenfield, Concetta Carestia. 1981. *Humanist and Scholastic Poetics, 1250-1500*. London: Associated University Presses.

Greffe, Florence, and Valérie Brousselle. 1997. *Documents du Minutier central des notaires de Paris: Inventaires après décès, tome deuxième (1547-1560)*. Paris: Archives nationales.

Grieco, Allen. 2006. "Meals." In *At Home in Renaissance Italy*, edited by Marta Ajmar-Wollheim and Flora Dennis, 244-53. London: V&A Publications.

Griffin, Clive. 2005. *Journey-Men Printers, Heresy, and the Inquisition in Sixteenth-Century Spain*. Oxford: Oxford University Press.

Griffiths, John. 1999. "Extremities: The Vihuela in Development and Decline." In *Luths et luthistes en Occident: Actes du colloque 13-15 mai 1998*, 51-61. Paris: Cité de la Musique.

Griffiths, John. 2009. "Hidalgo, Merchant, Poet, Priest: The Vihuela in the Urban Soundscape." *Early Music* 37: 355-66.

Grigoryan, Metaskya. 2014. "Beginnings of Early Armenian Printing in Venice and Rome in the Sixteenth Century: Reconsideration of Research Frameworks and Contexts." MA diss., Central European University, Budapest.

Groos, Arthur. 1992. "Constructing Nuremberg: Typological and Proleptic Communities in 'Die Meistersinger'." *19th Century Music* 16: 18-34.

Groote, Inga Mai. 2013a. *Ludwig Senfl: Zwischen Memoria, Markt und Musenkult*. Winterthur: Amadeus Verlag.

Groote, Inga Mai. 2013b. "'KinderMusic': Musiklehre und Allgemeinbildung für Chorknaben." In *Rekrutierung musikalischer Eliten: Knabengesang im 15. und 16. Jahrhundert*, edited by Nicole Schwindt, 111-41. Kassel: Bärenreiter.

Groote, Inga Mai. 2018. "Das 'Musicae Compendium latino germanicum' von Faber/Vulpius: Versuch einer Lese(r) geschichte." In *Melchior Vulpius. Leben, Werk, Wirkung*, edited by Maren Goltz and Kai Schabram, 75-86. Beeskow: ortus.

Groote, Inga Mai. Forthcoming. "Lutheranising through Music: Traces of the Confessional Soundscapes of Early Seventeenth-Century Wolfenbüttel and Braunschweig." In *Crossing Boundaries: Music and Conversion in the Early Modern City*, edited by Iain Fenlon, Marie-Alexis Colin, and Matthew Laube. Turnhout: Brepols.

Grotto, Giulio. 1590. *La Violina*. Ferrara: Vittorio Baldini.

Gschwend, Annemarie Jordan, and Kate Lowe. 2017. "A representação da Lisboa global." In *A Cidade Global: Lisboa no Renascimento / The Global City: Lisbon in the Renaissance*, edited by Annemarie Jordan Gschwend and K. J. P. Lowe, 14-31. Lisbon: Museu Nacional de Arte Antiga / Imprensa Nacional-Casa da Moeda.

Gualtieri, Guido. 1586. *Relationi della venuta degli ambasciatori giaponesi a Roma fino alla partita di Lisbona. Con le accoglienze fatte loro da tutti i Principi Christiani per dove sono passati.* Rome: Zannetti.

Guaman Poma de Ayala, Felipe. (1615) 1936. *Nueva corónica y buen gobierno*. Edited by Paul Rivet. Paris: Institut d'Ethnologie.

Guaman Poma de Ayala, Felipe. (1615) 1980. *El primer nueva corónica y buen gobierno*. 3 vols. Edited by John V. Murra and Rolena Adorno. Mexico City: Siglo Veintiuno.

Guarini, Battista. 1588. *Il Verato ovvero difesa di quanto ha scritto m. Giason Denores contra le tragicomedie, et le pastorali, in un suo discorso di poesia*. Ferrara: Caraffa.

Guarini, Battista. 1593. *Il Verato secondo, ovvero replica dell'Attizzato accademico ferrarese in difesa del Pastor fido*. Florence: Filippo Giunti.

Guarini, Battista. 1601. *Compendio della poesia tragicomica, tratto dai duo Verati*. Venice: Ciotti.

Guðmundsson, Guðlaugur R. 2000. *Skólalíf: Starf og siðir í latínuskólunum á Íslandi, 1552-1846*. Reykjavík: IÐNÚ.

Guerra, Enrica, ed. 2010. *Il carteggio tra Beatrice d'Aragona e gli Estensi (1476-1508)*. Rome: Aracne.

Guicciardini, Lodovico. 1567. *Decrittione […] di tutti e paesi bassi*. Antwerp: Guglielmo Silvio.

Guidobaldi, Nicoletta. 1992. "Il ritorno delle Muse nel Quattrocento." *RIdIM/RCMI Newsletter* 17: 15-24.

Gundersheimer, Werner L., ed. 1971. *The Dance of Death. 41 Woodcuts by Hans Holbein the Younger. Complete Facsimile of the Original 1538 French Edition*. New York: Dover Publications.

Gutierrez, Beniamino. 1938. *La prima ambasceria giapponese in Italia: Dall'ignorata cronaca di un diarista e cosmografo milanese della fine del XVI sec.* Milan: Perego.

Gutwirth, Eleazar. 1988. "Religión, historia y las Biblias Romanceadas." *Revista Catalana de Teologia* 13: 115-34.

Gutwirth, Eleazar. 1998. "Music, Identity and the Inquisition in Fifteenth-Century Spain." *Early Music History* 17: 161-81.

Gutwirth, Eleazar. 2004. "A Song and Dance: Transcultural Practices of Daily Life in Medieval Spain." In *Jews, Muslims and Christians in and around the Crown of Aragon: Essays in Honour of Professor Elena Lourie*, edited by Harvey J. Hames, 207-27. Leiden: Brill.

Gutwirth, Eleazar. 2014. "Models of Patronage in Medieval Spain." In *Patronage, Production, and Transmission of Texts in Medieval and Early Modern Jewish Cultures*, edited by Esperanza Alfonso and Jonathan Decter, 45-75. Turnhout: Brepols.

Gutwirth, Eleazar. 2015. "The *Most marueilous historie of the Iewes*: Historiography and the 'Marvelous' in the Sixteenth Century." In *In and Of the Mediterranean*, edited by Michelle M. Hamilton and Núria Silleras-Fernández, 157-82. Nashville: Vanderbilt University Press.

Gutwirth, Eleazar. 2015b. "Rabbi Mose Arragel and the Art of the Prologue in Fifteenth Century Castile" *Helmantica* 66: 187-212.

Gutwirth, Eleazar. 2016. "Musical Lives: Late Medieval Hispano-Jewish Communities." In *Companion to Music in the Age of the Catholic Monarchs*, edited by Tess Knighton, 579-616. Leiden: Brill.

Guzmán, Luis de. 1601. *Historia de las missiones que han hecho los religiosos de la Compañia de Iesus para predicar el sancto Euangelio en los reynos de Iapon / compuesta por el padre Luis de Guzman […]*. 2 vols. Alcalá: Biuda de Iuan Gracian.

Haar, James. 1974. "The Frontispiece of Gafori's Practica Musicae (1496)." *Renaissance Quarterly* 27: 7-22.

Haar, James. 1981. "Arie per cantar stanze ariostesche." In *L'Ariosto: La musica, i musicisti*, edited by Maria Antonella Balsano, 31-46. Florence: Olschki.

Haar, James. 1983. "The Courtier as Musician: Castiglione's View of the Science and Art of Music." In *Castiglione: The Ideal and the Real in Renaissance Culture*, edited by Robert W. Hanning and David Rosand, 65-189. New Haven: Yale University Press.

Haar, James. 2004. "From 'cantimbanco' to Court: The Musical Fortunes of Ariosto in Florentine Society." In *L'arme e gli amori: Ariosto, Tasso and Guarini in Late Renaissance Florence*, 2 vols, edited by Massimiliano Rossi and Fiorella Gioffredi Superbi, 2:179-97. Florence: Olschki.

Habermas, Jürgen. 1962. *Strukturwandel der Öffentlichkeit: Untersuchungen zu einer Kategorie der bürgerlichen Gesellschaft.* Neuwied: Luchterhand.

Habich, Georg. 1907. "Studien zur deutschen Renaissancemedaille: III. Friedrich Hagenauer." *Jahrbuch der preussischen Kunstsammlungen* 28: 181-98, 230-72.

Hackel, Heidi Brayman. 2005. *Reading Material in Early Modern England: Print, Gender, and Literacy*. Cambridge: Cambridge University Press.

Hackett, Frances. 1939. *Queen Anne Boleyn: A Novel.* N.P.: Doubleday, Doran & Company.

Haggh, Barbara. 1997. "New Publications in Dutch on Music before 1700 and a Newly Discovered 15th Century Dutch Manuscript with Songs." *Early Music* 25: 121-28.

Hahn, Philip. 2017. "The Emperor's Boot, or: Perceiving Public Rituals in the Urban Reformation." *German History* 35: 362-80.

Haines, John. 2001. "The Arabic Style of Performing Medieval Music." *Early Music* 29: 369-78.

Haines, John. 2008. "The Origins of the Musical Staff." *The Musical Quarterly* 91: 327-78.

Haines, John. 2014a. "Antiquarian Nostalgia and the Institutionalization of Early Music." In *The Oxford Handbook of Music Revival*, edited by Caroline Bithell and Juniper Hill, 73-93. New York: Oxford University Press.

Haines, John. 2014b. *Music in Films on the Middle Ages: Authenticity vs. Fantasy*. Routledge Research in Music 7. New York: Routledge.

Hall, Michael. 2014. *George Frederick Bodley*. New Haven: Yale University Press.

Halldórsson, Jón. 1916-18. *Skólameistarasögur*. Reykjavík: Sögufélag.

Hamling, Tara, and Catherine Richardson, eds. 2010. *Everyday Objects: Medieval and Early Modern Material Culture and Its Meanings*. New York: Routledge.

Hamm, Charles. 1968. "Musiche del Quattrocento in S. Petronio." *Rivista italiana di musicologia* 3: 215-32.

Hand, John Oliver. 1992. "Some Thoughts on the Iconography of the *Head of Christ* by Petrus Christus." *Metropolitan Museum Journal* 27: 7-18.

Hannes, Hellmut. 1990. "Der Pommersche Kunstschrank: Entstehung, Umfeld, Schicksal." *Baltische Studien* 76: 81-115.

Hannikainen, Jorma, and Erkki Tuppurainen. 2016. "Vernacular Gregorian Chant and Lutheran Hymn-Singing in Reformation-Era Finland." In *Re-Forming Texts, Music, and Church Art in the Early Modern North*, edited by Tuomas M. S. Lehtonen and Linda Kaljundi, 157-77. Amsterdam: Amsterdam University Press.

Harich-Schneider, Eta. 1973a. *A History of Japanese Music*. London: Oxford University Press.

Harich-Schneider, Eta. 1973b. "Renaissance Europe through Japanese Eyes: Record of a Strange Triumphal Journey." *Early Music* 1: 19-26.

Harms, Wolfgang, and Gilbert Heß, eds. 2009. *Joachim Camerarius d.J.: Symbola et emblemata tam moralia quam sacra: Die handschriftlichen Embleme von 1587*. Tübingen: Max Niemeyer Verlag.

Harris, Ann Sutherland, and Linda Nochlin. 1976. *Women Artists 1550-1950*. Los Angeles: Los Angeles County Museum of Art.

Harrison, Frank Ll., ed. 1956-61. *The Eton Choirbook, I-III*. Musica Britannica 10-12. London: Stainer & Bell.

Harrison, Frank Ll., and Peter M. Lefferts, eds. 1980. *Motets of English Provenance*. Polyphonic Music of the Fourteenth Century 15. Monaco: Editions L'Oiseau-Lyre.

Haskell, Harry. 1988. *The Early Music Revival: A History*. London: Thames & Hudson.

Haspels, Jan Jaap. 2006. *Royal Music Machines: Vijf eeuwen vorstelijk vermaak*. Zutphen: Walburg Press.

Hasse, Dag Nikolaus. 2016. *Success and Suppression: Arabic Sciences and Philosophy in the Renaissance*. Cambridge, MA: Harvard University Press.

Haug, Judith I. 2019. *Ottoman and European Music in ʿAlī Ufuḳī's Compendium, MS Turc 292: Analysis, Interpretation, Cultural Context*. Vol 1. Münster: Readbox Unipress.

Hayward, Maria. 2016. "In the Eye of the Beholder: 'Seeing' Textiles in the Early Modern Interior." *Textile History* 47: 27-42.

Heal, Ambrose. 1931. *The English Writing Masters and Their Copy-Books 1570-1800: A Biographical Dictionary and a Bibliography*. Cambridge: Cambridge University Press.

Heal, Bridget. 2007. *The Cult of the Virgin Mary in Early Modern Germany: Protestant and Catholic Piety, 1500-1648*. Cambridge: Cambridge University Press.

Heal, Bridget. 2017. *A Magnificent Faith: Art and Identity in Lutheran Germany*. Oxford: Oxford University Press.

Heartz, Daniel. 1969. *Pierre Attaingnant, Royal Printer of Music: A Historical Study and Bibliographical Catalogue*. Berkeley: University of California Press.

Heikkilä, Tuomas. 2010. "Asiakirjat ja kirjoitetut kielet." In *Kirjallinen kulttuuri keskiajan Suomessa*, edited by Tuomas Heikkilä, 331-49. Helsinki: Suomalaisen Kirjallisuuden Seura.

Helenius, Eva. 2007. "Albertus Pictor och musiken." In *Den mångsidige målaren: Vidgade perspektiv på Albertus Pictors bild- och textvärld*, edited by Jan Öberg, Erika Kihlman, and Pia Melin, 65-74. Stockholm: Runica et Mediaevalia.

Hellinga, W. G. 1962. *Copy and Print in the Netherlands*. Amsterdam: North-Holland Publishing.

Helms, Dietrich. "Die mehrstimmige Musik der Renaissance und der Begriff des 'Populären': eine Kritik." In *Kultur- und kommunikationshistorischer Wandel des Liedes im 16. Jahrhundert*, edited by Albrecht Classen, Michael Fischer, and Nils Grosch, 127-54. Münster: Waxmann.

Hendrix, Lee, and Thea Vignau-Wilberg. 1992. *Mira calligraphiae monumenta: A Sixteenth-Century Calligraphic Manuscript Inscribed by Georg Bocskay and Illuminated by Joris Hoefnagel*. Malibu: The J. Paul Getty Museum.

Hentzner, Paul. 1612. *Itinerarium Germaniae, Galliae, Angliae, Italiae, scriptum à Paulo Hentznero J C. Illustrissimi Monsterbergensium ac Olßnensium ducis, Caroli, sacri Rom. Imperij principis, & supremi per utramq[ue] Silesiam capitanei &c. consiliario, cum indice locorum, rerum atq[ue] verborum memorabilium*. Nuremberg: typis Abrahami Wagenmanni.

Herain, Jan. 1905. "Bronzová fontána v král. zahradě na hradě Pražském" ["Bronze Fountain in the Royal Garden at Prague Castle"]. In *Ze staré Prahy, II. [From Old Prague, II]*, 1-11. Prague: Společnost přátel starožitností českých [Society of friends of Czech antiques].

Herold, Eduard. 1884. *Malerische Wanderungen durch Prag. Band II: Die Burg*. Prague: Eduard Grégr.

Hewitt, Peter. 2011. "Shakespeare in 100 Objects: Vanitas." Shakespeare Birthplace Trust Explore Shakespeare Blog, 14 November. www.shakespeare.org.uk/explore-shakespeare/blogs/shakespeare-100-objects-vanitas.

Hewitt, Peter. 2014. "The Material Culture of Shakespeare's England: A Study of the Early Modern Objects in the Museum Collection of the Shakespeare Birthplace Trust." PhD diss., University of Birmingham.

Hicks, Andrew. 2017. *Composing the World: Harmony in the Medieval Platonic Cosmos*. Oxford: Oxford University Press.

Highlights of the Untermyer Collection. 1977. *Highlights of the Untermyer Collection of English and Continental Decorative Arts*. New York: Metropolitan Museum of Art.

Hiley, David. 2001. "Staff." *Grove Music Online*.

Hinn íslenzki Þursaflokkur. 1978. *Hinn íslenzki Þursaflokkur* (album). Reykjavík: Fálkinn.

Hinterkeuser, Guido. 2014. "Der Pommersche Kunstschrank in Berlin: Die Stationen bis zum Untergang." In *Wunderwelt: Der Pommersche Kunstschrank*, edited by Christoph Emmendörfer, 58-73. Berlin: Deutscher Kunstverlag.

Hipp, Hermann. 1979. *Studien zur "Nachgotik" des 16. und 17. Jahrhunderts in Deutschland, Böhmen, Österreich und der Schweiz*. Hannover: Böttger.

Hirsch, Martin. 2013. "*Vera Imago Ludovvici Senflii*: Die Medaillen auf Ludwig Senfl." In *Senfl-Studien 2*, edited by Stefan Gasch and Sonja Tröster, 3-22. Tutzing: Schneider.

Hjelmslev, Louis. 1941. *Breve fra og til Rasmus Rask*. Vol. 1. Copenhagen: Munksgaard.

Hlávková, Lenka, and Hana Vlhová-Wörner. 2014. "Hudba" ["Music"]. In *Husitské století* [*The Hussite Century*], edited by Pavlína Cermanová, Robert Novotný and Pavel Soukup, 474-89. Prague: Lidové noviny.

Hobbes, Thomas. 2004. *Leviathan or the Matter: Forme, & Power of a Common-Wealth Ecclesiasticall and Civill*. New York: Barnes and Nobles.

Hobson, James. 2015. "Musical Antiquarianism and the Madrigal Revival in England, 1726-1851." PhD diss., University of Bristol.

Hoffmann, Detlef. 1993. *Altdeutsche Spielkarten 1500-1650: Katalog der Holzschnittkarten mit deutschen Farben aus dem Deutschen Spielkarten-Museum Leinfelden-Echterdingen und dem Germanischen Nationalmuseum Nürnberg*. Nuremberg: Verlag des Germanischen Nationalmuseums.

Hofmann, Mara. 2019. "Brussels, Belgium, Bibliothèque Royal Albert Ier/Koninklijke Bibliotheek Albert I, MS 228." *The Production and Reading of Music Sources: Mise en Page in Manuscripts and Printed Books Containing Polyphonic Music, 1480-1530*. http://www.proms.ac.uk/object_part/51/.

Holeton, David R. 2019. "Singing the Utraquist Faith: A Theology of Selected Hymns from the Jistebnice Kancionál." In *Jistebnický kancionál. MS. Praha, Knihovna Národního muzea, II C 7. Kritická edice. 2. svazek. Cantionale/ The Jistebnice Kancionál. MS. Prague, National Museum Library, II C 7. Critical Edition. Volume 2. Cantionale*, edited by Hana Vlhová-Wörner, 61-64. Chomutov: Luboš Marek.

Holford-Strevens, Leofranc. 2006. "Sirens in Antiquity and the Middle Ages." In *Music of the Sirens*, edited by Linda Austern and Inna Naroditskaya, 16-51. Bloomington: Indiana University Press.

Hollstein, F. W. H. 1993. *The New Hollstein: Dutch and Flemish Etchings, Engravings and Woodcuts 1450-1700*. Roosendaal: Koninklijke Van Poll.

Holman, Peter. 1993. *Four and Twenty Fiddlers: The Violin at the English Court 1590-1640*. Oxford: Clarendon Press.

Holmes, Megan. 2013. *The Miraculous Image in Renaissance Florence*. New Haven: Yale University Press.

Holton, David, trans. 1991a. *Erotokritos*. Bristol: Bristol Classical.

Holton, David, ed. 1991b. *Literature and Society in Renaissance Crete*. Cambridge: Cambridge University Press.

Hoogvliet, Margriet. 2003. "Princely Culture and Catherine de Médicis." In *Princes and Princely Culture, 1450-1650: Volume One*, edited by Martin Gosman, Alasdair Macdonald, and Arjo Vanderjagt, 103-30. Leiden: Brill.

Hörmann, Leonhard. 1882. "Erinnerungen an das ehemalige Frauenkloster St. Katharina in Augsburg." *Zeitschrift des Historischen Vereins für Schwaben und Neuburg* 9: 357-86.

Hörmann, Leonhard. 1883. "Erinnerungen an das ehemalige Frauenkloster Katharina in Augsburg. II: Zur innern und besondern Geschichte des Klosters." *Zeitschrift des Historischen Vereins für Schwaben und Neuburg* 10: 301-44.

Horz, Andrea. 2013. "Imago Senflij: Komponieren im Zeitalter der Reformation." In *Senfl-Studien 2*, edited by Stefan Gasch and Sonja Tröster, 43-76. Tutzing: Schneider.

Howard, Deborah. 2013. "Contextualising Titian's *Sacred and Profane Love*: The Cultural World of the Venetian Chancery in the Early Sixteenth Century." *Artibus et Historiae* 67: 185-99.

Howard, Deborah, and Laura Moretti. 2009. *Sound and Space in Renaissance Venice: Architecture, Music, Acoustics*. New Haven: Yale University Press.

Howard, Deborah, and Laura Moretti, eds. 2012. *The Music Room in Early Modern France and Italy: Sound, Space and Object*. Oxford: Oxford University Press.

Hrdina, Karel and Bohumil Ryba, eds. 1951. Vavřinec z Březové. *Píseň o vítězství u Domažlic* [*The Song about the Victory at Domažlice*]. Prague: Orbis. http://libros.csic.es/product_info.php?products_id=927; http://libros.csic.es/product_info.php?products_id=928.

Huber, Alfons. 1995. "Die Restaurierung einer Rindentrompete aus dem 16. Jhdt." *Mitteilungen des österreichischen Restauratorenverbandes* 5: 25-29.

Hughes, Dom Anselm. 1924. "Sixteenth Century Service Music: The Tudor Church Music Series." *Music and Letters* 5: 145-54.

Huizinga, Johan. 1949. *Homo Ludens: A Study of the Play-Element in Culture*. Translated by R. F. C. Hull. London: Routledge and Kegan Paul.

Hunt, David. 2003. "The Association of the Lady and the Unicorn, and the Hunting Mythology of the Caucasus." *Folklore* 114: 75-90.

Huot, Sylvia. 1987. *From Song to Book: The Poetics of Writing in Old French Lyric and Lyrical Narrative Poetry*. Ithaca, NY: Cornell University Press.

Huot, Sylvia. 1993. *The Romance of the Rose and Its Medieval Readers*. Cambridge: Cambridge University Press.

Hyatt King, Alec. 1973. "The 500th Anniversary of Music Printing: The Gradual of c.1473." *The Musical Times* 114: 1220-23.

Ianello, Tiziana. 2012. "'L'Indiani gionsero qui sabato.' Riflessi ferraresi della prima missione giapponese alla Santa Sede (1585)." *Annali Online di Ferrara - Lettere* 1: 339-56.

Idel, Moshe. 2013. "The Tsadik and His Soul's Sparks." *Jewish Quarterly Review* 103: 196-240.

Ihde, Don. 2007. *Listening and Voice: Phenomenologies of Sound*. Albany, NY: State University of New York Press.

Ingold, Timothy. 2007. "Against Soundscape." In *Autumn Leaves: Sound and the Environment in Artistic Practice*, edited by Angus Carlyle, 11-13. Paris: Double Entendre.

Ingólfsson, Árni Heimir. 2003. "The Buchanan Psalter and Its Icelandic Transmission." *Gripla* 14: 7-46.

Ingólfsson, Árni Heimir. 2012. "Fimm 'Ütlensker Tonar' í Rask 98." *Gripla* 23: 7-52.

Ingram, Jeannine S., and Keith Falconer. 2001. "Salve regina." *Grove Music Online*.

Ingram, Sonja Stafford. 1973. "The Polyphonic *Salve Regina*, 1425-1550." PhD diss., University of North Carolina at Chapel Hill.

Intabolatura di liuto de diversi. 1536. *Intabolatura di liuto de diversi, con la bataglia, et altre cose bellissime, di m. Francesco da Milano, stampata nuovamente*. Venice: Marcolini.

Ircani Menichini, Paola. 2004. *Vita quotidiana e storia della SS. Annunziata di Firenze nella prima metà del Quattrocento*. Biblioteca della Provincia Toscana dei Servi di Maria 8. Florence: Convento della SS. Annunziata.

Isacoff, Stuart. 2009. *Temperament: How Music Became a Battleground for the Great Minds of Western Civilization*. New York: Vintage Books.

Isaiasz, Vera. 2012. "Early Modern Lutheran Churches: Redefining the Boundaries of the Holy and the Profane." In *Lutheran Churches in Early Modern Europe*, edited by Andrew Spicer, 17-38. Farnham: Ashgate.

ISO [International Organization for Standardization]. 2014. "Acoustics - Soundscape - Part 1: Definition and conceptual framework." *International Organization for Standardization*, https://www.iso.org/standard/52161.html.

Ivančević, Radovan. 1994. *Šibenska katedrala [The Cathedral of Šibenik]*. Šibenik: Gradska knjižnica "Juraj Šižgorić."

Jager, Eric. 2000. *The Book of the Heart*. Chicago: University of Chicago Press.

James, Aaron. 2014. "The Apotheosis of the *Salve regina* and the Purpose of Munich, Bayerische Staatsbibliothek, Mus.ms. 34." *Journal of the Alamire Foundation* 6: 33-68.

James, Montague Rhodes. 1895. *A Descriptive Catalogue of the Manuscripts in the Library of Eton College*. Cambridge: Cambridge University Press.

Japanese travellers. 2012. *Japanese Travellers in Sixteenth-Century Europe: A Dialogue Concerning the Mission of the Japanese Ambassadors to the Roman Curia (1590)*. Edited by Derek Massarella, translated by J.F. Moran. Farnham: Ashgate.

Jervis, Simon Swynfen. 2016. "Furniture at Hardwick Hall - I." In *Hardwick Hall: A Great Old Castle of Romance*, edited by David Adshead and David Taylor, 95-99. New Haven: Yale University Press.

Jewel, John. 1842. "Letter to Peter Martyr, 5 March 1560." In *The Zurich Letters [First Series]*, edited by Hastings Robinson, 70-72. Cambridge: Cambridge University Press.

Jochymczyk, Maciej, ed. 2018. *Jakub Gołąbek: Msze trzygłosowe / Jakub Gołąbek: The Masses for Three Voices*. Kraków: Musica Iagellonica.

Johnson, Edmond. 2017. "Arnold Dolmetsch's 'Green Harpsichord' and the Musical Arts and Crafts." *Keyboard Perspectives* 10: 145-67.

Jones, Nancy A. 1994. "Music and the Maternal Voice in *Purgatorio* XIX." In *Embodied Voices: Representing Female Vocality in Western Culture*, edited by Leslie C. Dunn and Nancy A. Jones, 35-49. Cambridge: Cambridge University Press.

Jones, R. O., and Carolyn R. Lee, eds. 1975. *Juan del Encina: Poesía lírica y cancionero musical*. Madrid: Castalia.

Jónsson, Már. 1998. *Árni Magnússon: ævisaga*. Reykjavík: Mál og menning.

Jordan, Annemarie. 2005. "Images of Empire: Slaves in the Lisbon Household and Court of Catherine of Austria." In *Black Africans in Renaissance Europe*, edited by Tom F. Earle and Kate J. P. Lowe, 155-80. Cambridge: Cambridge University Press.

Joseph, George Gheverghese. 2011. *The Crest of the Peacock: Non-European Roots of Mathematics*. 3rd edn. Princeton: Princeton University Press.

Judd, Cristle Collins. 1992. "Josquin des Prez: *Salve regina* (à 5)." In *Models of Musical Analysis: Music Before 1600*, edited by Mark Everist, 114-53. Oxford: Blackwell.

Jumeau-Lafond, Jean-David. 1997. "Le chœur sans paroles ou les voix du sublime." *Revue de Musicologie* 83: 263-79.

Jurgens, Madeleine. 1982. *Documents du Minutier central des notaires de Paris: Inventaires après décès, tome premier (1483-1547)*. Paris: Archives nationales.

Jütte, Daniel. 2015. "The Place of Music in Early Modern Italian Jewish Culture." In *Musical Exodus: Al-Andalus and*

Its Jewish Diasporas, edited by Ruth F. Davis, 45-61. Lanham: Rowman & Littlefield.

Juul, Hanne. 1993. *Hanne Juul* (album). Uddevalla: Liphone.

Juva, Mikko. 1952. "Jaakko Finno rukouskirjansa valossa." In *Ramus Virens: In honorem Aarno Maliniemi 9. maii 1952*, 72-109. Suomen Kirkkohistoriallisen Seuran Toimituksia 52. Helsinki: Suomen kirkkohistoriallinen seura.

Kaff, Brigitte. 1977. *Volksreligion und Landeskirche: Die evangelische Bewegung im bayerischen Teil der Diözese Passau.* Munich: Kommissionsbuchhandlung R. Wölfle.

Kagan, Richard L., ed. 1986. *Ciudades del Siglo de Oro: Las vistas españolas de Van den Wyngaerde*. Madrid: Ediciones El Viso.

Kagan, Richard. L. 2000. *Urban Images of the Hispanic World, 1493-1780*. New Haven: Yale University Press.

Kallio, Kati. 2016. "Changes in the Poetics of Song during the Finnish Reformation." In *Re-Forming Texts, Music, and Church Art in the Early Modern North*, edited by Tuomas M. S. Lehtonen and Linda Kaljundi, 125-56. Amsterdam: Amsterdam University Press.

Kallio, Kati, Tuomas M. S. Lehtonen, Senni Timonen, Irma-Riitta Järvinen, and Ilkka Leskelä. 2018. *Laulut ja kirjoitukset: Suullinen ja kirjallinen kulttuuri uuden ajan alun Suomessa*. Helsinki: Suomalaisen Kirjallisuuden Seura.

Kaltenbacher, Robert. 1904. "Der altfranzösische Roman Paris et Vienne." *Romanische Forschungen* 15: 321-688.

Kambe, Yukimi. 2000. "Viols in Japan in the Sixteenth and Early Seventeenth Centuries." *Journal of the Viola da Gamba Society of America* 37: 31-67.

Kamen, Henry. 1997. *Philip of Spain*. New Haven: Yale University Press.

Kammel, Frank Matthias. 2007. "Lebensgenuss, Analmetaphorik und moralisierender Spott: Eine Schnupftabakdose des späten 18. Jahrhunderts im kulturgeschichtlichen Kontext." *Anzeiger des Germanischen Nationalmuseums*: 137-60.

Kammerer, Elsa. 2013. *Jean de Vauzelles et le creuset lyonnais: Un humaniste catholique au service de Marguerite de Navarre entre France, Italie et Allemagne (1520-1550)*. Geneva: Droz.

Kammerlander, Monika. 2011. "Auswirkungen der strengen Klausur auf die Musikpflege der Salzburger Benediktinen-Abtei Nonnberg des 17./18. Jahrhunderts im Vergleich mit cisterciensischen Frauenklöstern." *Analecta Cisterciensia* 61: 79-99.

Kamper, Dietmar, and Christoph Wulf, eds. 1992. *Schweigen: Unterbrechung und Grenze der menschlichen Wirklichkeit*. Berlin: Dietrich Reimer.

Kanazawa, Masakata, ed. 1974. *Antonii Ianui Opera Omnia*. Corpus Mensurabilis Musicae 70. Neuhausen-Stuttgart: American Institute of Musicology.

Kanazawa, Masakata. 1978. "[Johannes] Martini and [Johannes] Brebis at the Estense Chapel." In *Essays Presented to Myron P. Gilmore*, 2 vols., edited by Sergio Bertelli and Gloria Ramakus, 2: 412-32. Florence: La Nuova Italia.

Kanazawa, Masakata. 2001. "Janue, Antonius." *Grove Music Online*.

Kaplanis, Tassos A. 2014. "The Scholar in His Study: Depictions of a Renaissance Tradition in Vitsentzos Kornaros's Erotokritos." In *His Words Were Nourishment and His Counsel Food: A Festschrift for David W. Holton*, edited by Efrosini Camatsos, Tassos A. Kaplanis, and Jocelyn Pye, 81-99. Newcastle: Cambridge Scholars Publishing.

Kastenholz, Richard. 2006. *Hans Schwarz: Ein Augsburger Bildhauer und Medailleur der Renaissance*. Munich: Deutscher Kunstverlag.

Kaufmann, Miranda. 2017. *Black Tudors: The Untold Story*. London: Oneword Publications.

Kelber, Moritz. 2018. *Die Musik bei den Augsburger Reichstagen im 16. Jahrhundert*. Munich: Allitera Verlag.

Kelber, Moritz. 2019. "Leviathan: Die Orgel als Herrschaftsinstrument." *Musiktheorie* 34: 83-94.

Kellman, Herbert. 1999. "Brussels, Bibliothèque royale de Belgique MS 9126." In *The Treasury of Petrus Alamire: Music and Art in Flemish Court Manuscripts 1500-1535*, edited by Herbert Kellman, 73. Ghent: Ludion.

Kellman, Herbert, ed. 1999. *The Treasury of Petrus Alamire: Music and Art in Flemish Court Manuscripts 1500-1535*. Ghent: Ludion.

Kelman, Ari. 2010. "Rethinking the Soundscape: A Critical Genealogy of a Key Term in Sound Studies." *Senses & Society* 5: 212-24.

Kendrick, Robert L. 1996. *Celestial Sirens: Nuns and Their Music in Early Modern Milan*. Oxford: Clarendon Press.

Kendrick, Robert L. 2002. *The Sounds of Milan, 1585-1650*. New York: Oxford University Press.

Kenter, Barry Allen. 2014. "Table for One or Shulhan Ihu 'Iqra: The Medieval Jewish Table." DHL diss., Jewish Theological Seminary, New York.

Kerovpyan, Aram. 1995-96. "Les Tbir: Les artisans du chant liturgique arménien." *Hask* 7-8: 367-75. Updated French translation: https://www.academia.edu/7072220/Les_Tbir_les_artisans_du_chant_liturgique_arm%C3%A9nien.

Kerovpyan, Aram. 1996. "Armenian Liturgical Chant: The System and Reflections on the Present Situation." *Saint Nerses Theological Review* 1: 25-42.

Kerovpyan, Aram. 2001. "Armenia, Republic of, II. Church Music." *Grove Music Online*.

Kessler, Herbert L. 2000. *Spiritual Seeing: Picturing God's Invisibility in Medieval Art*. Philadelphia: University of Pennsylvania Press.

Ketterer, Robert C. 1999. "Classical Sources and Thematic Structure in the Florentine Intermedi of 1589." *Renaissance Studies* 13: 192-222.

Kilgour, Maggie. 1991. *From Communion to Cannibalism: An Anatomy of Metaphors of Incorporation*. Princeton: Princeton University Press.

[Kilian, Wolfgang and Lucas Kilian]. 1612. *Musae IX. Viro Nob. Et Cl. Dn. Philip. Hainhofero Civi Aug. Vind. Eleg. Et Subtil. Art. Aestim. Et Patrexim. Dn. Plur. Col.* Augsburg: n.p.

Kilström, Bengt Ingmar. 1968. *Härkeberga kyrka*. Sveriges kyrkor 123. Stockholm: Almqvist och Wiksell.

King, John N. 2006. *Foxe's Book of Martyrs and Early Modern Print Culture*. Cambridge: Cambridge University Press.

Kinney, Daniel, and Elizabeth Styron. 2018. "Ovid Illustrated: The Reception of Ovid's *Metamorphoses* in Image and Text." http://ovid.lib.virginia.edu/ovidillust.html.

Kirkendale, Warren. 1972. "Franceschina, Girometta, and their Companions in a Madrigal 'a diversi linguaggi' by Luca Marenzio and Orazio Vecchi." *Acta musicologica* 44: 181-235.

Kirkendale, Warren. 1984. "*Circulatio*-Tradition, *Maria Lactans*, and Josquin as Musical Orator." *Acta Musicologica* 56: 69-92.

Kirkendale, Warren. 1988. "La Franceschina, la Girometta e soci in un madrigale 'a diversi linguaggi' di Luca Marenzio e Orazio Vecchi." In *Il madrigale tra cinque e seicento*, edited by Paolo Fabbri, 249-331. Bologna: Il Mulino.

Kirkman, Andrew, and Philip Weller. 2017. "Music and Image / Image and Music: The Creation and Meaning of Visual-Aural Force Fields in the Later Middle Ages." *Early Music* 45: 55-75.

Kirkman, Andrew, and Philip Weller. 2019. "English Alabaster Images as Recipients of Music in the Long Fifteenth Century: English Sacred Traditions in a European Perspective." In *English Alabaster Carvings and Their Cultural Contexts*, edited by Zuleika Murat, 93-126. Woodbridge: Boydell and Brewer.

Kirnbauer, Martin. 2015. "Petrucci in the Fifteenth Century: The Lute Duos." In *Venezia 1501: Petrucci e la stampa musicale*, edited by Giulio Cattin and Patrizia Dalla Vecchia, 591-607. Venice: Fondazione Levi.

Kizzire, Jessica. 2014. "'The Place I'll Return to Someday': Musical Nostalgia in *Final Fantasy IX*." In *Music in Video Games: Studying Play*, edited by K. J. Donnelly, William Gibbons, and Neil Lerner, 183-98. New York: Routledge.

Kline, Daniel T. 2013. *Digital Gaming Re-Imagines the Middle Ages*. New York: Routledge.

Knight, Frances. 2015. *Victorian Christianity at the Fin de Siècle: The Culture of English Religion in a Decadent Age*. London: I.B. Tauris.

Knighton, Tess. 1992. "Editorial." *Early Music* 20: 530-31.

Knighton, Tess. 2007. "Song Migration: The Case of *Adorámoste Señor*." In *Devotional Music in the Iberian World, 1450-1800*, edited by Tess Knighton and Álvaro Torrente, 53-76. Aldershot: Ashgate.

Knighton, Tess. 2018. "Orality and Aurality: Contexts for the Unwritten Musics of Sixteenth-Century Barcelona." In *Hearing the City in Early Modern Europe*, edited by Tess Knighton and Ascensión Mazuela-Anguita, 295-308. Turnhout: Brepols.

Knighton, Tess, and Ascensión Mazuela-Anguita, eds. 2018. *Hearing the City in Early Modern Europe*. Turnhout: Brepols.

Knighton, Tess, and Kenneth Kreitner. 2019. *The Music of Juan de Anchieta*. Abingdon: Routledge.

Knox, Dilwyn. 2000. "Civility, Courtesy and Women in the Italian Renaissance." In *Women in Italian Renaissance Culture and Society*, edited by Letizia Panizza, 2-17. Oxford: European Humanities Research Centre.

Knuutila, Jyrki. 1997. "Yxi wähä suomenkielinen wirsikirja, 1583." In *Vanhimman suomalaisen kirjallisuuden käsikirja*, edited by Tuija Laine, 136-38. Helsinki: Suomalaisen Kirjallisuuden Seura.

Kobayashi-Sato, Yoriko. 2010. "An Assimilation between Two Different Cultures: Japan and the West during the Edo Period." In *Artistic and Cultural Exchanges between Europe and Asia, 1400-1900: Rethinking Markets, Workshops and Collections*, edited by Michael North, 163-86. Farnham: Ashgate.

Kohl, Jeanette. 2010. "Icons of Chastity, 'Objets d'Amour': Female Renaissance Portrait Busts as Ambivalent Bodies." In *The Body in Early Modern Italy*, edited by Julia Hairston and Walter Stephens, 123-41. Baltimore: Johns Hopkins University Press.

Kolár, Jaroslav, Anežka Vidmanová, and Hana Vlhová-Wörner, eds. 2005. *Jistebnický kancionál. MS. Praha, Knihovna Národního muzea, II C 7. Kritická edice. 1. svazek. Graduale/ The Jistebnice Kancionál. MS. Prague, National Museum Library, II C 7. Critical Edition. Volume 1. Graduale.* Brno: Luboš Marek.

Koldewey, Friedrich. 1890. *Schulordnungen des Herzogtums Braunschweig (mit Ausschluß der Hauptstadt des Landes) vom Jahre 1248-1826*. Berlin: Hofmann.

Kornaros, Vitsentzos. 2004. *Erotokritos*. Edited and translated by Gavin Betts, Stathis Gauntlett, and Thanasis Spilias. Melbourne: Australian Association for Byzantine Studies.

Kornmeier, Uta. 2004. "Madame Tussaud's as a Popular Pantheon." In *Pantheons: Transformations of a Monumental Idea*, edited by Richard Wrigley and Matthew Craske, 147-66. Aldershot: Ashgate.

Koskinen, Ulla. 2010. "Aatelin aineellinen kulttuuri 1500-luvun lopulla – löytöjä Arwid Henrikinpoika Tawastin hämäläisten kartanoiden tilikirjoista." *Ennen ja Nyt*, January 10. http://www.ennenjanyt.net/2010/01/aatelin-aineellinen-kulttuuri-1500-luvun-lopulla/.

Kovacs, Susan R. 1994. "The French Lyric Collection from Manuscript to Print: Authorship, Arrangement, and Poetic Identity." PhD diss., New York University.

Kovacs, Susan R. 2001. "Staging Lyric Performance in Early Print Culture: The *Jardin de Plaisance et Fleur de Rhétorique* (c.1501-1502)." *French Studies* 55: 1-24.

Kozina, Jiří, and Markéta Kozinová. 2005. "The Nineteenth Century Discovery of the Jisteb- nice Kancionál and Its Subsequent Use." In *Jistebnický kancionál. MS. Praha, Knihovna Národního muzea, II C 7. Kritická edice. 1. svazek. Graduale/ The Jistebnice Kancionál. MS. Prague, National Museum Library, II C 7. Critical Edition. Volume 1. Graduale*, edited by Jaroslav Kolár, Anežka Vidmanová, and Hana Vlhová-Wörner, 29-36. Brno: Luboš Marek.

Kraemer, Gilles. 2008. "Les incroyables merveilles de la XXIe TEFAF." *Art et métiers du livre* 264: 12-13.

Kramer-Schlette, Carla. 1970. *Vier augsburger Chronisten der Reformationszeit: Die Behandlung und Deutung der Zeitgeschichte bei Clemens Sender, Wilhelm Rem, Georg Preu und Paul Hektor Mair*. Lübeck, Hamburg: Matthiesen.

Kranz, Annette. 2004. "Zur Portraitmedaille in Augsburg im 16. Jahrhundert." In *Die Renaissance-Medaille in Italien und Deutschland*, edited by Georg Satzinger, 301-42. Münster: Rhema.

Kravina, Chiara. 2018. "Tradizione e fortuna del *De re uxoria* di Francesco Barbaro." In *Acta Conventus Neo-Latini Vindobonensis: Proceedings of the Sixteenth International Congress of Neo-Latin Studies (Vienna 2015)*, edited by Astrid Steiner-Weber and Franz Römer, 412-22. Leiden: Brill.

Kren, Thomas, with Jill Burke, and Stephen J. Campbell, eds. 2018. *The Renaissance Nude*. Los Angeles: J. Paul Getty Museum.

Kreutziger-Herr, Annette. 2003. *Ein Traum vom Mittelalter: Die Wiederentdeckung mittelalterlicher Musik in der Neuzeit*. Vienna: Böhlau.

Kristeva, Julia. 1998. *Visions capitales*. Paris: Réunion des Musées Nationaux.

Krüger, Klaus. 2017. "Visions of Inaudible Sounds: Heavenly Music and Its Pictorial Representations." In *Voir l'au-delà: L'expérience visionnaire et sa représentation dans l'art italien de la Renaissance*, edited by Andreas Beyer, Philippe Morel, et al., 77-93. Turnhout: Brepols.

Krummel, D. W., and Stanley Sadie, eds. 1980. *Music Printing and Publishing*. London: Macmillan.

Kurvinen, P. J. I. 1929. *Suomen virsirunouden alkuvaiheet vuoteen 1640*. Helsinki: Suomalaisen Kirjallisuuden Seura.

Kushnatyan, Kristapor. 2016. *Armenian Monodic Music: The History and Theory*. Yerevan: Ankyunacar Publishing.

Küster, Konrad. 2016. *Musik im Namen Luthers: Kulturtraditionen seit der Reformation*. Kassel: Bärenreiter.

La Bibbia di Borso d'Este. 1997. *La Bibbia di Borso d'Este: Commentario al codice*. 2 vols. Modena: Franco Cosimo Panini.

La Malfa, Claudia. 2005. "A New Sketch by Filippino Lippi for the 'Assumption of the Virgin' in the Carafa Chapel." *Master Drawings* 43: 144-59.

Labowsky, Lotte. 1979. *Bessarion's Library and the Biblioteca Marciana: Six Early Inventories*. Rome: Edizioni di storia e letteratura.

Lach, David. 1965. "A Japanese Mission in Europe, 1584-86." In *Asia in the Making of Europe*. Vol. 1. *The Century of Discovery*, 688-706. Chicago: University of Chicago Press.

Lachèvre, Frédéric. 1922. *Recueils collectifs de poésies du XVIe siècle, du Jardin de Plaisance (1502) aux recueils de Toussaint du Bray (1609)*. Paris: E. Champion.

Ladis, Andrew. 2001. "The Music of Devotion: Image, Voice, and the Imagination in Domenico di Bartolo's Madonna of Humility." In *Visions of Holiness: Art and Devotion in Renaissance Italy*, edited by Andrew Ladis and Shelley E. Zuraw, 163-77. Athens, GA: Georgia Museum of Art, University of Georgia.

Lampadius, Auctor. 1541. *Compendium musices*. Bern: Apiarius.

Landau, Peter. 1975. *Jus patronatus: Studien zur Entwicklung des Patronats im Dekretalenrecht und der Kanonistik des 12. und 13. Jahrhunderts*. Cologne: Böhlau-Verlag.

Landersdorfer, Anton. 1986. *Das Bistum Freising in der bayerischen Visitation des Jahres 1560*. St Ottilien: EOS.

Landino, Cristoforo. 2001. *Comento sopra la Comedia*. 4 vols. Edited by Paolo Procaccioli. Rome: Salerno.

Lange-Krach, Heidrun, ed. 2019. *Maximilian I. (1459-1519): Kaiser, Ritter, Bürger zu Augsburg*. Regensburg: Schnell & Steiner.

Langeron, M. Olivier. 1851. "La trompette d'argent." *Mémoires de la Commission des antiquités de la Côte-d'Or*, 2nd ser. 14: 91-102.

Larson, Katherine R. 2019. *The Matter of Song in Early Modern England: Texts In and Of the Air*. Oxford: Oxford University Press.

Lasithiotakis, Michalis. 2008. "Apichisis tou Cortigiano tou B. Castiglione ston Erotokrito" [Λασσιθιοτάκης, Μιχάλης, "Απηχήσεις του Cortigiano του B. Castiglione στον Ερωτόκριτος"]. In *Pedia kie politismos stin Kriti: Vysantio – Venetokratia* [Παιδεία και πολιτισμός στην Κρήτη: Βυζάντιο – Βενετοκρατεία], edited by Ioannis Vassis, Stefanos Kaklamanis, and Marina Loukaki, 251-62. Herakleion: Panepistimiakes ekdosis Kritis.

Laube, Matthew. 2017. "Materializing Music in the Lutheran Home." *Past & Present* 243: 114-38.

Lawatsch Melton, Barbara. 2010. "Loss And Gain in a Salzburg Convent: Tridentine Reform, Princely Absolutism, and the Nuns of Nonnberg (1620 to 1696)." In *Enduring Loss in Early Modern Germany: Cross Disciplinary Perspectives*, edited by Lynne Tatlock, 259-80. Studies in Central European History 50. Leiden: Brill.

Lazzarini, Elena. 2010. *Nudo, arte e decoro: Oscillazioni estetiche negli scritti d'arte del Cinquecento*. Pisa: Pacini Editore.

Le Huray, Peter. 1967. *Music and the Reformation in England*. London: Herbert Jenkins.

Le Jardin de plaisance. 1910-25. *Le Jardin de plaisance et fleur de rhétorique: Reproduction en fac-similé de l'édition publiée par Antoine Vérard vers 1501*. 2 vols. Edited by Eugénie Droz and Arthur Piaget. Vol. 1 (facsimile). Paris: Firmin-Didot, 1910. Vol. 2 (Introduction and notes). Paris: Firmin-Didot, 1925.

Le Roy Ladurie, Emmanuel. 2000. *Le voyage de Thomas Platter, 1595-1599*. Paris: Fayard.

Leaver, Robin A. 1991. *Goostly Psalmes and Spiritual Songs*. Oxford: Oxford University Press.

Leaver, Robin A. 2007. *Luther's Liturgical Music: Principles and Implications*. Grand Rapids: William B. Eerdmans.

Leech-Wilkinson, Daniel. 2002. *The Modern Invention of Medieval Music: Scholarship, Ideology, Performance*. Cambridge: Cambridge University Press.

Lefebvre, Henri. 1991. *The Production of Space*. Translated by Donald Nicholson-Smith. Oxford: Blackwell.

Lehtonen, Tuomas M. S. 2016. "Pious Hymns and Devil's Music: Michael Agricola (c.1507-1557) and Jacobus Finno (c.1540-1588) on Church Song and Folk Beliefs." In *Re-Forming Texts, Music, and Church Art in the Early Modern North*, edited by Tuomas M. S. Lehtonen and Linda Kaljundi, 179-216. Amsterdam: Amsterdam University Press.

Lempiäinen, Pentti. 1988. "Ensimmäinen suomalainen virsikirja." In Jacobus Petri Finno, *Jaakko Finnon Virsikirja: Näköispainos ensimmäisestä suomalaisesta virsikirjasta sekä uudelleen ladottu laitos alkuperäisestä tekstistä ja sitä täydentävistä käsikirjoituksista*, edited by Pentti Lempiäinen, 358-87. Helsinki: Suomalaisen Kirjallisuuden Seura.

Lepine, Ayla. 2017. "Heaven and Earth in Little Space: G. F. Bodley at All Saints, Jesus Lane." *Noesis: Theology, Philosophy, Poetics* 3: 77-84.

Lessing, Julius, and Adolf Brüning, eds. 1905. *Der Pommersche Kunstschrank*. Berlin: Königliches Kunstgewerbe-Museum / Ernst Wasmuth.

Lesure, François. 1954. "La facture instrumentale à Paris au seizième siècle." *The Galpin Society Journal* 7: 11-52.

Levi D'Ancona, Mirella. 1977. *The Garden of the Renaissance: Botanical Symbolism in Italian Painting*. Florence: Olschki.

Levy, Evonne. 2004. *Propaganda and the Jesuit Baroque*. Berkeley: University of California Press.

Liebenwein, Wolfgang. 1993. "Die 'Privatisierung' des Wunders: Piero de' Medici in SS. Annunziata und San Miniato." In *Piero de' Medici, 'il Gottoso', 1416-1469: Kunst im Dienste der Mediceer / Art in the Service of the Medici*, edited by Andreas Beyer and Bruce Boucher, 251-90. Berlin: Akademie Verlag.

Liehm, Antonín J. 2016. *The Miloš Forman Stories*. Abingdon: Routledge.

Lind, Stephanie. 2020. "Music as Temporal Disruption in Assassin's Creed." *The Soundtrack* 11, no. 1/2: 57–73.

Lindmayr-Brandl, Andrea, Elisabeth Schmierer, and Joshua Rifkin. 2012-forthcoming. *Handbuch der Musik der Renaissance*. 7 vols. Laaber: Laaber-Verlag.

Lippincott, Kristen. 1987. "The Frescoes of the Salone dei Mesi in the Palazzo Schifanoia in Ferrara: Style, Iconography and Cultural Context." 2 vols. PhD diss., University of Chicago.

Liscia-Bemporad, Dora. 1996. "La cappella 'tedesca'." *MCM: La Storia delle Cose* 32: 14-16.

Litchfield, Malcolm. 1988. "Aristoxenus and Empiricism: A Reevaluation Based on His Theories." *Journal of Music Theory* 32: 51-73.

Little, Frances. 1941. "An Elizabethan Bed Valance." *The Metropolitan Museum of Art Bulletin* 36: 183-85.

Locke, Ralph P. 2015. *Music and the Exotic from the Renaissance to Mozart*. Cambridge: Cambridge University Press.

Lockwood, Lewis. 1984. *Music in Renaissance Ferrara 1400-1505: The Creation of a Musical Center in the Fifteenth Century*. Oxford: Oxford University Press.

Lockwood, Lewis. 2001. "Soggetto cavato." *Grove Music Online*.

Lodes, Birgit. 2006. "Senfl, Ludwig." *MGG Online*.

Lodes, Birgit. 2012. "Zur katholischen Psalmmotette der 1520er Jahre: Othmar Luscinius und die Fugger." In *Senfl-Studien 1*, edited by Stefan Gasch, Birgit Lodes and Sonja Tröster, 347-87. Tutzing: Hans Schneider.

Lodes, Birgit. 2013. "*Translatio panegyricorum*: Eine Begrüßungsmotette Senfls (?) für Kaiser Karl V. (1530)." In *Senfl-Studien 2*, edited by Stefan Gasch, and Sonja Tröster, 189-255. Tutzing: Schneider.

Lodes, Birgit. 2016. "'Mehrfacher Sinn': Jacob Obrechts Missa Salve diva parens und die Königskrönung Maximilians." *Musikleben des Spätmittelalters in der Region Österreich*. https://musical-life.net/essays/mehrfacher-sinn-jacob-obrechts-missa-salve-diva-parens-und-die-konigskronung-maximilians.

Lodes, Birgit. 2017. "Musik für Kaiser Karl V. (1530)." *Musikleben des Spätmittelalters in der Region Österreich*. http://www.musical-life.net/essays/musik-fur-kaiser-karl-v-1530.

Lofts, Norah. 1979. *Anne Boleyn*. New York: Coward, McCann & Geoghegan.

Lomazzo, Giovanni Paolo. 1584. *Trattato dell'arte della pittura, scoltura et architettura*. Milan: Paolo Gottardo Pontio.

Long, Michael. 2014. "Hearing Josquin Hearing Busnoys." In *The Cambridge History of Fifteenth-Century Music*, edited by Anna Maria Busse Berger and Jesse Rodin, 21-39. Cambridge: Cambridge University Press.

Lootens, Matthew. 2011. "Augustine." In *The Spiritual Senses: Perceiving God in Western Christianity*, edited by Paul L. Gavrilyuk and Sarah Coakley, 56-70. Cambridge: Cambridge University Press.

López-Gay, Jesús. 1970. *La liturgia en la misión del Japón del siglo XVI*. Rome: Università Gregoriana.

Lorenz, Detlev. 1992. *Fleischextrakt und große Oper: Die Reklame-Sammelbilder der Liebig-Gesellschaft zu Oper, Operette und Ballett*. Berlin: [Lorenz].

Lorenzetti, Stefano. 2011a. "Public Behaviour, Music and the Construction of Feminine Identity in the Italian Renaissance." *Recercare* 23: 7-34.

Lorenzetti, Stefano. 2011b. "'Cum tanta armonia, cum tanta incredibile sonoritate, cum tanta insueta proportione': La dialettica tra sensibile e sovrasensibile nella percezione della musica rinascimentale." In *Proportions: Science, musique, peinture & architecture: Actes du 51. Colloque international d'études humanistes, 30 juin - 4 juillet 2008*, edited by Sabine Rommevaux, Philippe Vendrix, and Vasco Zara, 199-215. Turnhout: Brepols.

Lorris, Guillaume de, and Jean de Meun. 1973-75. *Le Roman de la Rose*. 3 vols. Edited by Félix Lecoy. Paris: Champion.

Losty, J. P., and Malini Roy. 2013. *Mughal India: Art, Culture and Empire*. London: British Library.

Lovell, Percy. 1979. "'Ancient' Music in Eighteenth-Century England." *Music & Letters* 60: 401-15.

Lovrenović, Dubravko. 2011. "Bosnian 'School of Death': Interconfessionality of Stećci." *Ikon: Časopis za ikonografske studije* 4: 59-72.

Lowe, Barbara. 1957. "Early Records of the Morris in England." *Journal of the English Folk Dance and Song Society* 8: 61-82.

Lowe, Kate. 2005. "The Stereotyping of Black Africans in Renaissance Europe." In *Black Africans in Renaissance Europe*, edited by Tom F. Earle and Kate J. P. Lowe, 17-47. Cambridge: Cambridge University Press.

Lowinsky, Edward E. 1954. "Music in the Culture of the Renaissance." *Journal of the History of Ideas* 15: 509-53.

Lowinsky, Edward E. 1989a. "Cipriano de Rore's Venus Motet: Its Poetic and Pictorial Sources." In *Music in the Culture of the Renaissance and Other Essays*, 2 vols, edited by Bonnie J. Blackburn, 2:575-94. Chicago: Chicago University Press. (Originally published as: *Cipriano de Rore's Venus Motet: Its Poetic and Pictorial Sources*. Provo, UT: College of Fine Arts and Communications, 1986).

Lowinsky, Edward E. 1989b. "A Music Book for Anne Boleyn." In *Music in the Culture of the Renaissance and Other Essays*, 2 vols., edited by Bonnie J. Blackburn, 2:484-528. Chicago: University of Chicago Press. (Originally published in *Florilegium Historiale: Essays Presented to Wallace K. Ferguson*, edited by J. G. Rowe and W. H. Stockdale, 161-235. Toronto: University of Toronto Press, 1971).

Lozica, Ivan. 2007. "Karneval životinja." In *Kulturni bestijarij*, edited by Suzana Marjanović, and Antonija Zaradija Kiš, 203-14. Zagreb: Institut za etnologiju i folkloristiku; Hrvatska sveučilišna naklada.

Lubenow, Martin, ed. 2006. *Martin Peudargent: Musiker und Komponist am jülich-klevischen Hof. Gesamtausgabe*. Germersheim: Musiche Varie.

Ludolphy, Ingetraut. 2006. *Friedrich der Weise, Kurfürst von Sachsen, 1463-1525*. Leipzig: Universitätsverlag.

Lüdtke, Joachim. 2001. "'14. iuni. principium posui artis musicae': Die musikalische Ausbildung des Kaufmannssohns Philipp Hainhofer." In *Musikalischer Alltag im 15. und 16. Jahrhundert*, Trossinger Jahrbuch für Renaissancemusik 1, edited by Nicole Schwindt, 159-80. Kassel: Bärenreiter.

Lund, Engel. *Íslenzk þjóðlög valin og búin til prentunar af Engel Lund* (arr. Ferdinand Rauter). Reykjavík: Almenna bókafélagið.

Lundberg, Mattias. 2017. "Liturgical Singing in the Lutheran Mass in Early Modern Sweden and Its Implications for Clerical Ritual Performance and Lay Literacy." *Yale Journal of Music & Religion* 3, no. 1: 61-76.

Lupieri, Edmondo. 1988. *Giovanni Battista fra storia e leggenda*. Brescia: Paideia.

Lütteken, Laurenz. 2011. *Musik der Renaissance: Imagination und Wirklichkeit einer kulturellen Praxis*. Kassel: Bärenreiter.

MacCarthy, Evan A. 2014. "The Sources and Early Readers of Ugolino of Orvieto's *Declaratio Musice Discipline*." In *Beyond 50 Years of Ars Nova Studies at Certaldo. 1959-2009*, edited by Marco Gozzi, Agostino Ziino, and Francesco Zimei, 401-25. Lucca: Libreria Musicale Italiana.

Macchiarella, Ignazio. 1995. *Il falsobordone fra tradizione orale e tradizione scritta*. Lucca: Libreria Musicale Italiana.

MacGregor, Neil. 2010. *A History of the World in 100 Objects*. London: Penguin.

Macho, Thomas H. 1993. "Die Kunst der Pause: Eine musikontologische Meditation." *Paragrana: Internationale Zeitschrift für historische Anthropologie* 2: 104-16.

Madame Tussauds London. 1993. *Illustrated Guide*. N.P.: n.p.

Maffei, Celso. 1504. *Delitiosam explicationem de sensibilibus deliciis paradisi*. Verona: Lucas Antonius Florentinus.

Magno, Alessandro Marzo. 2013. *Bound in Venice: The Serene Republic and the Dawn of the Book*. Rome: Edizioni e/o.

Mährle, Wolfgang. 2019. "Der Tag des Gelehrten: Das 'Diarium' des Martin Crusius als frühneuzeitliches Selbstzeugnis." In *Spätrenaissance in Schwaben. Wissen – Literatur – Kunst*, edited by Wolfgang Mährle, 229-47. Stuttgart: Kohlhammer.

Mai, Paul. 1993. *Das Bistum Regensburg in der bayerischen Visitation von 1559*. Beiträge zur Geschichte des Bistums Regensburg 27. Regensburg: Verlag des Vereins für Regensburger Bistumsgeschichte.

Maldonado, Alonso. 1935. *Hechos del Maestre de Alcántara*. Edited by Antonio Rodríguez Moñino. Madrid: Revista de Occidente.

Maltezou, Cryssa, Angeliki Tzavara, and Despina Vlassi, eds. 2009. *I Greci durante la venetocrazia: Uomini, spazio, idee (XIII-XVIII), Atti del Convegno Internazionale di Studi, Venezia, 3-7 dicembre 2007*. Venice: Istituto Ellenico di Studi Bizantini e Postbizantini di Venezia.

Manassero, Roberto. 2017. "Mr Forman goes to America." In *Miloš Forman*, edited by Angelo Signorelli, 58-65. Bergamo: Bergamo Film Meeting.

Marcora, Carlo. 1962. "Il processo diocesano informativo sulla vita di s. Carlo per la sua canonizzazione." *Memorie storiche della diocesi di Milano* 9: 76-735.

Marcorin, Francesco. 2013. "Alcuni documenti inediti relativi alla facciata sanmicheliana di palazzo Bevilacqua a Verona." *Annali di Architettura* 25: 117-34.

Marcos Álvarez, Fernando. 2001. "Literatura y realidad: El ciego rezador." *Revista de Estudios Extremeños* 54: 219-32.

Marin, Louis. 1977. *Détruire la peinture*. Paris: Flammarion.

Marsh, Christopher. 2010. *Music and Society in Early Modern England*. Cambridge: Cambridge University Press.

Marshall, Melanie L. 2004. "Cultural Codes and Hierarchies in the Mid-Century Villotta." 2 vols. PhD diss., University of Southampton.

Marshall, Melanie L. 2015. "Voce Bianca: Purity and Whiteness in British Early Music Vocality." *Women and Music: A Journal of Gender and Culture* 19: 36-44.

Marshall, Peter, and Alexandra Walsham. 2006. "Migrations of Angels in the Early Modern World." In *Angels in the Early Modern World*, edited by Peter Marshall and Alexandra Walsham, 1-40. Cambridge: Cambridge University Press.

Martin, Thomas. 2013. "The Nude Figure in Renaissance Art." In *A Companion to Renaissance and Baroque Art*, edited by Babette Bohn and James M. Saslow, 402-21. Chichester: Wiley-Blackwell.

Martínez Gil, Carlos. 1993-94. *Catálogo de música del Archivo Parroquial (antigua colegiata) de Pastrana (Guadalajara)*. Universidad de Salamanca: Cursos de Doctorado Bienio, unpublished.

Martini, Emanuela. 2017. "Forman in Wonderland." In *Miloš Forman*, edited by Angelo Signorelli, 44-57. Bergamo: Bergamo Film Meeting.

Massarella, David. 2012. "The Japanese Embassy to Europe (1582-1590)." *The Journal of the Hakluyt Society* 25: 1-12.

Massing, Jean Michel. 2011. *The Image of the Black in Western Art*. Vol. 3/2: *From the "Age of Discovery" to the Age of Abolition: Europe and the World Beyond*. Cambridge, MA: Belknap Press.

Mathiesen, Thomas J. 1988. *Ancient Greek Music Theory: A Catalogue Raisonné of Manuscripts*. Répertoire International des Sources Musicales [RISM] B/XI. Munich: Henle.

Mathiesen, Thomas J. 1992. "Hermes or Clio? The Transmission of Ancient Greek Music Theory." In *Musical Humanism and Its Legacy: Essays in Honor of Claude V. Palisca*, edited by Nancy Kovaleff Baker and Barbara Russano Hanning, 3-35. Stuyvesant, NY: Pendragon Press.

Matut, Diana. 2017. "'Lid, ton, vayz – shir, nign, zemer': Der einstimmige jiddische Gesang im 15. und 16. Jahrhundert." In "Creatio ex unisono: Einstimmige Musik im 15. und 16. Jahrhundert," edited by Nicole Schwindt, special issue, *Trossinger Jahrbuch für Renaissancemusik* 13: 149-74.

Maué, Hermann. 2003. "Hagenauer, Friedrich." *Grove Art Online*.

Mavromatis, Giannis. 1982. *To protypo tou Erotokritou* [Μαυρομάτης, Γιάννης. Το πρότυπο του Ερωτοκρίτου]. Ioannina: Panepistimio Ioanninon.

Mayes, Stanley. 1956. *An Organ for the Sultan*. London: Putnam.

Maza, Francisco de la. 1945. "Fray Diego Valadés: Escritor y grabador franciscano del siglo XVI." *Anales del Instituto de Investigaciones Estéticas* 13: 15-44.

Mazuela-Anguita, Ascensión. 2015. "¿Bailes o aquelarres? Música, mujeres y brujería en documentos inquisitoriales del Renacimiento." *Bulletin of Spanish Studies: Hispanic Studies and Researches on Spain, Portugal and Latin America* 92, no. 5: 725-46.

McGeary, Thomas. 1995. "Giovanni Paolo Lomazzo on the Decoration of Organs and Musical Instruments." *The Organ Yearbook* 25: 33-48.

McGee, Timothy J. 1985. *Medieval and Renaissance Music: A Performer's Guide*. Toronto: University of Toronto Press.

McGee, Timothy J. 2003. "*Cantare all'improvviso:* Improvising to Poetry in Late Medieval Italy." In *Improvisation in the Arts of the Middle Ages and Renaissance*, edited by Timothy J. McGee, 31-70. Kalamazoo: Medieval Institute, Western Michigan University.

McGee, Timothy J. 2006/07. "Filippino Lippi and Music." *Renaissance and Reformation / Renaissance et Réforme* 30: 5-28.

McGowan, Margaret M. 1963. *L'art du ballet de cour en France, 1581-1643*. Paris: Éditions du Centre National de la Recherche Scientifique.

McGowan, Margaret M. 2008. *Dance in the Renaissance: European Fashion, French Obsession*. New Haven: Yale University Press.

McGuire, Brian Patrick. 1991. *The Difficult Saint: Bernard of Clairvaux and His Tradition*. Kalamazoo: Cistercian Publications.

McIver, Katherine A. 2014. "Visual Pleasures, Sensual Sounds: Music, Morality, and Sexuality in Paintings by Titian." In

Sexualities, Textualities, Art and Music in Early Modern Italy, edited by Linda L. Carroll, Melanie L. Marshall, and Katherine A. McIver, 13-22. Burlington, VT: Ashgate.

McKinnon, James W., and Robert Anderson. 2018. "Ovid." *Grove Music Online*.

Mearns, James. 1914. *The Canticles of the Christian Church Eastern and Western in Early Medieval Times*. Cambridge: Cambridge University Press.

Meconi, Honey. 2010. "Margaret of Austria, Visual Representation, and Brussels, Royal Library, Ms. 228." *Journal of the Alamire Foundation* 2: 11-36.

Medica, Massimo. 2008a. "Mantova, Ferrara e Roma: Il percorso di un artista 'cortigiano'." In *Giovanni Battista Cavalletto: Un miniatore bolognese nell'età di Aspertini*, edited by Marco Medica, 9-27. Cinisello Balsamo: Silvana.

Medica, Massimo. 2008b. "Giovanni Battista Cavalletto, *Allegoria I, Allegoria II*." In *Bonacolsi l'antico*, edited by Filippo Trevisani and Davide Gasparotto, 164-65. Milan: Electa.

Medici, Lorenzo de'. 1913-14. *Opere*. 2 vols. Edited by Attilio Simioni. Bari: Laterza.

Mei, Girolamo. 1602. *Discorso sopra la musica antica et moderna*. Venice: Ciotti.

Meitinger, Otto. 1970. "Die baugeschichtliche Entwicklung der Neuveste: Ein Beitrag zur Geschichte der Münchner Residenz." *Oberbayerisches Archiv* 92: 3-295.

Melin, Pia. 2006. "Fåfängans förgänglighet: Allegorin som livs- och lärospegel hos Albertus Pictor." PhD diss., University of Stockholm.

Meriani, Angelo. 2016. "Teoria e storia della musica greca antica alla scuola di Vittorino da Feltre." *Rivista di Cultura Classica e Medioevale* 78: 311-35.

Merkley, Paul A., and Lora L. M. Merkley. 1999. *Music and Patronage in the Sforza Court*. Studi sulla storia della musica in Lombardia 3. Turnhout: Brepols.

Merrifield, Ralph. 1987. *The Archaeology of Ritual and Magic*. London: Batsford.

Merryweather, James W. 2001. "Two-Chanter Bagpipes in England." *Galpin Society Journal* 54: 62-75.

Mersenne, Marin. 1636-37. *Harmonie universelle, contenant la théorie et la pratique de la musique*. 2 vols. Paris: Pierre Ballard.

Mersenne, Marin. 1637. *Seconde Partie de L'Harmonie Universelle*. Paris: Pierre Ballard.

Mersenne, Marin. 1648. *Harmonicorvm Libri XII*. Paris: Guillaume Baudry.

Merula, Pellegrino. 1627. *Santuario di Cremona [...]*. Cremona: for Bartolomeo and the heirs of Baruccio Zanni.

Messenger, Ruth. 1953. *The Medieval Latin Hymn*. Washington: Capital Press.

Messisbugo, Cristoforo. 1549. *Banchetti composizione di vivande e apparecchio generale*. Ferrara: Buglhat and Hucher.

Meucci, Renato. 2017. "Gabriele d'Annunzio e Arnold Dolmetsch, l'apostolo della musica antica." In *La Polifonica Ambrosiana (1947-1980): Musica antica nell'Italia del secondo dopoguerra*, edited by Livio Aragona and Claudio Toscani, 149-70. Lucca: Libreria Musicale Italiana.

Meyer-Baer, Kathi. 1970. *Music of the Spheres and the Dance of Death: Studies in Musical Iconology*. Princeton: Princeton University Press.

Mezzetti, Amalia. 1977. *Girolamo da Ferrara detto da Carpi: L'opera pittorica*. Milan: Silvana.

Mihulka, Antonín. 1935. "Královský letohrádek na hradě Pražském" ["The Royal Summer Palace at Prague Castle"]. In *Ročenka Kruhu pro pěstování dějin umění za rok 1934* [*Yearbook of the Circle for the Cultivation of Art History for 1934*], edited by Emanuel Poche, 73-93. Prague: Kruh pro pěstování dějin umění [Circle for the cultivation of art history].

Milano, Alberto. 1987. "Prints for Fans." *Print Quarterly* 4: 2-19.

Milano, Alberto, and Elena Villani. 1995. *Museo d'Arti Applicate, Raccolta Bertarelli: ventole e ventagli*. Milan: Mondadori Electa.

Milano, Ernesto. 1997. "La Bibbia di Borso d'Este: L'avventura di un codice." In *La Bibbia di Borso d'Este: Commentario al codice*, 1:15-72. Modena: Franco Cosimo Panini.

Miles, Margaret R. 2008. *A Complex Delight: The Secularization of the Breast, 1350-1750*. Berkeley: University of California Press.

Miller, Naomi. 2003. *Mapping the City: The Language and Culture of Cartography in the Renaissance*. London: Continuum.

Milsom, John. 2000. "Analyzing Josquin." In *The Josquin Companion*, edited by Richard Sherr, 431-84. Oxford: Oxford University Press.

Milsom, John. 2021. "The Music in Staff Notation." In *Music and Instruments of the Elizabethan Age: The Eglantine Table*, edited by Michael Fleming and Christopher Page, 69-100. Woodbridge: Boydell and Brewer.

Mina, Gabriele. 2000. *Il morso della differenza: Il dibattito sul tarantismo dal XV al XVI secolo*. Nardò: Besa.

Minagawa, Tatsuo. 1990. "Oratio Christianorum Occultorum in Japonia (16th Cent.)." In *Atti del XIV congresso della Società internazionale di musicologia: Trasmissione e recezione delle forme di cultura musicale*, edited by Angelo Pompilio, 39-43. Turin: Edizioni di Torino.

Minamino, Hiroyuki. 1997. "The First Japanese Lutenists." *Lute Society of America Quarterly* 32, no. 3: 19-20.

Minamino, Hiroyuki. 1999. "European Musical Instruments in Sixteenth-Century Japanese Paintings." *Music in Art* 24: 41-50.

Minor, Andrew C., and Bonner Mitchell. 1968. *A Renaissance Entertainment: Festivities for the Marriage of Cosimo I, Duke of Florence, in 1539*. Columbia, MO: University of Missouri Press.

Minor, Ryan. 2013. "Meistersinger von Nürnberg, Die." In *The Cambridge Wagner Encyclopedia*, edited by Nicholas Vazsonyi, 287-93. Cambridge: Cambridge University Press.

Mirimonde, Albert Pomme de. 1977. *Astrologie et musique*. Geneva: Minkoff.

Mirimonde, Albert Pomme de. 1978. "Les Vanités à personnages et à instruments de musique." *Gazette des Beaux-Arts*, 92: 115-30.

Molina, Mauricio. 2006. "Frame Drums in the Medieval Iberian Peninsula." PhD diss., The City University of New York.

Molina, Mauricio. 2010. *Frame Drums in the Medieval Iberian Peninsula*. Kassel: Reichenberger.

Möller, Hans-Herbert, ed. 1987. *Die Hauptkirche Beatae Mariae Virginis in Wolfenbüttel*. Hannover: Niedersächsisches Landesverwaltungsamt.

Molteni, Monica. 1999. *Cosmè Tura*. Milan: Federico Motta.

Monferrand, Jean-Charles, et al., eds. 2015. *La Muse et le Compas: Poétiques à l'aube de l'âge moderne*. Paris: Garnier.

Montagu, Jeremy. 1976. *The World of Medieval and Renaissance Musical Instruments*. Woodstock, NY: The Overlook Press.

Montagu, Jeremy. 2006. "Musical Instruments in the Macclesfield Psalter." *Early Music* 34: 189-204.

Moore, Kenneth J., Jayson Kerr Dobney, and E. Bradley Strauchen-Scherer. 2015. *Musical Instruments: Highlights of the Metropolitan Museum of Art*. New York: Metropolitan Museum Of Art.

Moran, J. F. 2001. "The Real Author of the *De Missione Legatorum Japonesium ad Roman Curiam ... Dialogus*: A Reconsideration." *Bulletin of Portuguese-Japanese Studies* 2: 7-21.

Morelli, Arnaldo. 1997. "Per ornamento e servicio: Organi e sistemazioni architettoniche nelle chiese toscane del Rinascimento." *I Tatti Studies* 7: 279-303.

Morelli, Arnaldo. 1998. "*Cantare sull'organo:* An Unrecognized Practice." *Recercare* 10: 183-208.

Morelli, Giovanni. 1987. "Gli 'arbundei' di Francesco Colonna (Le 'arie' di Polifilo)." In *La letteratura, la rappresentazione, la musica al tempo e nei luoghi di Giorgione, a cura di Michelangelo Muraro,* 163-75. Rome: Jouvence.

Morena, Francesco, ed. 2012. *Di linea e di colore: Il Giappone, le sue arti e l'incontro con l'Occidente / Line and Colour: Japanese Art and the European Connection*. Livorno: Sillabe.

Moreno Navarro, Isidoro. 1997. *La antigua hermandad de los negros de Sevilla: Etnicidad, poder, y sociedad en 600 años de historia*. Seville: Universidad de Sevilla.

Moretti, Laura. 2010. "Musica e architettura alla 'corte' di Alvise Cornaro nel primo Cinquecento." In *Proceedings of the International Conference 'I luoghi e la musica'*, edited by Fabrizio Pezzopane, 117-28. Rome: ISMEZ.

Moretti, Laura. 2015. "L'immagine della musica nello 'studio' del palazzo veronese di Mario Bevilacqua (1536-93)." *Music in Art* 40: 285-96.

Moretti, Laura. 2017. "The Palazzo, Collections, and Musical Patronage of Niccolò Gaddi (1536-1591)." *Journal of the History of Collections* 29: 189-207.

Moretti, Laura. 2020. *In the House of the Muses: Collection, Display and Performance in the Veronese Palace of Mario Bevilacqua (1536-93)*. London: Harvey Miller.

Morley, Thomas. 1597. *A Plain and Easy Introduction to Practical Music*. London: Peter Short.

Morolli, Gabriele, ed. 1998. *Michelozzo scultore e architetto, 1396-1472*. Florence: Centro Di.

Morton, Jonathan. 2018. *The* Romance of the Rose *in Its Philosophical Context: Art, Nature, and Ethics*. Oxford: Oxford University Press.

Moser, Fernando de Mello. 1966. "Liturgia e iconografia na interpretação do *Auto da Alma*." *Revista da Faculdade de Letras de Lisboa* 2: 88-112.

Moss, Ann. 1982. *Ovid in Renaissance France: A Survey of the Latin Editions of Ovid and Commentaries Printed in France before 1600*. London: The Warburg Institute.

Mossakowski, Stanisław. 2012. *King Sigismund Chapel at Cracow Cathedral (1515-1533)*. Kraków: IRSA, Zamek Królewski na Wawelu.

Motta, Emilio. 1887. "Musici alla corte degli Sforza: Ricerche e documenti milanesi." *Archivio storico lombardo*, Series II, 4: 29-64, 278-340, 514-61.

Mottola-Molfino, Alessandra, and Mauro Natali, eds. 1991. *Le Muse e il Principe: Arte di corte nel Rinascimento padano*. 2 vols. Modena: Franco Cosimo Panini.

Motture, Peta, and Michelle O'Malley, eds. 2010. *Re-Thinking Renaissance Objects: Design, Function and Meaning*. Oxford: Blackwell.

Müller-Blattau, Joseph. 1923/24. "Die musikalischen Schätze der Staats- und Universitätsbibliothek zu Königsberg i. Pr." *Zeitschrift für Musikwissenschaft* 6: 219-28.

Mulryne, J. R., Helen Watanabe-O'Kelly, and Margaret Shewring, eds. 2004. *Europa Triumphans: Court and Civic Festivals in Early Modern Europe*. Aldershot: Ashgate.

Mundt, Barbara. 2009. *Der Pommersche Kunstschrank des Augsburger Unternehmers Philipp Hainhofer für den gelehrten Herzog Philipp II. von Pommern*. Munich: Hirmer.

Munrow, David. 1976. *Instruments of the Middle Ages and Renaissance*. London: Oxford University Press.

Münzer, Hieronymus. 1987. *Viaje por España y Portugal: Reino de Granada*. Edited by Fermín Camacho Evangelista. Granada: Tat.

Murat, Zuleika. 2016. "Medieval English Alabaster Sculptures: Trade and Diffusion in the Italian Peninsula." *Hortus Artium Medievalium* 22: 399-413.

Murat, Zuleika. 2019. "Contextualizing Alabasters in Their Immersive Environment: The 'ancona d'allabastro di diverse figure' of the Novalesa Abbey: Meaning and Function." In *English Alabaster Carvings and Their Cultural Contexts*, edited by Zuleika Murat, 127-49. Woodbridge: Boydell and Brewer.

Muro, Gaspar. 1887. *Vida de la princesa de Éboli [...] illustrada con hojas, documentos inéditos, el retrato de la princesa de Éboli, grabados y facsimiles*. Madrid: Murillo.

Murray, Russell E., Susan Forscher Weiss, and Cinthya J. Cyrus. 2010. *Music Education in the Middle Ages and the Renaissance*. Bloomington: Indiana University Press.

Nádas, John. 2014. "Some New Documentary Evidence Regarding Heinrich Isaac's Career in Florence." In *Firenze e la musica: Fonti, protagonisti, committenza. Scritti in ricordo di Maria Adelaide Bartoli Bacherini*, edited by Cecilia Bacherini, Giacomo Sciommeri, and Agostino Ziino, 45-64. Rome: Istituto Italiano per la Storia della Musica.

Natif, Mika. 2018. *Mughal Occidentalism: Artistic Encounters between Europe and Asia at the Courts of India, 1580-1630*. Leiden: Brill.

Nave, Francine de, ed. 1996. *Antwerpse muziekdrukken: Vocale en instrumentale polyphonie (16de-18de eeuw.)*. Antwerp: Museum Plantin-Moretus en het Stedelijk Prentenkabinet Antwerpen.

Neilson, Katharine Bishop. 1972. *Filippino Lippi: A Critical Study*. Westport: Greenwood Press.

Nelson, Jonathan Katz. 1997. "The High Altar-Piece of SS. Annunziata in Florence: History, Form, and Function." *Burlington Magazine* 139: 84-94.

Nelson, Jonathan Katz. 2004. "I cicli di affreschi nelle Cappelle Carafa e Strozzi." In Patrizia Zambrano and Jonathan Katz Nelson, *Filippino Lippi*, 513-55. Milan: Electa.

Nelson, Jonathan Katz. 2011. "La cappella Carafa: Un nuovo linguaggio figurativo per la Roma del Rinascimento." In *Filippino Lippi e Sandro Botticelli nella Firenze del '400*, edited by Alessandro Cecchi, 41-49. Milan: 24 ore Cultura.

Nelson, Philip. 1920. "The Woodwork of English Alabaster Retables." *Transactions of the Historic Society of Lancashire and Cheshire* 72: 50-60.

Nery, Rui Vieira. 2003. Liner notes for *Villancicos y Danzas Criollas: De la Iberia Antigua al Nuevo Mundo: 1550-1750*. La Capella Reial de Catalunya, Hespèrion XXI, Jordi Savall. Alia Vox AV9834 (CD).

Nery, Rui Vieira. 2006. "From Prophecy to Tragedy." Liner notes to *Paraísos Perdidos*, Alia Vox AVSA9850A+B, 92-96.

Newbigin, Nerida. 1996. *Feste d'Oltrarno: Plays in Churches in Fifteenth-Century Florence*. 2 vols. Florence: Olschki.

Ng, Sebastian. 2015/16. "The Magnificent Reception of Japanese Travellers in Sixteenth-Century Europe." MA diss., Durham University.

Ni, Yibin. 2014. "The Iconographic Variations of Two Scenes from *Romance of the Western Chamber*." In *Performing Images: Opera in Chinese Visual Culture*, edited by Judith T. Zeitlin and Yuhang Li, 96-107. Chicago: Smart Museum of Art.

Nichols, John Gough, ed. 1848. *The Diary of Henry Machyn, Citizen and Merchant-Taylor of London, from AD 1550 to AD 1563*. Camden Society (Old Series) 42. London: JB Nichols.

Nichols, Stephen. 1992. "Commentary and/as Image." In "Commentary as Cultural Artifact," edited by Lee Patterson and Stephen Nichols, special issue, *South Atlantic Quarterly* 91: 965-92.

Nickel, Helmut. 1982. "About the Sequence of the Tapestries in 'The Hunt of the Unicorn' and 'The Lady with the Unicorn'." *Metropolitan Museum Journal* 17: 9-14.

Niemöller, Klaus Wolfgang. 1969. *Untersuchungen zu Musikpflege und Musikunterricht an den deutschen Lateinschulen vom ausgehenden Mittelalter bis um 1600*. Regensburg: Bosse.

Nocilli, Cecilia. 2007. "La danza en Las bodas de Camacho (Quijote, II, 19-21): Reelaboración coréutico-teatral de momos y moriscas." In *Cervantes y el Quijote en la música: Estudios sobre la recepción de un mito*, edited by Begoña Lolo, 595-608. Madrid: Centro de Estudios Cervantinos.

Nordera, Marina. 2017. "'Essere liberamente signore della sua persona e del suo piede': Corpo, gesto e genere nella danza italiana del XV secolo." In *Guglielmo Ebreo da Pesaro: La danza nel Quattrocento*, edited by Chiara Gelmetti and Alessandro Pontremoli, 99-110. Milan: AB Editore.

Norton, Elizabeth, ed. 2011. *Anne Boleyn in Her Own Words & the Words of Those Who Knew Her*. Stroud: Amberley.

Nowakowska, Natalia. 2011. "From Strassburg to Trent: Bishops, Printing and Liturgical Reform in the Fifteenth Century." *Past and Present* 213: 3-39.

Nugent, George. 1990. "Anti-Protestant Music for Sixteenth-Century Ferrara." *Journal of the American Musicological Society* 43: 228-91.

O'Brien, Grant. 1990. *Ruckers: A Harpsichord and Virginal Building Tradition*. Cambridge: Cambridge University Press.

Oen, Maria H. 2011. "The Origins of a Miraculous Image: Notes on the Annunciation Fresco in SS. Annunziata in Florence." *Konsthistorisk Tidskrift* 80: 1-22.

Oettinger, Rebecca Wagner. 2001. *Music as Propaganda in the German Reformation*. Aldershot: Ashgate.

Olsen, Dale. 2002. *Music of El Dorado: The Ethnomusicology of Ancient South American Cultures*. Gainesville: University Press of Florida.

Olson, Roberta J. M. 1981. "Brunelleschi's Machines of Paradise and Botticelli's Mystic Nativity." *Gazette des Beaux-Arts* 97: 183-88.

Olson, Vibeke. 2015. "Embodying the Saint: Mystical Visions, *Maria Lactans* and the Miracle of Mary's Milk." In *Matter of Faith: An Interdisciplinary Study of Relics and Relic Veneration in the Medieval Period*, edited by James Robinson, Lloyd de Beer, and Anna Harndon, 151-58. London: The British Museum.

Onians, Richard B. 1951. *The Origin of European Thought about the Body, the Mind, the Soul, the World, Time and Fate*. Cambridge: Cambridge University Press.

Orgel, Stephen. 1969. *Ben Jonson: The Complete Masques*. New Haven: Yale University Press.

Orgel, Stephen, and Roy Strong. 1973. *Inigo Jones: The Theatre of the Stuart Court*. London: Sotheby Parke Bernet.

Orth, Christoph. 2018. "Zwischen Italien und Innsbruck: Gereiste Objekte am Tiroler Hof in der Schilderung Philipp Hainhofers von 1628." In *Travelling Objects: Botschafter des Kulturtransfers zwischen Italien und dem Habsburgerreich*, edited by Gernot Mayer and Silvia Tammaro, 15-29. Vienna: Böhlau.

Ossi, Massimo. 2008. "Monteverdi, Marenzio, and Battista Guarini's *Cruda Amarilli*." *Music & Letters* 89: 311-36.

Ostermark-Johansen, Lene. 2015. "Enshrined in a Library Edition, and an Incubus to Get Rid of: Walter Pater's Renaissance around 1910." *19th Century Art Worldwide*, Summer. http://www.19thc-artworldwide.org/index.php/summer15/ostermark-johansen-on-walter-pater-s-renaissance-around-1910.

Otis, Jessica Marie. 2017. "'Sportes and Pastimes, done by Number': Mathematical Games in Early Modern England." In *Playthings in Early Modernity: Party Games, Word Games, Mind Games*, edited by Allison Levy, 131-44. Kalamazoo: Medieval Institute Publications.

Owen, Barbara, Peter Williams, and Stephen Bicknell. 2001. "Organ." *Grove Music Online*.

Owen, Dorothy M. 1971. *Church and Society in Medieval Lincolnshire*. Lincoln: Lincolnshire Local History Society.

Owens, Jessie Ann. 1990. "Music Historiography and the Definition of 'Renaissance'." *Notes* 47: 305-30.

Owens, Jessie Anne, and Martin Ruhnke. 2001. "Lampadius [Lampe], Auctor." *Grove Music Online*.

Pacciani, Riccardo. 2006. "L'œuvre architecturale d'Alberti à Florence." In *Alberti humaniste, architecte*, edited by Françoise Choay and Michel Paoli, 169-91. Paris: École Nationale Supérieure des Beaux-Arts.

Pagé, Camille. 1896-1905. *La coutellerie depuis l'origine jusqu'à nos jours*. 7 vols. Paris: Chatelleraut, Impr. H. Rivière.

Palencia, Alonso de. 1490. *Universal vocabulario en latín y en romance*. Seville: Paulus de Colonia.

Palerne, Jean. 1606. *Les peregrinations du S. Jean Palerne, [...] où est traicté de plusieurs singularités et antiquités remarquées és provinces d'Egypte, Arabie [...] Terre saincte, Surie, Natolie, Grece [...]*. Lyon: Jean Pillehotte.

Palisca, Claude V. 1985. *Humanism in Italian Renaissance Musical Thought*. New Haven: Yale University Press.

Palisca, Claude V. 1993. "Aristoxenus Redeemed in the Renaissance." *Revista de Musicología* 16: 1283-93.

Palisca, Claude V. 1994. "The Artusi-Monteverdi Controversy." In Claude V. Palisca, *Studies in the History of Italian Music and Music Theory*, 54-87. Oxford: Clarendon Press.

Palliser, David M. 2014. *Medieval York: 600-1540*. Oxford: Oxford University Press.

Panagiotakis, Nikolaos, ed. 1988. *Krìti, istorìa kai politismòs* [Παναγιωτάκης, Νικόλαος. Κρήτη, ιστορία και πολιτισμός]. Herakleion: Syndesmos topikon enoseon dìmeon kai kinotiton Kritis.

Panagiotakis, Nikolaos. 1989. *O poitìs tou Erotokrìtou kai alla venetokritikà meletìmata* [Παναγιωτάκης, Νικόλαος. Ο ποιητής του Ερωτοκρίτου και άλλα βενετοκρητικά μελετήματα]. Herakleion: Vikelaia Vivliothiki.

Panagl, Victoria. 2004. *Lateinische Huldigungsmotetten für Angehörige des Hauses Habsburg: Vertonte Gelegenheitsdichtung im Rahmen neulateinischer Herrscherpanegyrik*. Frankfurt am Main: Peter Lang.

Pane, Riccardo. 2011. *La Chiesa Armena: Storia, spiritualità, istituzioni*. Bologna: Edizioni Studio Domenicano.

Panofksy, Erwin. 1969. *Problems in Titian: Mostly Iconographic*. New York: New York University Press.

Panti, Cecilia. 2011. "Pregiudizi e miti sulla musica medievale, fra oblii e riscoperte." *Semicerchio* 44: 22-36.

Panzanelli, Roberta. 2008. "Introduction: The Body in Wax, the Body of Wax." In *Ephemeral Bodies: Wax Sculpture and the Human Figure*, edited by Roberta Panzanelli, 1-12. Los Angeles: The Getty Research Institute.

Pape, Dorothy R. 1991. *Der Vorläufer: Johannes der Täufer, Prophet und Wegbereiter des Herrn*. Translated by Katharina Goodwin. Stuttgart: Verlag Junge Gemeinde.

Parker, Geoffrey. 2014. *Imprudent King: A New Life of Philip II*. New Haven: Yale University Press.

Parker, Mike. 1958. "Punches and Matrices in the Museum Plantin Moretus." *Printing & Graphic Arts* 6: 53-66.

Parrello, Domenico. 2010. "*Ḳamsa* of Nezami." *Encyclopaedia Iranica*. https://iranicaonline.org/articles/kamsa-of-nezami.

Pasio, Francesco. 1604. *Lettera annua di Giappone scritta nel 1601 e mandata dal P. Francesco Pasio V. prouinciali. Al M.R.P. Claudio Acquauiua generale della Compagnia di Giesù*. Venice: Ciotti.

Peers, Glenn. 2001. *Subtle Bodies: Representing Angels in Byzantium*. Berkeley: University of California Press.

Pelc, Milan. 2007. *Renesansa* [*Renaissance*]. Zagreb: Ljevak.

Perella, Nicholas. 1973. *The Critical Fortune of Battista Guarini's Il Pastor Fido*. Florence: Olschki.

Pérez Priego, Miguel Ángel. 1991. *Juan del Encina: Teatro completo*. Madrid: Cátedra.

Perkins, Juliet, and T. F. Earle. 2009. "Portuguese Theatre in the Sixteenth Century: Gil Vicente and António Ferreira." In *A Companion to Portuguese Literature*, edited by Stephen Parkinson, Cláudia Pazos Alonso, and T. F. Earle, 56-71. Woodbridge: Boydell & Brewer/Tamesis.

Perkins, Leeman L. 1999. *Music in the Age of the Renaissance.* New York: Norton.

Perry, Marilyn. 1975. "A Greek Bronze in Renaissance Venice." *The Burlington Magazine* 117: 204-11.

Peters, Gretchen. 2012. *Musical Sounds in Late Medieval French Cities: Players, Patrons, and Politics.* Cambridge: Cambridge University Press.

Petersohn, Jürgen. 1997. "Die Reichsinsignien im Herrscherzeremoniell und Herrschaftsdenken des Mittelalters." In *Die Reichskleinodien: Herrschaftszeichen des Heiligen Römischen Reiches.* Göppingen: Gesellschaft für staufische Geschichte.

Pettegree, Andrew, et al., eds. 2007. *French Vernacular Books: Books Published in the French Language before 1601.* Leiden: Brill.

Peverada, Enrico. 1991. *Vita musicale nella chiesa ferrarese del Quattrocento.* Ferrara: Capitolo della Cattedrale di Ferrara.

Pfisterer, Ulrich. 2013. "Wettstreit der Köpfe und Künste: Repräsentation, Reproduktion und das neue Bildmedium der Medaille nördlich der Alpen." In *Wettstreit in Erz: Porträtmedaillen der deutschen Renaissance*, edited by Walter Cupperi, Martin Hirsch, Annette Kranz, and Ulrich Pfisterer, 15-27. Berlin: Deutscher Kunstverlag.

Philips, Helen. 1992. "Gardens of Love and the Garden of the Fall." In *A Walk in the Garden: Biblical, Iconographical and Literary Images of Eden*, edited by Paul Morris and Deborah Sawyer, 205-19. Sheffield: Sheffield Academic Press.

Picker, Martin. 1998. "*Liber selectarum cantionum* (Augsburg: Grimm & Wirsung, 1520): A Neglected Monument of Renaissance Music and Music Printing." In *Gestalt und Entstehung musikalischer Quellen im 15. und 16. Jahrhundert*, edited by Martin Staehelin, 149-67. Wiesbaden: Harrassowitz.

Picot, Émile. 1967. *Catalogue des livres composant la bibliothèque de Feu M. le Baron James de Rothschild.* 5 vols. 2nd edn. New York: Burt Franklin.

Pietschmann, Klaus, ed. 2008. *Das Erzbistum Köln in der Musikgeschichte des 15. und 16. Jahrhunderts: Kongressbericht Köln 2005.* Kassel: Merseburger.

Pietzsch, Gerhard. 1962. "Die Jülich'sche Hochzeit 1585." In *Studien zur Musikgeschichte des Rheinlandes: Karl Gustav Fellerer zum 60. Geburtstag*, edited by Herbert Drux, Klaus Wolfgang Niemöller, and Walter Thoene, 166-89. Köln: Arno Volk-Verlag.

Pilbeam, Pamela. 2003. *Madame Tussaud and the History of Waxworks.* London: Hambledon and London.

Pillinger, Renate. 2012. "Parola e silenzio nell'arte paleocristiana." In *Silenzio e Parola nella Patristica*, Studia Ephemeridis Augustinianum 127, 685-89. Rome: Institutum patristicum Augustinianum.

Pinto, Bernard. 1943. "Les instructions du Père Valignano pour l'ambassade japonaise en Europe (Goa, 23 décembre 1583)." *Monumenta Nipponica* 6: 391-403.

Pirker, Michael. 2001. "Janissary Music." *Grove Music Online.*

Pirrotta, Nino. 1969. *Li due Orfei: Da Poliziano a Monteverdi. Con un saggio critico sulla scenografia di Elena Povoledo.* Turin: ERI.

Plamenac, Dragan. 1981. "Su Julije Skjavetić (Giulio Schiavetti) e i *Motetti a cinque et a sei voci* del 1564: Annotazioni bibliografiche." *Subsidia Musica Veneta* 2: 21-38.

Plumley, Yolanda. 2013. *The Art of Grafted Song.* New York: Oxford University Press.

Poirier, John C. 2010. *The Tongues of Angels: The Concept of Angelic Languages in Classical Jewish and Christian Texts.* Tübingen: Mohr Siebeck.

Poklečki Stošić, Jasminka, ed. 2008. *Stećci.* Zagreb: Galerija Klovičevi Dvori.

Pokorny, Julius. n.d. a. "Root/lemma: gʷer-1, gʷer." *Indogermanisches Etymologisches Wörterbuch.* http://dnghu.org/indoeuropean.html.

Pokorny, Julius. n.d. b. "Root/lemma: (s)kel-1." *Indogermanisches Etymologisches Wörterbuch.* http://dnghu.org/indoeuropean.html.

Poliziano, Angelo. 2004. *Silvae.* Edited and translated by Charles Fantazzi. Cambridge, MA: Harvard University Press.

Polk, Keith. 1990. "Voices and Instruments: Soloists and Ensembles in the 15th Century." *Early Music* 18: 179-98.

Pollens, Stewart. 1997. "Flemish Harpsichords and Virginals in The Metropolitan Museum of Art: An Analysis of Early Alterations and Restorations." *The Metropolitan Museum Journal* 32: 85-110.

Pollens, Stewart. 1998. "Early Alterations Made to Ruckers, Chouchet and Grouwels Harpsichords in the Collection of the Metropolitan Museum of Art." In *Kielinstrumente aus der Werkstatt Ruckers: Zu Konzeption, Bauweise und Ravalement sowie Restaurierung und Konservierung*, edited by Christiane Rieche, 136-70. Halle an der Saale: Händel Haus.

Pomian, Krzysztof. 1987. *Collectionneurs, amateurs et curieux. Paris, Venise: XVIe-XVIIIe siècle.* Paris: Gallimard.

Pon, Lisa. 2015. "Raphael's Acts of the Apostles Tapestries for Leo X: Sight, Sound, and Space in the Sistine Chapel." *Art Bulletin* 97, no. 4: 388-408.

Potter, Pamela. 1994. "German Musicology and Early Music Performance, 1918-1933." In *Music and Performance during the Weimar Republic*, edited by Bryan Gilliam, 94-106. Cambridge: Cambridge University Press.

Powell, Michael. [1980]. *Alfred Deller. A Recorded Legacy 1949-1979*. York: Alfred Deller Memorial Trust.

Powers, Katherine. 2004. "Music-Making Angels in Italian Renaissance Painting: Symbolism and Reality." *Music in Art* 29: 52-63.

Prado-Vilar, Francisco. 2013. "Silentium: El silencio cósmico como imagen en la edad media y la modernidad." *Revista de poética medieval* 27: 21-43.

Praetorius, Michael. 1607. *Musarum Sioniarum: Motectae et psalmi latini*. Nuremberg: Wagenmann.

Premoli, Beatrice. 1991. "Note iconografiche a proposito di alcune moresche del Rinascimento italiano." In *La moresca nell'area mediterranea*, edited by Roberto Lorenzetti, 43-53. Bologna: Forni.

Primaudaye, Pierre de la. 1593. *L'Academie Francoise, de la philosophie humaine, deuxième livre*. Paris: Guillaume Chauderie [repr. Cologne: Chouët].

Primisser, Johann Baptist. 1777. *Kurze Nachricht von dem K.K. Raritätenkabinet zu Ambras in Tyrol*. Innsbruck: Wagner.

Protz, Albert. 1939. *Mechanische Musikinstrumente*. Kassel: Bärenreiter.

Pugh, Tison, and Angela Jane Weisl. 2012. *Medievalisms: Making the Past in the Present*. New York: Routledge.

Quiccheberg, Samuel. 1565. *Inscriptiones vel tituli theatri amplissimi*. Munich: Berg.

Quitslund, Beth. 2012. "Singing the Psalms for Fun and Profit." In *Private and Domestic Devotion in Early Modern England*, edited by Jessica Martin and Alec Ryrie, 237-58. Farnham: Ashgate.

Ragghianti, Carlo Ludovico. 1938. "Notizie e letture." *La critica d'Arte* 3: 15-16.

Rahn, Thomas. 2006. *Festbeschreibung: Funktion und Topik einer Textsorte am Beispiel der Beschreibung höfischer Hochzeiten (1568–1794)*. Tübingen: Max Niemeyer Verlag.

Ramakers, Bart. 2015. "Books, Beads and Bitterness: Making Sense of Gifts in Two Table Plays by Cornels Everaert." In *Discovering the Riches of the Word: Religious Reading in Late Medieval and Early Modern Europe*, edited by Sabrina Corbelli, Margriet Hoogvliet, and Bart Ramakers, 141-69. Leiden: Brill.

Ramdan, Marcel. 2016. "Zpívající fontána v Královské zahradě Pražského hradu" ["The Singing Fountain in the Royal Garden of Prague Castle"]. BA diss., Charles University, Prague.

Ramos de Pareja, Bartolomeo. 1482. *Musica practica*. Bologna: Baltasaris de Hiriberia.

Ramos López, Pilar. 2015. "The Spanish Prohibition on Women Listening to Music: Some Reflections on Juan Luis Vives and the Jewish and Muslim Legacy." In *New Perspectives on Early Music in Spain*, edited by Tess Knighton and Emilio Ros-Fábregas, 418-32. Kassel: Reichenberger.

Ramsay, Nigel. 1991. "Alabaster." In *English Medieval Industries: Craftsmen, Techniques, Products*, edited by John Blair and Nigel Ramsay, 29-40. London: Hambledon.

Randall, Lilian M. C. 1962. "The Snail in Gothic Marginal Warfare." *Speculum* 37: 358-67.

Randel, Don. 1976. "Al-Fārābī and the Role of Arabic Music Theory in the Latin Middle Ages." *Journal of the American Musicological Society* 29: 173-88.

Range, Matthias. 2012. "The Material Presence of Music in the Church: The Hanseatic City of Lübeck." In *Lutheran Churches in Early Modern Europe*, edited by Andrew Spicer, 197-220. Farnham: Ashgate.

Raninen, Sanna. 2018. "The Early History of Printed Folio Choirbooks: Production and Layout." In *The Production and Reading of Music Sources: Mise-en-page in Manuscripts and Printed Books Containing Polyphonic Music, 1480-1530*, edited by Thomas Schmidt and Christian Thomas Leitmeir, 117-49. Turnhout: Brepols.

Rasmussen, Mikael Bøgh. 2014. "Enemy Enticements: A Habsburg Artist in Süleyman's Capital City." *Calíope* 19: 159-95.

Rastall, Richard. 1977. "Music for a Royal Entry, 1474." *The Musical Times* 118: 463-66.

Razzi, Serafino. 1585. *Cento casi di coscienza*. Venice: Vincenti.

Read, Alexander. 1638. *The Manuall of the Anatomy, or Dissection of the Body of Man*. London: F. Constable.

Reale, Steven. 2014. "Transcribing Musical Worlds; or, is *L.A. Noire* a Music Game?" In *Music In Video Games: Studying Play*, edited by K. J. Donnelly, William Gibbons, and Neil Lerner, 77-103. New York: Routledge.

Redel, Carl Adolph. 1710. *Das Sehens-würdige Prag*. Nuremberg: Johann Friedrich Rüdiger.

Reed, Helen H., and Trevor J. Dadson. 2015. *La princesa de Éboli: Cautiva del rey: Vida de Ana de Mendoza y de la Cerda (1540-1592)*. Madrid: Centro de Estudios Europea Hispanica y Marcial Pons Historia.

Rees, Owen. 2007. "*The City Full of Grief*: Music for the Exequies of King Philip II." In *Music as a Social and Cultural Practice: Essays in Honour of Reinhard Strohm*, edited by Melania Bucciarelli and Berta Joncus, 119-34. Woodbridge: Boydell Press.

Rees, Owen. 2019. *The Requiem of Tomás Luis de Victoria (1603)*. Cambridge: Cambridge University Press.

Reese, Gustave. 1968. "Musical Compositions in Renaissance Intarsia." *Medieval and Renaissance Studies* 2: 74-97.

Refini, Eugenio. 2018. "La voix des sirènes: Réécritures du roman chevaleresque dans le théâtre musical du XVIIe siècle." In *Dramaturgies vagabondes, migrations romanesques: Croisements entre théâtre et roman (XVIe-XVIIe siècles)*, edited by Magda Campanini, 95-106. Paris: Honoré Champion.

Reichard, Tobias, Anno Mungen, and Alexander Schmidt, eds. 2018. *Hitler.Macht.Oper: Propaganda und Musiktheater in Nürnberg*. Petersberg: Michael Imhof.

Reichenhart, Emil. 1880. "Die lateinische Schule zu Memmingen im Reformationszeitalter." *Neue Jahrbücher für Philologie und Pädagogik* 50: 225-35, 273-80, 331-45, 401-12.

Reichert, Georg. 1953. "Martin Crusius und die Musik in Tübingen um 1590." *Archiv für Musikwissenschaft* 10: 185-212.

Relatione degli honori. 1585. *Relatione degli honori et accoglienze fatte dall'Illustrissima, et Serenissima Signoria di Venetia alli Signori Ambasciatori Giapponesi*. Cremona: Draconi.

Relatione del viaggio. 1585. *Relatione del viaggio et arriuo in Europa, et Roma de' Principi giapponesi, venuti a dare obedienza a Sua Santita l'anno MDLXXXV*. Venice: Meietto.

Rem, Wilhelm. 1896. "'Cronica newer geschichten', 1512-1527." In *Die Chroniken der schwäbischen Städte*. Vol. 5: *Augsburg*. Leipzig: S. Hirzel.

Resende, Garcia de, ed. 1516. *Cancioneiro Geral*. Almeirim: Hermão de Campos. http://purl.pt/12096/6.

Révah, Israel S. 1949. *Deux "autos" de Gil Vicente restitués à leur auteur*. Lisbon: Academia das Ciências de Lisboa.

Rey, Juan José, and Antonio Navarro. 1993. *Los instrumentos de pua en España: Bandurria, cítola y laúdes españoles*. Madrid: Alianza Editorial.

Reyna, Ferdinando. 1981. *Historia del ballet*. Barcelona: Daimon.

Reynolds, Dwight. 2013. "Arab Musical Influence on Europe: A Reassessment." In *A Sea of Languages: Literature and Culture in the Pre-Modern Mediterranean*, edited by Suzanne Akbari and Karla Mallette, 182-98. Toronto: University of Toronto Press.

Reynolds, Robert D. 2000. "Textless Choral Music." *The Choral Journal* 41: 19-34.

Richards, Jennifer, and Richard Wistreich. 2016. "The Anatomy of the Renaissance Voice." In *The Edinburgh Companion to the Critical Medical Humanities*, edited by Anne Whitehead and Angela Woods, 276-93. Edinburgh: Edinburgh University Press.

Ripin, Edwin. 1977. "Joes Karest's Virginal and the Flemish Tradition." In *Keyboard Instruments: Study of Keyboard Organology, 1500-1800*, edited by Edwin Ripin, 67-75. New York: Dover.

Rivani, Giovanni (alias Zan Badile). 1612. *È tanto tempo hormai*. Bologna: Bartolomeo Cochi.

Rivera, Isidro J. 2014. "Visualising the Passion in Andrés de Li's *Summa de paciencia*." *Revista Hispánica Moderna* 67: 55-72.

Roach, Joseph. 2007. *It*. Ann Arbor: University of Michigan Press.

Robertson, Anne Walters. 2015. "Affective Literature and Sacred Themes in Fifteenth-Century Music." In *The Cambridge History of Fifteenth-Century Music*, edited by Anna Maria Busse Berger and Jesse Rodin, 545-60. Cambridge: Cambridge University Press.

Robichaud, Denis J.-J. 2018. *Plato's Persona: Marsilio Ficino, Renaissance Humanism, and Platonic Traditions*. Philadelphia: University of Pennsylvania Press.

Robins, Brian. 2006. *Catch and Glee Culture in Eighteenth-Century England*. Woodbridge: Boydell and Brewer.

Robinson, Cynthia. 2013. *Imagining the Passion in a Multiconfessional Castile: The Virgin, Christ, Devotions and Images in the Fourteenth and Fifteenth Centuries*. University Park: Pennsylvania State University Press.

Rodrigues, Ana Maria, ed. 2010. *Os Negros em Portugal – sécs. XV a XIX*. Lisbon: Comissão Nacional para as Comemorações dos Descobrimentos Portugueses.

Roelvink, Véronique, and Egidius Kwartet. 2002. *Gegeven den Sangeren: Meerstemmige muziek bij de Illustre Lieve Vrouwe Broederschap te 's-Hertogenbosch in de Zestiende Eeuw*. 's-Hertogenbosch: Adr. Heinen.

Romanillos, José Luis, and Marian Harris Winspear. 2002. *The Vihuela de Mano and the Spanish Guitar: A Dictionary of the Makers of Plucked and Bowed Musical Instruments of Spain (1200-2002)*. Guijosa (Guadalajara): Sanguino Press.

Romeu Figueras, José. 1965. *La música en la corte de los Reyes Católicos*. Vols. 4/1-2: *Cancionero Musical de Palacio*. Monumentos de la Música Española. Vols. 14/1-2. Barcelona: Consejo Superior de Investigaciones Científicas (CSIC), Instituto Español de Musicología. Available online in open access, *Reedición digital*: Madrid, Editorial CSIC, 2015. Vol. 14/1: http://libros.csic.es/product_info.php?products_id=929, and vol. 14/2: http://libros.csic.es/product_info.php?products_id=930.

Romoli, Domenico. 1560. *La singolar dottrina*. Venice: Spineda.

Roper, Lyndal. 1989. *The Holy Household: Women and Morals in Reformation Augsburg*. Oxford: Clarendon Press.

Rose, Stephen. 2016. "Patriotic Purification: Cleansing Italian Secular Vocal Music in Thuringia, 1575-1600." *Early Music History* 35: 203-60.

Rosenberg, Charles M. 1981. "The Bible of Borso d'Este: Inspiration and Use." In *Cultura figurativa ferrarese tra XV e XVI secolo*, 51-73. Venice: Corbo e Fiore Editori.

Rosenzweig, Claudia. 2016. *"Bovo d'Antona" by Elye Bokher: A Yiddish Romance. A Critical Edition with Commentary*. Leiden: Brill.

Ros-Fábregas, Emilio. 2008. "Melodies for Private Devotion at the Castilian Court of Queen Isabel." In *Queen Isabel I of Castile: Power, Patronage, Persona*, edited by Barbara F. Weissberger, 83-107. London: Tamesis.

Ros-Fábregas, Emilio. 2012. "Cómo leer, cantar o grabar el Cancionero de Uppsala (1556): ¿de principio a fin?" *Revista de Musicología*, 35: 43-68.

Ros-Fábregas, Emilio. 2017. "Manuscripts of Polyphony from the Time of Isabel and Ferdinand." In *A Companion to Music in the Age of the Catholic Monarchs*, edited by Tess Knighton, 404-68. Leiden: Brill.

Ros-Fábregas, Emilio, and Fernando Sánchez-Pérez. *E-Mp II/1335 ("Cancionero Musical de Palacio")*. Books of Hispanic Polyphony. Edited by Emilio Ros-Fábregas. https://hispanicpolyphony.eu/source/13370.

Rospocher, Massimo. 2017. "The Battle for the Piazza: Creative Antagonism between Itinerant Preachers and Street Singers in Late Medieval and Early Modern Italy." In *Voices and Texts in Early Modern Italian Society*, edited by Stefano Dall'Aglio, Brian Richardson, and Massimo Rospocher, 212-28. London: Routledge.

Rossetti, Edoardo. 2019. "L''Isola beata' dei musici e degli aristocratici: Qualche appunto su gerarchie sociali e culturali nella Milano del Rinascimento." In *Codici per cantare: I Libroni del Duomo nella Milano sforzesca*, edited by Daniele V. Filippi and Agnese Pavanello, 53-87. Lucca: Libreria Musicale Italiana.

Rossi, Antonio, ed. 2005. *Serafino Aquilano: Sonetti e altre rime*. Rome: Bulzoni.

Rossi, Bastiano de'. 1589. *Descrizione dell'apparato e degli intermedi fatti per la commedia rappresentata in Firenze nelle nozze de Seren. D. Ferdinando Medici, e Madame Cristina di Loreno Gran Duchi di Toscana*. Firenze: Padovani 1589.

Rößler, Hans. 1966. *Geschichte und Strukturen der evangelischen Bewegung im Bistum Freising 1520-1571*. Nuremberg: Verein für Bayerische Kirchengeschichte.

Roth, Friedrich. 1900. "Eine lutherische Demonstration in der Münchner Augustinerkirche." *Beiträge zur bayerischen Kirchengeschichte* 6: 97-109.

Rothenberg, David J. 2011. *The Flower of Paradise: Marian Devotion and Secular Song in Medieval and Renaissance Music*. Oxford: Oxford University Press.

Röttinger, Heinrich. 1916. *Peter Flettners Holzschnitte*. Strasbourg: Heitz.

Rousseau, Vanessa. 2005. *Le goût du sang: Croyances et polémiques dans la chrétienté occidentale*. Paris: Armand Colin.

Rubin, Miri. 2009a. *Emotion and Devotion: The Meaning of Mary in Medieval Religious Cultures*. Budapest: Central European University Press.

Rubin, Miri. 2009b. *Mother of God: A History of the Virgin Mary*. New Haven: Yale University Press.

Rublack, Ulinka. 2013. "Matter in the Material Renaissance." *Past and Present* 219: 41-85.

Rudy, Kathryn M. 2016. *Rubrics, Images and Indulgences in Late Medieval Netherlandish Manuscripts*. Leiden: Brill.

Ruehl, Martin A. 2015. *The Italian Renaissance in the German Historical Imagination, 1860-1930*. Cambridge: Cambridge University Press.

Ruiz-de-Medina, Juan. 2003. "The Role of the Blind *Biwa Hōshi* Troubadours in the History of the Christian Mission in Japan." *Bulletin of Portuguese-Japanese Studies* 6: 107-45.

Ruiz Jiménez, Juan. 2019. "La transformación del paisaje sonoro urbano en la Granada conquistada (1492-1570)." In *Paisajes sonoros medievales*, edited by Gerardo Fabián Rodríguez and Gisela Coronado. Mar del Plata: Universidad Nacional de Mar del Plata, Facultad de Humanidades, GIEM.

Rümmler, Else. 1983. *Die Fürstlich Jülichsche Hochzeit zu Düsseldorf 1585: Das Fest und seine Vorgeschichte*. Düsseldorf: Verlag Hans Marcus.

Russell, Peter E. 1978. "La 'Poesía Negra' de Rodrigo de Reinosa." In Peter E. Russell, *Temas de La Celestina y Otros Estudios: del Cid al Quijote*, 377-406. Barcelona: Arie.

Rust, Jennifer R. 2013. "Reforming the Mystical Body: From Mass to Martyr in John Foxe's Acts and Monuments." *English Literary History* 80: 627-59.

Rutkowski, Henryk. 1996. "Zygmunt I Stary" ["Sigismund I the Old"]. In *Poczet królów i książąt polskich* [*Galaxy of Polish Kings and Princes*], 326-34. Warszawa: Czytelnik.

Ryan, William G., and Eamon Duffy, eds. 1993. *Jacobus de Voragine: Readings of the Saints*. 2 vols. Princeton: Princeton University Press.

Ryrie, Alec. 2013. *Being Protestant in Reformation Britain*. Oxford: Oxford University Press.

S. G. B. 1916. "An Old Flemish Spinet." *The Connoisseur: An Illustrated magazine for collectors* 45: 169.

Sahagún, Bernardino de. 1950-82. *Florentine Codex: General History of the Things of New Spain*. 3 vols./13 parts. Translated and edited by Arthur J. O. Anderson and Charles E. Dibble. Salt Lake City: University of Utah Press.

Sahagún, Bernardino de. 1993. *Bernardino de Sahagú's* Psalmodia Christiana (Christian Psalmody). Translated by Arthur J. O. Anderson. Salt Lake City: University of Utah Press.

Saïd, Edward. 1978. *Orientalism*. New York: Pantheon.

Salmen, Walter. 1982. *Musiker im Porträt 1: Von der Spätantike bis 1600*. Munich: Beck.

Salmen, Walter, ed. 1992. *Imperiale Musik von Schloß Ambras aus der Regierungszeit Karls V. und Ferdinands I.* Innsbruck: Helbling.

Salvatici, Luciano. 1999. *Posate, pugnali, coltelli da caccia del Museo Nazionale del Bargello*. Florence: Museo Nazionale del Bargello / SPES.

Sampson, Lisa. 2003. "The Mantuan Performance of Guarini's 'Pastor fido' and Representations of Courtly Identity." *The Modern Language Review* 98: 65-83.

Sand, Alexa. 2014. "*Materia Meditandi*: Haptic Perception and Some Parisian Ivories of the Virgin and Child, ca. 1300." *Different Visions: A Journal of New Perspectives on Medieval Art* 4: 1-28.

Sand, George. 1844. *Jeanne*. Brussels: Hauman.

Sanders, Ernest H. 2001. "Gymel." *Grove Music Online*.

Sanford, Martin, and John Blatchly, eds. 2012. *Thomas Fella of Halesworth, Suffolk, Draper and Writing Master, His Book of Divers Devices and Sorts of Pictures compiled between 1592 and 1598 with additions made at Dunwich in July 1622, with his setting up of the Robert Launce Charity in 1611*. Privately published in an edition of 300 copies.

Sanjian, Avedis K. 1999. "Introduction." In *Medieval Armenian Manuscripts at the University of California, Los Angeles*, edited by Avedis K. Sanjian, 1-44. Berkley: University of California Press.

Sansovino, Francesco. 1663. *Venetia città nobilissima et singolare descritta in XIIII libri da Francesco Sansovino: Con aggiunta di tutte le cose notabili della stessa città, fatte et occorse dall'anno 1580 fino al presente 1663 da D. Giustiniano Martinioni*. Venice: Curti.

Santoro, Caterina. 1961. *I registri delle lettere ducali del periodo sforzesco*. Milan: Castello Sforzesco.

Sassu, Giovanni. 2010. "Le ante d'organo di Cosmè Tura." In *Museo della Cattedrale di Ferrara: Catalogo generale*, edited by Berenice Giovannucci Vigi and Giovanni Sassu, 118-26. Ferrara: Edisai.

Saunders, A. C. de C. M. 1982. *A Social History of Black Slaves and Freedmen in Portugal 1441-1555*. Cambridge: Cambridge University Press.

Sautter, Cia. 2010. *The Miriam Tradition: Teaching Embodied Torah*. Urbana: University of Illinois Press.

Savage, Elizabeth. 2015a. "A Printer's Art: The Development and Influence of Colour Printmaking in the German Lands, c.1476-c.1600." In *Printing Colour 1400-1700: History, Techniques, Functions and Receptions*, edited by Ad Stijnman and Elizabeth Savage, 91-102. Leiden: Brill.

Savage, Elizabeth. 2015b. "Jost de Negker's Woodcut Charles V (1519): An Undescribed Example of Gold Printing." *Art in Print* 5: 9-15.

Savage, Elizabeth. 2018. *A Guide to Early German Colour Prints in the British Museum*. London: University of London Press.

Savall, Jordi. 1992. "Performing Early Spanish Music." *Early Music* 20: 649-53.

Savall, Jordi. 2006. "Lost Paradises." Liner notes to *Paraísos Perdidos*, Alia Vox AVSA9850A+B, 90-91.

Savoy, Bénédicte. 2014. "1934. Der Film zum Schrank." In *Wunderwelt: Der Pommersche Kunstschrank*, edited by Christoph Emmendörfer, 73-77. Berlin: Deutscher Kunstverlag.

Scalabrini, Giuseppe Antenore. 1773. *Memorie istoriche delle chiese di Ferrara*. Ferrara: Carlo Coatti.

Scappi, Bartholomeo. 1570. *Opera*. Venice: Tramezzino.

Scappi, Bartolomeo. 2008. *The Opera of Bartolomeo Scappi (1570): L'arte et prudenza d'un maestro Cuoco*. Translated by Terence Scully. Toronto: University of Toronto Press.

Schadendorf, Wulf. 1960. "Peter Flötners Spielkarten für Francesco d'Este." *Anzeiger des Germanischen Nationalmuseums 1954 bis 1959*: 143-65.

Schaller, Jaroslaus. 1794. *Beschreibung der königlichen Haupt- und Residenzstadt Prag sammt allen darinn befindlichen sehenswürdigen Merkwürdigkeiten. Erster Band*. Prague: Franz Geržabeck.

Schawe, Martin. 2001. *Staatsgalerie Augsburg: Altdeutsche Malerei in der Katharinenkirche*. Munich: Bayerische Staatsgemäldesammlungen.

Scher, Stephen K., ed. 1994. *The Currency of Fame: Portrait Medals of the Renaissance*. New York: Harry N. Abrams.

Schiltz, Katelijne. 2015. *Music and Riddle Culture in the Renaissance*. Cambridge: Cambridge University Press.

Schlagel, Stephanie P. 2002. "The Liber selectarum cantionum and the 'German Josquin Renaissance'." *Journal of Musicology* 19: 564-615.

Schlager, Karlheinz. 1968-87. *Alleluia Melodien*. 2 vols. Kassel: Bärenreiter.

Schlosser, Julius. 1920. *Die Sammlung alter Musikinstrumente: Beschreibendes Verzeichnis*. Kunsthistorisches Museum in Wien, Publikationen aus den Sammlungen für Plastik und Kunstgewerbe 3. Vienna: Schroll & Co.

Schlosser, Julius. (1908) 1978. *Kunst- und Wunderkammern der Spätrenaissance: Ein Beitrag zur Geschichte des Sammelwesens*. Braunschweig: Klinkhardt & Biermann.

Schmid, Ernst Fritz. 1941. "Hans Leo Hassler und seine Brüder." *Zeitschrift des Historischen Vereins für Schwaben* 54: 60-212.

Schmid, Ernst Fritz. 1948. "Vom Allgäuer Alphorn: Geschichten um ein altes Instrument." *Das schöne Allgäu* 12: 140-42.

Schmidt, Alexander. 1995. "'Wo Sachs gesungen hat': Zum Hans-Sachs-Gedenken in Nürnberg im 19. und 20. Jahrhundert." In *Hans Sachs im Schnittpunkt von Antike und Neuzeit: Akten des interdisziplinären Symposions vom 23./24. September 1994 in Nürnberg* (= Pirckheimer-Jahrbuch 1995), edited by Stephan Füssel, 157-87. Nuremberg: Hans Carl.

Schmitz, Hermann. 1981. *System der Philosophie*. Vol. 3: *Der Raum: Der Gefühlsraum*. Bonn: Bouvier.

Schneider Adams, L. 1976. "Donatello and Caravaggio: The Iconography of Decapitation." *American Imago* 33: 83-91.

Schneider, Federico. 2008. "Pastoral Therapies for the Heartbroken in Guarini's *Pastor Fido* and Monteverdi's *Book V*." *Quaderni d'italianistica* 29: 73-104.

Schoch, Rainer. 1993. "Aller Laster Anfang. Zur Ikonographie der Nürnberger Künstlerspielkarten." In Detlef Hoffmann, *Altdeutsche Spielkarten 1500-1650: Katalog der Holzschnittkarten mit deutschen Farben aus dem Deutschen Spielkarten-Museum Leinfelden-Echterdingen und dem Germanischen Nationalmuseum Nürnberg*, 55-80. Nuremberg: Verlag des Germanischen Nationalmuseums.

Schofield, Katherine Butler. 2010. "Reviving the Golden Age Again: 'Classicization,' Hindustani Music & the Mughals." *Ethnomusicology* 53: 484-517.

Schrade, Leo. 1953. "Renaissance: The Historical Conception of an Epoch." In *International Society for Music Research. Fifth Congress, Utrecht, 3-7 July 1952: Report*, 19-32. Amsterdam: Alsbach.

Schröter, Elisabeth. 1977. *Die Ikonographie des Themas Parnass vor Raffael*. Hildesheim: Georg Olms.

Schubert, Linda. 1998. "Plainchant in Motion Pictures: The 'Dies irae' in Film Scores." *Florilegium* 15: 207-29.

Schütte, Josef. 1980-85. *Valignano's Mission Principles for Japan*. Vol. 1: *From His Appointment as Visitor until His First Departure from Japan (1573-1582)*. Part 2: *The Solution (1580-1582)*. St Louis: Institute of Jesuit Sources.

Schwarz, Anton. 1845. "Der Kaisergarten in Prag." *Prag Beiblätter zu "Ost und West"* 63: 251; 64: 255-56; 65: 259-60.

Schwindt, Nicole. 2018. "Fünf Freunde: Bekannte und unbekannte Nachrichten zu Senfls Kollegen." In *Senfl-Studien 3*, edited by Stefan Gasch, Birgit Lodes, and Sonja Tröster, 1-18. Vienna: Hollitzer.

Scolieri, Paul A. 2013. *Dancing the New World: Aztecs, Spaniards, and the Choreography of Conquest*. Austin, TX: University of Texas Press.

Sehling, Emil, ed. 1957. *Die evangelischen Kirchenordnungen des XVI. Jahrhunderts*. Vol. 6/1: *Niedersachsen, 1. Hälfte: Die welfischen Lande; Die Fürstentümer Wolfenbüttel und Lüneburg mit den Städten Braunschweig und Lüneburg*. Tübingen: Mohr.

Seidel, Max, ed. 2010. *Le arti a Siena nel primo Rinascimento: Da Jacopo della Quercia a Donatello*. Milan: Motta.

Seipel, Wilhelm, ed. 2001. *Alle Wunder dieser Welt: Die kostbarsten Kunstwerke der Sammlung Erzherzog Ferdinands II. (1529-95)*. Vienna: Kunsthistorisches Museum.

Selmi, Elisabetta. 2001. *'Classici e moderni' nell'officina del Pastor Fido*. Alessandria: Edizioni dell'Orso.

Senfl, Ludwig. 1520. *Liber selectarum cantionum*. Augsburg: Grimm & Wirsung.

Serés, Guillermo. 2017. "La monarquía hispánica en la era del Espíritu Santo: El atrio de Valadés." *Hipogrifo: Revista de Literatura y Cultura del Siglo de Oro* 5: 261-82.

Serinus, Jason Victor. 2016. "The Mysteries of Hagia Sophia Revisited." *Stanford Live*. https://live.stanford.edu/blog/october-2016/mysteries-hagia-sophia-revisited.

Seroussi, Edwin. 2002. "More on Maimonides on Music." *Zutot*: 126-35.

Sewright, Kathleen Frances. 2008. "Poetic Anthologies of Fifteenth-Century France and their Relationship to Collections of the French Secular Polyphonic Chanson." PhD diss., University of North Carolina at Chapel Hill.

Shaw, Bernard. 1978. *How to Become a Music Critic*. Edited by Dan H. Laurence. New York: Da Capo Press.

Shaw, Brent D. 1996. "Body/Power/Identity: Passions of the Martyrs." *Journal of Early Christian Studies* 4: 269-312.

Shaw, Dougal. 2004. "Nothing but Propaganda? Historians and the Study of Early Modern Ritual." *Cultural and Social History* 1: 139-58.

Shay, Robert. 1996. "'Naturalizing' Palestrina and Carissimi in Late Seventeenth-Century Oxford: Henry Aldrich and His Recompositions." *Music & Letters* 77: 368-400.

Shephard, Tim. 2014. *Echoing Helicon: Music, Art and Identity in the Este Studioli, 1440-1530*. Oxford: Oxford University Press.

Shephard, Tim. 2015. "Noblewomen and Music in Italy, c.1430-1520: Looking past Isabella." In *Gender, Age and Musical Creativity*, edited by Catherine Howarth and Lisa Colton, 27-40. Farnham: Ashgate.

Shephard, Tim, Laura Ştefanescu and Serenella Sessini. 2017. "Music, Silence, and the Senses in a Late Fifteenth-Century Book of Hours." *Renaissance Quarterly* 70: 474-512.

Shephard, Tim, Sanna Raninen, Serenella Sessini and Laura Ştefănescu. 2020. *Music in the Art of Renaissance Italy 1420-1540*. London: Harvey Miller.

Shiloah, Amnon. 1979. *The Theory of Music in Arabic Writings, c. 900-1900*. Répertoire International des Sources Musicales [RISM] B/X. Munich: Henle.

Shuger, Deborah. 1999. "The 'I' of the Beholder: Renaissance Mirrors and the Reflexive Mind." In *Renaissance Culture and the Everyday*, edited by Patricia Fumerton and Simon Hunt, 21-41. Philadelphia: University of Pennsylvania Press.

Sidgwick, Emma. 2012. "Touching the Threshold to Creation: The Haemorrhoissa Motif (Mark 5:24b–34parr) between Anthropological Origin and Image Paradigm." PhD diss., KU Leuven.

Signer, Emanuel. 2020. "Tradition and Experimentation in Choirbooks Printed in Late Sixteenth- and Seventeenth-Century Italy." In *Sounding the Past: Music as History and Memory*, edited by Karl Kügle, 157-87. Turnhout: Brepols.

Silver, Larry. 2013. "The Face is Familiar: German Renaissance Portrait Multiples in Prints and Medals." *Word & Image* 19: 6-21.

Sisson, Rosemary Anne. 1972. "Catherine of Aragon." In *Plays of the Year: The Six Wives of Henry VIII*, edited by J. C. Trewin, 3-103. London: Paul Elek.

Skinner, David. 2017. "Context and Early Ownership." In *The Anne Boleyn Music Book (Royal College of Music MS 1070): Facsimile*, with introduction by Thomas Schmidt and David Skinner with Katja Airaksinen-Monier, 1-11. Oxford: DIAMM Publications.

Skjavetić, Julije. 1996. *Vokalne skladbe I. Duhovne: Moteti u 5 i 6 glasova* [*Vocal Woks I: Motets for 5 and 6 Voices*]. Edited by Lovro Županović. Zagreb: MIC.

Skjavetić, Julije. 2004. *Vokalne skladbe II. Svjetovne: Madrigali i gregeske* [*Vocal Woks II: Madrigals and Greghesche*]. Edited by Lovro Županović. Zagreb: Cantus.

Slim, H. Colin. 1984. "Music in Maiolica." *Early Music* 12: 371-73.

Šmahel, František. 1999. "Causa non grata: Premature Reformation in Hussite Bohemia". In *Proceedings of the Commission Internationale d'Histoire Ecclesiastique Comparée, Lublin 1996*, edited by Paweł Kras, Jerzy Kłoczowski, and Wojciech Polak, 224-31. Lublin: Instytut Europy Środkowo-Wschodniej.

Smart, William. 2010. "Sirens." In *The Classical Tradition*, edited by Anthony Grafton, Glenn W. Most, and Salvatore Settis, 887-88. Cambridge, MA: Harvard University Press.

Smith, Darwin. 2002. "Greban, Arnoul." In *Die Musik in Geschichte und Gegenwart. Zweite, neubearbeitete Ausgabe* [MGG], edited by Ludwig Finscher, vol. 7 (Personenteil), 1541-45. Kassel-Stuttgart-Weimar: Bärenreiter-Metzler.

Smith, Helmut Walser. 2017. "What Travelers Saw in Eighteenth-Century Germany." *Bulletin of the German Historical Institute* 61: 49-66.

Smith, Jeffrey Chipps. "Medals and the Rise of German Portrait Sculpture." In *Die Renaissance-Medaille in Italien und Deutschland*, edited by Georg Satzinger, 271-86. Münster: Rhema, 2004.

Smith, Mark M. 2007. *Sensing the Past: Seeing, Hearing, Smelling, Tasting, and Touching in History*. Berkeley: University of California Press.

Smoller, Laura A. 1986. "Playing Cards and Popular Culture in Sixteenth-Century Nuremberg." *The Sixteenth Century Journal* 17: 183-214.

Smythe, Barbara. 1926. "Music in the Divine Comedy: II." *Blackfriars* 7: 86-95.

Sölch, Brigitte. 2010. "Klöster und ihre Nachbarn – Konkurrenz im Blick? Neubauprojekte und Kapellenausstattungen des 16. Jahrhunderts in Augsburg am Beispiel der Dominikanerkirche St. Magdalena". In *Humanismus und Renaissance in Augsburg: Kulturgeschichte einer Stadt zwischen Spätmittelalter und Dreißigjährigem Krieg*, edited by Gernot Michael Müller, 491-526. Berlin: De Gruyter.

Sopta, Josip. 2001. "Šibenski biskupi na Tridenstkom saboru" ["The Šibenik Bishops at the Tridentine Council"]. In *Sedam stoljeća šibenske biskupije* [*Seven Centuries of Šibenik Bishopric*], edited by Vilijam Lakić, 237-49. Šibenik: Gradska knjižnica "Juraj Šižgorić."

Sotheby Parke Bernet & Co. 1983. *The Hever Castle Collection, the Property of the Lord Astor of Hever*. Vol. 2: *Works of Art Which Will Be Sold by Auction*. London: Sotheby Parke Bernet & Co.

Sotheby's. 2004. *Old Master Paintings Part Two: London July 8, 2004*. London: Sotheby's.

Soukup, Pavel. 2013. "Kauza reformace: Husitství v konkurenci reformních projektů" ["The Cause of the Reformation: Hussitism in Competition with Other Reform Projects"]. In *Heresis seminaria: Pojmy a koncepty v bádání o husitství* [*Heresis Seminaria: Ideas and Concepts in Research about Hussitism*], edited by Pavlína Rychterová and Pavel Soukup, 171-217. Prague: Filosofia.

Sousa, António Caetano de. 1745. *Provas da Historia Genealogica da Casa Real Portugueza*. 6 vols. Vol. 4. Lisbon: Régia Oficina Silviana, Academia Real.

Sparti, Barbara, ed. and trans. 1993. *Guglielmo Ebreo of Pesaro: De pratica seu arte tripudii/On the Practice or Art of Dancing*. Oxford: Clarendon Press.

Spector, Nancy. 2000. "Reinventing Realism." In *Sugimoto: Portraits*, edited by Tracey Bashkoff and Nancy Spector, 10-25. New York: Guggenheim Museum Publications and Harry N. Abrams.

Spence D. and Jesper Kyd. 2007. "Jesper Kyd and Assassin's Creed." *IGN*, 11 December. https://www.ign.com/articles/2007/12/12/jesper-kyd-and-assassins-creed?page=3.

Spenser, Edmund. 1590/96. *The Faerie Queene*. London: William Ponsonbie.

Sperling, Jutta. 2018. "Squeezing, Squirting, Spilling Milk: The Lactation of Saint Bernard and the Flemish *Madonna Lactans* (ca.1430-1530)." *Renaissance Quarterly* 71: 868-918.

Spohr, Arne. 2019. "'Mohr und Trompeter': Blackness and Social Status in Early Modern Germany." *Journal of the American Musicological Society*, 72: 619-63.

Sprague Smith, Carleton. 1965. "Table Blessings Set to Music." In *The Commonwealth of Music*, edited by Gustave Reese and Rose Brandel, 236-82. New York: Free Press.

Spring, Matthew. 2001. *The Lute in Britain*. Oxford: Oxford University Press.

Ştefănescu, Laura. 2020. "Staging and Painting the Heavens: Art, Theatre, and Music in Fifteenth-Century Florence." PhD diss., University of Sheffield.

Stein, Sigmund. 1957. "The Influence of Symposia Literature on the Literary Form of the Pesah Haggadah." *Journal of Jewish Studies* 7: 13-44.

Stell, Judith, and Andrew Wathey. 1981. "New Light on the Biography of John Dunstable?" *Music and Letters* 62: 60-63.

Stellfeld, J. A. 1949. *Bibliographie des Éditions Musicales Plantiniennes*. Brussels: Palais des Académies.

Stern, Moritz. 1922. *Lieder des venezianischen Lehrers Gumprecht von Szczebrszyn (um 1555)*. Berlin: Verlag Hausfreund.

Stevenson, Jill. 2010a. *Performance, Cognitive Theory, and Devotional Culture: Sensual Piety in Late Medieval York*. New York: Palgrave Macmillan.

Stevenson, Jill. 2010b. "Performance Literacy: Theorizing Medieval Devotional Seeing." In *Performance, Cognitive Theory, and Devotional Culture: Sensual Piety in Late Medieval York*, edited by Jill Stevenson, 15-43. New York: Palgrave Macmillan.

Stevenson, Robert. 1960. *Spanish Music in the Age of Columbus*. The Hague: Martinus Nijhoff.

Stevenson, Robert. 1964. "European Music in 16th-Century Guatemala." *The Musical Quarterly* 50: 341-52.

Stevenson, Robert. 1968. "The Afro-American Musical Legacy to 1800." *The Musical Quarterly* 54: 475-502.

Stevenson, Robert. 1968 and 1976. *Music in Aztec and Inca Territory*. Berkeley: University of California Press.

Stevenson, Robert. 1980. "Cuzco Cathedral: 1546-1750." *Inter-American Music Review* 2: 1-25.

Stipčević, Ennio. 1993. "La Serenissima, l'Istria e la Dalmazia – Contatti e interferenze musicali nel Cinque e Seicento." *International Review of the Aesthetics and Sociology of Music* 24: 23-44.

Stipčević, Ennio. 2016. *Renaissance Music and Culture in Croatia*. Turnhout: Brepols.

Stoichiţă, Victor Ieronim. 1978. "Deux œuvres ferraraises au Musée d'Art de la République Socialiste de Roumanie. Première partie: Qualche fabula antiqua et de bello significato." *Revue Roumaine d'Histoire de l'Art* 15: 19-52.

Stollberg-Rilinger, Barbara. 2015. *The Emperor's Old Clothes: Constitutional History and the Symbolic Language of the Holy Roman Empire*. Translated by Thomas Dunlap. New York: Berghahn.

Stoneman, Richard, Kyle Erickson, and Ian Netton, eds. 2012. *The Alexander Romance in Persia and the East*. Groningen: Barkhuis Publishing and Groningen University Library.

Stopp, John Frederick. 1974. *The Emblems of the Altdorf Academy: Medals and Orations 1577-1626*. London: Modern Humanities Research Association.

Stow, John, and Anthony Munday. 1618. *The Survay of London*. London: George Purslowe.

Stras, Laurie. 2017. "Cipriano de Rore and the Este Women." In *Cipriano de Rore: New Perspectives on His Life and Music*, edited by Jessie Ann Owens and Katelijne Schiltz, 85-92. Turnhout: Brepols.

Strauss, Walter Leopold. 1973. *Chiaroscuro: The Clair-Obscur Woodcuts by the German and Netherlandish Masters of the XVI and XVII Centuries: A Complete Catalogue with Commentary*. London: Thames and Hudson.

Strickland, Agnes. 1842. *Lives of the Queens of England, from the Norman Conquest; With Anecdotes of Their Courts, Now First Published from Official Records and Other Authentic Documents, Private as Well as Public*. Vol. 4. New Edition, with Corrections and Additions. London: Henry Colburn.

Strohm, Reinhard. 1993. *The Rise of European Music, 1380-1500*. Cambridge: Cambridge University Press.

Strohm, Reinhard. 2001. "Music, Humanism, and the Idea of a 'Rebirth' of the Arts." In *Music as Concept and Practice in the Late Middle Ages*, edited by Reinhard Strohm and Bonnie Blackburn, 346-406. Oxford: Oxford University Press.

Sturges, Robert S. 2015. "Things: Object and Agency in the Trial and Crucifixion Plays." In Robert S. Sturges, *The Circulation of Power in Medieval Biblical Drama*, 32-50. New York: Palgrave Macmillan.

Subirá, José. 1927. *La música en la casa de Alba: Estudios históricos y biográficos*. Madrid: n.p.

Subrahmanyam, Sanjay. 2002. "The Circulation of Musical Instruments in the Indian World, 1500-1800." *Oriente* 2: 76-83.

Suomalaisen Kirjallisuuden Seura. n.d. "Codices Fennici – Suomen keskiajan ja 1500-luvun käsikirjoitukset." https://www.codicesfennici.fi.

Svátek, Josef. 1899. *Ze staré Prahy: Obrazy děje- a místopisné s illustracemi K. Štapfra* [*From Old Prague: Historical and Topographical Pictures with Illustrations by K(arel) Štapfer*]. Prague: Jos. R. Vilímek.

Sweet, Rosemary. 2004. *Antiquaries: The Discovery of the Past in Eighteenth-Century Britain*. New York: Hambledon and London.

Sweet, Rosemary. 2008. "Antiquarianism and History." *Making History: The Changing Face of the Profession in Britain*. The Institute for Historical Research. http://www.history.ac.uk/makinghistory/resources/articles/antiquarianism.html.

Symondson, Anthony, and Arthur Bucknall. 2006. *Sir Ninian Comper: An Introduction to His Life and Work*. Reading: Spire.

Syson, Luke, and Dora Thornton. 2001. *Objects of Virtue: Art in Renaissance Italy*. London: British Museum.

Syson Carter, Françoise. 1987. "Celestial Dance: A Search for Perfection." *Dance Research: The Journal of the Society for Dance Research* 5: 3-17.

Taburet-Delahaye, Élisabeth, and Michel Pastoureau. 2013. *Les Secrets de la licorne*. Paris: Réunion des musées nationaux.

Takao, Makoto Harris. 2019. "'In Their Own Way': Contrafactal Practices in Japanese Christian Communities during the 16th Century." *Early Music* 47: 183-98.

Tallis, Thomas. 1993. *O Lord, in Thee is All My Trust*. Edited by John Milsom. Oxford: Oxford University Press.

Tanay, Dorit. 1999. *Noting Music, Marking Culture: The Intellectual Context of Rhythmic Notation*. [n.p.]-Holzgerlingen: American Institute of Musicology-Hänssler-Verlag.

Tanner, Marie. 1993. *The Last Descendant of Aeneas: The Hapsburgs and the Mythic Image of the Emperor*. New Haven: Yale University Press.

Taruskin, Richard. 2005. *The Oxford History of Western Music*. Vol 2: *Music in the Seventeenth and Eighteenth Centuries*. New York: Oxford University Press.

Taucci, Raffaello M. 1942. "La chiesa e il convento della SS. Annunziata di Firenze e i loro ampliamenti fino alla metà del secolo XV." *Studi Storici dell'Ordine dei Servi di Maria* 4: 99-126.

Taylor, Charles. 1989. *Sources of the Self: The Making of the Modern Identity*. Cambridge: Cambridge University Press.

Taylor, Jane H. M. 2007. *The Making of Poetry: Late-Medieval French Poetic Anthologies*. Turnhout: Brepols.

Tebbe, Karin, Ursula Timann, and Thomas Eser. 2007. *Nürnberger Goldschmiedekunst 1541-1868*. 2 vols. Nuremberg: Verlag des Germanischen Nationalmuseums.

Terra, José da Silva. 1996. "A datação do primeiro texto em 'língua de preto' na literatura portuguesa." *Diacrítica* 11: 513-27.

Thibault, Geneviève, and David Fallows, eds. 1991. *Chansonnier de Jean de Montchenu (Bibliothèque nationale, Rothschild 2973 [1.5.13]*. Paris: Publications de la Société Française de Musicologie.

Thibaut, Anton Friedrich Justus. 1825. *Ueber Reinheit der Tonkunst*. Heidelberg: I. B. C. Mohr.

Thibaut, Anton Friedrich Justus. 1877. *On Purity in Musical Art*. London: John Murray.

Thibaut, Anton Friedrich Justus. 1907. *Über Reinheit der Tonkunst. Neueste, den Text der ersten und zweiten Ausgabe erhaltende Auflage. Durch eine Biographie Thibauts sowie zahlreiche Erläuterungen und Zusätze vermehrt von Raimund Heuler*. Paderborn: Ferdinand Schöningh.

Thompson, John J. 2010. "Bagpipes and Patterns of Conformity in Late Medieval England." In *Everyday Objects: Medieval and Early Modern Material Culture and Its Meaning*, edited by Tara Hamling and Catherine Richardson, 221-30. Farnum: Ashgate.

Þorkelsson, Jón. 1906-13. *Diplomatarium Islandicum*. Vol. 8. Reykjavík: Hið íslenzka bókmentafélag.

Thornton, Dora. 1997. *The Scholar in His Study: Ownership and Experience in Renaissance Italy*. New Haven: Yale University Press.

Þorsteinsson, Bjarni. 1906-09. *Íslenzk þjóðlög*. Copenhagen: S.L. Møller.

Tiggemann, Hildegard. 2012. "Die Geschichte der großen Orgel in der Stadtkirche zu Bückeburg." In *Studien zur Musikgeschichte Bückeburgs vom 16. bis zum 20. Jahrhundert*, edited by Hildegard Tiggemann, 243-309. Hannover: Hahnsche Buchhandlung.

Tigrini, Orazio. 1588. *Il compendio della musica*. Venice: Amadino.

Timm, Erika. 1995. "Zur Frühgeschichte der jiddischen Erzählprosa: Eine neuaufgefundene Maise-Handschrift." *Beiträge zur Geschichte der deutschen Sprache und Literatur* 117: 243-80.

Tinctoris, Johannes. 1494. *Terminorum musice diffinitorium*. Treviso: Gerardus de Lisa.

Tinhorão, José Ramos. 1988. *Os negros em Portugal: Uma presença silenciosa*. Lisbon: Caminho.

Toft, Robert. 2014. *With Passionate Voice: Re-Creative Singing in 16th Century England and Italy*. Oxford: Oxford University Press.

Tomlinson, Gary. 1987. *Monteverdi and the End of the Renaissance*. Berkeley: University of California Press.

Tomlinson, Gary. 1993. *Music in Renaissance Magic: Toward a Historiography of Others*. Chicago: University of Chicago Press.

Tomlinson, Gary. 2007. *The Singing of the New World: Indigenous Voice in the Era of European Contact*. Cambridge: Cambridge University Press.

Tonietti, Tito. 2014. *And Yet It Is Heard: Musical, Multilingual and Multicultural History of Mathematical Sciences*. Basel: Springer.

Toniolo, Federica. 1997. "Descrizione delle miniature del primo volume della Bibbia." In *La Bibbia di Borso d'Este: Commentario al codice*, 1:155-237. Modena: Franco Cosimo Panini.

Toniolo, Federica. 1997a. "La Bibbia di Borso d'Este: Cortesia e Magnificenza a Ferrara tra Tardogotico e Rinascimento." In *La Bibbia di Borso d'Este: Commentario al codice*, 2:295-497. Modena: Franco Cosimo Panini.

Treccani degli Alfieri, Giovanni. 1942. *La Bibbia di Borso d'Este: Recupero e riproduzione con uno studio di Adolfo Venturi e sei tavole a colori*. Milan: Emilio Bestetti Edizioni d'Arte.

Tröster, Sonja. 2013. "Ein gestickter Stimmbuchsatz in Brüssel: Senfl mit Nadel und Faden." In *Senfl-Studien 2*, edited by Stefan Gasch and Sonja Tröster, 149-87. Tutzing: Schneider.

Tröster, Sonja. 2019a. "Bildnismedaille auf Ludwig Senfl." In *Maximilian I. (1459-1519): Kaiser, Ritter, Bürger zu Augsburg*, edited by Heidrun Lange-Krach, 321. Regensburg: Schnell & Steiner.

Tröster, Sonja. 2019b. *Senfls Liedsätze: Klassifikation und Detailstudien eines modellhaften Repertoires*. Vienna: Hollitzer.

Troiano, Massimo, 1569. *Dialoghi di Massimo Troiano: ne' quali si narrano le cose più notabili fatte nelle nozze dello prencipe Guglielmo VI conte palatino del Reno, e duca di Bauiera; e dell'illustriss. & eccell. madama Renata di Loreno*. Venice: Bolognino Zaltieri.

Trottein, Gwendolyn. 1993. *Les Enfants de Vénus: Art et astrologie à la Renaissance*. Paris: Editions de la Lagune.

Tuohy, Thomas. 1996. *Herculean Ferrara: Ercole d'Este (1471-1505) and the Invention of a Ducal Capital*. Cambridge: Cambridge University Press.

Tuppurainen, Erkki. 2005. "Hemminki Maskulaisen virsikirjaan liittyneet sävelmistöt." In *Soukat sanat maistaa suu: Hemminki Maskulaisen virsikirja 400 vuotta*, edited by Reijo Pajamo, 53-68. Hymnologian ja liturgiikan seuran vuosikirja. Helsinki: Multiprint.

Tuppurainen, Erkki, and Jorma Hannikainen. 2010. *Suomenkielisiä kirkkolauluja 1500-1600 -luvuilta*. Helsinki: Sibelius-Akatemia.

Turnbull, Stephen R., and Angus McBride. 2003. *The Hussite Wars, 1419-1436*. Oxford: Osprey.

Uluhogian, Gabriella. 2009. *Gli Armeni*. Bologna: Il Mulino.

Uluhogian, Gabriella. 2016. "Il Salterio di Abgar Toxateci (a. 1565) e l'avvio degli studi armenistici presso al Biblioteca Ambrosiana di Milano." In *Collectanea Armeniaca*, edited by Rosa Bianca Finazzi and Anna Sirinian, 313-37. Rome: Bulzoni.

Umiltà da Faenza. 2005. *Sermones: Le lezioni di una monaca*. Edited by Adele Simonetti. Translated by Lea Montuschi and Luigi G. G. Ricci. Florence: SISMEL, Edizioni del Galluzzo.

Updike, Daniel Berkeley. 1922. *Printing Types: Their History, Forms and Use*. 2 vols. Cambridge, MA: Harvard University Press.

Urkevich, Lisa. 2011. "Anne Boleyn's French Motet Book: A Childhood Gift." In *Ars musica septentrionalis*, edited by Frédéric Billiet and Barbara Haggh, 95-120. Paris: Presses de l'Université Paris-Sorbonne.

Utidjian, Haig. 2009. "Modality in the Hymns of the Armenian Church." In *Proceedings of the 10th WSEAS International Conference on Acoustics & Music: Theory & Applications*, edited by Nikos E. Mastorakis, Anca Croitoru, Valentina Emilia Balas, et al., 23-29. Stevens Point: World Scientific and Engineering Academy and Society.

Valadés, Didacus (Diego). 2003. *Retórica cristiana* (Perugia, 1579). Introduction by Esteban J. Palomera; caveat by Alfonso Castro Pallares; translation by Tarsicio Herrera Zapién. 2nd edn. Mexico City: Fondo de Cultura Económica.

Valier, Agostino. 1586. *Vita Caroli Borromei*. Verona: Discepolo.

[Valignano, Alessandro]. 1590. *De missione legatorum Iap. nensium ad Romanam curiam, rebusq; in Europa, ac toto itinere animaduersis dialogus ex ephemeride ipsorvm legatorvm collectvs, & in sermonem latinvm versvs ab Eduardo de Sande Sacerdote societatis Iesv, in domo Societatis Iesu*. Macau: in domo Societatis Iesu.

Valignano, Alessandro. 1946. *Il cerimoniale per i missionari del Giappone*. Edited by G. F. Schütte. Rome: Edizioni di Storia e Letteratura.

van Ooijen, David. 2011. "European Music in Japan in the 16th and 17th centuries." *FoMRHI Quarterly* 120: Comm 1955. https://www.fomrhi.org/vanilla/fomrhi/uploads/bulletins/Fomrhi-120/Comm%201955%20web%20version.pdf.

van Orden, Kate. 2001. "Female Complaintes: Laments of Venus, Queens, and City Women in Late Sixteenth-Century France." *Renaissance Quarterly* 54: 801-45.

van Orden, Kate. 2005. *Music, Discipline, and Arms in Early Modern France*. Chicago: University of Chicago Press.

van Orden, Kate. 2015. *Materialities: Books, Readers, and the Chanson in Sixteenth-Century Europe*. New York: Oxford University Press.

Vandervellen, Pascale. 2017. *The Golden Age of Flemish Harpsichord Making: A Study of the MIM's Ruckers Instruments*. Brussels: Musical Instruments Museum.

Vanhauwaert, Soetkin, and Georg Geml. 2015. "(Don't) Judge a Head by Its Cover: The Materiality of the Johannesschüssel as Reliquary." In *Late Medieval Devotions: Images, Instruments and the Materiality of Belief*, edited by S. Ryan and H. Laugerud, 104-20. Dublin: Four Courts Press.

Vanhulst, Henri. 1978. "Un succès de l'édition Musicale: Le 'Septiesme livre des chansons a quatre parties' (1560-1661/3)." *Revue Belge De Musicologie / Belgisch Tijdschrift Voor Muziekwetenschap* 32/33: 97-120.

Vanhulst, Henri. 1982. "L'instruction pour le cistre parue dans la version anversoise de 'l'Horutlus Citharae' (1582)." *Revue Belge de Musicologie / Belgisch Tijdschrift Voor Muziekwetenschap* 36/38: 65-87.

Vapaavuori, Hannu. 2003. "Vanhan virsikirjan sävelmistöt ja kirkkoveisuu." In *Ain' veisatkaam' Herral': Vanha virsikirja 300 vuotta*, edited by Reijo Pajamo, 45-54. Hymnologian ja liturgiikan seuran vuosikirja. Helsinki: Hymnologian ja liturgiikan seura.

Varese, Ranieri. 1985. "Un polittico inglese in alabastro." In *Il Museo Civico in Ferrara: Donazioni e restauri*, edited by Elena Bonatti, 124-28. Florence: Centro Di.

Vasari, Giorgio. 1550. *Le Vite de' piu eccellenti pittori, scultori et architettori*. Florence: Giunti.

Vasari, Giorgio. 1568. *Le Vite de' piu eccellenti pittori, scultori et architettori*. Florence: Giunti.

Vasari, Giorgio. 1878-85. *Le vite de' più eccellenti pittori, scultori ed architettori*. 9 vols. Edited by Gaetano Milanesi. Florence: G. C. Sansoni.

Vasić, Olivera. 2004. "Промене у игрању уз посмртни ритуал на примеру игре ситан танац и обичаја тужба: Прилог проучавању игара југозападне Србије" ["Changes in Funeral Ritual Dances Explained on the Example of the *Sitan Tanac* and the Custom *Tužba*: A Contribution to the Study of Dances of Southwestern Serbia"]. In Етнокореологија: Трагови [*Ethnochoreology Traces*], edited by Olivera Vasić, 1:58-65. Beograd: Art Grafik.

Veith, Ilza. 1965. *Hysteria: The History of a Disease*. Vol. 2. Chicago: University of Chicago Press.

Verdon, Timothy, ed. 2005. *Santissima Annunziata: Alla riscoperta delle chiese di Firenze*. Florence: Centro Di.

Vervliet, Hendrick D. L. 1968. *Sixteenth Century Printing Types of the Low Countries*. Amsterdam: Menno Hertzberger.

Vicentino, Nicola. 1555. *L'Antica musica ridotta alla moderna prattica*. Rome: Barre.

Vicentino, Nicola. 1996. *Ancient Music Adapted to Modern Practice*. Translated by Maria Rika Maniates. New Haven: Yale University Press.

Vidal, Auguste. 1903. "Les délibérations du conseil communal d'Albi de 1372 à 1388." *Revue des langues romanes* 46: 33-73.

Vignau-Wilberg, Thea. 2017. *Joris and Jacob Hoefnagel: Art and Science around 1600*. Berlin: Hatje Cantz Verlag.

Villanueva Serrano, Francesc. 2009. "Mateo Flecha el Viejo en la Catedral de Valencia: Sus dos períodos de magisterio de capilla (1526-1531? y 1539-1541) y su entorno musical." *Anuario Musical* 64: 57-108.

Villette, Jeanne. 1940. *L'ange dans l'art d'occident du XIIe au XVIe siècle: France, Italie, Flandre, Allemagne*. Paris: H. Laurens.

Virdung, Sebastian. 1511. *Musica getutscht und auszgezogen*. Basel: Michael Furter.

Virgil (Publius Vergilius Maro). 1469. *Opera*. Rome: Sweynheym and Pannartz.

Virtuaalikatedraali. n.d. "Virtuaalikatedraali." http://www2.siba.fi/virtuaalikatedraali/.

Visconti, Gaspare. 1979. *I canzonieri per Beatrice d'Este e per Bianca Maria Sforza*. Edited by Paolo Bongrani. Milan: Mondadori.

Vitiello, Maria. 2003. *Le architetture dipinte di Filippino Lippi: La Cappella Carafa a S. Maria Sopra Minerva in Roma*. Rome: Gangemi.

Vives, Juan Luis. 2000. *The Education of a Christian Woman: A Sixteenth-Century Manual*. Translated by Charles Fantazzi. Chicago: The University of Chicago Press.

Vlhová-Wörner, Hana, ed. 2019. *Jistebnický kancionál. MS. Praha, Knihovna Národního muzea, II C 7. Kritická edice. 2. svazek. Cantionale / The Jistebnice Kancionál. MS. Prague, National Museum Library, II C 7. Critical Edition. Volume 2. Cantionale*. Chomutov: Luboš Marek.

Vodovozova, Natalie. 1996. "A Contribution to the History of the *Villancico de Negros*." MA diss., University of British Columbia.

Voet, Leon. 1969-72. *The Golden Compasses: A History and Evaluation of the Printing and Publishing Activities of the Officina Plantaniana at Antwerp*. 2 vols. Amsterdam: Vagendt.

Voet, Leon. 1980-83. *The Plantin Press (1555-1589): A Bibliography of the Works Printed and Published by Christopher Plantin at Antwerp and Leiden*. 6 vols. Amsterdam: Van Hoeve.

Vogelsänger, Siegfried. 2013. "Dokumente zur Musik an der Wolfenbütteler Hauptkirche." In *Ruhm und Ehre durch Musik: Beiträge zur Wolfenbütteler Hof- und Kirchenmusik während der Residenzzeit*, edited by Rainer Schmitt, et al., 255-69. Wolfenbüttel: Kulturstadt Wolfenbüttel e.V.

Volterrani, Silvia. 1997. "Tasso e il canto delle Sirene." *Studi Tassiani* 45: 51-83.

"Vom Tage." 1878. "Vom Tage Aus der Hradschiner Hofburg." *Prager Tagblatt* 2 136, May 17, 1878: 3.

von Büren, Guido. 2010. "'… *wie sich bei sulchem mechtigen fursten wol gezimt*': Die 'Fürstlich Jülichsche etc. Hochzeit' von 1585 und die Festkultur der Renaissance." In *Städte, Höfe und Kulturtransfer: Studien zur Renaissance am Rhein*, edited by Stephan Hoppe, Alexander Markschies, and Norbert Nußbaum, 284-320. Regensburg: Schnell & Steiner.

von Stetten, Paul. 1779. *Kunst-Gewerb- und Handwerks-Geschichte der Reichs-Stadt Augsburg*. Augsburg: Conrad Heinrich Stage.

Voss, Angela. 2002. "Orpheus Redivivus: The Musical Magic of Marsilio Ficino." In *Marsilio Ficino: His Theology, His Philosophy, His Legacy*, edited by Michael J. B. Allen, Valery Rees, and Martin Davies, 227-41. Leiden: Brill.

Wackenroder, Wilhelm Heinrich. 1797. *Herzensergießungen eines kunstliebenden Klosterbruders*. Berlin: Johann Friedrich Unger.

Wade, Bonnie C. 1997. "When West Met East: The Organ as an Instrument of Culture." In *Festschrift für Christoph-Hellmut Mahling zum 65. Geburtstag*, 2 vols., edited by Axel Beer, Kristina Pfarr, and Wolfgang Ruf, 2:1479-89. Tutzing: Han Schneider.

Wade, Bonnie C. 1998. *Imaging Sound: An Ethnomusicological Study of Music, Art and Culture in Mughal India*. Chicago: University of Chicago Press.

Wall, John N. 2014. "Recovering Lost Acoustic Spaces: St Paul's Cathedral and Paul's Churchyard in 1622." *Digital Studies / le champ numérique*. https://www.digitalstudies.org/articles/10.16995/dscn.58/.

Warburg, Aby. (1895) 1999. "The Theatrical Costumes for the Intermedi of 1589." In Aby Warburg, *The Renewal of Pagan Antiquity*, 349-401. Santa Monica: Getty Research Institute for the History of Art and the Humanities.

Wardropper, Bruce W. 1950. "The Search for the Dramatic Formula for the Auto Sacramental." *Publications of the Modern Language Association* 65: 1196-211.

Warner, Marina. 1976. *Alone of All Her Sex: The Myth and the Cult of the Virgin Mary*. New York: Alfred A. Knopf.

Warnicke, Retha. 1985. "Anne Boleyn's Childhood and Adolescence." *The Historical Journal* 28: 939-52.

Waterhouse, David B. 1997. "Música dos bárbaros do sul no Japaão / Southern Barbarian Music in Japan." In *Portugal e o mundo o encontro de culturas na música / Portugal and the World: The Encounter of Cultures in Music*, edited by Salwa El-Shawan Castelo-Branco, 323-49 / 351-77. Lisbon: Publicações Dom Quixote.

Wathey, Andrew. 1985. "Dunstable in France." *Music and Letters* 67: 1-36.

Watson, Paul F. 1979. *The Garden of Love in Tuscan Art of the Early Renaissance*. Philadelphia: Art Alliance.

Weber, William. 1994. "The Intellectual Origins of Musical Canon in Eighteenth-Century England." *Journal of the American Musicological Society* 47: 488-520.

Weeks-Chapman, Catherine. 1964. "Andrea Antico." PhD diss., Harvard University.

Wegman, Rob C. 1996. "From Maker to Composer: Improvisation and Musical Authorship in the Low Countries, 1450-1500." *Journal of the American Musicological Society* 49: 409-79.

Weisbach, Werner. 1921. *Der Barock als Kunst der Gegenreformation*. Berlin: P. Cassirer.

Weiss, Susan F. 2010. "Vandals, Students, or Scholars? Handwritten Clues in Renaissance Music Textbooks." In *Music Education in the Middle Ages and the Renaissance*, edited by Russell E. Murray, et al., 207-46. Bloomington: Indiana University Press.

Weitlauff, Manfred. 2003. "Vom spätmittelalterlich-benediktinischen 'Damenstift' zur tridentinisch-'regulierten' Benediktinerinnenabtei: Kloster Frauenchiemsee im 17. Jahrhundert." In *Kloster Frauenchiemsee 782-2003: Kunst, Wirtschaft und Kultur einer altbayerischen Benediktinerinnenabtei*, edited by Walter Brugger and Manfred Weitlauff, 303-66. Weißenhorn: Anton H. Konrad Verlag.

Welch, Evelyn. 2009. "Art on the Edge: Hair and Hands in Renaissance Italy." *Renaissance Studies* 23: 241-68.

Welch, Stuart Cary. 1987. *The Emperors' Album: Images of Mughal India*. New York: Metropolitan Museum of Art.

Wellens, Robert. 1982. "Un épisode des relations entre l'Angleterre et les Pays-Bas au début du XVIe siècle: Le projet de mariage entre Marguerite d'Autriche et Henri VII." *Revue d'histoire moderne et contemporaine* 29: 267-90.

Wells-Cole, Anthony. 1997. *Art and Decoration in Elizabethan and Jacobean England: The Influence of Continental Prints, 1558-1625*. London: Paul Mellon Centre for Studies in British Art.

Welser, Marcus. (1595) 2014. *Chronica der weitberühmten Kaiserlichen freien und des H. Reichs Stadt Augsburg in Schwaben*. Frankfurt am Main: Christoph Egen.

Welzel, Barbara. 2005. "Widowhood: Margaret of York and Margaret of Austria." In *Women of Distinction: Margaret of York, Margaret of Austria*, edited by Dagmar Eichberger, 103-13. Leuven: Brepols-Davidsfonds.

Wenzel, Marian. 1965. *Ukrasni motive na stećcima / Ornamental Motifs on Tombstones from Medieval Bosnia and Surrounding Regions*. Sarajevo: Veselin Masleša.

Wesley, John. 1827. *The Journal of the Rev. John Wesley, A.M., Sometime Fellow of Lincoln College, Oxford*. Vol. 2: *From November 25, 1746, to May 5, 1760*. London: J. Kershaw.

Whittaker, Adam. 2018. "Musical Divisions of the Sacred and Secular in *The Hunchback of Notre Dame*." In *Recomposing the Past: Representations of Early Music on Stage and Screen*, edited by James Cook, Alex Kolassa, and Adam Whittaker, 89-106. New York: Routledge.

Widmann, Benedikt. 1889. "Die Kompositionen der Psalmen von Statius Olthof." *Vierteljahrsschrift für Musikwissenschaft* 5: 290-321.

Wijaczka, Jacek. 2019. *Albrecht von Brandenburg-Ansbach (1490-1568): Der letzte Hochmeister des Deutschen Ordens und der erste Herzog in Preußen*. Buskow: edition bodoni.

Wilhelmi, Thomas. 2011. "Crusius (Kraus), Martin." In *Frühe Neuzeit in Deutschland 1520-1620: Literaturwissenschaftliches Verfasserlexikon*, edited by Wilhelm Kühlmann, et al., 2:58-63. Berlin: De Gruyter.

Williamson, Beth. 2004. "Altarpieces, Liturgy, and Devotion." *Speculum* 79: 341-406.

Williamson, Beth. 2009. *The Madonna of Humility: Development, Dissemination and Reception, c. 1340-1400*. Woodbridge: The Boydell Press.

Williamson, Beth. 2013. "Sensory Experience in Medieval Devotion: Sound and Vision, Invisibility and Silence." *Speculum* 88: 1-43.

Williamson, Magnus. 1997. "*Pictura et scriptura*: The Eton Choirbook in Its Iconographical Context." *Early Music* 28: 359-80.

Williamson, Magnus. 2005. "Liturgical Polyphony in the Pre-Reformation English Parish Church: A Provisional List and Commentary." *Royal Musical Association Research Chronicle* 38: 1-43.

Williamson, Magnus, ed. 2010. *The Eton Choirbook: Facsimile and Introductory Study*. Oxford: DIAMM.

Williamson, Magnus. 2015. "The Fate of the Choirbook in Protestant Europe." *Journal of the Alamire Foundation* 7, no. 2: 117-131, 135.

Williamson, Paul, and Glyn Davies. 2014. *Medieval Ivory Carvings, 1200-1550*. 2 vols. London: V&A Publications.

Willis, Jonathan. 2010a. "'A Pottle of Ayle on Whyt Sonday': Everyday Objects and the Musical Culture of the Post-Reformation Parish Church." In *Everyday Objects: Medieval and Early Modern Material Culture and Its Meanings*, edited by Tara Hamling and Catherine Richardson, 211-20. Farnham: Ashgate.

Willis, Jonathan. 2010b. *Church Music and Protestantism in Post-Reformation England: Discourses, Sites and Identities*. Farnham: Ashgate.

Wilson, Blake. 1992. *Music and Merchants: The Laudesi Companies of Republican Florence*. Oxford: Clarendon Press.

Wilson, Blake. 2009. *Singing Poetry in Renaissance Florence: The "Cantasi Come" Tradition*. Florence: Olschki.

Wilson, Nick. 2014. *The Art of Re-Enchantment: Making Early Music in the Modern Age*. New York: Oxford University Press.

Winn, Mary Beth. 1997. *Anthoine Vérard: Parisian Publisher, 1485-1512*. Geneva: Droz.

Winternitz, Emanuel. 1963. "On Angel Concerts in the 15th Century: A Critical Approach to Realism and Symbolism in Sacred Painting." *The Musical Quarterly* 49: 450-63.

Wistreich, Richard. 2012. "Introduction: Musical Materials and Cultural Spaces." *Renaissance Studies* 26: 1-12.

Wistreich, Richard. 2017. "'Inclosed in this tabernacle of flesh': Body, Soul, and the Singing Voice." *Journal of the Northern Renaissance* 8. https://www.northernrenaissance.org/inclosed-in-this-tabernacle-of-flesh-body-soul-and-the-singing-voice/.

Wistreich, Richard. 2018. "Singing" and "Vocal Performance." In *The Cambridge Encyclopedia of Historical Performance in Music*, edited by Colin Lawson and Robin Stowell, 576-80 and 676-80. Cambridge: Cambridge University Press.

Wolff, Larry. 2012. *The Singing Turk: Ottoman Power and Operatic Emotions on the European Stage from the Siege of Vienna to the Age of Napoleon*. Stanford: Stanford University Press.

Wolfthal, Diane. 2018. "From Venus to Witches: The Female Nude in Northern Europe." In *The Renaissance Nude*, edited by Thomas Kren, Jill Burke, and Stephen Campbell, 81-116. Los Angeles: J. Paul Getty Museum.

Wolpe, Berthold. 1980. "John de Beauchesne and the First English Writing-Books." In *Scribes and Sources: Handbook of the Chancery Hand in the Sixteenth Century. Texts from the Writing Masters*, edited by A. S. Osley, 227-42. London: Faber and Faber.

Woodfield, Ian. 1984. *The Early History of the Viol*. Cambridge: Cambridge University Press.

Woodfield, Ian. 1990. "The Keyboard Recital in Oriental Diplomacy, 1520-1620." *Journal of the Royal Musical Association* 115: 33-62.

Woodfield, Ian. 1995. *English Musicians in the Age of Exploration*. Stuyvesant, NY: Pendragon Press.

Woolf, Virginia. 1940. *Roger Fry: A Biography*. London: Hogarth Press.

Wright, Craig. 1979. *Music at the Court of Burgundy, 1364-1419: A Documentary History*. Henryville: Institute of Mediaeval Music.

Wright, Owen. 1978. *The Modal System of Arab and Persian Music, A.D. 1250-1300*. Oxford: Oxford University Press.

Wright, Owen. 2004. "The Sight of Sound." *Muqarnas* 21: 359-71.

Wright, Owen. 2014. *Music Theory in Mamluk Cairo: The ġāyat al-maṭlūb fī ʿilm al-adwār wa-ʾl-ḍurūb by Ibn Kurr*. Farnham: Ashgate.

Yri, Kirsten. 2010. "Thomas Binkley and the Studio der Frühen Musik: Challenging 'the myth of Westernness.'" *Early Music* 38: 273-80.

Zamboni, Silla. 1975. *Pittori di Ercole I d'Este: Giovan Francesco Maineri, Lazzaro Grimaldi, Domenico Panetti, Michele Coltellini*. Ferrara: Cassa di risparmio di Ferrara.

Zambotti, Bernardino. 1934. *Diario ferrarese dall'anno 1476 sino al 1504*. Edited by Giuseppe Pardi. Rerum Italicarum Scriptores 24. Part 7. Bologna: Zanichelli.

Zanardi, Zita. 2009. *Le stagioni di un cantimbanco: Vita quotidiana a Bologna nelle opere di Giulio Cesare Croce*. Bologna: Editrice compositori.

Zanovello, Giovanni. 2014. "'In the Church and in the Chapel': Music and Devotional Spaces in the Florentine Church of Santissima Annunziata." *Journal of the American Musicological Society* 67: 379-428.

Zap, Karel Vladislav. 1848. *Průwodce po Praze: Potřebná příruční kniha pro každého, kdo se s pamětnostmi Českého hlawního města seznámiti chce* [*Guide to Prague: The Essential Handbook for Anyone Who Wants to Get Acquainted with the Monuments of the Bohemian Capital City*]. Prague: Bedřich Krečmár.

Zara, Vasco. 2010. "Dall'*Hypnerotomachia Poliphili* al Tempio di Salomone: Modelli architettonico-musicali nell'*Architecture harmonique* di René Ouvrard, 1679." In *La réception de modèles "cinquecenteschi" dans la théorie et les arts français du XVIIe siècle*, edited by Flaminia Barbati and Sabine Frommel, 131-56. Genève: Droz.

Zarlino, Gioseffo. 1558. *Le istitutioni harmoniche*. Venice: [n.p.].

Zarri, Gabriella, ed. 1996. *Donna, disciplina, creanza cristiana dal XV al XVII secolo: Studi e testi a stampa*. Rome: Edizioni di storia e letteratura.

Zecher, Carla. 2007. *Sounding Objects: Musical Instruments, Poetry, and Art in Renaissance France*. Toronto: University of Toronto Press.

Zeiller, Martin. 1632. *Itinerarium Germania Nov- Antiquae / Teutsches Reyßbuch durch Hoch und Nider Teutschland auch angräntzende / vnnd benachbarte Königreich / Fürstenthumb vnd Lande / als Vngarn / Siebenbürgen / Polen / Schweden / Dennemarck / etc. So vor alters zu Teutschland gerechnet worden sein*. Strasbourg: In Verlegung Lazari Zetzners Seligen Erbe.

Zemon Davis, Natalie. 1956. "Holbein's Pictures of Death and the Reformation at Lyons." *Studies in the Renaissance* 3: 97-130.

Zimmer, Gerhard, and Nele Hackländer, eds. 1997. *Der Betende Knabe: Original und Experiment*. Frankfurt: Peter Lang.

Županović, Lovro. 2001. "Crkvena glazba i crkveni glazbenici u Šibeniku" ["Church Music and Church Musicians in Šibenik"]. In *Sedam stoljeća šibenske biskupije* [*Seven Centuries of Šibenik Bishopric*], edited by Vilijam Lakić, 967-76. Šibenik: Gradska knjižnica "Juraj Šižgorić."

Zwolińska, Elżbieta. 1987. "Musica figurata in the Jagiellonian Mausoleum: Some Remarks on the Polyphony of Wawel Rorantists in the 16th Century." *Polish Art Studies* 8: 145-50.